Experimenting with the Mind

Readings in Cognitive Psychology

Lloyd K. Komatsu

Carleton College

Brooks/Cole Publishing Company
Pacific Grove, California

The trademark ITP is used under license.

Brooks/Cole Publishing Company
A Division of Wadsworth, Inc.

Printed in the United States of America

10 9 8 7 6 5 4 3 2 1

Library of Congress Cataloging-in-Publication Data
Experimenting with the mind : readings in cognitive psychology /
[edited by] Lloyd Komatsu.
    p. cm.
  Includes bibliographical references and index.
  ISBN 0-534-21600-5
  1. Cognitive psychology.   I. Komatsu, Lloyd.
BF201.E95   1994
153—dc20   93-23715
                                 CIP

Sponsoring Editor: *Vicki Knight*
Editorial Associate: *Lauri Banks Ataide*
Production Coordinator: *Fiorella Ljunggren*
Production: *Scratchgravel Publishing Services*
Manuscript Editor: *Barbara Kimmel*
Permissions Editor: *May Clark*
Interior Design: *Anne Draus, Scratchgravel Publishing Services*
Cover Design: *Vernon T. Boes*
Cover Photo: *C. Sloat, Phototake*
Art Coordinator: *Greg Draus, Scratchgravel Publishing Services*
Typesetting: *Scratchgravel Publishing Services*
Printing and Binding: *Malloy Lithographing, Inc.*

THIS BOOK IS PRINTED ON ACID-FREE RECYCLED PAPER

To my entire family, human and canine:

Kathie, Timmy, Tandy, Bussey, and Eskie

PREFACE

A large part of learning a science is learning what's done in that science and why. But textbooks often fail to describe experiments in the kind of detail that would allow students to think about them critically or to do their own replications, variations, or extensions of them. Textbooks also rarely convey the struggle and excitement to be found in the process of formulating research questions and designing, conducting, and analyzing experiments that address those questions. For these reasons, many who teach cognitive psychology would like to expose their students to the primary literature. Reading original research reports is often the only way to learn how science is actually done.

This volume brings together original reports of research from all areas of cognitive psychology. All of these articles were originally intended for a professional scientific audience, typically experimental psychologists. In many cases the intended audience was specifically cognitive psychologists. The advantage of this collection is that it provides students with the "real thing"—articles that at the time of their publication were on the cutting edge of research on cognition. The disadvantage is that many articles assume a background on the part of their readers that students learning cognitive psychology for the first time do not have. I've taken several steps to deal with this problem.

The introduction to the book includes brief overviews of experimental methodology, statistics, and conventions in the writing of psychological reports. In selecting articles for this collection, I've looked for those that present motivations and methods clearly. Some articles have been edited to exclude technical discussions or additional experiments that elaborate on the main point but are of limited use to, and are often confusing for, nonspecialist readers.

Each article, or reading, in this book is preceded by an introduction that provides a context for the research and explains concepts, terminology, or techniques that may be unfamiliar. Each introduction ends with something for the student to think about while reading the article. Each reading is followed by a postscript that summarizes more recent research in the area and points out related topics. Numerous references are cited to provide guidance for readers who want to pursue a topic in more depth. Questions that follow the postscript help students think critically about the experiment(s) they've just read.

I've tried to choose articles that collectively provide broad coverage of cognitive psychology without compromising excessively the goals of accessibility and affordability. The readings are organized into 10 chapters, falling into four parts.

Part I, Acquisition of Knowledge, consists of three chapters; the readings in these chapters deal with lower-level cognitive processes that bring information into the human information-processing system. Part II, Representation of Knowledge, offers readings in two chapters that explore various aspects of the knowledge that results from processing information. The three chapters in Part III, Higher-Order Processing of Knowledge, reflect some of the uses to which we put that knowledge: language and comprehension, reasoning and judgment, and problem solving. Finally, Part IV, Everyday Cognitive Experiences, consists of two chapters in which the readings have a more "applied" orientation to understanding cognitive phenomena. Although the organization of this volume and most of the readings reflect a traditional information-processing approach to cognition, a Gibsonian orientation can be found in Reading 7, a connectionist approach is taken in Readings 6 and 8, and a cognitive neuroscience perspective is adopted in Readings 15, 19, and 23.

A much appreciated faculty development grant from Carleton College supported the writing of part of this book. I would like to thank R. Dale Dick of the University of Wisconsin–Eau Claire, Terry R. Greene of Franklin and Marshall College, Steven Smith of Texas A & M University, and Lori R. Van Wallendael of the University of North Carolina at Charlotte, who reviewed the manuscript and offered constructive suggestions. I'm very grateful to Vicki Knight of Brooks/Cole, who helped me develop the idea for this book and provided guidance throughout the process of writing it. I appreciate the support and advice I received from Anne Draus of Scratchgravel and from Fiorella Ljunggren, Carline Haga, and May Clark, all of Brooks/Cole. I also appreciate Barbara Kimmel's keen eye for details and her efforts to improve my prose. Finally, and most of all, I thank Kathie Galotti for her moral support, her tolerance for books and journals strewn all about, and her many suggestions for readings. I urge other colleagues who may have suggestions to send their input to me via Brooks/Cole, and I thank all of them in advance.

Lloyd K. Komatsu

CONTENTS

Chapter Five / Concepts and Imagery 241

PART III / HIGHER-ORDER PROCESSING OF KNOWLEDGE 329

Chapter Six / Language and Comprehension 331

Chapter Seven / Reasoning and Judgment   **395**

Chapter Eight / Problem Solving   **421**

PART IV / EVERYDAY COGNITIVE EXPERIENCES   **449**

Chapter Nine / Everyday Memory and Judgment   **451**

Chapter Ten / Group and Individual Differences in Cognition   **515**

INTRODUCTION

to *Experimenting with the Mind*

Imagine yourself in a shopping mall. You see a man standing near one of the exits, scanning the faces of people as they approach. He looks briefly at his watch then starts looking at people again, alternating between looking at those close by and those down the walkway. At one point, he suddenly turns around to look at a group of people shouting greetings to one another. He looks at his watch again then looks around. He walks over to a map of the mall, looks at it for a while, looks up and around at the stores in the vicinity, then looks at the map again. He glances at his watch, purses his lips, and starts to study the people approaching the exit again. Then he walks over to a bank of phones, grabs a phone book, flips pages, pauses, and runs his finger down a page. Moving his lips slightly, he closes the book, moves over to a phone, and starts dialing. While holding the receiver, he turns to watch people as they approach the exit. Soon he's talking, but just for a few seconds. He hangs up, looks at his watch, and walks back to his post by the exit. He starts scanning again.

What's going on in this little scenario? Most people would suggest that the man was supposed to meet someone who was late. He scanned faces hoping to see the person approach. When he looked farther down the walkway, he was probably trying to see whether he could recognize the person's clothes or walk, because it's hard to make out faces at such a distance. At one point, a group of people meeting one another captured his attention. Then he checked the mall map to make sure he was in the right spot. After thinking about what to do next, he looked up a phone number, repeated it to himself to remember it while he got to a phone, and started calling. Someone answered and they talked. He went back to waiting. It seems to be a simple situation.

But consider the range of skills and abilities that our explanation suggests the man has. He must be able to remember an appointment (and believe others can, too). He must be able to read his watch and to recognize a face, and perhaps a walk, and must be able to focus his attention on different things. He must be able to make decisions, such as what to do next if a present course of action isn't satisfactory. He must be able to read a map and a phone book. He must be able to remember novel information like phone numbers, at least briefly. He must know the conventions of using a telephone. He must know how to talk and understand speech.

This list of skills and abilities that we attribute to the man is pretty long yet so familiar that we take it for granted. But if you think about it, it's rather odd that we're so sure he has these skills and abilities. None of them is directly observable—you can't see memory directly the way you can see hair color. What makes us so sure that they apply in this case? Our explanation, like all our everyday explanations about people's behavior, stems largely from our assumption that other people are like us; that they perceive, remember, and think; that they have minds.[1]

How do we know whether other people's minds work the way ours do? In fact, do we really know how our own minds work? How is it that we manage to shift our attention from one thing to another? How do we manage to recognize faces, read words, remember phone numbers, and figure out that someone must be waiting for someone who's late? We're able to do many things without quite being aware of how we do them. In a much broader sense than was popularized by Freud, we're unconscious of much that goes on in our minds. So how do we figure out how our minds and the minds of other people operate?

We usually depend on scientists to discover how things in the world work. But how can the mind be studied scientifically? As typically practiced, science assumes an objective and shared reality, something that exists independently of our perceiving or thinking about it. Science doesn't study individual experiences. In this sense, science is fundamentally a communal activity. For something to be studied scientifically and objectively, it must be open to examination by anyone with the right tools; and when it's examined by different people, everyone should obtain the same results. Scientifically studying something that is not directly observable poses a problem.

For a long time, particularly in America, psychologists concluded that the mind could not be studied scientifically. But the psychology that developed from that assumption had difficulty capturing the rich variety of human behaviors. Inspired in part by the rise of information theory and the development of the computer after World War II, psychologists began to develop theories and methods for a scientific study of the mind. By the late 1960s, the study of human cognition was an established and extremely energetic aspect

---

[1]Philosophers refer to this as the problem of other minds, and it's even more vexing than I make it out to be here. A discussion of this problem that's accessible and useful for students of cognitive psychology can be found in Churchland (1988).

of experimental psychology (see Gardner, 1985, and Lachman, Lachman, & Butterfield, 1979, for detailed histories of cognitive psychology; see Bruner, 1983, for a much more personal account).

The range of cognitive phenomena studied and our understanding of those phenomena have gained in richness tremendously over the past 30 to 40 years. There are still many things to be sorted out. But I think that people are natural problem solvers and that we find real excitement and satisfaction in discovery. This book is intended to help you develop the tools needed to participate in the challenge and excitement of discovering new things about the human mind.

ABOUT THIS BOOK

Today, a number of good textbooks on cognitive psychology are available. You may be using one of them in conjunction with this text. Why then have I put this collection together?

Textbooks summarize theories and research. Summaries of research necessarily leave out details. Often what's left out are details of the researcher's or researchers' thinking when designing the research and details of how the research was carried out. In contrast, this book gathers together original reports of research on central issues in cognitive psychology from the past 40 years. The focus of these reports is not to summarize some body of research but to present findings that were new when the articles were first written. When new findings are reported, presentation of details regarding the motivation for and methodology used in the research are crucial. Thus, what you'll find here that you won't find in textbooks are the details of how cognitive psychology research is actually carried out. But why should a student learning about cognitive psychology for the first time be concerned about such details?

I believe that a large part of learning cognitive psychology, as with learning any science, is learning how it is done. Scientific knowledge is not static; it doesn't just sit there waiting to be absorbed by students. Scientific knowledge is constantly being refined, elaborated, tested, and occasionally flipped on its head. Whether an experiment succeeds or fails in its attempt to add to our scientific knowledge often lies in the details of how it was carried out. To learn how to recognize and do good research, to be able to participate in the *science* of cognitive psychology, students must be exposed to the messy specifics of designing, executing, analyzing, and interpreting research.

In selecting articles for this collection, I've been motivated by several factors. First, as mentioned above, I've chosen original reports of research investigating central issues in cognitive psychology. Second, I've tried to choose articles that present their motivation and methods as clearly as possible. To this end, articles are sometimes edited to exclude technical discussions or experiments that provide only minor elaborations of the main point; such elements are often very difficult to follow or are of limited use for readers encountering these issues for the first time. Such exclusions are always noted, either in the introductions or in the body of the article itself. If you're particularly interested in the issues raised by an edited article, I urge you to read the article in its original published form; complete original references are always provided. I've also provided references for work that follows up on the research reported in the article or in related areas. Finally, I've tried to choose articles so that, taken as a whole, the collection provides broad coverage of many of the topics, theories, and methods that make up modern cognitive psychology. This collection is by no means exhaustive, but I think it represents a reasonable balance between the competing needs of coverage, accessibility, and affordability.

To benefit fully from reading original reports of research in experimental psychology, it's useful to have a background in statistics, methodology, and report writing. To help readers without such backgrounds, the last section of this introduction provides very brief sketches of those topics in "A Primer on Methodology, Statistics, and Research Reports."

The readings themselves are compiled in ten chapters, arranged into four parts. To oversimplify somewhat, three of the four parts can be described as dealing with the acquisition, storage, and manipulation of knowledge. The fourth deals with cognitive phenomena that are familiar in everyday life and with differences in cognition among people.

Part I, Acquisition of Knowledge, consists of three chapters. Chapter One (Sensory Register and Attention) deals with the earliest stages of information intake. These early stages happen so quickly, effortlessly, and naturally that they often appear to be automatic. But what exactly does it mean for something to be automatic? Automaticity is a somewhat complicated issue and is also covered in the first chapter. The readings in Chapter Two (Visual Perception) cover various aspects of how we recognize (attach meaning to) visual information. Midway through Chapter One, and certainly by the end of Chapter Two, it should become clear that the simple view of an orderly sequence of cognitive stages implied by the descriptive phrase *information intake* is inadequate for describing the processes that enable people to attend to and perceive the world around them. One of the lessons of the first two chapters is that people are not passive receivers of information but are instead active seekers and interpreters of information. Chapter Three (Episodic Memories) focuses on how people retain information about their experiences.

Part II, Representation of Knowledge, consists of three chapters. The readings in Chapter Four (Organization and Priming of Knowledge) report on studies aimed at understanding how knowledge is mentally organized and at illuminating the processes involved in retrieving specific pieces of knowledge. Because categorizing is such a basic and central aspect of cognition, most of Chapter Five (Concepts and Imagery) is devoted to the mental representation of categories. Chapter Five also includes a reading on the representation of visual and spatial information.

Part III, Higher-Order Processing of Knowledge, covers several of our more advanced cognitive abilities. Language is such an integral part of our mental life that we rarely note its complexity. Often, it's only when learning a new language that we realize that every language consists of a largely arbitrary set of sounds and words and a large number of difficult-to-state grammatical rules (each with a long list of apparent exceptions). Chapter Six (Language and Comprehension) deals with a selection of issues involved in using language, from the storage and retrieval of words to the comprehension of sentences, plus a discussion of what brain damage can tell us about language. Chapters Seven and Eight deal with several topics often referred to collectively as thinking. A theme that runs through the readings in Chapter Seven (Reasoning and Judgment) is that people's thinking does not correspond in any simple fashion to the various logical or statistical systems given in logic and statistics textbooks. But there is some systematicity to what we do, and psychologists have made progress in characterizing those processes. The readings in Chapter Eight (Problem Solving) are less easy to capture in a straightforward theme, but in one way or another they both touch upon the observation that the manner in which we think about a problem, or how we represent it to ourselves, plays a large role in whether we can solve it successfully.

Finally, the two chapters in Part IV, Everyday Cognitive Experiences, cover cognitive phenomena whose direct relations to everyday life are probably easily apparent. The readings in Chapter Nine (Everyday Memory and Judgment) report findings about situations people frequently encounter outside the laboratory that call for memory or judgment. In Chapter Ten (Group and Individual Differences in Cognition) the focus shifts away from descriptions of general principles of human cognition and toward describing and explaining differences in cognition among people.

A PRIMER ON METHODOLOGY, STATISTICS, AND RESEARCH REPORTS

The sketches provided here are very brief and simplified. For more detailed discussion, consult any of numerous books devoted to each of these topics.

Methodology

The typical cognitive psychology experiment begins with a hypothesis, a general statement about the relationship between two or more variables. The hypothesis is used to generate a prediction that, when subjects are given a particular task, manipulating one variable (called the independent variable) will affect subjects' behavior on another variable (called the dependent variable) in a way that can be measured.

For example, we may hypothesize that repeating a random sequence of numbers or letters helps us remember that sequence over short periods of time. The hypothesis makes a general statement about memorability and its relationship to repetition. From this we can generate a prediction that when subjects are asked to remember a phone number for two minutes (the subject's task), whether the subject is allowed to repeat the sequence silently during the two minutes (the independent variable) will affect the number of errors the subject makes in remembering the sequence at the end of the period (the dependent variable). So we design an experiment in which some subjects are allowed to repeat the phone number during the two-minute retention period and other subjects are prevented from doing so; then we measure subjects' accuracy in reporting the phone number. If the number of errors committed by the subjects who repeated the numbers is smaller than the number of errors committed by subjects prevented from doing so, then the prediction is correct and we say that the hypothesis was supported. If the number of errors in the two groups is the same, then the prediction is wrong and we reject the hypothesis.

Where does the hypothesis come from? Usually, a hypothesis is derived from a larger theory—in this case, a theory about memory and the factors that contribute to remembering a random sequence. Sometimes, hypotheses come from observations of the world. This latter possibility is the reason you may sometimes hear the charge (often from your grandmother) that psychologists only test things we know from common sense. The problem is that common sense is typically very vague about exactly which variables are related and in what way. Considering a few old aphorisms should make the problem with common sense clearer: "out of sight, out of mind" but "absence makes the heart grow fonder"; or "birds of a feather flock together" but "opposites attract." Testing hypotheses derived from observations is a way of systematizing our common-sense knowledge.

What makes a good test of a hypothesis? A good test is one in which the only variable that distinguishes the two groups is the independent variable identified by the prediction, because that increases the likelihood that, if a difference in behavior is found, the difference exists for the reason specified by the hypothesis (we can interpret the difference). If the subjects in the number repetition group all happened to be telephone operators whereas those in the other group were not, you'd worry about whether it was repetition or expertise that was responsible for their superior performance. A good test is also one that has reasonably wide generalizability to other situations. If all the subjects in both groups were telephone operators, the cause of the *difference* between the groups may be repetition, but it's highly questionable whether the same relationship between repetition and memorability would hold among non–telephone operators. On the other hand, because repeating telephone numbers to ourselves is a pretty common everyday occurrence, using telephone numbers as the stimuli and having subjects repeat them silently to themselves as the task is quite reasonable. However, sometimes, to ensure interpretability, experiments require that we use quite unnatural conditions (such as being in a soundproof room) or quite unnatural tasks (such as trying to make out letters that appear for a fraction of a second). There is often tension between making sure that results are obtained for the reasons we believe and making sure that the results obtained tell us something about the real world.

The kinds of experimental tasks and measures and the nonexperimental methods that cognitive psychologists use are too numerous to mention here. See Bower and Clapper (1989), Ericsson and Oliver (1988), Kintsch, Miller, and Polson (1984), and Massaro (1989) for fuller descriptions of cognitive psychology methodologies. Here is a description of a few of the kinds of measures that cognitive psychologists take.

We've already mentioned one kind of measure: number of errors. We give people a task and see what variables affect their accuracy. With some tasks, however, such as reading individual letters, subjects (at least, literate adults) typically make very few errors. In such cases, it's more useful to measure how long it takes people to do the task, a measure called reaction time. Reaction time frequently allows more sophisticated analyses of task performance but requires more sophisticated, and perhaps less natural, techniques than error measurements do. Also, notice that errors and reaction time are related: if subjects are simply told to react as fast as they can without concern for accuracy, they may ignore the task completely. Thus it's important when measuring reaction time that subjects' accuracy be high, so that you can be sure that they are actually doing the task you've set for them.

At the opposite end of the spectrum from tasks for which reaction time measures are useful are tasks for which verbal reports are useful. Whereas we have very little awareness of how we read individual letters—a task for which reaction time measures are well suited and verbal reports are useless—we have considerable awareness of how we go about solving reasoning problems, a task for which reaction times will vary wildly from trial to trial and are therefore difficult to use, but for which verbal reports are quite rich and useful. One thing to remember about verbal reports, however, is that they are essentially an introspective measure. With verbal reports, subjects tell us what they think, perhaps as they actually solve a problem, but it is unclear how accurate introspective reports are. Such reports need to be examined carefully and confirmed with other methods. However, the techniques for using verbal reports are often quite natural and easy to implement (although analyzing such reports can be very difficult).

Statistics

The statistics you'll encounter in these articles are of two basic types: descriptive and inferential. Descriptive statistics help summarize and make sense of sets of numbers. An average is a kind of descriptive statistic; it helps summarize a set of numbers by giving us a measure of what's called the central tendency of those numbers. The most familiar kind of average is called a mean; you add up all the numbers you're trying to summarize and divide by the number of numbers you added. The mean is symbolized in different articles as M or $\overline{X}$ (or on rare occasions, μ). Under different circumstances, different measures of central tendency are appropriate; you are likely to encounter not only the mean but also the median (the score above which half the results fall) and the mode (the most frequent score or answer).

Other common descriptive statistics measure the extent to which two sets of numbers vary with one another, called their correlation, or the amount of variability in a set of numbers. Just as different circumstances call for different measures of central tendency, different circumstances call for different measures of correlation. Most that you will encounter have the word *correlation* in their names and are symbolized as r; occasionally, however, you may find a reference to rho or Kendall's tau (symbolized τ). You'll encounter measures of variability like variance (symbolized as σ^2 or s^2) and standard deviation (σ or SD); both are measures of the extent to which scores tend to spread around the mean.

Inferential statistics help us decide when inferences to other situations are warranted by our results. Almost always, the inference we want to make is that two groups, or a set of groups, in an experiment are reliably different; the phrase usually used is that the difference is statistically significant.[2] A reliable difference is usually taken to be one for which there is likely to be a systematic reason. It is also a difference that you would be likely to find again if you were to repeat the same experiment with other subjects of the same kind. However, you need to bear in mind several important cautions here.

First, to say that there is likely to be a systematic reason does *not* guarantee that that reason is the one you think it is. For example, you might have subjects in one group memorize a list of words using technique A and those in a second group memorize the same list using technique B. If you find a statistically significant difference in the groups' performances, that does not necessarily mean it's because of the different techniques that were used. If the subjects in one group were familiar with all the words in the list and the subjects in the other group were not, then subjects in the first group will prob-

---

[2]Because the inferential statistics most commonly encountered in research on cognitive psychology are those that test whether differences are statistically significant, I'll discuss only those. However, the points and cautions described hold for statistics that test the significance of correlations and other cases as well.

ably perform better than those in the second regardless of the memorization technique used.

Second, the generalization that a statistically significant difference allows is technically very narrow. It implies that you'll find the difference with other subjects of the same kind in the same experiment. Statistics do not tell us how literally to take the terms *subjects of the same kind* and *same experiment*. For example, in most cognitive psychology experiments, subjects' shoe sizes do not matter, so we could probably generalize to other subjects that are like the original subjects in all respects except shoe size. Unfortunately, many subject characteristics such as age and sex fall into the category of "maybe mattering, and maybe not." The same problem holds with experiments. Does the time of day that the experiment was conducted matter? Must the stimuli be *exactly* the same? In most cases, the extent to which it is safe to generalize is a matter of judgment that depends on the particulars of the subjects and the experiment. For this reason, it is important that experimenters describe their subjects, materials, and procedure in rich detail. That way, the reader can decide for herself or himself what generalizations are reasonable.

Third, that a difference is statistically significant does *not* guarantee that it is important. In the memorization example, we could find a statistically significant difference with average scores in the two groups of 95.3 and 95.1 out of 100 if variability within each group were very low and the groups were very large, but rarely is a difference that small of any importance. Still, we can be reasonably sure that it is likely to hold up with other subjects of the same kind, and thus is said to be statistically significant. Whenever the word *significant* is used in an article, it is used in this sense, not the sense of importance.

Finally, notice that I consistently used the word *likely*. Statistics do not tell you whether groups are truly different. Statistics tell you how likely it would be for groups that are the same to have results that differ by as much as was observed. The problem is that random, irrelevant events can sometimes cause small differences in performance or behavior that lead to differences in results that aren't systematic in any way. For example, suppose you have three dogs that you teach to bark in unison and you measure how loud their unison bark is at the same time of day over several days. Even though you use the same three dogs and try to keep extraneous factors constant, the loudness of their unison bark will vary slightly from day to day. So we know that even without any systematic factors operating, results can differ, although they ought not differ by too much. Statistics allow us to estimate the probability that a particular difference would be observed if the groups were in fact the same.

A significant difference is one that is *not* likely to be found if the groups are in fact the same, and so it is safe to conclude that the groups are probably different, perhaps because of differences in subject characteristics or the different tasks or stimuli the groups were given.[3] How unlikely does it have to be that the groups are the same to safely conclude that the groups are likely to be different? The usual rule of thumb is that the statistic used should indicate that groups that are the same would differ by the observed amount fewer than 5 times out of 100. This is usually reported as "significant at the .05 level," or as $p < .05$ (where p stands for probability); $p < .01$ means that fewer than 1 time out of 100 would groups that were the same have results that differ this much.

Inferential statistics that you are likely to encounter, depending on the circumstances, include t-tests of various sorts, analysis of variance (ANOVA, sometimes called the F-test), sign and Kruskal–Wallis tests, and chi-square.

How to Read an Article Reporting an Experiment

You'll probably find it easier to understand the articles in this book (or any psychology article) if you're familiar with the different sections of an experimental report and the function of each. Most experimental reports in cognitive psychology adhere to the style specified by the American Psychological Association (APA) (American Psychological Association, 1983). Because the structure of articles is not completely rigid, the comments that follow may not apply to every article you encounter, but they provide good rules of thumb for getting the most from your reading of research articles.

The first section in the body of a paper is the introduction. The introduction lays out the issue under investigation and gives you some background: What theories have been or are being proposed? What evidence is available? What question remains to be answered? How can one go about addressing that question? What do the theories and evidence previously reported lead us to expect if we do that? In some cases, it's difficult to know what results can be expected on the basis of previous work. In that case, the introduction should explain what different results would mean. By the end of the introduction, you should have a pretty good idea about (1) the background on the problem; (2) the research question; (3) the general shape of the experiment to be reported, such as what kinds of subjects will be used or what variables are to be manipulated; (4) what results are expected; and (5) how those results would fit (or not fit) with and expand upon previous findings and theories. If any of these issues is not clear to you, take the time to review the introduction; otherwise, the rest of the report is not likely to make much sense to you.

---

[3]The technically correct manner of stating this is likely to strike nonstatisticians as double-talk, which I've tried to avoid. However, for the compulsive, this should be stated as "and so it is safe to reject the hypothesis that the groups do not differ."

The method section comes next. It specifies the subjects, materials, and procedures used in the experiment. By the end of the method section, you should be clear on who the subjects were. If the subjects were divided into groups, you should know how many groups there were and the basis for the groupings—such as ages or backgrounds of the subjects, or the kinds of tasks they were given. You should know what stimuli the subjects received, what the subjects were supposed to do, and the conditions under which they did them. In general, you should be able to imagine for yourself what it must have been like to actually carry out or be in the experiment. If you can't, it may be difficult to understand the results or discussion sections.

The results section follows the method section. You should make sure that you understand what was and was not found. Which variables had an effect and which did not? What was the pattern of results across the different kinds of subjects, different kinds of stimuli, or different kinds of tasks? Did the results turn out as expected? If not, in what way did they differ from the predictions? Carefully examine any tables and figures that are present. Read their titles, captions, and all labels and headings. These steps will help clarify your understanding of the research question and of the conclusions.

The final section is the discussion or conclusion. This section should relate the results actually obtained to the issues raised in the introduction. From the discussion, you should learn the answer to the research question that was posed, the implications of that finding for previous thinking about the problem being investigated, the limits or qualifications of those implications, and what can and cannot be concluded about the problem being investigated.

Remember that when you read the discussion section, what you are reading is the author or authors' interpretation of the results. Judge for yourself the persuasiveness of that interpretation. Keep in mind exactly what the results were. Think about how those results were obtained. Review what others have found or concluded. There are always more questions to be asked and investigated. Perhaps after reading some of these articles, you'll want to ask and test some of your own.

REFERENCES

American Psychological Association. (1983). *Publication manual of the American Psychological Association* (3rd ed.). Washington, DC: American Psychological Association.

Bower, G. H., & Clapper, J. P. (1989). Experimental methods in cognitive science. In M. I. Posner (Ed.), *Foundations of cognitive science* (pp. 245–300). Cambridge, MA: MIT Press.

Bruner, J. S. (1983). *In search of mind: Essays in autobiography.* New York: Harper & Row.

Churchland, P. M. (1988). *Matter and consciousness: A contemporary introduction to the philosophy of mind* (revised ed.). Cambridge, MA: MIT Press.

Ericsson, K. A., & Oliver, W. L (1988). Methodology for laboratory research on thinking: Task selection, collection of observations, and data analysis. In R. J. Sternberg & E. E. Smith (Eds.), *The psychology of human thought* (pp. 392–428). New York: Cambridge University Press.

Gardner, H. (1985). *The mind's new science: A history of the cognitive revolution.* New York: Basic Books.

Kintsch, W., Miller, J. R., & Polson, P. G. (Eds.) (1984). *Method and tactics in cognitive science.* Hillsdale, NJ: Erlbaum.

Lachman, R., Lachman, J. L., & Butterfield, E. C. (1979). *Cognitive psychology and information processing: An introduction.* Hillsdale, NJ: Erlbaum.

Massaro, D. W. (1989). *Experimental psychology: An information processing approach.* San Diego: Harcourt Brace Jovanovich.

Part I

The Acquisition of Knowledge

The three chapters in this first part deal with several of the basic cognitive structures and processes involved in acquiring and retaining information.

Chapter One (Sensory Register and Attention) focuses on how people take in information. Reading 1 deals with the sensory register, which (by hypothesis) is the cognitive structure that enables us to retain very briefly a rich (but uninterpreted) representation of visually presented information. Subsequent retention and interpretation of this information requires the application of attentional and other cognitive processes. Early work on attention (Readings 2 and 3) assumed that people are bombarded with information and that the function of attentional processes is to selectively allow only some of that information in the sensory register to proceed through the cognitive system. Later work (Reading 4) has assumed that people must actively pull information into the system and that our efficiency at doing so under particular circumstances depends on our prior experience with such circumstances. Note that in this latter perspective, it would be wrong to say that taking in information is the *first* step in a linear sequence of cognitive processes. Instead, the sequence of cognitive processes is more like a cycle, in which new information affects existing knowledge and existing knowledge affects the intake of new information (Neisser, 1976). This latter view—in which people are regarded as active seekers of information, whose existing knowledge affects the processing of that information—is echoed in many of the other readings in this volume.

Chapter Two (Visual Perception) focuses on the processes involved in visual recognition. Reading 5 explores the word-superiority effect, a phenomenon that poses problems for any view of people as passive recipients of information. Reading 6 presents a model that explains the word-superiority effect by describing one way in which existing knowledge might affect the process of pattern recognition. Reading 7 examines our recognition of movement.

The readings in Chapter Three (Episodic Memories) deal with what typically are called episodic memories (Tulving, 1972). Episodic memories are of "unique, concrete, personal, temporally dated events" (Tulving, 1986, p. 307). Thus, to remember that a particular list of words is relevant for a particular experiment or that you had quiche for lunch yesterday is to have an episodic memory.[1] Experiments have tested how we search (Reading 8), store, and retrieve (Readings 9, 10, and 11) episodic memories.

REFERENCES

McKoon, G., Ratcliff, R., & Dell, G. S. (1986). A critical evaluation of the semantic-episodic distinction. *Journal of Experimental Psychology: Learning, Memory, and Cognition, 12,* 295–306.

Neisser, U. (1976). *Cognition and reality.* San Francisco: W. H. Freeman.

Schacter, D. L. (1990). Memory. In M. I. Posner (Ed.), *Foundations of cognitive science* (pp. 683–725). Cambridge, MA: MIT Press.

Tulving, E. (1972). Episodic and semantic memory. In E. Tulving & W. Donaldson (Eds.), *Organization of memory* (pp. 381–403). New York: Academic Press.

Tulving, E. (1986). What kind of a hypothesis is the distinction between episodic and semantic memory? *Journal of Experimental Psychology: Learning, Memory, and Cognition, 12,* 307–311.

---

[1]The astute reader may notice that I describe here episodic *memories* without committing myself to the claim that episodic memories reside in a separate (that is, episodic) memory *system* or structure. Whether it is useful to talk about distinct memory systems is an area of lively debate (compare with McKoon, Ratcliff, & Dell, 1986; Schacter, 1990; Tulving, 1986).

CHAPTER ONE
Sensory Register and Attention

INTRODUCTION

Atkinson and Shiffrin (1968, 1971) presented a general theoretical framework integrating much of what was known at that time about how people acquire and retain information. Their theory—long one of the most influential in the field—proposed that human memory consists of three distinct structures: a sensory register, a short-term store (STS), and a long-term store (LTS). Evidence for a sensory register came from studies such as those reported in George Sperling's article, "The Information Available in Brief Visual Presentations."

This classic paper retains interest for a variety of reasons. First, it is an elegant argument for the existence of a very short-term visual register (dubbed "iconic memory" by Neisser, 1967), distinct from a general short-term store. Second, this paper is an example of how an objective method can be developed for confirming and exploring a phenomenon that we initially become aware of through introspection—in this case, the introspective experience that more information is available during a brief visual presentation than can usually be reported. Finally, this article describes a method, the method of partial report, that clearly demonstrates the wide applicability of a principle critical to the entire experimental method: estimating properties of a whole from properties of random samples of that whole.

Sperling used an instrument called a tachistoscope to present his stimuli to subjects. A tachistoscope has two or more fields, each of which holds a different display that can be illuminated and thus become visible for controlled periods. The first field to be illuminated typically displays a small dot or cross to indicate where the subject should focus his or her eyes (called the fixation point). The field with the fixation point is then darkened, and the field with the second display, the stimulus, is made visible. The presentation of the stimulus is terminated after a predetermined amount of time. It is also possible, although Sperling does not use the tachistoscope in this fashion, to have the tachistoscope terminate the stimulus and present other displays after the subject responds in some manner.

Several of Sperling's experiments and much of his technical discussion have been excluded from this selection. As you read this article, ask yourself what kind of general characterization can be made of the kinds of information that are and are not available in the visual register.

The Information Available in Brief Visual Presentations

George Sperling
Harvard University

How much can be seen in a single brief exposure? This is an important problem because our normal mode of seeing greatly resembles a sequence of brief exposures. Erdmann and Dodge (1898) showed that in reading, for example, the eye assimilates information only in the brief pauses between its quick saccadic movements. The problem of what can be seen in one brief exposure, however, remains unsolved. The difficulty is that the simple expedient of instructing the observer of a single brief exposure to report what he has just seen is inadequate. When complex stimuli consisting of a number of letters are tachistoscopically presented, observers enigmatically insist that they have seen more than they can remember afterwards, that is, report afterwards.[1] The apparently simple question: "What did you see?" requires the observer to report both what he remembers and what he has forgotten.

The statement that *more is seen than can be remembered* implies two things. First, it implies a memory limit, that is, a limit on the (memory) report. Such a limit on the number of items which can be given in the report following any brief stimulation has, in fact, been generally observed; it is called the span of attention, apprehension, or immediate-memory (cf. Miller, 1956b). Second, *to see more than is remembered* implies that more information is available during, and perhaps for a short time after, the stimulus than can be reported. . . .

In order to circumvent the memory limitation in determining the information that becomes available following a brief exposure, it is obvious that the observer must not be required to give a report which exceeds his memory span. If the number of letters in the stimulus exceeds his memory span, then he cannot give a whole report of all the letters. Therefore, the observer must be required to give only a partial report of the stimulus contents. Partial reporting of available information is, of course, just what is required by ordinary schoolroom examinations and by other methods of sampling available information.

An examiner can determine, even in a short test, approximately how much the student knows. The length of the test is not so important as that the student not be told the test questions too far in advance. Similarly, an observer may be "tested" on what he has seen in a brief exposure of a complex visual stimulus. Such a test requires only a partial report. The specific instruction which indicates which part of the stimulus is to be reported is then given only after termination of the stimulus. On each trial the instruction, which calls for a specified part of the stimulus, is randomly chosen from a set of possible

This paper is a condensation of a doctoral thesis (Sperling, 1959). For further details, especially on methodology, and for individual data, the reader is referred to the original thesis. It is a pleasure to acknowledge my gratitude to George A. Miller and Roger N. Shepard whose support made this research possible and to E. B. Newman, J. Schwartzbaum and S. S. Stevens for their many helpful suggestions. Thanks are also due to Jerome S. Bruner for the use of his laboratory and his tachistoscope during his absence in the summer of 1957. This research was carried out under Contract AF 33 (038)–14343 between Harvard University and the Operational Applications Laboratory, Air Force Cambridge Research Center, Air Research Development Command.

[Author] now at Bell Telephone Laboratories, Murray Hill, New Jersey.

[1]Some representative examples are: Bridgin (1933), Cattell (1883), Chapman (1930), Dallenbach (1920), Erdmann and Dodge (1898), Glanville and Dallenbach (1929), Külpe (1904), Schumann (1922), Wagner (1918), Whipple (1914), Wilcocks (1925), Woodworth (1938).

SOURCE: *Psychological Monographs, 74*(11, Whole No. 498), 1960. Copyright 1960 by the American Psychological Association. Reprinted by permission of the author.

instructions which cover the whole stimulus. By repeating the interrogation (sampling) procedure many times, many different random samples can be obtained of an observer's performance on each of the various parts of the stimulus. The data obtained thereby make feasible the estimate of the total information that was available to the observer from which to draw his report on the average trial.

The time at which the instruction is given determines the time at which available information is sampled. By suitable coding, the instruction may be given at any time: before, during, or after the stimulus presentation. Not only the available information immediately following the termination of the stimulus, but a continuous function relating the amount of information available to the time of instruction may be obtained by such a procedure.

Many studies have been conducted in which observers were required to give partial reports, that is, to report only on one aspect or one location of the stimulus. In prior experiments, however, the instructions were often not randomly chosen, and the set of possible instructions did not systematically cover the stimulus. The notions of testing or sampling were not applied.[2] It is not surprising, therefore, that estimates have not been made of the total information available to the observer following a brief exposure of a complex stimulus. Furthermore, instructions have generally not been coded in such a way as to make it possible to control the precise time at which they were presented. Consequently, the temporal course of available information could not have been quantitatively studied. In the absence of precise data, experimenters have all too frequently assumed that the time for which information is available to the observer corresponds exactly to the physical stimulus duration. Wundt (1899) understood this problem and convincingly argued that, for extremely short stimulus durations, the assumption that stimulus duration corresponded to the duration for which stimulus

information was available was blatantly false, but he made no measurements of available information.

The following experiments were conducted to study quantitatively the information that becomes available to an observer following a brief exposure. Lettered stimuli were chosen because these contain a relatively large amount of information per item and because these are the kind of stimuli that have been used by most previous investigators. The first two experiments are essentially control experiments; they attempt to confirm that immediate-memory for letters is independent of the parameters of stimulation, that it is an individual characteristic. In the third experiment the number of letters available immediately after the extinction of the stimulus is determined by means of the sampling (partial report) procedure described above. The fourth experiment explores decay of available information with time. The fifth experiment examines some exposure parameters. In the sixth experiment a technique which fails to demonstrate a large amount of available information is investigated. The seventh experiment deals with the role of the historically important variable: order of report.

GENERAL METHOD

Apparatus. The experiments utilized a Gerbrands tachistoscope.[3] This is a two-field, mirror tachistoscope (Dodge, 1907b), with a mechanical timer. Viewing is binocular, at a distance of about 24 inches. Throughout the experiment, a dimly illuminated fixation field was always present.

The light source in the Gerbrands tachistoscope is a 4-watt fluorescent (daylight) bulb. Two such lamps operated in parallel light each field. The operation of the lamps is controlled by the microswitches, the steady-state light output of the lamp being directly proportional to the current. However, the phosphors used in coating the lamp continue to emit light for some time after the cessation of the current. This afterglow in the lamp follows an exponential decay function consisting of two parts: the first, a blue component, which accounts for about 40% of the en-

---

[2]The experiments referred to are (cf. Sperling, 1959): Külpe (1904), Wilcocks (1925), Chapman (1932), Long, Henneman, and Reid (1953), Long and Lee (1953a), Long and Lee (1953b), Long, Reid, and Garvey (1954), Lawrence and Coles (1954), Adams (1955), Lawrence and Laberge (1956), Broadbent (1957a).

[3]Ralph Gerbrands Company, 96 Ronald Road, Arlington 74, Massachusetts.

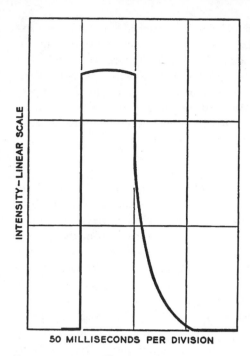

FIGURE 1   A 50-millisecond light flash, such as was used in most of the experiments. (Redrawn from a photograph of an oscilloscope trace)

ergy, decays with a time constant which is a small fraction of a millisecond; the decay constant of the second, yellow, component was about 15 msec. in the lamp tested. Figure 1 illustrates a 50-msec. light impulse on a linear intensity scale. The exposure time of 50 msec. was used in all experiments unless exposure time was itself a parameter. Preliminary experiments indicated that, with the presentations used, exposure duration was an unimportant parameter. Fifty msec. was sufficiently short so that eye movements during the exposure were rare, and it could conveniently be set with accuracy.

Stimulus materials.   The stimuli used in this experiment were lettered 5 × 8 cards viewed at a distance of 22 inches. The lettering was done with a Leroy No. 5 pen, producing capital letters about 0.45 inch high. Only the 21 consonants were used, to minimize the possibility of Ss interpreting the arrays as words. In a few sets of cards the letter Y was also omitted. In all, over 500 different stimulus cards were used.

There was very little learning of the stimulus materials either by the Ss or by the E. The only learning that was readily apparent was on several stimuli that had especially striking letter combinations. Except for the stimuli used for training, no S ever was required to report the same part of any stimulus more than two or three times, and never in the same session.

Figure 2 illustrates some typical arrays of letters. These arrays may be divided into several categories: (*a*) stimuli with 3, 4, 5, 6, or 7 letters normally spaced on a single line; (*b*) stimuli with six letters closely spaced on a single line (6-massed); (*c*) stimuli having two rows of letters with three letters in each row (3/3), or two rows of four letters each (4/4); (*d*) stimuli having three rows of letters with three letters in each row (3/3/3). . . .

R N F	K L B
	Y N X
X V N K H	X M R J
	P N K P
L Q D K K J	T D R
	S R N
	F Z R
Z Y V V F F	7 I V F
	X L 5 3
	B 4 W 7

FIGURE 2   Typical stimulus materials. Col. 1: 3, 5, 6, 6-massed. Col. 2: 3/3, 4/4, 3/3/3, 4/4/4 L&N.

In addition to stimuli that contained only letters, some stimuli that contained both letters and numbers were used. These had eight (4/4 L&N . . .) and twelve symbols (4/4/4 L&N . . .) respectively, four in each row. Each row had two letters and two numbers—the positions being randomly chosen. The S was always given a sample stimulus before L&N stimuli were used and told of the constraint above. He was also told that O when it occurred was the number "zero" and was not considered a letter. . . .

Subjects.   The nature of the experiments made it more economical to use small numbers of trained *Ss* rather than several large groups of untrained *Ss*. Four of the five *Ss* in the experiment were obtained through the student employment service. The fifth *S* (RNS) was a member of the faculty who was interested in the research. Twelve sessions were regularly scheduled for each *S*, three times weekly.

Instructions and trial procedures.   *S* was instructed to look at the fixation cross until it was clearly in focus; then he pressed a button which initiated the presentation after a 0.5-sec. delay. This procedure constituted an approximate behavioral criterion of the degree of dark adaptation prior to the exposure, namely, the ability to focus on the dimly illuminated fixation cross.

Responses were recorded on a specially prepared response grid. A response grid appropriate to each stimulus was supplied. The response grid was placed on the table immediately below the tachistoscope, the room illumination being sufficient to write by. The *Ss* were instructed to fill in all the required squares on the response grid and to guess when they were not certain. The *Ss* were not permitted to fill in consecutive X's, but were required to guess "different letters." After a response, *S* slid the paper forward under a cover which covered his last response, leaving the next part of the response grid fully in view.

Series of 5 to 20 trials were grouped together without a change in conditions. Whenever conditions or stimulus types were changed, *S* was given two or three sample presentations with the new conditions or stimuli. Within a sequence of trials, *S* set his own rate of responding. The *Ss* (except ND) preferred rapid rates. In some conditions, the limiting rate was set by the *E*'s limitations in changing stimuli and instruction tones. This was about three to four stimuli per minute.

Each of the first four and last two sessions began with and/or ended with a simple task: the reporting of all the letters in stimuli of 3, 4, 5, and 6 letters. This procedure was undertaken in addition to the usual

runs with these stimuli to determine if there were appreciable learning effects in these tasks during the course of the experiment and if there was an accuracy decrement (fatigue) within individual sessions. Very little improvement was noted after the second session. This observation agrees with previous reports (Whipple, 1914). There was little difference between the beginning and end of sessions.

Scoring and tabulation of results.   Every report of all *Ss* was scored both for total number of letters in the report which agreed with letters in the stimulus and for the number of letters reported in their correct positions. Since none of the procedures of the experiments had an effect on either of these scores independently of the other, only the second of these, *letters in the correct position*, is tabulated in the results. This score, which takes position into account, is less subject to guessing error,[4] and in some cases it is more readily interpreted than a score which does not take position into account. As the maximum correction for guessing would be about 0.4 letter for the 4/4/4 (12-letter) material—and considerably less for all other materials—no such correction is made in the treatment of the data. In general, data were not tabulated more accurately than 0.1 letter.

Data from the first and second sessions were not used if they fell below an *S*'s average performance on these tasks in subsequent sessions. This occurred for reports of five and of eight (4/4) letters for some *Ss*. A similar criterion applied in later sessions for tasks that were initiated later. In this case, the results of the first "training" session(s) are not incorporated in the total tabulation if they lie more than 0.5 letter from *S*'s average in subsequent sessions.

---

[4]If there are a large number of letters in the stimulus, the probability that these same letters will appear somewhere on the response grid, irrespective of position, becomes very high whether or not *S* has much information about the stimulus. In the limit, the correspondence approaches 100% provided only that the relative frequency of each letter in the response matches its relative frequency of occurrence in the stimulus pack. If the response is scored for both letter *and* position, then the percent guessing correction is independent of changes in stimulus size.

EXPERIMENT 1: IMMEDIATE-MEMORY

When an *S* is required to give a complete (whole) report of all the letters on a briefly exposed stimulus, he will generally not report all the letters correctly. The average number of letters which he does report correctly is usually called his *immediate-memory span* or *span of apprehension for that particular stimulus material under the stated observation conditions.* An expression such as immediate-memory span (Miller, 1956a) implies that the number of items reported by *S* remains invariant with changes in stimulating conditions. The present experiment seeks to determine to what extent the span of immediate-memory is independent of the number and spatial arrangement of letters, and of letters and numbers on stimulus cards. If this independence is demonstrated, then the qualification "for that particular stimulus material" may be dropped from the term immediate-memory span when it is used in these experiments.

Procedure.   *S*s were instructed to write all the letters in the stimulus, guessing when they were not certain. All 12 types of stimulus materials were used. At least 15 trials were conducted with each kind of stimulus with each *S*. Each *S* was given at least 50 trials with the 3/3 (6-letter) stimuli which had yielded the highest memory span in preliminary experiments. The final run made with any kind of stimulus was always a test of immediate-memory. This procedure insured that *S*s were tested for memory when they were maximally experienced with a stimulus.

Results.   The lower curves in Figure 3 represent the average number of letters correctly reported by each *S* for each material.[5] The most striking result is that immediate-memory is constant for each *S*, being nearly independent of the kind of stimulus used. The immediate-memory span for individual *S*s ranges from approximately 3.8 for JC to approximately 5.2 for NJ with an average immediate-memory span for all *S*s of about 4.3 letters. (The upper curves are discussed later.)

---

[5] See Sperling (1959) for tables giving the numerical values of all points appearing in this and in all other figures.

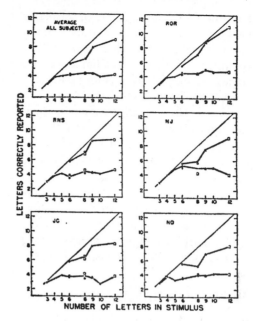

FIGURE 3   "Channel capacity curves." Immediate-memory and letters available (output information) as functions of the number of stimulus letters (input information). Lower curves = immediate-memory (Exp. 1); upper curves = letters available immediately after termination of the stimulus; diagonal lines = maximum possible score (i.e., input = output). Code: × = letters on one line; + = 6-massed; o = 3/3, 4/4, 5/5; △ = 3/3/3, □ = 4/4 L&N, 4/4/4 L&N.

The constancy which is characteristic of individual immediate-memory curves of Figure 3 also appears in the average curve for all *S*s. For example, three kinds of stimuli were used that had six letters each: six letters normally spaced on one line, 6-massed, and 3/3-letters (see Figure 2). When the data for all *S*s are pooled, the scores for each of these three types of materials are practically the same: the range is 4.1–4.3 letters. The same constancy holds for stimuli containing eight symbols. The average number of letters correctly reported for each of the two different kinds of eight letter stimuli, 4/4, 4/4 L&N, is nearly the same: 4.4, 4.3, respectively.

Most *S*s felt that stimuli containing both letters and numbers were more difficult than those containing letters only. Nevertheless, only NJ showed an objective deficit for the mixed material.

In conclusion, the average number of correct letters contained in an S's whole report of the stimulus is approximately equal to the smaller of (a) the number of letters in the stimulus or (b) a numerical constant—the span of immediate-memory—which is different for each S. The use of the term immediate-memory span is therefore justified within the range of materials studied. This limit on the number of letters that can be correctly reported is an individual characteristic, but it is relatively similar for each of the five Ss of the study. . . .

[In Experiment 1, Sperling presents the stimuli for .05 sec (500 msec.). In Experiment 2, he shows that the number of letters that subjects report correctly does not change with exposure durations ranging from .015 to .5 secs (150 to 500 msecs.).]

EXPERIMENT 3: PARTIAL REPORT

Experiments 1 and 2 have demonstrated the span of immediate-memory as an invariant characteristic of each S. In Experiment 3 the principles of testing in a perceptual situation that were advanced in the introduction are applied in order to determine whether S has more information available than he can indicate in his limited immediate-memory report.

The S is presented with the stimulus as before, but he is required only to make a partial report. The length of this report is four letters or less, so as to lie within S's immediate-memory span. The instruction that indicates which row of the stimulus is to be reported is coded in the form of a tone. The instruction tone is given after the visual presentation. The S does not know until he hears the tone which row is called for. This is therefore a procedure which samples the information that S has available after the termination of the visual stimulus .

Procedure.   Initially, stimulus materials having only two lines were used, that is, 3/3 and 4/4. The S was told that a tone would be sounded, that this tone would come approximately simultaneously with the exposure, and that it would be either a high tone (2500 cps) or a low tone (250 cps). If it were a high tone, he was to write only the upper row of the stimulus; if a low tone, only the lower row. He was then shown a sample card of 3/3 letters and given several high and low tones. It was suggested that he keep his eyes fixated on the fixation point and be equally prepared for either tone. It would not be possible to out-guess the E who would be using a random sequence of tones.

The tone duration was approximately 0.5 sec. The onset of the tone was controlled through the same microswitch that controlled the off-go of the light, with the completion of a connection from an audio-oscillator to the speaker. Intensity of the tone was adjusted so that the high (louder) tone was "loud but not uncomfortable."

In each of the first two sessions, each S received 30 training trials with each of the materials 3/3, 4/4. In subsequent sessions Ss were given series of 10 or more "test" trials. Later, a third, middle (650 cps) tone was introduced to correspond to the middle row of the 3/3/3 and 4/4/4 stimuli. The instructions and procedure were essentially the same as before.

In any given session, each tone might not occur with equal frequency for each type of stimulus. Over several sessions, usually two, this unequal frequency was balanced out so that an S had an exactly equal number of high, medium, and low tones for each material. If an S "misinterpreted" the tone and wrote the wrong row, he was asked to write what he could remember of the correct row. Only those letters which corresponded to the row indicated by the tone were considered.

Treatment of the data.   In the experiments considered in this section, S is never required to report the whole stimulus but only one line of a possible two or three lines. The simplest treatment is to plot the percentage of letters correct. This in fact, will be done for all later comparisons. The present problem is to find a reasonable measure to enable comparison between the partial report and the immediate-memory data for the same stimuli. The measure, *percent correct*, does not describe the results of the immediate-memory experiments parsimoniously. In Experiment 1 it was shown that Ss report a constant number of letters, rather than a constant percentage of letters in the stimulus. The measure, *number of letters correct*, is inappropriate to the partial report data because the number of letters which *S* reports is limited by the *E* to at most three or four. The most reasonable procedure is to treat the partial report as a random sample of the letters which the *S* has available. Each partial report represents a typical sample of the number of letters *S* has available for report. For example, if an *S* is correct about 90% of the time when he is reporting three out of nine letters, then he is said to have 90% of the nine letters—about eight letters—available for partial report at the time the instruction tone is given.

In order to calculate the number of available letters, the average number of letters correct in the partial report is multiplied by the number of equiprobable (nonoverlapping), partial reports. If there are two tones and two rows, multiplication is by 2.0; if three, by 3.0. As before, only the number of correct letters in the correct position is considered.

Results.   The development of the final, stable form of the behavior is relatively rapid for *Ss* giving partial reports. The average for all *Ss* after 30 trials (first session) with the 3/3 stimuli was 4.5; on the second day the average of 30 more trials was 5.1. On the third day *Ss* averaged 5.6 out of a possible six letters. Most of the improvement was due to just one *S*: ND who improved from 2.9 to 5.8 letters available. In the 3/3/3 stimulus training, all *Ss* reached their final value after the initial 40 trials on the first day of training. The considerable experience *Ss* had acquired with the partial reporting procedure at this time may account for the quick stabilization. NJ, whose score was 7.7 letters available on the first 20 trials, was given almost 150 additional trials in an unsuccessful attempt to raise this initial score.

In Figure 3 the number of letters available as a function of the number of letters in the stimulus are graphed as the upper curves. For all stimuli and for all *Ss*, the available information calculated from the partial report is greater than that contained in the immediate-memory report. Moreover, from the divergence of the two curves it seems certain that, if still more complex stimuli were available, the amount of available information would continue to increase.

The estimate above is only a lower bound on the number of letters that *Ss* have available for report after the termination of the stimulus. An upper bound cannot be obtained from experiments utilizing partial reports, since it may always be argued that, with slightly changed conditions, an improved performance might result. Even the lower-bound measurement of the average available information, however, is twice as great as the immediate-memory span. The immediate-memory span for the 4/4/4 (12-letters and numbers) stimuli ranges from 3.9 to 4.7 symbols for the *Ss*, with an average of 4.3. Immediately after an exposure of the 4/4/4 stimulus material, the number of letters available to the *Ss* ranged from 8.1 (ND) to 11.0 (ROR), with an average of 9.1 letters available. . . .

EXPERIMENT 4: DECAY OF AVAILABLE INFORMATION

. . . It was established in Experiment 3 that more information is available to the *Ss* immediately after termination of the stimulus than they could report. It remains to determine the fate of this surplus information, that is, the "forgetting curve." The partial report technique makes possible the sampling of the available information at the time the instruction signal is given. By delaying the instruction, therefore, decay of the available information as a function of time will be reflected as a corresponding decrease in the accuracy of the report.

Procedure.   The principal modification from the preceding experiment is that the signal tone, which indicates to the *S* which row is to be reported, is given at various other times than merely "zero delay" following the stimulus off-go. The following times of indicator tone onset relative to the stimulus were explored: 0.05 sec. before stimulus onset (−0.10 sec.), ±0.0-, +0.15-, +0.30-, +0.50-, +1.0-sec. delays after stimulus off-go. The stimuli used were 3/3, 4/4.

The *Ss* were given five or more consecutive trials in each of the above conditions. These trials were always preceded by at least two samples in order to familiarize *S* with the exact time of onset. The particular delay of the instruction tone on any trial was thus fixed rather than chosen randomly. The advantages of this procedure are (*a*) optimal performance is most likely in each delay condition, if *S* is prepared for that precise condition (cf. Klemmer, 1957), (*b*) minimizing delay changes makes possible a higher rate of stimulus presentations. On the other hand, a random sequence of instruction tone delays would make it more likely that *S* was "doing the same thing" in each of the different delay conditions.

The sequence in which the different delay conditions followed each other was chosen either as that given above (ascending series of delay conditions) or in the reverse order (descending series). Within a session, a descending series always followed an ascending series and vice versa, irrespective of the stimulus materials used. At least two ascending and two descending series of delay conditions were run with each *S* and with each material after the initial training (Experiment 3) with that material. This number of trials insures that for each *S* there are at least 20 trials at each delay of the indicator tone. . . .

[In the first series of analyses of Experiment 4, Sperling analyzes how subjects' strategies change with more practice and with different stimulus conditions, focusing first on one subject, ROR.]

ROR's performance is analyzable in terms of two kinds of observing behavior (strategies) which the situation suggests. He may follow the instruction, given by *E* prior to training, that he pay equal attention to each row. In this case, errors are evenly distributed between rows. Or, he may try to anticipate the signal by guessing which instruction tone will be presented. In this case, *S* is differentially prepared to report one row. If the signal and *S*'s guess coincide, *S* reports accurately; if not, poorly. . . .

. . . The accuracy of report resulting from the first of these behaviors (equal attention) is correlated with the delay of the instruction tone; it is associated with the *S*s initially giving equal attention to all parts of the stimulus. The accuracy of the other kind of report (guessing) is uncorrelated with the delay of the instruction; it is characterized by *S*s' differential preparedness for some part of the stimulus (guessing). Equal attention observing is selected for further study here. The preceding experiment suggests three modifications that would tend to make equal attention observing more likely to occur, with a corresponding exclusion of guessing.

1. The use of stimuli with a larger number of letters, that is, 3/3/3 and 4/4/4. Differential attention to a constant small part of the stimulus is less likely to be reinforced, the larger the stimulus. The use of three tones instead of two diminishes the probability of guessing the correct tone.

2. Training with instruction tones that begin slightly before the onset of the stimulus. It is not necessary for *S* to guess in this situation since he can succeed by depending upon the instruction tone alone. This situation not only makes equal attention likely to occur, but differentially reinforces it when it does occur. . . .

3. The *E* may be able to gain *verbal* control over *S*s' modes of responding. Initially, however, even *S* cannot control his own behavior exactly. This suggests a limit to what *E* can do. For example, frequently *S*s reported that, although they had tried to be equally prepared for each row, after some tones they realized that they had been selectively prepared for a particular row. This comment was made both when the tone and the row coincided and (more frequently) when they differed.

Some verbal control is, of course, possible. An instruction that was well understood was:

> You will see letters illuminated by a flash that quickly fades out. This is a visual test of your ability to read letters under these conditions, not a test of your memory. You will hear a tone during the flash or while it is fading which will indicate which letters you are to attempt to read. Do not read the card until you hear the tone [etc.].

The instruction was changed at the midway point in the experiment. The *S* was no longer to do as well as he could by any means, but was limited to the procedure described above. Part 2 of this experiment, utilizing 9- and 12-letter stimuli, was carried out with the three modifications suggested above.

Results.   The results for 3/3/3 and 4/4/4 letters and numbers are shown for each individual *S* in Figures 4 and 5. The two ordinates are linearly related by the equation:

$$\frac{\text{percent correct}}{100} \times \text{no. letters in stimulus}$$

= letters available

Each point is based on all the test trials in the delay condition. The points at zero delay of instructions for NJ and JC also include the training trials, as these Ss showed no subsequent improvement.

The data indicate that, for all Ss, the period of about one sec. is a critical one for the presentation of the instruction to report. If Ss receive the instruction 0.05 sec. before the exposure, then they give accurate reports: 91% and 82% of the letters given in the report are correct for the 9- and 12-letter materials, respectively. These partial reports may be interpreted to indicate that the Ss have, on the average, 8.2 of 9 and 9.8 of 12 letters available. However, if the instruction is delayed until one sec. after the exposure, then the accuracy of the report drops 32% (to 69%) for the

9-letter stimuli, and 44% (to 38%) for the 12-letter stimuli. This substantial decline in accuracy brings the number of *letters available* very near to the number of letters that Ss give in immediate-memory (whole) reports.

The decay curves are similar and regular for each S and for the average of all Ss. Although individual differences are readily apparent, they are small relative to the effects of the delay of the instruction. For example, when an instruction was given with zero delay after the termination of the stimulus, the *least* accurate reports by any Ss are given by ND, who has 8.1 letters available immediately after the termination of the stimulus. With a one-sec. delay of instructions, the *most* accurate reports were given by JC, who has only 5.1 letters available at this time.

In Figure 3, in which whole reports and partial reports were compared, only that particular partial report was considered in which the instruction tone followed the stimulus with zero delay. It is evident from this experiment that the zero delay instruction is unique only in that it is the earliest possible "after" instruction, but not because of any functional difference.

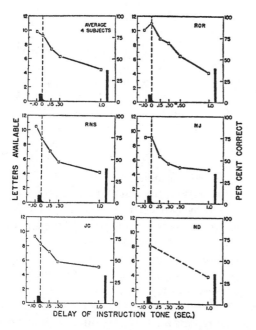

FIGURE 4   Decay of available information: nine (3/3/3) letters. Light flash is shown on same time scale at lower left. Bar at right indicates immediate-memory for this material.

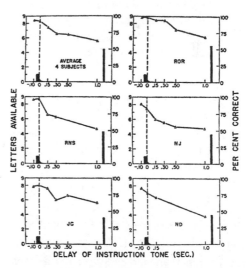

FIGURE 5   Decay of available information: twelve (4/4/4) letters and numbers. Light flash is shown on same time scale at lower left. Bar at right indicates immediate-memory for this material.

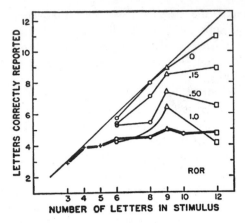

FIGURE 6   Immediate-memory and available information. The parameter is the time at which available information is sampled (delay of instruction). Heavy line indicates immediate-memory for the same materials. One subject (ROR).

In Figure 6, therefore, the 0.15-, 0.50-, and 1.00-sec. instruction delays are also plotted for one *S*, ROR. . . . Figure 6 clearly highlights the significance of a precisely controlled coded instruction, given within a second of the stimulus off-go, for the comparison of partial and immediate-memory reports. One second after termination of the stimulus, the accuracy of ROR's partial reports is no longer very different from the accuracy of his whole reports. . . .

[In Experiment 5, Sperling compares subjects' performance when presentation of the stimulus is followed by a bright light (a procedure now called masking; see Introduction to Reading 5) and when stimulus presentation is followed by a dark (post-exposure) field. He finds that performance suffered overall, and it didn't matter whether stimuli were exposed for 150 or for 500 msecs.]

EXPERIMENT 6: LETTERS AND NUMBERS

In Experiment 3 partial reports were found to be uniformly more accurate than whole reports. In one case, stimuli of eight letters were used and only one row of four letters was reported. Designating the letters to be reported by their location is only one of a number of possible ways. In the following experiment, a quite similar set of stimuli is used; each stimulus has two

letters and two numbers in each of the two rows. The partial report again consists of only four symbols, but these are designated either as letters or as numbers rather than by row. In addition, a number of controls which are also relevant to Experiment 3 are conducted.

Procedure

I. Training: The *Ss* were given practice trials with the instruction: "Write down only the numbers if you hear a short pip (tone 0.05-sec. duration) and only the letters if you hear the long tone (0.50-sec. duration)." The tones were then given with zero delay following the stimulus off-go. The stimuli were 4/4 L&N.

II. In the following session, tests were conducted with five different instructions:

1. Letters only—Instructions given well in advance of stimulus to write only the letters in the following card(s). (8 trials)

2. Numbers only—Write only the numbers in the following card(s). (8 trials)

3. Top only—Write only the top row in the following card(s). (4 trials)

4. Bottom only—Write only the bottom row in the following card(s). (4 trials)

5. Instruction tone—Write either letters or numbers as indicated by tone. Tone onset 0.05 sec. before stimulus onset. (16 trials) ROR was also given additional trials at longer delay times.

Results.   The results are illustrated in Table 1. For purposes of comparison, the number of correct letters is multiplied by two when an instruction was used which required *S* to report only four of the eight symbols of the stimulus. This includes instructions given well in advance of the stimulus. All measures, then, have 8.0 as the top score and are thus equivalent within a scale factor to percent correct measures. The range is 0–8 instead of 0–100. Scores which are based on partial reports are therefore directly comparable to the partial report scores (letters available) obtained in Experiments 3, 4, and 5.

When stimuli consist of letters and numbers, but *Ss* report only the letters or only the numbers, then

TABLE 1   Comparison of Five Procedures

Subject	Letters Only	Numbers Only	Average L&N	Instr. Tone −0.10	Immediate-Memory	One Row Only
RNS	5.0	4.5	4.8	4.3	4.6	7.3
ROR	6.5	6.5	6.5	6.3	4.5	7.3
ND	3.5	3.8	3.6	4.1	4.1	7.5
NJ	4.0	5.0	4.5	4.6	4.3	—
JC	3.3	4.0	3.6	3.4	4.1	8.0
Mean	4.5	4.8	4.6	4.5	4.3	—

Note—Average letters and/or numbers available (fraction of letters—numbers—correct in partial report × number of symbols in stimulus). Stimuli: eight (4/4) letters and numbers.

the Ss' partial reports are only negligibly more accurate than their whole reports of the same stimuli. The average number of letters available (calculated from the partial report) is just 0.2 letter above the immediate-memory span for the same material. For practical purposes, the partial report score is the same score that Ss would obtain if they wrote all the letters and numbers they could (that is, gave a whole report) but were scored only for letters or only for numbers, independently by the experimenter. The partial report of letters only (or of numbers only) does not improve even when the instruction is given long in advance verbally instead of immediately before the exposure by a coded signal tone.

The estimate of the number of available letters and numbers which is obtained from the partial report of letters (or numbers) only is also the same as the estimate that would be obtained if, on each trial, Ss wrote only one row—either the top or the bottom —according to their whim. Reporting only one row of four letters and numbers is a task at which the Ss succeed with over 90% accuracy. Even if they are scored for the whole stimulus, by arbitrarily reporting only one row they would still achieve a score of almost 50% correct or almost four letters available. This is why no delay series were conducted. If Ss had ignored the instruction to write only the letters (or numbers) and had written only a single row on each trial, they would have shown less than a 0.5 letter decrement, no matter what the delay of the instruction. . . .

Whether the Ss would have shown improvement with a large amount of additional training in the partial report of letters or numbers cannot be stated. Table 1 shows that, when Ss are required in advance to report only one row, this task is trivial. The substantial advantage of partial reports of rows (report by position) over partial reports of numbers or letters (report by category) when the instruction is given verbally long in advance of the exposure is retained even when the instruction is coded and given shortly after the exposure.

The failure in Experiment 6 to detect a substantial difference in accuracy between partial reports of only letters (or only numbers) and whole reports clearly illustrates that partial reports by position are more effective for studying the capacity of short-term information storage than partial reports by category. . . .

[In Experiment 7, Sperling uses stimuli with two rows of letters. Rather than requiring a partial report, Sperling requires a whole report, with the tone indicating which row is to be reported first. He finds in this experiment that performance on the signaled row (which was the first of two rows reported) was lower than in experiments in which the signaled row was the only row to be reported. Furthermore, in this whole report experiment, Sperling does not find a consistent effect of delay in tone presentation.

In his discussion, Sperling raises a number of technical issues and discusses his findings in relation to earlier findings in a number of areas.]

SUMMARY AND CONCLUSIONS

When stimuli consisting of a number of items are shown briefly to an observer, only a limited number of the items can be correctly reported. This number defines the so-called "span of immediate-memory." The fact that observers commonly assert that they can *see* more than they can *report* suggests that memory sets a limit on a process that is otherwise rich in available information. In the present studies, a sampling procedure (partial report) was used to circumvent the limitation imposed by immediate-memory and thereby to show that at the time of exposure, and for a few tenths of a second thereafter, observers have two or three times as much information available as they can later report. The availability of this information declines rapidly, and within one second after the exposure the available information no longer exceeds the memory span.

Short-term information storage has been tentatively identified with the persistence of sensation that generally follows any brief, intense stimulation. In this case, the persistence is that of a rapidly fading, visual image of the stimulus. Evidence in support of this hypothesis of visual information storage was found in introspective accounts, in the type of dependence of the accuracy of partial reports upon the visual stimulation, and in an analysis of certain response characteristics. These and related problems were explored in a series of seven experiments.

An attempt was first made to show that the span of immediate-memory remains relatively invariant under a wide range of conditions. Five practiced observers were shown stimuli consisting of arrays of symbols that varied in number, arrangement, and composition (letters alone, or letters and numbers together). It was found (Experiments 1 and 2) that each observer was able to report only a limited number of symbols (for example, letters) correctly. For exposure durations from 15 to 500 msec., the average was slightly over four letters; stimuli having four or fewer letters were reported correctly nearly 100% of the time.

In order to circumvent the immediate-memory limit on the (whole) report of what has been seen, observers were required to report only a part—designated by location—of stimuli exposed for 50 msec. (partial report). The part to be reported, usually one out of three rows of letters, was small enough (three to four letters) to lie within the memory span. A tonal signal (high, middle, or low frequency) was used to indicate which of the rows was to be reported. The *S* did not know which signal to expect, and the indicator signal was not given until after the visual stimulus had been turned off. In this manner, the information available to the *S* was sampled immediately after termination of the stimulus.

Each observer, for each material tested (6, 8, 9, 12 symbols), gave partial reports that were more accurate than whole reports for the same material. For example, following the exposure of stimuli consisting of 12 symbols, 76% of the letters called for in the partial report were given correctly by the observers. This accuracy indicates that the total information available from which an observer can draw his partial report is about 9.1 letters (76% of 12 letters). This number of randomly chosen letters is equivalent to 40.6 bits of information, which is considerably more information than previous experimental estimates have suggested can become available in a brief exposure. Furthermore, it seems probable that the 40-bit information capacity observed in these experiments was limited by the small amount of information in the stimuli rather than by a capacity of the observers.

In order to determine how the available information decreases with time, the instruction signal, which indicated the row of the stimulus to be reported, was delayed by various amounts, up to 1.0 sec. (Experiment 4). The accuracy of the partial report was shown to be a sharply decreasing function of the delay in the instruction signal. Since, at a delay of 1.0 sec., the accuracy of the partial reports approached that of the whole reports, it follows that the information in excess of the immediate-memory span is available for less than a second. In contrast to the partial report, the accuracy of the whole report is not a function of the time at which the signal to report is given (Experiment 7).

The large amount of information in excess of the immediate-memory span, and the short time during which this information is available, suggests that it may be stored as a persistence of the sensation resulting from the visual stimulus. In order to explore further this possibility of visual information storage, some parameters of visual stimulation were studied. A decrease of the exposure duration from 50 to 15 msec. did not substantially affect the accuracy of partial reports (Experiment 5). On the other hand, the substitution of a white post-exposure field for the dark field ordinarily used greatly reduced the accuracy of both partial and whole reports. The ability of a homogeneous visual stimulus to affect the available information is evidence that the process depends on a persisting visual image of the stimulus.

Whether other kinds of partial reports give similar estimates of the amount of available information was examined by asking observers to report by category rather than by location. The observer reported numbers only (or the letters only) from stimuli consisting of both letters and numbers (Experiment 6). These partial reports were no more accurate than (whole) reports of all the letters and numbers. The ability of observers to give highly accurate partial reports of letters designated by location (Experiment 3), and their inability to give partial reports of comparable accuracy when the symbols to be reported are designated as either letters or numbers, clearly indicates that all kinds of partial reports are not equally suitable for demonstrating the ability of observers to retain large amounts of information for short time periods.

In the final study (Experiment 7), the order of report was systematically varied. Observers were instructed to get as many letters correct as possible, but the order in which they were to report the letters was not indicated until after the exposure. An instruction tone, following the exposure, indicated which of the two rows of letters on the stimulus was to be reported first. This interference with the normal order of report reduced only slightly the total number of letters that were reported correctly. As might be expected, the first row—the row indicated by the instruction tone—was reported more accurately than the second row (order effect). There was, however, a strong tendency for the top row to be reported more accurately than the bottom row (position effect). Although, as a group, the observers showed both effects, some failed to show either the order or the position effect, or both. The fact that, for some observers, order and po-

sition are not correlated with response accuracy suggests that order of report, and position, are not the major *causes* of, nor the necessary conditions for, response accuracy. The high accuracy of partial report observed in the experiments does not depend on the order of report or on the position of letters of the stimulus, but rather it is shown to depend on the ability of the observer to read a visual image that persists for a fraction of a second after the stimulus has been turned off.

REFERENCES

Adams, J. S. The relative effectiveness of pre- and post-stimulus setting as a function of stimulus uncertainty. Unpublished master's dissertation, Department of Psychology, University of North Carolina, 1955.

Alpern, M. Metacontrast. *J. Opt. Soc. Amer.*, 1953, 43, 648–657.

Baxt, N. Über die Zeit welche nötig ist damit ein Gesichtseindruck zum Bewusstsein kommt und über die Grösse (Extension) der bewussten Wahrnehmung bei einem Gesichtseindrucke von gegebener Dauer. *Pflüger's Arch. ges. Physiol.*, 1871, 4, 325–336.

Berry, W., & Imus, H. Quantitative aspects of the flight of colors. *Amer. J. Psychol.*, 1935, 47, 449–457.

Bidwell, S. On the negative after-images following brief retinal excitation. *Proc. Roy. Soc. Lond.*, 1897, 61, 268–271.

Bridgin, R. L. A tachistoscopic study of the differentiation of perception. *Psychol. Monogr.*, 1933, 44(1, Whole No. 197), 153–166.

Broadbent, D. E. Immediate memory and simultaneous stimuli. *Quart. J. exp. Psychol.*, 1957, 9, 1–11. (a)

Broadbent, D. E. A mechanical model for human attention and memory. *Psychol. Rev.*, 1957, 64, 205–215. (b)

Broadbent, D. E. *Perception and communication.* New York: Pergamon, 1958.

Cattell, J. McK. Über die Trägheit der Netzhaut und des Sehcentrums. *Phil. Stud.*, 1883, 3, 94–127.

Chapman, D. W. The comparative effects of determinate and indeterminate aufgaben. Unpublished doctor's dissertation, Harvard University, 1930.

Chapman, D. W. Relative effects of determinate and indeterminate "Aufgaben." *Amer. J. Psychol.*, 1932, 44, 163–174.

Cohen, L. D., & Thomas, D. R. Decision and motor components of reaction time as a function of anxiety level and task complexity. *Amer. Psychologist,* 1957, 12, 420. (Abstract).

Dallenbach, K. M. Attributive vs. cognitive clearness. *J. exp. Psychol.,* 1920, 3, 183–230.

Diefendorf, A. R., & Dodge, R. An experimental study of the ocular reactions of the insane from photographic records. *Brain,* 1908, 31, 451–489.

Dodge, R. An experimental study of visual fixation. *Psychol. Monogr.,* 1907, 8 (4, Whole No. 35). (a)

Dodge, R. An improved exposure apparatus. *Psychol. Bull.,* 1907, 4, 10–13. (b)

Erdmann, B., & Dodge, R. *Psychologische Untersuchungen über das Lesen auf experimenteller Grundlage.* Halle: Niemeyer, 1898.

Glanville, A. D., & Dallenbach, K. M. The range of attention. *Amer. J. Psychol.,* 1929, 41, 207–236.

Goldiamond, I. Operant analysis of perceptual behavior. Paper read at Symposium on Experimental Analysis of Behavior, APA Annual Convention, 1957.

James, W. *The principles of psychology.* New York: Holt, 1890.

Klemmer, E. T. Simple reaction time as a function of time uncertainty. *J. exp. Psychol.,* 1957, 54, 195–200.

Klemmer, E T., & Loftus, J. P. *Numerals, nonsense forms, and information.* USAF Cambridge Research Center, Operational Applications Laboratory, Bolling Air Force Base, 1958. (Astia Doc. No. AD110063)

Külpe, O. Versuche über Abstraktion. In *Bericht über den erste Kongress für experimentelle Psychologie.* Leipzig: Barth, 1904. Pp. 56–68.

Ladd, G. T. *Elements of physiological psychology: A treatise of the activities and nature of the mind.* New York: Scribner, 1889.

Lawrence, D. H., & Coles, G. R. Accuracy of recognition with alternatives before and after the stimulus. *J. exp. Psychol.,* 1954, 47, 208–214.

Lawrence, D. H., & Laberge, D. L. Relationship between accuracy and order of reporting stimulus dimensions. *J. exp. Psychol.,* 1956, 51, 12–18.

Lindsley, D. B., & Emmons, W. H. Perception time and evoked potentials. *Science,* 1958, 127, 1061.

Long, E. R., Henneman, R. H., & Reid, L. S. Theoretical considerations and exploratory investigation of "set" as response restriction: The first of a series of reports on "set" as a determiner of perceptual responses. *USAF WADC tech. Rep.,* 1953, No. 53–311.

Long, E. R., & Lee, W. A. The influence of specific stimulus cuing on location responses: The third of a series of reports on "set" as a determiner of perceptual responses. *USAF WADC tech. Rep.,* 1953, No. 53–314. (a)

Long, E. R., & Lee, W. A. The role of spatial cuing as a response-limiter for location responses: The second of a series of reports on "set" as a determiner of perceptual responses. *USAF WADC tech. Rep.,* 1953, No. 53–312. (b)

Long, E. R., Reid, L. D., & Garvey, W. D. The role of stimulus ambiguity and degree of response restriction in the recognition of distorted letter patterns: The fourth of a series of reports on "set" as a determiner of perceptual responses. *USAF WADC tech. Rep.,* 1954, No. 54–147.

Luce, D. R. *A survey of the theory of selective information and some of its behavioral applications.* New York: Bureau of Applied Social Research, 1956.

McDougall, W. The sensations excited by a single momentary stimulation of the eye. *Brit. J. Psychol.,* 1904, 1, 78–113.

Miller, G. A. Human memory and the storage of information. *IRE Trans. Information Theory,* 1956, IT-2, No. 3, 129–137. (a)

Miller, G. A. The magic number seven, plus or minus two: Some limits on our capacity for processing information. *Psychol. Rev.,* 1956, 63, 81–97. (b)

Miller, G. A., & Nicely, P E. An analysis of perceptual confusions among some English consonants. *J. Acoust. Soc. Amer.,* 1955, 27, 338–352

Pieron, H. L'évanouissement de la sensation lumineuse: Persistance indifferenciable et persistance totale. *Ann. Psychol.,* 1934, 35, 1–49.

Pollack, I. The assimilation of sequentially-encoded information. *Hum. Resources Res. Lab. memo Rep.,* 1952, No. 25.

Pritchard, R. M. Visual illusions viewed as stabilized retinal images. *Quart. J. exp. Psychol.,* 1958, 10, 77–81.

Quastler, H. Studies of human channel capacity. In H. Quastler, *Three survey papers.* Urbana, Ill.: Control Systems Laboratory, Univer. Illinois, 1956. Pp. 13–33.

Schumann, F. Die Erkennung von Buchstaben und Worten bei momentaner Beleuchtigung. In *Bericht über den erste Kongress für experimentelle Psychologie.* Leipzig: Barth, 1904. Pp. 34–40.

Schumann, F. The Erkennungsurteil. *Z. Psychol.* 1922, 88, 205–224.

Sperling, G. Information available in a brief visual presentation. Unpublished doctor's dissertation, Department of Psychology, Harvard University, 1959.

Sperling, G. Afterimage without prior image. *Science,* 1960, 131, 1613–1614.

Von Helmholtz, H. *Treatise on Physiological optics.* Vol. II. *The sensations of vision* (Transl. from 3rd German ed.) Rochester, New York: Optical Society of America, 1924–25.

Wagner, J. Experimentelle Beitrage zur Psychologie des Lesens. *Z. Psychol.,* 1918, 80, 1–75.

Weyer, E. M. The Zeitschwellen gleichartiger und disparater Sinneseindrucke. *Phil. Stud.,* 1899, 15, 68–138.

Whipple, G. M. *Manual of physical and mental tests.* Vol. I. *Simpler processes.* Baltimore: Warwick & York, 1914.

Wilcocks, R. W. An examination of Külpe's experiments on abstraction. *Amer. J. Psychol.* 1925, 36, 324–340.

Woodworth, R. S. *Experimental psychology.* New York: Holt, 1938.

Wundt, W. Zur Kritik tachistosckopischer Versuche. *Phil. Stud.* 1899, 15, 287–317.

Wundt, W. *An introduction to psychology.* London: Allen & Unwin, 1912.

POSTSCRIPT

Sperling's description of iconic memory has been confirmed by researchers using methods other than partial report (for example, Averbach & Sperling, 1961; Haber & Standing, 1969). Also relevant to Atkinson and Shiffrin's (1968) claims about a sensory register is the evidence Darwin, Turvey, and Crowder (1972) found for an auditory sensory register [dubbed "echoic" memory by Neisser (1967)] using the method of partial report. (The existence and characterization of echoic memory has been especially controversial; see Ashcraft, 1989.)

It should be noted that Haber (1983) argues that our theories of perception and information processing do not require a distinct sensory register. Although he does not dispute the experimental evidence for iconic memory, Haber argues that such evidence comes from highly artificial experiments (comparable only to vision in a thunderstorm), and that most everyday visual perception can be understood without appealing to a high capacity, very short-term, "precategorical" sensory register. Haber's article is accompanied by comments from a large number of psychologists, including Sperling himself. Most of the commentators disagree with at least some part of Haber's argument. One interesting contrary view is that the phenomena often explained by appealing to iconic memory are actually due to the operation of two or more distinct components (Coltheart, 1980; Irwin & Yeomans, 1986; Mewhort, Campbell, Marchetti, & Campbell, 1981). Although highly technical, Haber's article and the accompanying responses are well worth reading for insight into how psychologists construct arguments and judge theories.

FOR FURTHER THOUGHT

1. Sperling describes his apparatus and stimuli in a great deal of detail. Why is this so important in these experiments?
2. In experiments requiring partial report, Sperling was careful to make sure that every row was sampled the same number of times over a series of sessions. Why was this important?
3. How was the number of available letters estimated from the number of letters given in the partial report? Suppose there were a condition in which the subject was given 4 rows of 4 letters each, and on any given trial, the subject was asked to report one specific row. If, under these conditions, the subject correctly reported an average of 3.52 letters (88%), what would you estimate the total number of available letters to be?
4. Sperling points out that the guessing strategy is uncorrelated with the delay of the instruction (the tone telling the subject which row to report). Why is that?
5. Why is the best estimate of the duration of iconic memory given by the cue-delay at which the results obtained by the partial report and full report methods converge, and not when the percent correct for partial report reached a certain level (say, 50%)?
6. In Experiment 6, Sperling found that telling subjects to report only the letters or only the numbers was not as useful a cue for a partial report as telling them to report only one row or another. What does that imply about the information available in the icon?
7. Why does Sperling use so few subjects? Do you think that fact calls his results into question? Why or why not? If it does, what would running more subjects tell you?

REFERENCES

Ashcraft, M. H. (1989). *Human memory and cognition.* Glenview, IL: Scott, Foresman.

Atkinson, R. C., & Shiffrin, R. M. (1968). Human memory: A proposed system and its control processes. In K. W. Spence & J. T. Spence (Eds.), *The psychology of learning and motivation: Vol. 2* (pp. 89–195). New York: Academic Press.

Atkinson, R. C., & Shiffrin, R. M. (1971, August). The control of short-term memory. *Scientific American,* pp. 82–90.

Averbach, E., & Sperling, G. (1961). Short-term storage of information in vision. In C. Cherry (Ed.), *Information theory* (pp. 196–211). Washington, DC: Butterworth.

Coltheart, M. (1980). Iconic memory and visible persistence. *Perception & Psychophysics, 27,* 183–228.

Darwin, C. J., Turvey, M. T., & Crowder, R. G. (1972). The auditory analogue of the Sperling partial report procedure: Evidence for brief auditory storage. *Cognitive Psychology, 3,* 255–267.

Haber, R. N. (1983). The impending demise of the icon: A critique of the concept of iconic storage in visual information processing. *Behavioral and Brain Sciences, 6,* 1–54.

Haber, R. N., & Standing, L. G. (1969). Direct measures of short-term visual storage. *Quarterly Journal of Experimental Psychology, 21,* 43–54.

Irwin, D. E., & Yeomans, J. M. (1986). Sensory registration and informational persistence. *Journal of Experimental Psychology: Human Perception and Performance, 12,* 343–360.

Mewhort, D. J. K., Campbell, A. J., Marchetti, F. M., & Campbell, J. I. D. (1981). Identification, localization, and "iconic" memory: An evaluation of the bar-probe task. *Memory & Cognition, 9,* 50–67.

Neisser, U. (1967). *Cognitive psychology.* New York: Appleton-Century-Crofts.

INTRODUCTION

"Some Experiments on the Recognition of Speech, with One and with Two Ears" by E. Colin Cherry introduces a method used by many early studies of attention. In this method, two messages—which can consist of continuous prose, unconnected sentences, or unconnected strings of words—are presented to subjects either binaurally or dichotically via headphones. In binaural presentation, both messages are presented to both ears so that the messages are superimposed on one another and seem to originate in the middle of the subject's head. Typically, the experimenter then examines how well the subject is able to separate the two messages. In dichotic presentation, one message is presented to each ear so that the messages are discrete and appear to come from different directions. With dichotic presentation, subjects typically are asked to shadow, or repeat aloud, the message presented to one ear. The experimenter then examines how much the subject knows about the message that was not shadowed (presented to the unattended ear).

When Cherry's article was written, (neo-)behaviorism dominated American psychology, and cognitive psychology had not been formally established. Cherry's work here follows in the traditions of both human engineering, which studies how machines should be designed so people could use them most effectively, and communication theory, which studies the transmission of information. Cherry's guiding metaphor was that people can be seen as channels through which messages are transmitted. Therefore, Cherry had little interest in the listeners' subjective experiences and instead was concerned with the conditions under which and the manner in which people's ability to pass on a message accurately would break down.

Work preceding Cherry's had focused on people's ability to deal with simultaneously presented nonspeech sounds that differ in frequency or duration. In the first series of experiments reported here, Cherry examines people's ability to deal with the binaural presentation of two messages that differ only in transition probabilities. *Transition probability* is the likelihood that a stimulus (in this case, a word) with a particular characteristic will be followed by another stimulus with a particular characteristic. For example, it is generally very likely in natural speech that a word spoken in a female voice will be followed by another word spoken in a female voice or that a word in English will be followed by another word in English. More important, certain words are much more likely to be followed by some words than by others. For example, *the* is much more likely to be followed by *cat* than by *on*.

Before you read this article, imagine yourself in situations in which you are confronted with simultaneous messages, such as at a party where many people are speaking at the same time. What variables make it easier or harder for you to focus on a particular person's message? What information do you pick up from the speech of people you are not attending to? Determine whether Cherry investigates all the variables you identified and whether his results agree with your intuitions.

Some Experiments on the Recognition of Speech, with One and with Two Ears

E. Colin Cherry

Imperial College, University of London, and Research Laboratory of Electronics, Massachusetts Institute of Technology

1. INTRODUCTION

The experiments described herein are intended as a small contribution to the solution of the general problem of the recognition of speech. They are designed to be essentially objective and behavioristic; that is, the "subject" under test (the listener) is regarded as a transducer whose responses are observed when various stimuli are applied, whereas his subjective impressions are taken to be of minor importance.

A great deal of work has been done relating to aural discrimination, mostly using two kinds of stimulus: (a) pure tones, which may be regarded as separable in frequency, and (b) acoustic "clicks," or impulses, considered as separable in time.[1] It is suggested that a third kind of discrimination is possible and amenable to experimental treatment, namely statistical separation. Speech signals form stimuli in this class, and we appear to possess powers of such discrimination. For example, we decide that a person is speaking English and not, say, French; again we can listen to one speaker when another is speaking simultaneously. These are acts of recognition and discrimination.

The tests to be described are in two groups. In the first, two different spoken messages are presented to the subject simultaneously, using both ears. In the second, one spoken message is fed to his right ear and a different message to his left ear. The results, the subject's spoken reconstructions, are markedly different in the two cases; so also are the significances of

This work, supported in part by the Signal Corps, the Air Materiel Command, and the U.S. Office of Naval Research, was carried out by the author at M.I.T. while there as a Visiting Professor under a Fulbright grant, and is presented with the kind permission of Professor J. B. Wiesner.

[1]M. R. Rosenzweig, Am. J. Physiol. **167**, No. 1 (October, 1951).

SOURCE: *The Journal of the Acoustical Society of America,* 25(5), September 1953, pp. 975–979. Copyright 1953 by the American Institute of Physics. Reprinted by permission.

these results. Before examining such possible significance, it will be better to describe some of the experiments.

2. THE SEPARATION OF TWO SIMULTANEOUSLY SPOKEN MESSAGES

The first set of experiments relates to this general problem of speech recognition: how do we recognize what one person is saying when others are speaking at the same time (the "cocktail party problem")? On what logical basis could one design a machine ("filter") for carrying out such an operation? A few of the factors which give mental facility might be the following:

(a) The voices come from different directions.
(b) Lip-reading, gestures, and the like.
(c) Different speaking voices, mean pitches, mean speeds, male and female, and so forth.
(d) Accents differing.
(e) Transition-probabilities (subject matter, voice dynamics, syntax . . .).

All of these factors, except the last (e), may, however, be eliminated by the device of recording two messages on the same magnetic-tape, spoken by the same speaker. The result is a babel, but nevertheless the messages may be separated.

The logical principles involved in the recognition of speech seem to require that the brain have a vast "store" of probabilities, or at least of probability-rankings. Such a store enables prediction to be made, noise or disturbances to be combatted, and maximum-likelihood estimates to be made. Shannon[2] has already reported that prediction is readily possible in the case of printed language, and has described experiments in which a subject is required to guess the successive letters or words of a hidden written message; our present experiments are somewhat analogous, but are carried out with speech, at normal rates of speaking.

Those holding the strict behaviorist view may rightly object that it is inadmissible to speak of "stor-

age of probability-rankings in the brain," because these are not directly observable; the only probabilities which can be discussed are those of the subject's responses. Acknowledging this, we may turn the problem around from one of psychology to one of engineering and ask: On what logical principles could one design a machine whose reaction, in response to speech stimuli, would be analogous to that of a human being? How could it separate one of two simultaneous spoken messages? The tests described here merely purport to show that we ourselves have such power, with the suggestion that we can assess probability-rankings of words, phonemic sounds, syntactical endings, and other factors of speech.

In the first experiment the subject is presented with the two mixed speeches recorded on tape and is asked to repeat one of them word by word or phrase by phrase. He may play the tape as many times as he wishes and in any way. His task is merely to separaate one of the messages. He repeats the various identified portions verbally, but is not allowed to write them down.

The following is one example of two messages, showing his reconstructions; the subject matters are markedly distinct in this case.

Message 1(a) "It may mean that our religious convictions,

legal systems and politics have been so successful in

accomplishing their ends during the past two thousand years,
    AIMS
that there has been no need to change our outlooks about

them. Or it may mean that the outlook has not changed for

other reasons. I will leave the first hypothesis to those who are
    BELIEVE IN   AND IN
willing to defend it, and choose the second. As the reader may

have guessed, I am interested in learning how obsolete

structure of languages preserves obsolete metaphysics."

Message 1(b) "This very brief discussion will serve to give a

slight indication of the really complex nature of the causes

and uses of birds' colors, and may serve to suggest a few of the

many possibilities that may underlie them. There is a very

great opportunity here for close and careful observation of

[2]C. E. Shannon, Bell System Tech. J. XXX, 50 (1951).

the habits of birds in a free state, with a view to shedding light on these problems. But the observer, in interpreting what he sees, must ever be on his guard lest he lose sight of alternative explanation."

The phrases recognized have been underlined and error indicated by the sub-scripts. No transpositions of phrases between the messages occurred in this example; in other examples extremely few transpositions arose, but where they did they could be highly probable from the text. The next example illustrates this point (indicated by asterisks).

Message 2(a) "He came out of nowhere special; a cabin like
FROM
any other out West. His folks were nobody special; pleasant,
HE SPOKE TO
hardworking people like many others. Abe was a smart boy but not too smart. He could do a good day's work on the farm, though he'd just as soon stand around and talk. He told
funny* stories; he was strong and kind. He'd never try to hurt
PROFESSIONAL TRAINING
you, or cheat you, or fool you. Young Abe worked at odd jobs and read law books at night. Eventually he found his way into
WAR
local politics. And it was then that people, listening* to his
LEADING POSITION IN THE WORLD
speeches, began to know there was something special about
NOTICE
Abe Lincoln. Abe talked about running a country as though it
THE
were something you could do. It was just a matter of people
HE
getting along. He had nothing against anybody, rich or poor, who went his own way and let the other fellow go his. No
GO
matter how mixed up things got, Abe made you feel that the answer was somewhere among those old rules that everybody
AMONGST
knows: no hurting, no cheating, no fooling."

Notice here the recognition in phrases, the highly likely errors and transpositions and the consistency of any initial grammatical mistake. Similar factors were observed in all the samples taken.

At the subjective level the subject reported very great difficulty in accomplishing his task. He would shut his eyes to assist concentration. Some phrases were repeatedly played over by him, perhaps 10 to 20 times, but his guess was right in the end. In no cases were any long phrases (more than 2 or 3 words) identified wrongly.

Message 2(b) "In attaining its present* position, the institution
SPECIAL
has constantly kept before it three objectives—the education of men, the advancement of knowledge and service to
industry* and the nation. It aims to give its students such a
OTHERS
combination of humanistic, scientific and professional training as will fit them to take leading positions in a world in
THE
which science, engineering and architecture are of basic importance. This training is especially planned to prepare
HAS BEEN
students, according to their desires and aptitudes, to become practicing engineers or architects, investigators, business executives or teachers. The useful knowledge and mental
AND
discipline gained in this training are, however, so broad and fundamental as to constitute an excellent general preparation for other careers.* Realizing that the institution trains for life
PEOPLE GETTING ALONG   TRAINING
and for citizenship as well as for a career, its Staff seeks to
ASSOCIATIONSHIP(?)
cultivate in each student a strong character, high ideals, and a sense of social responsibility, as well as a keen intellect."

In a variation of the experiment the subject was given a pencil and paper, and permitted to write down the words and phrases as he identified them. Subjectively speaking, his task then became "very much easier." Times were shortened. It appears that the long-term storage provided assists prediction.

Numerous tests have been made, using pairs of messages of varying similarity. Some test samples consisted of adjacent paragraphs out of the same book. The results were consistently similar; the messages were almost entirely separated.

However, it was considered possible to construct messages which could not be separated with such a low frequency of errors. Such a test is described in the next Section.

3. INSEPARABLE SPOKEN MESSAGES. USE OF CLICHÉS OR "HIGHLY-PROBABLE PHRASES"

As a final test in this series, using the same speaker recorded as speaking two different messages simultaneously, a pair of messages was composed which could not be separated by the listening subject. The messages were composed by selecting, from reported speeches in a newspaper, 150 clichés and stringing them together with simple conjunctions, pronouns, etc., as continuous speeches. For example, a few of the clichés were:

(1) I am happy to be here today,
(2) The man in the street,
(3) Stop beating about the bush,
(4) We are on the brink of ruin,

and the like. The corresponding sample of one speech was as follows:

"I am happy to be here today to talk to the man in the street. Gentlemen, the time has come to stop beating about the bush—we are on the brink of ruin, and the welfare of the workers and of the great majority of the people is imperiled," and so forth.

It is remarkably easy to write such passages by the page.[3] Now a cliché is, almost by definition, a highly probable chain of words, and on the other hand the transition probability of one cliché following another specific one is far lower. The subject, as he listened to the mixed speeches in an endeavor to separate one of them was observed to read out complete clichés at a time; it appeared that recognition of one or two words would insure his predicting a whole cliché. But he picked them out in roughly equal numbers from both speeches; in such artificially constructed cases, message separation appeared impossible. The speeches were of course read with normal continuity, and with natural articulatory and emotional properties, during their recording.

It is suggested that techniques such as those described in the preceding sections may be extended so that they will shed light on the relative importance of the different types of transition probabilities in recog-

nition. For instance, speeches of correct "syntactical structure" but with no meaning and using few dictionary words may readily be constructed. [Lewis Carroll's "Jabberwocky" is such an instance; similarly, "meaningful" speeches with almost zero (or at least unfamiliar) syntactical or inflexional structure (Pidgin English).][4] Again continuous speaking of dictionary words, which are relatively disconnected, into "meaningless phrases" is possible; the word-transition probabilities may be assessed *a priori,* with the assistance of suitable probability tables. Further experiments are proceeding.

4. UNMIXED SPEECHES; ONE IN THE LEFT EAR AND ONE IN THE RIGHT

The objective, and subjective, results of a second series of tests were completely different. In these tests one continuous spoken message was fed into a headphone on the subject's left ear and a different message applied to the right ear. The messages were recorded, using the same speaker.

The subject experiences no difficulty in listening to either speech at will and "rejecting" the unwanted one. Note that aural directivity does not arise here; the earphones are fixed to the head in the normal way. To use a loose expression, the "processes of recognition may apparently be switched to either ear at will." This result has surprised a number of listeners; although of course it is well known to anyone who has made hearing tests. It may be noteworthy that when one tries to follow the conversation of a speaker in a crowded noisy room, the instinctive action is to turn one ear toward him, although this may increase the difference between the "messages" reaching the two ears.

The subject is instructed to repeat one of the messages concurrently while he is listening[5] and to make no errors. Surprising as it may seem this proves easy; his words are slightly delayed behind those on the record to which he is listening. One marked characteristic of his speaking voice is its monotony. Very little emotional content or stressing of the words oc-

---

[3]Comment upon this fact has appeared in the *New Yorker* under the name of Mr. Arbuthnot.

[4]Editor's note: Bracketed material is Cherry's own comment.

[5]D. E. Broadbent, J. Exptl. Psychol., 43 (April 1952).

curs at all. Subjectively, the subject is unaware of this fact. Also he may have very little idea of what the message that he has repeated is all about, especially if the subject matter is difficult. But he has recognized every word, as his repeating proves.

But the point of real interest is that if the subject is subsequently asked to repeat anything of what he heard in his other (rejected-message) ear, he can say little about it at all, except possibly that sounds were occurring.

Experiments were made in an attempt to find out just what attributes, if any, of the "rejected" message are recognized.

5. LANGUAGE OF "REJECTED" EAR UNRECOGNIZED

In a further set of tests the two messages, one for the right ear and one for the left, started in English. After the subject was comfortably repeating his right-ear message, the left-ear message was changed to German, spoken by an Englishman. The subject subsequently reported, when asked to state the language of the "rejected" left-ear message, that he "did not know at all, but assumed it was English." The test was repeated with different, unprepared listeners; the results were similar. It is considered unfair to try this particular test more than once with the same listener.

It was considered that a further series of tests might well indicate the level of recognition which is attained in the "rejected" ear, raising the questions, Is the listener aware even that it is human speech? male or female? and the like.

6. WHAT FACTORS OF THE "REJECTED" MESSAGE ARE RECOGNIZED?

In this series of tests the listening subjects were presented at their right-hand ears with spoken passages from newspapers, chosen carefully to avoid proper names or difficult words, and again instructed to repeat these passages concurrently without omission or error. Into their left ears were fed signals of different kinds, for different tests, but each of which started and ended with a short passage of normal English speech in order to avoid any troubles that might be involved in the listener's "getting going" on the test.

The center, major, portions of these rejected left-ear signals thus reached the listener while he was steadily repeating his right-ear message.

Again no one listening subject was used for more than one test; none of them was primed as to the results to be expected. The center, major, portions of the left-ear signals for the series of tests were, respectively:

(a) Normal male spoken English—as for earlier tests.
(b) Female spoken English—high-pitched voice.
(c) Reversed male speech (i.e., same spectrum but no words or semantic content).
(d) A steady 400-cps oscillator.

After any one of these tests, the subject was asked the following questions:

(1) Did the left-ear signal consist of human speech or not?
(2) If yes is given in answer to (1), can you say what it was about, or even quote any words?
(3) Was it a male or female speaker?
(4) What language was it in?

The responses varied only slightly. In no case in which normal human speech was used did the listening subjects fail to identify it as speech; in every such instance they were unable to identify any word or phrase heard in the rejected ear and, furthermore, unable to make definite identification of the language as being English. On the other hand the change of voice—male to female—was nearly always identified, while the 400-cps pure tone was always observed. The reversed speech was identified as having "something queer about it" by a few listeners, but was thought to be normal speech by others.

The broad conclusions are that the "rejected" signal has certain statistical properties recognized, but that detailed aspects, such as the language, individual words, or semantic content are unnoticed.

7. SIMILAR MESSAGES IN THE TWO EARS, BUT WITH TIME DELAY BETWEEN THEM

Subjectively speaking, the effect of listening normally, with both ears, to a single message is a very different sensation from that of listening with one ear to one of two different messages as in the earlier tests. This raises the question of how we correlate the signals reaching our two ears so that we are able to decide to listen either to both at the same time (when identical or "correlated") or only to one, rejecting the other.

This question suggested the following experiment. Suppose we apply identical messages to the two ears of a listening subject, but with a very long delay between them. What will be the effect if this delay is steadily reduced, as the message proceeds, until eventually the two ears are stimulated simultaneously and identically?

Preliminary experiments suggest that the basis of correlation (using the word in the popular not the mathematical sense) of the messages reaching the two ears depends upon the magnitude of the delay between the ears. When this is very short, of the order of milliseconds, there will exist a considerable connection between the actual sounds, or their spectra; but with longer delays, of the order of seconds, the relation is more a semantic one, or one of word and phrase identification.

The following experiment was carried out with a number of subjects. A long passage of speech was recorded on magnetic tape and subsequently run through two reproducing machines in cascade, with a length of tape between them. The subject, who was unprimed as to the nature and purpose of the experiment, was instructed in exactly the same way as in the earlier experiments; namely, he was asked to repeat the message reaching his right ear, without omission or error. As he was doing this the two machines were slowly pushed together, reducing the delay between the ears. At some stage the subject would exclaim: "My other ear is getting the same thing" or some equivalent remark. Some of them said nothing until asked afterwards and then stated the word or words first recognized as being the same. Nearly all subjects reported that they had recognized words or phrases, at some stage, in the rejected ear message as being the same as those in the accepted ear message.

The surprising thing here is that such words were recognized at all, because in earlier tests, using different texts for the two ears, not a single word of the rejected ear was identified. The delay at which recognition first occurred in the present tests varied considerably between the different listeners acting as subjects but mostly lay between 6 sec and 2 sec.

Experiments of a similar nature, but using very short delays of the orders of milliseconds or tens of milliseconds, are not reported here in connection with the present study. They are of interest mainly for the subjective effects produced.

8. THE SWITCHING OF ONE MESSAGE PERIODICALLY BETWEEN THE TWO EARS

This experiment was suggested by the results of earlier ones described in Secs. 4, 5, and 6. When listening to and repeating concurrently a message received in one ear while a different message is being presented to the other ear, it is found that a very short time interval is required to transfer the attention from the one ear to the other. Thus it was thought that, if a single message was switched between the ears at approximately the time period of this reaction time (not under the control of the listening-speaking subject), his recognition facility might be completely confounded and he would be unable to repeat the words.

A long sample of English speech was recorded on tape and subsequently applied to the right or left headphone of the subject, alternately, by an automatic switch which could be thrown (a) randomly and (b) periodically, at any required rate. When the switching speed was very slow (say a 1-sec period) the subject repeated 100 percent correctly; when very fast (say $1/20$–$1/50$-sec period) most subjects repeated the majority of the words, though they varied in their ability considerably, reporting that they listened as though to both ears simultaneously. The point that matters is that an optimum period of switching could be found at which the fraction of words repeated by the subjects was a minimum. The flatness of this minimum varied between the subjects; the approximate average value of the minimum switching rate was $1/6$–$1/7$ sec, for a complete cycle of switching.

Somewhat surprisingly, little difference in the results was found between the uses of random and periodic switching; so the former was abandoned. The variations between the subjects in their abilities, the flatness of the minima, and other factors tended to make such experiments rather inconclusive. Instead, therefore, a method of switching was sought which could virtually stop any subject repeating any of the words. It was found that if, while the reversing switch was in operation, a very short gap of silence was introduced, the effect upon the subject's responses was most marked. The switching cycle was thus: right ear/silence/left ear/silence—periodically, at about 6 to 7 cps. The silence interval needed to be no greater than 10 msec.

A comparison measurement was made with each subject. Firstly, the earphone signals were not reversed, though the silence gap was introduced; the subjects thus listened to both ears, with the periodic (<10 msec) interval as interruption. Word scores were 95 to 100 percent correct. Then the reversal of the earphones was introduced; the word scores fell to less than 20 percent correct.

It may be considered that these results might be accounted for by the inherent noise introduced by the switching interruption of the speech; there are several factors which assist in denying this.

(a) The noise is at extremely low level when the switching rate is as slow as 6 to 7 per sec.
(b) A subject might get a high score with a silence gap of <1 msec but this would inevitably fall if the gap was opened. The noise is substantially unchanged.

(c) Miller and Licklider's results of experiments[6] carried out with periodically interrupted speech (both ears simultaneously) show that a 6-cps interruption of 50 percent of the time, that is, square-wave modulation of the speech, gave a word-articulation score as high as 75 percent; the noise introduced presumably being much the same as in our present experiment. The test material was somewhat different in their case, being individual monosyllabic words, not connected speech.

ACKNOWLEDGMENTS

Acknowledgments of the very great assistance offered by many patient subjects is gratefully made. The author wishes also to thank Professor J. B. Wiesner, Massachusetts Institute of Technology, and Professor Willis Jackson, Imperial College, London, for their assistance in affording the necessary facilities.

---

[6]G. A. Miller and J. C. R. Licklider, J. Acoust. Soc. Am., 22, 167 (1950).

POSTSCRIPT

In this article, Cherry does not offer an explanation of why he obtained the results that he did. Instead, he simply presents a series of studies that explore the effects of different variables on subjects' ability to reconstruct or shadow a message, and then he offers certain general summaries of his results.

However, on the basis of this work (and other work, in some cases using other techniques), Donald Broadbent (1954, 1957, 1958) developed a filter theory of attention. Broadbent suggested that people can transmit (attend to) only one message or channel at a time. What happens, Broadbent thought, is that people identify the physical properties of all incoming messages and then attend to one message on the basis of its physical characteristics, such as the direction from which it comes or the pitch of the voice in which it is spoken. Broadbent viewed attention metaphorically as a physical channel that allows one message to enter and filters out others. Such nonselected messages are stored in a temporary memory buffer. If not retrieved from that buffer within a short time period, none of the nonphysical properties of the unattended message will be available to the subject.

Perhaps most significantly for us, however, Broadbent made a clean break with the conceptual framework existing at the time, and he defined *attending to* a message as allowing it into consciousness. Subsequent work on attention and its relationship to consciousness is discussed in the following articles in this chapter.

FOR FURTHER THOUGHT

1. Notice that in the first experiment, subjects often managed to get only snippets of a message rather than the entire message; they also made frequent errors. Are the snippets received just random bits and pieces? If not, how can they be characterized? Did subjects' errors occur at random? If not, can you see any pattern to when subjects were likely to make errors or what their errors were likely to be based on?
2. What effect did being allowed to write things down have for subjects in the binaural presentation experiments? Keeping in mind that subjects were given the opportunity to listen to the messages several times, what light does that shed on how subjects were doing the task?
3. Do the results with clichés support your answers to questions 1 and 2? If so, how, and if not, how not?
4. Cherry notes that, when shadowing in the dichotic presentation experiments, subjects often spoke in a monotone. Does this suggest anything about how they were processing the information to which they were attending?
5. Make a list summarizing (1) the characteristics of the nonattended message that subjects in Cherry's experiment did and did not recognize and (2) the effects of time delays between the messages.
6. What are the implications of the results from Cherry's last experiment, in which only one message is used but is switched from ear to ear, sometimes preceded by a slight pause?

REFERENCES

Broadbent, D. E. (1954). The role of auditory localization in attention and memory span. *Journal of Experimental Psychology, 47,* 191–196.

Broadbent, D. E. (1957). A mechanical model of human attention and immediate memory. *Psychological Review, 64,* 205–215.

Broadbent, D. E. (1958). *Perception and communication.* New York: Pergamon Press.

INTRODUCTION

In "Contextual Cues in Selective Listening," Anne Treisman presents some data that prove problematic for Broadbent's (1958) filter theory of attention (see the Postscript to Reading 2). She also suggests a modification of that theory.

The need for such a modification first became apparent with findings reported by Moray (1959). Recall that Cherry (Reading 2) found that subjects knew very little about the message in the unattended ear beyond certain of its gross physical characteristics, such as pitch. According to Broadbent's filter theory, this lack of knowledge resulted because the unattended message had been filtered out. But Moray found that certain important words, including highly emotional terms or the subject's name, were sometimes noticed even when they occurred in the unattended ear. If messages in the unattended ear are filtered out, how can specific words get through? And what does it mean for a word to be "important"?

Treisman uses Cherry's dichotic presentation technique (described in the Introduction to Reading 2) to test whether importance is a long-term property of words or whether it can be raised temporarily within a particular context if its occurrence is highly probable in that context. Treisman manipulates the probability of occurrence by using stimuli in which words are embedded in prose text or in word strings that approximate real sentences.

Treisman uses two kinds of prose text and two levels of statistical approximation to English. In a second-order approximation (as in "was he went to the newspaper is in deep and"; Miller & Selfridge, 1950), each word is followed by a word that could follow it in a real sentence. However, outside of this restriction on the words that immediately follow one another, there are no constraints on word order. In an eighth-order approximation, every sequence of eight words would make sense in a real sentence, but there are no constraints outside each sequence of eight. The effect is like a run-on sentence that keeps losing track of where it is headed.

As you read this article, see whether you can figure out what the different kinds of stimuli would suggest about the variables that affect word importance.

Contextual Cues in Selective Listening

Anne M. Treisman

Institute of Experimental Psychology, University of Oxford

INTRODUCTION

Cherry (1953) found that subjects, when asked to "shadow"—or repeat aloud continuously as they heard it—a passage of prose given to one ear, remained almost completely unaware of the content, though not of the presence of another passage in the other ear; they noticed gross changes of pitch or loudness, but not the introduction of a foreign language or of reversed speech. He concluded that only certain statistical properties of the sounds were analyzed, but none of the meaning of the words. Moray (1959) studied in more detail the nature of the attention "barrier." He found that subjects, given a recognition test, failed to show any trace of repeated lists of words given to the rejected ear, and that when they were given a specific set to listen, for example for numbers, they were no more likely to hear them than if they were given more general instructions. The only signals which were sometimes heard were the subjects' own names. He suggested that some kind of analysis was carried out prior to the level of the selective filter, but that only "important" or affective signals were allowed to pass.

It has been shown that dichotic localization of the sound sources is a very effective cue for selective attention (Broadbent, 1954); if both passages are given to both ears it becomes very much more difficult for subjects to separate out the two passages, at least on the first trial (Cherry, 1953). Another factor which plays an important part in "shadowing" tasks is redundancy in the message itself. Moray and Taylor (1958) asked subjects to repeat as they heard them passages composed of statistical approximations to English (made up using Miller's technique (1950))

and found that the number of words omitted was logarithmically related to the order of approximation to English. The higher the transition probabilities between the words, the more likely they were to be heard and correctly repeated.

The aim of the present experiment was to discover whether this type of contextual cue, or expectancy based on transition probabilities between words, would be strong enough to override the dichotic localization cues; whether, if words were made highly probable instead of "important" (as in Moray's experiment), they would also be allowed through the selective attention filter, despite the fact that they came from the rejected ear.

METHOD

The apparatus used was a Brenell Mark 5 two-channel tape-recorder, the output from each track of the tape going through independent amplifiers to separate earpieces of a pair of headphones. Each subject was asked to equalize the intensities of the two passages.

The passages recorded were fifty words long and were of four different kinds: (*a*) narrative passages from a novel (*Lord Jim* by Conrad), (*b*) extracts from a technical discussion of language (from *Signs, Language and Behaviour* by C. Morris), (*c*) eighth order statistical approximations to English, (*d*) second order approximations to English. There were twelve passages of types (*a*), (*c*) and (*d*) and four of type (*b*). The passages were recorded in pairs, one on each track of the tape, in the following arrangements:—

a–b, b–a, a–c, c–a, a–d, d–a, c–d, d–c, c–c, d–d;

two examples of each pair were used, and the order was randomized. At some point in each recording between the twentieth and the thirty-fifth word, the passages were switched from one track to the other, so that each recording consisted of, on one track, the first part of passage 1 and the second part of passage 2, and, on the other track, the first part of passage 2 and the second part of passage 1. The switches from top to bottom and bottom to top track of the tape-recorder were made to coincide and any pause or change of tone was, as far as possible, avoided. The following example, an "*a–d*" pair, is typical:—

1st track. "While we were talking she would come and go with rapid glances at us

2nd track. "The camera shop and boyhood friend from fish and screamed loudly

leaving on her passage an impression of grace and / is idiotic idea of

singing men and then it was jumping in the tree / charm and a
distinct

almost there is cabbage a horse which was not always be the set

suggestion of watchfulness. Her manner presented a curious combination

works every evening is heaviest with bovine eyes looking sideways. . . ."

of shyness and audacity. Every pretty smile was succeeded swiftly by a . . ."

The 18 subjects were undergraduates or research students. They were all given three practice passages of 100 words to shadow. They were then given the passages described above, one track to each ear, and were asked to repeat as they heard it whatever came through one of the two headphones: some were asked to listen to the right and some the left ear.

Six subjects were also given a control series (half of them before the experimental series and half after it). Here the top track was exactly the same as that described above, but on the bottom track a different and irrelevant passage of narrative was recorded, so that the subjects still heard the break in context, but the passage was not switched and continued on the other ear.

Their responses were recorded and later scored for any words repeated from the wrong ear. These were arranged in three categories: intrusions from the wrong ear made within five words before the break in context; intrusions within five words after the break and intrusions elsewhere in the passages. Subjects were also asked if they noticed anything about the rejected passages at the end of the experiment.

RESULTS

There were relatively very few changes to the wrong passage: no subjects changed ears for the whole of the second part to follow contextual rather than localization cues. Three subjects never transferred to the wrong passage. However, fifteen of them did repeat just one or two words on one or more occasions from the rejected ear (the average number of words, for these fifteen subjects, out of twenty 50-word passages being about six). But, when asked afterwards, only one subject had any idea that the passages had been switched to opposite ears, and only two thought they might have said one or two words from the wrong ear. The one who realized the passages had changed sides suddenly commented towards the end of the series, "That time the right ear suddenly wanted to take over." All the other subjects described the rejected passage as "just noise," "perhaps English," or made similar comments. Several noticed that some at least of the passages they were repeating had a break in the context, which they found rather disturbing, and all realized that some (the statistical approximations) were more disconnected than others. Seven subjects were also given, after the other passages, two more where message 1 was in a woman's voice and message 2 in a man's voice. All of these noticed that the voices switched to opposite ears, although they did not transfer with them in what they were repeating.

The six subjects who did the control series did not insert any of the words which followed after the break in the original passage, so that it is confirmed that in the actual experiment, subjects were genuinely transferring to the other channel and repeating words heard on the side to be rejected.

The number of words repeated from the wrong channel in the "switched" case did seem to bear some relation to the redundancy of the prose. In the results these intrusions are classified by the nature of the material to or from which the transfer was made.

The differences between the conditions were tested, using Student's "t" method, to see which were statistically significant.

Intrusions *from* passage on rejected ear.

After break.   Novel > 8th order.
            Significantly $p = 0.01$ $t = 3.2$
                different

            Novel > 2nd order
            Significantly $p = 0.01$ $t = 3.6$
                different

            8th order 2nd order
            Not significantly different.

Before break.   None significantly different.

Not at break.   None significantly different.

Intrusions *to* passage on accepted ear.

None significantly different, except Before break, 2nd order > 8th order, just significantly different, $p = 0.05$, $t = 2.6$.

Subjects were significantly more likely to repeat words from the rejected passage after the break if the context they were following was the narrative prose from a novel than if it was a statistical approximation to English, but no difference was seen between the 8th order passages and the less redundant 2nd order ones. There were some, though considerably fewer, intrusions before the break; this was possible because when subjects shadow they are repeating two or three words behind the recorded ones. When all intrusions in the five words preceding the break in context were summed and compared with all intrusions not at the break, divided by eight (to give equal numbers of words which could potentially have been transferred), the difference was statistically significant ($p = 0.01$ level). Here, the contextual constraints of the passage which has just come to the right ear from the wrong one seem to work retrospectively, applying transition probabilities in the reverse direction. (Goldman-Eisler (1957) has shown that this is possible, using Shannon's (1949) guessing technique.) There were not enough of these intrusions to show any statistically significant differences between types of prose, although the numbers show the same trend as those coming after the break.

When the results were tabulated in terms of the numbers of intrusions *to* a certain type of passage, there were no significant differences between the different types of prose in intrusions after the break, or intrusions not at the break, perhaps because there were two factors acting in opposite directions: the greater the redundancy the less likely subjects were to leave the correct passage, but also the greater would be the disruption of transition probabilities when the break in context came. In number of intrusions before the break, there were just significantly more from 2nd order approximation to English than from 8th order, presumably an effect of its lower redundancy.

A few examples of the kinds of intrusion that occurred were:—

(1) "...I SAW THE GIRL / song was WISHING..."
    ...me that bird   / JUMPING in the street...

(2) "...SITTING AT A MAHOGANY / three POSSIBILITIES..."
    ...let us look at these   / TABLE with her head...

(3) "...THE GROWL OF THE/ "GOAT" (go to) swim fast DURING THE..."
    ...book is she went to / thunder INCREASED STEADILY and the...

(4) "...NEWER techniques will / FOR A MOMENT NOT DARING..."
    ...left, while I STOOD / be especially serviceable...

The words in capital letters were those spoken by the subjects.

DISCUSSION

This experiment has confirmed the finding that when the two ears are used as the two channels in a selective listening task, subjects remain almost completely unaware of the content of the rejected passage. Moreover, it seems that contextual cues are not sufficient to make subjects change permanently to the second channel in order to follow the sense of the passage, or even to make them aware of what is being said there. However (using the terms and type of model put forward by Broadbent in his book, *Perception and Communication*) the "selective filter" does seem occasionally to allow one or two highly probable words through from the rejected channel, when the transition probabilities on the correct channel are suddenly contradicted.

The fact that subjects nearly all believe these words came from the same accepted channel makes it seem unlikely that the selective filter has been, as it

TABLE 1

The table shows $\dfrac{\text{Number of intrusions}}{\text{Number of words} \times \text{Number of passages} \times \text{Number of subjects}}$.

1. Intrusions *from* passage on rejected ear.

	(a) Novel	(b) Technical Prose	(c) 8th Order	(d) 2nd Order
After break	$\dfrac{27}{5 \times 6 \times 15}$ (6%)	$\dfrac{10}{5 \times 2 \times 15}$ (6.7%)	$\dfrac{9}{5 \times 6 \times 15}$ (2%)	$\dfrac{8}{5 \times 6 \times 15}$ (1.8%)
Before break	$\dfrac{8}{5 \times 6 \times 15}$ (1.8%)	$\dfrac{1}{5 \times 2 \times 15}$ (0.7%)	$\dfrac{2}{5 \times 6 \times 15}$ (0.4%)	$\dfrac{4}{5 \times 6 \times 15}$ (0.9%)
Not at break	$\dfrac{3}{40 \times 6 \times 15}$ (0.08%)	$\dfrac{2}{40 \times 2 \times 15}$ (0.17%)	$\dfrac{1}{40 \times 6 \times 15}$ (0.03%)	$\dfrac{8}{40 \times 6 \times 15}$ (0.22%)

2. Intrusions *to* passage on accepted ear.

	(a) Novel	(b) Technical Prose	(c) 8th Order	(d) 2nd Order
After break	$\dfrac{19}{5 \times 6 \times 15}$ (4.2%)	$\dfrac{9}{5 \times 2 \times 15}$ (6%)	$\dfrac{16}{5 \times 6 \times 15}$ (3.6%)	$\dfrac{10}{5 \times 6 \times 15}$ (2%)
Before break	$\dfrac{4}{5 \times 6 \times 15}$ (0.9%)	$\dfrac{2}{5 \times 2 \times 15}$ (0.4%)	$\dfrac{1}{5 \times 6 \times 15}$ (0.2%)	$\dfrac{8}{5 \times 6 \times 15}$ (1.8%)
Not at break	$\dfrac{4}{40 \times 6 \times 15}$ (0.11%)	$\dfrac{2}{40 \times 2 \times 15}$ (0.17%)	$\dfrac{2}{40 \times 6 \times 15}$ (0.06%)	$\dfrac{6}{40 \times 6 \times 15}$ (0.16%)

were, reset momentarily for a different channel. Shadowing experiments suggest that there is a single channel system for analyzing meaning, presumably comprising the matching of signals with some kind of "dictionary" and its store of statistical probabilities and transition probabilities gradually learned through continual use of the language. If this is so, one should be able to avoid the "identification paradox" pointed out by Moray (1959). To explain his finding that subjects sometimes hear their own names when they occur in the rejected message, he suggests that there must be some kind of pattern analysis prior to the filter. Instead, one can suppose that in the "dictionary" or store of known words, some units or groups have permanently lower thresholds for activation, or are permanently more readily available than others; such might be "important" words, a person's own name, or perhaps danger signals (such as "look out" or "fire"); others would be lowered temporarily by in-

coming signals on some kind of conditional probability basis (along the lines suggested for a learning machine by Uttley (1955)). Thus, for instance, if the three words " I sang a" were heard, the stored trace of the word "song" in the dictionary would have its threshold considerably lowered. The thresholds might of course also be altered in the same way by other types of contextual constraint, by the selection of a verbal category, for example, as in Bruce's experiment (1956) on recognition of words masked by noise. Here the knowledge of the class of words (for example "types of food") allowed them to be recognized at a considerably lower signal-to-noise ratio.

In using the word "threshold" in this context, it is not necessarily meant to imply an intensity threshold, which might be one possibility, but simply that the unit is more or less likely to be activated by incoming signals, or that it is made more or less quickly available. Now if the selective mechanism in

attention acts on all words not coming from one particular source by "attenuating" rather than "block-
ing" them, that is, it transforms them in such a way
that they become less likely to activate dictionary
units, it might still allow the above classes of words,
with their thresholds which were originally exceptionally low, to be heard. It is suggested that what
happens in the experiment described here might be
as follows: for the first word after the passages have
been switched, two units will be activated in the dictionary, one by the signal from the "selected" ear and
the other by the summated effect of the "attenuated"
signal from the rejected ear and the lowered threshold due to transition probabilities following the previous word. Either of these units may be chosen for
the response, or neither (many subjects in fact omitted words after the break, perhaps because they had
no cues to decide between the two active units). For
the second word after the break, the situation is
rather different. The transition probabilities will be
lowering the thresholds of units following both the
units which were last active, but the signals coming
in will not be equally effective, since the filter is still
operating to favor the selected channel. Thus at either the second or perhaps the third word, the subject will return to the correct ear, and the transition
probabilities will be consistent with this until the end
of the passage (Figure 1).

An alternative hypothesis is that the rejected
messages are sampled or monitored occasionally. If
the signals in the brief sample happened to coincide
with a unit in the word-matching system which had
been made more sensitive or more available by high
transition probabilities, it might emerge in the final
response. If not, the competing favored signal from
the selected ear would be the one repeated.

Either of these two possibilities seems a more
economical system than any reduplication of analysis
before and after the selective filter. Something along
these lines also seems necessary to explain why not
only a few "important" words, such as one's own
name, may be heard from the rejected ear, but also
any word which has been made contextually highly
probable. If Moray wanted his suggested analyzing
mechanism prior to the selective barrier to cope with
all these possibilities, it would need to be as complex

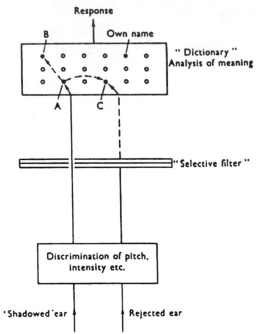

The thresholds of words B and C are lowered by their high
transition probability after word A.   Word C is also activated
by the "attenuated" signal from the rejected ear and is sometimes heard.

FIGURE 1

as the one he places after it, at the level of conscious
perception.

This might also provide an alternative way of explaining responses to classes of words, such as may
occur in perceptual defense experiments. Broadbent
(1958) suggests that the filter may be set to select
classes of words; but it is difficult to see how a word
can be recognized as belonging to a class on the basis
of its meaning (the only characteristic common to the
class) without already having been analyzed individually. An alternative explanation would be that within
the "dictionary decoding system" all words belonging
to a certain class might have their thresholds raised or
lowered relatively to the others. This differs from
Broadbent's hypothesis simply in that the selective filter is here confined to acting on "physical" cues of intensity, time or frequency differences, while selection
according to characteristics of meaning is done in advance within the analyzing or "P" system.

The writer would like to thank Professor R. C. Oldfield who supervised the research, Dr. R. Davis for his helpful criticism and the Medical Research Council for financial assistance. She is also grateful to all the volunteer subjects for their help.

REFERENCES

Broadbent, D. E. (1954). The role of auditory localization in attention and memory span. *J. exp. Psychol.*, 47, 191–6.

Broadbent, D. E. (1958). *Perception and Communication.* London.

Bruce, D. J. (1956). In *Information Theory.* Edited by E. C. Cherry, London.

Cherry, C. (1953). Some experiments on the recognition of speech with one and with two ears. *J. acoust. Soc. Amer.*, 25, 975–9.

Goldman-Eisler, F. (1957). Speech production and language statistics. *Nature,* 28, 1497.

Miller, G. A. and Selfridge, J. (1950). Verbal content and the recall of meaningful material. *Amer. J. Psychol.*, 63, 176–95.

Moray, N. and Taylor, A. M. (1958). The effect of redundancy in shadowing one of two dichotic messages. *Language and Speech,* 1, 102–9.

Moray, N. (1959). Attention in dichotic listening: affective cues and the influence of instructions. *Quart. J. exp. Psychol.*, 11, 56–60.

Uttley, A. M. (1955). The conditional probability of signals in the nervous system. *Radar Research Establishment Memo. No.* 1109.

POSTSCRIPT

Treisman's attenuation theory, as do Broadbent's filter theory and the late selection theory proposed by Deutsch and Deutsch (1963), falls into the category of bottleneck theories of attention. Such theories portray the human information processing system as multichannel at its earliest stage or stages, and single-channel thereafter. Thus the system is viewed as having a bottleneck that results in only some information receiving complete processing. Bottleneck theories differ in the placement of the bottleneck (in Broadbent and Treisman, the bottleneck is placed after registering simple physical characteristics but before identification; in Deutsch and Deutsch, it is placed after identification but before preparation of a response) and in what they hypothesize happens to nonselected information (in Broadbent and Deutsch and Deutsch, it is completely filtered out; in Treisman, it is attenuated).

Studies investigating the placement of the bottleneck (Corteen & Wood, 1972; Deutsch, Deutsch, Lindsay, & Treisman, 1967; Norman, 1968; Treisman, 1964; Treisman & Geffen, 1967) have suggested that early selection occurs with some tasks, whereas late selection occurs with others. People also can handle multiple messages as easily as they can single messages, given the right tasks and enough practice (see also Kerr, 1973). As Moray (1967) has pointed out, these facts are difficult to reconcile with the bottleneck view.

Furthermore, Kahneman (1973) has noted that bottleneck theories focus only on the *selective* aspect of attention. But attention has an intensive, or effortful, aspect to it as well. It takes a certain amount of effort to recognize the word *dyslexia* or to memorize a list.

To account for these observations, Kahneman (1973) developed a capacity view of attention to complement the bottleneck view. Kahneman begins by assuming that people's capacity for doing mental work is limited. To pay atention to something is to allocate this limited capacity to, or expend some mental effort on, that thing. This view of attention has been eloborated by a number of authors. For example, Johnston and Heinz (1978) and Yantis and Johnston (1990) describe how capacity may be allocated differentially to different stages, depending on the task at hand. Norman and Bobrow (1975) refine the notion of capacity, suggesting that there are a variety of cognitive resources, rather than a single resource called attentional capacity, to be allocated (see also Hirst & Kalmar, 1987; Navon, 1984, criticizes the resource idea).

Recognizing that attention involves the allocation of capacity or resources has had at least four consequences for theories of attention. First, it has prompted a shift toward seeing humans as active information processors rather than as passive conduits of information. Attention is no longer seen as simply determining what information is to be allowed in and what is to be filtered out. Attention is now seen as determining what information is to receive further processing, or further allocations of capacity or resources (see Neisser, 1976, and Neisser & Becklen, 1975). Second, this recognition has provided a theoretical framework for discussing individual differences in attention (Hunt, Pellegrino, & Yee, 1989). Third, given that allocation of attentional capacity may be guided in part by unconscious processes (see Neisser, 1967, or Treisman, 1986, 1988, for example), a wedge has been driven between attention and consciousness; now consciousness is seen either as depending on attention or as being a specific form of attention rather than as synonymous with attention. Finally, the capacity, or resources, view has led to the identification of tasks that can be performed without attention (in the sense of not consuming any capacity); such tasks are said to be automatic. A great deal of recent work in attention has focused on automaticity and its development (Logan, 1988; Schneider & Shiffrin, 1977; Shiffrin & Schneider, 1977; Spelke, Hirst, & Neisser, 1976 [see Reading 4]; Treisman, Vieira, & Hayes, 1992; see Kahneman & Treisman, 1984, and Schneider, Dumais, & Shiffrin, 1984, for reviews). Treisman's recent work (Treisman, 1986, 1988), sometimes called feature-integration theory, describes the role of preattentive and focused attentional processes in the visual perception of objects.

For very useful reviews of attention (including the neurobiology of attention), see Allport (1989) or chapters in LeDoux and Hirst (1986).

FOR FURTHER THOUGHT

1. Does Triesman's theory explain why her subjects sometimes shadowed the wrong ear without realizing it? If so, how?
2. Does Triesman's theory explain why subjects would shadow the wrong ear only for a short period of time? If so, how?
3. Does Triesman's theory explain the results obtained by Cherry (Reading 2) when he switched a single message from ear to ear, sometimes preceded by a brief pause?
4. How does Treisman's modification of Broadbent's theory differ from Moray's? What advantages does Treisman suggest her alternative presents?

REFERENCES

Allport, A. (1989). Visual attention. In M. I. Posner (Ed.), *Foundations of cognitive science* (pp. 631–682). Cambridge, MA: MIT Press.

Broadbent, D. E. (1958). *Perception and communication.* New York: Pergamon Press.

Corteen, R. S., & Wood, B. (1972). Autonomic responses to shock-associated words in an unattended channel. *Journal of Experimental Psychology, 94,* 308–313.

Deutsch, J. A., & Deutsch, D. (1963). Attention: Some theoretical considerations. *Psychological Review, 70,* 80–90.

Deutsch, J. A., Deutsch, D., Lindsay, P. H., & Treisman, A. M. (1967). Comments on "Selective attention: Perception or response?" and reply. *Quarterly Journal of Experimental Psychology, 19,* 362–367.

Hirst, W., & Kalmar, D. (1987). Characterizing attentional resources. *Journal of Experimental Psychology: General, 116,* 68–81.

Hunt, E., Pellegrino, J. W., & Yee, P. L. (1989). Individual differences in attention. In G. H. Bower (Ed.), *The psychology of learning and motivation* (Vol. 24, pp. 285–310). New York: Academic Press.

Johnston, W. A., & Heinz, S. P. (1978). Flexibility and capacity demands of attention. *Journal of Experimental Psychology: General, 107,* 420–435.

Kahneman, D. (1973). *Attention and effort.* Englewood Cliffs, NJ: Prentice-Hall.

Kahneman, D., & Treisman, A. M. (1984). Changing views of attention and automaticity. In R. Parasuraman & R. Davies (Eds.), *Varieties of attention* (pp. 29–61). New York: Academic Press.

Kerr, B. (1973). Processing demands during mental operations. *Memory & Cognition, 1,* 401–412.

LeDoux, J. E., & Hirst, W. (Eds.) (1986). *Mind and brain: Dialogues in cognitive neuroscience.* New York: Cambridge University Press.

Logan, G. D. (1988). Toward an instance theory of automatization. *Psychological Review, 95,* 492–527.

Moray, N. (1959). Attention in dichotic listening: Affective cues and the influence of instructions. *Quarterly Journal of Psychology, 11,* 56–60.

Moray, N. (1967). Where is capacity limited? A survey and a model. *Acta Psychologica, 27,* 84–92.

Navon, D. (1984). Resources: A theoretical soupstone. *Psychological Review, 91,* 216–234.

Neisser, U. (1967). *Cognitive psychology.* New York: Appleton-Century-Crofts.

Neisser, U. (1976). *Cognition and reality.* San Francisco: W. H. Freeman.

Neisser, U., & Becklen, R. (1975). Selective looking: Attending to visually specified events. *Cognitive Psychology, 7,* 480–494.

Norman, D. A. (1968). Toward a theory of memory and attention. *Psychological Review, 75,* 522–536.

Norman, D. A., & Bobrow, D. G. (1975). On data limited and resource limited processes. *Cognitive Psychology, 7,* 44–64.

Schneider, W., Dumais, S. T., & Shiffrin, R. M. (1984). Automatic and control processing and attention. In R. Parasuraman & R. Davies (Eds.), *Varieties of attention* (pp. 1–27). New York: Academic Press.

Schneider, W., & Shiffrin, R. M. (1977). Controlled and automatic human information processing: I. Detection, search and attention. *Psychological Review, 84,* 1–66.

Shiffrin, R. M., & Schneider, W. (1977). Controlled and automatic human information processing: II. Perceptual learning, automatic attending, and a general theory. *Psychological Review, 84,* 127–190.

Spelke, E., Hirst, W., & Neisser, U. (1976). Skills of divided attention. *Cognition, 4,* 215–230.

Treisman, A. M. (1964). Verbal cues, language and meaning in selective attention. *American Journal of Psychology, 77,* 206–219.

Treisman, A. (1986, November). Features and objects in visual processing. *Scientific American,* pp. 114B–125.

Treisman, A. (1988). Features and objects: The fourteenth Bartlett Memorial Lecture. *Quarterly Journal of Experimental Psychology, 40A,* 201–237.

Treisman, A. M., & Geffen, G. (1967). Selective attention: Perception or response? *Quarterly Journal of Psychology, 19,* 1–17.

Treisman, A. M., Vieira, A., & Hayes, A. (1992). Automaticity and preattentive processing. *American Journal of Psychology, 105,* 341–362.

Yantis, S., & Johnston, J. C. (1990). On the locus of visual selection: Evidence from focused attention tasks. *Journal of Experimental Psychology: Human Perception and Performance, 16,* 135–149.

INTRODUCTION

The early bottleneck theories of attention implicitly accepted the assumption that attention and consciousness are the same thing. But the capacity model of attention (see the Postscript to Reading 3) allows for some attentional processes to be unconscious—in particular, those that determine what subsequent processing will focus on. It seems quite safe to say that, for most people, consciousness is limited; we can only consciously think about one thing or a very few things at the same time. But if consciousness and attention are not the same thing, this leaves open the question of whether there is a fixed limit to *attentional* capacity in the way there seems to be for the capacity of *consciousness*. In other words, is it possible to simultaneously pay attention to more things than we can keep in consciousness at once? This is one of the issues addressed by Elizabeth Spelke, William Hirst, and Ulric Neisser in "Skills of Divided Attention."

A second issue Spelke and her associates address is the definition of automaticity. In the Postscript to Reading 3, we defined a task as automatic if its performance does not consume attentional capacity. One problem with this definition is that it does not tell us how to determine whether a particular task is in fact performed automatically—that is, without consuming attentional resources. To do so, we must operationalize the notion of automaticity. Posner and Snyder (1975) did just that, providing a list of operational indicants that a task is performed automatically. These indicants include occurring without intention, occurring without conscious awareness, and occurring without causing interference in other mental tasks (Posner & Snyder, 1975, p. 56). Although these indicants are commonly accepted, Spelke and her colleagues suggest that the Posner and Snyder criteria are unsatisfactory. The alternative they propose is responsible for the presence of the word *skills* in the title of their paper.

As you read this article, try to think of a task you seem to be able to do automatically and simultaneously with other tasks. Have you always been able to do that task automatically? If not, how did you come to be able to do it and another task simultaneously? And what changes, if any, have there been in how you do the task, now that it is automatic?

Skills of Divided Attention

Elizabeth Spelke, William Hirst, and Ulric Neisser

Cornell University

The study of divided attention has a long history. Most early psychologists, like their contemporary counterparts, believed that consciousness could only be directed to a single activity at a time. Conscious attention to two different actions performed at the same time was thought to be possible only if they were coordinated into a single, higher-order activity, or attended to in rapid alternation. Otherwise, it was assumed that at least one of them was being carried out "automatically," without conscious control (James, 1890; Woodworth, 1921).

Early investigators attempted to explore the limits of consciousness by combining diverse tasks while introspecting on their performance. Paulhan (1887) recited one poem while writing another, or while executing mathematical calculations. Solomons and Stein (1896) and later Downey and Anderson (1915) practiced reading stories while writing at dictation, and noted the changes that occurred in their conscious awareness of the act of writing. These studies did not always support the view that consciousness is unitary. Experimenter/subjects variously reported that one activity was performed unconsciously (Solomons & Stein, 1896), that attention alternated between the two activities (Paulhan, 1887), and that a genuine division of attention was accomplished (Downey & Anderson, 1915).

Modern studies of attention have avoided the dependence on introspection which characterizes the early work. In addition, however, they have usually divorced attention from action. Division of attention has not been defined by simultaneous directed activity, but by concurrent processing in two distinct "channels." In experiments on selective listening, for example, subjects are usually asked to shadow only one of two verbal messages; the other is to be "ignored." Processing of the secondary input may be assessed by testing memory for the words on the "unattended channel" (Glucksberg & Cowen, 1970; Norman, 1969), by measuring autonomic responses to those words (Corteen & Wood, 1972), or by observing the facilitory and inhibitory effects of the secondary message on the focal task (Lewis, 1970). Only a few studies have required subjects to perform two simultaneous tasks (e.g., Allport, Antonis & Reynolds, 1972; Shaffer, 1975; see also Welford, 1968). None of these have examined changes in dual task performance with practice (but see Underwood, 1974).

Our research revives the tradition of earlier experiments on divided attention. Specifically, it replicates and extends the work of Leon M. Solomons and Gertrude Stein at the Harvard Psychological Laboratory (Solomons & Stein, 1896). We have studied the development of skills for attending to and acting on two simultaneous messages. Two subjects, Diane and John, participated in this three-part study. As they read short stories to themselves, John and Diane first practiced writing unrelated words at dictation. When their reading speed stabilized, they were asked to detect semantic relations among the dictated words. Finally, they were asked to categorize words in a manner which forced them to use semantic information. By giving the subjects extensive practice, while gradually increasing the demands of the writing task, we

Some of these results were reported at the American Psychological Association, Chicago, August, 1975.

The names of the two senior authors are listed in a randomly chosen order; they contributed equally to this work. Reprint requests may be addressed to any of the authors at the Department of Psychology, Uris Hall, Cornell University, Ithaca, NY 14853.

SOURCE: *Cognition, 4,* 1976, pp. 215–230. Copyright 1976 by Elsevier Sequoia S.A., Lausanne. Reprinted by permission.

were able to produce very substantial increases in their ability to perform two complex and meaningful activities at the same time.

METHOD

Diane and John, respectively a graduate student in Biology and a Cornell Hotel School undergraduate, were recruited through the Cornell Student Employment Office. They worked for five one-hour sessions a week over a period of about seventeen weeks, paid by the hour. In each session, they read short stories while writing at dictation. The stories ranged in length from 700 to 5000 words, and were selected from collections of works by American, English, and translated European writers. Words for the dictation lists were selected randomly without replacement from the norms of Kucera and Francis (1967). The principal dependent variables were reading speed, reading comprehension, dictation rate, and recognition memory for the dictated words. The procedure varied considerably in the different phases of the experiment, and will be described phase by phase. A full chronology of the study appears in Table 1.

I. SIMULTANEOUS READING AND WRITING

After two pre-experimental sessions to be described below, the first phase of the experiment was devoted to practicing the dual task. Diane and John participated together in 29 one-hour sessions spread over six weeks. In each session, they silently read three short stories while writing words dictated by the experimenter (WH or ES). As soon as both of them had finished writing a given word, the next word was dictated. The average rate of dictation was about 10 words per minute. They wrote on plain paper, moving their hands vertically down the page for each new word. On reaching the bottom of the page, they turned to a new sheet of paper and continued to write. Except when they changed sheets, the subjects rarely looked at their writing.

There were three kinds of reading trials in this phase, given in random order. In a *control trial* (one each week), Diane and John each read one short story from beginning to end without any concurrent writing. At the end of the story they received a comprehension test. Comprehension questions were prepared by the first two authors. Memory for the

TABLE 1   Chronology of the Study

Sessions 1–29	Practice: 14 trials per week of reading while writing at dictation—10 full experimental trials, 4 recognition trials, and 1 control trial.
Sessions 30–35	Controlled testing: 1 full experimental, 1 recognition, and 1 control trial per day.
Sessions 36–43	Dictation with embedded lists of related words: Sentences, words from semantic categories, words from syntactic classes, or rhymes. Subjects were not forewarned that the dictated words would be structured in any way.
Sessions 44–46	Dictation with embedded lists of related words: Subjects were asked to look for and report the occurrence of any structured sublists. (A one-week vacation followed session 46.)
Sessions 47–49	Retraining (comprehension trials only).
Sessions 50–55	Controlled testing of reading comprehension by means of free and cued recall of the stories.
Sessions 56–61	Dictation of categorizable lists, in which subjects either wrote the dictated word or the name of its category.
Sessions 62–68	Continuation of sessions 44–46.
Sessions 69–74	Continued practice of reading while categorizing dictated words, as in sessions 56–61 (Diane only).
Sessions 75-80	Controlled testing of reading while categorizing dictated words.
Session 81	Writing at dictation while reading aloud.
Sessions 82–85	Writing at dictation while shadowing.

important details of plot and character was assessed by 8 to 15 short answer questions (e.g., "What did Laura say to the dead man at the cottage?" was a question pertaining to the story, "The Garden Party," by Katherine Mansfield). In a *full experimental trial* (ten each week), the subjects copied dictated words while reading stories; on the average about 60 words were dictated during a single story. As in the control trials, they read the stories to completion and were given comprehension tests. In a *recognition trial* (four each week), reading was interrupted after exactly 40 words had been dictated, and there was no comprehension test. Instead, a test of recognition memory for the dictated words was immediately administered. Recognition tests consisted of 20 randomly selected words from the dictated list, and 20 other words, (which were never dictated) from the same norms. The lists were read aloud by the experimenter; Diane and John indicated (in writing) whether they recognized each item as having been on the dictated list.

Throughout the experiment, instructions emphasized the importance of writing all the dictated words, of comprehending the stories, and of reading as rapidly as possible. On the other hand, we did not encourage John and Diane to try to remember the dictated words. They were never told in advance whether reading comprehension or word recognition would be tested. At the end of each week, they were shown how much they had progressed and were encouraged to read still more rapidly.

In two pre-experimental sessions, we assessed the subjects' normal reading speed and comprehension as well as their recognition memory for dictated words. In each of these sessions, conducted before Diane and John knew the nature of the main experiments, they read two short stories and copied two lists of 40 words from dictation on separate, alternating trials. John read at an average of 483 words per minute (wpm) and answered 73% of the comprehension questions correctly; Diane read 351 wpm and correctly answered 90% of the questions. John correctly recognized an average of 87.5% of the dictated words, with a false alarm rate of 2.5%; Diane recognized 77.5% of them, with 5% false alarms.

The levels of comprehension manifested in the pre-experimental sessions were little affected by the simultaneous dictation task introduced in the main experiment. Comprehension was high even in the first session. Both Diane and John's comprehension improved somewhat over the course of the practice sessions (Table 2, line 1). The rate at which words were written (and hence the rate at which they were dictated) showed no systematic change. Recognition of the words dictated on experimental trials also showed little change with practice. Recognition memory was somewhat poorer than in the pre-

TABLE 2   Comprehension and Recognition Memory on Experimental Trials (Sessions 1–35)

		Sessions						
		1–5	*6–10*	*11–15*	*16–20*	*21–25*	*26–29*	*30–35* (Testing)
Comprehension[a]	Diane	83.4	86.8	86.5	100.0	99.6	97.6[b]	99.2[c]
(% Correct)	John	75.0	70.3	71.6	82.2	89.5	84.3[b]	86.3[c]
Recognition[d]	Diane	0.72	0.76	0.88	0.70	0.80	0.82	0.76
p (hit)	John	0.61	0.66	0.68	0.71	0.68	0.72	0.70
Recognition[d]	Diane	0.23	0.18	0.19	0.25	0.26	0.28	0.33
p (false alarm)	John	0.02	0.04	0.09	0.10	0.15	0.12	0.12

[a]Each score is the mean of 10 trials, except as noted.
[b]Each score is the mean of 8 trials.
[c]Each score is the mean of 12 trials.
[d]Each score is the mean of 4 trials.

experimental sessions, especially for John (Table 2, lines 2 and 3). The quality of the subjects' handwriting deteriorated rapidly in the first week of practice and then improved, appearing normal by the fourth week. Omissions and misspellings were rare throughout.

Reading speeds dropped sharply on the first full experimental trials, as was expected, but soon began to increase. By about the fourth week, they began to approach normal levels (Figure 1). There was a great deal of variability from one trial to the next. In part, this must have been due to the varying strategies and motivations of our subjects. A more obvious source of variability, however, was the relative difficulty of the stories being read. In particular, some authors seemed to demand slower reading than others.

In the seventh week, a different procedure was adopted to confirm that Diane and John could indeed read just as fast while taking dictation as on control trials. This second phase of the experiment involved six sessions. Each day the subjects read three stories by the same author: one in a full experimental trial, one under control conditions, and one for a recognition test. The stories which Diane read on control trials were read by John on experimental trials, and vice versa. Summary results for this phase appear in the last column of Table 2. A day-by-day comparison of experimental and control trials, presented in Table 3, reveals no systematic differences. Diane and John read as quickly, and apparently as effectively, while taking dictation as when they read alone.

Some weeks later, in sessions 50–55, we attempted a stricter test of reading comprehension. In each of six sessions, five control and five full experimental trials were followed by a demanding probed-recall test of memory for selected episodes from the story read on that trial. The episodes, which ranged in length from 192 to 410 words, were divided into "idea units": 14 to 43 idea units per episode. For example, from the sentence, "When he heard the whistle of the northbound train arriving from Los Angeles, he led the girl to the window" we extracted the idea units, "when he heard the whistle of the northbound train," "the train arrived from Los Angeles," and "he led the girl to the window." After each story, Diane and John were first asked to give a written account of the episode in as much detail as they could. Then they answered probing questions about all the ideas that had been left out of their recalls. One question served as a cue for each omitted idea unit. For example, the last cue for the sentence above was "Where did he lead the girl?"

This procedure revealed no decrement in comprehension or memory that could be attributed to the added task of writing from dictation. John's mean probed comprehension, in terms of the proportion of "idea units" recalled, was 0.90 on experimental trials and 0.88 on control trials. Diane's probed comprehension was 0.94 on experimental and 0.95 on control trials. Their initial free recall scores (the percentage of idea units recalled before the probing questions) were about 20 percentage points lower in all conditions.

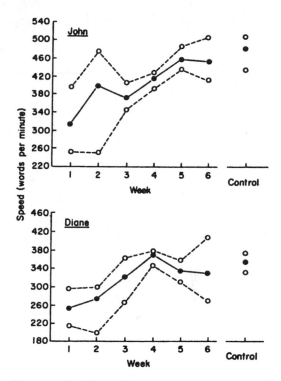

FIGURE 1   Reading speeds during the practice phase: weekly means and interquartile ranges

TABLE 3   Controlled Testing of Reading Speed and Comprehension

	Reading Speed (wpm)		Reading Comprehension (% correct)	
Session	Experimental	Control	Experimental	Control
Diane				
30	336.7[a]	331.0	100	100
31	365.8	354.9	100	100
32	302.1	330.8	100	100
33	322.2	297.6	100	100
34	358.2	325.2	100	100
35	303.6	332.4	95	95
$\overline{X}$	331.43	328.65	99.17	99.17
John				
30	485.5	593.3	100	100
31	412.1	502.0	90	100
32	573.5	555.0	82.5	80
33	477.6	471.6	65	95
34	468.0	380.4	100	100
35	450.0	441.8	80	100
$\overline{X}$	477.78	490.68	86.25	95.83

[a]Each score is based on 1 trial.

II. DETECTION OF STRUCTURED SUBLISTS

The observations reported so far establish that John and Diane could copy dictated words while reading with normal speed and comprehension, but they give little indication of how much information the subjects picked up from the dictated words. In the second part of the study, we explored the degree to which they analyzed and understood the words they wrote.

In these sessions, the subjects were observed individually and no recognition or control trials were administered. Instead, John and Diane were asked to report any of the dictated words, or any "general properties" of the list, which they remembered. They were also asked why they thought they remembered what they did. Lengthy stories were used (three per session) so that we could dictate lists of 80 to 100 words without interruption. Unknown to the subjects, the lists were no longer entirely random. Each included a sublist of 20 consecutive words that were interrelated in one of four ways. On the first day, the words of the sublist all came from the same super-

ordinate category: the three trials used the categories "furniture," "vehicles," and "dwellings," respectively. On the second day, the sublist words all came from one of three syntactic classes: plural nouns, past tense verbs, and adjectives. On the third and fourth days, consecutive words in the sublists formed sentences. These six 20-word lists each included two to five sentences, three to ten words long. On the fifth day, the words of the sublists rhymed: each consisted of 20 words rhyming with the words "board," "bee," and "bean," respectively. The category sublists were taken from the Battig and Montague (1969) norms; the others were constructed ad hoc by the authors. Each sublist appeared after the first 35 to 45 random words in the longer list.

Of the several thousand words dictated in this phase, only 35 were spontaneously recalled. The subjects gave several reasons for these recalls. In six cases, the word had some personal significance: Diane recalled "diameter," which she at first thought was her own name, and John recalled several words related to his studies, such as "luncheon" and "finances." In ten cases, the word recalled was semantically or phonetically related to the story being read. John noticed "ecumenical" while reading a story about a priest, and "aversion" while reading the word "version." In six cases, one of the subjects was uncertain about exactly what word the experimenter had said, and he "had to think about it." No reasons were given for the recall of the remaining 13 words.

The subjects seemed completely unaware of the presence of the sublists on the first four days of this phase. Neither of them noted the existence of the categories, the consistent syntactic classes, or the sentences. Neither recalled more than two words from any sublist. The single exception was the phrase "muddy water" from the sentence "Dogs drink muddy water." Both subjects reported this phrase, but assumed that juxtaposition of words was accidental. This failure to notice the list structures is quite striking. As a control, we asked each of three naive subjects to copy one of the 80-word lists from dictation without looking at it, and subsequently to report such words and general properties as he could remember. Each type of list was read to one subject. Those who were given category and sentence lists noticed the structure immediately, though the subject who was given 20 words from the same syntactic class, plural nouns, did not.

The effect of the rhyming list, given on the fifth day, was very different. Both John and Diane noticed the rhymes on the first trial (as did another naive control subject).

After these sessions, we showed Diane and John the 15 sublists they had copied and asked if they remembered noticing anything about them. They confirmed that they had not. Indeed, they were not easily convinced that these lists had actually been dictated. They found it hard to believe, for example, that they had copied "trolley, skates, truck, horse, airplane, tractor, car, rocket, bike, taxi, scooter, jet, trailer, subway, tank, feet, cab, ship, tricycle, van" without noticing the category.

In the final ten sessions of this phase, we determined whether the subjects, now alerted to the possible presence of structure in the dictated lists, could detect it on request. Each day, they read two very long stories (4500 to 7000 words); 200 or more words were dictated during each story. Five ten-word sublists were embedded in each (otherwise random) dictation list. One such sublist consisted of words from a particular category, one of words from a given syntactic class, one of rhyming words, and two of sentences. The order of sublists, and their positions in the 200 word list, were randomly determined. As always, Diane and John were encouraged to read at their normal rate with full comprehension. In addition, they were asked to indicate whenever they had noticed a sublist by interrupting the experimenter and telling him the basis of the relation among the words (e.g., "sentence," "clothing").

These final sessions were originally planned to take only three days, which immediately followed the earlier sessions in phase II. Five weeks later, in sessions 62–68, we returned to this task to obtain more information about performance under these conditions.

The subjects proved to be quite good at detecting the structured sublists once the task had been set for them. Rhymes were always, and superordinate category lists nearly always, detected. Diane identified rhyming sublists after only 3.2 words had been dictated, on the average, and category lists after an average of 5.0 words. John detected rhyming and category lists after 2.3 and 3.1 words, respectively. Sentences were detected most of the time (42 of 69 times by Diane, 41 of 55 by John), and syntactic class lists about half the time. Diane and John were slightly outperformed by two control subjects, who each copied three of our lists from dictation under the same instructions but without simultaneous reading.

The reading speed of both subjects dropped when this phase began, and again when it was resumed (Table 4). John's reading speed recovered rapidly, while Diane's increased more gradually. By the final sessions they read at rates comparable to those exhibited during the controlled testing of sessions 30–35. Diane's comprehension was high throughout these sessions; John's declined and then recovered. The initial decline in reading performance indicates that the demand to report structure from the dictated list was not fully compatible with the reading and copying skills that the subjects had developed in the preceding sessions.

TABLE 4   Reading Speed and Comprehension While Detecting Structured Sublists

	Diane			John	
Sessions	Speed	Comprehension		Speed	Comprehension
44	252.3[a]	92		388.5	42
45	339.4	100		500.1	78
46	409.5	100		442.8	100
(...)					
62	283.0	100		385.7	72
63	299.4	95		531.6	60
64	326.4	100		403.0	98
65	310.5	100		474.0	98
66	360.6	100		520.8	100
67	342.6	100		655.2	78
68	325.5	95		448.5	100

[a]Each score is the mean of 2 trials.

The fact that the subjects did not read with normal speed or with full comprehension on some of these trials suggested a further analysis. Were they more sensitive to relations among words on trials in which they read more slowly, or more superficially? We made a separate tabulation of the structure-detection data for those trials on which normal speed and 90% comprehension were achieved, and for the remaining trials. No systematic differences appeared.

III. READING WHILE CATEGORIZING WORDS

Judging from their ability to detect the structured sublists in the final sessions of the second phase, Diane and John appeared able to read and write simultaneously while understanding both the stories they read and the words they wrote. In order to obtain clearer evidence about the ability to extract meaning from the dictated words, a new task was introduced. On some trials, Diane and John were asked to write the names of superordinate categories to which the words belonged, rather than the words themselves.

In this phase, every dictated list consisted exclusively of words from one or the other of two semantic categories, such as "animals" and "furniture." Differ-

ent categories, either from Battig and Montague (1969) or devised by the authors, were used on each trial. We announced the names of the two categories immediately before the start of each trial.

The first six sessions consisted of four kinds of trials. On "word trials," John and Diane wrote the words that were dictated. On "category trials," they wrote the name of the superordinate. Word and category trials both used the fully categorizable lists described above. Every trial was followed either by a reading comprehension or a word recognition test. Recognition tests consisted of 20 randomly selected items from the dictation list and 20 distractors, never dictated, from the same semantic categories. Each of the six sessions consisted of one category trial with a comprehension test, one category trial with a recognition test, and one word trial. The word trial was followed equally often by a recognition or a comprehension test.

Reading comprehension and recognition memory were unaffected by the new categorization task (Table 5a). Reading speed dropped markedly for both subjects on the first few sessions of the categorization trials (Figure 2). By the end of these six sessions, only John appeared to have reached normal speed; Diane was given additional practice, with categorization trials only, for six sessions.

TABLE 5   Comprehension and Recognition Memory: Categorization Phase

a. Sessions 56–61

		Category Trials[a]	Word Trials[b]
Comprehension	Diane	98	100
(% correct)	John	88	80
Recognition	Diane	0.91	0.83
p (hit)	John	0.86	0.86
Recognition	Diane	0.23	0.28
p (FA)	John	0.12	0.17

b. Sessions 75–80

		Category Trials[c]	Control Trials[d]
Comprehension	Diane	100	100
(% correct)	John	81	88

[a]Each score is the mean of 6 trials.
[b]Each score is the mean of 3 trials.
[c]Each score is the mean of 36 trials.
[d]Each score is the mean of 6 trials.

By the end of her additional practice sessions, Diane too appeared to achieve normal reading speed while categorizing words (Figure 2). The final six sessions of the categorization phase attempted to verify that both subjects were reading as well while categorizing as they did normally. In each two hour session, the subjects read seven stories by the same author. Each session consisted of six category trials with comprehension tests and one control trial (with no writing at dictation). Reading comprehension appeared little affected by the writing task (Table 5b). Diane read with full comprehension, both on categorization and on control trials. John's comprehension on control trials exceeded his comprehension on categorization trials slightly, but both sets of scores were within his usual range. Reading speed also appeared unaffected by simultaneous categorization (Figure 2). After sixteen weeks' practice, Diane and John were able to categorize words semantically while reading at normal speed, and probably with normal comprehension.

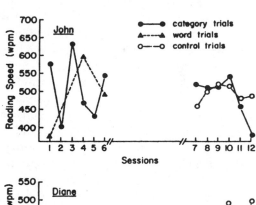

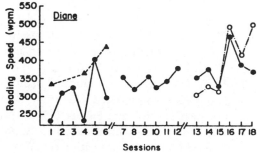

FIGURE 2   Reading speeds during the categorization phase

DISCUSSION

Diane and John appear able to copy words, detect relations among words, and categorize words for meaning, while reading as effectively and as rapidly as they can read alone. What accounts for their surprising abilities? We conclude this report by considering several possible descriptions of the attentional skills that they acquired.

Following Paulhan (1887), one might suggest that Diane and John rapidly "alternated their attention" between the tasks, making use of redundancies in the stories they read to avoid any decrement in performance. This hypothesis is not directly tested in our work, and indeed it may not be testable at all. Our results do show, however, that this hypothetical alternation would have to occur so rapidly as to take no measurable amount of time. Paulhan never predicted (or achieved) this degree of efficiency in any of the task combinations he studied.

The other traditional explanation for our results was first offered by Solomons and Stein (1896). These authors suggested that one learns to read and write simultaneously by training attention away from one of the tasks: one learns to write "automatically." Automaticity is a widely used concept in the literature on human performance, and it has been assessed by a number of different criteria. Solomons and Stein judged the automaticity of their behavior introspectively: they considered their writing to be "automatic" when they ceased to be aware of it. Introspections do not always agree, however, and Downey and Anderson (1915) reported no full loss of consciousness when they read and wrote together. The introspective reports of Diane and John were no more decisive. They sometimes reported that they thought clearly about each dictated word, repeating it to themselves while copying it. On other occasions, however, they said that they were unaware of even writing.

A more objective "operational indicant" of automatic processing has been suggested in a recent theoretical discussion by Posner and Snyder (1975). An activity or a mental process might be called "automatic" if it caused no interference with a concurrent attentive activity. By this criterion, Diane and John's writing would seem to be "automatic" by definition.

An interference criterion of automaticity becomes more interesting when we ask if our subjects' writing at dictation would interfere with concurrent activities other than the one on which they were trained. We did explore two transfer tasks in the final week of study: the subjects wrote at dictation while reading aloud (for one day) and while shadowing prose (for four days). Writing at dictation caused a decrement both in reading aloud and in shadowing prose, but not if they shadowed single letters (Shaffer, 1975). And the interference began to decrease with practice.

We do not regard these transfer tasks as a definitive test of the automaticity of writing by the interference criterion. Indeed, we doubt that any definitive test will be possible. Whether or not a given response interferes with a given task depends on the nature of the response and the nature of the task. Typists appear to type "automatically" from written copy if they shadow prose, but not if they shadow single letters (Shaffer, 1975). An examination of subjects' performance on a wide range of dual tasks need not converge in any simple way on a unitary conception of attention or capacity.

A third conception of automatism, which we prefer, would term behavior "automatic" if it did not involve certain high-order attentional skills. We suggest that attention be regarded as a matter of extracting meaning from the world, and perceiving the significance of events. Attention is involved in comprehending what one reads or hears, or in following any meaningful event over time. Our results suggest that the writing skills developed by John and Diane in the first eight weeks were not of this kind. Since they failed to notice sentences and categories in the dictated lines, they were evidently copying the words without much semantic analysis. In this sense, their writing might be called "automatic." As the demands of the experiment changed and the subjects were given additional practice, however, they gradually learned to analyze the dictated words semantically and to detect simple sentential relations among them. Finally, both subjects succeeded in categorizing dictated words with no loss of reading speed or comprehension. By our definition, their writing was no longer "automatic," as it had been in earlier stages of practice.

Since we did not dictate connected discourse to our subjects, we do not know whether they would have become able to read normally while following another meaningful sequence over time. That achievement remains to be demonstrated. It seems clear, however, that they understood both the text they were reading and the words they were copying. In at least this limited sense, they achieved a true division of attention: they were able to extract meaning simultaneously from what they read and from what they heard.

Our results suggest that attention itself is based on developing situation-specific skills. Particular instances of attentive performance should not be taken to reflect universal and unchanging capacities. Performance necessarily depends on one's knowledge about a particular set of tasks and situations, and one's skills for coping with them. Although individual strategies may have their own limitations, there are no obvious, general limits to attentional skills. Studies of attention which use unpracticed subjects, and infer mechanisms and limitations from their performance, will inevitably underestimate human capacities. Indeed, people's ability to develop skills in specialized situations is so great that it may never be possible to define general limits on cognitive capacity.

REFERENCES

Allport, D. A., Antonis, B., & Reynolds, P. (1972) On the division of attention: A disproof of the single channel hypotheses. Q. J. exp. Psychol., 24, 225–235.

Battig, W. F., & Montague, W. E. (1969) Category norms for verbal items in 56 categories: A replication and extension of the Connecticut Category Norms. J. exp. Psychol. Monograph, 80, No. 3, Part 2.

Corteen, R. S., & Wood, B. (1972) Autonomic responses to shock-associated words in an unattended channel. J. exp. Psychol., 94, 308–313.

Downey, J. E., & Anderson, J. E. (1915) Automatic writing. Amer. J. Psychol., 26, 161–195.

Glucksberg, S., & Cowen, G. N., Jr. (1970) Memory for nonattended auditory material. Cog. Psychol, 1, 149–156.

James, W. (1890) The principles of Psychology, Vol. 1. New York, Henry Holt and Co.

Kucera, H., & Francis, W. N. (1967) Computational analysis of present-day American English. Providence, Brown University Press.

Lewis, J. L. (1970) Semantic processing of unattended messages using dichotic listening. J exp. Psychol, 85, 225–228.

Norman, D. A. (1969) Memory while shadowing. Q. J. exp. Psychol., 21, 85–93.

Paulhan, F. (1887) La simultanéité des actes psychiques. Revue Scientifique, 13, 684–689.

Posner, M. I., & Snyder, C. R. R. (1975) Attention and cognitive control. In R. Solso (Ed.), Information Processing and Cognition: The Loyola Symposium. Potomac, MD, Lawrence Erlbaum Associates.

Shaffer, L. H. (1975) Multiple attention in continuous verbal tasks. In P. Rabbitt & S. Dornic (Eds.), Attention and Performance V. New York, Academic Press.

Solomons, L., & Stein, G. (1896) Normal motor automatism. Psychol. Rev., 3, 492–512.

Underwood, G. (1974) Moray vs. the rest: The effects of extended shadowing practice. Q. J. exp. Psychol., 26, 368–372.

Welford, A. T. (1968) Fundamentals of skill. London, Methuen.

Woodworth, R. S. (1921) Psychology: A study of mental life. New York, Henry Holt and Co.

POSTSCRIPT

Note that, in this article, Spelke, Hirst, and Neisser deal with the Posner and Snyder operational criteria for automaticity; they do not deal directly with the possibility that certain processes, perhaps through practice, come to require no attentional capacity to perform (compare LaBerge & Samuels, 1974; Shiffrin & Schneider, 1977; Treisman, Vieira, & Hayes, 1992). Nor do the authors completely eliminate the possibility that Diane and John were just shifting their focus rapidly from one task to another. However, in a subsequent paper (Hirst, Spelke, Reaves, Caharack, & Neisser, 1980), they take up both these possibilities and reject them.

The Spelke, Hirst, and Neisser view of attention emphasizes the fact that we often manage to do several things at once, rather than the fact that we tend to select and process only some of the information available in our environment. In this view, processing the information presented by the environment in particular ways (including selecting it out of the environment in the first place) can be seen as posing specific challenges to the information processor. Overcoming these challenges requires the development of certain skills, which has several consequences. First, it implies that becoming more skillful at meeting a particular challenge may reflect either increased efficiency at applying a certain skill or the development of a completely different way of approaching the challenge. Second, because different combinations of tasks or different kinds of information present different challenges, the implication is that being skilled at dealing with one task or one kind of information does not guarantee being able to deal with it in the context of other tasks or other kinds of information. This means that limitations on how much we can do at once may be not so much a matter of limitations in attentional or conscious capacity as of limitations in the skills we have at a particular time.

FOR FURTHER THOUGHT

1. What do introspective reports from earlier studies on divided attention, and from Diane and John, suggest? Why do Spelke, Hirst, and Neisser reject such reports?
2. Why do the authors reject Posner and Snyder's definition of automaticity based on interference among tasks?
3. How is Spelke, Hirst, and Neisser's description of attention different from that offered by bottleneck theories? How is it different from that offered by a capacity theory?
4. Identify an example of the practice phenomenon examined by Spelke and her associates (such as driving a car). Explain how the bottleneck, capacity, and attentional-skills theories would explain that phenomenon.

REFERENCES

Hirst, W., Spelke, E. S., Reaves, C. C., Caharack, G., & Neisser, U. (1980). Dividing attention without alternation or automaticity. *Journal of Experimental Psychology: General, 109,* 98–117.

LaBerge, D., & Samuels, S. J. (1974). Toward a theory of automatic information processing in reading. *Cognitive Psychology, 6,* 293–323.

Posner, M. I., & Snyder, C. R. R. (1975). Attention and cognitive control. In R. L. Solso (Ed.), *Information processing and cognition: The Loyola symposium* (pp. 55–85). Hillsdale, NJ: Erlbaum.

Shiffrin, R. M., & Schneider, G. E. (1977). Controlled and automatic human information processing: II. Perceptual learning, automatic attention, and general theory. *Psychological Review, 84,* 127–190.

Treisman, A. M., Vieira, A., & Hayes, A. (1992). Automaticity and preattentive processing. *American Journal of Psychology, 105,* 341–362.

CHAPTER TWO
Visual Perception

INTRODUCTION

In a 1968 article, Gerald Reicher conclusively demonstrated that when viewing time is very limited, people identify individual letters more accurately when the letters are presented in the context of a word than they do when letters are presented alone. In this excerpt from "Processes in Word Recognition," Daniel Wheeler identifies and tests five different hypotheses to account for this word-superiority effect.

Wheeler identifies studies such as reported in this article as descending from work by Howes and Solomon (1951), who had found that the amount of time a word must be presented for it to be accurately identified (its visual duration threshold) is less, on average, for frequently encountered words than it is for infrequently encountered words. (The "on average" is noteworthy, because the visual duration threshold for any given word varies among subjects. Some subjects need considerably longer exposures than others do to read a word accurately.)

Traditionally, in experiments of this kind, an instrument called a tachistoscope is used to present stimuli for very brief periods of times (see the Introduction to Reading 1 for a description). Work by Sperling (1960; see Reading 1) and others, however, indicates that information about the stimulus remains available for some time after the termination of the display; a visual representation of the stimulus seems to linger for a certain period. Presenting another display immediately afterward erases or masks this lingering icon (Neisser, 1967). Hence, to limit the availability of the information in the stimulus to the time during which it is actually displayed, it is important that the stimulus field be followed by a masking field.

Two points should be noted about the study reported here. First, rather than using a tachistoscope, Wheeler used a computer that presented the different displays in sequence. Second, he adjusted the duration of the stimulus display for each subject so that the subject's accuracy would be about 75% overall. Thus the duration of the stimulus display was different for different subjects.

In this excerpt, some of the more technical aspects of the article have been left out, including a lengthy discussion about serial position effects and latency results. Read very carefully through each of the hypotheses that Wheeler identifies in his introduction. As you read the rest of the article, ask yourself which hypothesis each experimental manipulation is directed toward, what the possible outcomes are, and what each outcome would mean.

Processes in Word Recognition

Daniel D. Wheeler

Mental Health Research Institute, The University of Michigan

This decade has provided a number of advances in our understanding of how humans process visual information. On the experimental side, Sperling (1960) and Averbach and Coriell (1961) have demonstrated the existence and general nature of the icon (Neisser, 1967). . . . The theoretical advances have included the development of a number of pattern recognition models (Uhr, 1966; Selfridge, 1966). . . . The stimuli used in most of this work were letters, either singly or in arrays, rather than words.

The major line of recent work on word recognition has been fairly independent of the other work on visual information processing. It traces back to Howes and Solomon's (1951) demonstration that the visual duration thresholds for words are a function of word frequency. There has been a major theoretical controversy over whether the word frequency effect reflects some basic property of the perceptual mechanism or whether the effect is attributable to a response bias from the subjects' greater tendency to use high frequency words. Broadbent (1967) and Morton (1968) have tested a number of specific models from two classes, guessing models and signal detection models. In general, their analyses of data from auditory perception of words in noise support a signal detection model with a criterion shift towards more frequent words.

A tacit assumption [in this work] is that the perceptual aspects of word recognition can be understood in terms of individual letter recognition. Only very general interactions among letters should occur from changes in attention or overall contrast. Other than these effects, perception of one letter (or extraction of information from the letter) should be independent of perception of the others. The effects of set, word frequency, etc., are introduced by a decision mechanism which takes advantage of the redundancy of words.

This independence assumption is challenged by Reicher's (1968) study of word recognition. Reicher probed the accuracy of the recognition of the individual letters of a word in a tachistoscopic exposure by giving the subject a forced-choice test between two letters, one of which appeared in the stimulus. Normally the redundancy of English words would prevent this probe technique from being specific to a single letter of the stimulus because the identity of a letter can often be inferred from the other letters of the word. Reicher eliminated the effects of redundancy by having both alternatives form a word with the remaining letters. For example, *D* and *K* might be the alternatives for testing the fourth position of the stimulus *WORD*. The untested three letters *WOR* should contribute no information to the choice between *D* and *K* since *WORK* is also a common English word.

Reicher's main finding was that performance on the forced-choice tests of letter recognition was more

This article is a modified version of a Ph.D. dissertation submitted to The University of Michigan. I would like to thank my Committee, Robert A. Bjork, James C. Greeno, and Wilfred M. Kincaid, and especially my Chairman, Walter Reitman, for their help and encouragement. I am indebted to Jonathan Baron, Donald Broadbent, Jerry Gardner, George Mandler, Arthur Melton, and Donald Norman for comments and discussion. The late Peter Headly deserves considerable credit for programming the experimental system. Mrs. Billie Lawson and Miss Judith Brunclik helped devise the stimulus materials. Mrs. Joan McClain did a wonderful job of typing everything through at least three versions of the paper. This work was supported by USPHS Grant No. MH12160, which I should like to acknowledge with appreciation.

[Author] now at the University of Texas at Austin.

accurate when the stimulus was a four-letter word than when it was either a single letter or a nonsense quadrigram. Since the subjects did not know until after the presentation of the stimulus what letter position would be tested, the strong word superiority effect means that subjects recognized all four letters of the word with a higher probability of being correct than they had on a single letter alone.

Figure 1 shows examples of the experimental materials used by Reicher. On each trial the fixation point was displayed until the subject initiated the stimulus exposure. One of the six types of stimulus displays was then briefly exposed and then immediately replaced by the masking field with the alternatives. The position of the alternatives marked the position of the probed letter in the word.

Reicher found that performance, as measured by the proportion of correct choices, was better with word stimuli than either single letters or quadrigrams by about 8%. . . . Performance on the quadrigrams was worst, but apparently not significantly worse than on single letters. . . .

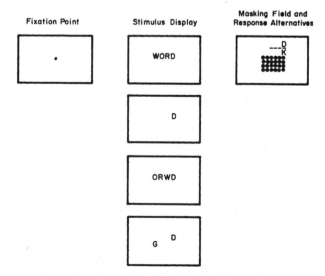

FIGURE 1 Examples of tachistoscopic displays used by Reicher (1968, Figure 2). The stimulus display always consisted of either one or two stimuli of the same type, words, letters, or quadrigrams.

Implications of Reicher's Results

At first glance, Reicher's experimental paradigm appears to provide a test of the serial versus parallel processing issue in the organization of visual information processing in humans. The simple versions of parallel and serial models make different predictions about the results of Reicher's experiment. Most serial processing models for the readout of information from the visual image or icon would predict that subjects in Reicher's experiment should do best on the single letter stimuli. With more than one letter to process, the average amount of processing per letter during the limited iconic duration must decrease.

The simple parallel models usually assume that the letter units are processed independently at the same time. There should be no difference in the processing of single letters alone and in a word. Performance in Reicher's experiment should be the same with letter and word stimuli.

Neither prediction is consistent with the obtained results. Neither model has any mechanism that would explain the superiority of performance on words. As soon as a mechanism is added to account for more accurate performance on meaningful words, either model can fit the observed data.

There are two ways around this theoretical impasse. One can hypothesize separate factors or processes which account for the superiority of words without changing the basic pattern recognition models. These are generally consistent with either parallel or serial models and can be included in the models without drastic changes. Or one can modify the basic pattern recognition models by dropping the independence assumption and proposing some interactive recognition system in its place. The first approach leads to testable hypotheses and simpler models. It will be attempted first.

Hypotheses for Separate Mechanisms

The five hypotheses discussed below all suggest mechanisms or processes that could be included in either a serial or parallel model to account for the word superiority effect.

1. *Interference hypothesis.* In Reicher's experiment, the presentation of the stimulus display was terminated by the onset of a field containing both the mask and the two choice alternatives. The subject then had to recognize the two choice letters before he could decide between them. Some of Reicher's subjects reported that the choice letters interfered with the recognition of the stimulus. Reicher argued that the recognition of the single letter choice alternatives would interfere with the recognition of the single letter stimuli more than with the recognition of the word stimuli. This would be true if, for instance, the interference occurred in that part of the pattern recognition process which involved access to memory to find the stored representation of the object identified. Such interference would result in better performance on words.

This hypothesis can easily be tested. The interference should not occur if the recognition of the alternatives is separated in time from the recognition of the stimulus. This can be accomplished by delaying the presentation of the alternatives until the recognition of the stimulus is completed. Thus if the hypothesis is correct the difference between the performance on words and letters should disappear when the presentation of the choices is delayed sufficiently.

2. *Preprocessing hypothesis.* A number of pattern recognition models have postulated a stage of preprocessing which comes before the actual pattern recognition process (see Uhr, 1966). This stage is supposed to isolate and normalize the size, position, etc., of the stimulus to be recognized. In order to control for differential sensitivity within the foveal area, Reicher presented his single letter stimuli at the same position they would have appeared at had they been in the corresponding word. Since the words were centered with respect to the fixation point, the positions of the single letter stimuli had to vary. This might cause the preprocessing stage to take longer to isolate the single letter stimuli in the visual field. Thus there would be less time remaining before the icon faded for the actual pattern recognition system to work on the single letter stimuli.

The positional uncertainty of the single letter stimuli can be eliminated by positioning the single letter stimuli at a constant position in the visual field defined by the fixation point. If the superiority of performance on word stimuli is a result of the additional preprocessing required to locate letter stimuli in the visual field, the effect should disappear when the positional uncertainty of the letters is eliminated. This manipulation does not, however, control for variation in foveal sensitivity. As a further check on a possible preprocessing stage and the effects of positional uncertainty, another condition could be run so the words rather than the letters have positional uncertainty. Each word could be presented with the letter being tested positioned at the fixation point. Thus the position of the whole word would vary as a function of the position of the letter being tested. When compared with single letters in the constant position, performance on words should be worse than on single letters if the preprocessing and positional uncertainty hypothesis is correct.

3. *Focusing hypothesis.* There may be some idiosyncratic properties of individual words that cause the pattern recognizing mechanism to focus on those aspects of a word which contain the most information that distinguishes the presented word from other words. These aspects are likely to be in those letter positions for which there are alternative letters that can be switched to form similar words. This is, of course, exactly where the stimuli were tested in Reicher's experiment. The appropriate control is to choose the stimulus words so that they have an alternative for every letter position. For example, *READ* can be changed one letter at a time to form *HEAD*, *ROAD*, *REND*, and *REAL*. If the effect holds over all positions in the same word, it is hard to see how a focusing mechanism could account for Reicher's results.

4. *Response bias hypothesis.* If subjects see some of the letters of a word stimulus, but not the letter tested, they are probably more likely to guess the alternative that forms the more frequent word with those letters [they have] recognized. Reicher does not mention any control of word frequency. The simplest control for a possible response bias effect of word frequency is to use both words as stimuli. If one subject

gets the stimulus *READ* with choices *R* and *H*, another subject should get *HEAD* with the same choices. Any improvement in performance on the more frequent words will be canceled by poorer performance on the other words.

5. *Word frequency hypothesis.* The effects of word frequency need not be limited to a guessing process that would produce a response bias. Recognition involves the access to the subject's long-term memory for the object being recognized. Access may be easier for more frequent words. Thus performance on the TAME/TAMP pair would be worse than on the pair of more frequent words CARE/CAKE.

Single letters can be considered as low frequency words. The letter *E* is the most frequent letter in English, but appears alone as a unit only in such unusual contexts as "row *E*" on a theater ticket. Thus a word frequency effect might explain the superiority of performance on words.

The crucial data for a test of this hypothesis is the performance on the single letters *I* and *A*. These letters are also high frequency English words. Both are among the 500 most frequent words in the Thorndike-Lorge (1944) count. If the superiority of performance on words is attributable only to the fact that they appear more frequently on the average than the letters appear as units, then the performance on the single letters (words) *I* and *A* should be as good as the performance on high frequency words.

EXPERIMENTAL METHOD

The tests of the five hypotheses were carried out in a single experiment. The experimental paradigm was very similar to that used by Reicher (1968). . . .[However], the use of the position of the alternatives to mark the position of the critical letter of the stimulus, . . . if Reicher's mask field is effective, . . . should be of little use to the subject. . . . [This aspect] of Reicher's experiment [was] eliminated. . . .

Apparatus and Experimental Setting

The experimental equipment consisted of a Digital Equipment Corporation PDP-8 computer connected to a Tektronix Model 611 storage scope. The computer was programmed to display a series of four visual fields on the scope, making it much like a four-channel tachistoscope.

The display scope and response keys were in an experimental room separate from the computer and teletype. The subjects were run individually, seated in front of a panel on which the response keys were mounted. The display scope was positioned at eye level on a wheeled cart behind the panel. This allowed the distance from the subject to be adjusted so that the mask field subtended an angle of 2½ degrees for each subject. A 7½ watt nightlight provided dim overall illumination for the experimental room, sufficient for the dark-adapted subjects to see the response keys, yet not so much that the subjects could see their reflection in the glass scope face. An intercom allowed the experimenter in the computer room to communicate with the subject. . . .

Figure 2 shows the physical arrangement of the display fields. The sequence of events during each trial was as follows: First the fixation point was displayed. Then the subject initiated the trial by pressing a key with his left hand. The fixation point disappeared, and the stimulus field was displayed for the length of time specified. . . . Immediately after the offset of the stimulus the mask field was displayed. The mask field consists of a random pattern of dots, different on each trial. After the choice delay interval

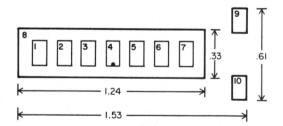

FIGURE 2   Arrangement of the display fields on the face of the scope. The dimensions are in inches. The letter position areas are .11 × .16 in. Field 1: The fixation point appeared at the bottom of area 4. Field 2: The stimulus appeared in letter positions 1–7. Field 3: A masking pattern of random dots covered area 8. Field 4: The choices were displayed in letter positions 9 and 10 as the masking pattern remained on.

(possibly 0 sec), the two choices appeared to the right of the mask field. Both the mask and the choice fields remained on until the subject pressed one of the response keys. The average rate was approximately one trial per 5½ sec.

One disadvantage of the computer-operated experimental apparatus was that the brightness of the display scope could not be controlled precisely. The brightness adjustment on the scope provided only coarse control; small changes in the knob position caused large changes in the brightness. Furthermore, the brightness of the scope drifted over time. Fortunately, the drift was slow and of relatively small magnitude.

Materials

The test of the focusing hypothesis requires that we use words that can be tested in every letter position, i.e., words that have an alternative that forms another meaningful word in each letter position. These words will be called base words. The test of the response bias hypothesis requires that the alternative for every test also be tested. Thus the stimulus words were made up in sets of five, one base word and four alternatives. An example of a base word is *READ*, with the alternatives *HEAD*, *ROAD*, *REND*, and *REAL*.

Forty-eight nonoverlapping sets of five words were found with the aid of a crossword puzzle dictionary of four-letter words. Each set of five words provided 16 test items: four tests of the base word (once in each letter position); four tests of the alternative words; and eight single letter items constructed from the word items. The single letter items were formed by removing the three untested letters of the word items. The single letter remaining was used with the same alternatives as the original word. Table 1 shows how the 16 items were formed and divided into groups. It would not be wise to give the same subject all 16 items, especially the four tests of the base word. Thus the items were divided into four groups. Into each group went a test of one of the positions of the base word, the test of the alternative formed from a different position of the key word, and two single letter items.

TABLE 1   Construction of 16 Items from a Single Base Word, *READ*

| Type | Stimulus | Choices | | Stimulus Group |
		Correct	Incorrect	
4 tests of base word	READ	R	H	1
	READ	E	O	2
	READ	A	N	3
	READ	D	L	4
Alternative words	HEAD	H	R	3
	ROAD	O	E	4
	REND	N	A	1
	REAL	L	D	2
Single letter items from base word	R	R	H	2
	E	E	O	3
	A	A	N	4
	D	D	L	1
Single letter items from alternative words	H	H	R	4
	O	O	E	1
	N	N	A	2
	L	L	D	3

Note: Items are divided into four groups so that each subject is tested on only one item of each type.

Each group was balanced so that each letter position was tested equally often on both base words and alternatives. Since there were 48 different base words, a complete group consisted of 192 (4 × 48) items.

Another group of 192 items was constructed for use in estimating the exposure duration required to obtain the desired percentage correct for each subject. This group also consisted of half words and half single letters. All four-letter positions were tested equally often, and none of the words used overlapped those in the fully balanced groups. A small group of 20 items was constructed to serve as examples during the instructions.

The test of the preprocessing hypothesis requires different ways of placing the words and letters into the seven positions of the display field (see Figure 2). Both words and letters could vary in position or remain constant. When word position was constant, the four letters were placed in positions three through six. When the word position was varied, it was placed in the field so that the tested letter appeared in position four. Letters in constant position appeared in position four. When letters varied, they appeared in the position in which they would have been in the word from which they were derived (see Table 2). . . .

The letter or word shift variable was the only difference among the three experimental conditions.

The other independent variables were manipulated within subjects. Three values of choice delay time were used to provide the test of the interference hypothesis. The time between the stimulus offset/mask onset and the presentation of the choice letters was 0, 1, or 2 sec.

The independent variables within each condition were completely counterbalanced so that each level of each variable was tested equally often with each possible combination of levels of the other variables. The balanced variables were the following: (a) word or letter stimulus, (b) choice delay time, (c) base word or alternative word, and (d) letter position of the tested letter. There are 2 × 3 × 2 × 4 = 48 combinations; each subject was tested four times on each combination for a total of 192 trials.

The 192 items were divided into two matched sets of 96. The items were randomized within each set of 96. Twelve different randomized orders were used, four in each condition.

Procedure

Each subject was run for one experimental session lasting approximately 1 hr. The session began with an instructional group of 20 trials, with display times beginning at $\frac{1}{2}$ sec and decreasing to 25 msec. As the

TABLE 2 Arrangement of the Stimuli in the Display Field for the Three Conditions

Letter Position Tested	Condition			Correct Choice	Incorrect Choice
	Letter Shift	No Shift	Word Shift		
1	_ _ H E A D _ _ _ H _ _ _ _	_ _ H E A D _ _ _ _ H _ _ _	_ _ _ H E A D _ _ _ H _ _ _	H	R
2	_ _ R O A D _ _ _ _ O _ _ _	_ _ R O A D _ _ _ _ O _ _ _	_ _ R O A D _ _ _ _ O _ _ _	O	E
3	_ _ R E N D _ _ _ _ _ N _ _	_ _ R E N D _ _ _ _ N _ _ _	_ R E N D _ _ _ _ _ N _ _ _	N	A
4	_ _ R E A L _ _ _ _ _ _ L _	_ _ R E A L _ _ _ _ L _ _ _	R E A L _ _ _ _ _ _ L _ _ _	L	D

Note: When words were shifted, the letter tested was always placed at the fixation point. When letters were shifted, they were placed in the same position in which they had appeared in the word from which they were derived.

subject worked through these items, the experimenter explained the procedure. The following points were emphasized: (*a*) the stimulus would always be a single letter or a four-letter English word, (*b*) they were to perform as accurately as possible and guess when necessary, and (*c*) they were to work at a rate they found comfortable. The experimenter left the room as the subject finished the instructional trials.

The subject then worked through four sets of 96 items, with a 2-min break between each set. The exposure duration was varied in the first two sets. Performance on these sets was used to estimate the exposure duration which would result in 75% correct performance on the remaining sets. The last two sets of 96 were from the matched groups of base words and alternatives. Only the data from the last two sets were used in the complete analysis. The exposure time for the fourth set was adjusted if performance on the third set was not in the range of 15 to 39% errors. An adjustment was necessary for 13 of the 36 subjects.

At the conclusion of the experiment, the subjects were interviewed to obtain their general reactions, to check on the strategies the subjects may have used, and to test their awareness of the positional shifts (if any) in their condition.

Subjects

Subjects were 36 paid volunteers from the Mental Health Research Institute subject pool. Most were college students. Each served for one experimental session, approximately 1 hr long. Six male and six female subjects served in each of the three conditions. Subjects were assigned to conditions by a rotating scheme in the order in which they participated in the experiment.

RESULTS

Overall Results

Performance on words was consistently better than performance on single letter items in all three conditions. The average difference in performance, in favor of words, is 10%. Table 3 shows both the overall results and the breakdown by condition. . . .

TABLE 3   Percent Correct Responses by Condition

Condition	Percent Correct		Word-Letter Difference
	Words	Letters	
Letter shift	72.5	65.8	6.7
No shift	80.8	67.5	13.3
Word shift	74.9	65.0	9.9
Mean	76.1	66.1	10.0

Note: 1,152 observations per entry.

. . . A check using Kincaid's (1962) method of combining contingency tables[1] showed that the difference between the performance on words and letters within the letter shift condition was significant at the .001 level. The larger differences in the other groups were significant beyond the .001 level. [Excluded here is a discussion of the slight differences in results that can be observed among the different conditions. Wheeler's conclusions are that those differences are an artifact (an uninteresting side-effect) of the criterion-setting procedure and that there is a sizeable word-superiority effect in all three conditions.]

Tests of Specific Hypotheses

1. *Interference hypothesis.* Within each condition, three delay times (0, 1, and 2 sec) were used between the onset of the mask and the presentation of the choices. If the process of recognizing the alternatives interferes with the still proceeding process of recognizing the stimulus when the delay time is zero, the interference should be reduced and performance should improve when the delay times are longer. Furthermore, the improvement should be greater for letters than for words because the single letter choices are more similar to the single letter stimuli than to the word stimuli.

The data shown in Figure 3 confirm this prediction. For the letter items, the delay time had a signifi-

---

[1]All significance levels reported in this work were obtained by this method unless otherwise stated. A sign test (Siegel, 1956) was used only when Kincaid's method was difficult to apply.

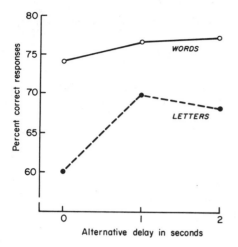

FIGURE 3   Percent correct by alternative delay for letter and word items.

cant (.001 level) effect on performance. The percent correct was lowest at the zero delay interval, where the interference should have been strongest. Performance on the word items increased slightly as the delay time increased, but the increase was not significant ($.10 > p > .05$).

Despite this confirmation of the interference effect, that effect is not sufficient to account for the word superiority effect. As Figure 3 clearly shows, there was still a considerable difference in performance in favor of the words beyond the zero delay point. Within the 1 and 2 sec delay items, the mean percentages of correct responses were 77.1% for words and 69.1% for letters. The difference of 8.0% is significant at the .001 level.

The word superiority effect with choice delays of 1 and 2 sec was significant within each of the three conditions. This eliminates the possibility that the interference effect interacting with the conditions could explain the word superiority effect. The smallest difference among the conditions was 5.2%, significant at the .025 level. . . .

2. Preprocessing hypothesis.   If the variance in the letter position causes the word superiority effect by slowing down a preprocessing mechanism in the human pattern recognition system, the effect should disappear when the variance in the letter position is eliminated. Thus the hypothesis predicts that the word superiority effect should appear in only the letter shift condition of the present experiment. In fact, performance on letters was poorer than on words in the other conditions as well, even though the letters appeared in a constant position in those conditions. The preprocessing hypothesis can be rejected.

3. Focusing hypothesis.   The operation of a focusing or attention directing mechanism should not improve the forced-choice performance on word items when each word is tested in all four letter positions. Thus if the hypothesis is correct, the word superiority effect should not be found with base words (words tested in all positions) in the present experiment. The word superiority effect should be found only with the alternatives to the base words.

Table 4 shows the percentage correct for the base words and alternative words. The difference between them is not significant. Performance on both base words and alternative words is significantly (.001 level) better than performance on single letters, even by a simple sign test. The focusing hypothesis can be rejected.

TABLE 4   Percent Correct Responses for Base Words and Alternative Words

	Percent Correct	
Condition	*Base Words*	*Alternative Words*
Letter shift	72.4	72.6
No shift	80.4	81.2
<u>Word shift</u>	<u>73.4</u>	<u>76.4</u>
Overall	75.4	76.7

Note: 576 observations per entry.

4. Response bias hypothesis.   If the word superiority effect is simply the result of a response bias established by the untested letters of the words towards the correct alternative, the effect should be reversed when the stimuli are changed so that the other alternative becomes correct. The net effect in favor of words should disappear when both alternatives are tested, as in this experiment. The strong word superiority effect shown in the overall results (see Table 3) demonstrates that the response bias hypothesis cannot be the correct explanation.

5. *Word frequency hypothesis.*   The critical data for a test of the hypothesis that the word superiority effect is due to the higher frequency of words as units than letters as units is the performance on the single letters *I* and *A*. Both of these are also high frequency words, within the top category in the Thorndike-Lorge (1944) count. Table 5 shows the percentage correct for *I*'s and *A*'s as single letters and for words in which the letters *I* and *A* were tested. In both cases performance on the four-letter words is better than performance on the single letters *I* and *A*. A sign test showed these differences to be significant, at the .002 level for *A*'s and beyond the .001 level for *I*'s and for the combined data. The combined performance on *A*'s and *I*'s is slightly worse than the average percent correct for all letters (see Table 3). These results show that the word superiority effect cannot be explained in terms of a word frequency effect. . . .

TABLE 5   Percent Correct Responses on Tests of *A* and *I*

| | Context | | |
Letter Tested	Word	Single Letter	N
A	78.4	70.1	351
I	80.9	59.7	225
Combined	79.3	65.6	576

Subjective Reports

In answer to a question about the strategies they used to improve performance, only a few subjects failed to report things that they were doing to help identify the stimulus. More complex strategies included rehearsing the stimulus on the longer delay trials, trying to avoid looking at the choices until the stimulus had been identified, and trying to take in the whole field, as one subject had learned to do in a speed reading course.

The strategies reported did not attempt to take advantage of the differences among the conditions.

Perhaps this is because only a couple of subjects figured out correctly the shifts of words or letters relative to the fixation point. Most were not at all aware of the relative positions.

About half the subjects thought that they did better on word items than on letters, and a quarter of them thought they did better on letters. Of the three subjects who actually did better on letter items, two thought they did better on words and one didn't know. A few subjects had difficulty answering which item type they did better on because at the exposure durations used they were not able to tell the letter and word items apart.

DISCUSSION

All five of the initial hypotheses have been rejected as complete explanations of the word superiority effect. Performance on words was consistently better than on single letters in all cases, despite the controls suggested by the five hypotheses. It seems appropriate to stop trying to explain away the phenomenon and, instead, to consider the implications for models of the human recognition system.

The major conclusion to be drawn from the strength and persistence of the word superiority effect, as shown in Reicher's (1968) experiment and the experiment reported here, is that word recognition cannot be analyzed into a set of independent letter recognition processes. There is an interaction among the letters such that the context of the other letters of a meaningful word improves recognition despite the control of letter redundancy. It is not a general effect from the context of other letters; Reicher showed that the context of a nonsense quadrigram did not improve performance.

The Serial versus Parallel Issue

The results of this experiment are not directly relevant to the serial versus parallel issue. The latency data are consistent with either type of model. It is difficult to imagine how a serial model could account for improved performance on four-letter words since the four letters would take longer to be read off the rapidly fading icon. But such a model cannot be ruled out.

The parallel-serial issue can be restated in terms of the size of the perceptual recognition unit. At some level the aspects of the visual stimulus are processed simultaneously as a unit (i.e., in parallel). This parallel level might be at the stage where individual points are analyzed into lines. In most serial models for words or letter arrays, the processing of the letter features is assumed to be in parallel, but the letters are processed in serial. In even the most radical parallel model, a level is reached at which processing is serial. No one proposes that we read a whole paragraph in parallel. Thus there is not really a dichotomy between serial and parallel processing models. Each model should be specified by the largest unit which is processed in parallel, i.e., at the same time. This unit might be considered the perceptual unit. Possible unit sizes for verbal materials include the letter, spelling-unit, syllable, word, and phrase.

A perceptual unit size can also be based on nonindependence of the sort demonstrated in this experiment. The perceptual unit can be considered the highest level in which facilitative interactions of the lower level units occur in both directions. The mutual facilitation is assumed to occur only when the lower units are processed together as a perceptual unit. For example, an experiment on the perception of word pairs like *TOP HAT* might show that the presence of the first word enhanced recognition of the second, but not vice versa. This would suggest that the first word is processed separately, prior to the second. Thus the perceptual unit would have to be smaller than the word pair. If the results showed mutual facilitation, a perceptual unit size of word pairs or larger would be indicated. Of course, redundancy and set effects would have to be eliminated.

The word superiority results can be interpreted as demonstrating that the perceptual units are larger than single letters. The single letters interact to facilitate performance on words. The perceptual units might be words, but the data do not require this. Any unit size of diagram or spelling pattern or larger would account for the word superiority effect.

Whether the perceptual units defined in these two ways coincide remains to be seen.

Feature Analysis

Many models of letter recognition have assumed that the recognition process is based on the extraction of the distinctive features of the stimulus. The extracted features are then used by some decision process to categorize the stimulus. In Selfridge's (1966) "Pandemonium" the lowest level demons are the feature extractors. The operators of Uhr and Vossler's (1963) model extract features from the pattern being recognized. Rumelhart's (1970) components in his multicomponent theory are equivalent to features. The attributes input to the logogen in Morton's (1969) model can also be considered as features.

The feature framework treats individual letters as bundles of features. The features are usually identified with visually apparent attributes of the letters, such as "curved shape on top." Words consist of a sequence of letter bundles of features. The pattern recognition system operates by extracting features from the stimulus and applying a decision procedure to determine the identity of the stimulus. If processing time were available, sufficient features would be extracted for the system to identify the stimulus with very little probability of error. In a tachistoscopic recognition situation, not all of the features of each bundle can be extracted. Errors will result when the features needed for a particular decision fail to be extracted.

A simple specific version of a feature model is one that postulates that the extraction of features from all bundles proceeds in parallel such that in a limited exposure a proportion of the features in each bundle would be extracted. Thus when the stimulus *LOVE* is presented, or when *L* is presented alone, the bundle for the *L* should contain the same proportion of features. Performance should be the same for both cases. Yet the experimental results show that the decision between the alternatives *D* and *L* is more likely to be correct when the stimulus was the whole word *LOVE,* than when it was the single letter *L.* The simple model must be modified to account for these results.

More Features

Perhaps more features relevant to the D versus L decision can be extracted from the word stimulus than from the single letter. The problem then becomes one of identifying the source of the additional features. It is unlikely that increasing the number of letters in the stimulus increases the rate at which features are extracted from each bundle. The attention assumptions so important in Rumelhart's (1970) multicomponent model would predict just the opposite. As the number of letters in the stimulus array increases, the amount of attention or feature extracting capacity available for each bundle should decrease. In addition to being implausible, the extraction of more features per bundle with multiletter stimuli would predict better performance on quadrigrams than on single letters unless other changes were also made in the model. Reicher (1968) showed that performance on quadrigrams was not better than on letters.

The experiment reported here eliminated two hypotheses that otherwise would have been considered as the source of the additional features. These are the focusing and response bias hypotheses. The focusing hypothesis supposes that the additional features are extracted at the tested position at the expense of not extracting as many features from other letter positions. The response bias hypothesis suggests that the feature bundles for the untested letters of the word stimuli, i.e., OVE, are, in fact, relevant to the decision between the D and L alternatives. Both of these hypotheses were eliminated by the use of carefully balanced stimulus sets.

There are additional possibilities for the source of more features relevant to the choice between the response alternatives if the restriction of features to letter bundles is relaxed. With multiletter stimuli there could be additional features extracted from the various combinations of letters, independent of the specific letter features. Any feature extracted from a letter combination including the tested letter might be relevant to the choice between the two alternatives. The additional information available from these features would enable the subject to perform better on words than on letters. . . .

Feature Selection

The extraction of more features in the case of word stimuli is not the only way to account for superior performance on words. Of the features extracted from the feature bundle for the letter L, only a few may be relevant to the decision between the alternatives L and D. The others are features on which both L and D have the same value. Instead of extracting more features in order to get more relevant features, the extraction process could be selective with word stimuli such that of the features extracted for a given exposure time, more will be relevant to the choice between the alternatives. In order for this to explain the superiority of the word stimuli, the features extracted from the irrelevant letters OVE must direct the extraction of features from the L such that the features which distinguish LOVE from other words ending in OVE are more likely to be extracted. Since the superiority of words is evident at all letter positions at once, each letter must simultaneously, before it is identified, both affect and be affected by the features extracted from other letter positions. . . .

Verbal Coding with Information Loss

The preceding two models have attempted to account for superior performance on word stimuli by postulating a source for additional information in the case of word stimuli. The same information difference can be obtained by proposing that information is lost in the case of single letter stimuli. This information loss could occur in the process of categorizing or producing a verbal code for either the word or letter stimulus. All we need to suppose is that the system has only a single verbal code, either a word name or a letter name, available at the point the decision is made between the two forced-choice alternatives.

An example will make this alternative clear. Suppose the single letter L is presented and sufficient features are extracted to limit the possible letters that it could be to the set B, E, M, and L. If this information is available at the time of a forced-choice decision between D and L, the correct choice will be made. But if the system must code the feature information into a verbal code before the forced-choice decision, the system would lose the information needed for that decision except when *L* happened to be the code selected.

Now suppose that the stimulus *LOVE* is presented and that the same features are extracted from the *L* as before. The possible letters for the first position of the word are the same set as before, *B, E, M,* and *L.* But the system now has some basis for selecting among these letters. It looks for a word code which simultaneously satisfies the constraints provided by all four letter positions. The actual stimulus word, *LOVE,* will, of course, satisfy all the constraints.

There may be other words that satisfy all the constraints provided by the features extracted from all letter positions. With *M* as a possibility for the first letter position, *MOVE* is another solution to the simultaneous constraints. *LONE* and *LOSE* are solutions if *N* and *S* are possibilities for the third letter position. Although there may be several solutions, there is likely to be in each letter position some possible letters that do not enter into any of the solutions. In the first position of the example, the letters *B* and *E* may not appear in any of the solutions. When a word is selected from the set of solutions to the simultaneous constraints to be the verbal code for that item, it is more likely to include the letter *L* than in the case where a letter was selected from the set of four possible letters to be the verbal code for the single letter stimulus. Thus the word code is more likely to retain the information from the feature analysis that allows a correct choice to be made between the alternatives *D* and *L*.

The simultaneous constraints model is almost identical to the fragment theory of Newbigging (1961) and the sophisticated guessing model of Broadbent (1967). But the general notion of information loss in coding is also consistent with the signal detection models of Broadbent (1967) and Morton (1968, 1969).

An additional attraction of the simultaneous constraints model is that it is easy to qualitatively account for the increase in processing time as word length increases. On a more abstract level, the model consists of two stages. The first is a feature extraction stage in which the processing is, presumably, in parallel. The second stage uses the features to find, construct, or otherwise determine a code for the stimulus. . . .

Conclusions

The three models account for superior performance on words by postulating (*a*) more features from digrams or larger units, (*b*) selection of features for greater efficiency, and (*c*) information loss in verbal coding. Experimental tests of the models are difficult to make. The first two could be distinguished if the features could be identified. Eleanor Gibson has made some progress with confusion matrix methods of identifying the distinctive features used in the recognition of single letters (see Gibson, Schapiro, and Yonas, unpublished), but the techniques are not sufficient for a test of the models. The verbal coding model makes one easily testable prediction.[2] Performance on the forced-choice task with letter stimuli, when corrected for guessing, should be no better than performance when the subject reports a single letter without having alternatives to choose from. This test, of course, would not give direct evidence about the word processing.

REFERENCES

Averbach, E., & Coriell, A. S. Short term memory in vision. *Bell System Technical Journal,* 1961, 40, 309–328.

Broadbent, D. E. Word-frequency effect and response bias, *Psychological Review,* 1967, 74, 1–15.

Conrad, R. Acoustic confusions in immediate memory. *British Journal of Psychology,* 1964, 55, 75–84.

Estes, W. K., & Taylor, H. A. A detection method and probabilistic models for assessing information processing from brief visual displays. *Proceedings of the National Academy of Sciences,* 1964, 52(2), 446–454.

Estes, W. K., & Taylor, H. A. Visual detection in relation to display size and redundancy of critical elements. *Perception and Psychophysics,* 1966, 1, 91–16.

Feigenbaum, E. A. The simulation of verbal learning behavior. In E. A. Feigenbaum and J. Feldman (Eds.), *Computers and Thought.* New York: McGraw-Hill, 1963.

Gibson, E. J., Schapiro, F., & Yonas, A. Confusion matrices for graphic patterns obtained with a latency measure. Unpublished manuscript, Cornell University.

---

[2]Pointed out by Gordon H. Bower, personal communication.

Howes, D. H., & Solomon, R. L.. Visual duration threshold as a function of word probability. *Journal of Experimental Psychology,* 1951, 41, 401–410.

Kincaid, W. M. The combination of 2 × *m* contingency tables. *Biometrics,* 1962, 18, 224–228.

Morton, J. A retest of the response-bias explanation of the word frequency effect. *British Journal of Mathematical and Statistical Psychology,* 1968, 21, 21–33.

Morton, J. Interaction of information in word recognition. *Psychology Review,* 1969, 76, 165–178.

Neisser, U. *Cognitive Psychology.* New York: Appleton-Century-Crofts, 1967.

Newbigging, P. L. The perceptual re-integration of frequent and infrequent words. *Canadian Journal of Psychology,* 1961, 15, 123–132.

Reicher, G. M. Perceptual recognition as a function of meaningfulness of stimulus material. Technical Report No. 7, 1968, The University of Michigan, Human Performance Center.

Rumelhart, D. E. A multicomponent theory of the perception of briefly exposed visual displays. *Journal of Mathematical Psychology,* 1970, 7, 191–218.

Selfridge, O. G. Pandemonium: A paradigm for learning. In L. Uhr (Ed.), *Pattern recognition.* New York: Wiley, 1966.

Siegel, S. *Nonparametric statistics for the behavioral sciences.* New York: McGraw-Hill, 1956.

Sperling, G. The information available in brief visual presentations. *Psychological Monographs,* 1960, 74(11).

Stewart, M. L., James, C. T., & Gough, P. B. Word recognition latency as a function of word length. Paper presented at Midwestern Psychological Association Convention, May, 1969.

Thorndike, E. L., & Lorge, I. *The teacher's word book of 30,000 words.* New York: Teachers College Press, 1944.

Uhr, L.. Pattern recognition. In L. Uhr (Ed.), *Pattern recognition.* New York: Wiley, 1966.

Uhr, L., & Vossler, C. A pattern-recognition program that generates, evaluates and adjusts its own operators. In E. A. Feigenbaum and J. Feldman (Eds.), *Computers and thought.* New York: McGraw-Hill, 1963.

Wolford, G. L., Wessel, D. L., & Estes, W. K. Further evidence concerning scanning and sampling assumptions of visual detection models. Technical Report No. 126, 1968, Stanford University, Institute for Mathematical Studies in the Social Sciences.

POSTSCRIPT

Wheeler's experiments disconfirm each of his hypotheses. Later experimenters (for example, Baron & Thurston, 1973; Johnston, 1978) tested other hypotheses. The results of all these experiments suggest that when a letter occurs in a word or in a pronounceable nonword, it really does somehow become easier to perceive than when it occurs in isolation. Similar results have been found for words presented in braille (Krueger, 1982) and for stimuli that are presented in type too small to see easily (Prinzmetal, 1992). It has also been shown that it is possible to obtain a word-*inferiority* effect under some conditions (Chastain, 1986).

Wheeler is primarily interested in ruling out various nonperceptual explanations for the word-superiority effect. He does not really explore the implications of these results for a theory of visual perception, although he does mention Selfridge's Pandemonium model (see Selfridge & Neisser, 1960, for a very readable account of the model). The Pandemonium model suggests that certain units in the visual system, so-called feature detectors, are sensitive to the presence of particular features of a stimulus when it occurs at particular locations in the visual field. Thus, one such unit may be sensitive to horizontal lines in the middle of the field whereas another might be sensitive to horizontal lines at the top of the field or to vertical lines in the middle of the field. When a feature detector detects the presence of the feature to which it is sensitive, its activity level increases, which in turn increases the activity level of particular other higher-order units to which it is connected. These higher-order units, or letter detectors, are connected to precisely those feature detectors that are sensitive to features present in the letters to which the letter detectors correspond. Thus there might be an *H* letter detector, which would be connected to the feature detector sensitive to horizontal lines in the middle of the field (among other features). Much work in neurophysiology has been taken to be consistent with models like Pandemonium, at least at the level of feature detectors (see reviews in Hubel, 1982, and various chapters in LeDoux & Hirst, 1986, and in Spillmann & Werner, 1990).

Phenomena such as the word-superiority effect that demonstrate that the context in which an item is embedded can have an effect on its recognition, however, have been taken by most psychologists (such as Neisser, 1967; Pinker, 1985) as posing a problem for models such as Pandemonium, in which information flows in just one direction (that is, from feature detectors to letter detectors but not vice versa). Most attempts to explain the word-superiority effect assume that information flows both from the bottom up (from specific details to larger patterns) and from the top down (from larger patterns to specific details). Paap, Newsome, McDonald, and Schvaneveldt (1982) describes one such attempt; see Reading 6 for another.

FOR FURTHER THOUGHT

1. See whether you can describe each of the hypotheses tested by Wheeler, explain which data bear on each, and determine why each is ruled out by that data.
2. The hypotheses developed and tested by Wheeler are alternatives to a hypothesis that he does not test. What is that untested hypothesis? How would it explain the word-superiority effect? Why does Wheeler not test it?
3. Why did Wheeler adjust the presentation time for each subject? Does doing this present any difficulties in interpreting his results?
4. Wheeler suggests that his data do not completely rule out a serial model. Can you describe a serial model that could account for Wheeler's data? Is there another experiment that could rule out that alternative?

5. Is it possible to develop a bottom-up model of perception (one in which information flows in just one direction) that might account for the word-superiority data? What would it look like? Is that alternative satisfactory? Why or why not?

REFERENCES

Baron, J., & Thurston, I. (1973). An analysis of the word-superiority effect. *Cognitive Psychology, 4,* 207–228.

Chastain, G. (1986). Word-to-letter inhibition: Word-inferiority and other interference effects. *Memory & Cognition, 14,* 361–368.

Howes, D. H., & Solomon, R. L. (1951). Visual duration threshold as a function of word probability. *Journal of Experimental Psychology, 41,* 401–410.

Hubel, D. H. (1982). Exploration of the primary visual cortex, 1955–1978. *Nature, 299,* 515–524.

Johnston, J. C. (1978). A test of the sophisticated guessing theory of word perception. *Cognitive Psychology, 10,* 123–154.

Krueger, L. E. (1982). A word-superiority effect with print and braille characters. *Perception & Psychophysics, 31,* 345–352.

LeDoux, J. E., & Hirst, W. (Eds.). (1986). *Mind and brain: Dialogues in cognitive neuroscience.* New York: Cambridge University Press.

Neisser, U. (1967). *Cognitive psychology.* New York: Appleton-Century-Crofts.

Paap, K. R., Newsome, S. L., McDonald, J. E., & Schvaneveldt, R. W. (1982). An activation-verification model for letter and word recognition: The word-superiority effect. *Psychological Review, 89,* 573–594.

Pinker, S. (1985). Visual cognition: An introduction. In S. Pinker (Ed.), *Visual cognition* (pp. 1–63). Cambridge, MA: MIT Press.

Prinzmetal, W. (1992). The word-superiority effect does not require a T-scope. *Perception & Psychophysics, 51,* 473–484.

Selfridge, O. G., & Neisser, U. (1960, August). Pattern recognition by machine. *Scientific American,* pp. 60–68.

Sperling, G. (1960). The information available in brief visual presentations. *Psychological Monographs, 74* (Whole No. 498).

Spillmann, L., & Werner, J. S. (Eds.). (1990). *Visual perception: The neurophysiological foundations.* San Diego: Academic Press.

INTRODUCTION

James McClelland and David Rumelhart introduce a sophisticated computer model to account for the word-superiority effect—and for context effects on letter perception more generally—in their article "An Interactive Activation Model of Context Effects in Letter Perception: Part I. An Account of Basic Findings." This article was originally published in conjunction with a second article (Rumelhart & McClelland, 1982). Together, these two articles present one of the earliest accounts of the sort now called connectionist, or parallel distributed processing. The connectionist approach is characterized by the use of a large number of relatively simple processing units that support a wide variety of cognitive functions, including letter recognition. A large number of connections link these units, allowing activation (and inhibition) to flow among many units and in many directions, all in parallel.

This extended excerpt should give you a good flavor of how connectionist models integrate the top-down and bottom-up flows of information to explain the basic word-superiority phenomena. Excluded here are McClelland and Rumelhart's discussion of related formulations (such as the neural-like model of Szentagothai & Arbib, 1975, and Morton's 1969 logogen model) and their account of a variety of other results observed with the word-superiority effect, such as of nonword contexts. Also excluded are many of the technical (mathematical) details originally presented.

As you read this article, think about how this explanation of the word-superiority effect compares with the sorts of explanations Wheeler considers (see Reading 5). Connectionist explanations are often described as being a different *kind* of explanation than are the more common cognitivist explanations. How would you characterize the differences between the explanation given here and those described by Wheeler? the similarities?

An Interactive Activation Model of Context Effects in Letter Perception: Part 1. An Account of Basic Findings

James L. McClelland and David E. Rumelhart

University of California, San Diego

As we perceive, we are continually extracting sensory information to guide our attempts to determine what is before us. In addition, we bring to perception a wealth of knowledge about the objects we might see or hear and the larger units in which these objects co-occur. As one of us has argued for the case of reading (Rumelhart, 1977), our knowledge of the objects we might be perceiving works together with the sensory information in the perceptual process. Exactly how does the knowledge that we have interact with the input? And how does this interaction facilitate perception?

... We have attempted to take a few steps toward answering these questions. We consider one specific example of the interaction of knowledge and perception—the perception of letters in words and other contexts. In [this article] we examine the main findings in the literature on perception of letters in context and develop a model called the interactive activation model to account for these effects. ...

BASIC FINDINGS ON THE ROLE OF CONTEXT IN PERCEPTION OF LETTERS

The notion that knowledge and familiarity play a role in perception has often been supported by experiments on the perception of letters in words (Bruner, 1957; Neisser, 1967). It has been known for nearly 100 years that it is possible to identify letters in words more accurately than letters in random letter sequences under tachistoscopic presentation conditions (Cattell, 1886; see Huey, 1908, and Neisser, 1967, for reviews). However, ... it has been possible until recently to imagine that the context in which a letter was presented influences only the accuracy of postperceptual processes and not the process of perception itself.

The perceptual advantage of letters in words. The seminal experiment of Reicher (1969) suggests that context does actually influence perceptual processing. ...

Reicher's (1969) finding seems to suggest that perception of a letter can be facilitated by presenting it in the context of a word. It appears, then, that our knowledge about words can influence the process of perception. Our model presents a way of bringing such knowledge to bear. The basic idea is that the presentation of a string of letters begins the process of activating detectors for letters that are consistent with the visual input. As these activations grow stronger, they begin to activate detectors for words that are consistent with the letters, if there are any. The active word detectors then produce feedback, which rein-

Preparation of this article was supported by National Science Foundation Grants BNS-76-14830 and BNS-79-24062 to J. L. McClelland and Grant BNS-76-15024 to D. E. Rumelhart, and by the Office of Naval Research under contract N00014-C-0323. We would like to thank Don Norman, James Johnston, and members of the LNR research group for helpful discussions of much of the material covered in this article.

Requests for reprints may be sent to James L. McClelland or David E. Rumelhart at Department of Psychology, C-009, University of California, San Diego, La Jolla, California 92093.

forces the activations of the detectors for the letters in the word. Letters in words are more perceptible, because they receive more activation than representations of either single letters or letters in an unrelated context.

Reicher's basic finding has been investigated and extended in a large number of studies, and there now appears to be a set of important related findings that must also be explained. . . .

Role of patterned masking.   The word advantage over single letters and nonwords appears to depend upon the visual masking conditions used (Johnston & McClelland, 1973; Massaro & Klitzke, 1979; see also Juola, Leavitt, & Choe, 1974; Taylor & Chabot, 1978). The word advantage is quite large when the target appears in a distinct, high-contrast display followed by a patterned mask of similar characteristics. However, the word advantage over single letters is actually reversed, and the word advantage over nonwords becomes quite small when the target is indistinct, low in contrast, and/or followed by a blank, nonpatterned field.

Extension to pronounceable pseudowords.   The word advantage also applies to pronounceable nonwords, such as *REET* or *MAVE*. A large number of studies (e.g., Aderman & Smith, 1971; Baron & Thurston, 1973; Spoehr & Smith, 1975) have shown that letters in pronounceable nonwords (also called pseudowords) have a large advantage over letters in unpronounceable nonwords (also called unrelated letter strings), and three studies (Carr, Davidson & Hawkins, 1978; Massaro & Klitzke 1979; McClelland & Johnston, 1977) have obtained an advantage for letters in pseudowords over single letters. . . .

To be successful, any model of word perception must provide an account not only for Reicher's (1969) basic effect but for these related findings as well. Our model accounts for all of these effects. We begin by presenting the model in abstract form. We then focus on the specific version of the model implemented in our simulation program and consider some of the details. Subsequently, we turn to detailed considerations of the findings we have discussed in this section.

THE INTERACTIVE ACTIVATION MODEL

We approach the phenomena of word perception with a number of basic assumptions that we want to incorporate into the model. First, we assume that perceptual processing takes place within a system in which there are several levels of processing, each concerned with forming a representation of the input at a different level of abstraction. For visual word perception, we assume that there is a visual feature level, a letter level, and a word level, as well as higher levels of processing that provide "top–down" input to the word level.

Second, we assume that visual perception involves parallel processing. There are two different senses in which we view perception as parallel. We assume that visual perception is spatially parallel. That is, we assume that information covering a region in space at least large enough to contain a four-letter word is processed simultaneously. In addition, we assume that visual processing occurs at several levels at the same time. Thus, our model of word perception is spatially parallel (i.e., capable of processing several letters of a word at one time) and involves processes that operate simultaneously at several different levels. Thus, for example, processing at the letter level presumably occurs simultaneously with processing at the word level and with processing at the feature level.

Third, we assume that perception is fundamentally an *interactive* process. That is, we assume that "top–down" or "conceptually driven" processing works simultaneously and in conjunction with "bottom–up" or "data driven" processing to provide a sort of multiplicity of constraints that jointly determine what we perceive. Thus, for example, we assume that knowledge about the words of the language interacts with the incoming featural information in codetermining the nature and time course of the perception of the letters in the word.

Finally, we wish to implement these assumptions by using a relatively simple method of interaction between sources of knowledge whose only "currency" is simple excitatory and inhibitory activations of a neural type.

Figure 1 shows the general conception of the model. Perceptual processing is assumed to occur in

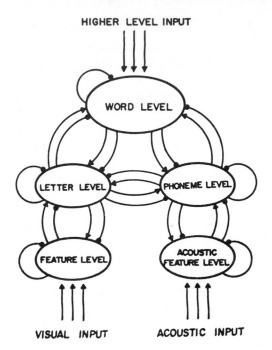

FIGURE 1 A sketch of some of the processing levels involved in visual and auditory word perception, with interconnections.

a set of interacting levels, each communicating with several others. Communication proceeds through a spreading activation mechanism in which activation at one level spreads to neighboring levels. The communication can consist of both excitatory and inhibitory messages. Excitatory messages increase the activation level of their recipients. Inhibitory messages decrease the activation level of their recipients. The arrows in the diagram represent excitatory connections, and the circular ends of the connections represent inhibitory connections. The intralevel inhibitory loop represents a kind of lateral inhibition in which incompatible units at the same level compete. For example, since a string of four letters can be interpreted as at most one four-letter word, the various possible words mutually inhibit one another and in that way compete as possible interpretations of the string.

It is clear that many levels are important in reading and perception in general, and the interactions among these levels are important for many phenom-

ena. However, a theoretical analysis of all of these interactions introduces an order of complexity that obscures comprehension. For this reason, we have restricted the present analysis to an examination of the interaction between a single pair of levels, the word and letter levels. We have found that we can account for the phenomena reviewed above by considering only the interactions between letter level and word level elements. Therefore, for the present we have elaborated the model only on these two levels, as illustrated in Figure 2. We have delayed consideration of the effects of higher level processes and phonological processes, and we have ignored the reciprocity of activation that may occur between word and letter levels and any other levels of the system. . . .

Specific Assumptions

Representation assumptions. For every relevant unit in the system we assume there is an entity called a *node*. We assume that there is a node for each word we know, and that there is a node for each letter in each letter position within a four-letter string.

The nodes are organized into levels. There are *word level* nodes and *letter level* nodes. Each node has connections to number of other nodes. The nodes to which a node connects are called its *neighbors*. Each connection is two-way. There are two kinds of connections: *excitatory* and *inhibitory*. If two nodes suggest each other's existence (in the way that the node for the word *the* suggests the node for an initial *t* and vice versa), then the connections are excitatory. If two nodes are inconsistent with one another (in the way that the node for the word *the* and the node for the word *boy* are inconsistent), then the relationship is inhibitory. Note that we identify nodes according to the units they detect, printing them in italics; stimuli presented to the system are in uppercase letters.

Connections may occur within levels or between adjacent levels. There are no connections between nonadjacent levels. Connections within the word level are mutually inhibitory, since only one word can occur at any one place at any one time. Connections between the word level and letter level may be either inhibitory or excitatory (depending on whether the letter is a part of the word in the appropriate letter

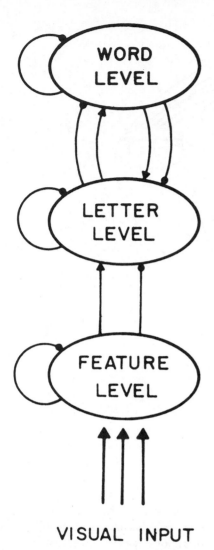

FIGURE 2   The simplified processing system.

position). We call the set of nodes with excitatory connections to a given node its *excitatory neighbors* and the set of nodes with inhibitory connections to a given node its *inhibitory neighbors.*

A subset of the neighbors of the letter *t* is illustrated in Figure 3. Again, excitatory connections are represented by the arrows ending with points, and inhibitory connections are represented by the arrows ending with dots. We emphasize that this is a small subset of the neighborhood of the initial *t*. The pic-

ture of the whole neighborhood, including all the connections among neighbors and their connections to their neighbors, is much too complicated to present in a two-dimensional figure.

Activation assumptions.   There is associated with each node a momentary activation value. This value is a real number, and for node i we will represent it by $a_i(t)$. Any node with a positive activation value is said to be *active*. In the absence of inputs from its neighbors, all nodes are assumed to decay back to an inactive state, that is, to an activation value at or below zero. This resting level may differ from node to node and corresponds to a kind of a priori bias (Broadbent, 1967) determined by frequency of activation of the node over the long term. Thus, for example, the nodes for high-frequency words have resting levels higher than those for low-frequency words. In any case, the resting level for node i is represented by r_i. For units not at rest, decay back to the resting level occurs at some rate θ_i.

When the neighbors of a node are active, they influence the activation of the node by either excitation or inhibition, depending on their relation to the node. These excitatory and inhibitory influences combine by a simple weighted average to yield a net input to the unit, which may be either excitatory (greater than zero) or inhibitory. . . . Inactive nodes have no influence on their neighbors. Only nodes in an active state have any effects, either excitatory or inhibitory. . . .

Input assumptions.   Upon presentation of a stimulus, a set of featural inputs is made available to the system. Each feature in the display will be detected with some probability p. For simplicity it is assumed that feature detection occurs, if it is to occur at all, immediately after onset of the stimulus. The probability that any given feature will be detected is assumed to vary with the visual quality of the display. Features that are detected begin sending activation to all letter nodes that contain that feature. All letter level nodes that do not contain the extracted feature are inhibited.

It is assumed that features are binary and that we can extract either the presence or absence of a particular feature. So, for example, when viewing the

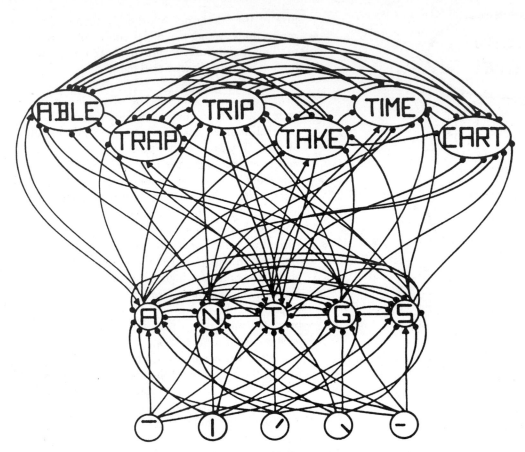

FIGURE 3 A few of the neighbors of the node for the letter *T* in the first position in a word, and their interconnections.

letter *R* we can extract, among other features, the presence of a diagonal line segment in the lower right corner and the absence of a horizontal line across the bottom. In this way the model honors the conceptual distinction between knowing that a feature is absent and not knowing whether a feature is present. . . .

On making responses. One of the more problematic aspects of a model such as this one is a specification of how these relatively complex patterns of activity might be related to the content of percepts and the sorts of response probabilities we observe in experiments. We assume that responses and perhaps the contents of perceptual experience depend on the temporal integration of the pattern of activation over all of the nodes. The integration process is assumed to

occur slowly enough that brief activations may come and go without necessarily becoming accessible for purposes of responding or entering perceptual experience. However, as the activation lasts longer and longer, the probability that it will be reportable increases. . . .

Most of the experiments we will be considering test subjects' performance on one of the letters in a word or other type of display. In accounting for these results, we have adopted the assumption that responding is always based on the output of the letter level, rather than the output of the word level or some combination of the two. The forced choice is assumed to be based only on this letter-level information. The subject compares the letter selected for the appropriate position against the forced-choice alternatives. If the letter selected is one of the alternatives, then that alternative is chosen in the forced choice. If it is not one of the alternatives, then the model assumes that one of the alternatives would simply be chosen at random.

One somewhat problematical issue involves deciding when to read out the results of processing and select response letters for each letter position. When a target display is simply turned on and left on until the subject responds, and when there is no pressure to respond quickly, we assume that the subject simply waits until the output strengths have reached their asymptotic values. However, when a target display is presented briefly followed by a patterned mask, the activations produced by the target are transient, as we shall see. Under these conditions, we assume that the subject learns through experience in the practice phase of the experiment to read out the results of processing at a time that allows the subject to optimize performance. For simplicity, we have assumed that readout occurs in parallel for all four letter positions.

The Operation of the Model

Now, consider what happens when an input reaches the system. Assume that at time t_0 all prior inputs have had an opportunity to decay, so that the entire system is in its quiescent state, and each node is at its resting level. The presentation of a stimulus initiates a process in which certain features are extracted and excitatory and inhibitory pressures begin to act upon the letter-level nodes. The activation levels of certain letter nodes are pushed above their resting levels. Others receive predominantly inhibitory inputs and are pushed below their resting levels. These letter nodes, in turn, begin to send activation to those word-level nodes they are consistent with and inhibit those word nodes they are not consistent with. In addition, within a given letter position channel, the various letter nodes attempt to suppress each other, with the strongest ones getting the upper hand. As word-level nodes become active, they in turn compete with one another and send feedback down to the letter-level nodes. If the input features were close to those for one particular set of letters and those letters were consistent with those forming a particular word,

the positive feedback in the system will work to rapidly converge on the appropriate set of letters and the appropriate word. If not, they will compete with each other, and perhaps no single set of letters or single word will get enough activation to dominate the others. In this case the various active units might strangle each other through mutual inhibition.

At any point during processing, the results of perceptual processing may be read out from the pattern of activations at the letter level into a buffer, where they may be kept through rehearsal or used as the basis for overt reports. The accuracy of this process depends on a running average of the activations of the correct node and of other competing nodes.

Simulations

Although the model is in essence quite simple, the interactions among the various nodes can become complex, so that the model is not susceptible to a simple intuitive or even mathematical analysis. Instead, we have relied on computer simulations to study the behavior of the model and to see if it is consistent with the empirical data. . . .

For purposes of these simulations, we have made a number of simplifying assumptions. These additional assumptions fall into three classes: (a) discrete rather than continuous time, (b) simplified feature analysis of the input font, and (c) a limited lexicon.

The simulation operates in discrete time slices, or ticks, updating the activations of all of the nodes in the system once each cycle on the basis of the values on the previous cycle. Obviously, this is simply a matter of computational convenience and not a fundamental assumption. We have endeavored to keep the time slices "thin" enough so that the model's behavior is continuous for all intents and purposes.

Any simulation of the model involves making explicit assumptions about the appropriate featural analysis of the input font. We have, for simplicity, chosen the font and featural analysis employed by Rumelhart (1970) and by Rumelhart and Siple (1974), illustrated in Figure 4. Although the experiments we have simulated employed different type fonts, we assume that the basic results do not depend on the particular font used. The simplicity of the

ABCDEFGHI
JKLMNOPQR
STUVWXYZ

FIGURE 4   The features used to construct the letters in the font assumed by the simulation program, and the letters themselves. (From "Process of Recognizing Tachistoscopically Presented Words" by David E. Rumelhart and Patricia Siple, *Psychological Review*, 1974, *81*, 99–118. Copyright 1974 by the American Psychological Association. Reprinted by permission.)

FIGURE 5   A hypothetical set of features that might be extracted on a trial in an experiment on word perception.

present analysis recommends it for the simulations, though it obviously skirts several fundamental issues about the lower levels of processing.

Finally, our simulations have been restricted to four-letter words. We have equipped our program with knowledge of 1,179 four-letter words occurring at least two times per million in the Kucera and Francis (1967) word count. Plurals, inflected forms, first names, proper names, acronyms, abbreviations, and occasional unfamiliar entries arising from apparent sampling flukes have been excluded. This sample appears to be sufficient to reflect the essential characteristics of the language and to show how the statistical properties of the language can affect the process of perceiving letters in words.

An Example

Let us now consider a sample run of our simulation model. The parameter values employed in the example are those used to simulate all the experiments discussed in the remainder of Part 1. These values are described in detail in the following section. For the purposes of this example, imagine that the word *WORK* has been presented to the subject and that the subject has extracted those features shown in Figure 5. In the

first three letter positions, the features of the letters *W*, *O*, and *R* have been completely extracted. In the final position a set of features consistent with the letters *K* and *R* have been extracted, with the features that would disambiguate the letter unavailable. We wish now to chart the activity of the system resulting from this presentation. Figure 6 shows the time course of the activations for selected nodes at the word and letter levels, respectively.

At the word level, we have charted the activity levels of the nodes for the words *work, word, wear,* and *weak*. Note first that *work* is the only word in the lexicon consistent with all the presented information. As a result, its activation level is the highest and reaches a value of .8 through the first 40 time cycles. The word *word* is consistent with the bulk of the information presented and therefore first rises and later is pushed back down below its resting level, as a result of competition with *work*. The words *wear* and *weak* are consistent with the only letter active in the first letter position, and one of the two active in the fourth letter position. They are also inconsistent with the letters active in Positions 2 and 3. Thus, the activation they receive from the letter level is quite weak, and they are easily driven down well below zero, as a result of competition from the other word units. The activations of these units do not drop quite as low, of course, as the activation level of words such as *gill*, which contain nothing in common with the presented information. Although not shown in Figure 6, these words attain near-minimum activation levels of about −.20 and stay there as the stimulus stays on. Returning to *wear* and *weak,* we note that these words are equally consistent with the presented information

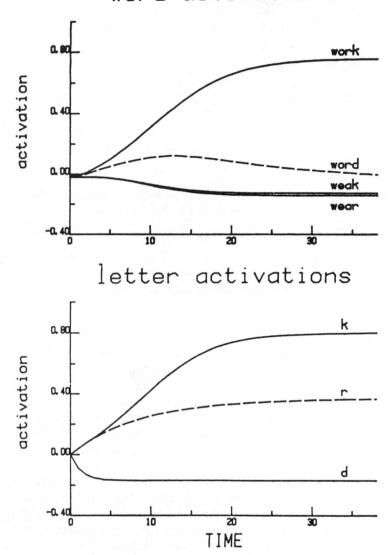

FIGURE 6   The time course of activations of selected nodes at the word and letter levels after extraction of the features shown in Figure 5.

and thus drop together for about the first 9 time units. At this point, however, the word *work* has clearly taken the upper hand at the word level, and produces feedback that reinforces the activation of the final *k* and not the final *r*. As a result, the word *weak* receives more activation from the letter level than the word *wear* and begins to gain a slight advan-

tage over *wear*. The strengthened *k* continues to feed activation into the word level and strengthen consistent words. The words that contain an *R* continue to receive activation from the *r* node also, but they receive stronger inhibition from the words consistent with a *K* and are therefore ultimately weakened, as illustrated in the lower panel of Figure 6.

The strong feature–letter inhibition ensures that when a feature inconsistent with a particular letter is detected, that letter will receive relatively strong net bottom–up inhibition. Thus in our example, the information extracted clearly disconfirms the possibility that the letter *D* has been presented in the fourth position, and thus the activation level of the *d* node decreases quickly to near its minimum value. However, the bottom–up information from the feature level supports either a *K* or an *R* in the fourth position. Thus, the activation of each of these nodes rises slowly. These activations, along with those for *W*, *O*, and *R*, push the activation of *work* above zero, and it begins to feed back; by about Time Cycle 4, it is beginning to push the *k* above the *r* (because *WORR* is not a word). Note that this separation occurs just before the words *weak* and *wear* separate. It is the strengthening of *k* due to feedback from *work* that causes them to separate.

Ultimately, the *r* reaches a level well below that of *k* where it remains, and the *k* pushes toward a .8 activation level. As discussed below, the word-to-letter inhibition and the letter-to-letter inhibition have both been set to 0. Thus, *k* and *r* both co-exist at moderately high levels, the *r* fed only from the bottom up, and the *k* fed from both bottom up and top down.

Finally, consider the output values for the letter nodes *r*, *k*, and *d*. Figure 7 shows the output values for the simulation. The output value is the probability that if a response was selected at time *t*, the letter in question would be selected as the output or response from the system. As intended, these output values grow somewhat more slowly than the values of the letter activations themselves but eventually, as they reach and hold their asymptotic values, come to reflect the activations of the letter nodes. Since in the absence of masking subjects can afford to wait to read out a response until the output values have had a chance to stabilize, they would be highly likely to choose the letter *K* as the response.

Although this example is not very general in that we assumed that only partial information was available in the input for the fourth letter position, whereas full information was available at the other letter positions, it does illustrate many of the important characteristics of the model. It shows how ambiguous sensory information can be disambiguated

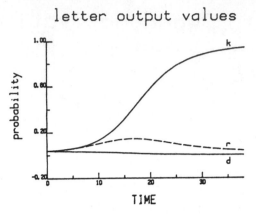

FIGURE 7   Output values for the letters *r*, *k*, and *d* after presentation of the display shown in Figure 5.

by top–down processes. Here we have a very simple mechanism capable of applying knowledge of words in the perception of their component letters.

Parameter Selection

Once the basic simulation model was constructed, we began a lengthy process of attempting to simulate the results of several representative experiments in the literature. Only two parameters of the model were allowed to vary from experiment to experiment: (a) the probability of feature extraction and (b) the timing of the presentation of the masking stimulus if one was used.

The probability of feature extraction is assumed to depend on the visual characteristics of the display. In most of the experiments we will consider, a bright, high-contrast target was used. Such a target would produce perfect performance if not followed by a patterned mask. In these cases probability of feature extraction was fixed at 1.0 and the timing of the target offset and coincident mask onset typically was adjusted to achieve 75% correct performance over the different experimental conditions of interest. In simulating the results of these experiments, we likewise varied the timing of the target offset/mask onset to achieve the right average correct performance from the model.

In some experiments no patterned mask was used, and performance was kept below perfect levels by using a dim or otherwise degraded target display. In these cases the probability of feature extraction was set to a value less than 1.0, which produces about the right overall performance level.

The process of exploring the behavior of the model amounted to an extended search for a set of values for all the other parameters that would permit the model to simulate, as closely as possible, the results of all the experiments to be discussed. . . . To constrain the search, we adopted various restrictive simplifications. First we assumed that all nodes have the same maximum activation value. In fact, the maximum was set to 1.0, and served to scale all activations within the model. The minimum activation value for all nodes was set at −.20, a value that permits rapid reactivation of strongly inhibited nodes. The decay rate of all nodes was set to the value of .07. This parameter effectively serves as a scale factor that determines how quickly things are allowed to change in a single time slice. The .07 value was picked after some exploration, since it seemed to permit us to run our simulations with the minimum number of time slices per trial, at the same time as it minimized a kind a reverberatory oscillation that sets in when things are allowed to change too much on any given time cycle. We also assigned the resting value of zero to all of the letter nodes. The resting value of nodes at the word level was set to a value between −.05 and 0, depending on word frequency.

We have assumed that . . . the excitatory connections between all letter nodes and all of the relevant word nodes are equally strong, independent of the identity of the words. Thus, for example, the degree to which the node for an initial *t* excites the node for the word *tock* is exactly the same as the degree to which it excites the node for the word *this,* in spite of a substantial difference in frequency of usage. To further simplify matters, the word-to-letter inhibition was also set to zero. This means that feedback from the word level can strengthen activations at the letter level but cannot weaken them. . . .

The values of the remaining parameters were fixed at the values given in Table 1. It is worth noting the differences between the feature–letter influences and the letter–word influences. The feature–letter inhibition is 30 times as strong as the feature–letter excitation. This means that all of the features detected

TABLE 1 Parameter Values Used in the Simulations

Parameter	Value
Feature–letter excitation	.005
Feature–letter inhibition	.15
Letter–word excitation	.07
Letter–word inhibition	.04
Word–word inhibition	.21
Letter–letter inhibition	0
Word–letter excitation	.30

must be compatible with a particular letter before that letter will receive net excitation (since there are only 14 possible features, there can only be a maximum of 13 excitatory inputs whenever there is a single inhibitory input). The main reason for choosing this value was to permit the presentation of a mask to clear the previous pattern of activation. On the other hand, the letter–word inhibition is actually somewhat less than the letter–word excitation. When only one letter is active in each letter position, this means that the letter level will produce net excitation of all words that share two or more letters with the target word. Because of these multiple activations, strong word–word inhibition is necessary to "sharpen" the response of the word level, as we will see. In contrast, no such inhibition is necessary at the letter level. For these reasons, the letter–letter inhibition has been set to 0, whereas the word–word inhibition has been set to .21. . . .

APPLICATION OF THE SIMULATION MODEL TO SEVERAL BASIC FINDINGS

We are finally ready to see how well our model fares in accounting for the findings of several representative experiments in the literature. In discussing each account, we will try to explain not only how well the simulation works but why it behaves as it does. As we proceed through the discussion, we will have occasion to describe several interesting synergistic properties of the model that we did not anticipate but discovered as we explored the behavior of the system. As mentioned previously, the actual parameters used in both the examples that we will discuss and in the simulation results we will report are those summarized in

Table 1. We will consider the robustness of the model, and the effects of changes in these parameters, in the discussion section at the end [of this excerpt].

The Word Advantage and the Effects of Visual Conditions

As we noted previously, word perception has been studied under a variety of different visual conditions, and it is apparent that different conditions produce different results. The advantage of words over non-words appears to be greatest under conditions in which a bright, high-contrast target is followed by a patterned mask with similar characteristics. The word advantage appears to be considerably less when the target presentation is dimmer or otherwise degraded and is followed by a blank white field.

Typical data demonstrating these points (from Johnston & McClelland, 1973) are presented in Table 2. Forced-choice performance on letters in words is compared to performance on letters embedded in a row of number signs (e.g., *READ* vs. *#E##*). The number signs serve as a control for lateral facilitation or inhibition. This factor appears to be important under dim-target/blank-mask conditions.

Target durations were adjusted separately for each condition, so that it is only the pattern of differences within display conditions that is meaningful. The data show that a 15% word advantage was obtained in the bright-target/patterned-mask condition and only a 5% word advantage in the dim-target/ blank-mask condition. Massaro and Klitzke (1979) obtained about the same size effects. Various aspects of these results have also been corroborated in two other studies (Juola et al., 1974; Taylor & Chabot, 1978).

TABLE 2   Effect of Display Conditions on Proportion of Correct Forced Choices in Word and Letter Perception (From Johnston & McClelland, 1973)

	Display Type	
Visual Condition	Word	Letter with Number Signs
Bright target/patterned mask	.80	.65
Dim target/blank mask	.78	.73

To understand the difference between these two conditions it is important to note that in order to get about 75% correct performance in the no-mask condition, the stimulus must be highly degraded. Since there is no patterned mask, the iconic trace presumably persists considerably beyond the offset of the target. It is our assumption that the effect of the blank mask is simply to reduce the contrast or the icon by summating with it. Thus, the limit on performance is not so much the amount of time available in which to process the information as it is the quality of the information made available to the system. In contrast, when a patterned mask is employed, the mask produces spurious inputs, which can interfere with the processing of the target. Thus, in the bright-target/patterned-mask conditions, the primary limitation on performance is the amount of time that the information is available to the system in relatively legible form rather than the quality of the information presented. This distinction between the way in which blank masks and patterned masks interfere with performance has previously been made by a number of investigators, including Rumelhart (1970) and Turvey (1973). We now consider each of these sorts of conditions in turn.

Word perception under patterned-mask conditions. When a high-quality display is followed by a patterned mask, we assume that the bottleneck in performance does not come in the extraction of feature information from the target display. Thus, in our simulation of these conditions, we assume that all of the features presented can be extracted on every trial. The limitation on performance comes from the fact that the activations produced by the target are subject to disruption and replacement by the mask before they can be translated into a permanent form suitable for overt report. This general idea was suggested by Johnston and McClelland (1973) and considered by a number of other investigators, including Carr et al. (1978), Massaro and Klitzke (1979), and others. On the basis of this idea, a number of possible reasons for the advantage for letters in words have been suggested. One is that letters in words are for some reason translated more quickly into a nonmaskable form (Johnston & McClelland, 1973; Massaro & Klitzke, 1979). Another is that words activate representations removed from the direct effects of visual patterned masking (Carr et al., 1978; Johnston & McClelland, 1973, 1980; McClelland, 1976). In the interactive activation model, the reason letters in words fare better than letters in nonwords is that they benefit from feedback that can drive them to higher activation levels. As a result, the

probability that the activated letter representation will be correctly encoded is increased.

To understand in detail how this account works, consider the following example. Figure 8 shows the operation of our model for the letter *E* both in an unrelated (#) context and in the context of the word *READ* for a visual display of moderately high quality.

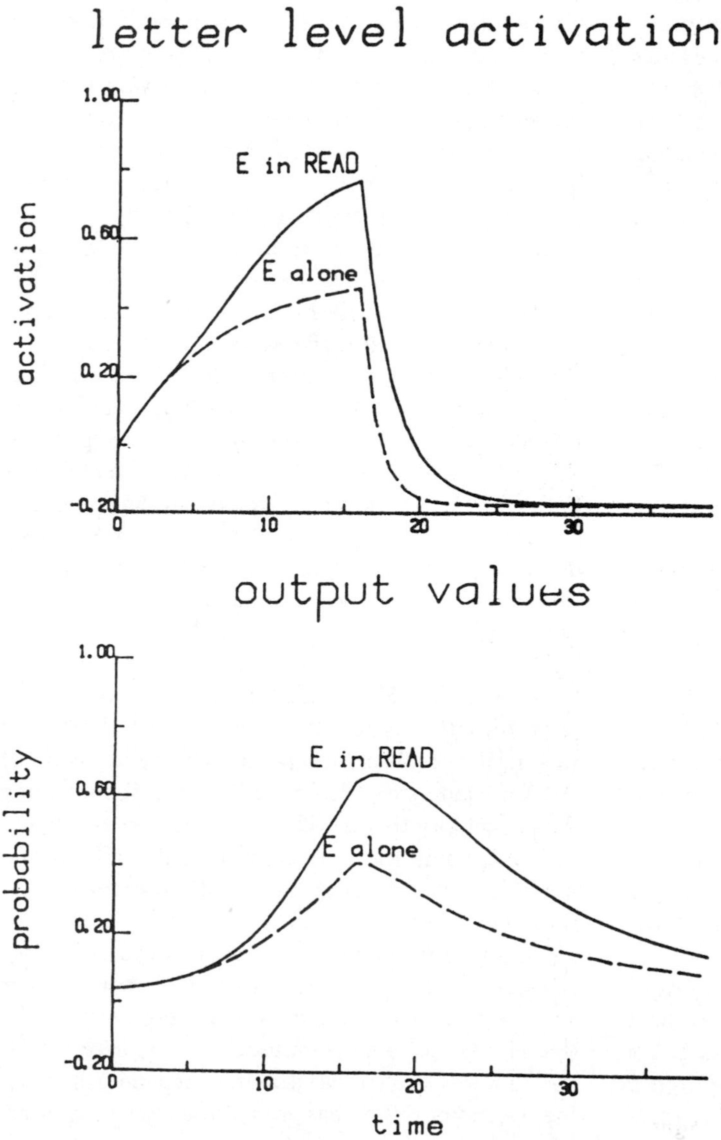

FIGURE 8   Activation functions (top) and output values (bottom) for the letter *E*, in unrelated context and in the context of the word *READ*.

We assume that display conditions are sufficient for complete feature extraction, so that only the letters actually contained in the target receive net excitatory input on the basis of feature information. After some number of cycles have gone by, the mask is presented with the same parameters as the target. The mask simply replaces the target display at the feature level, resulting in a completely new input to the letter level. This input, because it contains features incompatible with the letter shown in all four positions, immediately begins to drive down the activations at the letter level. After only a few more cycles, these activations drop below resting level in both cases. Note that the correct letter was activated briefly, and no competing letter was activated. However, because of the sluggishness of the output process, these activations do not necessarily result in a high probability of correct report. As shown in the top half of Figure 8, the probability of correct report reaches a maximum after 16 cycles at a performance level far below the ceiling.

When the letter is part of the word (in this case, *READ*), the activation of the letters results in rapid activation of one or more words. These words, in turn, feed back to the letter level. This results in a higher net activation level for the letter embedded in the word. . . .

[Our] simulation replicated the experimental data shown in Table 2 quite closely. Accuracy on the forced choice was 81% correct for the letters embedded in words and 66% correct for letters in an unrelated (#) context. . . .

Perception of letters in words under conditions of degraded input.   In conditions of degraded (but not abbreviated) input, the role of the word level is to selectively reinforce possible letters that are consistent with the visual information extracted and that are also consistent with the words in the subject's vocabulary. Recall that the task requires the subject to choose between two letters, both of which (on word trials) make a word with the rest of the context. There are two distinct cases to consider. Either the featural information extracted from the to-be-probed letter is sufficient to distinguish between the alternatives, or it is not. Whenever the featural information is consistent with both of the forced-choice alternatives, any feedback will selectively enhance both alternatives and will not permit the subject to distinguish between them. When the information extracted is inconsistent with one of the alternatives, the model produces a word advantage. The reason is that we assume forced-choice responses are based not on the feature information itself but on the subject's best guess about what letter was actually shown. Feedback from the word level increases the probability of correct choice in those cases where the subject extracts information that is inconsistent with the incorrect alternative but consistent with the correct alternative and a number of others. Thus, feedback would have the effect of helping the subject select the actual letter shown from several possibilities consistent with the set of extracted features. Consider again, for example, the case of the presentation of *WORD* discussed above. In this case, the subject extracted incomplete information about the final letter consistent with both *R* and *K*. Assume that the forced choice the subject was to face on this trial was between a *D* and a *K*. The account supposes that the subject encodes a single letter for each letter position before facing the forced choice. Thus, if the features of the final letter had been extracted in the absence of any context, the subject would encode *R* or *K* equally often, since both are equally compatible with the features extracted. This would leave the subject with the correct response some of the time. But if *R* were chosen instead, the subject would enter the forced choice between *D* and *K* without knowing the correct answer directly. When the whole word display is shown, the feedback generated by the processing of all of the letters greatly strengthens the *K*, increasing the probability that it will be chosen over the *R* and thus increasing the probability that the subject will proceed to the forced choice with the correct response in mind.

Our interpretation of the small word advantage in blank-mask conditions is a specific version of the early accounts of the word advantage offered by Wheeler (1970) and Thompson and Massaro (1973) before it was known that the effect depends on masking. Johnston (1978) has argued that this type of account does not apply under patterned-mask conditions. We are suggesting that it does apply to the small word advantage obtained under blank-mask conditions like those of the Johnston and McClelland (1973) experiment. We will see below that the model offers a different account of performance under patterned-mask conditions.

We simulated our interpretation of the small word advantage obtained in blank-mask conditions in the following way. A set of 40 pairs of four-letter words that differed by a single letter was prepared. The differing letters occurred in each position equally often. From these words corresponding control pairs were generated in which the critical letters from the word pairs were presented in nonletter contexts (#s). Because they were presented in nonletter contexts, we assumed that these letters did not engage the word processing system at all.

Each member of each pair of items was presented to the model four times, yielding a total of 320 stimulus presentations of word stimuli and 320 presentations of single letters. On each presentation, the simulation sampled a random subset of the possible features to be detected by the system. The probability of detection of each feature was set at .45. As noted previously, these values are in a ratio of 1 to 30, so that if any one of the 14 features extracted is inconsistent with a particular letter, that letter receives net inhibition from the features and is rapidly driven into an inactive state.

For simplicity, the features were treated as a constant input, which remained on while letter and word activations (if any) were allowed to take place. At the end of 50 processing cycles, which is virtually asymptotic, output was sampled. Sampling results in the selection of one letter to fill each position; the selected letter is assumed to be all the subject takes away from the target display. As described previously, the forced choice is assumed to be based only on this letter identity information. The subject compares the letter selected for the appropriate position against the forced-choice alternatives. If the letter selected is one of the alternatives, then that alternative is selected. If it is not one of the alternatives, then one of the two alternatives is simply picked at random.

The simulation produced a 10% advantage for letters in words over letters embedded in number signs. Probability-correct forced choice for letters em-

bedded in words was 78% correct, whereas for letters in number signs, performance was 68% correct.

The simulated results for the no-mask condition clearly show a smaller word advantage than for the patterned-mask case. However, the model produces a larger word advantage, which is observed in the experiment (Table 2). As Johnston (1978) has pointed out, there are a number of reasons why an account such as the one we have offered would overestimate the size of the word advantage. First, subjects may occasionally be able to retain an impression of the actual visual information they have been able to extract. On such occasions, feedback from the word level will be of no further benefit. Second, even if subjects only retain a letter identity code, they may tend to choose the forced-choice alternative that is most similar to the letter encoded—instead of simply guessing—when the letter encoded is not one of the two choices. This would tend to result in a greater probability of correct choices and less of a chance for feedback to increase accuracy of performance. It is hard to know exactly how much these factors should be expected to reduce the size of the word advantage under these conditions, but they would certainly bring it more closely in line with the results.

Perception of Letters in Regular Nonwords

One of the most important findings in the literature on word perception is that an item need not be a word in order to produce facilitation with respect to unrelated letter or single letter stimuli. . . .

Our model produces the facilitation for pseudowords by allowing them to activate nodes for words that share more than one letter in common with the display. When they occur, these activations produce feedback which strengthens the letters that gave rise to them just as in the case of words. These activations occur in the model if the strength of letter-to-word inhibition is reasonably small compared to the strength of letter-to-word excitation.

To see how this takes place in detail, consider a brief presentation of the pseudoword *MAVE* followed by a patterned mask. (The pseudoword is one used by Glushko, 1979, in developing the idea that partial activations of words are combined to derive

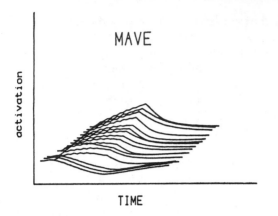

FIGURE 9   Activation at the word level upon presentation of the nonword *MAVE*.

pronunciations of pseudowords.) As illustrated in Figure 9, presentation of *MAVE* results in the initial activation of 16 different words. Most of these words, like *have* and *gave*, share three letters with *MAVE*. By and large, these words steadily gain in strength while the target is on and produce feedback to the letter level, sustaining the letters that supported them.

Some of the words are weakly activated for a brief period of time before they fall back below zero. These typically are words like *more* and *many*, which share only two letters with the target but are very high in frequency, so they need little excitation before they exceed threshold. But soon after they exceed threshold, the total activation at the word level becomes strong enough to overcome the weak excitatory input, causing them to drop down just after they begin to rise. Less frequent words sharing two letters with the word displayed have a worse fate still. Since they start out initially at a lower value, they generally fail to receive enough excitation to reach threshold. Thus, when there are several words that have three letters in common with the target, words that share only two letters with the target tend to exert little or no influence. In general then, with pronounceable pseudo-word stimuli, the amount of feedback—and hence the amount of facilitation—depends primarily on the activation of nodes for words that share three letters with a displayed pseudoword. It is the nodes for these words that primarily interact with the activations

generated by the presentation of the actual target display. In what follows we will call the words that have three letters in common with the target letter string the neighbors of that string.

The amount of feedback a particular letter in a nonword receives depends, in the model, on two primary factors and two secondary factors. The two primary factors are the number of words in the neighborhood that contain the target letter and the number of words that do not. In the case of the *M* in *MAVE*, for example, there are seven words in the neighborhood of *MAVE* that begin with *M*, so the *m* node gets excitatory feedback from all of these. These words are called the "friends" of the *m* node in this case. Because of competition at the word level, the amount of activation that these words receive depends on the total number of words that have three letters in common with the target. Those that share three letters with the target but are inconsistent with the *m* node (e.g., *have*) produce inhibition that tends to limit the activation of the friends of the *m* node, and can thus be considered its "enemies." These words also produce feedback that tends to activate letters that were not actually presented. For example, activation from *have* produces excitatory input to the *h* node, thereby producing some competition with the *m* node. These activations, however, are usually not terribly strong. No one word gets very active, and so letters not in the actual display tend to get fairly weak excitatory feedback. This weak excitation is usually insufficient to overcome the bottom–up inhibition acting on nonpresented letters. Thus, in most cases, the harm done by top–down activation of letters that were not shown is minimal.

A part of the effect we have been describing is illustrated in Figure 10. Here, we compare the activations of the nodes for the letters in *MAVE*. Without feedback, the four curves would be identical to the one single-letter curve included for comparison. So although there is facilitation for all four letters, there are definitely differences in the amount, depending on the number of friends and enemies of each letter. Note that within a given pseudoword, the total number of friends and enemies (i.e., the total number of words with three letters in common) is the same for all the letters.

letter level

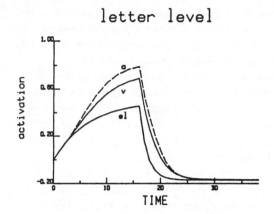

FIGURE 10   Activation functions for the letters *a* and *v* on presentation of *MAVE*. (Activation function for *e* is indistinguishable from function for *a*, and that for *m* is similar to that for *v*. The activation function for a single letter (sl), or a letter in an unrelated context is included for comparison.)

There are two other factors that affect the extent to which a particular word will become active at the word level when a particular pseudoword is shown. Although the effects of these factors are only weakly reflected in the activations at the letter level, they are nevertheless interesting to note, since they indicate some synergistic effects that emerge from the interplay of simple excitatory and inhibitory influences in the neighborhood. These are the *rich-get-richer effect* and the *gang effect*. The rich-get-richer effect is illustrated in Figure 11, which compares the activation curves for the nodes for *have*, *gave*, and *save* under presentation of *MAVE*. The words differ in frequency, which gives the words slight differences in baseline activation. What is interesting is that the difference gets magnified so that at the point of peak activation there is a much larger difference. The reason for the amplification can be seen by considering a system containing only two nodes, *a* and *b*, starting at different initial positive activation levels, *a* and *b* at time *t*. Let us suppose that *a* is stronger than *b* at *t*. Then at $t + 1$, *a* will exert more of an inhibitory influence on *b*, since inhibition of a given node is determined by the sum of the activations of all nodes other than itself. This advantage for the initially more active nodes

the "rich get richer" effect

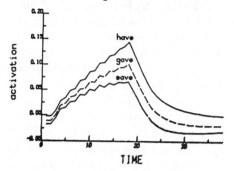

FIGURE 11   The rich-get-richer effect. (Activation functions for the nodes for *have*, *gave*, and *save* under presentation of *MAVE*.)

is compounded further in the case of the effect of word frequency by the fact that more frequent words creep above threshold first, thereby exerting an inhibitory effect on the lower frequency words when the latter are still too weak to fight back at all.

Even more interesting is the gang effect, which depends on the coordinated action of a related set of word nodes. This effect is depicted in Figure 12. Here, the activation curves for the *move*, *male*, and *save* nodes are compared. In the language, *move* and *male* are of approximately equal frequency, so their activations start out at about the same level. But they soon pull apart. Similarly, *save* starts out below *move* but

the "gang" effect

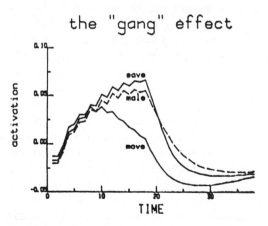

FIGURE 12   The gang effect. (Activation functions for *move*, *male*, and *save* under presentation of *MAVE*.)

soon reaches a higher activation. The reason for these effects is that *male* and *save* are both members of gangs with several members, whereas *move* is not. Consider first the difference between *male* and *move*. The reason for the difference is that there are several words that share the same three letters with *MAVE* as *male* does. In the list of words used in our simulations, there are six. These words all work together to reinforce the *m*, and *a*, and the *e* nodes, thereby producing much stronger reinforcement for themselves. Thus, these words make up a gang called the *ma_e* gang. In this example, there is also a *_ave* gang consisting of 6 other words, of which *save is* one. All of these work together to reinforce the *a, v,* and *e.* Thus, the *a* and *e* are reinforced by two gangs, whereas the letters *v* and *m* are reinforced by only one each. Now consider the word *move*. This word is a loner; there are no other words in its gang, the *m_ve* gang. Although two of the letters in *move* receive support from one gang each, and one receives support from both other gangs, the letters of *move* are less strongly enhanced by feedback than the letters of the members of the other two gangs. Since continued activation of one word in the face of the competition generated by all of the other partially activated words depends on the activations of the component letter nodes, the words in the other two gangs eventually gain the upper hand and drive *move* back below the activation threshold.

As our study of the *MAVE* example illustrates, the pattern of activation produced by a particular pseudoword is complex and idiosyncratic. In addition to the basic friends and enemies effects, there are also the rich-get-richer and the gang effects. These effects are primarily reflected in the pattern of activation at the word level, but they also exert subtle influences on the activations at the letter level. In general though, the main result is that when the letter-to-word inhibition is low, all four letters in the pseudoword receive some feedback reinforcement. The result, of course, is greater accuracy of reporting letters in pseudowords compared to single letters. . . .

DISCUSSION

The interactive activation model does a good job of accounting for the results in the literature on the perception of letters in words and nonwords. The model provides a unified explanation of the results of a variety of experiments and provides a framework in which the effects of manipulations of the visual display characteristics used may be analyzed. . . .

One issue that deserves some consideration is the robustness of the model. To what extent do the simulations depend upon particular parameter values? What are the effects of changes of the parameter values? These are extremely complex questions, and we do not have complete answers. However, we have made some observations. First, the basic Reicher (1969) effect can be obtained under a very wide range of different parameters, though of course its exact size will depend on the ensemble of parameter values. However, one thing that seems to be important is the overpowering effect of one incompatible feature in suppressing activations at the letter level. Without this strong bottom–up inhibition, the mask would not effectively drive out the activations previously established by the stimulus. Second, performance on pronounceable nonwords depends on the relative strength of letter–word excitation compared to inhibition and on the strength of the competition among word units. Parameter values can be found which produce no advantage for any multiletter strings except words, whereas other values can be found that produce large advantages for words, pseudowords, and even many nonword strings. . . .

It thus appears that relatively strong feature–letter inhibition is necessary, but at the same time, relatively weak letter–word inhibition is necessary. This discrepancy is a bit puzzling, since we would have thought that the same general principles of operation would have applied to both the letter and the word level. A possible way to resolve the discrepancy might be to introduce a more sophisticated account of the way masking works. It is quite possible that new inputs act as position-specific "clear signals," disrupting activations created by previous patterns in corresponding locations. Some possible physiological mechanisms that would produce such effects at lower processing levels have been described by Weisstein, Ozog, and Szoc (1975) and by Breitmeyer and Ganz (1976), among others. If we used such a mechanism to account for the basic effect of masking, it might well be possible to lower the feature–letter inhibition considerably. Lowering feature–letter inhibition would then necessitate strong letter–letter inhibition, so that letters that exactly match the input would be able to dominate those with only partial matches. With these changes the letter and word levels would indeed operate by the same principles. . . .

In all but one of the experiments we have simulated, the primary (if not the only) data for the experiments were obtained from forced choices between pairs of letters, or strings differing by a single letter. In these cases, it seemed to us most natural to rely on the output of the letter level as the basis for responding. However, it may well be that subjects often base their responses on the output of the word level. Indeed, we have assumed that they do in experiments like the Broadbent and Gregory (1968) study, in which subjects were told to report what word they thought they had seen. This may also have happened in the McClelland and Johnston (1977) and Johnston (1978) studies, in which subjects were instructed to report all four letters before the forced choice on some trials. Indeed, both studies found that the probability of reporting all four letters correctly for letters in words was greater than we would expect given independent processing of each letter position. It seems natural to account for these completely correct reports by assuming that they often occurred on occasions where the subject encoded the item as a word. Even in experiments where only a forced choice is obtained, on many occasions subjects may still come away with a word, rather than a sequence of letters.

In the early phases of the development of our model, we explicitly included the possibility of output from the word level as well as the letter level. We assumed that the subject would either encode a word, with some probability dependent on the activations at the word level or, failing that, would encode some letter for each letter position dependent on the activations at the letter level. However, we found that simply relying on the letter level permitted us to account equally well for the results. In essence, the reason is that the word-level information is incorporated into the activations at the letter level because of the feedback, so that the word level is largely redundant. In addition, of course, readout from the letter level is necessary to the model's account of performance with nonwords. Since it is adequate to account for all of the forced-choice data, and since it is difficult to

know exactly how much of the details of free-report data should be attributed to perceptual processes and how much to such things as possible biases in the readout processes and so forth, we have stuck for the present with readout from the letter level. . . .

REFERENCE NOTES

1. Hinton, G. E. Relaxation and its role in vision. Unpublished doctoral dissertation, University of Edinburgh, Scotland, 1977.
2. Rumelhart, D. E. *A multicomponent theory of confusion among briefly exposed alphabetic characters* (Tech. Rep. 22). San Diego: University of California, San Diego, Center for Human Information Processing, 1971.

REFERENCES

Adams, M. J. Models of word recognition. *Cognitive Psychology,* 1979, *11,* 133–176.

Aderman, D., & Smith, E. E. Expectancy as a determinant of functional units in perceptual recognition. *Cognitive Psychology,* 1971, *2,* 117–129.

Anderson, J. A. Neural models with cognitive implications. In D. LaBerge & S. J. Samuels (Eds.), Basic processes in reading: *Perception and comprehension.* Hillsdale, N.J.: Erlbaum, 1977.

Anderson, J. A., Silverstein, J. W., Ritz, S. A., & Jones, R. S. Distinctive features, categorical perception, and probability learning: Some applications of a neural model. *Psychological Review,* 1977, *84,* 413–451.

Baron, J., & Thurston, I. An analysis of the word-superiority effect. *Cognitive Psychology,* 1973, *4,* 207–228.

Bouwhuis, D. G. *Visual recognition of words.* Eindhoven, The Netherlands: Greve Offset B. V., 1979.

Breitmeyer, B. G., & Ganz, L. Implications of sustained and transient channels for theories of visual pattern masking, saccadic suppression, and information processing. *Psychological Review,* 1976, *83,* 1–36.

Broadbent, D. E. Word-frequency effect and response bias. *Psychological Review,* 1967, *74,* 1–15.

Broadbent, D. E., & Gregory, M. Visual perception of words differing in letter digram frequency. *Journal of Verbal Learning and Verbal Behavior,* 1968, *7,* 569–571.

Bruner, J. S. On perceptual readiness. *Psychological Review,* 1957, *64,* 123–152.

Carr, T. H., Davidson, B. J., & Hawkins, H. L. Perceptual flexibility in word recognition: Strategies affect orthographic computation but not lexical access. *Journal of Experimental Psychology: Human Perception and Performance,* 1978, *4,* 674–690.

Cattell, J. M. The time taken up by cerebral operations. *Mind,* 1886, *11,* 220–242.

Estes, W. K. The locus of inferential and perceptual processes in letter identification. *Journal of Experimental Psychology: General,* 1975, *1,* 122–145.

Glushko, R. J. The organization and activation of orthographic knowledge in reading words aloud. *Journal of Experimental Psychology: Human Perception and Performance,* 1979, *5,* 674–691.

Grossberg, S. A theory of visual coding, memory, and development. In E. L. J. Leeuwenberg & H. R. M. Buffart (Eds.), *Formal theories of visual perception.* New York: Wiley, 1978.

Havens, L. L., & Foote, W. E. The effect of competition on visual duration threshold and its independence of stimulus frequency. *Journal of Experimental Psychology,* 1963, *65,* 5–11.

Hinton, G. E., & Anderson, J. A. (Eds.). *Parallel models of associative memory.* Hillsdale, N. J.: Erlbaum, 1981.

Holender, D. Identification of letters in words and of single letters with pre- and postknowledge vs. postknowledge of the alternatives. *Perception & Psychophysics,* 1979, *25,* 214–318.

Huey, E. B. *The psychology and pedagogy of reading.* New York: Macmillan, 1908.

Johnston, J. C. *The role of contextual constraint in the perception of letters in words.* Unpublished doctoral dissertation. University of Pennsylvania. 1974.

Johnston, J. C. A test of the sophisticated guessing theory of word perception. *Cognitive Psychology,* 1978, *10,* 123–154.

Johnston, J. C., & McClelland, J. L. Visual factors in word perception. *Perception & Psychophysics,* 1973, *14,* 365–370.

Johnston, J. C., & McClelland, J. L. Perception of letters in words: Seek not and ye shall find. *Science,* 1974, *184,* 1192–1194.

Johnston, J. C., & McClelland, J. L. Experimental tests of a hierarchical model of word identification. *Journal of Verbal Learning and Verbal Behavior,* 1980, *19,* 503–524.

Juola, J. F., Leavitt, D. D., & Choe, C. S. Letter identification in word, nonword, and single letter displays. *Bulletin of the Psychonomic Society,* 1974, *4,* 278–280.

Kohonen, T. *Associative memory: A system-theoretic approach.* West Berlin: Springer-Verlag, 1977.

Kucera, H., & Francis, W. *Computational analysis of present-day American English.* Providence, R.I.: Brown University Press, 1967.

LaBerge, D., & Samuels, S. Toward a theory of automatic information processing in reading. *Cognitive Psychology,* 1974, *6,* 293–323.

Levin, J. A. *Proteus: An activation framework for cognitive process models (ISI/WP-2).* Marina del Rey, Calif.: Information Sciences Institute, 1976.

Luce, R. D. *Individual choice behavior.* New York: Wiley, 1959.

Manelis, L. The effect of meaningfulness in tachistoscopic word perception. *Perception & Psychophysics,* 1974, *16,* 182–192.

Massaro, D. W., & Klitzke, D. The role of lateral masking and orthographic structure in letter and word recognition. *Acta Psychologica,* 1979, *43,* 413–426.

McClelland, J. L. Preliminary letter identification in the perception of words and nonwords. *Journal of Experimental Psychology: Human Perception and Performance,* 1976, *1,* 80–91.

McClelland, J. L. On the time relations of mental processes: An examination of systems of processes in cascade. *Psychological Review,* 1979, *86,* 287–330.

McClelland, J. L., & Johnston, J. C. The role of familiar units in perception of words and nonwords. *Perception & Psychophysics,* 1977, *22,* 249-261.

Morton, J. Interaction of information in word recognition. *Psychological Review,* 1969, *76,* 165–178.

Neisser, U. *Cognitive psychology.* New York: Appleton-Century-Crofts, 1967.

Newbigging, P. L. The perceptual reintegration of frequent and infrequent words. *Canadian Journal of Psychology.* 1961, *15,* 123–132.

Reicher, G. M. Perceptual recognition as a function of meaningfulness of stimulus material. *Journal of Experimental Psychology,* 1969, *81,* 274–280.

Rumelhart, D. E. A multicomponent theory of the perception of briefly exposed visual displays. *Journal of Mathematical Psychology,* 1970, *7,* 191–218.

Rumelhart, D. E. Toward an interactive model of reading. In S. Dornic (Ed.), *Attention and performance IV.* Hillsdale, N.J.: Erlbaum, 1977.

Rumelhart, D. E., & McClelland, J. L. An interactive activation model of context effects in letter perception: Part 2. The contextual enhancement effect and some tests and extensions of the model. *Psychological Review,* in press.

Rumelhart, D. E., & Siple, P. The process of recognizing tachistoscopically presented words. *Psychological Review,* 1974, *81,* 99–118.

Spoehr, K., & Smith, E. The role of orthographic and phonotactic rules in perceiving letter patterns. *Journal of Experimental Psychology: Human Perception and Performance,* 1975, *1,* 21–34.

Szentagothai, J., & Arbib, M. A. *Conceptual models of neural organization.* Cambridge, Mass.: MIT Press, 1975.

Taylor, G. A., & Chabot, R. J. Differential backward masking of words and letters by masks of varying orthographic structure. *Memory & Cognition,* 1978, *6,* 629–635.

Thompson, M. C., & Massaro, D. W. Visual information and redundancy in reading. *Journal of Experimental Psychology,* 1973, *98,* 49–54.

Turvey, M. On peripheral and central processes in vision: Inferences from an information-processing analysis of masking with patterned stimuli. *Psychological Review,* 1973, *80,* 1–52.

Weisstein, N., Ozog, G., & Szoc, R. A comparison and elaboration of two models of metacontrast. *Psychological Review,* 1975, *82,* 325–343.

Wheeler, D. Processes in word recognition. *Cognitive Psychology,* 1970, *1,* 59-85.

POSTSCRIPT

For a very useful and readable summary of letter perception, see Crowder and Wagner (1992). Bruce and Green (1990) and Gordon (1989) provide comprehensive reviews of theory and research on visual perception, and Sekuler and Blake (1990) provide clear coverage of all aspects of perception.

The full flowering of the connectionist approach came with the publication in 1986 of the two-volume *Parallel Distributed Processing* (McClelland, Rumelhart, & the PDP Research Group, 1986; Rumelhart, McClelland, & the PDP Research Group, 1986; but see also Hinton and Anderson, 1981). Although that two-volume work is still the standard reference on connectionism, many students who wish to learn more about connectionism may be daunted by more than 1100 pages of highly technical reading. Such students may prefer Rumelhart (1989) or, particularly, Bechtel and Abrahamsen (1991), Martindale (1991), or Quinlan (1991). In many ways, however, the connectionist approach is difficult to appreciate fully without actually exploring and testing computer simulations that implement connectionist models. The interested reader is therefore referred to McClelland and Rumelhart (1988), which includes a number of simulation exercises and programs that can be run on personal computers. Nonconnectionist computer models of visual processes have also been developed. Some of these are described by Poggio (1984) and Stillings et al. (1987).

Connectionist models are often described as being neural-like. This should not be taken to mean that the units in connectionist models behave in exactly the same fashion as neurons do. But some neural network models of visual processes (see Carpenter & Grossberg, 1991) do try to limit the kinds of processing each unit is called upon to play so that they are within the capacities of neurons or small sets of neurons.

The presymbolic orientation of connectionists has come under heavy criticism as being unilluminating as an explanation of human cognition (Fodor & McLaughlin, 1990; Fodor & Pylyshyn, 1988; Pinker & Mehler, 1988); however, it has been defended equally vociferously (see various articles in Davis, 1992; Smolensky, 1987, 1988). Lately, several authors have attempted a reconciliation between connectionist and classical cognitivist approaches (for instance, Bechtel & Abrahamsen, 1991; Clark, 1989; McCloskey, 1991).

FOR FURTHER THOUGHT

1. In what sense or senses does McClelland and Rumelhart's model operate in parallel? In what sense or senses is it interactive?
2. Summarize the key assumptions about letter perception that McClelland and Rumelhart make in their model. For what parameters must values be assigned or fixed? On what basis do McClelland and Rumelhart assign the values for those parameters?
3. What is a cycle in the operation of a connectionist network? When does the cycling stop?
4. We often fail to notice ambiguities in word meanings when they occur in certain contexts. For example, the word *bank* in the sentence "He left his money at the bank" is ambiguous; it can refer either to a financial institution or to the side of a river. But that ambiguity is rarely noticed. See whether you can develop a connectionist explanation of this phenomenon.
5. The connectionist network described here deals only with the visual perception of letters. Could it be adapted to account for the auditory perception of words? If not, why not? If so, how, and would such a network be able to account for the "cocktail party" effect discussed by Treisman (Reading 3)?

REFERENCES

Bechtel, W., & Abrahamsen, L. (1991). *Connectionism and the mind: An introduction to parallel processing in networks.* Cambridge, MA: Basil Blackwell.

Bruce, V., & Green, P. R. (1990). *Visual perception: Physiology, psychology, and ecology* (2nd ed.), Hove, United Kingdom: Erlbaum.

Carpenter, G. A., & Grossberg, S. (Eds.). (1991). *Pattern recognition by self-organizing neural networks.* Cambridge, MA: MIT Press.

Clark, A. (1989). *Microcognition: Philosophy, cognitive science, and parallel distributed processing.* Cambridge, MA: MIT Press.

Crowder, R. G., & Wagner, R. K. (1992). *The psychology of reading* (2nd ed.). New York: Oxford University Press.

Davis, S. (1992). *Connectionism: Theory and practice.* New York: Oxford University Press.

Fodor, J. A., & McLaughlin, B. P. (1990). Connectionism and the problem of systematicity: Why Smolensky's solution doesn't work. *Cognition, 35,* 183–204.

Fodor, J. A., & Pylyshyn, A. W. (1988). Connectionism and cognitive architecture. *Cognition, 28,* 3–71.

Gordon, I. E. (1989). *Theories of visual perception.* Chichester, GB: Wiley.

Hinton, G. E., & Anderson, J. A. (Eds.) (1981). *Parallel models of associative memory.* Hillsdale, NJ: Erlbaum.

Martindale, C. (1991). *Cognitive psychology: A neural-network approach.* Pacific Grove, CA: Brooks/Cole Publishing Co.

McClelland, J. L., & Rumelhart, D. E. (1988). *Explorations in Parallel Distributed Processing: A handbook of models, programs, and exercises.* Cambridge, MA: MIT Press.

McClelland, J. L., Rumelhart, D. E., & the PDP Research Group (1986). *Parallel Distributed Processing: Explorations in the microstructure of cognition (Vol. 2): Psychological and biological models.* Cambridge, MA: MIT Press.

McCloskey, M. (1991). Networks and theories: The place of connectionism in cognitive science. *Psychological Science, 2,* 387–395.

Morton, J. (1969). Interaction of information in word recognition. *Psychological Review, 76,* 165–178.

Pinker, S., & Mehler, J. (Eds.) (1988). *Connections and symbols.* Cambridge, MA: MIT Press.

Poggio, T. (1984, April) Vision by man and machine. *Scientific American,* pp. 106–116.

Quinlan, P. (1991). *Connectionism and psychology.* Chicago: University of Chicago Press.

Rumelhart, D. E. (1989). The architecture of mind: A connectionist approach. In M. I. Posner (Ed.), *Foundations of cognitive science* (pp. 133–159). Cambridge, MA: MIT Press.

Rumelhart, D. E., & McClelland, J. L. (1982). An interactive activation model of context effects in letter perception: Part 2. The contextual enhancement effect and some tests and extensions of the model. *Psychological Review, 89,* 60–94.

Rumelhart, D. E., McClelland, J. L., & the PDP Research Group (1986). *Parallel distributed processing: Explorations in the microstructure of cognition: Vol. 1. Foundations.* Cambridge, MA: MIT Press.

Sekuler, R., & Blake, R. (1990). *Perception* (2nd ed.). New York: McGraw-Hill.

Smolensky, P. (1987). The constituent structure of mental states: A reply to Fodor and Pylyshyn. *Southern Journal of Philosophy, 26,* 137–160.

Smolensky, P. (1988). On the proper treatment of connectionism. *Behavioral and Brain Sciences, 11,* 1–74.

Stillings, N. A., Feinstein, M. H., Garfield, J. L., Rissland, E. L., Rosenbaum, D. A., Weisler, S. E., & Baker-Ward, L. (1987). *Cognitive science: An introduction.* Cambridge, MA: MIT Press.

Szentagothai, J., & Arbib, M. A. (1975). *Conceptual models of neural organization.* Cambridge, MA: MIT Press.

INTRODUCTION

Although being able to recognize static stimuli (stimuli such as printed letters that do not change as we're looking at them) is an important aspect of human visual perception, much of the information that makes up our visual experience is dynamic, changing over time because of either changes in our viewing position, movement of the stimuli, or both. Lynn Kozlowski and James Cutting study a very simple dynamic display in "Recognizing the Sex of a Walker from a Dynamic Point-Light Display."

For these experiments, Kozlowski and Cutting put reflective tape on various joints of some men and women and videotaped them as they walked. By playing back the resulting tapes on a television monitor, with the brightness diminished and contrast heightened, and then videotaping the resulting image with a second video recorder, they created films on which the only thing that could be seen were bright spots moving against a black background. Thus the only visual information available to subjects viewing these films was the pattern of movements among the spots; none of the information we typically think of as being useful for recognizing people or determining their sex (what Kozlowski and Cutting refer to as familiarity cues) was present. Kozlowski and Cutting's references to "visual angle" in descriptions of the stimuli refer to the *size* of those stimuli; see the introduction to Reading 21 for further explanation of visual angles.

As you read this article, ask yourself: What information is present in these displays? What kind of information can movement patterns convey? How do they convey that information? What must our visual system be doing to pick up and make use of that information?

Recognizing the Sex of a Walker from a Dynamic Point-Light Display

Lynn T. Kozlowski and James E. Cutting
Wesleyan University

The present set of experiments was prompted by two films by Gunnar Johansson (Maas & Johansson, 1971a, 1971b). Point-light sources are attached to the joints of a person and the surround darkened. When the individual walks, runs, rides a bicycle, or does pushups, only an array of correlated movements among lights can be seen. What is seen, however, is not what is experienced. There is absolutely no doubt that this conflation of lights is a human being.

Johansson has explored the general aspects of this technique (Johansson, 1973), has emphasized its significance for any theory of visual perception (Johansson, 1974, 1975), and has begun to write a calculus for biological motion perception (Johansson, 1973, 1976). We, on the other hand, have become interested in the phenomenon itself. We have shown that an array of dynamic point-lights mounted on a walker is sufficient for recognizing and identifying oneself and one's friends (Cutting & Kozlowski, 1977). Provoked by the success of that demonstration, we looked for more general aspects of recognition. One question on a study guide circulated with Johansson's films interested us: Is it possible to recognize the sex of a walker from these dynamic displays? By asking the question, Maas and Johansson imply that it is. We sought to confirm their suspicion,

to determine to what degree such recognition occurs, and to explore some of the parameters of sex recognition without familiarity cues.

EXPERIMENT 1: DYNAMIC DISPLAYS

Method

We employed the second of Johansson's (1973) techniques: glassbead retroreflective tape wrapped around joints, videotape recording equipment, and bright lights focused on the walking area and mounted very close to the lens of a television camera. The contrast of the resulting image on the television monitor is turned to maximum, and the brightness to minimum so that only the reflectant patches are seen.

Six Wesleyan University undergraduates, three males and three females, served as walkers. Each had a normal gait. All were approximately the same height (1.63 to 1.73 m) and weight (55 to 68 kg). All wore blue jeans and a dark turtleneck shirt during the recording session. Five-centimeter-wide commercially available reflectant tape was wrapped around their wrists, around their arms just above the elbow, around their ankles, and around their legs just above the knee. Patches of tape, 5 × 15 cm, were attached to their belts at the hips and to their shoulders as epaulets, half on the shoulder and half on the upper arm. Each walked at his or her own pace for several minutes until we were satisfied that he or she was not "performing" before the camera. We videotaped side views of the individuals as they walked in a straight line in front of the camera, about 8 m from the lens at the closest point. Each walked back and forth 10 times. Both head and feet were well within the pic-

This research was sponsored by research grants from Wesleyan University to both authors. We thank Robert J. White for technical assistance, Deborah A. Cassidy for assistance in running experiments, and Catharine D. Barclay and Kendall J. Bryant for assistance in statistical analysis. James E. Cutting is also a member of the Haskins Laboratories. Requests for reprints should be sent to L. T. Kozlowski, Department of Psychology, Wesleyan University, Middletown, Connecticut 06457.

SOURCE: *Perception and Psychophysics, 21*(6), 1977, pp. 575–580. Reprinted by permission of Psychonomic Society, Inc.

tured frame. There was no reflectant tape on the head. Each walker was on camera for five strides ($\pm\frac{1}{4}$ stride) for each pass across the viewing field. The camera was fixed in position and did not pan to follow the walker. Walkers were videotaped individually.

Presentation order of all 60 tokens (6 walkers, 10 times each) was randomized by recording onto a second videotape. The dubbing procedure involved two helical-scan videotape recorders, a monitor connected to one recorder on which the source tape was played, and a television camera focused on the monitor and connected to the second tape recorder, on which the test tape was recorded. Test trials were recorded by locating the particular trial to be dubbed from the source tape (a process aided by an audio channel recorded onto it after the recording session), playing that trial on the source videotape recorder and recording it on the other. This sequence was repeated until all trials were recorded. Each trial consisted of the individual walking across the screen from left to right, a brief pause of 3 to 5 sec, and then the same individual walking from right to left. An interval of 15 to 20 sec occurred between trials to insure that both video recorders reached the same speed and that no "flop-over" of image on the monitor occurred within a trial. This same videotape sequence was used by Cutting and Kozlowski (1977).

The videotape dubbing procedure degraded the stimuli somewhat, but to our advantage. The point-lights "bloomed" slightly, becoming larger and more circular. Static approximations to our dynamic stimuli can be seen in Figure 1. Each of the six walkers is portrayed in a cluster of four point-light configurations. Those on the top of each cluster show the individual walking from left to right, those on the bottom from right to left. The two configurations on the left of each of the clusters portray the walker at a time when arms and legs are most outstretched, and those to the right at a time when the body is most aligned, on one stiff leg with the other knee slightly raised. Walkers 1, 2, and 3 are females; 4, 5, and 6 are males.

Thirty Wesleyan University undergraduates, 15 males and 15 females, were paid to view the test sequence. They sat 2 to 4 m from the monitor in groups of six or less. For each trial they wrote down M or F to indicate the sex of the walker, and used a 5-point

FIGURE 1   Static approximations of the dynamic stimuli for the six walkers.

unipolar scale to indicate confidence in their judgments. Visual angle, measured vertically, was between about 2° and 4° for each viewer.

Results and Discussion

As shown in Table 1, Walkers 4, 5, and 6 were correctly identified as male on an average of 72% of all trials, and Walkers 2 and 3 were correctly identified as female on 67% of all trials. Walker 1, however, proved to be an anomaly: She was identified as female only 32% of all trials, a result of the same magnitude as the others but in the wrong direction. This fact is considered in more depth in Experiments 3, 4, and 5. There was no effect of the sex of the viewer in this or in any other experiment in this paper.

Figure 2 shows the mean percent correct identification as a function of the raters' confidence in their guesses. The anomalous walker is omitted from the data, in order to indicate the confidence effect more clearly. If this walker is included, the pattern of results is still statistically reliable, though the mean decreases by about 10 points at each level of confidence. When not at all confident the raters' performance is not better than chance, 55% [t(29) = 1.0, n.s.]; when most confident, it is an impressive 87% [t(29) = 9.1, p<.001]. The linear trend is robust [F(1,90) = 12.3,

TABLE 1   Percent Correct Identification of Sex for Each of the Six Walkers in Experiments 1 and 2

	Female Walkers			Male Walkers			
	1	2	3	4	5	6	Mean
Dynamic Displays (Experiment 1)	32*†	67*	64*	62*	73*	81*	63*
Static Displays (Experiment 2)	41	50	50	49	40*†	46	46

*p < .05 by two-tailed *t* tests

†These results are significant in the opposite direction.

p < .01], without higher order components. It suggests that the compelling nature of the general percept of a person walking (Johansson, 1973) is extended to judgments of the walker's sex. Remember, no feedback was given at any time during this or any other experiment in this paper.

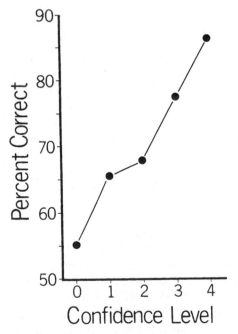

FIGURE 2   Mean correct identification of the sex of walkers as a function of confidence in the judgment.

EXPERIMENT 2: STATIC DISPLAYS

It is clear that a dynamic display of point-lights is sufficient for recognizing the sex of a walker. Next, we sought to determine if similar static displays would do as well.

Method

Four photographs were taken of stopped images of each walker, as shown in Figure 1. All four comprised a set and were mounted on cardboard in the same arrangement as in the figure. Five photocopies were made of each set. Twenty different Wesleyan University undergraduates, 10 males and 10 females, performed two tasks: (a) each looked at one sheet and guessed what the point-light displays represented, and (b) after being told that the dots represented walkers, they sorted the 30 sheets (6 walkers, 5 copies of each set) into two piles, male and female. They were not told how many walkers were in the sample.

Results and Discussion

When first presented with the static displays, only one subject guessed that they represented people. The most common responses were that the pictures were constellations of stars or Christmas tree lights. Thus, the impression of a person walking in a static array is not compelling or immediate, although it is compelling and immediate in the Johansson dynamic-array experiments. Johansson's (1976) more recent work corroborates this result. He found that very brief presentations (100 msec) of people walking or running were not identifiable as people, whereas longer presentations (≥ 200 msec) were.

When sorting the displays according to sex of walker, the subjects fared no better. They yielded an overall performance of only 46%, slightly, but not significantly, less than chance [t(19) = 1.6, n.s.]. Intrawalker reliability was very low. In Table 1, performance on each of the six walkers in static presentation is shown against the data of Experiment 1 for dynamic presentation. All differences are 9% or greater and all are statistically reliable.

In summary, then, viewers can recognize the sex of a walker from a dynamic display without familiarity cues, but not from four static displays taken out of the dynamic sequence.

EXPERIMENTS 3 AND 4: DYNAMIC DISPLAYS VARYING ARMSWING AND WALKING SPEED

Next, we turned our efforts toward the discovery of cues for the judgment of a walker's sex. Our approach was to investigate why the sex of Walker 1 was misidentified, in the hope that general principles might arise. Inspection of the stimuli suggested two possibilities. First, the female walkers had more pronounced armswing than the males, as can be seen in Figure 1. Moreover, Walker 1 had the least armswing of the women. Second, the women in our sample (Walkers 1, 2, and 3) walked faster than the men (4, 5, and 6). We timed each walker during each pass across the monitor in the test tape used in Experiment 1 and found that they averaged 2.61, 2.57, 2.53, 2.71, 3.04, and 2.75 sec for Walkers 1 through 6, respectively. Notice that the distributions of walking times do not overlap, and that Walker 1 is the slowest of the women. These two cues, armswing and walking speed, are correlated in natural gait. For example, the faster one walks the more one generally pumps his or her arms. Nevertheless, in Experiment 3 we isolated armswing as distinct from walking speed, and in Experiment 4 we attempted to isolate walking speed from armswing.

Method

Walkers 1, 2, 4, and 6 were brought back for another recording session. Thus, though our sample of walkers is smaller still, we retained two males and two females. For Experiment 3, five types of armswing were recorded: a "normal" armswing,[1] two smaller-than-normal armswings, and two larger-than-normal armswings. The smaller-than-normal armswings had the walkers (a) walk with their hands in the front pockets of their jeans, and (b) walk with hands at their sides using as little armswing as possible without stiffening the muscles of the upper body. The two larger-than-normal armswings were (a) just slightly larger than normal, and (b) very exaggerated, with the front arm (elbow to wrist) always reaching the horizontal with each stride. Large and exaggerated armswings were standardized simply through the judgments of the authors at the time of recording.

In Experiments 4, five walking speeds were recorded: the normal walking speed, two slower-than-normal speeds, and two faster-than-normal speeds. The normal speed was determined by matching metronome pulses against the walker's pace. The pulse was varied until each walker declared that he or she was most comfortable walking at a particular rate. Slower speeds were 8 and 16 strides/min slower than the normal; faster speeds were 8 and 16 strides/min faster than normal. In all cases, the individuals walked with the beat of the metronome. The normal speeds for Walkers 1, 2, 4, and 6 were 104, 108, 104, and 96 paces/min, respectively.

Test tapes were recorded in the same manner as in Experiment 1, except that only two tokens of each walker were used in each condition and only left-to-right passes across the monitor screen were used. On each experimental tape, tokens were mixed and presented in a 40-item sequence. As a group, 30

---

[1]People differ greatly in the amount they swing their arms when they walk. Moreover, it is not uncommon to discover considerable asymmetries: A given individual may swing one arm through 60° of an arc while holding the other arm almost motionless. Our six walkers appeared to have symmetrical walks and armswings, and we did not coach them to make their walks "more normal." Nonetheless, the data of these experiments when taken together hint at the possibility of asymmetries for Walker 1.

Wesleyan undergraduates (15 males and 15 females) were paid to view the video test tape for Experiment 3. As a group, 28 members of a psychology class (10 males and 18 females) viewed the sequence for Experiment 4. Each viewer wrote down M or F to indicate the sex of the walker for each trial. Confidence measures were also taken, but, since they revealed nothing different from the previous studies, they will not be discussed.

Results and Discussion

In Experiment 3, armswing had no clear effect on judgments except that nonnormal armswings tended to interfere with identifiability. When the individual walked with normal armswing, sex identification was comparable with that of previous experiments with this stimulus sample, 65% [t(29) = 4.1, p < .001]. With hands in pockets, walker's sex was only 46% identifiable; with hands at sides, it was only 54% identifiable, and for armswing very exaggerated, it was only 55% identifiable. None of these results differs significantly from chance. Only with armswings slightly larger than normal was the walker's sex identifiable at a rate greater than chance, 59% [t(29) = 2.6, p < .011, but at a level reduced from that for normal armswing. Increasing armswing did not make walkers appear more feminine; nor did decreasing armswing make them appear more masculine. Summed across the five armswing conditions, the sex of each walker was correctly identified 33%, 66%, 54%, and 70% for Walkers, 1, 2, 4, and 6, respectively. These percentages are comparable to those in Experiment 1.

In Experiment 4, walking speed did have a small effect, as shown in Table 2. For the two men, the manipulation interfered with correct identification. That is, although the men were always identified as male from the dynamic display, conditions of both faster- and slower-than-normal impeded viewer performance. For the two women, on the other hand, increase in walking speed was associated with greater correct identification. This linear trend was statistically reliable [F(1,10) = 6.2, p < .05]. However, the trend for males and females together is not significant.

Since these two studies were, in part, prompted by the results of our anomalous walker, Walker 1, in-

TABLE 2 Percent Correct Identification of Male and Female Walkers at Five Walking Speeds

	Walking Speed (strides/min deviation from normal)				
	−16	−8	0	+8	+16
Female Walkers	44	38*†	57*	57*	66*
Male Walkers	69*	77*	78*	65*	70*
Mean	56	57	67*	61*	68*

*p < .05, two-tailed t test.

†Significant and in the opposite direction.

spection of her results seemed warranted. Oddly enough, when walking with normal armswing or at normal speed she failed to be identified as either male or female, thus not entirely replicating her results from Experiment 1. Having her walk faster did make her appear somewhat feminine (57% correct identification), but this effect was not statistically reliable.

EXPERIMENT 5: DYNAMIC DISPLAYS WITH CERTAIN JOINTS NOT REPRESENTED

The results of Experiments 3 and 4 suggest that more or less holistic aberrations of normal gait either have little influence on the viewer performance for these dynamic displays or actually impede viewer performance. In no case did either the manipulation of armswing or walking speed systematically improve the identifiability of all walkers' sex. In Experiment 5, we examine information in the normal gait, but with less displayed to the viewer. Our hope was to determine the locus of information important to the viewer. In other words, which joints are necessary for the identification of a walker's sex, and which, if any, are sufficient?

Method

Walkers 1, 2, 4, and 6 were employed again. Source videotapes were recorded for this experiment at the same time as those for Experiments 3 and 4.

Seven configurations of lights were used for each walker. For notational purposes, we will designate the

TABLE 3   Percent Correct Identification of Sex of Walker for Each of Seven Dynamic Point-Light Configurations

Body Portion		Female Walkers		Male Walkers		
		1	2	4	6	Mean
Lower Body	A		61*	60*	39*†	54
	HA		59*	55*	55	56
	HNA		62*	42*†	62*	55
Upper Body	SER	53	62*	65*	65*	61*
	SERH	59*	69*	69*	84*	70
Full Body	SERHA	59*	72*	66*	72*	67*
	SERHNA	60*	77*	67*	78*	70*
Mean		58*	66*	60*	65*	

Note—S = shoulder, E = elbows, R = wrists, H = hip, N = knees, A = ankles.

*p < .05, two-tailed t test.

†These results are in the opposite direction.

shoulder as S, the elbows E, the wrists R, the hip H, the knees N, and the ankles A. Three configurations included information only about the lower body—A, HA (hip and ankles), and HNA (for hip, knees, and ankles).[2] Two others contained information only about the upper body—SER (for shoulder, elbows, and wrists) and SERH (shoulder, elbows, wrists, and hip). A sixth configuration portrayed information about all joints except the knees (SERHA), and a seventh included all joints (SERHNA).

The preparation of the test tape was identical to that in Experiments 3 and 4. All token types were blocked by configuration. The test tape began with six practice trials of Walkers 3 and 5 with lights on all joints, followed by a random sequence of A (ankles alone), then random sequences of SER, HA, SERH, HNA, SERHA, and SERHNA, in that order. Due to an error made during the recording session, all tokens of Walker 1 in A, HA, and HNA configurations were lost.

As a group, members of an introductory psychology class viewed the test sequence. There were 132

males and 127 females, for a total of 259 viewers. They watched the sequence on one of two monitors placed at the front of a lecture hall. Visual angle for viewers was between about 0°20' and 3°0'. Each viewer wrote down M or F to indicate the sex of the walker.

Results and Discussion

Overall, the viewers could identify the sex of the walkers 63% of the time [t(258) = 10.2, p < .001]. In each of the separate conditions, the viewers were able to identify the walkers correctly (see the last column of Table 3). Correlated t tests revealed that, on the average, upper-body and full-body conditions were significantly more identifiable than lower-body conditions (all ps < .01)[3]: Armswing information, as suggested by the results of Experiment 3, appears to be especially helpful. There were no significant differences among lower-body conditions: Adding hips and knees to ankles did not increase accuracy of guessing. However, adding to upper body information (SER) any information about the lower body (SERH, SERHA, and SERHNA) significantly increased accuracy (ps < .01). It appears that, roughly speaking, any

[2]Strictly speaking, the HA and HNA conditions do give some upper body information. Even though no tape was mounted on the arm, it still occluded the reflectant patch at the waist during part of every stride. The occlusion gives some information about the velocity of the pendular movement of the arms, and thus some information about movement in the torso.

[3]For these comparisons, the means of Walkers 2, 4, and 6 were used.

joint is sufficient and no joint is necessary for the recognition of a walker's sex.

Interestingly, Walker 1, the formerly anomalous subject of Experiment 1, became identifiable as a female (although in her SER condition she is the only walker not different from chance). Perhaps her walk when viewed from her right side is reliably more "feminine" than when viewed from her left side. (Both were used in Experiment 1, but only the former in Experiments 3, 4, and 5.) In addition, since the recording session for the last three experiments occurred at a different time from that for the first study, her mood, her walking speed, or even the exact location of the reflectant tape might have changed enough to cause these effects. Other anomalies in these data, that Walker 6's ankles and Walker 4's legs appear feminine, are perhaps best attributable to the particular sequence of trials. Given the state of our knowledge, we believe that it is uninteresting and unrewarding to try to develop an ideographic approach to the study of gait. Therefore, such reversals in the data will not be discussed further. Only the nomothetic trends are considered.

Since the study was conducted in a large lecture hall and the visual angle of the stimuli varied from $3°0'$ to $0°20'$ for the observers, we decided to evaluate the accuracy of guesses as a function of distance from the stimuli. The rows of seats were divided into three sections: near, halfway, and far. Guessing for these groups was, respectively, 65%, 62%, and 61% correct [linear trend, $F(1,219) = 5.49$, $p < .02$]. It is noteworthy that even the far group was well above chance in the estimation of the sex of the walkers.

GENERAL DISCUSSION AND SUMMARY

The point of this investigation was not to study sex. We are not interested in why males and females walk differently, whether through socialization or through biomechanical differences. Instead, we have used sex as a convenient, pervasive, and abstract source of structural information. Shaw, McIntyre, and Mace (1974) argue that a successful study of event must consider two issues: the underlying dynamic aspect of the event, or the *transformational invariant*, and the underlying unity of the structures involved, or the *structural invariant*. Walking, of course, is our transformational invariant, and sex part of the structural invariant.

In Experiment 1 we confirm the suspicions of Maas and Johansson. That is, viewers can recognize the sex of a walker from a dynamic point-light display. Given information about the shoulder, elbows, wrists, hip, knees, and ankles, recognition appears to hover around 70%. Experiment 2 emphasizes that it is the dynamic nature of the display which is important: Recognition of the sex of a walker is simply not possible from four static arrays taken from the dynamic sequence.

In Experiments 3 and 4, we demonstrated that there is a certain "grammar" to an individual's natural walk and that violation of it decreases the identifiability of the sex of the walker. Change in movement of the hands and arms during walking detracts from the overall strength and integrity of the percept. In other words, we violated the nature of the transformational invariant to some small degree. Deviation in the walker's speed from that which is normal also disrupts the transformational invariant, although in a less clear fashion.

In Experiment 5, we found, essentially, that no clue is necessary for identification. It would appear that any light on joints of the upper body or any of the lower body may be absent. Moreover, it appears that any cue is sufficient. Most surprising to us was that ankles alone yielded greater-than-chance performance. We anticipated that the hip would be particularly important. By itself, it proved not to be, but in conjunction with information from the upper body it enhances the percept.

Viewers immediately recognize the pendular motion of a few lights as a person walking. No feedback is required, not even for them to make reasonably accurate guesses as to the sex of the walker. Walking appears to be a holistic act. Information as abstract as the sex of the walker appears to be distributed through all the movement.

REFERENCES

Cutting. E., & Kozlowski, L. T. Recognizing friends by their walk: Gait perception without familiarity cues. *Bulletin of the Psychonomic Society*, 1977, 9, 353–356.

Johansson, G. Visual perception of biological motion and a model for its analysis. *Perception & Psychophysics,* 1973, 14, 201–211.

Johansson, G. Projective transformations as determining visual space perception. In R. B. MacLeod & H. L. Pick (Eds.), *Perception: Essays in honor of J. J. Gibson.* Ithaca, NY: Cornell University Press, 1974.

Johansson, G. Visual motion perception. *Scientific American,* 1975, 232(6), 76–89.

Johansson, G. Spatio-temporal differentiation and integration in visual motion perception. *Psychological Research,* 1976, 38, 379–393.

Maas J. B., & Johansson, G. *Motion perception I: 2-dimensional motion perception.* Boston: Houghton Mifflin, 1971 (film). (a)

Maas, J. B., & Johansson, G. *Motion perception II: 3-dimensional motion perception.* Boston: Houghton Mifflin, 1971 (film). (b)

Shaw, R. E., McIntyre, M., & Mace, W. M. The role of symmetry in event perception. In R. B. MacLeod & H. L. Pick (Eds.), *Perception: Essays in honor of J. J. Gibson.* Ithaca, NY: Cornell University Press, 1974.

POSTSCRIPT

In subsequent work on this topic, Cutting and his colleagues (Barclay, Cutting, & Kozlowski, 1978; Cutting, Proffitt, & Kozlowski, 1978; Kozlowski & Cutting, 1978) showed (1) that the most important information for determining the sex of a walker is likely to be the relative amount of movement at the shoulders and hips (more hip than shoulder in women, more shoulder than hip in men), and (2) that subjects need between 1.6 and 2.7 secs (approximately two steps) of such information to make a determination of sex. One particularly interesting result is that if the displays are turned upside down, subjects are likely to guess the wrong sex (Barclay et al., 1978). This suggests that the information we make use of involves not only the amount of movement in the lights but also the spatial relationships among them (Cutting, 1981). Much of the more recent work on gait perception has used light displays generated by computers (Cutting 1978a, 1978b; Cutting, Moore, & Morrison, 1988). This gives experimenters more precise control over the displays and allows for independent manipulation of factors that typically go together when a real person walks (Todd, 1983). The technique can even be used to test infants' ability to recognize walking figures (Bertenthal, 1993; Bertenthal, Proffitt, & Kramer, 1987).

As mentioned in the introduction to this article, the work reported here focuses on what in the visual display stays the same (remains invariant) as the observer and elements in the environment move about. This approach, which emphasizes the fact that our visual systems evolved in a dynamic environment, is generally associated with the approach of the late J. J. Gibson and his colleagues and is sometimes called an ecological approach to visual perception, or ecological optics (Reed & Jones, 1982). One of the main arguments made in this approach is that the environment continually and directly (without laborious computation) "affords" us certain information impossible to capture with static stimuli (Cutting, 1986; Gibson, 1979; Michaels & Carello, 1981). This argument has been both strongly criticized (Fodor & Pylyshyn, 1981) and strongly defended (Glotzbach, 1992; Turvey, Shaw, Reed, & Mace, 1981). Much of the work in ecological optics is quite technical, but you can get a good flavor of it from Bruce and Green (1990) or Gordon (1989). The latter two references and Sekuler et al. (1990) also discuss more general issues in the perception of motion.

FOR FURTHER THOUGHT

1. Why did Kozlowski and Cutting use walkers who were all approximately the same height and weight? What implications does this have for the generalizability of their results?
2. In discussing their second experiment, Kozlowski and Cutting cite results from Johansson (1976) indicating that if subjects see only 100 msec of a dynamic display, they don't recognize the display as depicting people, but if they see 200 msec or more, they do. In what way are these results relevant and not relevant to the point Kozlowski and Cutting are trying to make in Experiments 1 and 2?
3. What do Kozlowski and Cutting mean when they say (in discussing Experiment 5) that "any joint is sufficient and no joint is necessary for the recognition of a walker's sex"? Which of their data are consistent and which are inconsistent with this generalization?
4. What do Kozlowski and Cutting mean when they say "walking appears to be a holistic act"? What data contribute to this conclusion, and why?
5. Generate two examples each of transformational and structural invariants.

REFERENCES

Barclay, C. D., Cutting, J. E., & Kozlowski, L. T. (1978). Temporal and spatial factors in gait perception that influence gender recognition. *Perception & Psychophysics, 23,* 145–152.

Bertenthal, B. I. (1993). Infants' perception of biomechanical motions: Intrinsic image and knowledge-based constraints. In C. Granrud (Ed.), *Visual perception and cognition in infancy* (pp. 175–214). Hillsdale, NJ: Erlbaum.

Bertenthal, B. I., Proffitt, D. R., & Kramer, S. J. (1987). Perception of biomechanical motions by infants: Implementation of various processing constraints. *Journal of Experimental Psychology: Human Perception and Performance, 13,* 577–585.

Bruce, V., & Green, P. R. (1990). *Visual perception: Physiology, psychology, and ecology* (2nd ed.). Hove, United Kingdom: Erlbaum.

Cutting, J. E. (1978a). Generation of synthetic male and female walkers through manipulation of a biomechanical invariant. *Perception, 7,* 393–405.

Cutting, J. E. (1978b). A program to generate synthetic walkers as dynamic point-light displays. *Behavior Research Methods and Instrumentation, 10,* 91–94.

Cutting, J. E. (1981). Coding theory adapted to gait perception. *Journal of Experimental Psychology: Human Perception and Performance, 7,* 71–87.

Cutting, J. E. (1986). *Perception with an eye for motion.* Cambridge, MA: MIT Press.

Cutting, J. E., Moore, C., & Morrison, R. (1988). Masking the motions of human gait. *Perception & Psychophysics, 44,* 339–347.

Cutting, J. E., Proffitt, D. R., & Kozlowski, L. T. (1978). A biomechanical invariant for gait perception. *Journal of Experimental Psychology: Human Perception and Performance, 4,* 357–372.

Fodor, J. A., & Pylyshyn, Z. W. (1981). How direct is visual perception? Some reflections on Gibson's "ecological approach." *Cognition, 9,* 139–196.

Gibson, J. J. (1979). *The ecological approach to visual perception.* Boston: Houghton Mifflin.

Glotzbach, P. A. (1992). Determining the primary problem of visual perception: A Gibsonian response to "correlation" objection. *Philosophical Psychology, 5,* 69–94.

Gordon, I. E. (1989). *Theories of visual perception.* Chichester, GB: Wiley.

Kozlowski, L. T., & Cutting, J. E. (1978). Recognizing the gender of walkers from point-lights mounted on ankles: Some second thoughts. *Perception & Psychophysics, 23,* 459.

Michaels, C. F., & Carello C. (1981). *Direct perception.* Englewood Cliffs, NJ: Prentice-Hall.

Reed, E., & Jones, R. (Eds.) (1982). *Reasons for realism: Selected essays of James J. Gibson.* Hillsdale, NJ: Erlbaum.

Sekuler, R., Anstis, S., Braddick, O. J., Brandt, T., Movshon, J. A., & Orban, G. (1990). The perception of motion. In L. Spillmann & J. S. Werner (Eds.), *Visual perception: The neurophysiological foundations.* San Diego: Academic Press.

Todd, J. T. (1983). Perception of gait. *Journal of Experimental Psychology: Human Perception and Performance, 9,* 31–42.

Turvey, M. T. , Shaw, R. E. , Reed, E. S. , & Mace, W. M. (1981). Ecological laws of perceiving and acting: In reply to Fodor and Pylyshyn (1981). *Cognition, 9,* 237–304.

CHAPTER THREE
Episodic Memories

READING 8

INTRODUCTION

"Memory-Scanning: Mental Processes Revealed by Reaction-Time Experiments" summarizes a large body of work conducted in the 1960s by Saul Sternberg (Sternberg, 1966, 1967, 1969). This work explores some of the cognitive processes people are able to apply to information in short-term memory; specifically, how they decide whether it contains some piece of information. Sternberg's work has been tremendously influential for at least three reasons.

First, in this work Sternberg develops a method for using reaction time—the time it takes to perform a very simple task under a particular set of conditions—to understand a particular cognitive process. Actually, as Sternberg points out, the significance of reaction times for understanding the nature of cognitive processes had been recognized a hundred years earlier by the Dutch physiologist F. C. Donders. The use of reaction times was abandoned, however, when critical flaws with Donders' approach became apparent at the beginning of the 20th century. Sternberg's revision, which has been called the method of additive factors, overcomes these flaws.

A second reason for the importance of this work is that Sternberg makes a very strong case for concluding that people decide whether some piece of information is being held in short-term memory (such as whether the letter *A* is in a previously memorized list of letters) by examining every item in short-term memory, one item at a time. At first, this conclusion may seem very surprising. But Sternberg suggests that it is also quite sensible if one is trying to design an efficient search mechanism.

Third, Sternberg's work is influential because it suggests an instance in which a cognitive process proceeds not only without conscious awareness but also in a fashion that contradicts what awareness we do have. When people introspect about what they do when they search short-term memory, they usually report that they either check all the items at once or that they check one item at a time and stop when they find the desired piece of information. On the basis of his experiments, Sternberg argues that neither report is accurate.

In this selection, Sternberg's discussion and evidence about the relationship between short-term and long-term memories, the effects of different kinds of information (for instance, faces rather than letters or digits), the determination of where in a memorized list an item is found (what Sternberg calls context), and the difference between recall and recognition of context information have been excluded. As you read this article, consider the following questions: Does it make sense for us not to have conscious access to certain cognitive processes? Why or why not? If we don't have conscious access to certain cognitive processes, how can we be sure about the nature of those processes? What roles does consciousness play in cognition?

Memory-Scanning: Mental Processes Revealed by Reaction-Time Experiments

Saul Sternberg

One of the oldest ideas in experimental psychology is that the time between stimulus and response is occupied by a train of processes or *stages*—some being mental operations—which are so arranged that one process does not begin until the preceding one has ended. This *stage theory* implies that the reaction-time (RT) is a *sum,* composed of the durations of the stages in the series, and suggests that if one could determine the component times that add together to make up the RT, one might then be able to answer interesting questions about mental operations to which they correspond. The study of RT should therefore prove helpful to an understanding of the structure of mental activity.

The use of results from RT experiments to study stages of information processing began about a century ago with a paper, "On the Speed of Mental Processes," by F. C. Donders (1868). It was in this paper

that Donders introduced the *subtraction method*—a method for analyzing the RT into its components and thereby studying the corresponding stages of processing.

1. DECOMPOSING RT BY THE SUBTRACTION METHOD

To use the subtraction method one constructs two different tasks in which RT can be measured, where the second task is thought to require all the mental operations of the first, plus an additional inserted operation. The difference between mean RTs in the two tasks is interpreted as an estimate of the duration of the inserted stage, as shown in Figure 1. This interpretation depends on the validity of both the stage theory and an *assumption of pure insertion* which states that changing from Task 1 to Task 2 merely inserts a new processing stage without altering the others.

For example, Wundt (1880, pp. 247–260) developed an application in which RTs were measured when a subject had to respond after he had identified a stimulus, and also when he had to respond after merely detecting its presence. The difference was used as an estimate of the identification time. In this instance the stages shown in Figure 1 might be (a) stimulus detection, (b) stimulus identification, and

Most of the research reported in this paper was supported by Bell Telephone Laboratories and conducted in its Behavioral and Statistical Research Center at Murray Hill, N. J. The work reported as Exp. 4 was done in collaboration with A. M. Treisman of the University of Oxford. I am grateful to C. S. Harris, T. K. Landauer, H. Rouanet, and R. Teghtsoonian for helpful criticisms of the manuscript, and to L. D. Harmon for discussion leading to Exp. 5. R. E. Main assisted with Exps. 4 and 5, B. Barkow with Exps. 7 and 8, and B. A. Nasto with Exps. 4, 5, 7, and 8.

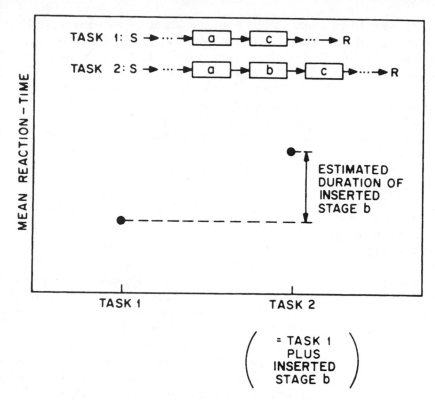

FIGURE 1   Donders' subtraction method. Hypothetical stages between stimulus (*S*) and response (*R*) are represented by *a, b,* and *c*.

(c) response organization. In an earlier application, Donders (1868) had compared mean RTs in a simple-reaction task (one stimulus and response) and a choice-reaction task (multiple stimuli and responses); he regarded the difference as the duration of the stages of stimulus discrimination and response selection.

This kind of enterprise occupied many psychologists during the last quarter of the nineteenth century. Much of their work was summarized by J. Jastrow (1890) in a popular treatise on *The Time Relations of Mental Phenomena.*

Around the turn of the century the subtraction method became the subject of criticism for two main reasons. First, the differences in mean RT that were observed in some applications varied excessively from subject to subject, and from laboratory to laboratory. In retrospect, this seems to have been caused by the use of tasks and instructions that left the subject's choice of "processing strategy" relatively uncontrolled.[1] Second, introspective reports put into question the assumption of pure insertion, by suggesting that when the task was changed to insert a stage, other stages might also be altered. (For example, it was felt that changes in stimulus-processing requirements might also alter a response-organization stage.) If so, the difference between RTs could not be identified as the duration of the inserted stage. Because of these difficulties, Külpe, among others, urged caution in

---

[1]For example, Cattell (1886, p. 377) reported that "I have not been able myself to get results by [Wundt's] method. I apparently either distinguished the impression and made the motion simultaneously, or if I tried to avoid this by waiting until I had formed a distinct impression before I began to make the motion, I added to the simple reaction not only a perception, but a volition."

the interpretation of results from the subtraction method (1895, Secs. 69, 70). But it appears that no tests other than introspection were proposed for distinguishing valid from invalid applications of the method.

A stronger stand was taken in later secondary sources. For example, in a section on the "discarding of the subtraction method" in his *Experimental Psychology* (1938, p. 309), R. S. Woodworth queried "[Since] we cannot break up the reaction into successive acts and obtain the time of each act, of what use is the reaction-time?" And, more recently, D. M. Johnson said in his *Psychology of Thought and Judgment* (1955, p. 5), "The reaction-time experiment suggests a method for the analysis of mental processes which turned out to be unworkable."

Nevertheless, the attempt to analyze RT into components goes on, and there has been a substantial revival in the last few years in the use of RT as a tool for the study of mental processes ranging from perceptual coding to mental arithmetic and problem-solving.[2] The work on memory retrieval described here is part of this revival, and is based heavily on Donders' stage theory. Modern styles of experimentation and data analysis lead to applications of the stage theory that seem to withstand the early criticisms, and to tests of validity other than introspection.

I shall describe experiments on retrieval from memory that have led to the discovery of some relatively simple search processes. My aim is to convey the general outline rather than the details of this work, so the picture I paint will be somewhat simplified; there will be little discussion of alternative explanations that have been considered and rejected. Such discussions can be found in Sternberg (1966, 1967a, b, and 1969).

The purpose of most of these experiments has been to study the ways in which information is retrieved from memory when learning and retention are essentially perfect. The method is to present a list of items for memorization that is short enough to be within the immediate-memory span. The subject is then asked a question about the memorized list; he answers as quickly as he can, and his delay in responding is measured. By examining the pattern of his RTs, while varying such factors as the number of items in the list and the kind of question asked, one can make inferences about the underlying retrieval processes. Since the aim has been to understand error-free performance, conditions and payoffs are arranged so that in most experiments the responses are almost always correct.

2. JUDGING PRESENCE VERSUS ABSENCE IN A MEMORIZED LIST

The flavor of this approach will become clearer as we consider a particular experiment. Figure 2 shows the paradigm of an *item-recognition task*. The stimulus ensemble consists of all potential test stimuli. From among these, a set of s elements is selected arbitrarily and is defined as the *positive set*; these items are presented as a list for the subject to memorize. The remaining items are called the *negative set*. When a test stimulus is presented, the subject must decide whether it is a member of the positive set. If it is, he makes a *positive response* (e.g., saying "yes" or operating a particular lever). If not, he makes a *negative response*. The measured RT (sometimes referred to as *response latency*) is the time from test-stimulus onset to response.

Within the item-recognition paradigm, different procedures can be used. One of them, shown at the top of Figure 3, is the *varied-set procedure*. Here, the subject must memorize a different positive set on each trial. In one experiment (Exp. 1), for example, the stimulus ensemble consisted of the ten digits. On each trial a new positive set, ranging randomly over trials from one to six different digits, was presented sequentially at a rate of 1.2 seconds per digit. Two seconds after the last digit in the set was displayed, a warning signal appeared, followed by a visually presented test digit. The subject pulled one lever, making a positive response, if the test stimulus was contained in the memorized list. He pulled the other lever, making a negative response, if it was not. After responding to the test stimulus the subject recalled the list. This forced him to retain the items in the presented

---

[2]See, e.g., Egeth, 1966; Hochberg, 1968; Nickerson, 1967; Posner & Mitchell, 1967; Restle & Davis, 1962; Smith, 1967; Suppes & Groen, 1966.

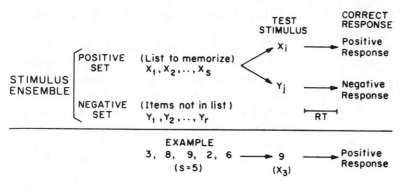

FIGURE 2   Paradigm of item-recognition task (Exps. 1–5).

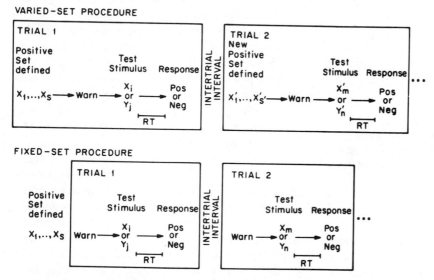

FIGURE 3   Varied-set and fixed-set procedures in item-recognition. A *Y* represents an item in the negative set. Primes are used in representing trial 2 of the varied-set procedure to show that both the items in the positive set $(X_1, \ldots, X_s)$ and its size(s) may change from trial to trial.

order, and prevented him from working with the negative set rather than the positive. Regardless of the size of the positive set, the two responses were required equally often. As in the other experiments I shall describe, subjects were relatively unpracticed. The error rate in this kind of experiment can be held to 1 or 2 percent by paying subjects in such a way as to penalize errors heavily while rewarding speed.

Averaged data from eight subjects are shown in Figure 4. Mean RT is plotted as a function of the number of symbols in memory—that is, the number of digits in the positive set that the subject committed to memory at the start of the trial.

These data are typical for item-recognition experiments. They show, first, a linear relation between mean RT and the size of the positive set. Second, the latencies of positive and negative responses increase at approximately the same rate. The slope of the line fitted to the means is 38 msec per item in memory; its zero-intercept is about 400 msec. (It happens to be

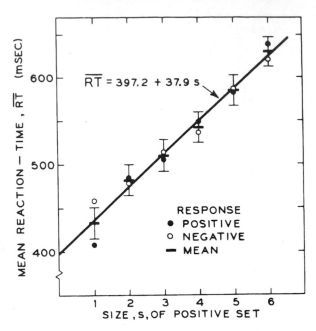

FIGURE 4   Results of Exp. 1: Item-recognition with varied-set procedure. Mean latencies of correct positive and negative responses, and their mean, as functions of size of positive set. Averaged data from eight subjects, with estimates of $\pm\sigma$ about means, and line fitted by least squares to means.

true in these data that latencies of positive and negative responses have approximately the same *values:* the two latency functions have not only the same slope but also the same zero-intercept. This is not a general finding, but results from the particular conditions in this experiment. By varying the relative frequency with which positive and negative responses are required, for example, one can vary the relation between their latencies. But as relative frequency is varied the *slopes* of the two latency functions remain equal and unchanged.) Before considering the interpretation of these findings, we turn to some general matters regarding search processes.

3. TWO TYPES OF SERIAL SEARCH

Let *serial search* (or *scanning)* be a process in which each of a set of items is compared one at a time, and no more than once, to a target item. Linear RT-func-

tions, as in Figure 4, suggest that subjects in the item-recognition task use a serial search process whose mean duration increases by one unit for each additional comparison. The purpose of the search is to determine whether an agreement (or *match*) exists between the test item and any of the items in the memorized set. Two types of serial search that might serve this purpose need to be considered. In *self-terminating serial search,* the test stimulus is compared successively to one item in memory after another, either until a match occurs (leading to a positive response), or until all comparisons have been completed without a match (leading to a negative response). In *exhaustive serial search,* the test stimulus is compared successively to *all* the memorized items. Only then is a response made—positive if a match has occurred, and negative otherwise. A self-terminating search might require a separate test, after each comparison, to ascertain whether a match had occurred, rather than only one such test after the entire series. On the other hand, an exhaustive search must involve more comparisons, on the average, than a search that terminates when a match occurs.

Suppose that the average time from the beginning of one comparison to the beginning of the next is the same for each comparison in the series, and is not influenced by the number of comparisons to be made. Then the durations of both kinds of search will increase linearly with the number of memorized items (*list length*). There are, however, important differences. In an exhaustive search the test stimulus is compared to all items in memory before each positive response as well as before a negative response. Hence, the rate at which RT increases with list length—the slope of the RT-function—is the same for positive and negative responses. In contrast, a self-terminating search stops in the middle of the list, on the average, before positive responses, but continues through the entire list before negatives. The result is that as list length is increased, the latency of positive responses increases at half the rate of the increase for negatives. This difference between the two kinds of search is illustrated on the left side of Figure 5.

A second difference between the two types of search, illustrated on the right side of Figure 5, is in the serial-position functions for positive responses. In a simple exhaustive search neither the order of search

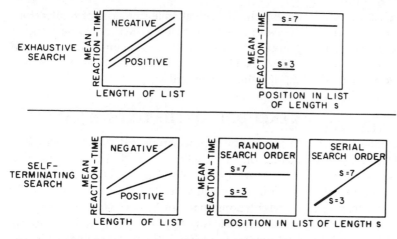

FIGURE 5   Some properties of exhaustive (top) and self-terminating (bottom) serial search. Left: Theoretical RT-functions (mean latencies of positive and negative responses as functions of length of list). Right: Theoretical serial-position functions (mean latency of positive responses as a function of serial position of test item in a list of given length).

nor the position of the matching item in the list should have any effect on the RT, since all items are compared. A self-terminating search that occurred in a random order, or started at a random point, also would produce flat serial-position curves. But if a self-terminating search started consistently with the first item, and proceeded serially, then the serial-position curves would increase linearly. (If, in addition, list length influenced *only* the search process, then the curves for different list lengths would be superimposed: for example, the time to arrive at the second item in a memorized list would be independent of the length of the list.) Increasing serial-position functions are therefore sufficient (but not necessary) evidence for inferring that a search process is self-terminating.

4. HIGH-SPEED EXHAUSTIVE SCANNING

The serial-position curves actually observed in the item-recognition experiment described in Section 2 were relatively flat.[3] Together with this finding, the

linearity of the latency functions and the equality of their slopes for positive and negative responses indicate an exhaustive search. The data show also that memory-scanning can proceed at a remarkably high rate. The slope of the mean RT-function, which is an estimate of the time per comparison, was 38 msec, indicating an average scanning rate between 25 and 30 digits per second.

Perhaps because of its high speed, the scanning process seems not to have any obvious correlate in conscious experience. Subjects generally say either that they engage in a self-terminating search, or that they know immediately, with no search at all, whether the test stimulus is contained in the memorized list.

Is high-speed scanning used only when a list has just been memorized and is therefore relatively unfamiliar? The results discussed so far (Figure 4) are from the varied-set procedure (Figure 3), in which

---

[3]Several investigators have, however, reported marked recency effects in item-recognition tasks: RTs were shorter for test stimuli later in the list (Corballis, 1967; Morin, DeRosa & Stultz, 1967; Morin, DeRosa & Ulm, 1967). Without embellishment a theory of

exhaustive scanning cannot, of course, handle such findings. The salient procedural characteristics of experiments that produce such recency effects seem to be a fast rate of list presentation and a short interval (less than 1 sec) between the last item in the list and the test item. Findings of Posner, *et al.* (1969), indicate that in this range the time interval between successive stimuli may critically influence the nature and duration of comparison operations.

the subject must memorize a new positive set on each trial, and is tested only three seconds after its presentation. How is the retrieval process changed when a person is highly familiar with a particular positive set and has had a great deal of practice retrieving information from it? At the bottom of Figure 3 is shown the *fixed-set procedure* in the item-recognition paradigm, in which the same positive set is used for a long series of trials. For example, in one experiment (Exp. 2) subjects had 60 practice trials and 120 test trials for each positive set. On the average test trial, a subject had been working with the same positive set for ten minutes, rather than three seconds. The sets were sufficiently well learned that subjects could recall them several days later. Sets of one, two, and four digits were used. There were six subjects.

Results are shown in Figure 6, and are essentially identical to those from the varied-set procedure. The RT data are linear, the slopes for positive and negative responses are equal, and the average slope is 38 msec per digit. The small difference between the zero-intercepts in the two experiments is not statistically significant. The remarkable similarity of results from the two procedures indicates that the same retrieval process was used for both the unfamiliar and the well-learned lists. . . .

[Section 5 is deleted.]

6. ENCODING OF THE TEST STIMULUS

In the scanning process inferred from these experiments, some internal representation of the test stimulus is compared to internal representations of the items in the positive set. What is the *nature* of the representations that can be compared at such high speed? Another way to phrase the question is to ask how much processing of the test stimulus occurs before it is compared to the memorized items.

Various considerations lead one to expect a good deal of preprocessing. For example, the idea that items held in active memory are retained as acoustic or articulatory representations of their spoken names introduces the possibility that the test stimulus is processed to the point of naming, and that the name of the test stimulus is compared to the names of the items in the positive set. But two points should be kept in mind regarding this possibility. First, it would require that stored names could be scanned much faster than they could be covertly articulated, since the scanning rate is about four times as fast as people can say names of digits to themselves. Second, unlike other forms of preprocessing, such as image-sharpening or feature-extraction, preprocessing a character to the point of identification or naming would itself require the retrieval of information from memory—that information which relates the character to its name.

In one experiment bearing on this question (Exp. 3), I degraded the test stimulus by superimposing a pattern that had been adjusted to increase the RT without substantially altering the error rate. I then examined the effect of stimulus quality on the function that relates mean RT and the size of the positive set. It is shown below that this effect would depend on the nature of the internal representation of the test stimulus.

Figure 7 shows idealized data from a scanning experiment. The zero-intercept corresponds to the total duration of all processes that occur just once, regardless of the size of the positive set—such as the en-

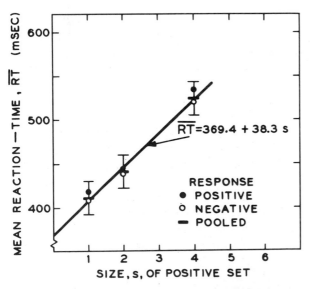

$$\overline{RT} = 369.4 + 38.3 \, s$$

RESPONSE
- • POSITIVE
- ○ NEGATIVE
- ▬ POOLED

FIGURE 6   Results of Exp. 2: Item-recognition with fixed-set procedure. Mean latencies of correct positive, negative, and pooled responses as functions of size of positive set. Averaged data from six subjects, with estimates of ±σ about pooled means, and line fitted by least squares to those means. For each set size positive responses were required on 27% of the trials.

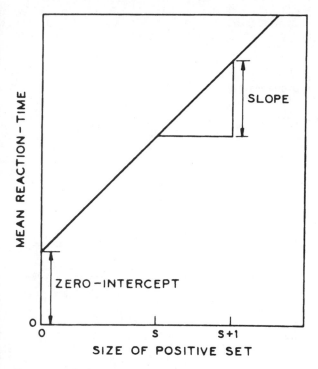

FIGURE 7 Idealization of mean RT-function from an item-recognition task.

coding of the test stimulus to form its representation, and the organization and execution of the motor response. The slope, on the other hand, measures the duration of processes that occur once for each member of the positive set—the comparison operation, and the time to switch from one item to the next.[4] Figure 8 shows a flow diagram of some hypothetical stages between test stimulus and response. The height of a box represents the mean duration of that stage. An effect of stimulus degradation on the *stimulus-encoding stage*, which generates the stimulus representation, would increase the zero-intercept of the RT-function. An effect on the *serial-comparison stage*

would increase the slope, since a time increment would be added for each item compared.

Consider two extreme possibilities: First, suppose that the encoding stage did nothing other than transmit an unprocessed image, or direct copy, of the test stimulus. Then degradation could influence only the comparison operation, which occurs once for each member of the positive set; only the slope of the RT-function would change, as in Panel A of Figure 9. At the other extreme, suppose that the representation produced by the encoding stage was the *name* of the test stimulus. The input to the serial-comparison stage would be the same, whether or not the test stimulus had been degraded by a superimposed visual pattern; hence degradation could not influence this stage. (For the serial-comparison stage to be influenced by visual degradation, its input would have to be visual, in the sense of embodying details of the physical stimulus pattern that are not present in the mere name of the stimulus.) Only the encoding stage, then, could be influenced by degradation; and since encoding takes place just once, only the zero-intercept of the RT-function would change, as in Panel B of Figure 9. (The absence of a change in slope, however, does not necessarily imply a nonvisual stimulus-representation; the representation could be visual, but highly processed.)

In Exp. 3 each of twelve subjects had positive sets of one, two, and four digits, with test stimuli *intact* in some blocks of trials, and in others *degraded* by a superimposed checkerboard pattern. Intact and degraded numerals are shown in Figure 10.

The fixed-set procedure was used. Results for the two sessions are shown separately in Figure 11. Consider first the data from the second session, on the right-hand side of the figure. Latencies of positive and negative responses have been averaged together. The functions for degraded and intact stimuli are almost parallel, but there is a large effect on the zero-intercept, closely approximating the pattern shown in Panel B of Figure 9. This indicates that degradation had a large influence on the stimulus-encoding stage, and that the representation generated was sufficiently processed that the serial-comparison stage could proceed as rapidly with degraded as with intact stimuli. The stimulus representation was either nonvisual or, if visual, sufficiently refined in the second session to eliminate any effect of degradation.

---

[4]This analysis assumes that the mean durations of comparisons leading to matches and to mismatches are equal. Without this assumption all the statements here (and elsewhere in the paper) are correct, except that the slope of the RT-function measures the mean duration of only those comparisons that lead to mismatches, together with the time to switch from one comparison to the next. Any difference between durations of the two kinds of comparison would contribute to a difference between zero intercepts of the latency functions for positive and negative responses.

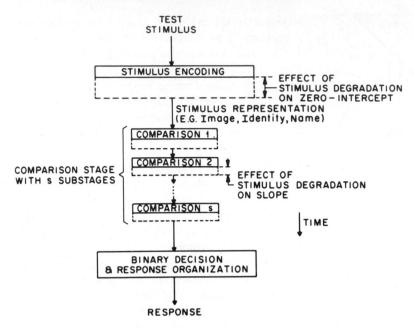

FIGURE 8   Some hypothetical stages and substages in item-recognition, and two possible effects of test-stimulus quality on stage and substage durations. Height of box represents mean duration of that stage or substage.

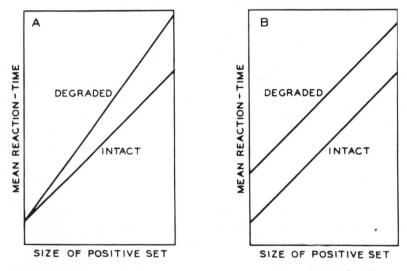

FIGURE 9   Two possibilities for the effect of test-stimulus quality on the RT-function. A: Quality influences comparison stage only. B: Quality influences encoding stage only.

FIGURE 10   Photographs of intact and degraded numerals used Exp. 3. Numerals were about 0.6 in. high and were viewed from a distance of about 29 in. Degraded numerals were somewhat more discriminable than they appear in the black-and-white photograph, possibly because of a slight color difference between numerals and checkerboard.

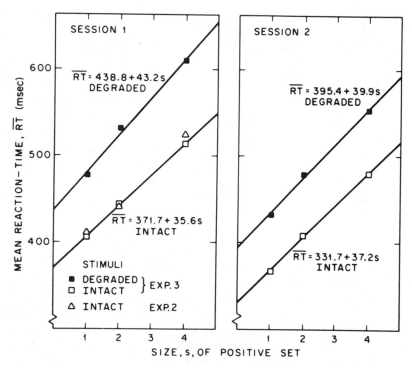

FIGURE 11   Results of Exp. 3: Effect of stimulus quality on item-recognition. Mean RT, based on pooled data from positive and negative responses, as a function of size of positive set for intact and degraded test stimuli. Left-hand and right-hand panels show data from Sessions 1 and 2, respectively. Averaged data from 12 subjects, with lines fitted by least squares. In all conditions positive responses were required on 27% of the trials. Triangles show results from Exp. 2 (Figure 6), which was similar.

The data from this session are an instance of the *additivity* of two effects on RT. There is no interaction between the effect of set size and the effect of stimulus quality; instead, the effect of each of these factors on mean RT is independent of the level of the other. Such additivity supports the theory of a sequence of stages, one stage influenced by stimulus quality and the other by set size (see Section 7).

Now let us consider the data from the first session, shown on the left-hand side of Figure 11. Here, where subjects have not yet had much practice with the superimposed checkerboard, there is a 20% increase in the slope of the RT-function, as well as an increase in its zero-intercept. This pattern agrees with neither of the pure cases of Figure 9. Stimulus quality apparently *can* influence the duration of comparison operations; hence, the output of the encoding stage must be sensitive to degradation. Findings from the two sessions imply, then, that although the stimulus representation is highly processed, it embodies physical attributes of the test stimulus, rather than being a name or identity. That is, the test-stimulus representation is visual. The memory representations of the positive set that are used in the serial-comparison stage must therefore also be visual, to make comparison possible. Hence, although items in the positive set appear to be represented as covertly-spoken names in the course of their rehearsal, this is not the only form in which they are available.

What changed between the first and second sessions so as to virtually eliminate the influence of stimulus quality on the slope of the RT-function? Since the scanning rate with intact stimuli and the effect of degradation on the zero-intercept are approximately the same in the two sessions, it seems unlikely that the type of representation changed. For the present, my interpretation is that the encoding stage became more efficient at removing the effects of the fixed degrading pattern.

Additional support for the idea that the memory representations scanned in the item-recognition task have sensory characteristics, rather than being completely abstracted from the physical stimuli, comes from two other studies. In the first, Chase and Calfee (1969) created four different conditions in the varied-set procedure by representing both the positive set

and the test stimulus either visually or aurally. When the set and test item were presented in different modalities, the slope of the RT-function increased by about 30%, indicating a slower scanning rate. If abstract representations were being compared in the same-modality conditions, then the change to different-modality conditions should have altered only the zero-intercept, as in Figure 9B. In the second study, Posner, *et al.* (1969), concluded that when a single letter is presented *aurally* for memorization, the decision whether a *visual* test-letter is the "same" is facilitated by the internal generation of a visual representation of the memorized letter, which obviates the need to identify the test letter. . . .

7. A TEST OF THE STAGE THEORY

The work described above is grounded on Donders' stage theory. That is, as in his subtraction method, the effects on mean RT of changes in experimental conditions (factors) have been attributed to the selective effects of these factors on hypothetical processing stages between stimulus and response. How can we ensure that such inferences are not open to the classical criticism of the subtraction method, that even if information processing *is* organized in functionally different stages, factor effects may not be selective? One answer, of course, is that the test of a method's applicability is whether it produces results that fit together and make sense. But there are two other arguments as well.

The first stems from replacement of the assumption of pure insertion by a weaker and more plausible *assumption of selective influence*. Instead of requiring that a change in the task insert or delete an entire processing stage without altering others, the weaker assumption requires only that it influence the *duration* of some stage without altering others. One example is illustrated in Figure 12. To estimate the comparison time by the subtraction method, one would have studied Task 2, in which the positive set has one member, and compared it to a Task 1. Task 1 would have been constructed to measure the zero-intercept directly, by deleting the entire comparison stage. But I suspect that there *is* no appropriate Task 1, in which

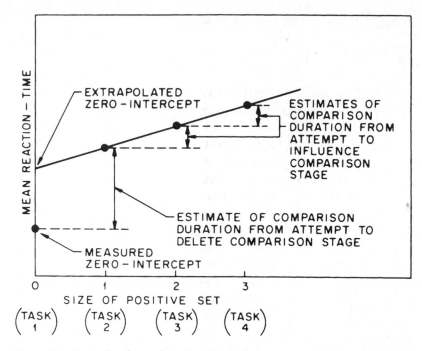

FIGURE 12   Example of error from hypothetical attempt to estimate comparison time by deleting the comparison stage altogether, as in the subtraction method, and to use a measured zero intercept. Attempt fails because *deletion* of comparison stage changes the demands placed on other stages, whereas *variation* of the number of comparisons, s, $(s \geq 1)$ does not.

deletion of all comparisons would leave the other stages of processing invariant. In this instance, then, the assumption of pure insertion is probably invalid. This is why the important RT-differences in the experiments described above were those between Tasks 2 and 3, 3 and 4, and so on, whose interpretation required only that the comparison stage be selectively *influenced* by set size. Similarly, in studying the pre-processing of the stimulus, instead of entirely eliminating the need to discriminate the stimulus (in an effort to *delete* the hypothetical encoding stage) I examined the effects of making its discrimination more or less difficult, thereby varying the amount of work the stage had to accomplish. Of course, one result of using a factor that influences but does not insert a stage is that we have no estimate of the stage's total duration.

But that seems to be of less interest than whether there is such a stage, what influences it, what it accomplishes, and what its relation is to other stages.[5]

In a given experimental situation the validity of even the weaker assumption of selective influence must be checked, however. We can distinguish those situations where one of the assumptions—influence or insertion—holds, by testing the additivity of the effects of two or more factors on mean RT (Sternberg, 1969). It is this test that provides the second and most telling way of dealing with the classical criticism.

[5]This alternative was preferred by Cattell, 1886, who argued (p. 378) "I do not think it is possible to add a perception to the reaction without also adding a will-act. We can however change the nature of the perception without altering the will-time, and thus investigate with considerable thoroughness the length of the perception time." But he suggested no way to test these assertions.

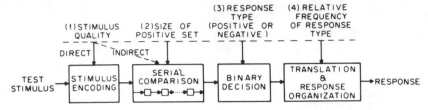

FIGURE 13   Four processing stages in item-recognition. Above the broken line are shown the four factors examined. Below the line is shown the decomposition of RT inferred from additive relations between factor pairs 1&2, 1&3, 2&3, 2&4, and 3&4, the linear effect of factor 2, and other considerations. (The indirect effect of factor 1 on the comparison stage, and the resulting interaction of factors 1&2, is seen in unpracticed subjects only.)

Consider a pair of hypothetical stages and a pair of experimental factors, with each factor inserting or selectively influencing one of the stages. Because stage durations are additive (by definition), the changes in mean RT produced by such factors should be independent and additive. That is, the effect of one factor will be the same at all levels of the other, when the response is measured on a scale of time or its (arithmetic) mean."[6]

In experiments with the fixed-set procedure I have examined four factors, which are listed above the broken line in Figure 13. The additivity of five of the six possible factor pairs has been tested and confirmed (1&2, after a session of practice, 1&3, 2&3, 2&4, and 3&4). These instances of additivity support the assumption that the factors selectively influence different stages of processing and, *a fortiori*, confirm the existence of such stages. Another instance of additivity, and the one on which inferences about the structure of the comparison stage strongly depend, is represented by the linearity of the effect of set size: the effect of adding an item to the positive set is independent of the number of items already in the set. Together with other considerations (discussed in Sternberg, 1969) these findings lead to the analysis

into processing stages and substages shown below the broken line in Figure 13. . . .[7]

[Sections 8 through 10 are not reprinted.]

11. AN EXPLANATION OF EXHAUSTIVENESS

As mentioned in Section 3, an exhaustive search must involve more comparisons, on the average, than a search that terminates when a match occurs. The exhaustiveness of the high-speed scanning process therefore appears inefficient, and hence implausible. Why continue the comparison process beyond the point at which a match occurs? Figure 14 illustrates a system in which an exhaustive search could be more efficient than a self-terminating one for performance in an item-recognition task. A representation of the test stimulus is placed in a comparator. When the scanner is being operated by the "central processor" or "homunculus," H, it delivers memory representa-

---

[6]Discussions of various other aspects and modern versions of the subtraction method, including considerations of validity, may be found in Hohle, 1967; McGill & Gibbon, 1965; McMahon, 1963; Smith, 1968; Sternberg, 1964; Sternberg, 1969; and Taylor, 1966.

[7]The linear interaction between stimulus quality and set size in Session 1 is attributed to an "indirect" influence of stimulus quality on the duration of the second stage, by way of its effect on the output of the first stage (see Section 6, and Sternberg, 1967b). Thus one may sometimes infer a separate stage even when its output is not invariant with respect to a factor that influences its duration, and when as a consequence there is a failure of additivity. In this instance the inference is justified by the form of the interaction (a *linear* increase in the effect of degradation with set size), and the structure of the comparison stage (inferred to be a series of substages).

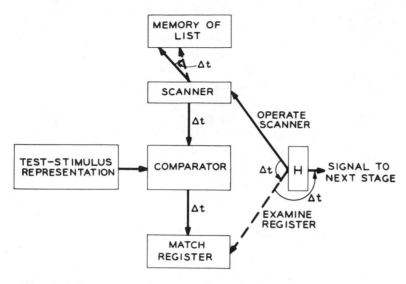

FIGURE 14   A system in which exhaustive scanning could be more efficient than self-terminating scanning. Some loci of possible time delays are represented by Δts.

tions of the items in the list, one after another, to the comparator. If and when a match occurs a signal is delivered to the match register. The important feature of the system is that the homunculus can *either* operate the scanner *or* examine the register. It cannot engage in both of these functions at once, and switching between them takes time.

In this kind of system, if the switching time is long relative to the scanning rate, and if the list is sufficiently short, then an exhaustive search (in which the match register must be examined only once) is more efficient than a self-terminating one (where the register would have to be examined after each comparison). The surprisingly high speed of the scanning process may therefore be made possible by its exhaustiveness. But such a system might have at least one important limitation. After the search was completed, there might be no information available (without further reference to the memory of the list) as to the location in the list of the item that produced the match. The limitation would create no difficulty if the response required of the subject depended only on the presence or absence of an item in the list and not on its location, as in the item-recognition task. But the

possibility that high-speed scanning does not yield location information does suggest an experiment to test this theory of exhaustiveness. Suppose we require a subject to give a response that *does* depend on where in the list a matching item is located. Then after each comparison, with information still available as to the location of the item just compared to the test stimulus (e.g., preserved by the position of the scanner in Figure 14), it would have to be determined whether this item produced a match (by the homunculus switching from scanner to register). Scanning should then be slower than when only presence or absence has to be judged; it should also be self-terminating, since further comparisons after a match had been detected would be superfluous. Such a process will be called *scanning to locate*.

12. RETRIEVAL OF CONTEXTUAL INFORMATION BY SCANNING TO LOCATE

In Figure 15 is shown the paradigm of a *context-recall task*, one of the experiments devised to test these ideas (Exp. 6). On each trial the subject memorized a new random list of from three to seven different digits,

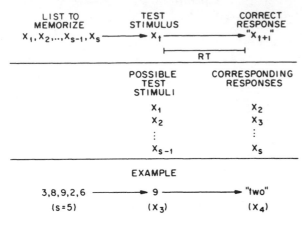

FIGURE 15   Paradigm of Exp. 6: Context-recall.

presented visually one after another. The length of the list was varied at random from trial to trial. After a delay and a warning signal, a test item was presented, randomly selected from among all the digits in the list except the last. The test item, then, was always present in the list. The correct response was the spoken name of the item that followed the test item in the memorized list. The idea was that in order to make this response—that is, to recall an item defined by its contextual relation to the test item—the location of the test item in the list might first have to be determined. As in the other experiments described, subjects were encouraged to respond as rapidly as possible, while attempting to maintain a low error rate.

Two aspects of the data are of particular interest: the relation between mean RT and list length; and the relation, for a list of given length, between RT and the serial position of the test item in the list.

Data averaged over six subjects are shown in Figure 16. Consider first Panel A. The bars show the percentage of wrong responses, which rises to 25% for lists of length 7. This is much higher than one would like, given an interest in error-free performance. The effect of list length on mean RT is roughly linear, suggesting a scanning process. (Even closer approximations to linearity have been found in other similar experiments.) With a slope of 124 msec per item, the fitted line is much steeper than the corresponding RT-function in the item-recognition task.

To interpret the slope, we have first to establish if the process is self-terminating, as expected. Evidence on this point is provided by the average serial-position functions shown in Panel B. For each list length, mean RT is plotted as a function of the serial position of the test item in the memorized list. These functions are all increasing, suggesting a self-terminating process that tends to start at the beginning of the list and proceed in serial order.

Now we can interpret the slope of the function in Panel A, if we assume that list length influences only the scanning stage. . . . Since an average of about half the items in a list have to be scanned before a match occurs, the slope represents half of the time per item, and implies a scanning rate of about 250 msec per item, or four items per second, in scanning to locate an item in a memorized list. Scanning to locate is therefore about seven times as slow as the high-speed scanning process used to determine the presence of an item in a list. The slowness of the search, and the fact it is self-terminating, lend support to the explanation (Section 11) of the exhaustiveness of the high-speed process. Scanning to locate seems to be fundamentally different from scanning for presence. . . .[8]

SUMMARY

I have reviewed informally eight experiments on the retrieval of information from human memory, whose interpretation depended on inferences from the structure of RT data to the organization of mental processes. [Only four experiments are reprinted here.] The experiments have led to the discovery of two kinds of memory search that people use in the retrieval of information from short memorized lists.

---

[8]Alternative explanations of the dissimilarity of the two kinds of scanning are possible, of course. One interesting alternative (which existing data cannot reject) is that memory representations that can carry order information are different from those that need only carry item information, and that the observed differences in retrieval result from the fact that different kinds of memory representations are being scanned. However, for this alternative explanation to apply to Exp. 1 (in which subjects had to recognize an item and then recall the entire list in order), it must be possible for both kinds of memory representation to be maintained simultaneously.

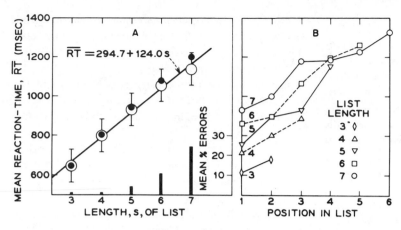

FIGURE 16   Results of Exp. 6: Context-recall. Averaged data from six subjects. A: Effect of list length on percent errors (bars), on mean latency of correct responses (open circles) with estimates of ±σ and line fitted by least squares, and on mean RT of all responses (filled circles). B: Relation between mean RT of correct responses and serial position of the test item in lists of five lengths.

One is a high-speed exhaustive scanning process, used to determine the *presence* of an item in the list; the other is a slow self-terminating scanning process used to determine the *location* of an item in the list. Among other substantive implications of the experiments are: (1) Apparently one *must* scan a list serially to retrieve information from it, even when it is contained in active memory. There is no evidence in any of these data that one can "think about" more than one thing at a time, and thereby simultaneously compare a set of memorized items to a test item. (2) On the other hand, even a well-learned list can be made more readily available by being maintained in active memory. (3) Despite the possibility that retention may depend on a rehearsal process involving covert speech, visual rather than auditory memory representations are used for comparison to representations of visual stimuli. (4) The same search process can be involved in both recall and recognition tasks. [The last implication follows from experiments not reprinted here.]

Many of the inferences from the data were based on a proposal first made by Donders (1868) that the time between stimulus and response be regarded as the sum of the durations of a series of processing stages. Donders' *subtraction method* depends on this *stage theory*, together with an *assumption of pure insertion* which states that a change in the subject's task can cause the insertion of an additional processing stage without altering the other stages. It was the questioning of this assumption, and the absence of any objective tests of its validity, that led to the decline of the subtraction method in the late nineteenth century.

The present paper advocates retaining the idea of stages of processing. But it shows how the insertion assumption can sometimes be replaced by a weaker *assumption of selective influence,* and how the validity of either assumption for a given experiment can be tested by determining whether the effects of experimental factors on RT are additive. The main ideas are: (1) if separate stages between stimulus and response have been correctly identified, then for each of these stages it may be easier to find a factor that *influences* it without altering other stages than to find one that *inserts* it without altering other stages; and (2) these factors would then have additive effects on mean RT. The discovery of several sets of such additive factors was critical in the interpretation of the experiments described.

REFERENCES

Atkinson, R. C. & Shiffrin, R. M. Human memory: a proposed system and its control processes. In K. W. Spence and J. T. Spence (Eds.), *The psychology of learning and motivation: Advances in research and theory.* Vol. 2. New York: Academic Press, 1968. Pp. 89–195.

Baddeley, A. D. The influence of acoustic and semantic similarity on long-term memory for word sequences. *Quart. J. exp. Psychol.,* 1966, *18,* 302–309.

Broadbent, D. E. *Perception and communication.* London: Pergamon Press, 1958.

Cattell, J. McK. The perception time. *Mind,* 1886, *11,* 377-392. Reprinted in *James McKeen Cattell, Man of science.* Lancaster, Pa.: The Science Press, 1947.

Chase, W. G. & Calfee, R. C. Modality and similarity effects in short-term recognition memory. *J. exp. Psychol.,* 1969, *81,* 510–514.

Cohen, R. L. & Johansson, B. S. Some relevant factors in the transfer of material from short-term to long-term memory. *Quart. J. exp. Psychol.,* 1967, *19,* 300–308.

Conrad, R. Acoustic confusions in immediate memory. *Brit. J. Psychol.,* 1964, *55,* 75–84.

Corballis, M. C. Serial order in recognition and recall. *J. exp. Psychol.,* 1967, *74,* 99–105.

Crowder, R. G. Short-term memory for words with a perceptual-motor interpolated activity. *J. verb. Learn. verb. Behav.,* 1967, *6,* 753–761.

Donders, F. C. Over de snelheid van psychische processen. Onderzoekingen gedaan in het Physiologisch Laboratorium der Utrechtsche Hoogeschool, 1868–1869, Tweede reeks, II, 92–120. Transl. by W. G. Koster in W. G. Koster (Ed.), *Attention and performance II.* Acta Psychol., 1969, *30,* 412–431.

Egeth, H. E. Parallel versus serial processes in multidimensional stimulus discrimination. *Percept. & Psychophys.,* 1966, *1,* 245–252.

Glanzer, M. & Cunitz, A. R. Two storage mechanisms in free recall. *J. verb. Learn. verb. Behav.,* 1966, *5,* 351–360.

Hochberg, J. In the mind's eye. In R. N. Haber (Ed.), *Contemporary theory and research in visual perception.* New York: Holt, Rinehart & Winston, 1968. Pp. 309–331.

Hohle, R. H. Component process latencies in reaction times of children and adults. In L. P. Lipsett and C. C. Spiker (Eds.), *Advances in child development and behavior.* Vol. 3. New York: Academic Press, 1967. Pp. 225–261.

Jastrow, J. *The time-relations of mental phenomena. Fact & theory papers No. VI.* New York: N.D.C. Hodges, 1890.

Johnson, D. M. *The psychology of thought and judgment.* New York: Harper, 1955.

Külpe, O. *Outlines of psychology.* New York: MacMillan, 1895.

Landauer, T. K. Rate of implicit speech. *Percept. mot. Skills,* 1962, *15,* 646.

Landauer, T. K. & Freedman, J. L. Information retrieval from long-term memory: category size and recognition time. *J. verb. Learn. verb. Behav.,* 1968, *7,* 291–295.

McGill, W. J. & Gibbon, J. The general gamma distribution and reaction times. *J. math. Psychol.,* 1965, *2,* 1–18.

McMahon, L. E. Grammatical analysis as part of understanding a sentence. Unpublished doctoral dissertation, Harvard University, 1963.

Miller, G. A. *Psychology, the science of mental life.* New York: Harper & Row, 1962.

Morin, R. E., DeRosa, D. V., & Stultz, V. Recognition memory and reaction time. In A. F. Sanders (Ed.), *Attention and performance.* Acta Psychol., 1967, *27,* 298–305.

Morin, R. E., DeRosa, D. V., & Ulm, R. Short-term recognition memory for spatially isolated items. *Psychon. Sci.,* 1967, *9,* 617–618.

Neisser, U. *Cognitive psychology.* New York: Appleton-Century-Crofts, 1967.

Newell, A. & Simon, H. A. Computers in psychology. In R. D. Luce, R. R. Bush and E. Galanter (Eds.), *Handbooks of mathematical psychology.* Vol. 1. New York: Wiley, 1963. Pp. 361–428.

Nickerson, R. S. Categorization time with categories defined by disjunctions and conjunctions of stimulus attributes. *J. exp. Psychol.,* 1967, *73,* 211–219.

Posner, M. I. Short-term memory systems in human information processing. In A. F. Sanders (Ed.), *Attention and performance.* Acta Psychol., 1967, *27,* 267–284.

Posner, M. I., Boies, S. J., Eichelman, W. H., & Taylor, R. L. Retention of visual and name codes of single letters. *J. exp. Psychol. Monogr.,* 1969, *79,* No. 1, Part 2, 1–16.

Posner, M. I. & Mitchell, R. F. Chronometric analysis of classification. *Psychol. Rev.,* 1967, *74,* 392–409.

Posner, M. I. & Rossman, E. Effect of size and location of informational transforms upon short-term retention. *J. exp. Psychol.,* 1965, *70,* 496–505.

Restle, F. & Davis, J. H. Success and speed of problem solving by individuals and groups. *Psychol. Rev.*, 1962, *69*, 520–536.

Rock, I. A neglected aspect of the problem of recall: The Höffding function. In J. M. Scher (Ed.), *Theories of the mind.* New York: Free Press, 1962. Pp. 645–659.

Sanders, A. F. Rehearsal and recall in immediate memory. *Ergonomics*, 1961, *4*, 25–34.

Slamecka, N. J. Serial learning and order information. *J. exp. Psychol.*, 1967, *74*, 62–66.

Smith, E. E. Effects of familiarity on stimulus recognition and categorization. *J. exp. Psychol.*, 1967, *74*, 324–332.

Smith, E. E. Choice reaction time: an analysis of the major theoretical positions. *Psychol. Bull.*, 1968, *69*, 77–110.

Sperling, G. The information available in brief visual presentations. *Psychol. Monogr.*, 1960, *75* (11, Whole No. 498).

Sperling, G. A model for visual memory tasks. *Hum. Factors*, 1963, *5*, 19–31.

Sternberg, S. Stochastic learning theory. In R. D. Luce, R. R. Bush and E. Galanter (Eds.), *Handbook of mathematical psychology.* Vol. 2. New York: Wiley, 1963. Pp. 1–120.

Sternberg, S. Estimating the distribution of additive reaction-time components. Paper presented at the meeting of the Psychometric Society, Niagara Falls, Ont., October 1964.

Sternberg, S. High-speed scanning in human memory. *Science*, 1966, *153*, 652–654.

Sternberg, S. Retrieval of contextual information from memory. *Psychon Sci.*, 1967, *8*, 55–6. (a)

Sternberg, S. Two operations in character-recognition: Some evidence from reaction-time measurements. *Percept. & Psychophys.*, 1967, *2*, 45–53. (b)

Sternberg, S. The discovery of processing stages: Extensions of Donders' method. In W. G. Koster (Ed.), *Attention and performance II. Acta Psychol.*, 1969, *30*, 276–315.

Suppes, P. & Groen, G. Some counting models for first-grade performance data on simple addition facts. Technical Report 90, Institute for Mathematical Studies in the Social Sciences, Stanford University, 1966.

Taylor, D. H. Latency components in two-choice responding. *J. exp. Psychol.* 1966, *72*, 481–488.

Waugh, N. C. & Norman, D. A. Primary memory. *Psychol. Rev.*, 1965, *72*, 89–104.

Wickelgren, W. A. Auditory or articulatory coding in verbal short-term memory. *Psychol. Rev.*, 1969, *76*, 232–235.

Woodworth, R. S. *Experimental psychology.* New York: Holt, 1938.

Wundt, W. *Grundzüge der physiologischen Psychologie*, Vol. II, 2nd ed. Leipzig: Engelmann, 1880.

Yonas, A. The acquisition of information-processing strategies in a time-dependent task. Unpublished doctoral dissertation, Cornell University, 1969.

POSTSCRIPT

Sternberg's conclusions about how search in short-term memory takes place have been modified and extended by some (for example, DeRosa & Tkacz, 1976; Raeburn, 1974) and have remained somewhat controversial (see Baddeley, 1976; Sternberg, 1975; and Wickelgren, 1979, for discussion). In particular, the set-size effect—reaction time increasing as a linear function of set size—has been closely examined (Diener, 1988; Stadler & Logan, 1989).

The use of reaction times for studying particular kinds of cognitive processes, however, has become a commonly accepted practice since this article was written (Welford, 1980; for a much more technical treatment of reaction times, see Luce, 1986). The more general issue of serial versus parallel processing and how they can be distinguished empirically also remains controversial (Townsend, 1990).

FOR FURTHER THOUGHT

1. If search were parallel, what would be the relationship between set size and reaction time? Is this relationship affected by whether the item being searched for is in the list or not?
2. If search were serial but self-terminating, what would be the relationship between set size and reaction time? Is this relationship affected by whether the item being searched for is in the list or not? Is this relationship affected by where the item being searched for is in the list?
3. What assumption does Sternberg make to explain why scanning of short-term memory is serial and exhaustive? Under what circumstances does Sternberg suggest that search is self-terminating?
4. How does Sternberg's assumption of selective influence differ from Donders' assumption of pure insertion? What are the consequences of those differences?
5. The conclusions Sternberg is led to by his reaction-time data contradict most people's introspections about what they're doing when they search short-term memory. What does this observation suggest about the proper use of introspective data and reaction-time data? Is one kind of data always to be preferred over the other, or does it depend on the particular task and context? If preference depends on task and content, under what kinds of circumstances is which kind of data to be preferred?

REFERENCES

Baddeley, A. D. (1976). *The psychology of memory*. New York: Basic Books.

DeRosa, D. V., & Tkacz, S. (1976). Memory scanning of organized visual material. *Journal of Experimental Psychology: Human Learning and Memory, 2,* 688–694.

Diener, D. (1988). Absence of the set-size effect in memory-search tasks in the absence of a preprobe delay. *Memory & Cognition, 16,* 367–376.

Luce, R. D. (1986). *Response times: Their role in inferring elementary mental organization*. New York: Oxford University Press.

Raeburn, V. P. (1974). Priorities in item recognition. *Memory & Cognition, 2,* 663–669.

Stadler, M. A., & Logan, G. D. (1989). Is there a search in fixed-set memory search? *Memory & Cognition, 17,* 723–728.

Sternberg, S. (1966). High-speed scanning in human memory. *Science, 153,* 652–654.

Sternberg, S. (1967). Retrieval of contextual information from memory. *Psychonomic Science, 8,* 55–56.

Sternberg, S. (1969). The discovery of processing stages: Extensions of Donders' method. In W. G. Koster (Ed.), *Attention and performance II, Acta Psychologica, 30,* 276–315.

Sternberg, S. (1975). Memory scanning: New findings and current controversies. *Quarterly Journal of Experimental Psychology, 27,* 1–32.

Townsend, J. T. (1990). Serial vs. parallel processing: Sometimes they look like Tweedledum and Tweedledee but they can (and should) be distinguished. *Psychological Science, 1,* 46–54.

Welford, A. T. (Ed.) (1980). *Reaction times.* New York: Academic Press.

Wickelgren, W. A. (1979). *Cognitive psychology.* Englewood Cliffs, NJ: Prentice-Hall.

INTRODUCTION

In "Word Length and the Structure of Short-Term Memory," Alan Baddeley, Neil Thomson, and Mary Buchanan explore some of the characteristics of short-term memory, building on the working-memory model introduced by Baddeley and Hitch (1974).

The working-memory model is a modification and elaboration of the concept of a short-term memory store (STS) described by Atkinson and Shiffrin (1968, 1971). Atkinson and Shiffrin describe the STS as a structure that stores a limited amount of information for a limited amount of time. They derived this characterization of STS from (among other things) experiments examining memory span and free recall.

In a memory-span task, a person is given a relatively short series of items, such as seven unrelated words, and is then asked to repeat the items back in the same order. People generally are able to repeat back successfully between five and nine items (Miller, 1956). However, memory span is decreased if the pronunciations of the items share the same basic speech sound units—phonemes (Conrad, 1964)—or if people repeat a word or sound over and over while remembering the items, a procedure called articulatory suppression (Levy, 1971; Murray, 1968). Such findings have suggested that STS allows for the storage of 7 ± 2 "chunks" of information in acoustic, articulatory, or phonemic form (Atkinson & Shiffrin, 1968).

In a free-recall task, a person is given a relatively long series of items, such as 20 unrelated words, and is then asked to repeat the items back in any order. The free-recall task shows that the memorability of an item is affected by its serial position, its location in the original list. People generally are more successful at remembering the items that occur early or late in the list (the primacy and recency effects, respectively) than they are at remembering those in the middle (see Reading 10).

Atkinson and Shiffrin claimed that both memory span and recency effects arise from information being stored in and retrieved from STS. Baddeley and Hitch (1974) argued that memory span and recency arise from different aspects of a working-memory system consisting of a "central executive" processor plus several passive stores, including a phonemic buffer. Specifically, Baddeley and Hitch suggested that recency effects arise from the retrieval strategies carried out by the central executive, and memory-span effects arise from the characteristics of the phonemic buffer. In the article that follows,

Baddeley, Thomson, and Buchanan explore the characteristics of the phonemic buffer.

As you read this article, ask yourself: How is the Baddeley and Hitch characterization of short-term memory different from that of Atkinson and Shiffrin (1968)? Do these experiments address that difference?

Word Length and the Structure of Short-Term Memory

Alan D. Baddeley

Medical Research Council, Applied Psychology Unit

Neil Thomson and Mary Buchanan

University of Stirling, Scotland

Miller (1956) has suggested that the capacity of short-term memory is constant when measured in terms of number of chunks, a chunk being a subjectively meaningful unit. Because of the subjective definition of a chunk, this hypothesis is essentially irrefutable unless an independent measure of the nature of a chunk is available. Typically this problem has been avoided by making the simplifying assumption that such experimenter-defined units as words, digits, and letters constitute chunks to the subject. Hence, although Miller's hypothesis is not refutable in the absence of an independent measure of a chunk, it is meaningful to test a weaker version, namely that the capacity of short-term memory is a constant number of items, where items are defined experimental units. Words represent one commonly accepted type of item, and in this case, the chunking hypothesis would predict that the capacity of short-term memory, as measured in words, should be constant regardless of the size or duration of the words used.

A number of studies testing this hypothesis have used the recency effect in free recall as an estimate of short-term memory capacity. Craik (1968) found no reliable effect of word length on performance in the free recall of separate groups of words comprising one to five syllables. This invariance held true whether performance was measured in terms of either raw scores, or estimates of primary memory and secondary memory components. This result was replicated and extended by Glanzer and Razel (1974) who observed a recency effect which was constant when measured in number of items, even when an item comprised a whole proverb rather than a single word. They concluded from their study that short-term or primary memory has a capacity of two items regardless of item duration or complexity.

Miller's generalization, however, was based on the memory span paradigm, and it is questionable whether recency and span depend on the same memory mechanisms. There is indeed a growing body of evidence suggesting that the recency effect in

We are grateful to the Social Science Research Council and the Medical Research Council for financial support. We thank Ronald Bidgood for running Experiment VII, Rob Baker for phonetic advice, and Graham Hitch for many useful discussions.

Dr. Baddeley's address is: Medical Research Council, Applied Psychology Unit, Cambridge, CB2 2EF, England.

SOURCE: *Journal of Verbal Learning and Verbal Behavior, 14,* 1975, pp. 575–589. Copyright 1975 by Academic Press, Inc. Reprinted by permission.

free recall is basically unrelated to short-term memory as measured by memory span. Such evidence includes:

(1) Craik's (1970) observation that a subject's memory span correlates more highly with the secondary memory than the primary memory component of free recall.

(2) Memory span shows clear evidence of speech coding, being impaired by both phonemic similarity (Conrad, 1964; Baddeley, 1966) and articulatory suppression (Levy, 1971). This is not the case for the recency effect in free recall which is unaffected by either phonemic similarity (Craik & Levy, 1970; Glanzer, Koppenaal, & Nelson, 1972) or articulatory suppression (Richardson & Baddeley, 1975).

(3) Baddeley and Hitch (1974) have shown unimpaired recency in free recall for subjects performing a concurrent memory span task involving the retention of a sequence of six digits. Since the memory span task did not interfere with recency, it is difficult to maintain the view that the two tasks are based on the same limited-capacity system.

Studies investigating the effect of word length on memory span do not in general support the weak version of Miller's hypothesis. Thus, unpublished work by Laughery, Lachman, and Dansereau (Note 1) and by Standing, Bond, and Smith (Note 2) have reported poorer performance in a memory span task when longer words are used. Mackworth (1963) found a high correlation between reading rate and memory span for a wide range of materials, including pictures, letters, digits, shapes, and colors. This result could be interpreted in terms of word length as a determinant of memory span, with reading rate providing an indirect measure of word length. The situation is, however, complicated by the fact that subjects in some cases were asked to label pictures, and in others to read words so that it is not clear whether the result is due to articulation time or to difficulty in retrieving the correct verbal label. Watkins and Watkins (1973) present the clearest published evidence for an effect of word length on memory span, in a study primarily concerned with the modality effect. They found evidence for a word length effect on earlier serial positions, but observed that the modality effect (the enhanced recall of auditorily presented items) did not interact with word length. They suggest that the word length effect observed may have been due to the greater difficulty of perceiving their four-syllable words which were presented at a 1/sec rate.

These studies do not support the hypothesis that memory span capacity is a constant number of items. However, it is always possible to save the item-based hypothesis by questioning the assumption that words constitute items. Given evidence that short-term memory is a speech-based system, it could be reasonably argued that its capacity should be measured in more basic speech units such as syllables or phonemes. The experiments that follow aim first to study the influence of word-length on memory span, secondly to explore the relative importance of number of syllables and temporal duration of a word as determinants of span, and thirdly to explore the implications of this for the question of whether the underlying memory system is time-based or item-based.

EXPERIMENT I

This study compared the memory span of subjects for sets of long and short words of comparable frequency of occurrence in English. One set comprised eight monosyllables, namely, *sum, hate, harm, wit, bond, yield, worst,* and *twice.* The other set comprised eight five-syllable words, namely *association, opportunity, representative, organization, considerable, immediately, university,* and *individual.*

Method

Five list lengths were used, comprising sequences of four, five, six, seven, and eight words. Eight sequences of each length were made up from the pool of short words, and eight from the pool of long words. In both cases, sequences were generated by sampling at random without replacement from the appropriate pool of words. All subjects were tested on both long and short words, and all received the sequences in ascending order of list length, beginning with sequences of four words and proceeding up to the point at which they failed on all eight sequences, whereupon testing on the pool of words in question was discontinued.

Half the subjects began with the pool of long words, and half with the short words.

The words were read to the subject at a 1.5-sec rate, with each list being preceded by the spoken warning "Ready." Subjects were allowed 15 sec to recall the words verbally in the order presented. Subjects were allowed to familiarize themselves with the two pools of words at the beginning of the experiment, and these two pools remained visible to the subjects on prompt cards throughout the experiment. Several different prompt cards with the words in differing orders were used in this and subsequent experiments so as to prevent the subjects from using location on the card as a cue. The subjects were eight undergraduate or postgraduate students from the University of Stirling.

Results and Discussion

Performance was scored in terms of number of sequences recalled completely correctly (i.e., all the items correct and in the correct order). Figure 1 shows the level of performance at each sequence length for the long and the short words. There is a

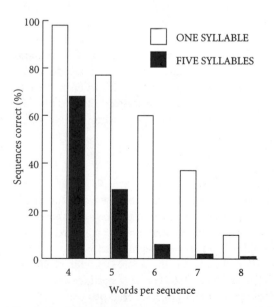

FIGURE 1   Effect of word length on memory span. Mean percentage recall of long and short words as a function of sequence length.

very clear advantage to the short word set which occurs at all sequence lengths and is characteristic of all eight subjects tested.

There is little doubt that the sample of short words used results in better memory span performance than the sample of long words. However, it is arguable that polysyllabic words tend to be linguistically different from monosyllables. In particular, our polysyllables tended to be of Latin origin, compared to the monosyllables which seemed to comprise simpler words of Anglo–Saxon origin. Experiment II attempted to avoid this problem by using words from a single category, country names, a sample of material unlikely to come from any single language source.

EXPERIMENT II

Method

Sequences of five words were constructed by sampling without replacement from each of two pools. The pool of short words comprised the country names *Chad, Chile, Greece, Tonga, Kenya, Burma, Cuba, Malta,* while the long names were *Somaliland, Afghanistan, Venezuela, Czechoslovakia, Yugoslavia, Ethiopia, Nicaragua,* and *Australia.* The names were selected on the basis of their probable familiarity to the subjects, and because they had a similar frequency of repetition of initial and final letters within the pool. Subjects were tested on a total of eight sequences of five short names and eight sequences of five long names. Eight undergraduate subjects were tested using the same presentation procedure as Experiment I.

Results and Discussion

Table 1 shows the mean number of sequences recalled completely correctly, and the mean number of items recalled in the appropriate serial position, for long and short names. On both these scores all eight subjects showed a clear word length effect. Since the material in this study was very different at a linguistic level from the material used in the previous study, and since the effect is very large in both cases, it is clear that the word length effect is a robust phenomenon of some generality.

TABLE 1   Mean Number of Sequences and Items Correctly Recalled as a Function of Word Length in Experiment II

	Short Names		Long Names	
	Mean	SD	Mean	SD
Sequences correct				
Max = 8	4.50	2.00	.88	1.27
Items correct				
Max = 5	4.17	.71	2.80	.24

However, in these and all previous experiments investigating the effect of word length, two major variables are confounded, namely a word's spoken duration and the number of syllables it contains. The results could therefore indicate either that memory span is limited in the number of items it can hold, with the item being the syllable, or that the temporal duration of the words determines the size of memory span. The latter possibility might be predicted by decay theory (Broadbent, 1958) which assumes that forgetting occurs as a function of time. Many studies have attempted to test the theory by measuring performance as a function of presentation rate, and while some studies report enhanced performance with rapid presentation as predicted by decay theory (Conrad & Hille, 1958), others have found the opposite (Sperling & Speelman, 1970). However, in none of these studies was the subject prevented from rehearsing, and this makes interpretation of the results difficult as the subject is effectively re-presenting the list to himself at a rate of his own choosing. This problem can be avoided by allowing the subject to rehearse while using lists of long- and short-duration words. As [fewer] long words than short words can be rehearsed in a given period of time, a word duration effect will be predicted by decay theory (Sperling, 1963). On the other hand, a simple displacement or interference model would predict an effect of number of items, but not duration. Thus, the hypothesis that short-term memory capacity is a constant number of items, where the syllable is the item, predicts no word length effect for words matched for syllable number, but differing in spoken duration. Decay theory, on the other hand, predicts that the amount recalled will be a function of word duration. The next experiment tests these predictions.

EXPERIMENT III

Method

Two pools of disyllabic words, matched for frequency, were produced such that one set tended to have a longer duration when spoken normally. The long word set comprised: *Friday, coerce, humane, harpoon, nitrate, cyclone, morphine, tycoon, voodoo*, and *zygote*, and the short words were *bishop, pectin, ember, wicket, wiggle, pewter, tipple, hackle, decor*, and *phallic*. The words were recorded by a female experimenter onto magnetic tape, which then played through an oscillograph. This plots the wave-form of the signal against time, allowing the duration of the utterance to be measured. The mean duration of the long words was 0.77 sec, and of the short words, 0.46 sec.

From each pool of words, 10 lists of five words were constructed by sampling at random without replacement. The twenty lists were divided into four blocks of five, two comprising lists of short duration words and two of long duration words. A Latin square design was then used to present the blocks in counterbalanced order to each of the 12 subjects. Words were read at a 2-sec rate, and subjects were required to recall verbally at the same rate, paced by a metronome. Recall was paced so as to ensure that the mean delay between input and recall was comparable for long and short words (Conrad & Hille, 1958). Subjects were familiarized with the set of words and with the procedure, and were instructed to commence recall as soon as the last item in each list had been presented. Twelve undergraduates from the University of Stirling served as subjects.

Results and Discussion

Figure 2 shows the mean number of words correctly recalled as a function of serial position. A three-way analysis of variance involving subjects, word length, and serial position showed significant effects of word length, $F(1, 11) = 11.33$, $p < .01$, serial position, $F(4, 44) = 36.82$, $p < .001$, and a significant interaction between word length and serial position, $F(4, 44) = 3.28$, $p < .05$. Analysis by t test showed that the word length effect was significant for serial positions 1, 2, and 3, but not for positions 4 and 5.

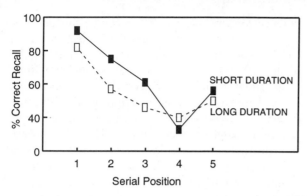

FIGURE 2   Mean recall of disyllabic words of long and short temporal duration.

These results are very similar to those of Watkins and Watkins (1973) showing a word length effect only for the earlier serial positions; this could reflect the masking of an underlying word length effect by the modality effect. However, the experiment differs from the Watkins and Watkins study in using words which are matched for number of syllables, but differ in spoken duration. As such, the results are consistent with the hypothesis that short-term memory holds a constant number of syllables.

The last version of Miller's weakened hypothesis to be investigated is that short-term memory holds a constant number of phonemes. In the last experiment, there was a clear tendency for the long words to have more constituent phonemes, thus the result is open to the interpretation that the word length effect represents a limit to the number of phonemes that can be held. Experiment IV compares performance on sets of words which are matched for number of constituent phonemes, but which differ in duration. Decay theory again predicts a difference in performance in favor of the short duration words.

EXPERIMENT IV

Two sets of words were generated with the following constraints: They differed in spoken duration; they were equal in number of syllables; they were matched for word frequency; and they were equal in number of phonemes (with Scottish pronunciation). Given all these constraints, the previous sets of words reduced from 10 to five; details are given in Table 2. Sequences of five words were produced, and the experiment per-

TABLE 2   Details of Words Used in Experiment IV

	Words	Frequency	Number of Phonemes	Duration (sec)
Long	Coerce	1	5	.80
	Harpoon	1	6	.75
	Friday	40	5	.70
	Cyclone	3	6	.88
	Zygote	—	5	.90
Short	Wicket	1	5	.50
	Pectin	1	6	.60
	Bishop	40	5	.28
	Pewter	3	6	.40
	Phallic	—	5	.42

formed using a procedure identical to that in Experiment III, except that the presentation and paced recall rate was increased to 1 sec per word. Eight Scottish undergraduates served as subjects.

Results and Discussion

Subjects recalled a mean of 61.6% of the long words and 72.2% of the short. A three-way analysis of variance showed a significant effect of word length, $F(1, 7) = 18.9$, $p < .01$, and of serial position, $F(4, 28) = 38.06$, $p < .001$, but no interaction between serial position and word length, $F(4, 28) = 0.55$, $p > .05$.

It is clear then that word duration may influence span when the number of both syllables and phonemes is held constant. The absence of an interaction between word length and serial position is puzzling in view of the previous result; it may be due to either the change in material, or more likely, the change in presentation and recall rate. However, despite this minor discrepancy between experiments III and IV, both seem to concur in suggesting that the temporal duration of items is a powerful determinant of memory span. Before finally dismissing the hypothesis that short-term memory capacity is a constant number of items, a procedural point that could have distorted the results should be mentioned. In both experiments the same experimenter read out the words and it is possible that some incidental feature of her mode of delivery produced the observed effect. To avoid this possibility, the experiment was repeated using visual presentation at a 2-sec rate and to our dismay, a statistically reliable word length effect was not observed.

However, a closer examination of the data revealed that most subjects did show the predicted effect, but that two out of eight did substantially better on the long words. On testing a further set of subjects and asking them how they remembered the material, it was found that those who did best on the short words reported using a rehearsal strategy, whilst those who did better on the long words reported using an imagery strategy. Use of this latter strategy was facilitated by the fact that the presentation rate had been reduced to 2 sec/word in order to obviate perceptual difficulties. As the subject of investigation is the articulatory short-term memory system, it is reasonable to instruct subjects to use a rehearsal strategy in order to avoid this difficulty. The next experiment, then, is a replication of the previous one, but using visual presentation with an instruction to the subjects to rehearse.

EXPERIMENT V

The same material and design were used as in the previous experiment, except that the material was presented visually on flash cards at a 2-sec rate, and recall was unpaced. The duration of the words was also measured in a different way. The duration of a word is determined by two sets of variables, the acoustic nature of the word and the subjects' articulatory rate. The latter variable has been shown to be very stable over a wide range of conditions within a subject, but to vary considerably between subjects (Goldman-Eisler, 1961), and, as decay theory assumes rehearsal rate determines performance, the subject's rather than the experimenter's pronunciation of the words was used.

Two different estimates of rehearsal rate were made. In the first of these, subjects were timed for reading the 10 five-word lists in each condition, as quickly as they could out loud, the 50 words being typed out in two columns. This was done four times for each word length after the memory task, times being recorded by stopwatch. The times so obtained were transformed into reading rate (RR) scores in

units of words per second. The second estimate of rehearsal rate involved requiring the subject to repeat continuously three of the words from one of the pools out loud. Subjects did this as quickly as they could, and were timed by stopwatch for 10 repetitions of the three words. For each condition, they did this four times, always with a different set of three words, and always after the memory task. These times were transformed into articulatory rate scores (AR) in units of words per second. Half the subjects did the reading rate test first, and half the articulatory rate test first. The subjects, who were instructed to remember the lists by repeating the words to themselves, were eight members of the Applied Psychology Unit subject panel who were paid for their services.

Results and Discussion

Subjects recalled a mean of 53.4% of the long words correctly and in the right order, and 71.7% of the short words. Analysis of variance showed that there was a significant effect of word length. $F(1, 7) = 15.14$, $p < .01$, indicating that the word duration effect is not dependent on auditory presentation. There was again a significant effect of serial position, $F(4, 28) = 14.79$, $p < .001$, but the interaction between word length and serial position failed to reach significance, $F(4, 28) = 2.43$, $.05 < p < .1$. These results are again inconsistent with the hypothesis that short-term memory capacity is a constant number of items. An alternative view, that short-term memory is a time-based system, will next be explored and the adequacy of decay theory in this context empirically investigated.

Let us assume that the memory system underlying the word length effect exhibits trace decay, but that rehearsal may revive a decaying trace. It then follows that the amount recalled will be a function of rehearsal rate. Thus, if it can be assumed that reading rate (RR) and articulation rate (AR) are good estimates of rehearsal rate, then it should be possible to use them as predictors of memory span. Table 3 shows the ratio of memory span to reading rate and to articulation rate across conditions. A Wilcoxon matched pairs test showed that there was no effect of conditions for either the memory span–reading rate ratio, $T = 9$, $N = 8$, $p > .05$, or for the memory span–

TABLE 3   Ratio of Memory Score to Reading Rate and to Articulation Rate for Subjects in Experiment V

Subject	Memory Score Reading Rate		Memory Score Articulation Rate	
	$K_L{}^a$	$K_S{}^b$	$K_L{}^a$	$K_S{}^b$
1	1.78	1.70	1.48	1.43
2	1.72	1.42	.93	.93
3	1.55	1.80	1.15	1.14
4	1.43	1.83	1.34	1.48
5	1.30	1.46	1.14	1.32
6	1.68	1.95	1.40	1.79
7	1.38	1.59	1.24	1.00
8	2.15	1.63	1.95	1.36
Mean	1.62	1.67	1.33	1.31

[a]K_L = Constant for long words.
[b]K_S = Constant for short words.

articulation rate ratio, $T = 10$, $N = 6$, $p > .05$. In short, Table 3 indicates that a subject can recall as many words as he can read in 1.6 sec, or can articulate in 1.3 sec. The next experiment explored this relationship in more detail using five different word lengths rather than two.

EXPERIMENT VI

Method

Five pools of 10 words were constructed. Each pool comprised one word from each of 10 semantic categories, the items being matched as closely as possible for familiarity to the subjects. The sets differed in comprising words of either one, two, three, four, or five syllables, as may be seen in Table 4.

From each pool, 10 lists of five words were produced by sampling at random without replacement. The 50 lists were then presented visually on video tape in completely random order; hence subjects were unaware on any given trial what set would be used and so were unlikely to use a different strategy for words of different length. Half the subjects received Lists 1–25 first, and half Lists 26–50 first. Words were written on cards and presented at a 2-sec rate by a card changer which was viewed by a video camera and recorded. A card containing a row of asterisks served as a warning that the list was about to appear. Twelve seconds were allowed for spoken recall.

Reading rate was measured in this experiment by requiring the subjects to read lists of 50 words comprising five occurrences of each item in a given set. The words were typed in uppercase in random order in two columns on a sheet of paper. Subjects were instructed to read the lists aloud as quickly as they could, consistent with pronouncing each word correctly. Their reading times were measured by stopwatch. Subjects read each list a total of four times, twice before beginning the memory task and twice after completing it. Half the subjects began both tests by reading the one-syllable list and proceeding up to the five-syllable list, while the remainder of the subjects were tested in the reverse order. The subjects, who were tested individually, comprised 14 members of the Applied Psychology Unit's panel who were paid for their services.

TABLE 4   Pools of Words, Matched For Conceptual Class; Used in Experiment VI

		Number of Syllables		
1	2	3	4	5
Stoat	Puma	Gorilla	Rhinoceros	Hippopotamus
Mumps	Measles	Leprosy	Diphtheria	Tuberculosis
School	College	Nursery	Academy	University
Greece	Peru	Mexico	Australia	Yugoslavia
Crewe	Blackpool	Exeter	Wolverhampton	Weston-Super-Mare
Switch	Kettle	Radio	Television	Refrigerator
Maths	Physics	Botany	Biology	Physiology
Maine	Utah	Wyoming	Alabama	Louisiana
Scroll	Essay	Bulletin	Dictionary	Periodical
Zinc	Carbon	Calcium	Uranium	Aluminium

Results

Figure 3 shows the effect of word length on mean percentage of words correctly recalled in the appropriate position, and mean reading rate.

Memory scores. Analysis of variance showed a significant effect of condition, $F(4, 52) = 36.70$, $p < .001$, and of subjects, $F(13, 52) = 11.84$, $p < .001$. A Newman–Keuls test between conditions showed that words of one or two syllables were better recalled than words of three or four, which in turn were better than five-syllable words ($p < .05$ in each case).

Reading rate. Analysis of variance showed a significant effect on conditions, $F(4, 52) = 244.02$, $p < .001$. A Newman–Keuls test between conditions showed that each condition was significantly different from every other one ($p < .01$ in each case).

The next set of analyses tested the prediction made by decay theory, that the ratio of memory span

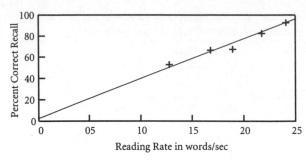

FIGURE 4   The relationship between reading rate and recall observed in Experiment VI.

to reading rate is constant across conditions. Figure 4 shows memory span plotted as a function of reading rate, the line being fitted by the method of least squares. The slope of the line is 1.87, and the intercept on the ordinate 0.17. The standard error of the estimate is 0.10. The value of the intercept differs significantly from zero, $t(3) = 3.71$, $p < .05$. Thus the results are well described by the function $S = c + kR$, where S is the memory span, R is reading rate, and k and c are constants.

One final question of interest is whether such a relationship holds across subjects as well as across word samples, or in other words as to whether fast readers are also good memorizers. This proved to be the case; there was a substantial correlation between memory span and reading rate, $r(13) = .685$, $p < .005$.

Discussion

The results show that the manipulations were effective in producing sets of words of different spoken duration, and that memory score for these words was well predicted by their duration. It has also been shown that fast readers tend to be good memorizers. The relationship between reading rate and memory span thus appears to be remarkably straightforward. Again the ratio of reading rate to span is approximately constant, indicating in the present study that subjects are able to remember as much as they can read out in 1.8 sec. At this stage of research, however, it is probably imprudent to generalize this result too widely. There are many variables which change memory span, but which are unlikely to change read-

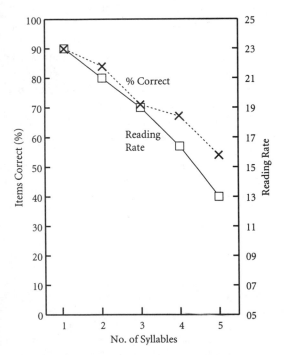

FIGURE 3   Mean reading rate and percentage correct recall of sequences of five words as a function of word length.

ing rate (e.g., list length, word meaningfulness, interpolated delay). It would be of interest to know whether these variables have an effect on the slope, as predicted by decay theory, or on the intercept of the function. Only if the intercept stays consistently near to zero for a variety of conditions can the simple form of decay theory under discussion be accepted. The main result of the experiment however, when seen in conjunction with the previous studies, is that short-term memory capacity, as measured by memory span, is constant when measured in units of *time*, not in units of structure.

The time-based system, which presumably underlies the effects observed, is broadly consistent with a decay theory component of short-term forgetting. Decay theory ascribes to rehearsal the role of reviving a decaying trace, and it is this function of rehearsal that requires the prediction of a word length effect. It follows that if rehearsal could be prevented then, providing the presentation rate was the same for both long and short words, no word length effect should occur. The next experiment was designed to test this prediction. The technique used to stop rehearsal was that of articulatory suppression (Murray, 1968) in which the subject is required to articulate an irrelevant item during presentation of the list.

EXPERIMENT VII

In this experiment, the recall of visually presented lists of long and short words was compared under two conditions: (1) with the subject remaining silent during list input and being free to rehearse, and (2) with the subject required to articulate an irrelevant sequence of items. The design thus involved four conditions, comprising two word lengths in each of two presentation conditions.

Method

Two pools of 10 words each were produced, one of one-syllable words and one of five-syllable words, matched for word frequency. From each pool 16 five-word lists were constructed by sampling at random without replacement. Each set of 16 lists was divided into two equal blocks and a Latin square used to determine order of presentation of the blocks. All subjects did all conditions. The lists were presented at a 1.5-sec rate on a memory drum, and subjects were instructed to recall the items in the order presented. In the suppression conditions, subjects counted repeatedly from one to eight, keeping rate of articulation as constant as possible at about three digits per second. They began counting before the list appeared and stopped to recall as soon as the last item had been presented. In the no-suppression condition, subjects were simply told to try to remember the words. The subjects, 12 undergraduate students from the University of Stirling, were familiarized with the pools of words before being tested.

Results and Discussion

Figure 5 shows the mean percentage of words recalled in the correct serial position as a function of word length for the two presentation conditions. Analysis of variance showed a significant effect of word length.

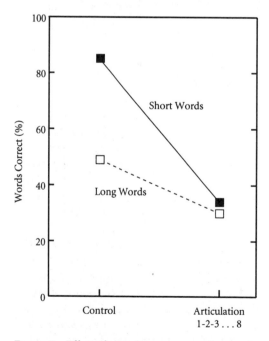

FIGURE 5   Effect of articulatory suppression on the word length effect. The influence of articulatory suppression on the recall of auditorily presented long and short words.

$F(1, 11) = 17.73$, $p < .005$, of suppression, $F(1, 11) = 67.89$, $p < .001$, and a significant interaction between word length and suppression, $F(1, 11) = 16.30$, $p < .005$. The data may be summarized by saying that the word length effect disappears under suppression. Thus, these results are consistent with decay theory if it can be assumed that suppression stops rehearsal. Unfortunately, this latter assumption is open to dispute, since the effects of suppression seem to be dependent on presentation modality (Levy, 1971; Peterson & Johnson, 1971). In particular, suppression has been shown to have a large effect on visually presented material, but little effect on auditorily presented material. It would seem unlikely that suppression stops rehearsal with visual presentation, but not with auditory. An alternative explanation might be to assume that suppression stops the transformation of a visual stimulus into a phonemic code. Thus, given that the word length effect is mediated by a system employing a speech code, and that under suppression, visually presented material does not enter this system, we have an alternative explanation for the above results. Experiment VIII was designed to throw light on this issue.

EXPERIMENT VIII

This was essentially a replication of the previous experiment, with the addition of a condition involving auditory presentation. This expanded the design into a $2 \times 2 \times 2$ design, with two levels of word length (one and five syllables), two articulatory conditions (suppression and no suppression), and two presentation modes (auditory and visual). All subjects did all conditions, with the number of replications per condition being reduced to five. The experiment was run in two halves, with the four conditions of one modality in each half. Half the subjects did the visual conditions first, and half the auditory conditions first. Within a modality, the order of the conditions was determined by a Latin square. New pools of words were used, taken from the one- and five-syllable pools of Experiment VI. Presentation rate was slowed to 2 sec; in the auditory condition, the lists were read to the subject, whilst in the visual condition, the lists were presented on a memory drum. In all conditions,

recall was verbal. In all other respects the procedure was as for the previous experiment: the subjects were 16 members of the Applied Psychology Unit panel who were paid for their services.

Results and Discussion

The mean percentage of words correctly recalled in the appropriate serial position is shown in Figure 6. Analysis of variance showed significant effects of word length, $F(1, 15) = 14.02$, $p < .005$, suppression $F(1, 15) = 85.68$, $p < .001$, and modality, $F(1, 15) = 39.66$, $p < .001$. The interaction between word length and modality was significant, $F(1, 15) = 8.81$, $p < .01$, as was the suppression $\times$ modality interaction, $F(1, 15) = 33.13$, $p < .001$. The remaining two-way interaction, word length $\times$ suppression, just failed to reach significance $F(1, 15) = 4.49$, $.05 < p < .10$. The three-way interaction did reach significance, $F(1, 15) = 6.23$, $p < .05$. This last result indicates that the

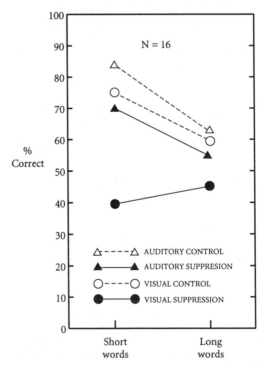

FIGURE 6   The influence of articulatory suppression on the recall of long and short words as a function of modality of presentation.

change in the word length effect produced by suppression is different in the two presentation modalities. Specifically, the word length effect is abolished by suppression in the visual modality, but is unchanged in the auditory modality.

The results demonstrate very clearly how the effects of suppression change with presentation modality and provide support for the view that suppression stops the visual to auditory transformation. These results can still be fitted into the simple decay and rehearsal hypothesis, but only if the assumption is made that articulatory suppression does not prevent rehearsal, but simple inhibits the translation of visual material into a phonemic code.

GENERAL DISCUSSION

The experiments described have shown: (1) That memory span is sensitive to word length across a range of verbal materials. (2) That when number of syllables and number of phonemes are held constant, the word length effect remains. (3) A systematic relationship between articulation time and memory span, such that memory span is equivalent to the number of words which can be read out in approximately 2 sec. (4) That memory span is correlated with reading rate across subjects. (5) That articulatory suppression abolishes the word length effect when material is presented visually.

We shall discuss the implications of these results for existing empirical generalizations about memory, and will then attempt to fit them into a conceptual framework.

The most obvious implication of these results is for Miller's (1956) suggestion that memory span is limited in terms of number of chunks of information, rather than their duration. It suggests a limit to the generality of the phenomenon which Miller discusses, but does not, of course, completely negate it. The question remains as to how much of the data subsumed under Miller's original generalization can be accounted for in terms of temporal rather than structural limitations. Consider, for example, the tendency for subjects' memory span for letter sequences to vary with order of approximation to English. McNulty (1966) has shown that higher orders of approxima-

tion to English lead to higher memory span performance when measured in terms of number of letters recalled, but not when measured in terms of number of adopted chunks. It seems highly probable that sequences which can be reduced to a relatively small number of chunks (e.g., THEMILEAKE) will be not only well remembered, but also spoken much more rapidly than sequences which cannot be reduced in this way (e.g., YVSPCWUECR). Such a view has, of course, been explored in some detail by Glanzer and Clark (1962) in connection with the recall of verbally recodable visual patterns. Both letter sequences and the types of pattern used by Glanzer and Clark are encodable into articulatory sequences which can be produced within the 1- to 2-sec limit implied by our results. It would clearly be desirable to explore the relationship between articulation time and memory for materials such as approximations to English prose, which are broadly consistent with Miller's chunking hypothesis (Tulving & Patkau, 1962) but which would seem likely to involve articulation times considerably in excess of 2 sec.

A second general point arises from the contrast between the recency effect in free recall, which apparently shows no word length effect (Craik, 1968; Glanzer & Razel, 1974), and the memory span task, which clearly does show such an effect. This fits in with the general pattern of results mentioned in the Introduction, suggesting that memory span relies on phonemic coding, whereas recency does not. This provides further evidence for the suggestion that the two reflect quite different underlying memory processes. Since most current views of the nature of short-term memory assumed a common primary memory system underlying both, it is unclear how they would interpret the word length effect.

One approach which does not have this drawback is the framework suggested by Baddeley and Hitch (1974), who explicitly postulate a working memory system which is responsible for performance on memory span tasks, but is not responsible for the recency effect in free recall. The formulation is based on a range of experiments in which subjects were required to perform reasoning, prose comprehension, or free recall learning tasks while simultaneously holding sequences of up to six random digits in short-term memory. In general, the results suggested that subjects could hold up to three items with virtually no effect on performance, but when required to remember six items, a decrement appeared. A tentative formulation was suggested in terms of a working memory system which acts as a central executive, and a supplementary articulatory rehearsal loop with a capacity of about three items.

Most of the experiments in the present series fit neatly into this broad framework, on the assumption that the word length effect is the result of the limited capacity of the rehearsal loop. Looked at from this viewpoint, our data suggest that the articulatory loop system is time-based, and hence has a temporally limited capacity. When access to the loop is prevented by articulatory suppression, memory depends entirely on the capacity of the executive working memory system, which is not phonemically based, and does not have the same temporal limitation as the articulatory loop. The tendency for memory span to be impaired by phonemic similarity among the items to be remembered can also be attributed to the operation of the articulatory rehearsal system. As in the case of the word length effect, the phonemic similarity effect disappears when articulatory suppression occurs with visually presented material (Levy, 1971). Finally, the existence of patients who have drastically impaired digit span, and yet who appear to show none of the general cognitive impairments that might be anticipated from most views of the role of short-term memory (Shallice & Warrington, 1970), can readily be accounted for within this framework if it is assumed that such patients are defective in the operation of the articulatory rehearsal system, while having the executive component of the working memory system intact.

One of our results however does present a problem for such a view. This is raised by the observation that the word length effect does occur despite articulatory suppression, provided the material is presented auditorily. Levy (1971) has shown a similar pattern of results for phonemic similarity, with the similarity effect disappearing under suppression when visual presentation is used, but not when the presentation is auditory. On the straightforward assumption of an articulatory rehearsal loop which is entirely synonymous with subvocalization, it should follow that

suppression effects could not be avoided by auditory presentation. Experiment VIII, however, suggests that although articulatory suppression produces an overall impairment in performance with auditory presentation, it does not influence the word length effect. This would therefore seem to point to articulation as being a means of converting the visual stimulus into a phonemic code which may be accepted by some form of storage system. With auditory presentation, the material is presumably already encoded in an appropriate form, and can be fed into the supplementary system without the need for articulation. The fact that articulatory suppression still impairs performance, even with auditory presentation, may imply either that there is an additional advantage to be gained by articulation, or simply that the task of suppression provides a secondary task which takes up some of the general processing capacity which might otherwise be devoted to remembering the items presented.

Suppose one tentatively assumes a supplementary phonemically based store, what might its other characteristics be? Could it, for example, be equivalent to the precategorical acoustic store suggested by Crowder and Morton (1969)? This seems unlikely for two reasons: First because the word length effect occurs with visual presentation, provided suppression is avoided, whereas the precategorical acoustic store does not appear to be operative unless auditory presentation is used. Secondly, Watkins and Watkins (1973) have presented evidence suggesting that the precategorical acoustic store is not sensitive to the effect of word length; if this is so, it can clearly not be used to explain the word length effect. An alternative is to suggest that the system is an output buffer of some type: A limited-capacity story for holding the motor program necessary for the verbal production of letter names has been suggested by Sperling (1963). It seems plausible to assume that some form of buffer store is necessary for the smooth production of speech; and indeed the existence of the eye–voice span in reading points to some such temporary storage process (Morton, 1964), since what the reader is saying when reading aloud lags consistently behind the point at which he is fixating. Such a buffer system would need to be separate from the act of articulation, since it is presumably necessary to set up new articulatory programs while existing programs are operating. On this interpretation, therefore, articulatory programs can be set up or at least primed, either by the act of overt or covert articulation, or indirectly through auditory stimulation. It is tentatively suggested that such a system may be necessary for fluent speech, and may have the supplementary advantage of providing an additional backup system for the immediate retention of phonemically codable material. Such a view is clearly very tentative and leaves unspecified the complex problem of how such a store might be interfaced with the other components of the system so as to account for even the basic phenomena of the memory span. It does, however, have the advantage of linking together the existing data in a way which is both internally consistent and also likely to generate testable hypotheses.

REFERENCES

Baddeley, A. D. Short-term memory for word sequences as a function of acoustic, semantic and formal similarity. *Quarterly Journal of Experimental Psychology,* 1966, 18, 362–365.

Baddeley, A. D. & Hitch, G. Working memory. In G. A. Bower (Ed.), *The psychology of learning and motivation.* New York: Academic Press, 1974, Vol. 8.

Broadbent, D. E. *Perception and communication.* London: Pergamon Press, 1958.

Conrad, R. Acoustic confusion in immediate memory. *British Journal of Psychology,* 1964, 55, 75–84.

Conrad R., & Hille, B. A. The decay theory of immediate memory and paced recall. *Canadian Journal of Psychology,* 1958, 12, 1–6.

Craik, F. I. M. Two components in free recall. *Journal of Verbal Learning and Verbal Behavior,* 1968, 7, 996–1004.

Craik, F. I. M. The fate of primary memory items in free recall. *Journal of Verbal Learning and Verbal Behavior,* 1970, 9, 143–148.

Craik, F. I. M., & Levy, B. A. Semantic and acoustic information in primary memory. *Journal of Experimental Psychology,* 1970, 86, 77–82.

Crowder, R. G., & Morton, J. Precategorical acoustic storage (PAS). *Perception & Psychophysics,* 1969, 5, 365–373.

Glanzer, M., & Clark, W. H. Accuracy of perceptual recall: An analysis of organization. *Journal of Verbal Learning and Verbal Behavior,* 1962, 1, 289–299.

Glanzer, M., Koppenaal, L., & Nelson, R. Effects of relations between words on short-term storage and long-term storage. *Journal of Verbal Learning and Verbal Behavior,* 1972, 8, 435–447.

Glanzer M., & Razel, M. The size of the unit in short-term storage. *Journal of Verbal Learning and Verbal Behavior,* 1974, 13, 114–131.

Goldman-Eisler, F. The significance of changes in rate of articulation. *Language and Speech,* 1961, 4, 171–174.

Levy, B. A. The role of articulation in auditory and visual short-term memory. *Journal of Verbal Learning and Verbal Behavior,* 1971, 10, 123–132.

Mackworth, J. F. The relation between the visual image and post-perceptual immediate memory. *Journal of Verbal Learning and Verbal Behavior,* 1963, 2, 75–85.

McNulty, J. A. The measurement of "adopted chunks" in free recall learning. *Psychonomic Science,* 1966, 4, 71–72.

Miller, G. A. The magical number seven, plus or minus two: Some limits to our capacity for processing information. *Psychological Review,* 1956, 63, 81, 97.

Morton, J. The effects of context upon speed of reading, eye movements and eye-voice span. *Quarterly Journal of Experimental Psychology,* 1964, 16, 340-354.

Murray, D. J. Articulation and acoustic confusability in short-term memory. *Journal of Experimental Psychology,* 1968, 78, 679–684.

Peterson, L. R., & Johnson, S. F. Some effects of minimizing articulation on short-term retention. *Journal of Verbal Learning and Verbal Behavior,* 1971, 10, 346–354.

Richardson, J. T. E., & Baddeley, A. D. The effect of articulatory suppression in free recall. *Journal of Verbal Learning and Verbal Behavior,* 1977, 14, 623–629.

Shallice, T. & Warrington, E. K. Independent functioning of verbal memory stores: A neuropsychological study. *Quarterly Journal of Experimental Psychology,* 1970, 22, 261–273.

Sperling, G. A model for visual memory tasks. *Human Factors,* 1963, 5, 19–31.

Sperling, G., & Speelman, R. G. Acoustic similarity and auditory short-term memory: Experiments and a model.

In D. A. Norman (Ed.), *Models of human memory*, New York: Academic Press, 1970.

Tulving, E., & Patkau, J. E. Concurrent effects of contextual constraint and word frequency on immediate recall and learning of verbal material. *Canadian Journal of Psychology*, 1962, 16, 83–95.

Watkins, M. J., & Watkins, O. C. The postcategorical status of the modality effect in serial recall. *Journal of Experimental Psychology*, 1973, 99, 226–230.

REFERENCE NOTES

1. Laughery, K. R., Lachman, R., & Dansereau, D. D. Short-term memory: Effects of item-pronunciation time. (Unpublished.)
2. Standing, L., Bond, B., & Smith, P. The memory span. (Unpublished.)

POSTSCRIPT

This article makes clear that Atkinson and Shiffrin's (1968, 1971) STS and Baddeley and Hitch's (1974) working-memory proposals differ in their characterization of the capacity limitations of short-term memory. In general, however, the differences between the two proposals are characterized better as changes in emphasis than as radical reworkings. The differences are highlighted by the choices of labels, such as *short-term store* versus *working memory* and by Baddeley's preference for talking about a working-memory *system*.

Atkinson and Shiffrin, it should be noted, did characterize STS as a working memory where information is held and manipulated by various control processes under the conscious control of the person. (In Atkinson and Shiffrin's theory, control processes such as rehearsal were contrasted with permanent, unalterable, and relatively passive structures like STS.) However, the use of the label *STS* emphasizes its storage function. Although Baddeley (1986, 1990) agrees that parts of the working-memory system store small amounts of information for a limited amount of time, the label he uses emphasizes its role in the manipulation of information.

Perhaps more important, Baddeley's model explains short-term memory phenomena in terms of a multicomponent working-memory system, rather than a single structure, consisting of a central executive and a number of slave systems. (Although only the phonemic buffer or phonological loop is mentioned in this article, Baddeley and his colleagues have also argued for a visuo-spatial sketch pad; see Farmer, Berman, & Fletcher, 1986; Logie, 1986). Baddeley describes the central executive as an "attentional system [that] supervises and coordinates" the slave systems (Baddeley, 1990, p. 71). Most phenomena, such as recency, are thought to arise from the processes selected and executed by the central executive, rather than directly reflecting the characteristics of the slave systems (see Greene, 1986, for further discussion of recency as a strategic, rather than a storage, effect).

Although the working-memory formulation has been extremely useful for understanding a variety of cognitive tasks, it has been criticized for its lack of specificity (for example, Parkin, 1988). Clearly, this is work in progress.

FOR FURTHER THOUGHT

1. According to Baddeley, Thomson, and Buchanan, what's wrong with Miller's (1956) 7 ± 2 characterization of short-term memory capacity?
2. What problem in Experiment I prompted Experiment II? Keeping in mind that Miller claimed that short-term memory capacity is 7 ± 2 meaningful chunks of information, what potential problem is there with the stimuli used in Experiment II? Did the authors address that problem?
3. What would you predict about memory span for a list of words that were difficult to pronounce (because they were in an unfamiliar foreign language or because they involved difficult sound sequences) compared to a list of easy-to-pronounce words, given the authors' findings in these experiments? Why? (See Naveh-Benjamin & Ayres, 1986, for related experiments.)
4. According to the authors, what is the function of the limited-capacity phonemically based store?

REFERENCES

Atkinson, R. C., & Shiffrin, R. M. (1968). Human memory: A proposed system and its control processes. In K. W. Spence & J. T. Spence (Eds.), *The psychology of learning and motivation: Vol. 2* (pp. 89–195). New York: Academic Press.

Atkinson, R. C., & Shiffrin, R. M. (1971, August). The control of short-term memory. *Scientific American*, pp. 82–90.

Baddeley, A. D. (1986). *Working memory*. Oxford: Oxford University Press.

Baddeley, A. D. (1990). *Human memory: Theory and practice*. Boston: Allyn & Bacon.

Baddeley, A. D., & Hitch, G. (1974). Working memory. In G. A. Bower (Ed.), *The psychology of learning and motivation: Vol. 8* (pp. 47–89). New York: Academic Press.

Conrad, R. (1964). Acoustic confusion in immediate memory. *British Journal of Psychology, 55*, 75–84.

Farmer, E. W., Berman, J. V., & Fletcher, Y. L. (1986). Evidence for a visuo-spatial scratch pad in working memory. *Quarterly Journal of Experimental Psychology, 38A*, 675–688.

Greene, R. L. (1986). Sources of recency effects in free recall. *Psychological Bulletin, 99*, 221–228.

Levy, B. A. (1971). The role of articulation in auditory and visual short-term memory. *Journal of Verbal Learning and Verbal Behavior, 20,* 123–132.

Logie, R. H. (1986). Visuo-spatial processes in working memory. *Quarterly Journal of Psychology, 38A,* 229–247.

Miller, G. A. (1956). The magical number seven, plus or minus two: Some limits to our capacity for processing information. *Psychological Review, 63,* 81–97.

Murray, D. J. (1968). Articulation and acoustic confusability in short-term memory. *Journal of Experimental Psychology, 78,* 679–684.

Naveh-Benjamin, M., & Ayres, T. J. (1986). Digit span, reading rate, and linguistic relativity. *Quarterly Journal of Experimental Psychology, 38A,* 739–751.

Parkin, A. J. (1988). Review of *Working Memory. Quarterly Journal of Experimental Psychology, 40A,* 187–189.

INTRODUCTION

Atkinson and Shiffrin (1968, 1971) proposed that human memory could be understood as having three different kinds of stores: a sensory register, a short-term store (STS), and a long-term store (LTS). In this view, different processes under the conscious control of the subject manipulate information in each of the stores and cause information to either remain in a particular store or become available in another.

The distinction between short-term, or primary, memory and long-term, or secondary, memory has been familiar to psychologists at least since James (1890/1983). Although some argued through the early part of the 1960s that short-term memory phenomena can result from a unitary system (see Melton, 1963), Atkinson and Shiffrin, as did most at the time (such as Neisser, 1967, and Waugh & Norman, 1965), argued that a short-term/long-term distinction accounted for the available evidence more parsimoniously. Included among the data then (or soon) available were findings showing that brain damage can selectively disrupt STS, LTS, or the processes that operate on them (Baddeley & Warrington, 1970; Milner, 1967; Shallice & Warrington, 1970; see Squire, 1987, for a general review of neurological aspects of memory).

Although Atkinson and Shiffrin identified several processes, most attention was focused on rehearsal, the process thought to be responsible for maintaining information in STS and (consequently) making it available to LTS. In "Rehearsal Processes in Free Recall: A Procedure for Direct Observation," Dewey Rundus and Richard Atkinson examine this hypothesis directly in an extremely clear and straightforward manner (see also Fischler, Rundus, & Atkinson, 1970; Rundus, 1971). The experiment makes use of the "talk aloud" method, in which the subject is asked to externalize (verbalize aloud) whatever she or he is doing. Note that this is effectively an introspective method that makes the subjects' introspections—or at least, those introspections that are easy to verbalize—available to the experimenter.

As you read this article, ask yourself whether, based on your own experience, rehearsing aloud a list of to-be-remembered words leads to something different than silently rehearsing a list does. If so, why? (Rundus and Atkinson presented the items to be remembered to their subjects twice. In this excerpt, references to the second presentation have been omitted.)

Rehearsal Processes in Free Recall: A Procedure for Direct Observation

Dewey Rundus and Richard C. Atkinson

Stanford University

In a free-recall task S is presented with a word list for study and then asked to recall in any order as many words as possible. As the list is presented, S presumably engages in some form of rehearsal of the list items which may be the formation of mnemonics, visual imagery, repetition (either overt or covert), or a combination of these. The nature of the rehearsal process is then inferred from the results of the free-recall test. This study attempts to make the rehearsal process directly observable by instructing S to rehearse using overt repetition of items from the list and recording the rehearsal. Thus, it should be possible to relate the observed rehearsal process to recall of items from the list.

One finding appearing consistently across many variations of the free-recall task is a U-shaped relationship between the probability of recalling an item and that item's serial position in the study list (e.g., Tulving, 1968). Items presented at the beginning or at the end are better recalled than items in the middle of the study list. The high probability of recall for items from the beginning of the list has been labeled the primacy effect, while the high probability of recall for the last items presented has been termed the recency effect.

One approach to the analysis of the effects of input position on recall has been the division of memory into a short-term store (STS) and a long-term store (LTS). The STS may be viewed as a temporary memory store in which information about recently presented items is maintained in a highly available state. While items are present in STS, they may be rehearsed. The result of this rehearsal is the accumulation of information about the items in the more permanent LTS. It is tempting to attribute the high probability of recall for items presented at the end of a study list to the availability of information about these items in STS. Experiments by Postman and Phillips (1965) and Glanzer and Cunitz (1966) support this assumption. In their experiments an unrelated mathematics task was interpolated between the study of a list and a free-recall test on that list. This interpolated task could be expected to disrupt any ongoing rehearsal and allow information about items in STS to decay. The effect of the interpolated task was to eliminate the recency effect while having essentially no effect on primacy.

What may be said about an item no longer retrievable from STS? One approach to this problem (Atkinson & Shiffrin, 1968; Atkinson & Wickens, 1970; Shiffrin & Atkinson, 1969) is to assume that while an item resides in STS it may be entered into a rehearsal buffer where it is rehearsed in conjunction with a limited number of other recently presented items. Rehearsal of an item serves two purposes: the item is maintained in the highly available STS and rehearsal results in the transfer of information about the item to LTS. The amount of information transferred is thus related to the duration of the item's residence in the buffer. The choice of items to be maintained in the buffer is under the control of S; however, since the buffer is assumed to be of a fixed size (determined by the nature of the material being studied and the length of the study period), the entry of a new item into a full

This research was sponsored by the National Aeronautics and Space Administration Grant No. NGR-05-020-244, and by a National Science Foundation graduate fellowship to the first author.

buffer necessitates the deletion of one of the items currently residing there. Since information transfer to LTS occurs only while an item resides in STS, items that are retained in STS via rehearsal for long periods of time will accrue more LTS information (and consequently have a higher probability of recall) than items whose residence in STS is brief.

By recording *S*'s rehearsal as the study list is being presented, the relationship between the amount of rehearsal accorded an item and its probability of recall can be specified. It will also be possible to observe which items are being rehearsed at the conclusion of list presentations and relate their presence in the final rehearsal set to the recency effect. . . .

METHOD

Eight Stanford students served as paid *Ss* for two 1-hour sessions with one day intervening between sessions. Nine lists of 20 nouns with frequencies of occurrence from 5 to 20 per million (Thorndike & Lorge, 1944) were presented to each *S*, four lists during the first session and five lists during the second session.[1] Three trials were given on each list. A trial involved presentation of the list (randomized on each presentation) followed by a 2-minute written free-recall test on that list. Items were displayed singly on cards, each card being shown for 5 seconds. A tone followed each 5-second interval and signaled the display of a new card. The *Ss* were instructed to study by repeating aloud items from the current list during the 5-second study intervals. There were no restrictions placed on the choice of items to be rehearsed or the rate of rehearsal as long as *S*'s rehearsal filled the interval. A tape recording was made of *S*'s rehearsal on every trial.

RESULTS

The recorded rehearsal protocols were coded numerically and analyzed on a computer. The tone pulses that had served to signal the display of a new item were used to partition the recorded rehearsal from each trial into rehearsal sets (RS). A RS was associated with each item of the list and consisted of all rehearsals occurring while that item was being presented. Thus, the tenth RS includes the rehearsals that occurred while the card bearing the tenth list item was being shown. The size of a RS was taken to be the number of different items in [the] RS. If an item was repeated more than once in a given RS, each rehearsal was counted in determining the total number of rehearsals accorded the item but not in the measure of the size of RS. The only rehearsals that were not items from the list being studied (less than 1% of the rehearsals) were variants of items from that list. These rehearsals were not included in the analysis. The first list of the first session for each *S* was treated as a practice list and not analyzed. The results reported are based on the first . . . presentation of each of five uncategorized lists.

Although not explicitly instructed to do so, *Ss* always rehearsed each newly presented item at least once while the item was being shown. Several other results concerning the makeup of RS during the initial presentation of a list are shown in Table 1. The mean number of rehearsals per RS as a function of its serial position in the study list is shown in the second column. With the exception of the first RS, the mean number of rehearsals appears roughly constant over all list positions. The third column gives the mean size of RS as a function of serial position. The size of RS is necessarily one for the first RS and is seen to rise rapidly to a maximum of 3.5 with a gradual decline toward the end of the list. Although mean RS size rises to a fairly stable value, inspection of individual *S* protocols showed that the actual size of RS varied from 1 to 8 items (e.g., for the first presentation of List 9 to the eighth *S*, the size of RS for serial positions 1 to 20 was observed to be 1,2,2,3,3,1,2,3,1,3,5,4,3,2,4,5,3,3,3,2). The mean number of rehearsals accorded to each item in RS as a function of the serial position of the RS is shown in the fourth column. With the exception of the first few list positions the mean number of rehearsals per item in RS appears quite constant. Items were usually rehearsed in more than one RS. The last column shows the mean number of different RSs in which an item appeared as a function of the serial input position of that item. The number of RSs in which the

---

[1]Three of the lists presented were chosen so as to contain categories. Data from these lists will not be considered here.

TABLE 1   Changes in the Rehearsal Set (RS) as a Function of Serial Position in the Study List

Serial Position m	Number of Rehearsals in RS	Number of Different Items in RS	Number of Repetitions per Item in RS	Number of RSs in Which Item m Appears
1	3.5	1.0	3.5	6.5
2	4.3	1.9	2.3	5.3
3	4.9	2.7	1.8	5.0
4	4.9	3.2	1.5	4.4
5	4.7	3.5	1.4	3.6
6	4.9	3.5	1.3	3.2
7	4.8	3.4	1.4	3.2
8	4.6	3.3	1.4	2.6
9	4.4	3.2	1.4	2.8
10	4.5	3.4	1.3	3.0
11	4.4	3.1	1.4	2.5
12	4.5	3.2	1.4	2.3
13	4.2	3.0	1.4	2.3
14	4.4	3.0	1.5	2.4
15	4.2	3.0	1.4	1.9
16	4.4	3.1	1.4	1.7
17	4.1	3.0	1.4	1.9
18	4.0	2.7	1.5	1.7
19	4.4	2.7	1.6	1.6
20	4.6	2.9	1.6	1.0

item was included decreases steadily with serial position to a value of one for the final item presented. An item's residence in RSs was not always continuous; that is, an item might be rehearsed in one or more consecutive RSs, then be absent from one or more RSs, and finally reappear in a latter RS. The probabilities of return were .140, .038, .033, .021, and .014 for items absent from 1, 2, 3, 4, and 5 intervening RSs, respectively. Items which appeared in the final RS prior to testing were recalled with probability .92. It is interesting to note that the probability of recall for the final item of the list was the same as that for any other item present in the final RS.

Recall of an item following the first presentation of a list will be denoted as R_1. . . . The solid curve of Figure 1 is a plot of the mean probability of an R_1 response, $P(R_1)$, for an item as a function of its serial input position. The resulting U-shaped curve shows definite primacy and recency effects, with the primacy effect being somewhat more pronounced than that found in other free-recall tests (Postman & Phillips, 1965; Glanzer & Cunitz, 1966). Also shown in Figure 1 is a plot of the mean number of rehearsals given to an item during the first presentation of a list. Number of rehearsals is seen to be quite high for the early items of the list and to decrease steadily as a function of serial position.

Figure 2 presents $P(R_1)$ for an item as a function of the number of rehearsals of the item. The only items included in this analysis were those having their last rehearsal in the fourteenth through the seventeenth RS. This assured that the items were not in the RS immediately prior to testing and minimized any possible interaction between number of rehearsals and the time elapsing between the final rehearsal and the test. The $P(R_1)$ is seen to increase as the number of rehearsals increases. A similar increasing function was found when the data were further restricted to those presented in serial positions 8 to 14, indicating that the result is not an artifact of the high mean number of rehearsals accorded to items from the beginning of the list. . . .

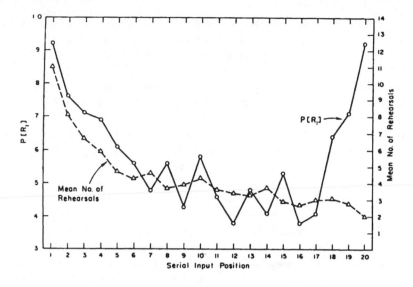
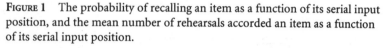

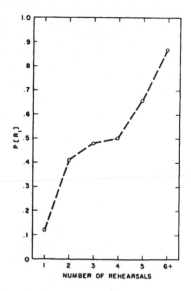

FIGURE 1   The probability of recalling an item as a function of its serial input position, and the mean number of rehearsals accorded an item as a function of its serial input position.

FIGURE 2   The probability of recalling an item as a function of the number of rehearsals of that item.

DISCUSSION

Several interesting features of the rehearsal process were observed in this study. The mean size of RS increased rapidly to a fairly stable level as the study list was being presented. Thus for analysis of the mean data, the RS could be assumed to have a fixed size and be only partially filled as the first items were presented. Items from the beginning of the study list received many more rehearsals and appeared in more RSs than did items from the remainder of the list; however, in spite of the limited rehearsal accorded items from the end of the list these items were recalled quite well.

As mentioned earlier, the U-shaped curve relating serial input position to probability of recall has been observed in a wide variety of free-recall tasks. A dual-storage model of memory might explain this result by assuming that recall of an item is a function of the information about that item which is retrievable from both STS and LTS. Because there are fewer items competing for S's attention at the beginning of list presentation, it might be expected that more information is accumulated about these items in LTS. The most re-

cently presented items have less opportunity to be stored in LTS; however, they should be retrievable from STS. Thus, the recency effect is a STS phenomenon while primacy is due to the fact that more LTS information accrues for the early items. The results presented in Figure 1 indicate that items presented early in the study list are accorded more rehearsal than items appearing subsequently. Figure 2 shows that probability of recall for an item is an increasing function of rehearsal for the item. It was also found that all items present in the final RS were recalled with a high probability; in fact, the last item presented had the same probability of recall as any other item that was included in the last RS. These results provide correlational support for the interpretation of the serial position curve provided by at least one class of dual-storage models (Atkinson & Shiffrin, 1968). . . .

The main purpose of this study was to provide a means of observing the rehearsal processes involved in the study of a free-recall list and to relate the observed rehearsal to the recall of individual items from that list. These observations have provided support for two important assumptions of the class of dual-storage models discussed by Atkinson and Shiffrin (1968). Probability of recall was indeed found to correlate with amount of rehearsal, and items in the final rehearsal set were recalled with high probability. In conclusion, it should be noted that the procedure used in this study is not only applicable to results concerning the probability of recall of items, but should also be of use in the investigation of ordering and clustering effects in both categorized and uncategorized lists.

REFERENCES

Atkinson, R. C., & Shiffrin, R. M. Human memory: A proposed system and its control processes. In K. W. Spence and J. T. Spence (Eds.), *The psychology of learning and motivation: Advances in research and theory,* Vol. II. New York: Academic Press, 1968.

Atkinson, R. C., Wickens, T. D. Human memory and the concept of reinforcement. In R. Glaser (Ed.), *The nature of reinforcement.* Columbus, Ohio: Merrill Publishing Co., 1970.

Glanzer, M., & Cunitz, A. R. Two storage mechanisms in free recall. *Journal of Verbal Learning and Verbal Behavior,* 1966, 5, 351–360.

Postman, L., & Phillips, L. W. Short term temporal changes in free recall. *Quarterly Journal of Experimental Psychology,* 1965, 17, 132–138.

Shiffrin, R. M., & Atkinson, R. C. Storage and retrieval processes in long-term memory. *Psychological Review,* 1969, 76, 179–193.

Thorndike, E. L., & Lorge, I. *The teacher's wordbook of 30,000 words.* New York: Teachers College, 1944.

Tulving, E. Theoretical issues in free recall. In T. R. Dixon and D. L. Horton (Eds.), *Verbal behavior and general behavior theory.* New Jersey: Prentice-Hall, 1968.

POSTSCRIPT

Although the claim that rehearsal is a key to long-term retention of information received considerable support (as in Brodie & Prytulak, 1975), some studies have indicated that maintaining information in STS through rehearsal may not be sufficient for long-term retention of that information. Craik and Watkins (1973), for example, had subjects rehearse aloud words in a list for varying amounts of time. After a couple of minutes of conversation, the subjects were unexpectedly asked to recall as many words in the list as possible (this is called incidental learning because the subjects were not told that they would be tested). Contrary to the Atkinson and Shiffrin theory, Craik and Watson did not find a relation between amount of rehearsal or time in STS and successful retrieval on the surprise test.

This finding led some to make a distinction between maintenance, or Type I, and elaborative, or Type II, rehearsal (Craik & Lockhart, 1972; see Glenberg & Adams, 1978, and Glenberg, Smith, & Green, 1977, for discussion and clarification of the distinction). This distinction was part of a more general theory suggesting that different processes achieve different levels or depths of processing and, consequently, vary in their effectiveness in achieving long-term remembering (see Craik & Tulving, 1975; Hyde & Jenkins, 1973). The levels-of-processing view does not deny a distinction between long-term and short-term memory, but it explains that distinction in terms of differences in the *processes* that operate in human remembering rather than in terms of different memory *stores* (Cermak & Craik, 1979; Craik & Lockhart, 1972; Craik & Tulving, 1975). In other words, certain processes are thought to lead to better long-term retention than other processes are. This levels-of-processing view, however, has come under considerable criticism, in part because its claims are difficult to define and test precisely (Baddeley, 1978, 1990; Nelson, 1977; but see Parkin, 1979).

Incidentally, Kellas, McCauley, and McFarland (1975) found that Rundus and Atkinson's use of the "talk aloud" method may have affected how their subjects performed the task. When these researchers compared subjects who rehearsed aloud with those who rehearsed silently, they found that those who rehearsed silently required less practice time to achieve a given accuracy level. Kellas, McCauley, and McFarland argued that subjects who had to talk aloud were probably less flexible in their use of rehearsal strategies than were silent rehearsers, perhaps because of the extra processing load posed by talking aloud.

FOR FURTHER THOUGHT

1. In plotting the relationship between number of rehearsals and probability of recall, Rundus and Atkinson did not include items receiving their last rehearsal after the seventeenth RS. Why? They also repeated their analyses only for items presented in serial positions 8 to 14. Why did they do that additional analysis?
2. Why is it that items early in the list receive so many rehearsals whereas items thereafter do not? Why is it that the last few items in the list do not receive a high number of rehearsals either?
3. What is implied by the observation that the RS typically consists of about four or five rehearsals? (Keep in mind that the number of rehearsals is not to be confused with the number of repetitions of an item; see the column labeled "Number of repetitions per item in RS" in Table 1.) What do you think would happen to that number if subjects were not required to verbalize their rehearsal? Do you think that the main findings of this experiment would change much if the number of rehearsals in each RS were different?
4. What is implied by the observation that the RS typically has about three items in it (assuming that three or more items have been presented)? How does that number interact with the number of rehearsals subjects did in each RS? Should the length of the words given affect this number?
5. In general, the later in the list the item appeared, the fewer RSs in which it appeared. Why does this happen? How might you test your idea?

REFERENCES

Atkinson, R. C., & Shiffrin, R. M. (1968). Human memory: A proposed system and its control processes. In K. W. Spence & J. T. Spence (Eds.), *The psychology of learning and motivation: Vol. 2* (pp. 89–195). New York: Academic Press.

Atkinson, R. C., & Shiffrin, R. M. (1971, August). The control of short-term memory. *Scientific American*, pp. 82–90.

Baddeley, A. D. (1978). The trouble with levels: A re-examination of Craik and Lockhart's framework for memory research. *Psychological Review, 85*, 139–152.

Baddeley, A. D. (1990). *Human memory: Theory and practice.* Boston: Allyn & Bacon.

Baddeley, A. D., & Warrington, E. K. (1970). Amnesia and the distinction between long- and short-term memory. *Journal of Verbal Learning and Verbal Behavior, 9*, 176–189.

Broadbent, D. E. (1958). *Perception and communication.* London: Pergamon Press.

Brodie, D. A., & Prytulak, L. S. (1975). Free recall curves: Nothing but rehearsing some items more or recalling them sooner? *Journal of Verbal Learning and Verbal Behavior, 14*, 549–563.

Cermak, L. S., & Craik, F. I. M. (Eds.) (1979). *Levels of processing in human memory.* Hillsdale, NJ: Erlbaum.

Craik, F. I. M., & Lockhart, R. S. (1972). Levels of processing: A framework for memory research. *Journal of Verbal Learning and Verbal Behavior, 11*, 671–684.

Craik, F. I. M., & Tulving, E. (1975). Depth of processing and the retention of words in episodic memory. *Journal of Experimental Psychology: General, 104*, 268–294.

Craik, F. I. M., & Watkins, M. J. (1973). The role of rehearsal in short-term memory. *Journal of Verbal Learning and Verbal Behavior, 12*, 599–607.

Fischler, I., Rundus, D., & Atkinson, R. C. (1970). Effects of overt rehearsal processes on free recall. *Psychonomic Science, 19*, 249–250.

Glenberg, A., & Adams, F. (1978). Type I rehearsal and recognition. *Journal of Verbal Learning and Verbal Behavior, 17*, 455–464.

Glenberg, A., Smith, S. M., & Green, C. (1977). Type I rehearsal: Maintenance and more. *Journal of Verbal Learning and Verbal Behavior, 6*, 339–352.

Hyde, T. S., & Jenkins, J. J. (1973). Recall for words as a function of semantic, graphic, and syntactic orienting tasks. *Journal of Verbal Learning and Verbal Behavior, 12*, 471–480.

James, W. (1890/1983). *The principles of psychology.* Cambridge, MA: Harvard University Press.

Squire, L. R. (1987). *Memory and brain.* New York: Oxford University Press.

Kellas, G., McCauley, C., & McFarland, C. E., Jr. (1975). Reexamination of externalized rehearsal. *Journal of Experimental Psychology: Human Learning and Memory, 104*, 84–90.

Melton, A. W. (1963). Implications of short-term memory for a general theory of memory. *Journal of Verbal Learning and Verbal Behavior, 2*, 1–21.

Milner, B., (1967). Amnesia following operation on the temporal lobes. In O. C. Zangwill & C. W. M. Whitty (Eds.), *Amnesia* (pp. 109–133). Washington, DC: Butterworth.

Neisser, U. (1967). *Cognitive psychology.* New York: Appleton-Century-Crofts.

Nelson, T. O. (1977). Repetition and depth of processing. *Journal of Verbal Learning and Verbal Behavior, 16,* 151–171.

Parkin, A. J. (1979). Specifying levels of processing. *Quarterly Journal of Experimental Psychology, 31,* 175–195.

Rundus, D. (1971). Analysis of rehearsal processes in free recall. *Journal of Experimental Psychology, 89,* 63–77.

Shallice, T., & Warrington, E. K. (1970). Independent functioning of verbal memory stores: A neuropsychological study. *Quarterly Journal of Experimental Psychology, 22,* 261–273.

Squire, L. R. (1987). *Memory and brain.* New York: Oxford University Press.

Waugh, N. C., & Norman, D. A. (1965). Primary memory. *Psychological Review, 72,* 89–104.

INTRODUCTION

Three principles that various researchers have argued affect long-term memorability of episodic information—depth of processing, encoding specificity, and distinctiveness—come together in Ronald Fisher and Fergus Craik's article "Interaction between Encoding and Retrieval Operations in Cued Recall."

The depth- or levels-of-processing principle, first proposed by Craik and Lockhart (1972; see also the Postscript to Reading 10), focuses on how the way in which someone thinks about or encodes some event, as opposed to how much the event is thought about, affects how well that event is remembered. Using an incidental learning paradigm in which subjects are not told specifically to remember all the information given, Craik and Tulving (1975) found support for this view; some kinds of processing in fact seemed to lead to better long-term remembering. Hyde and Jenkins (1973) found similar evidence with an intentional learning paradigm.

The encoding-specificity principle (Thomson & Tulving, 1970; Tulving & Osler, 1968; Tulving & Thomson, 1973), in contrast, focuses on the relationship between encoding and retrieval. Tulving and his colleagues found that the effectiveness of a particular kind of retrieval cue, such as a hint or a stimulus that requires a particular response, depends on how the information was originally encoded. Successful retrieval requires that some of the information present during encoding also be present during retrieving.

Finally, the distinctiveness or uniqueness principle (Moscovitch & Craik, 1976) focuses on how easily the information to be remembered can be distinguished from other information a person possesses. This implies that a retrieval cue is more effective if it is uniquely associated with the information to be remembered, and that the retrieval cue–information-to-be-remembered chunk is distinct from other information in memory.

In this article, Fisher and Tulving investigate how depth of processing, encoding specificity, and distinctiveness interact with one another. As you read it, ask yourself: In what ways do these experiments capture everyday remembering? In what ways do they not?

Interaction between Encoding and Retrieval Operations in Cued Recall

Ronald P. Fisher and Fergus I. M. Craik

University of Toronto, Canada

Craik and Lockhart (1972) suggested that the memory of an event was a function of the "depth" to which the event was initially processed. In this scheme, deeper levels of processing are those concerned with semantic and associative analyses of the stimulus. Some empirical support for these notions was provided by Craik and Tulving (1975). In their experiments, subjects were asked questions about a series of words in an incidental learning paradigm. Before each word was presented, the subject was asked a question, either about the word's physical features (e.g., "Is the word in capital letters?"), its phonemic features (e.g., "Does the word rhyme with chair?"), or its semantic features (e.g., "Is the word a type of animal?"). By Craik and Lockhart's formulation, the physical, phonemic, and semantic questions induce progressively deeper levels of processing; it was thus expected that the semantic questions would be associated with the highest level of performance in a subsequent memory test. This expectation was upheld with both recall and recognition measures and under both incidental and intentional learning conditions.

Although Craik and Tulving's (1975) results lend strong support to the levels-of-processing approach, there is one major deficiency in that approach if it is to lead to a complete account of memory processes; the deficiency is the absence of any specification of retrieval processes. Tulving (1974) has stressed that memory must be viewed as a joint function of stored information (the memory trace) and information provided to the subject at retrieval (the retrieval cue). So far, the levels-of-processing view has yielded some insights into relations between encoding operations and memory performance but has generated little work on possible interactions between the results of various encoding operations and retrieval processes. Although Craik and Tulving's results were interpreted as reflecting encoding variations, it is logically possible that encoding was equivalent under the various experimental conditions and that the differences arose at retrieval. For example, when subjects are given a free-recall or recognition task, they may typically adopt a semantic retrieval mode; that is, they may retrieve stored events in terms of their semantic characteristics. If this is so, it is plausible that the relatively poor performance following structural and phonemic decisions in Craik and Tulving's experiments was due to a mismatch between encoding and retrieval operations. This line of reasoning suggests that if subjects were induced to adopt structural or phonemic retrieval modes following structural or phonemic encoding, respectively, performance in these conditions would be brought up to the level of the semantic condition.

One purpose of the present series of experiments was to obtain evidence on this alternative account of Craik and Tulving's (1975) results. The method used was to gain some control of both encoding and

This research was supported by Grant A8261 from the National Research Council of Canada to the second author. The authors are grateful for many helpful discussions of these ideas with colleagues; we are especially grateful to Endel Tulving for his very useful comments on an earlier draft.

Requests for reprints should be sent to Ronald P. Fisher, Department of Psychology, Erindale College, University of Toronto, Mississauga, Ontario, Canada L5L 1C6.

SOURCE: *Journal of Experimental Psychology: Human Learning and Memory*, 3(6), 1977, pp. 701–711. Copyright 1977 by the American Psychological Association. Reprinted by permission.

retrieval processes through manipulation of the input context (by asking different types of questions or by presenting the target word with a rhyming or associated word) and through manipulation of the output context (by presenting different types of retrieval cues). If the alternative account is valid, then matching the nature of input and output contexts should equate memory performance in all cases.

A related purpose of the present experiments was to explore possible relations between the levels-of-processing notions and the encoding-specificity principle (Tulving & Thomson, 1973). This principle states: "Specific encoding operations performed on what is perceived determine what is stored, and what is stored determines what retrieval cues are effective in providing access to what is stored" (Tulving & Thomson, 1973, p. 369). The levels-of-processing manipulations reported by Craik and Tulving (1975) provide powerful examples of ways in which the nature of stored information may be influenced. In these experiments it seems likely that the qualitative nature of the encoded trace is affected by input conditions and that the memory trace of the encoded word is biased to contain more sensory, phonemic, or semantic information, depending on the questions asked during the encoding phase. If this is so, it follows from the encoding-specificity principle that the most effective retrieval cue will differ in these three encoding conditions. It is thus possible (as outlined above) that the differential retention observed by Craik and Tulving following different encoding conditions does not primarily reflect differential durability of the traces, as suggested by Craik and Lockhart (1972), so much as differential compatibility of trace and cue information. One possibility to be examined in the present experiments is that at retrieval, differently encoded traces are all still present in the memory system and can potentially give rise to equal levels of retention, provided the optimal retrieval cue is provided. The alternative outcome—superior retention levels for deeper processing even when retrieval cues are optimized—would support the original suggestion by Craik and Lockhart that deeper processing supports superior levels of retention.

A further issue relating encoding specificity to levels of processing will be examined in light of the present experiments; the notion is that the specificity of encoded information, and thus the effectiveness of a given retrieval cue, increases at deeper levels of encoding. This suggestion is made on the basis of several other ideas and assumptions. For example, Moscovitch and Craik (1976) made the case for "deeper" semantic encodings being more distinctive; whereas phonemic encodings are formed from a limited vocabulary of speech sounds, the possibilities for combining and recombining "semantic elements" are very much greater. It follows from this idea that a phonemic retrieval cue will tend to elicit many encoded traces, since the cue information pertains to many traces, whereas information in a semantic retrieval cue relates more specifically to a smaller number of traces. That is, there is greater functional cue overload (Baddeley, 1968; Watkins & Watkins, 1975) for shallow traces. It is thus assumed that the effectiveness of a retrieval cue is positively correlated with the extent to which information in the cue duplicates information in the trace and is negatively correlated with the extent to which information in the target trace duplicates information in other traces. From these background ideas, it is reasonable to suggest that the specificity of encoded information, and thus the effectiveness of a compatible retrieval cue, should increase at deeper levels of encoding.

A final major theoretical implication of the present results concerns the conceptual difference between the notion of "depth" in the levels-of-processing framework and the "strength" of memory traces as described by Wickelgren (1970) and others. Whereas differences in strength presumably refer to quantitative differences—a stronger memory trace has more of the same mnemonic attributes—Craik and Lockhart (1972) stressed qualitative differences between traces encoded at different levels. If the latter view is correct, interactions should occur between type of encoding and type of retrieval cue; that is, no absolute value of memorability can be given to any particular encoded event, since memory performance will depend on the interaction of trace information and retrieval cue information (Tulving, 1974). In the light of depth-of-processing and encoding-specificity views, it is perfectly plausible to conceive of two encoded traces, one of which yields the higher recall probability in one retrieval environment but the lower recall probability in a second retrieval environment. It is difficult to see how a theory that postulates a fixed value of strength could cope with this result.

These issues were examined by manipulating the qualitative nature of both the trace and the retrieval cue. Experiment 1 examined interactions between type of encoding operation and type of retrieval cue in the incidental learning paradigm reported by Craik and Tulving (1975). Experiments 2 and 3 extended the generality of the findings by using an intentional learning paradigm and by systematically varying the similarity between the encoding context and the retrieval cue.

EXPERIMENT 1

In Experiment 1, three types of encoding were induced by asking subjects a question about each word before it was presented. The paradigm is described more fully by Craik and Tulving (1975). In the present case, the three types of questions used were (a) rhyme (Does the word rhyme with the following word:————?); (b) category (Does the word belong to the following category:————?); and (c) sentence (Does the word fit into the following sentence:————?). In terms of levels of processing, the rhyme encoding represents the shallowest level; there are no theoretical grounds for distinguishing which of (b) and (c) represents the deeper level. In all cases, half of the questions led to a positive response and half to a negative response (that is, on half of the trials the word did not rhyme with the given word, fit the category, or complete the sentence). The combinations of three question types and two response types yielded six different encoding conditions.

Subjects were told that they were participating in a perception/reaction time experiment. At the beginning of each trial they were shown a card with a question printed on it. After studying the question, the subject looked into a tachistoscope. The word was then exposed for .2 sec. On reading the word, the subject immediately pressed one of two telegraph keys to indicate his or her response. After completing 72 such trials, the subject was unexpectedly given a stack of 72 retrieval cue cards and was asked to recall

as many of the tachistoscopically exposed words as possible. Each retrieval cue correctly referred to only one item and either repeated the same information that had been presented as a question at input or gave information of a different type. Thus, a word might be encoded in terms of a category but cued by a rhyme.

Method

The subjects were 20 undergraduates of both sexes, who were paid for their services. Each subject was tested individually. The words used here were 72 common concrete nouns, between four and six letters in length. For each word, three retrieval cues were formed—a rhyme, a category, and a sentence frame. The three cue types were orthogonally combined with the six encoding conditions (three Question Types × Yes/no) to form 18 encoding–retrieval combinations, with each combination occurring four times per subject. Four presentation formats were devised; 5 subjects were tested on each format. In each format, 12 words fell into each of the six encoding conditions. These groups of 12 were further split down into three groups of 4 words that were later cued either by a rhyme, a category, or a sentence

In Format 1, the 72 words were randomly assigned to the resulting 18 combinations of encoding and retrieval conditions, 4 words to each condition. In Format 2, each word retained the same "level" of encoding and retrieval, but each positive response was changed to a negative response and vice versa. In Format 3, the 72 words were allocated to new encoding–retrieval conditions. Format 4 replicated Format 3, but with response type changed.

At the time of retrieval, the subject was presented with a stack of 72 retrieval cue cards, each of which was a valid cue for one of the 72 words shown in the encoding phase. Of the 72 cues, 24 were rhymes, 24 were categories, and 24 were sentences with 1 word missing. Thus, like the encoding questions, retrieval cues were rhymes, categories, or sentences. It should be stressed that the retrieval cues (with certain exceptions) were *not* identical to the encoding questions for any one subject. Typically, a word was encoded under one condition (e.g., rhymes with brain?—TRAIN) and retrieved with a different, but valid, retrieval cue (e.g., form of transport). Similarly, words whose associated questions yielded negative responses in the encoding phase were given valid (that is, correct) cues at retrieval. The three exceptions to the general rule of cues being different from encoding questions were rhyme-positive followed by a rhyme cue, category-positive followed by a category cue, and sentence-positive followed by a sentence cue. In these three cases, the retrieval cue was identical to the encoding question; thus three conditions involved intralist cues and the remaining conditions involved extralist cues.

Results and Discussion

The probabilities of cued recall under the different encoding–retrieval combinations are shown in Table 1. The results are shown separately for positive and negative answers to the initial encoding questions. In the case of positive responses, recall was higher for the semantic encoding conditions (category and sentence) than for the rhyme condition; also, performance was somewhat higher when semantic retrieval cues were presented. An analysis of variance on the data for positive responses in Table 1 showed significant effects due to encoding conditions, $F(2, 38) = 48.5$, $p < .01$, and to retrieval conditions, $F(2, 38) = 3.37$, $p < .05$. However, the most striking feature of the data is the presence of a strong interaction between encoding questions and retrieval cues; this interaction was also statistically reliable, $F(4, 76) = 29.61$, $p < .01$. Thus, for each encoding condition, the highest recall probability was obtained when the retrieval cue was identical to that used during study.

These results have implications for the theoretical issues raised in the introduction. First, when the qualitative nature of retrieval was manipulated by varying the type of retrieval cue provided, recall levels were highest when the retrieval cue was identical to the encoding question. Thus, in line with Tulving and Thomson's (1973) findings, retrieval cues were typically most effective when the encoded trace had been biased at input to contain the same type of information as contained in the cue. However, provision of the encoding question as a cue did not equate recall in all cases; cued recall in the sentence-encoding/sentence-cue condition was approximately twice as high as recall in the rhyme-encoding/rhyme-cue condition. Given that the same pattern of results was obtained in the present experiment (in which retrieval mode was controlled) and in the experiment reported by Craik and Tulving (1975), the argument that the "levels-of-processing" effects reported by Craik and Tulving were due to a mismatch between encoding and retrieval operations is seriously weakened. When a word was encoded in a rhyme context, a rhyme cue was most effective; but even in this optimal retrieval context, performance was much lower than that exhibited by appropriately cued "deeper" encodings. To describe the pattern of results for positive responses in Table 1 adequately, the notions of depth of processing and encoding–retrieval compatibility are both required (cf. Nelson, Wheeler, Borden, & Brooks, 1974, who also suggest the use of both principles to complement each other). Finally, it may be noted that the data for positive responses are quite incompatible with the view that memory traces differ only in "strength"; performance levels under each encoding

TABLE 1   Proportions of Words Recalled as a Function of Encoding Question and Retrieval Cue (Experiment 1)

	Encoding Question							
	Positive Responses				Negative Responses			
Retrieval Cue	Rhyme	Category	Sentence	M	Rhyme	Category	Sentence	M
Rhyme	.40	.43	.29	.37	.26	.28	.28	.27
Category	.15	.81	.46	.47	.10	.28	.11	.16
Sentence	.10	.50	.78	.46	.08	.18	.08	.11
M	.22	.58	.51		.15	.25	.16	

condition do not reflect some absolute level but depend strongly on the type of retrieval cue used.

The data shown on the right-hand side of Table 1 are the cued-recall probabilities of words that were encoded in the context of questions that yielded negative responses. Since the retrieval cues were valid for the target words in all cases, they were necessarily extralist cues in all conditions in negative-response questions. The pattern of results is quite different from the pattern for positive responses in Table 1. First, there is no easily interpreted effect of type of encoding question; although the differences between encoding conditions were found by analysis of variance to be statistically reliable, $F(2, 38) = 6.16$, $p < .01$, the sentence condition gave very similar results to the rhyme condition. This attenuation of the levels-of-processing effect in the case of negative responses is similar to the results found under cued-recall conditions in previous experiments (Craik & Tulving, 1975, Experiment 8; Moscovitch & Craik, 1976). The analysis of variance yielded a main effect of cue condition, $F(2, 38) = 7.49$, $p < .01$, which is due largely to the higher recall of words with rhyme cues. Critically important for the present argument, there was no significant interaction between encoding question and retrieval cue, $F(4, 76) = 1.21$, $p > .25$.

The pattern of results in Table 1 for negative responses is interpreted as showing that when the encoded word and its encoding question are not "congruent" (Craik & Tulving, 1975; Schulman, 1974), the word's encoded trace is largely unaffected by the nature of the context. In this case, cued-recall performance appears to be determined to a large extent by the a priori effectiveness of particular cues to elicit the target words—in the present experiment, rhyme cues were apparently more effective cues than were other cue types. That is, since the encoding context had little effect in biasing the words' encoding, no interaction with cue type occurred. It should be noted, however, that when the positive responses in Table 1 are contrasted with the negative responses, the different pattern of results is not due simply to the presence of intralist cues in the negative diagonal cells for the positive responses. The table shows that each cell for the positive responses has a higher value than the corresponding cell for negative responses. Thus, the

congruent contexts in the positive-response data apparently added some encoded information that was later beneficial to cued recall. The increment was relatively slight in the case of rhyme encodings but substantial in most cases with category or sentence encoding. The increment was highest, of course, when the word was cued by its original encoding question (the negative diagonal of the positive responses in Table 1).

Overall, the results of Experiment 1 are similar to findings reported by Craik and Tulving (1975) and Moscovitch and Craik (1976); namely, the provision of more effective retrieval cues was especially beneficial to congruent and to highly elaborated traces. Craik and Tulving (1975, Experiment 7) manipulated the encoding context for single words by providing sentence frames of different degrees of complexity. When free recall of the target words was compared to cued recall, it was found that reproviding the non-congruent sentence frames as cues did not increase retention above the free-recall level. When the word and the sentence frame were congruent, however, reproviding the frame did boost recall, and the benefit was greatest with the most complex sentences. Moscovitch and Craik reported the related result that the benefit of cued over free recall was greater at deeper levels of processing; again, cues had relatively little effect on noncongruent encodings. Both these sets of data and the results from the present experiment suggest that the effectiveness of a cue depends not only on its presence during encoding but also on its integration with the target event; given that congruence or integration, the cue is most effective when the original encoding was "deep" or elaborate.

In summary, Experiment 1 has shown that the "levels-of-processing" effect demonstrated by Craik and Tulving (1975) is not an artifact caused by a mismatch between encoded information and the retrieval cue; the depth-of-processing effect remains strong (for positive responses at least) when retrieval is biased to be compatible with encoding. The presence of a strong interaction between encoding and cuing conditions provides severe difficulties for strength theories of memory—retention level is not absolute for any encoding but depends critically on the retrieval environment; the present results thus provide further evidence for the arguments against strength theory advanced by Anderson and Bower (1972) and by Tulving and Thomson (1973). The data from negative responses yielded a rather different pattern. In this case, the only major effect was that of cue type. When the word and its context are not congruent, the effect of encoding question and the encoding–retrieval interaction are largely absent. Discussion of further theoretical issues is deferred until the remaining experiments are described.

Experiment 1 embodied two major procedural weaknesses. First, retrieval cues apparently differed in their a priori effectiveness—Table 1 negative-response data show that the rhyme cues used were associated with generally higher levels of recall than were the semantic cues. Second, the results were somewhat difficult to interpret, owing to the use of both intralist and extralist cues. In Experiment 2, cues were first equated for "retrieval potency" to remove one source of confusion. In Experiment 3, cues were again equated, and in addition, the use of extralist cues was extended.

EXPERIMENT 2

The essential purpose of Experiment 2 was to replicate the interaction between type of encoding question and type of retrieval cue in a slightly different paradigm, using materials equated for the a priori effectiveness of the cues.

Method

In the first phase of the study, a pool of 56 words was formed such that each word could be generated with approximately equal facility from a rhyme cue and a semantically associated cue. This was accomplished by starting with a larger pool of 96 words, each of which had a potential rhyme cue and a potential semantic cue. Two sets of booklets were constructed, one containing the 96 rhyme cues and the other containing the 96 associative cues. The booklets were then distributed to 70 undergraduates in a classroom situation; half received the rhyme words with instructions to generate rhymes to each cue word during successive 10-sec intervals, and half of the subjects received the

associative cues with instructions to generate semantic associates during the 10-sec intervals. The point, of course, was to determine the probability of generating the original word from the cue. Subjects were encouraged to respond with as many rhymes (or associates) as they could generate within the allotted time. The original word was considered to have been generated if it appeared in any output position. Typically, subjects generated 2–4 words per cue. Finally, 56 words were selected to be used in the experiment proper. These words were chosen so that (a) for each word the probability of generating it from the rhyme cue was roughly equal to the probability of generating it from the associative cue (the average difference between these probabilities, disregarding sign, was .10), and also (b) for the group of words the probabilities of rhyme and associate generation were as close as possible. For the rhyme and association cues as groups, the mean probabilities (and standard deviations) of generating the target words were .16 $(SD = .12)$ and .15 $(SD = .13)$, respectively.

Thirty-two paid undergraduates were presented with a list of 64 word pairs. Each word pair contained one word in capital letters, the to-be-remembered word, and printed above it in lowercase letters, the context word. This context word either rhymed with, or was associatively related to, the target word as in $\frac{hat}{CAT}$ or $\frac{dog}{CAT}$ The subjects were instructed to learn the target words but to use the context words as an aid to remembering the target words (Tulving & Thomson, 1973). The 64 word pairs contained 4 untested primacy buffer items, 56 items to be tested later, and 4 untested recency buffer items. The pairs were presented visually at a 4-sec rate.

Following the last word pair, the test format was explained: The experimenter presented a series of 56 retrieval cues, each of which either rhymed with, or was associatively related to, only 1 of the target words. The relationship of each cue to its target word was made clear on each trial. Thus, for example, $\frac{dog}{CAT}$ during encoding was later cued by "associated with dog" (cf. Arbuckle & Katz, 1976, where the cue–target relationship was unclear to the subject at the time of test). Each retrieval cue was presented for 10 sec, during which time the subject attempted to recall the appropriate target word. A response was scored correct only if the appropriate target word was recalled; thus, if the subject wrote down a target word that was not specified by that particular retrieval cue, it was scored as incorrect (such instances were extremely rare, however).

For each subject, half of the target words were presented in a rhyme context and half in an associative context; half of the retrieval cues were rhymes and half were associates. The resulting 4 combinations of Encoding Context × Retrieval Cue appeared 14 times each per subject. The assignment of target words to experimental conditions was counterbalanced across subjects. When the retrieval cue level matched the encoding-context level (e.g., rhyme encoding and rhyme retrieval) the retrieval cue was identical to the encoding context. Half of the subjects were given the list of target words in one order and half in the reverse order. The test order always matched the presentation order so that study–test lag was constant for all items.

In summary, the encoding of common words was biased by means of context words that either rhymed with, or were associated with, the target words. In contrast to Experiment 1, learning was intentional in the present experiment; also, all words and encoding contexts were congruent. At test, the target words were cued either by the context word (intralist cues) or by the alternative cue (extralist cues). The point of the study was to obtain further information on interactions between level of processing and encoding-retrieval compatibility.

Results and Discussion

The results are shown in Table 2. The table shows that while there is an overall superiority of semantic encoding over rhyme encoding and a superiority of semantic cues over rhyme cues, both effects are qualified by an interaction between encoding and retrieval conditions. That is, semantic cues are superior for semantic encodings, whereas rhyme cues are superior for rhyme encodings. The reliability of these effects was assessed by means of analysis of variance. The effect of encoding condition was statistically reliable, $F(1, 31) = 16.13$, $p < .01$, as was the effect of retrieval condition, $F(1, 31) = 24.55$, $p < .01$. The interaction

TABLE 2 Proportions of Words Recalled as a Function of Encoding Context and Retrieval Cue (Experiment 2)

Retrieval Cue	Encoding Context		
	Rhyme	Associate	M
Rhyme	.26	.17	.21
Associate	.17	.44	.30
M	.21	.30	

between encoding and retrieval conditions was also statistically significant, $F(1, 31) = 80.9$, $p < .01$.

From these results, it is concluded that the compatibility between encoding conditions and cue conditions is a critically important determinant of recall. The present pattern of results thus confirms the findings from Experiment 1 (Table 1) and replicates previous results showing interactions between encoding and retrieval conditions (Arbuckle & Katz, 1976; Brooks, 1974; Tulving & Osler, 1968; Owings, Note 1). However, the present results also show that when encoding and cue conditions are optimally matched, the semantic encoding/semantic cue combination is associated with higher levels of retrieval than is the combination of rhyme encoding and rhyme cue (Brooks, 1974; Nelson et al., 1974). Thus again, both notions of depth of processing (or *type* of encoding) and encoding–cue compatibility are necessary to describe the results. Experiment 3 explores the further case in which both intralist cues and extralist cues within an encoding domain were utilized.

EXPERIMENT 3

In Experiment 3, the encoding of each word was again biased to emphasize its semantic or phonemic features by means of an accompanying context word. At retrieval, three different types of cues were used: first, identical cues—the same word that accompanied the target word at input; second, similar cues—in this case the cue was of the same type (for example, a semantic relationship) as that induced at input; third, different cues—in this case retrieval cues represented the alternative relationship to the target words to that emphasized at input. All cues were equated for their prior likelihood of generating the target word. Again, the purpose of Experiment 3 was to explore the possible interactions between depth of processing at input and the compatibility of encoding and retrieval cue at output.

Method

Twenty-four undergraduates were presented with 62 pairs of words, visually, at a 4-sec rate. The subjects were instructed to learn the word in capital letters in each pair but also to pay attention to the accompanying context word in lowercase letters "since it may help you to remember the word." Half of the context words rhymed with the target word and half of the context words were high associates of the target word. Of the 62 words presented, 4 were untested primacy buffer items and 4 were untested recency items. Immediately following presentation of all 62 pairs, the 54 middle items were tested by presenting one of the three types of cue, at the rate of 10 sec per cue. Each of the 54 cues was meant to refer to only one of the test items, and was either the *identical* word present at input, a cue word bearing a *similar* relation (rhyme or associate) to the target word, or a word bearing a *different* relation to the target word (e.g. rhyme cue for a target word encoded in the presence of an associate). Thus, if the presented pair was HAIL (pail), the identical cue was "rhymes with pail," the similar retrieval cue was "rhymes with bail," and the different cue was "associated with snow." If the encoding context was HAIL (sleet) the identical cue was "associated with sleet," the similar cue was "associated with snow," and the different retrieval cue was "rhymes with bail."

The words and cues were those used in Experiment 2. The three types of cue were equated for potency—that is, for the a priori likelihood of generating the target word from the cue. Thus, there were two types of encoding context (rhyme and associate) and three levels of similarity between the encoding context and the retrieval cue (identical, similar, and different). The two independent variables—encoding context and similarity between encoding and cue—were factorially combined in a within-subjects design. Assignment of target words to experimental condition was counterbalanced across subjects.

Results

Table 3 shows the probability of cued recall under the various experimental conditions. Clearly, the similarity of the cue to the original encoding had an effect on recall; the more similar the cue, the higher the level of recall. Also, there was an effect of depth of processing in that, at each level of similarity between encoding context and cue, the associative encoding yielded the higher level of recall. Finally, there is apparently an interaction between encoding type and similarity of cue to encoding context, since the superiority of associative over rhyme context is greater at higher degrees of similarity. These impressions were confirmed by an analysis of variance; the effects of encoding context, $F(1, 22) = 18.7$, $p < .01$; similarity of cue to encoding context, $F(2, 44) = 19.1$, $p < .01$; and the interaction between similarity and encoding context, $F(2, 44) = 6.71$, $p < .01$, were all statistically reliable.

TABLE 3   Proportions of Words Recalled as a Function of Encoding Context and Similarity Between Encoding Context and Retrieval Cue

	Encoding Context		
Encoding/Retrieval Similarity	Rhyme	Associate	M
Identical	.24	.54	.39
Similar	.18	.36	.27
Different	.16	.22	.19
M	.19	.37	

The results of Experiment 3 thus confirm that both type of encoding and similarity of cue to encoding context play a major role in determining the level of recall. The results also show that the superiority of semantic over phonemic processing is greatest when the identical cue is used; thus, when retrieval conditions are optimized by re-presenting the context word as a cue, the semantic–phonemic difference is increased, not decreased. This finding again speaks against the possibility that the advantage to semantic encoding lies with its differential compatibility with spontaneously generated retrieval cues. Viewed from a slightly different angle, the interaction shown in

Table 3 could be described as showing that the beneficial effects of similarity between encoding context and cue are greatest with deep, semantic encodings.

The interaction between encoding type and cue type persists under conditions of extralist cuing (*similar* and *different* conditions in Table 3). When *similar* rhymes and associates were used as cues, recall was .18 and .36 for the rhyme and association encoding conditions, respectively. When *different* cues were used, the corresponding figures were .16 and .22. These results again disconfirm the idea that semantic encodings are simply "stronger" than phonemic encodings; recall performance depends on both encoding condition and the cue used.

One final point may be made about the results shown in Table 3. The notion that memory performance depends on the reinstatement of the encoding context at retrieval seems generally accepted (Melton, 1963; Tulving & Thomson, 1973); a strong version of this notion might state that reinstatement of the learning context is the *only* important factor, and that performance is a function of how completely the original context is reinstated at retrieval. However, the data in Table 3 do not support the strong version of the reinstatement notion. Although it is obviously difficult to compare differences in similarity of input context to retrieval cue between rhyme and associative encodings, it seems reasonable to conclude that the *identical* cue in the rhyme condition is more like its encoding context than is the *similar* cue in the associative condition. Yet the rhyme–*identical* condition is associated with a substantially lower level (.24) of cued recall than the associate–*similar* condition (.36). An even stronger comparison may be made between the rhyme–*identical* and associate–*different* conditions; the similarity between cue and encoding context must presumably be stronger in the former case, yet cued-recall levels are virtually identical. These comparisons lead to the conclusion that both the qualitative nature of the encoding and the degree of overlap between encoding context and cue are important determiners of recall. In general, the pattern of results observed in Experiment 3 is similar to that found by Brooks (1974), with the exception that rhymes were relatively better cues in Brooks's study. We believe that this is due to the different methods used to equate the preexperimental potency of the rhyme and associate cues, with the result that Brooks's rhyme cues were relatively more potent—preexperimentally—than ours.

GENERAL DISCUSSION

The questions posed in the introduction have mostly been answered during discussion of the separate experiments; however, the points will be restated briefly and their theoretical implications considered. First, the present results again emphasize the need to take qualitative differences into account when describing the phenomena of memory. In the present experiments, as in previous studies (Craik & Tulving, 1975; Hyde & Jenkins, 1969, 1973), qualitative differences in encoding and retrieval operations had large effects on performance. Further, it was found that the retention levels associated with a particular type of encoding were not fixed but depended heavily on the type of retrieval cue used. This observed interaction between trace information and cue information fits well with Tulving's (1974) views of cue-dependent forgetting but is apparently incompatible with a unidimensional strength view of memory. Second, the present results disconfirmed the possibility that the lower levels of retention associated with phonemic and structural encoding observed in previous experiments were due to a mismatch between encoded information and the retrieval operations typically utilized. In the present studies, when retrieval cues were made compatible with the encoded information, differences between phonemic and semantic encodings were enhanced, not diminished. Whereas the optimal situation for high levels of memory performance appears to involve semantic encodings in conjunction with identical semantic retrieval cues, it was also found that the retention of phonemically encoded items was highest when identical phonemic cues were provided at retrieval. Both the qualitative nature of the encoding and the degree of compatibility between encoding and cue are apparently necessary to give an adequate account of memory processes. No one factor in isolation—the type of encoding, the type of cue, or the compatibility between encoding and cue—is by itself sufficient to describe performance.

Experiment 3 showed that the beneficial effects of similarity between input context and retrieval cue were greater with semantic encodings than with phonemic encodings. This interaction between depth of processing and differences in retrieval conditions was also reported by Moscovitch and Craik (1976). They found that the difference in free-recall levels between phonemic and semantic encodings was increased under cued recall conditions; also, the semantic superiority was increased when each encoded word had its own unique cue compared to the situation in which several words shared each cue. Cued recall and unique links between target word and cue may both be regarded as examples of "good" retrieval conditions, and both were differentially beneficial to semantic encodings. Moscovitch and Craik suggested that deeper, semantic encodings establish a higher potential ceiling on performance and that retrieval conditions determine the extent to which that potential is realized. By this argument, semantic encodings stand to gain more, so to speak, as retrieval conditions improve. In the present experiments, retrieval conditions were manipulated by varying the similarity between encoding and retrieval contexts; it is suggested that these results may also be viewed as examples of differentially effective retrieval conditions tapping the greater potential of semantic encodings to different extents. Finally, in this section, it should be noted that the foregoing discussion applies only to cases in which the target item is congruent with the context; in cases where the target cannot be readily integrated with the context, manipulations of retrieval conditions have relatively little effect (negative responses in Table 1 of the present study; Craik & Tulving, 1975, Experiment 7; Moscovitch & Craik, 1976, Experiment 1).

What is the reason for the higher levels of retention associated with semantic encodings? Craik and Lockhart (1972) suggested that the traces of deeper encodings decayed less rapidly, that such encodings were more durable in the system. An alternative description, which now seems preferable, is that semantic encodings are typically more distinctive, more discriminable from other memory traces. The importance of uniqueness or "isolation" in episodic memory was stressed by Koffka (1935) in a discussion of Von Restorff's experiments; more recently, the notion that deeper, semantic encodings are more dis-

tinctive was advanced by Klein and Saltz (1976). Both Lesgold and Goldman (1973) and Moscovitch and Craik (1976) explicitly manipulated uniqueness and found greater uniqueness in encoding to be associated with higher levels of recall. Further, Moscovitch and Craik found that the beneficial effects of uniqueness were restricted to semantic encodings; uniqueness did not benefit phonemic encodings. This last finding echoes the results and conclusions of Jacoby (1974) and of Nelson and his colleagues (Nelson & Borden, in press ; Nelson et al., 1974); these workers suggested that phonemic encodings are less modified by the specific encoding context than are semantic encodings and that phonemic encodings are less distinctive. The greater distinctiveness of semantic encodings will only benefit memory, however, if the modifying context is present at both encoding and at retrieval (Nelson & Borden, in press; Tulving & Thomson, 1973). Two further implications of this view are, first, that if semantic encodings are made more similar to one another, they will be remembered little better than phonemic encodings (Moscovitch & Craik, 1976, Experiment 2); second, that the retrieval of phonemic encoding is less affected than is the retrieval of semantic encodings by changes in retrieval context (Experiment 3 in the present series).

In conclusion, a final link between notions of levels of processing and encoding specificity is speculatively suggested by the results of Experiment 3. It seems possible, as outlined above, that deeper encodings are more discriminable from other traces; they are relatively unique and contain more specific information and less general, shared information than shallow encodings. If this description is accurate, it follows that shallow encodings may be elicited to some extent by a relatively broad range of retrieval cues, whereas deep encodings require specific cue information for successful retrieval. On the other hand, successful retrieval of a deep encoding will entail a fuller and more adequate reinstatement of the original event. That is, there may be a trade-off between shallow and deep encodings such that the information in shallow encodings can rarely be used to recreate the original percept clearly (due to the similarity of shallow encodings to other traces in the system), but this degree of remembering may be accomplished with the help of a broad range of cues. Deep encodings require more specific cues before the percept is elicited to any extent, but remembering is excellent when that specific cue is provided.

REFERENCE NOTE

1. Owings, R. A. *Levels of processing, encoding specificity, and retrieval of semantically, phonetically, and graphically encoded words.* Manuscript submitted for publication, 1977.

REFERENCES

Anderson, J. R., & Bower, G. H. Recognition and retrieval processes in free recall. *Psychological Review*, 1972, *79*, 97–123.

Arbuckle, T. Y., & Katz, W. A. Structure of memory traces following semantic and nonsemantic orientation tasks in incidental learning. *Journal of Experimental Psychology: Human Learning and Memory*, 1976, *2*, 362–369.

Baddeley, A. D. How does acoustic similarity influence short-term memory? *Quarterly Journal of Experimental Psychology*, 1968, *20*, 249–264.

Brooks, D. H. *The processing of word features in cued recall.* Unpublished doctoral dissertation, University of South Florida, 1974.

Craik, F. I. M., & Lockhart, R. S. Levels of processing: A framework for memory research. *Journal of Verbal Learning and Verbal Behavior*, 1972, *11*, 671–684.

Craik, F. I. M., & Tulving, E. Depth of processing and the retention of words in episodic memory. *Journal of Experimental Psychology: General*, 1975, *104*, 268–294.

Hyde, T. S., & Jenkins, J. J. Differential effects of incidental tasks on the organization of recall of a list of highly associated words. *Journal of Experimental Psychology*, 1969, *82*, 472–481.

Hyde, T. S., & Jenkins, J. J. Recall for words as a function of semantic, graphic, and syntactic orienting tasks. *Journal of Verbal Learning and Verbal Behavior*, 1973, *12*, 471–480.

Jacoby, L. L. The role of mental contiguity in memory: Registration and retrieval effects. *Journal of Verbal Learning and Verbal Behavior*, 1974, *13*, 483–496.

Klein, K., & Saltz, E. Specifying the mechanisms in a levels-of-processing approach to memory. *Journal of Experimental Psychology: Human Learning and Memory*, 1976, *2*, 671–679.

Koffka, K. *Principles of Gestalt psychology.* New York: Harcourt, Brace, 1935.

Lesgold, A. M., & Goldman, S. R. Encoding uniqueness and the imagery mnemonic in associative learning. *Journal of Verbal Learning and Verbal Behavior*, 1973, *12*, 193–202.

Melton, A. W. Implications of short-term memory for a general theory of memory. *Journal of Verbal Learning and Verbal Behavior*, 1963, *2*, 1–21.

Moscovitch, M., & Craik, F. I. M. Depth of processing, retrieval cues, and uniqueness of encoding as factors in recall. *Journal of Verbal Learning and Verbal Behavior*, 1976, *15*, 447–458.

Nelson, D. L., & Borden, R. C. Encoding and retrieval effects of dual sensory–semantic cues. *Memory & Cognition*, in press.

Nelson, D. L., Wheeler, J. W., Jr., Borden, R. C., & Brooks, D. H. Levels of processing and cuing: Sensory versus meaning features. *Journal of Experimental Psychology*, 1974, *103*, 971–977.

Schulman, A. Memory for words recently classified. *Memory & Cognition*, 1974, *2*, 47–52.

Tulving, E. Cue-dependent forgetting. *American Scientist*, 1974, *62*, 74–82.

Tulving, E., & Osler, S. Effectiveness of retrieval cues in memory for words. *Journal of Experimental Psychology*, 1968, *77*, 593–601.

Tulving, E., & Thomson, D. M. Encoding specificity and retrieval processes in episodic memory. *Psychological Review*, 1973, *80*, 352–373.

Watkins, O. C., & Watkins, M. J. Buildup of proactive inhibition as a cue-overload effect. *Journal of Experimental Psychology: Human Learning and Memory*, 1975, *104*, 442–452.

Wickelgren, W. A. Multitrace strength theory. In D. A. Norman (Ed.), *Models of human memory.* New York: Academic Press, 1970.

POSTSCRIPT

Tulving (1979) argues that results such as those obtained by Fisher and Craik in this selection can be explained just in terms of encoding specificity—that is, that one does not have to appeal to additional levels-of-processing or distinctiveness effects. Craik (1979), however, has defended the interpretation presented here. Both might agree, however, that the effects of distinctiveness and levels of processing on memory can only be understood in the context of recognizing the crucial role played by the relationship between information initially encoded and information available at the time of retrieval—the encoding-specificity principle (cf. Craik, 1979, and Jacoby & Craik, 1979).

Some (such as Postman, 1975) have questioned the generality of the encoding-specificity principle. However, a variety of experiments (reviewed in Tulving, 1983) support its broad applicability. In fact, one problem with the encoding-specificity principle is that it is unclear exactly how it can be falsified (Tulving, 1983). For example, if a retrieval cue fails to facilitate remembering, it is entirely consistent with the encoding-specificity principle to maintain that the cue had not been encoded, not that the principle has failed. Despite this problem, Tulving and others (for example, Baddeley, 1990) believe that the encoding-specificity principle remains an important concept.

FOR FURTHER THOUGHT

1. In their introduction, Fisher and Craik argue that because the levels-of-processing approach does not take into account processes at retrieval, the Craik and Tulving (1975) results might have been explainable by the encoding-specificity principle. What assumption must be made for the encoding-specificity principle to explain the Craik and Tulving (1975) results? How should the experiments reported in Fisher and Craik's study have turned out to support that possibility? What do their results suggest instead?

2. In their introduction, Fisher and Craik argue that the distinctiveness principle suggested by Moscovitch and Craik (1976) may explain why deeper processing leads to better memorability. Describe this explanation in your own words. What do Fisher and Craik's results suggest about this explanation?

3. What did Fisher and Craik find with negative responses in Experiment 1? How do they explain this result? Is this result predicted by the levels-of-processing, encoding-specificity, or distinctiveness principles? Does it pose a problem for these principles?

4. What two changes distinguished Experiment 2 from Experiment 1? Which alternative hypotheses (explanations other than those Fisher and Craik wished to put forward) did Experiment 2 eliminate?
5. What new information was gained from Experiment 3?

REFERENCES

Baddeley, A. D. (1990). *Human memory: Theory and practice.* Boston: Allyn & Bacon.

Craik, F. I. M. (1979). Levels of processing: Overview and closing comments. In L. S. Cermak & F. I. M. Craik (Eds.), *Levels of processing and human memory* (pp. 447–461). Hillsdale, NJ: Erlbaum.

Craik, F. I. M., & Lockhart, R. S. (1972). Levels of processing: A framework for memory research. *Journal of Verbal Learning and Verbal Behavior, 11,* 671–684.

Craik, F. I. M., & Tulving, E. (1975). Depth of processing and the retention of words in episodic memory. *Journal of Experimental Psychology: General, 104,* 268–294.

Hyde, T. S., & Jenkins, J. J. (1973). Recall for words as a function of semantic, graphic, and syntactic orienting tasks. *Journal of Verbal Learning and Verbal Behavior, 12,* 471–480.

Jacoby, L. L., & Craik, F. I. M. (1979). Effects of elaboration of processing at encoding and retrieval: Trace distinctiveness and recovery of initial context. In L. S. Cermak & F. I. M. Craik (Eds.), *Levels of processing and human memory* (pp. 1–21). Hillsdale, NJ: Erlbaum.

Moscovitch, M., & Craik, F. I. M. (1976). Depth of processing, retrieval cues, and uniqueness of encoding as factors in recall. *Journal of Verbal Learning and Verbal Behavior, 15,* 447–458.

Postman, L. (1975). Tests of the generality of the principle of encoding specificity. *Memory & Cognition, 3,* 663–672.

Thomson, D. M., & Tulving, E. (1970). Associative encoding and retrieval: Weak and strong cues. *Journal of Experimental Psychology, 86,* 255–262.

Tulving, E. (1979). Relation between encoding specificity and levels of processing. In L. S. Cermak & F. I. M. Craik (Eds.), *Levels of processing and human memory* (pp. 405–428). Hillsdale, NJ: Erlbaum.

Tulving, E. (1983). *Elements of episodic memory.* New York: Oxford University Press.

Tulving, E., & Osler, S. (1968). Effectiveness of retrieval cues in memory for words. *Journal of Experimental Psychology, 77,* 593–601.

Tulving, E., & Thomson, D. M. (1973). Encoding specificity and retrieval processes in episodic memory. *Psychological Review, 80,* 352–373.

Part II

Representation of Knowledge

The two chapters in Part II deal with various issues regarding the mental representation of knowledge. Chapter Four (Organization and Priming of Knowledge) focuses on two issues. The first issue is how the organization of our knowledge affects the ease with which we are able to answer different kinds of questions. Reading 12 describes a model of knowledge about objects whereas Reading 13 describes one of events. The second issue addressed in Chapter Four is the phenomenon of *priming*, which cognitive psychologists often use to examine how we organize and access knowledge. Reading 14 examines one form of priming—called semantic or associative priming—and Reading 15 examines another—called perceptual, repetition, or direct priming. Reading 15 also demonstrates how useful neuropsychological data are for extending our understanding of knowledge organization.

A third issue in the mental representation of knowledge deals with the kinds of knowledge being represented. One basic kind of knowledge we have is knowledge about categories. If we did not categorize objects or events, we would find it difficult to reason about or interact with our environment efficiently: our thinking about each novel object or event would have to start from scratch every time. On the other hand, once we categorize a novel object as a chair, we know a lot about it. But just what do we know about it?

What kinds of information do we store about categories, and what are the implications of placing something in a mental category? Three of the readings in Chapter Five (Concepts and Imagery) look at different aspects of these questions. The experiments in Reading 16 argue strongly against the view that once we identify two items as instances of the same concept, we treat them equivalently (that is, once we know that two objects are both chairs, we treat them in exactly the same fashion). The experiments in Reading 17 examine the nature of the different levels of abstraction we can use to categorize an object (for example, as an animal versus a dog versus a golden retriever) and the effects that different individuals' knowledge about an area has on what is their most natural or basic level of abstraction. Reading 18 describes a computer model that demonstrates how our knowledge about categories and about individual members of categories can be integrated.

In addition to knowledge about categories, people have knowledge about visual characteristics and spatial relationships. Reading 19 presents evidence that different parts of the brain are responsible for representing and/or processing visual and spatial knowledge.

CHAPTER FOUR
Organization and Priming of Knowledge

INTRODUCTION

In "Retrieval Time from Semantic Memory" Allan Collins and M. Ross Quillian describe and test a model of the knowledge, called semantic memory, that people use to verify the truth of certain simple factual statements. It is an early and extremely influential example of a computer model adapted as a description of human cognition.

Collins and Quillian's model makes certain structural and processing assumptions. It assumes that semantic memory is structured as a network consisting of nodes (which may be of one or many different kinds) and paths between nodes (which may also be of one or many kinds). In Collins and Quillian's network, there are two kinds of nodes—set nodes, such as *bird*, and property nodes, such as *wings*—and the paths are unidirectional and all of one kind (called *pointers*). For example, according to this model, our knowledge of canaries—our semantic memory representation of canaries—consists of a set node labeled *canary* and the set of pointers that lead from the canary node to other set and property nodes. (For examples of two very different kinds of network approaches, ACT* and PDP, see Anderson, 1983, and Reading 6 or 18, respectively.)

Because this model was originally developed as a method for representing semantic memory in a computer with limited memory, it places a premium on economy of representation. This economy is achieved through the use of two structural principles: strict hierarchical organization and placement of properties at their highest level of generalizability. Although Collins and Quillian focus on describing and testing predictions derived from these two principles, they recognize that these principles may not apply to all words or to all people. Nevertheless, the model has come to be known as the hierarchical network model.

The basic processing assumption made by this model is that it takes a certain amount of time to trace over a path from one node to another. Using several more specific processing assumptions (described in their introduction), Collins and Quillian test the applicability of this model as a description of human semantic memory for a limited set of words. As you read, ask yourself: How general is Collins and Quillian's model? Is the approach taken here appropriate for other kinds of tasks, such as deciding which of two animals is bigger, or for other kinds of categories and properties?

Retrieval Time from Semantic Memory

Allan M. Collins and M. Ross Quillian
Bolt Beranek and Newman, Inc.

Quillian (1967, 1969) has proposed a model for storing semantic information in a computer memory. In this model each word has stored with it a configuration of pointers to other words in the memory; this configuration represents the word's meaning. Figure 1 illustrates the organization of such a memory structure. If what is stored with canary is "a yellow bird that can sing" then there is a pointer to bird, which is the category name or *superset* of canary, and pointers to two *properties,* that a canary is yellow and that it can sing. Information true of birds in general (such as that they can fly, and that they have wings and feathers) need not be stored with the memory node for each separate kind of bird. Instead, the fact that a canary can fly can be inferred by retrieving that a canary is a bird and that birds can fly. Since an ostrich cannot fly, we assume this information is stored as a property with the node for ostrich, just as is done in a dictionary, to preclude the inference that an ostrich can fly. By organizing the memory in this way, the amount of space needed for storage is minimized.

If we take this as a model for the structure of human memory, it can lead to testable predictions about retrieving information. Suppose a person has only the information shown in Figure 1 stored on each of the nodes. Then to decide "A canary can sing," the person need only start at the node canary and retrieve the properties stored there to find the statement is true. But, to decide that "A canary can fly," the person must move up one level to bird before he can retrieve the property about flying. Therefore, the person should require more *time* to decide that "A canary can fly" than he does to decide that "A canary can sing." Similarly, the person should require still longer to decide that "A canary has skin," since this fact is stored with his node for animal, which is yet another step removed from canary. More directly, sentences which themselves assert something about a node's supersets, such as "A canary is a bird," or "A canary is an animal," should also require decision times that vary directly with the number of levels separating the memory nodes they talk about.

A number of assumptions about the retrieval process must be made before predictions such as those above can be stated explicitly. First, we need to assume that both retrieving a property from a node and moving up a level in a hierarchy take a person time. Second, we shall assume that the times for these two processes are additive, whenever one step is dependent on completion of another step. This assumption is equivalent to Donders' assumption of additivity (Smith, 1968) for the following two cases: (a) When moving up a level is followed by moving up another level, and (b) when moving up a level is followed by retrieving a property at the higher level. Third, we assume that the time to retrieve a property from a node is independent of the level of the node, although different properties may take different times to retrieve from the same node. It also seems reasonable to assume that searching properties at a node and moving up to the next level occur in a parallel rather than a serial manner, and hence are not

This research was supported by the Aerospace Medical Research Laboratories, Aerospace Medical Division, Air Force Systems Command, Wright-Patterson Air Force Base, Ohio, under Contract No. F33615-67-C-1982 with Bolt Beranek and Newman, Inc. and also partly by Advanced Research Projects Agency, monitored by the Air Force Cambridge Research Laboratories, under Contract No. F19628-68-C-0125.

SOURCE: *Journal of Verbal Learning and Verbal Behavior, 8,* 1969, pp. 240–247. Copyright © 1969 by Academic Press, Inc. Reprinted by permission.

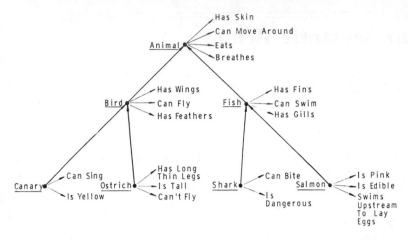

FIGURE 1   Illustration of the hypothetical memory structure for a 3-level hierarchy.

additive. However, this assumption is not essential, and our reasons for preferring it are made clear in the Discussion section.

We have labeled sentences that state property relations P sentences, and those that state superset relations S sentences. To these labels numbers are appended. These indicate the number of levels the model predicts it would be necessary to move through to decide the sentence is true. Thus, "A canary can sing" would be a P0 sentence, "A canary can fly" would be a P1 sentence, and "A canary has skin" would be a P2 sentence. Similarly, "A canary is a canary" would be an S0 sentence, "A canary is a bird" would be an S1 sentence, and "A canary is an animal" would be an S2 sentence.

It follows from the assumptions above that the time differences predicted for P0, P1, and P2 sentences are entirely a result of moving from one level in the hierarchy to the next. Thus, the increase in time from S0 to S1 should be the same as from P0 to P1 since both increases are a result of moving from level 0 to level 1. Likewise, the time increase from S1 to S2 should equal the time increase from P1 to P2. In fact, if we assume that the time to move from one level to the next is not dependent on which levels are involved, all the time increases (from P0 to P1, P1 to P2, S0 to S1, and S1 to S2) should be equal.

Recently, reaction time (RT) has been used as a measure of the time it takes people to retrieve infor-

mation from memory. By constructing a large number of true sentences of the six types discussed and interspersing these with equal numbers of false sentences, we can measure the reaction time for Ss to decide which sentences are true and which are false. Thus, this method can be used to test the prediction we have derived from the model and our assumptions about the retrieval process.

A caution is in order here: Dictionary definitions are not very orderly and we doubt that human memory, which is far richer, is even as orderly as a dictionary. One difficulty is that hierarchies are not always clearly ordered, as exemplified by dog, mammal, and animal. Subjects tend to categorize a dog as an animal, even though a stricter classification would interpose the category mammal between the two. A second difficulty is that people surely store certain properties at more than one level in the hierarchy. For example, having leaves is a general property of trees, but many people must have information stored about the maple leaf directly with maple, because of the distinctiveness of its leaf. In selecting examples, such hierarchies and instances were avoided. However, there will always be Ss for whom extensive familiarity will lead to the storing of many more properties (and sometimes supersets) than we have assumed. By averaging over different examples and different subjects, the effect of such individual idiosyncrasies of memory can be minimized.

METHOD

Three experiments were run, with eight Ss used in each experiment. The Ss were all employees of Bolt Beranek and Newman, Inc. who served voluntarily and had no knowledge of the nature of the experiment. Because of a faulty electrical connection, only three Ss gave usable data in Expt. 3. The same general method was used for all three experiments, except in the way the false sentences were constructed.

Apparatus.   The sentences were displayed one at a time on the cathode ray tube (CRT) of a DEC PDP-1 computer.[1] The timing and recording of responses were under program control.[2] Each sentence was centered vertically on one line. The length of line varied from 10 to 34 characters (approximately 4–11° visual angle). The S sat directly in front of the CRT with his two index fingers resting on the two response buttons. These each required a displacement of ¼ inch to trigger a microswitch.

Procedure.   The sentences were grouped in runs of 32 or 48, with a rest period of approximately 1 min between runs. Each sentence appeared on the CRT for 2 sec, and was followed by a blank screen for 2 sec before the next sentence. The S was instructed to press one button if the sentence was generally true, and the other button if it was generally false, and he was told to do so as accurately and as quickly as possible. The S could respond anytime within the 4 sec between sentences, but his response did not alter the timing of the sentences. Each S was given a practice run of 32 sentences similarly constructed.

Sentences.   There were two kinds of semantic hierarchies used in constructing sentences for the experiments, 2-level and 3-level. In Figure 1, a 2-level hierarchy might include bird, canary, and ostrich and their properties, whereas the whole diagram represents a 3-level hierarchy. A 2-level hierarchy included true P0, P1, S0, and S1 sentences; a 3-level hierarchy

included true P2 and S2 sentences as well. Examples of sentence sets with 2-level and 3-level hierarchies are given in Table 1.[3] As illustrated in Table 1, equal numbers of true and false sentences were always present (but in random sequence) in the sentences an S read. Among both true and false sentences, there are the two general kinds: Property relations (P), and superset relations (S).

In Expt 1, each S read 128 two-level sentences followed by 96 three-level sentences. In Expt 2, each S read 128 two-level sentences, but different sentences from those used in Expt 1. In Expt 3, a different group of Ss read the same 96 three-level sentences used in Expt 1. Each run consisted of sentences from only four subject-matter hierarchies.

To generate the sentences we first picked a hierarchical group with a large set of what we shall call *instances* at the lowest level. For example, baseball, badminton, etc. are instances of the superset game. Different instances were used in each sentence, because repetition of a word is known to have substantial effects in reducing RT (Smith, 1967). In constructing S1 and S2 sentences, the choice of the category name or superset was in most cases obvious, though in a case such as the above 2-level example, sport might have been used as the superset rather than game. To assess how well our choices corresponded with the way most people categorize, two individuals who did not serve in any of the three experiments were asked to generate a category name for each S1 and S2 sentence we used, e.g., "tennis is _____ ." These two individuals generated the category names we used in about ¾ of their choices, and only in one case, "wine is a drink" instead of "liquid," was their choice clearly not synonymous.

In generating sentences that specified properties, only the verbs "is," "has," and "can" were used, where "is" was always followed by an adjective, "has" by a noun, and "can" by a verb. To produce the P0 sentence one of the instances such as baseball was chosen

---

[1]Now at the University of Massachusetts, Amherst.

[2]The authors thank Ray Nickerson for the use of his program and for his help in modifying it to run on BBN's PDP-1.

[3]To obtain the entire set of true sentences for Expt 1 order NAPS Document NAPS-00265 from ASIS National Auxiliary Publications Service, c/o CCM Information Sciences, Inc., 22 West 34th Street, New York, New York 10001; remitting $1.00 for microfiche or $3.00 for photocopies.

TABLE 1   Illustrative Sets of Stimulus Sentences

	Sentence Type	True Sentences	Sentence Type[a]	False Sentences
Expt 1, 2-level				
	P0	Baseball has innings	P	Checkers has pawns
	P1	Badminton has rules	P	Ping pong has baskets
	S0	Chess is chess	S	Hockey is a race
	S1	Tennis is a game	S	Football is a lottery
Expt 1, 3-level				
	P0	An oak has acorns	P	A hemlock has buckeyes
	P1	A spruce has branches	P	A poplar has thorns
	P2	A birch has seeds	P	A dogwood is lazy
	S0	A maple is a maple	S	A pine is barley
	S1	A cedar is a tree	S	A juniper is grain
	S2	An elm is a plant	S	A willow is grass
Expt 2, 2-level				
	P0	Seven-up is colorless	P0	Coca-cola is blue
	P1	Ginger ale is carbonated	P1	Lemonade is alcoholic
	S0	Pepsi-cola is Pepsi-cola	S0	Bitter lemon is orangeade
	S1	Root beer is a soft drink	S1	Club soda is wine

[a] There were no distinctions as to level made for false sentences in Expt 1.

that had a property (in this case innings) which was clearly identifiable with the instance and not the superset. To generate a P1 or P2 sentence, we took a salient property of the superset that could be expressed with the restriction to "is," "has," or "can." In the first example of Table 1, rules were felt to be a very salient property of games. Then an instance was chosen, in this case badminton, to which the P1 property seemed not particularly associated. Our assumption was that, if the model is correct, a typical S would decide whether badminton has rules or not by the path, badminton is a game and games have rules.

In Expt 1, false sentences were divided equally between supersets and properties. No systematic basis was used for constructing false sentences beyond an attempt to produce sentences that were not unreasonable or semantically anomalous, and that were always untrue rather than usually untrue. In Expt 2, additional restrictions were placed on the false sentences. The properties of the false P0 sentences were chosen so as to contradict a property of the instance itself. In example 3 of Table 1, "Coca-cola is blue" contradicts a property of Coca-cola, that it is brown or caramel-colored. In contrast, the properties of false P1 sentences were chosen so as to contradict a

property of the superset. In the same example, alcoholic was chosen, because it is a contradiction of a property of soft drinks in general. The relation of elements in the false S0 and S1 sentences can be illustrated by reference to Figure 1. The false S0 sentences were generated by stating that one instance of a category was equivalent to another, such as "A canary is an ostrich." The false S1 sentence was constructed by choosing a category one level up from the instance, but in a different branch of the structure, such as "A canary is a fish."

The sequence of sentences the S saw was randomly ordered, except for the restriction to four hierarchies in each run. The runs were counterbalanced over Ss with respect to the different sentence types, and each button was assigned true for half the Ss, and false for the other half.

RESULTS AND DISCUSSION

In analyzing the data from the three experiments, we have used the mean RT for each S's correct responses only. Error rates were on the average about 8% and tended to increase where RT increased.

Deciding a Sentence Is True

The data from all three experiments have been averaged in Figure 2. To evaluate the differences shown there for true sentences, two separate analyses of variance were performed: One for the 2-level runs and one for the 3-level runs. For the 2-level data the difference between P sentences and S sentences was significant, $F(1, 60) = 19.73$, $p < .01$, the difference between levels was significant, $F(1, 60) = 7.74$, $p < .01$, but the interaction was not quite significant, $F(1, 60) = 2.06$. For the 3-level data, the difference between P and S sentences was significant, $F(1, 60) = 27.02$, $p < .01$, the difference between levels was significant, $F(2, 60) = 5.68$, $p < .01$, and the interaction was not significant, $F < 1$.

Our prediction was that the RT curves for P0, P1, and P2 sentences and for S0, S1, and S2 sentences should be two parallel straight lines. The results are certainly compatible with this prediction, except for the S0 point, which is somewhat out of line. It was anticipated that presenting the entire sentence on the CRT at one time would permit the Ss to answer the S0 sentences, e.g., "A maple is a maple," by pattern matching. That they did so was substantiated by spontaneous reports from several Ss that on the S0 sentences they often did not even think what the sentence said. Overall, the underlying model is supported by these data.

It can also be concluded, if one accepts the model and disregards the S0 point as distorted by pattern matching, that the time to move from a node to its superset is on the order of 75 msec, this figure being the average RT increase from P0 to P1, P1 to P2, and S1 to S2. The differences between S1 and P1 and between S2 and P2, which average to about 225 msec, represent the time it takes to retrieve a property from the node at the level where we assume it is stored.

We have assumed that retrieval of properties at a node and moving up to the superset of the node are parallel processes, but this was not a necessary assumption. In actual fact the computer realization of the model completes the search for properties at a node *before* moving up one level to its superset. If the property search is assumed to be complete before moving up to the next level, then the 75 msec would have to be divided into two processes: (a) The time spent searching for properties, and (b) the time to

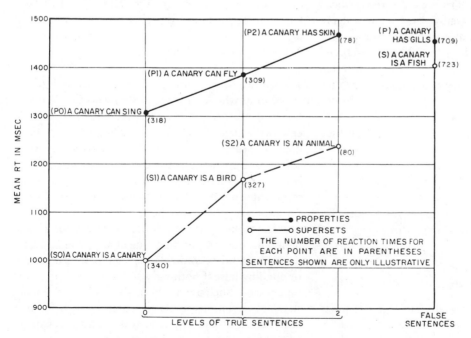

FIGURE 2   Average reaction times for different types of sentences in three experiments.

move up to the superset. If such an assumption is made, then there is no clear prediction as to whether the increases for P sentences should parallel the increases for S sentences. If, given an S-type sentence, the *S* could dispense with process (a) above, then the slope of the curve for S sentences would be less than for P sentences; if he could not, then the prediction of two parallel lines would still hold. However, the fact that the time attributable to retrieving a property from a node is much longer than the time to move from one node to the next suggests that the processing is in fact parallel. It is unlikely that a search of all the properties at a node could be completed before moving up to the next level in less than 75 msec, *if* it takes some 225 msec actually to retrieve a property when it is found at a node. This might be reasonable if most of the 225 msec was spent in verification or some additional process necessary when the search at a node is successful, but attributing most of the 225 msec to such a process involves the unlikely assumption that this process takes much longer for P sentences than for S sentences. If it were the same for both sentence types, then it would not contribute to the difference (the 225 msec) between their RTs.

Since any other systematic differences between sentence types might affect RTs, we did three further checks. We computed the average number of letters for each sentence type and also weighted averages of the word-frequencies based on the Thorndike-Lorge (1944) general count. Then we asked four *S*s to rate how important each property was for the relevant instance or superset, e.g., how important it is for birds that they can fly. In general, we found no effects that could account for the differences in Figure 2 on the basis of sentence lengths, frequency counts, or subject ratings of importance. The only exception to this is that the higher frequency of superset words such as bird and animal in the predicates of S1 and S2 sentences may have lowered the averages for S1 and S2 sentences relative to those for P sentences.

Deciding a Sentence Is False

There are a number of conceivable strategies or processes by which a person might decide a sentence is false. All of these involve a search of memory; they fall into two classes on the basis of how the search is assumed to terminate.

The Contradiction Hypothesis. Under this hypothesis, false responses involve finding a contradiction between information stored in memory and what the statement says. For example, if the sentence is "Coca-cola is blue," the *S* searches memory until he finds a property of Coca-cola (that it is brown or caramel colored) which contradicts the sentence.

The Contradiction Hypothesis was tested by the construction of false sentences for Expt 2. We predicted that the RT increase from P0 to P1 found for true sentences might also be found for false sentences. The difference found was in the right direction, but it was negligibly small (7 msec). Similarly, it was thought that if *S*s search for a contradiction, false S0 sentences should produce faster times than the false S1 sentences since there is one less link in the path between the two nodes for an S0 sentence. (This can be seen by comparing the path in Figure 1 between canary and ostrich as in S0 sentences to the path between canary and fish as in S1 sentences.) The difference turned out to be in the opposite direction by 59 msec on the average, $t(7) = 2.30$, $p < .1$. If anything, one should conclude from the false S0 and S1 sentences in Expt 2 that the closer two nodes are in memory, the longer it takes to decide that they are not related in a stated manner.

The Unsuccessful Search Hypothesis. This is a generalization of what Sternberg (1966) calls the "self-terminating search," one of the two models he considered with regard to his RT studies of short-term memory search. Under this hypothesis an *S* would search for information to decide that a given sentence is true, and, when the search fails, as determined by some criterion, he would respond false. One possible variation, suggested by the longer RTs for false responses, would be that *S*s search memory for a fixed period of time, responding true at any time information is found that confirms the statement is true, and responding false if nothing is found by the end of the time period. Such a hypothesis should lead to smaller standard deviations for false sentences than for true sentences, but the opposite was found for Expt 2, where it could be checked most easily.

The Search and Destroy Hypothesis.   We developed another variation of the Unsuccessful Search Hypothesis after the Contradiction Hypothesis proved unsatisfactory and Ss had been interrogated as to what they thought they were doing on false sentences. Under this hypothesis we assume the S tries to find paths through his memory which connect the subject and predicate of the sentence (e.g., the path "canary "→ bird → animal → has skin" connects the two parts of "A canary has skin"). Whenever he finds such a path he must check to see if it agrees with what is stated in the sentence. When the S has checked to a certain number of levels or "depth" (Quillian, 1967), all connections found having been rejected, the S will then respond false. Under this hypothesis, the times for false sentences will be longer, in general, and highly variable depending upon how many connective paths the S has to check out before rejecting the statement. For instance, assuming people know Coca-cola comes in green bottles, a statement such as "Coca-cola is blue" would on the average take less time than "Coca-cola is green." This is because the S would have to spend time checking whether or not the above path between Coca-cola and green (i.e., that its bottles are green) corresponds to the relation stated in the sentence.

This hypothesis would explain the longer times in Expt 2 for sentences such as "A canary is an ostrich" as compared with "A canary is a fish" in terms of the greater number of connections between canary and ostrich that presumably would have to be checked out. This difference in the number of connections would derive from the greater number of properties that are common to two nodes close together in the network, such as canary and ostrich, than are common to nodes further apart and at different levels, such as canary and fish.

Finding contradictions can be included in this hypothesis, as is illustrated with "Gin is wet." Here the S might make a connection between gin and wet through the path "gin is dry and dry is the opposite of wet." Seeing the contradiction, he rejects this as a basis for responding true, but continues to search for an acceptable path. In this example, if he searches deep enough, he will find the path "gin is liquor, and liquor is liquid, and liquid is wet" which is, in fact, what the sentence requires. The point we want to em-phasize here is that even though a contradiction can be used to reject a path, it cannot be used to reject the truth of a statement.

There are certainly other possible hypotheses, and it is possible that a combination of this hypothesis with the Contradiction Hypothesis may be necessary to explain false judgments. Needless to say, the process by which a person decides that a statement is false does not seem to be very simple.

CONCLUSION

In a computer system designed for the storage of semantic information, it is more economical to store generalized information with superset nodes, rather than with all the individual nodes to which such a generalization might apply. But such a storage system incurs the cost of additional processing time in retrieving information. When the implications of such a model were tested for human Ss using well-ordered hierarchies that are part of the common culture, there was substantial agreement between the predictions and the data.

There is no clear picture that emerges as to how people decide a statement is false. Our current hypothesis, that people must spend time checking out any interpretations that are possible (see the discussion of the Search and Destroy Hypothesis), should be testable, but even corroborative evidence would not clear up many of the questions about such decisions.

The model also makes predictions for other RT tasks utilizing such hierarchies. For instance, if Ss are given the task of deciding what common category two instances belong to, then RT should reflect the number of supersets the S must move through to make the decision. (Consider fish and bird, vs. shark and bird, vs. shark and canary; see Figure 1.) Such RT differences should parallel those in our data. Furthermore, if utilizing a particular path in retrieval increases its accessibility temporarily, then we would expect prior exposure to "A canary is a bird" to have more effect in reducing RT to "A canary can fly" than to "A canary can sing." There are many similar experiments which would serve to pin down more precisely the structure and processing of human semantic memory.

REFERENCES

Quillian, M. R. Word concepts: A theory and simulation of some basic semantic capabilities. *Behavioral Sci.*, 1967, 12, 410–430.

Quillian, M. R. The Teachable Language Comprehender: A simulation program and theory of language. *Communications Assn. Comp. Mach.*, 1969, (In press).

Smith, E. E. Effects of familiarity on stimulus recognition and categorization. *J. exp. Psychol.*, 1967, 74, 324–332.

Smith, E. E. Choice reaction time: An analysis of the major theoretical positions. *Psychol. Bull.*, 1968, 69, 77–110.

Sternberg, S. High-speed scanning in human memory. *Science*, 1966, 153, 652–654.

Thorndike, E. L. and Lorge, I. *The teacher's word book of 30,000 words.* New York: Columbia Univ. Press, 1944.

POSTSCRIPT

Recent studies have demonstrated that people's semantic memories are not arranged strictly hierarchically (see Rips, Shoben, & Smith, 1973, for example), nor are properties placed at the highest level of generality (for instance, Conrad, 1972). In a subsequent clarification and revision (Collins & Loftus, 1975), Collins argued that those assumptions were merely a simplification, never a key part of the Collins and Quillian model, and he suggested that they be abandoned.

Collins and Loftus (1975) propose a "spreading activation" model, in which paths are no longer unidirectional (and so are not called pointers). Instead, "activation" (so called because retrieval of a node involves activating it above some criterial level) can—and does—spread in all directions, with the level of activation diminishing with increasing distance from the initiating node. In addition, the Collins and Loftus model does not limit the nodes connected to one another to those that bear set subset or category property relationships to one another. Paths exist between every two associated nodes. Thus, between "peanut butter" and "jelly," there is a path that activation can travel. Collins and Loftus also stress that not all paths are equal; activation spreads more quickly and easily along some paths than it does along others, although it is difficult to offer an a priori principle for predicting which paths are which.

Unlike Collins and Quillian's original hierarchical network model—at least as it is usually interpreted—the Collins and Loftus spreading activation model is compatible with the large body of data about semantic memory gathered in the 1970s and 1980s, including such effects as priming and typicality (Reading 14 and Reading 16, respectively; see Chang, 1986, for a review). In fact, the spreading activation model has been roundly criticized for having too much flexibility; it is difficult to use the model to predict specific outcomes and rule out others (Johnson-Laird, Herrmann, & Chaffin, 1984; Smith, 1978), a requirement for an adequate scientific theory.

FOR FURTHER THOUGHT

1. Place *penguin* and *robin* in the sample portion of the network described in the article. What kinds of properties would you have to add to make the network deal with these two new instances of bird, and where would you place those properties? Why do you place them where you do?
2. What assumptions do Collins and Quillian make about the time it takes to trace over different paths? Would the credibility of the model be substantially damaged if those assumptions turned out not to be true?
3. What evidence leads Collins and Quillian to believe that tracing over different paths takes place in parallel, rather than serially? What would those results be if tracing over different paths did take place serially?
4. What three hypotheses do Collins and Quillian propose to explain what takes place when a subject is given a false sentence? What assumptions do those hypotheses make? What grounds are there for preferring one over another?
5. What kinds of relationships do you think are necessary for a complete account of semantic memory (aside from those captured in the Collins and Quillian model)? Could those relationships be added to this model without violating its assumptions?

REFERENCES

Anderson, J. R. (1983). *The architecture of cognition.* Cambridge, MA: Harvard University Press.

Chang, T. M. (1986). Semantic memory: Facts and models. *Psychological Bulletin, 99,* 199–220.

Collins, A. M., & Loftus, E. F. (1975). A spreading-activation theory of semantic processing. *Psychological Review, 82,* 407–428.

Conrad, C. (1972). Cognitive economy in semantic memory. *Journal of Experimental Psychology, 92,* 149–154.

Johnson-Laird, P. N., Herrmann, D. J., & Chaffin, R. (1984). Only connections: A critique of semantic networks. *Psychological Bulletin, 96,* 292–315.

Rips, L. J., Shoben, E. J., & Smith, E. E. (1973). Semantic distance and the verification of semantic relations. *Journal of Verbal Learning and Verbal Behavior, 12,* 1–20.

Smith, E. E. (1978). Theories of semantic memory. In W. K. Estes (Ed.), *Handbook of learning and cognitive processes* (Vol. 6, pp. 1–56). Hillsdale, NJ: Erlbaum.

INTRODUCTION

Although much of the research on how people organize their knowledge of the world focuses on knowledge about objects, a great deal of research has also been performed on people's knowledge of everyday activities. One popular view suggests that such knowledge is organized into structures called scripts (Schank & Abelson, 1977). Valerie Abbott, John Black, and Edward Smith investigate the nature of some scripts in their article "The Representation of Scripts in Memory."

Because Abbott, Brown, and Smith are unusually thorough in their explication of the theoretical and empirical background to their work, that background is not repeated here. However, their reporting of results might benefit from some explanation.

When psychologists manipulate more than one variable in an experiment—such as both the instructions and the stimulus—they often use an ANOVA, or F-test, to analyze their results. The F-test allows them to decide whether it is safe to conclude that the effects observed with their subjects are likely to generalize to other subjects of the same sort. This procedure is called analyzing by subjects or analyzing with subjects as random effect. There is often an overlooked constraint to such a conclusion, however; it applies only to other subjects using the same stimuli (and the same instructions, and so on). Often, we would like to know whether the effects observed with a particular set of stimuli can be generalized safely to other similar stimuli. In that case, the analysis must be done by stimuli or with stimuli as random effect. An analysis by stimuli is similarly constrained; it applies only to other stimuli using the same subjects (and the same instructions, and so on). In their report, Abbott, Black, and Smith report the results of F-tests both by subjects and by stimuli.

The authors' third experiment, in which they essentially combined the conditions of the first two experiments, has been excluded. Also excluded is a speculative section of the general discussion in which the authors compare the hierarchy of event knowledge to object taxonomies (hierarchical classification systems, as in animal-dog-poodle; see Readings 12 and 17) and to object partonomies (hierarchical part/whole systems, as in dog-head-nose; see Reading 12). Finally, an appendix that appeared in the original article giving the text of a story used in Experiment 3 has been excluded.

The Representation of Scripts in Memory

Valerie Abbott
University of Illinois at Chicago

John B. Black
Yale University

Edward E. Smith
Bolt Beranek and Newman, Inc.

People use what they know about the real world to understand both actual events and events in stories. That people have such knowledge is hardly controversial. What is debatable is how this knowledge is organized in memory. Since events are themselves sequential, it would seem that their representations should also be temporally organized. The research reported here indicates that knowledge about events, that appears to be entirely sequential is, in fact, also hierarchical.

PRIOR KNOWLEDGE AND UNDERSTANDING

When reading a text, people utilize their prior knowledge of the subject matter covered in the text. This prior knowledge plays an important part in facilitating the understanding processes of the reader. People read much faster and understand better than would be possible if each unit of information were processed in isolation without referring to prior knowledge to help decide what connection the item has with the rest of the passage. Consider, for example, what happens to reading speed and comprehension when one studies a difficult article in an unfamiliar field. The actual words used may not be unfamiliar and the sentences not particularly complicated, but reading is much slower than normal, and later recall is difficult.

This point is supported by a substantial body of experimental research. Dooling and Lachman (1971), and Bransford and Johnson (1972) found that subjects remembered a text much better when they knew what topics were being discussed; that is, subjects remembered more when they knew what prior knowledge to use in understanding the text. Similarly, Black and Bern (1981) found that memory was better when readers could use their prior knowledge to make inferences providing causal connections between the statements in a story. Bransford and Johnson (1973) and Thorndyke (1976) found that subjects claimed on a memory test to have previously read statements that were in fact inferences they had made, using real world knowledge, to understand the text. Graesser, Hoffman, and Clark (1980) found that the familiarity of the subject matter in a text was an important determinant of reading speed, and Miller and Kintsch (1981) found that parts of a text that were predictable from previous knowledge were read faster than those that were unpredictable. Thus, effects of knowledge on reading have been found in studies measuring amount remembered, memory distortions, and reading time. (See Black (1984) for a survey.)

This research was supported by a grant from the Sloan Foundation, U.S. Public Health Service Grants MH-19705 and MH-36586, and by the National Institute of Education under Contract US-HEW-C-400-81-10030. Experiments 1 and 2 are based on a master's thesis presented to the University of Illinois at Chicago in partial fulfillment of the requirements for the master's degree. We thank Lawrence Birnbaum and Brian Reiser for helpful discussions of the ideas presented in this paper and insightful comments on earlier drafts. Robert Abelson was of great assistance in the statistical analysis of the results reported here. Requests for reprints should be addressed to John B. Black, Department of Psychology, Yale University, Box 11A Yale Station, New Haven, Conn. 06520.

One particular kind of knowledge that adult members of our society possess is knowledge about commonplace events such as going to restaurants and visiting doctors. Typically, a written account of such an event is incomplete. So much is left out that the account would be incomprehensible if the written description were the reader's only source of information. People use their knowledge both to fill in the gaps found in these narratives, and to anticipate what will come next at each point in the narrative. The contrast between having knowledge applicable to understanding an account of an event and not having such knowledge is illustrated by the difference in the comprehensibility of the following two sequences:

(1) George entered the department store. He picked out some shoes. He paid the cashier.
(2) George entered the doctor's office. He ordered a salad. He took careful notes.

The statements in the first episode all refer to the stereotyped series of activities typically performed when one goes shopping. The second episode does not refer to any body of knowledge shared by most people. In the first story, it is easy to fill in the gaps between the actions explicitly stated with other activities that are part of the same sequence. Each sentence can be anticipated on the basis of the preceding sentences. For example, George must have found the shoe department and put on the new pair of shoes; probably someone said "Cash or charge?" to him. In the second story, however, it is much more difficult to find sensible actions to connect the stated actions and there is no way to correctly predict what actions might come next.

The information used for filling in gaps and expecting further inputs does not come from the individual sentences but from the overall bodies of knowledge to which they refer. Some quite different actions would be expected to follow the act of picking out a pair of shoes if it were a part of getting dressed in the morning rather than part of buying apparel. This example illustrates the point made by Schank and Abelson (1977) and Schank (1982) among others, that people must use the information they receive in reading to make available from memory more general information that will guide processing of further

inputs. Examples like the sequences above indicate the importance of accounting for the ability to accomplish this task in any valid language understanding theory. Memory must be organized so that relevant general information can be accessed from the input material.

At the same time, the memory organization must provide for inferences on a useful level of abstraction. Very abstract information, while providing a general framework for interpreting input, does not provide specific enough information to aid in understanding a detailed input. It should be possible to use the knowledge accessed from information in a text to find more specific predictions for processing later input.

An efficient memory organization for processing events should also represent temporal relationships among pieces of information. This would limit the possibilities for what is expected next. When one is reading a story about a shopping trip, if the shopper has found the item she desires, then the reader would anticipate information about paying for the item rather than entering a store.

Schank and Abelson (1977) have characterized a knowledge structure called a "script" that is an organization of information that allows access of relevant information during reading while ignoring irrelevant information. Scripts are intended to represent knowledge about events that are so well practiced in everyday life that their performance is stereotyped. Eating in restaurants, grocery shopping, and visiting doctors' offices are three situations about which we could expect people to have knowledge in the form of a script. A script for a commonplace event consists, in part, of the ordered sequence of actions and the standard characters and objects involved in the event. If people's knowledge about stereotypic situations is standardized, this would be an ideal sort of knowledge for experimental work on the use of information from long term memory during reading, because anyone coming into an experiment could be expected to possess the same information in his or her memory. This information would have been naturally acquired over the person's lifetime and, hence, would more likely be representative of the usual knowledge the person uses to interact with the world than would information acquired in the course of an experiment.

PREVIOUS RESEARCH ON SCRIPTS

Recently, the knowledge that people possess about commonplace events has been explored experimentally. In this section and the next, we selectively review those experiments concerning scriptal knowledge that are directly relevant to our own experiments. For a more extensive review, see Abelson (1981).

Investigations of people's knowledge of commonplace events have concluded that the actions in scripts are linked together in memory as sets; that is, when some of the actions in the set are accessed, so are the others. Bower, Black, and Turner (1979) provided two kinds of evidence for this conclusion. First, when they asked a group of 30 or so people to list the typical actions that make up such events as *going to a restaurant* or *getting up in the morning,* they found that only three or four of every hundred actions mentioned were mentioned by only one person and that many actions were referred to by more than half the subjects. These results show that there exists a commonly agreed upon group of actions that comprise these situations. Second, when given a memory test on stories that contained some of the actions from a script, subjects falsely remembered having seen the other actions in the script. Thus the script actions tended to be evoked together both when subjects were asked about what typically happens in a situation and when they read a story about that situation.

Smith, Adams, and Schorr (1978) also found that subjects falsely remembered omitted script actions after having read some of the actions in the script. In an additional study of time taken to recognize previously presented sentences, Smith et al. found that increasing the number of unrelated actions that subjects had to memorize slowed recognition time for each item. However, increasing the number of script actions subjects had to remember did not slow down recognition of the items. An explanation of this result is that items in the same script are linked in such a way that they are accessed together. Requiring subjects to remember a few more script items does not cause them to expend extra effort for retrieval.

Scripts are sets of actions, but they are not unstructured sets. In particular, scripts are ordered sets of actions. Bower et al. (1979) found that when subjects were asked to remember stories that presented some actions out of order, they tended to recall the stories with those actions shifted closer to their proper places in the sequence. Lichtenstein and Brewer (1980) obtained the same results when subjects viewed videotapes with actions that deviated from the standard order. Galambos and Rips (1982), using similar bodies of knowledge, have shown that when subjects try to determine the order in which two actions normally occur in a sequence, the decision takes longer if the two statements are close together in a temporal ordering than if they are far apart. All of these results indicate that temporal ordering is reflected in the memory representation for such events.

In addition to being ordered sets, actions in scripts seem to cluster together into closely interrelated subsets. Schank and Abelson (1977) termed these clusters "scenes." Bower et al. (1979) provided some evidence for a division of scripts into scenes. In particular, they found that when subjects had to divide a story into groups of statements that "go together," they divided the stories into chunks corresponding to scenes. Subjects agreed to a great extent on the location of the chunk boundaries, so there is evidence that the substructures involved are consistent across subjects. However, unlike the other characteristics of knowledge about scripted events described above, Bower et al. did not provide any evidence for the use of scenes in understanding stories. The experiments we report below provide some evidence that this characteristic of scripts is also used in understanding.

SERIAL VERSUS HIERARCHICAL MEMORY STRUCTURES

There is more than one way that information concerning commonplace events may be arranged in memory so that it fits the constraints of being accessed as a set, having temporal ordering, and being divided into scene substructures. One possibility is that actions involved in the event may be arranged using a simple serial ordering with markers to indicate scene boundaries. Another possibility is that people's knowledge of commonplace events may be arranged hierarchically in memory. In this section we indicate some processing consequences of these two hypotheses that will allow us to distinguish them experimentally.

An essential characteristic of a serially ordered scheme for representing events in memory is that each item in the representation be linked with the one preceding and the one succeeding it in time. Since knowledge about the event is linked together this way, and thus is set apart as a unit from other information in memory, the entire representation should be dominated by a header that denotes the unit–event as a whole.

Serial organization can explicitly maintain temporal ordering in memory and connect related information into a set that can be accessed as a whole. Each action sets up the conditions necessary for the next action, and these enabling relations link actions in a particular serial order. A serial organization does not provide a natural way of representing the substructures that seem to be characteristic of people's knowledge of commonplace events, but markers indicating substructure boundaries can be used for this purpose.

Another way in which information in memory may be organized so that it is accessed as a set with substructures is as a hierarchical structure instead of an ordered list. At the top of this hierarchy for an event is an action that summarizes the whole event (e.g., *Visit Restaurant*), which we will call a *script header*. The overall event is broken into superordinate actions, which we will call *scene headers* (e.g., *Eating, Ordering*). Each superordinate node is then broken down into a detailed set of *scene actions*. These actions are linked to the rest of the hierarchy through their scene headers. The scene actions dominated by different scene headers are not directly linked with each other, but are indirectly linked via the superordinate network of scene headers. Figure 1 illustrates a representation of this kind.

A strict hierarchical organization connects related information into a set that can be accessed as a whole and that provides a natural way of representing scene substructures, but this kind of organization is not able to represent the knowledge people have about the temporal order of events. The modification of the strict hierarchical organization shown in Fig-

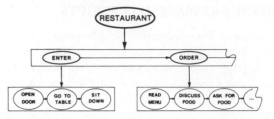

FIGURE 1   Hierarchically organized representation of the Restaurant script.

ure 1 would, however, allow items under a superordinate to be organized temporally with respect to each other. This modification adds temporal or enablement links between the various scene headers in a script, and between the actions subordinate to a particular scene header, but would not do violence to the basic notion that actions dominated by different scene headers are linked through only those scene headers. The experiments reported here provide evidence that the organization of common events in memory is such a modified hierarchy rather than a serial ordering.

As support for the hierarchical organization in Figure 1, consider the mixed history of studies attempting to demonstrate that people use the temporal information in a script when reading a script-based story. These experiments (e.g., Bower et al., 1979) focused on the time taken to read a target line in a script-based story, and studied this time as a function of whether the activities instantiated in the target and the line preceding it are far apart in the underlying script. To illustrate, consider the following vignette.

(1) John went to a restaurant.
(2) John ate his meal with gusto.
(target) (3) John paid the check and left.

There is relatively little "gap" between the script activities in the target line and the one preceding it— "pay the check" and "eat the meal." In contrast, there is a substantial gap between the target and preceding lines in the following:

(1) John went to a restaurant.
(2) John deliberated about his order.
(target) (3) John paid the check and left.

The basic prediction tested in these studies was that it should take longer to read a target line the greater the gap between the script activities mentioned in it and the preceding line (e.g., it should take longer to read "John paid the check and left" in the second vignette than in the first). This was the prediction because (i) using a script to understand a story presumably involves searching through the script for activities that match the story lines, and (ii) if the script activities are represented temporally, the duration of this search should increase with the number of script activities that intervene between the last activity matched and the one matching the present story line (Cullingford, 1978).

Early experiments failed to find the predicted effect of gap size. In Bower et al. (1979), for example, while reading time increased with initial increases in gap size, further increases in gap size led to a decrease in reading time. A close examination of these studies, however, suggested that the failure to find the expected results was due to a failure to appreciate the hierarchical structure of scripts. In some of the Bower et al. stories, different lines seem to describe actions at two different hierarchical levels, the scene header and scene action levels. Successive lines in these stories, therefore, sometimes required the reader to switch levels, which might have obscured the desired effect.

To overcome this problem, Smith (1981) varied gap size in stories that included either only scene headers (e.g., "Frank wanted to go to the movies. He bought tickets. He watched the movie."), or only scene actions (e.g., "Allan was going to buy tickets for a movie. He walked over to the ticket counter. He waited in line."). For the scene header stories, the time to read the target line increased monotonically with gap size. For the scene action stories, while reading time increased with an initial increase in gap size, a further increase in gap size led to a small and nonsignificant decrease in reading time. Thus, for scene actions, while there was a failure to find a strictly monotonic effect of gap size, there was no evidence for real nonmonotonicity.

In sum, that there was a monotonic effect of gap size for scene header stories, and a gap size effect with no real nonmonotonicity for scene action stories, implies that the temporal order of events is a part of the representation that people use in reading stories about events. This is evidence for the presence of some serial organization in these representations. However, that gap size effects are found only when the level of story events is held constant supports the hypothesis that these representations are also hierarchically structured.

EXPERIMENT 1: MEMORY FOR SINGLE- SCRIPT STORIES

The story comprehension process utilizing a serially organized representation is quite similar to one utilizing a hierarchically organized representation. Each story statement is read and the script structure is scanned for a path connecting the currently matched action with the preceding one. The script actions that comprise the connecting path are then inferred to have occurred even though they were not mentioned explicitly in the story. However, due to a difference between the pattern of inferences expected with the hierarchy and with the serial chain, hierarchical organization allows the processing to be more efficient. With the hierarchical representation, the scene header for each scene is always inferred in reading a story about a scripted event because it is on any path through the script, whereas the scene actions need not always be inferred. With the serial chain, all of these actions are always inferred because there is only one path through the script—namely, the one including all the actions. Therefore, our hierarchical representation for scripts predicts an asymmetry in inferencing of scene headers and scene actions: processing scene actions causes their scene headers to be inferred, but not vice versa. A serial chain representation, on the other hand, makes no such prediction, so we have an empirical distinction between the two representations that can be tested in a recognition memory task.

In this experiment, we varied whether the scene actions and scene headers were present or absent in target scenes of script-based stories. We compared the rate of falsely recognizing test items that were scene headers of presented scene actions with the false recognition rate for items that were scene actions of presented scene headers. In particular, we were interested in two effects:

(1) The effect of presenting a scene action on subjects' ratings of likelihood that they have seen its scene header.

(2) The effect of presenting a scene header on subjects' ratings of likelihood that they have seen its scene action.

A hierarchical network hypothesis predicts that the effect in (1) would be greater than that in (2). A serial ordering hypothesis does not predict any difference.

Method

Subjects.   Subjects were 32 undergraduate students who participated to fulfill a course requirement.

Materials.   We constructed four stories from scripts in such a way that we could manipulate independently the presence or absence of a header and action in at least one scene. The four stories were about *going to a restaurant, attending a lecture, visiting a doctor's office,* and *grocery shopping.* The target scene (i.e., the scene in each story chosen for variation) was moderately important; that is, statements corresponding to its header and actions had moderately high production frequencies in script norms (Bower et al., 1979). Each target scene was at least five statements long; this length further insured that the target scene was an important part of the story. The target scenes appeared in the stories in one of four forms:

(1) Nothing from the scene was mentioned.
(2) Only the scene header was mentioned.
(3) Only one scene action was mentioned.
(4) Both the scene header and one scene action were mentioned.

These forms provided the four conditions of the experiment. In particular, they represent the orthogonal manipulation of the presence or absence of the scene headers and scene actions. The rest of each story was composed by stating all the nontarget scene actions and scene headers produced by more than 25% of subjects in the Bower et al. norms. Some additional material was also included to make the stories more readable. One of the stories used, *Going to a Restaurant,* is shown in Table 1.

TABLE 1   Text of Going to a Restaurant

When they got home after shopping, Mary and her friend were hungry, so they decided to go to a restaurant. They called to make a reservation and drove to the restaurant.

Mary opened the door of the restaurant. They went inside. Mary gave the reservation name to the hostess. The table was not ready yet, so they had to wait to be seated. In a few minutes they went to their table. They were seated.

Scene action:	They discussed what they wanted to eat.
Scene header:	They ordered their meal.

They put their napkins on their laps. The waitress brought them their appetizers and refilled their water glasses. They drank water and ate their appetizers. When their meal arrived, they ate their food. When they were finished, they decided to forget their diets and order dessert. They ate the dessert. It was getting late, so they asked for the check. The check came. They figured out the tip and left it on the table. Mary paid the check. They went to the checkroom and got their coats. They left the restaurant.

Note. The target scene is enclosed in a box. Different versions of the story included the scene action alone, the scene header alone, both, or neither.

Regardless of which version of a story the subjects received, they all took the same recognition test. There were 20 recognition items for each story, 9 of which were always old (i.e., appeared in the story), for example, "In a few minutes they went to their table"; and 9 of which were always new, for example, "They heard the telephone ringing." The 9 new items were statements that could have been in the story, but were not, and were also not implied by the story. The other 2 items were the scene action and the scene header from the target scene; "They discussed what they wanted to eat" and "They ordered their meal." Whether these items were new or old depended on the experimental condition.

Procedure.   Each subject read one story in each of the four versions. Across subjects, each version was read by eight subjects. Subjects were given 2 minutes to read each story, and were then asked to write one sentence describing what they expected to happen next in the story. They were given 30 seconds to make this extrapolation. (This extrapolation provided a cover task and was designed to encourage the subjects to process the material meaningfully.) Subjects then performed an unrelated intervening task for 20 minutes. After this, subjects were presented with an unexpected recognition test for the stories. The recognition items were blocked by story title. Subjects were asked to rate each item on a seven point scale according to how likely it seemed that the item was stated in the story, where "7" indicated certainty that the item had not been stated and "1" indicated certainty that it had been stated.

Results and Discussion

As predicted by the hierarchical hypothesis, there was an asymmetry in inferencing favoring the scene headers over the scene actions. Figure 2 gives the mean recognition ratings for the scene headers and scene actions. The data are collapsed over story topic, but are given separately for each story version.

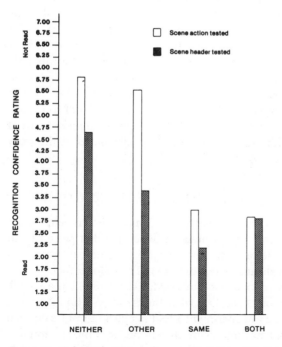

FIGURE 2   Subjects' ratings of recognition items for Experiment 1. Here "1" means certainty the item was read. "7" means certainty the item was not read.

The "NEITHER" condition consists of subjects' ratings for scene headers and scene actions when neither had been stated in the story. The "OTHER" condition consists of ratings for the scene action when only the scene header had been stated in the story, and for the scene header when only the scene action had been read. In the "SAME" condition were subjects' ratings for items when the identical item had actually been presented, and the other possible item from the same scene had not. The "BOTH" condition contains subjects' ratings for each item when both scene header and scene action were read.

A comparison of ratings in the NEITHER and OTHER conditions in Figure 2 indicates that presentation of a scene header did not affect ratings for the scene action from the same scene, but presentation of a scene action did affect ratings for the scene header from the same scene. This asymmetry argues strongly against serial organization and for hierarchical organization. The difference between ratings in the NEITHER and OTHER conditions for scene action test items was negligible—only 0.28 point on the scale. Ratings for scene actions when none were presented were well below the 7.0 maximum possible on the rating scale, so a ceiling effect for these items cannot be used to explain this result. For scene headers the difference was a much larger 1.24 points. Thus, scene headers show a tendency to be inferred by subjects when they read an action from the same scene. For scene actions, such a tendency was not evident.

The interaction between test item type (scene header or scene action) and condition was significant by subject ($F(2,56) = 4.97$, $p = .010$), but not by story ($F(1,3) < 1$). This interaction was mostly due to the results for the OTHER condition, in which ratings for scene headers and scene actions diverged compared to the NEITHER, SAME, and BOTH conditions in which both test item types were given more similar ratings. This is exactly the pattern of ratings we would expect if subjects infer scene headers when presented with scene actions, but fail to infer scene actions when presented with scene headers. A linear × quadratic comparison to test whether ratings diverge significantly in the OTHER condition was significant by subjects ($F(1,28) = 5.88$, $p = .021$). This comparison was not significant by stories ($F(1,3) < 1$) because we were only able to use four stories, but three of the four stories used in this experiment showed the expected pattern.

The problem with the other story may have been our unfortunate choice of a scene action for the critical scene. The subjects objected to this statement, rating it as probably not seen even when it was presented explicitly in the story. The predictions of either structural hypothesis rest on the assumption that when an item is presented there is a reasonable chance that it will be processed and remembered. If it is not, it is not clear that the item can be expected to have an effect on the processing and remembering of other items.

Also more consistent with a hierarchical than with a serial ordering hypothesis is the fact that the scene headers received higher confidence ratings (3.21) than the scene actions (4.25). There was also a significant main effect of test item type ($F(1,28) = 32.48$, $p < .001$ by subjects; $F(1,3) = 6.42$, $p = .086$ by materials). According to the hierarchical hypothesis, scene headers are in a privileged position determined structurally. Processing has to pass through a scene header whenever one of its scene actions is mentioned. Also, as was seen in the Smith (1981) study described above, scene headers are temporally linked, so a scene header is on a direct path through a representation between its two neighboring scene headers. These superordinate items should have more chances to be processed than the more subordinate scene action items and consequently should be more likely to be included in the memory representation for an event. In order to account for this scene header superiority, the serial ordering hypothesis would have to maintain additionally that some actions have memory attributes that make their base level of response higher. There is no reason to believe such an ad hoc claim, so the serial ordering hypothesis cannot parsimoniously account for the results. In an overall analysis of critical items, there was a main effect of presentation condition ($F(3,84) = 23.69$, $p < .001$ by subjects; $F(3,9) = 13.93$, $p < .001$ by materials). Not surprisingly, both scene headers and scene actions were rated as more likely to have been seen when they were presented (SAME and BOTH conditions) than when they were not (NEITHER and OTHER conditions) ($F(1,28) = 65.10$, $p < .001$ by subjects; ($F(1,3) = 28.46$, $p = .016$ by materials).

An alternative hypothesis about our results that must be considered is that they are due to a general strategy on the part of the subjects to remember only general information. This alternative can be rejected because the scene headers and scene actions were rated essentially the same in the BOTH condition. If subjects were simply biased against responding positively to detailed test statements or in favor of translating all input into general terms, this bias should not have vanished when one scene header and one scene action from a scene were presented.

The results for the noncritical items (which were the same in all the conditions) did not interact with the experimental conditions. Subjects gave average ratings of 2.03 to noncritical veridical items and ratings of 6.28 to noncritical distractor items. Ratings for these items did not vary with which version of the story the subject received (for veridical items $F(3,93) < 1$; for distractor items $F(3,93) < 1$). In the NEITHER condition (the condition in which critical items were not presented and hence were always distractors), noncritical distractor items were rejected by subjects with more certainty than critical items ($F(1,31) = 10.93$, $p = .002$). Thus, the critical items showed more of a tendency to be inferred than did noncritical distractors. Recall that the noncritical distractor items were designed not to be inferable from the stories, whereas the scene headers and scene actions were inferable using the script. Also, as is to be expected, the critical items in the NEITHER condition were more likely to be rejected than noncritical veridical items that were actually stated in the story ($F(1,31) = 87.41$, $p < .001$).

EXPERIMENT 2: MULTISCRIPT STORIES

The results of Experiment 1 indicate that people have memory representations for events that permit them to infer abstract knowledge (scene headers) from input details (scene actions). This allows them to use general bodies of knowledge to provide a framework for understanding what they read. We found no evidence in Experiment 1 that people infer more detailed information when they read general statements. However, surely there are limits to this process of generalization. If contact is made only with more abstract knowledge, inferences quickly become so general as to be useless. There must be some way to facilitate inference on a useful level, one which is specific enough to provide useful expectations, but not so specific that the expectations are likely to be wrong.

In studies that bear on this problem, Rosch, Mervis, Gray, Johnson, and Boyes-Braem (1976) found that for natural object categories, there is a basic level of classification at which people prefer to describe and think about objects. For example, in most contexts people prefer to classify an object as an *apple* rather than more generally as a *fruit* or more specifically as a *MacIntosh apple*. This idea of a basic level may carry over to knowledge about situations like going to a restaurant or visiting a doctor (Abbott & Black, 1980). If there is a basic level of abstraction for situation knowledge, then people might prefer to infer actions on that level when actions at a more abstract or a more specific level are presented.

Experiment 2 was designed to test this possibility. It essentially repeated Experiment 1, but with everything moved up one level of abstraction. Instead of varying presence versus absence of scene headers and scene actions as Experiment 1 did, Experiment 2 varied presence or absence of script headers and scene headers. Recall that a script header is a reference to a whole script (e.g., "Joe ate at a restaurant"), while a scene header is a reference to a scene (e.g., "Joe ordered a meal"). If there is in fact a basic level of representation for scriptal situations it would likely correspond to the scene header level because inferences on this level would yield fairly specific predictions about what was to follow in a story without generating inferences so specific that there would be a high probability that they were wrong. Thus, presentation of a script header might cause its scene headers to be processed and possibly be included as part of the memory representation.

Generalization from input material would always facilitate linking that material with more abstract information in a subject's memory. That is, inferring from a statement such as "Joe ordered a meal" that Joe was in a restaurant would make available general information about restaurants that could be useful in processing the rest of the story. Therefore, when a scene header is mentioned, we expect script headers to be inferred and included as part of the memory representation.

At this higher level, then, we did not expect to find the superordinate-subordinate asymmetry in inferencing that we found in Experiment 1. Generalization of input information would still occur, and if the scene header level was the most useful or basic level for situation knowledge, then people would show a tendency to infer information about events at that level.

Method

Subjects.   Subjects were 32 Yale undergraduate students who participated to fulfill a course requirement.

Materials.   We wrote two multiscript stories. One was about the activities of a student during a day; the other was about the experiences of a man going to a city to meet a friend who was arriving by plane. These stories were entitled *The Day* and *The Trip*. The stories were constructed so that each would contain references to eight stereotyped situations (scripts) in addition to sentences added to flesh out the stories and make them more readable. Two statements were chosen from an account of each of the eight target situations, one a script header and the other a scene header. For example, in the restaurant situation, the reference to the script header was "He ate dinner at a fancy restaurant" and the scene header was "He ordered a gourmet meal and some wine." The story versions varied according to whether both or neither the script header or the scene header was presented for a given situation. Two scripts were presented in each condition in each story, the order of conditions counterbalanced over subjects. . . . One of the stories used, *The Day,* [appeared in the appendix to the original article].

The recognition test for each story contained the same items for all subjects, and the order of items was randomized for each subject. There were 48 items on the test for each story, 24 of which had been present in the story and 24 of which were new. Both the script header and the scene header from each situation appeared on the recognition test. Thus, there were 16 items that were always old, 16 items that were always new, and 16 items that were old or new depending on the condition. This last group of 16 was made up of the eight script headers and eight scene headers for events in the story.

Procedure. Each subject was presented with one version of each story. Half the subjects read *The Day* first and the other half read *The Trip* first. Subjects were instructed to read each story carefully so that they could answer questions about it later, and were allowed to read at their own rate. They were then given an unrelated intervening task to perform for 20 minutes, after which they were given the recognition test for the first story, and were asked to rate each recognition item on a 1–7 scale according to how likely it seemed to them that the item was in the story ("7" indicated certainty that the item had not been stated and "1" indicated certainty that it had been stated). The recognition test for the second story followed immediately. Subjects were self-paced throughout the recognition portion of the experiment.

Results and Discussion

Results. As we expected, the results of the recognition tests show that presentation of scene headers led to false recognition of script headers, and presentation of script headers led to false recognition of scene headers. In other words, there was no inferencing asymmetry at this level as there was at the lower level of abstraction.

The mean confidence ratings for the recognition test of critical items in each event condition are presented in Figure 3. The open bars in the figure present the ratings for the scene headers in the various event conditions and the dotted bars present the ratings for the script headers.

The difference in ratings of test items between the NEITHER and OTHER conditions (from 5.19 to 4.26) shows that false recognition increased for these items when another item from the script was mentioned ($F(1,31) = 36.25$, $p < .001$ by subjects; $F(1,15) = 18.11$, $p = .001$ by materials) . This result, along with the lack of an interaction between test item type and condition for these two conditions ($F(1,31) < 1$ by subjects; $F(1,15) < 1$ by materials), indicates not

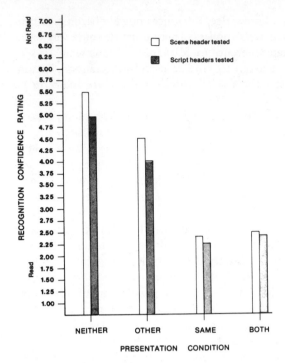

FIGURE 3   Subjects' ratings of recognition items for Experiment 2. Here "1" means certainty the item was read, "7" means certainty the item was not read.

only that more general knowledge structures were sought for interpretation of input material, but also that people infer more detailed information than they have actually read. Not only did false alarming occur for script headers when their scene headers were read, but there was also false alarming to scene headers when their script headers were read in the story. This lends credence to our claim that scene headers occupy a privileged position in the representation of knowledge about situations, in that the inferencing asymmetry favoring more general items found in Experiment 1 does not occur when script headers are the more specific items.

Overall, the script header statements were rated slightly more likely (3.35) to have been seen than the scene header statements (3.72). Although rather small, this difference was statistically significant ($F(1,31) = 21.10$, $p < .001$ by subjects; $F(1,15) = 11.64$, $p = .004$ by materials). However, this difference disappears in the "SAME" and "BOTH" conditions, which indicates that subjects were as likely to recognize a scene header as a script header when they were stated in the story.

The effect of presentation conditions was significant overall ($F(3,93) = 113.54$, $p < .001$ by subjects; $F(3,45) = 74.76$, $p < .001$ by materials). Items were rated more likely to have been read when they were actually presented (SAME and BOTH conditions) than when they were not (NONE and OTHER conditions) ($F(1,31) = 217.45$, $p < .001$ by subjects; $F(1,15) = 120.24$, $p < .001$ by materials).

For noncritical items, subjects gave average ratings of 2.14 to items they had seen, and average ratings of 5.41 to items they had not seen. These ratings are in an acceptable range and are comparable to the ratings of critical items in the NEITHER and BOTH conditions. . . .

[Experiment 3 has been omitted.]

GENERAL DISCUSSION

The Case for Hierarchical Representations

We can now combine the results from Experiments 1 through 3, along with previous work, to yield a coherent picture of how scripts are represented in memory and how such representations are used to understand stories.

Previous work has shown that people utilize temporal ordering information in representations of events to guide their inference processes. The Smith (1981) study in particular demonstrated that when subjects do not have to switch hierarchical levels in reading stories, they take longer to read a sentence the more separated it is from the preceding sentence in the temporal sequence of the script. Thus, serial organization is indicated in representations of scripts, since the length of the search necessary to connect two items on the same level of abstraction depends on their distance apart in the script. However, since this effect of temporal order seems to occur only in those experiments where subjects read stories at a constant level of abstraction, serial organization alone cannot describe people's representations of events; rather, the representation must distinguish between different levels.

These results suggest a hierarchical arrangement for information about events in memory. Additional

support for this suggestion comes from a number of other sources in both cognitive psychology and artificial intelligence. Many theories of memory for stories propose a hierarchical structure for stories (e.g., Rumelhart, 1977; Thorndyke, 1977; Mandler & Johnson, 1977). The basic finding related to these theories is that people remember events high in the story hierarchies better than those at lower levels. Thus event hierarchies have proven to be a useful representation for predicting the probability of remembering the statements in stories. Black and Bower (1980) have characterized stories in terms of problem solving hierarchies. They found that actions that lead to successful resolution of problems, or that are high in the action hierarchy, were better remembered than unsuccessful attempts and actions low in the hierarchy. Lichtenstein and Brewer (1980) found that such a hierarchical representation is also consistent with people's memory for videotaped events. Their study suggested that actions are more strongly linked to their superordinates than to the actions temporally contiguous with them in the sequence.

The question of why scripts should be organized hierarchically has been addressed specifically in the artificial intelligence literature. Sacerdoti (1974) argued that a hierarchical network of actions is the most efficient representation for use in planning how to accomplish a goal. In particular, he was concerned with endowing a robot with enough problem solving ability to enable it to interact with a simple world. He found that using a hierarchical representation in planning actions was more efficient for a problem solver than arranging the planning actions at a single level of detail because it allowed the robot to avoid wasting time worrying about details of plan execution when there was a flaw in the plan at a more general level. So, in addition to aiding a person's understanding of the actions of others, hierarchically structured information can be used to guide the person's own actions.

Experiment 1 turned up an asymmetry in inferencing. When a scene action was mentioned in a story, its scene header was likely to be inferred and stored as part of the memory for the story; on the other hand, mentioning the corresponding scene header did not lead to the subordinate scene action being inferred and stored in memory. We claim this asymmetry occurs because the scene actions are linked to the rest of the script only via their scene headers. Thus whenever a path is constructed between two story statements involving actions from different scenes of the script, these scene headers must be part of the path. This is further evidence for hierarchical organization in representation of scripts. A result from Experiment 2, that a script header is inferred when a scene header is mentioned in a story, shows that the generalization expected from a hierarchical representation extends to the script header level.

Combining the results of previous work with the results of Experiments 1 and 2, we can see that an appropriate representation for scripted events must combine an overall hierarchical organization with temporal connections between items under a given superordinate. Such a representation is illustrated in Figure 1. In this representation the script header, *Restaurant,* is related as a superordinate to the scene headers, *Enter, Order, Eat,* and so on. These scene headers are connected serially with each other. Each scene header stands in a superordinate relation to its scene actions. These, in turn, are interconnected serially. This representation would allow generalizing inferences to be made, while allowing the effect of serial order seen in the Smith (1981) study.

The results of Experiment 2 indicated that the asymmetry in inferencing does not occur if one moves up a level in the event hierarchy. Specifically, mentioning script headers in a story leads to their scene headers being inferred and stored in memory and mentioning scene headers in a story leads to their script headers being stored. This result suggests that people are able to infer more detailed information from general information when the detailed inference is at the scene header level. Experiment 3 confirmed that these results were not peculiar to the conditions presented in Experiments 1 and 2. It reaffirmed our contention that inferences are most likely to be made at the scene header level.

Given the results of these experiments, it would be possible to maintain that this is not the only level at which these inferences are made. We have not given subjects the opportunity to falsely recognize script headers when only more abstract items have been presented. Under most circumstances it is difficult to imagine that a restaurant experience would be

inferred on the mention of a social occasion. However, situations could probably be constructed in which this could happen. The general point of these investigations is that people are capable of using hierarchical structures in their representations of events in order to generalize detailed input or specify abstract input so that expectations can be generated at a useful level. The degree of flexibility people have in deciding which level of abstraction will yield the most useful expectations is left to future research.

Nevertheless, mention of a script header evokes the scene headers, and this evocation is neither in the direction necessary for generalization of input material nor essential for connection with earlier stated actions. Its functionality, we believe, stems from the need to supply expectations that facilitate connection with subsequently stated action. For this purpose, scene headers appear to be the level that people prefer or find most useful to think about script events, at least when they read stories about the events and are not specifically encouraged to concentrate on any one level. In this way it is similar to the basic level of abstraction that Rosch et al. (1976) found for natural object categories. This similarity is explored in the next section [omitted]. . . .

In sum, because of the difference in domains, one should be cautious in importing details of the analysis of object taxonomies to deal with event knowledge. A more useful analogy may be with object partonomies. However, the utility of the "basic level" concept applied to object taxonomies, partonomies, or scripts is the same. Items at the "basic level" should provide useful inferences for the task at hand. The behavior of subjects in our experiments leads to the conclusion that scene headers are basic for event knowledge, in that they provide inferences that are specific enough to provide useful information, but not so detailed as to provide information that is possibly erroneous and probably irrelevant.

CONCLUDING COMMENTS

Our finding that only part of a script gets inferred during reading and stored in memory is different from previous conceptions that assumed all actions in a script were inferred (e.g., Bower et al., 1979). An approach compatible with our results is the memory organization packet framework proposed by Schank (1982). In particular, Schank proposed that large scale knowledge structures like scripts are constructed when needed from smaller packets of information. In these terms, the representation of scripts we have described in this paper proposes that scripts are a hierarchically organized network of memory packets with a top level packet corresponding to a script header that indexes the scene header dominated packets. These lower level packets are composed of the scene actions that further detail the scene headers. Each packet contains information about the temporal ordering of its component parts. These packets are assembled during understanding into whatever combination is needed to understand the particular story being read.

Thus our results seem most consistent with a more flexible, generative representation for scripts than the rather rigid structures previously proposed. We have argued that a hierarchical network of organized information packets that can be combined in appropriate sequences is the best event representation for use in comprehension of events. . . .

REFERENCES

Abbott, V., & Black, J. B. (1980). *The representation of scripts in memory.* (Tech. Rep. No. 5) Cognitive Science Program, Yale University.

Abelson, R. P. (1981). Psychological status of the script concept. *American Psychologist, 36,* 715–729.

Andersen, E. S. (1975). Lexical universals in body-part terminology. In *Universals of human language,* Stanford, CA: Stanford Univ. Press, 1975.

Black J. B. (1984). Understanding and remembering stories. In J. R. Anderson and S. M. Kosslyn (Eds.), *Essays on learning and memory.* San Francisco: Freeman.

Black, J. B., & Bern, H. (1981). Causal coherence and memory for events in narratives. *Journal of Verbal Learning and Verbal Behavior, 20,* 267–275.

Black, J. B., & Bower, G. H. (1980). Story understanding as problem-solving. *Poetics, 9,* 223–250.

Bower, G. H., Black, J. B., & Turner, T. J. (1979). Scripts in text comprehension and memory. *Cognitive Psychology, 11,* 177–220.

Bransford, J. D., & Johnson, M. K. (1972). Contextual prerequisites for understanding: Some investigations of comprehension and recall. *Journal of Verbal Learning and Verbal Behavior, 11,* 717–726.

Bransford, J. D., & Johnson, M. K. (1973). Considerations of some problems of comprehension. In W. G. Chase (Ed.), *Visual Information Processing,* New York: Academic Press.

Brown, C. H. (1976). General principles of human anatomical partonomy and speculations on the growth of partonomic nomenclature. *American Ethnologist, 3,* 400–424.

Cullingford, R. E. (1978). *Script application: Computer understanding of newspaper stories.* (Tech. Rep. No. 116) Department of Computer Science, Yale University.

Dooling, D. J., & Lachman, R. (1971). Effects of comprehension on retention of prose. *Journal of Experimental Psychology, 88,* 216–222.

Galambos, J. A., & Rips, L. J. (1982). Memory for routines. *Journal of Verbal Learning and Verbal Behavior, 21,* 260–281.

Graesser, A. C., Hoffman, N. L., & Clark, L. F. (1980). Structural components of reading time. *Journal of Verbal Learning and Verbal Behavior, 19,* 131–151.

Lichtenstein, E. H., & Brewer, W. F. (1980). Memory for goal-directed events. *Cognitive Psychology, 12,* 412–445.

Mandler, J. M., & Johnson, N. S. (1977). Remembrance of things parsed: Story structure and recall. *Cognitive Psychology, 9,* 111–151.

Miller, G. A., & Johnson-Laird, P. N. (1976). *Language and perception.* Cambridge, MA: Harvard Univ. Press.

Miller, J. R., & Kintsch, W. (1981). Knowledge-based aspects of prose comprehension and readability. *Text, 3,* 215–232.

Murphy, G. L., & Smith, E. E. (1982). Basic-level superiority in picture categorization. *Journal of Verbal Learning and Verbal Behavior, 21,* 1–20.

Rosch, E., Mervis, C. B., Gray, W., Johnson, D., & Boyes-Braem, P. (1976). Basic objects in natural categories. *Cognitive Psychology, 8,* 382–439.

Rumelhart, D. E. (1977). Understanding and summarizing brief stories. In *Basic processing in reading, perception, and comprehension,* Hillsdale, NJ: Erlbaum.

Sacerdoti, E. (1974). Planning in a hierarchy of abstraction spaces. *Artificial Intelligence, 9,* 119–135.

Schank, R. C. (1982). *Dynamic memory: A theory of reminding and learning in computers and people.* New York: Cambridge Univ. Press.

Schank, R. C., & Abelson, R. P. (1977). *Scripts, plans, goals, and understanding.* Hillsdale, NJ: Erlbaum.

Smith, E. E. (1981, May). *Studying on-line comprehension of stories.* Paper presented at the Cognitive Science Colloquium, Yale University.

Smith, E. E., Adams, N., & Schorr, D. (1978). Fact retrieval and the paradox of interference. *Cognitive Psychology, 10,* 438–464.

Thorndyke, P. W. (1976). The role of inferences in discourse comprehension. *Journal of Verbal Learning and Verbal Behavior, 15,* 437–446.

Thorndyke, P. W. (1977). Cognitive structures in the comprehension and memory of narrative discourse. *Cognitive Psychology, 9,* 77–110.

Tversky, B., & Hemenway, K. (in press). Objects, parts, and categories. *Journal of Experimental Psychology: General.*

POSTSCRIPT

As originally conceived, scripts were thought to represent the full sequences of relatively complicated events (see Schank & Abelson, 1977). For example, the restaurant script would specify the sequence of events from deciding to go to a restaurant through going in, deciding what to order, ordering, eating, and paying. However, subsequent work by Schank (Schank, 1982; Schank, Collins, & Hunter, 1986) and Black and his colleagues (this reading; Bower, Black, & Turner, 1979) has led to the conclusion that people's event knowledge is in fact highly flexible and unlikely to be stored directly in units as large and as complex as scripts. This conclusion implies that the units of event knowledge stored directly in memory represent relatively small sequences of behaviors. For example, we may represent going to the dentist as a collection of small units more like scene headers than like scripts: waiting in the waiting room, climbing into a special chair when it's your turn, and so on. These knowledge units are put together into a linear sequence only in response to a particular situation, such as when actually visiting the dentist. Furthermore, a given knowledge unit may be elicited by different situations. Thus, the waiting-in-a-waiting-room unit may be elicited both by a visit to the dentist and by a visit to the doctor; the climbing-into-a-special-chair unit may be elicited both by a visit to the dentist and by a visit to the hair stylist.

Schank (1982; Schank et al., 1986) argues that if we frequently combine certain knowledge units, we may store information about these combinations in a special knowledge structure called a memory organization packet (or MOP). Unlike a script, a MOP does not directly contain all the information about how an event proceeds. Instead, it is more like an outline that orders other information in the proper combinations and sequences to capture only as much detail as is necessary about complex but common sequences of behavior. One advantage of MOPs is that their outlinelike nature makes them easier to modify in response to a new experience or a novel situation. A second advantage of the MOP approach is that it is consistent with the viewpoint that memory is reconstructive (see Reading 30). A third advantage is that MOPs fit very naturally with the evidence—including that presented by Reading 13—that our knowledge of events is hierarchically organized.

The script approach to knowledge about event categories is closely related to the schema approach to knowledge of object (and other) categories. For a classic description of schemas, see Rumelhart (1980) or the Introduction to Reading 32.

FOR FURTHER THOUGHT

1. What kind of evidence leads Abbott, Black, and Smith (and other researchers whose work they summarize) to conclude that certain common sequences of actions are linked together into organized units (scripts) in memory? Are such units supposed to exist for all kinds of events? If not, to what kinds of events are they limited?

2. On what grounds do the authors argue that a modified hierarchical representation of scripts is more efficient than a purely serial one is? Give examples of situations that demonstrate the efficiency of a hierarchical representation. How do the authors explain results such as those they obtained by Galambos and Rips (1982) and Smith (1981), which suggest that it takes people longer to relate events that are temporally distant from one another in a sequence than it does to relate events that are temporally close?

3. In your own words, explain why "an asymmetry in inferencing favoring scene headers over scene actions" constitutes support for the hierarchical hypothesis. Describe the asymmetry in terms of the results for the NEITHER and OTHER conditions in Experiment 1. What do the results for the SAME and BOTH conditions tell us?

4. How do Abbott, Black, and Smith rule out the possibility that subjects were more certain about having seen scene headers than they were about having seen scene actions simply because people tend to remember general information better than they do specific information?

5. Why did the authors expect the inferencing asymmetry results of Experiment 1 to be eliminated in Experiment 2? What do their results for Experiment 2 imply?

REFERENCES

Bower, G. H., Black, J. B., & Turner, T. F. (1979). Scripts in memory for text. *Cognitive Psychology, 11,* 177–220.

Rumelhart, D. E. (1980). Schemata: The building blocks of cognition. In R. J. Spiro, B. C. Bruce, & W. F. Brewer (Eds.), *Theoretical issues in reading comprehension* (pp. 33–58). Hillsdale, NJ: Erlbaum.

Schank, R. C. (1982). *Dynamic memory: A theory of reminding and learning in computers and people.* New York: Cambridge University Press.

Schank, R. C., & Abelson, R. P. (1977). *Scripts, plans, goals, and understanding.* Hillsdale, NJ: Erlbaum.

Schank, R. C., Collins, G. C., & Hunter, L. E. (1986). Transcending inductive category formation in learning. *Behavioral and Brain Sciences, 9,* 639–686.

INTRODUCTION

Priming occurs when our processing of a word affects how we process a sub-sequently presented word. When the two words are semantically associated as *dog* and *bark* are, the processing of the first word—called the prime—gen-erally facilitates our processing of the second word—the target. Thus, if we are asked to make some decision about the word *bark,* we respond somewhat more quickly if we've just seen the word *dog* than we would otherwise. When the two words are unrelated, as *dog* and *folder* are, no facilitation of our pro-cessing occurs. When the words are "near misses," as with *dog* and *meow,* the effect can be inhibitory; that is, our response to the word *meow* may be slower than usual.

In "Semantic Priming and Retrieval from Lexical Memory: Evidence for Facilitatory and Inhibitory Processes," James Neely argues that two processes are involved in priming effects: location shifting and spreading activation. Both location shifting and spreading activation assume that when we see or hear a word, a mental representation of that word, called a logogen, is acti-vated. Both processes also assume that we become consciously aware of a word when activation of its logogen reaches a certain threshold level. Finally, both location shifting and spreading activation assume that the organization of logogens can be described using a spatial metaphor: the more highly asso-ciated two words are in meaning, the "closer" their logogens are.

Location shifting explains priming in terms of the time it takes to shift attention from one logogen to another. Facilitation occurs between semanti-cally associated words because our attention needs to be shifted only a rela-tively short distance. Inhibition can occur if our attention is misleadingly shifted to a remote logogen. *Spreading activation* explains priming as an un-conscious, effortless, relatively fast spread of activation from an activated logogen to its near neighbors, rather than as a conscious, effortful, relatively slow process of shifting attention (see the Postscript to Reading 12 for a dis-cussion of spreading activation). This automatic spreading of activation is al-ways predicted to have a facilitating effect.

Whereas earlier research argued for one process or the other, Neely ar-gues that priming is best explained by combining both location shifting *and* spreading activation. His two-factor model predicts that facilitation will al-ways occur when the target and the prime are related; inhibition will occur only when a "near miss" prime appears far enough in advance of a target to give the relatively slow location-shifting process time to shift attention to a remote logogen. If the time between the presentations of the "near miss" prime and the target is too short (measured from the start of the presentation of the prime to the start of the presentation of the target, and called the stimulus onset asynchrony, or SOA), then attention does not have time to be shifted away, and no inhibition occurs (only spreading activation operates).

Neely's experiment is extremely clever and rather complicated, and the results are not exactly as predicted by two-factor theory. As you read this article, ask yourself the following questions. What do each of these two processes predict will happen when you immediately follow the presentation of the word *dog* with a related word like *bark?* What do they predict when *folder* or a simple string of letters like *XXXXX* is followed by *bark?* What actually happens?

Semantic Priming and Retrieval from Lexical Memory: Evidence for Facilitatory and Inhibitory Processes

James H. Neely
Yale University

In the lexical decision task, a subject must decide as quickly as possible whether a visually presented letter string is a common English word or nonword. A commonly obtained finding (e.g., Meyer & Schvaneveldt, 1971; Meyer, Schvaneveldt, & Ruddy, [References] Note 1) is that subjects are quicker to respond that a target letter string (e.g., NURSE) is a word when the immediately prior target was a semantically related word (i.e., DOCTOR) than when the

This research was supported by Grant 40310X to Dr. Michael I. Posner from the National Science Foundation and was conducted while Dr. Posner was a Visiting Professor at Yale and while the author was a National Science Foundation predoctoral fellow. I am indebted to Dr. Robert G. Crowder, Dr. Alice F. Healy, and Dr. Posner for several interesting discussions about this research. Requests for reprints should be sent to the author, who is now at the Department of Psychology, University of South Carolina, Columbia, South Carolina 29208.

immediately prior target was a semantically unrelated word (e.g., BREAD). Schvaneveldt and Meyer (1973) have proposed two models, each of which can account for this semantic-facilitation effect. Both models share the assumption that, in terms of a spatial metaphor, the logogens for semantically related words are located nearer each other in semantic memory than are the logogens for semantically unrelated words (cf. Morton, 1970). According to the *spreading excitation* model, when a stimulus word activates its logogen, this activation spreads to adjacent, semantically related logogens but not to remote, semantically unrelated logogens. Thus, if a word that is to be processed is presented before there has been a complete decay of the logogen activation produced by a previously presented semantically related word, the activation level in the logogen of the to-be-processed word will initially be higher (due to the activation

SOURCE: *Memory & Cognition*, 4(5), 1976, pp. 648–654. Reprinted by permission of Psychonomic Society, Inc.

that has spread to it) than it would have been had it been preceded by a semantically unrelated word; the result will be a facilitation in its processing. According to the *location shifting* model, a limited-capacity attentional mechanism can "read out" the information stored at only those logogens upon which it is focused, and it must therefore be shifted before the information stored at an unattended logogen can be analyzed in preparation for response initiation. Thus, in terms of the location shifting model, the semantic-facilitation effect occurs because attention "traverses a shorter distance" when it shifts between semantically related logogens than when it shifts between semantically unrelated logogens.

Meyer, Schvaneveldt, and Ruddy (Note 1) conducted a lexical decision experiment designed to distinguish between these two models. Within each triplet of successively presented items, an item could be a word semantically related to another word in the triplet (R items), a word semantically unrelated to other words in the triplet (U items), or a nonword (N items). The spreading excitation model predicts that the reaction times (RTs) to the second R item in a RUR triplet should be faster than RTs to the comparable item in the UUU control triplet—to the degree that the excitation spreading from the first R word's logogen has not dissipated during the time required for the response to the intervening U word. On the other hand, the location shifting model predicts that the RTs to the second R item of the RUR triplet should *never* be faster than the RTs to the comparable item in the UUU control triplet, since in both the RUR and UUU triplets the necessary shift in attention between the second and third items would always be between semantically unrelated items. The results were that RTs to the second R item in the RUR triplets were faster than the RTs to the comparable item in the UUU triplets, thus supporting the spreading excitation model. Schvaneveldt and Meyer (1973) obtained similar results in a simultaneous presentation paradigm and concluded that the semantic-facilitation effect in the lexical decision task should be attributed to spreading activation rather than to location shifting.

Quite recently, Posner and Snyder (1975a) have taken exception to Schvaneveldt and Meyer's (1973) conclusion that a limited-capacity attentional mecha-

nism is not involved in the semantic-facilitation effect. In their theorizing, rather than viewing spreading activation and limited-capacity attention as mutually exclusive processes, as Schvaneveldt and Meyer (1973) have viewed them, Posner and Snyder (1975a) have assumed that spreading activation and limited-capacity attention can operate in conjunction with each other to modulate performance. Thus, from Posner and Snyder's theoretical perspective, although the Meyer et al. (Note 1) and the Schvaneveldt and Meyer (1973) data did indeed provide evidence for spreading activation, they did not rule out a contribution of the limited-capacity attentional mechanism to the semantic-facilitation effect obtained in the lexical decision task. In fact, since a decay of spreading activation was not sufficient to explain the complete loss of facilitation that was obtained for RNR triplets in the Meyer et al. experiment, Posner and Snyder argued that the Meyer et al. results actually suggested that the semantic-facilitation effect in the lexical decision task is due to the operation of *both* a limited-capacity attentional mechanism and a spreading activation process.

The purpose of the present experiment was to examine further the roles of limited-capacity attention and spreading activation in the semantic-facilitation effect in the lexical decision task. A crucial feature of the design of the present experiment is that, following the recommendation of Posner and Snyder (1975a), the target word to which the subject was to make a lexical decision was preceded by a semantically neutral warning prime consisting of a series of Xs (Condition NX) on some trials and by either a semantically related word prime (Condition R) or a semantically unrelated word prime (Condition U) on other trials. The importance of including an NX warning prime which does not direct the limited-capacity attentional mechanism to a specific set of word logogens nor activate, via spreading activation, the logogen for the target word is that it provides a baseline for assessing the limited-capacity attentional effects and the spreading activation effects produced by the U and R word primes, with their warning signal effects (cf. Posner & Boies, 1971) partialled out. In terms of the cost-benefit nomenclature adopted by Posner and Snyder (1975b), if RTs to the target letter string are faster when the target follows a word prime than when it follows the NX prime, the word prime is said to have facilitated the processing of the target item; if, on the other hand, RTs to the target letter string are slower when the target follows a word prime than when it follows the NX prime, the word prime is said to have inhibited the processing of the target.

If the semantic-facilitation effect is replicated in the present experiment, subjects should be much faster in responding "word" to a word target in Condition R than in Condition U. More importantly, if, in comparison to Condition NX, subjects are slower to respond "word" to the word targets in Condition U, the limited-capacity attentional mechanism would be implicated in the semantic-facilitation effect because, in the Posner-Snyder theory, inhibition is produced by misdirected attention (due to its limited capacity) but is not produced by spreading activation.[1] If, on the other hand, there are no differences in the RTs to the word targets in Conditions NX and U, the semantic-facilitation effect could be solely attributed to spreading activation, as Schvaneveldt and Meyer (1973) have suggested. The stimulus onset asynchrony (SOA) between the prime and the target was also varied in the present experiment in order to chart the time course of the facilitation and inhibition effects (should they be obtained). The Posner-Snyder theory predicts that the facilitation in Condition R should build up faster than the inhibition in Condition U, because spreading-activation facilitation is fast and automatic, while inhibition depends on the slower and more deliberate commitment of conscious attention.

Another important feature of the design of the present experiment is that it uses words other than the target words themselves as primes to activate, via spreading activation in Condition R, the logogen for the target word. This eliminates the opportunity for the subject to respond to the target on the basis of a physical match or mismatch between the target and the priming word. This is important because the inhibition obtained in the Posner and Snyder (1975b) experiments could have been produced by such a

physical-match strategy rather than by a general inhibition associated with misdirected attention, as predicted by the Posner-Snyder theory. Because of the evidence for a physical-match strategy obtained in their experiments, Posner and Snyder (1975a, b) acknowledged that their theory would be more strongly supported if an inhibition effect was obtained in an experiment in which the prime and the target were not physically identical. If, in the present experiment, an inhibition effect was obtained in Condition U and this effect was to be attributed to a general inhibition effect associated with the operation of limited-capacity attention, the processing of the nonword targets should also be inhibited by the word primes. This prediction is based on the assumption that part of the limited capacity of the attentional mechanism is depleted by the decision to focus attention and the act of focusing attention (cf. LaBerge, 1973). Thus, independently of the location shifting metaphor, which may be inappropriate for N-target trials (see, however, Meyer & Schvaneveldt, 1971) and NX-prime trials, an inhibition effect is predicted for the N targets solely on the basis of the word prime's depleting more attentional capacity than the X prime, because its presentation results in the subject's performing the capacity-consuming operation of focusing his attention on semantically related logogens.[2]

METHOD

Design

As noted above, the dependent variable was the time to decide whether or not a target letter string was an English word. On half of the trials the target letter string was a common English word (W) and on half of the trials, a nonword (N). Immediately prior to the presentation of the target letter string, a prime was shown for 360, 600, or 2,000 msec. (Since SOA and prime duration were confounded, it should be noted that in Posner and Snyder's (1975b) Experiment 1,

---

[1]Collins and Loftus (1975, p. 411) have made a similar assumption in their spreading-activation theory of semantic memory.

[2]Since a priming word itself never appeared as a target and the subject was not required to respond overtly to the priming word, it is assumed that the subject would not continue to focus his attention on the logogen for the word prime itself, but would instead use the word prime to direct his attention to semantically related logogens.

the facilitation and inhibition effects depended only on SOA, not on prime duration.) The SOAs were chosen to be considerably longer than those used by Posner and Snyder (1975b) because it was thought that a substantial amount of time would be required for the subject to read a priming word selected from a large stimulus set, i.e., the English lexicon, and for the subject to use that priming word to direct his attention to semantically related logogens rather than focusing his attention on the logogen for the priming word itself. (See Footnote 2.) As defined above, there were three kinds of primes for the W targets: R, U, and NX. Since the R and U distinction was a pseudo-distinction for the N targets, data from all word-prime N-target trials were collapsed into a single word-prime (WP) condition. In short, for the W targets the complete design was a 3 (prime duration) by 3 (prime type) design and, for the N targets, it was a 3 (prime duration) by 2 (prime type, WP vs. NX) design, with each subject receiving each of the nine W conditions and each of the six N conditions.

Stimulus Materials and List Construction

The priming words and the target words for the R-W conditions were chosen from an atlas of normative free association data (Shapiro & Palermo, 1968) such that, when the priming word served as a stimulus, the target word was given as the primary associate at least 40% of the time. For the U-W conditions, the priming words were reshuffled so that they did not appear on the same trial as did their primary responses. For the WP-N conditions, the priming words were chosen from the Kucera and Francis (1967) norms, so that they were matched on frequency with the priming words for the R-W and U-W conditions. The N targets were constructed from words drawn from the set of remaining words in the Shapiro and Palermo norms by changing one letter in each of the words (e.g., BRUSH to GRUSH and CREDIT to CREMIT). James (1975) has argued that, when pronounceable nonword targets such as these are used, the subject cannot classify words and nonwords on the basis of structural differences and must, therefore, "look up" the meaning of the word targets in order to make his lexical decision.

A base list consisting of six blocks of 42 trials was formed using these materials. The W targets for the first three blocks of 126 total trials were chosen from the 126 response terms taken from the associative norms. Since there were only 63 N targets from which to choose, a W or N target was "randomly" chosen such that in the first three blocks there were 63 W targets and 63 N targets, with no repetitions of a W or N target. The remaining 63 W targets appeared in the second three blocks and the 63 N targets used in the first three blocks were used once again. Thus, each N target occurred twice in the whole list, once in the first three blocks and once in the second three blocks, but no *word* appeared twice in the experiment, either as a target or as a prime. The priming conditions were randomly assigned to the targets, with the constraint that within each block of 42 trials there were 7 instances each of the R-W, U-W, NX-W, and NX-N conditions and 14 instances of the WP-N condition. Two other base lists were derived from the first base list by reassigning primes, so that across the three lists each W target occurred in all three priming conditions and each N target occurred in both the WP and the NX conditions. The order of presentation of the targets remained the same for the three base lists. Three additional lists (for a total of six base lists) were constructed from the three base lists by interchanging the targets in the first three blocks with those targets in the same serial position in the second three blocks.

The SOAs were blocked such that, in the first three blocks, the SOA was 360 msec in one block, 600 msec in another block, and 2,000 msec in the remaining block, and likewise for the second three blocks. A base order of SOAs was developed by "randomly" assigning SOAs to blocks such that no two successive blocks were assigned the same SOA. Two other SOA orders were derived from it such that, across the three SOA orders, each of the six blocks was assigned to each of the SOAs.

Each of the 18 lists (6 base lists × 3 SOA orders) was preceded by an identical practice block of 28 trials with 14 W targets and 14 N targets. There were no instances of the R-W condition in the practice list. Furthermore, the SOA was always 2,000 msec for the first block of 14 trials and 360 msec for the second block of 14 trials. Although there were no 600 msec

SOAs in the practice list, subjects were told that they would receive three different SOAs in the experiment but that they would be given only the long and short SOAs in the practice block.

Each of the six blocks of 42 trials in the test sequence was preceded by two practice trials with no instances of Condition R-W. The two practice trials preceding each block were different for each block but identical for all 18 lists.

Procedure

Eighteen members of the Yale community were paid $2 each for their participation in the 1-h session. All subjects were native English speakers and each subject was tested individually. Each subject was read general instructions describing the task and was told that the word targets were common English words, so that the experiment would not be a vocabulary or spelling test. The subject was told to make fewer than 10% errors and to fixate his vision on both the priming slide and the target slide as long as it remained displayed. The subject was also told that he should try to avoid anticipating if a trial was going to contain a word or nonword target, since this was randomly determined, and that the experimenter would read out the RT for each trial so the subject could try to improve his times.

Each trial consisted of two slides, the priming slide and the target slide, successively rear projected on translucent Mylar near the center of a 12.0 × 16.0 cm aperture. The priming event and the target event occurred in identical positions in the aperture. The offset of the priming slide was followed immediately by the onset of the target slide, which remained exposed until the subject responded by pressing one of two keys. The subject began each trial with the index finger of each hand resting on its corresponding key. For half of the subjects, the "word" response was assigned to the dominant hand and the "nonword" response to the nondominant hand; for the other half of the subjects, the opposite assignment was made. During the 9-sec intertrial interval, subjects were informed of their RT for the previous trial and were told whether or not they had made an error. The prime durations were controlled by Lafayette shutters and BRS digibit solid state timers; RTs were measured

to the nearest millisecond by a Hunter Model 1520 timer.

After the instructions were read, the 28 practice trials were given. There was a 30-sec intertrial interval between the 14th and 15th practice trials to allow the experimenter to change the SOA from 2,000 to 360 msec. After the practice list, the slide trays and the SOA were changed. This required about 2 min and then the first block began. All six blocks were separated by this 2-min change-over period and, before each block began, the subject was told whether the SOA for that block would be the long, medium, or short time interval.

RESULTS

Word Target Data

Figure 1 displays the mean RTs for correct responses to the W targets for the different prime-type conditions as a function of SOA, with the mean percentage of errors given in parentheses. The number of observations upon which each of these means was based varied between 233 and 245. The most salient aspect of the W-target data is that a large semantic-facilitation effect was obtained, i.e., RTs in Condition R were, on the average, 54 msec faster than RTs in Condition U. More importantly, this semantic-facilitation effect was attributable to an average inhibition effect of 16 msec in Condition U (as compared to Condition NX) and an average facilitation effect of 38 msec in Condition R (as compared to Condition NX). The inhibition effect seen in Condition U remained relatively constant as a function of SOA, while the facilitation effect seen in Condition R increased from 17 msec for the 360-msec SOA to 56 msec for the 2,000-msec SOA. Another point of interest is that, for all three priming conditions, RTs tended to be fastest at the 600-msec SOA, a result that is in accord with the finding of Posner and Boies (1971) that a warning signal speeds up responses most at SOAs near 500 msec.

These conclusions were generally supported by a 2 (half of session) by 3 (prime type) by 3 (SOA) by 18 (subjects) analysis of variance. There was a highly significant effect of prime type [$F(2,32) = 62.1$, $p < .001$, $MSe = 1,318$]. Subsequent t tests, using the appropriate error term from the overall analysis of variance as

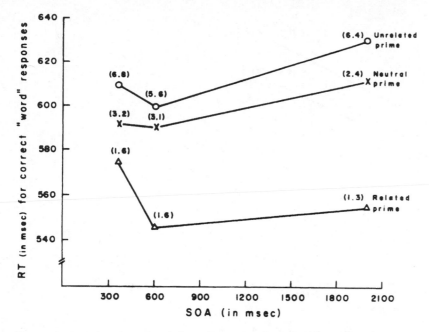

FIGURE 1   Reaction times (RTs) (in milliseconds) for correct responses in the word-target conditions as a function of stimulus onset asynchrony (SOA). Mean percentage errors are given in parentheses.

the error estimate, indicated that there was a statistically significant inhibition effect in Condition U [t(32) = 3.14, p < .01] and a statistically significant facilitation effect in Condition R [t(32) = 7.69, p < .001]. Fourteen subjects showed an inhibition effect for Condition U, and all 18 subjects demonstrated a facilitation effect in Condition R. Although the effect of SOA was not statistically reliable [F(2,32) = 2.36, MSe = 4,863], the interaction of SOA by Prime Type did reach conventional levels of statistical reliability [F(4,64) = 2.97, p < .05, MSe = 1,709]. The facilitation effect for Condition R was smaller at the 360-msec SOA than at the 600-msec and 2,000-msec SOAs [t(64) = 2.42, p < .01; t(64) = 4.04, p < .001, respectively]. The Session Half by Prime Type interaction yielded F(2,32) = 5.45, p < .01, MSe = 1,537, with the facilitation effect for Condition R being larger in the second half of the session than in the first half (48 vs. 28 msec) [t(32) = 2.68, p < .01], and the inhibition effect for Condition U being larger in the second half of the session than in the first half (23 vs. 8 msec) [t(32) = 1.99, p < .06].

Since error rates were so low (3.6% overall), they were not subjected to an analysis of variance. Thus, the only point that needs to be made concerning the error rates is that there was no evidence for a speed-accuracy tradeoff, since there were more errors (6.3%) in Condition U than in Condition NX (2.9%) and fewest errors (1.5%) in Condition R.

Nonword Target Data

Figure 2 displays the mean RTs for correct responses to the N targets for the two prime-type conditions as a function of SOA, with the mean percentage of errors given in parentheses. The number of observations upon which each of the WP and NX means was based varied between 464 and 471 and between 230 and 232, respectively. There are two points of interest in the data in Figure 2. First, RTs in the WP condition were, on the average, 12 msec faster than in the NX condition, and this facilitation effect increased with increasing SOAs. Second, RTs were fastest for both priming conditions at the 600-msec SOA.

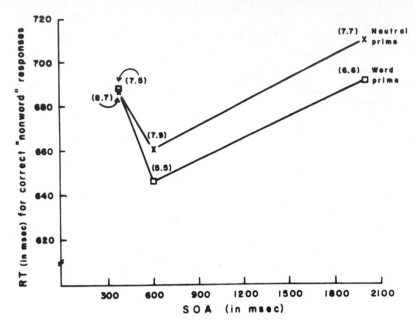

FIGURE 2   Reaction times (RTs) (in milliseconds) for correct responses in the nonword-target conditions as a function of stimulus onset asynchrony (SOA). Mean percentage errors are given in parentheses.

The statistical reliability of these effects was assessed with a 2 (half of session) by 2 (prime type) by 3 (SOA) by 18 (subjects) analysis of variance. The facilitation effect in Condition WP was statistically significant [$F(1,16) = 6.43$, $p < .05$, MSe = 1,200], with 14 of the 18 subjects showing the effect. However, the amount of facilitation produced by the word primes was not significantly greater for the 600- and 2,000-msec SOAs than for the 360-msec SOA [$F(2,32) < 1$, MSe = 3,685], nor did the amount of facilitation differ for the two halves of the session [$F(1,16) = 3.75$, $p > .05$, MSe = 1,546]. The only other effect to reach conventional levels of statistical significance was the effect of SOA [$F(2,32) = 6.96$, $p < .01$, MSe = 5,000]. The RTs were faster at the 600-msec SOA than at the 360-msec SOA [$t(32) = 1.87$, $p < .05$, one-tailed] or the 2,000-msec SOA [$t(32) = 2.55$, $p < .05$]. As noted above, this result is in accord with the findings of Posner and Boies (1971).

As with the word data, the error rates did not provide any evidence for a speed-accuracy tradeoff,

since there were fewer errors (6.5%) in Condition WP than in Condition NX (8.1%).

DISCUSSION

The results of the present experiment, taken in conjunction with the results of Meyer et al. (Note 1) and Schvaneveldt and Meyer (1973), suggest that there may be two reasons why subjects are faster to respond that a target letter string is a word when it follows a semantically related priming word than when it follows a semantically unrelated priming word: (1) Activation spreads from the logogen for the priming word to the logogens for semantically related words, and (2) the subject uses the priming word to direct his limited-capacity attention to logogens for words that are semantically related to the priming word. Within the framework of the Posner-Snyder (1975a) theory, evidence that the subject is using the prime to direct his attention comes from two sources. First, subjects were slower to respond that a target was a word when it followed a semantically unrelated priming word than when it followed a neutral warning signal. Such an effect would occur if the subject used the prime to direct his attention to semantically related logogens, since his attention would then be misdirected when the target was a semantically unrelated word. Second, the findings that the amount of inhibition seen in Condition U and the amount of facilitation seen in Condition R both increased with practice are congruent with the limited-capacity attention interpretation because, as subjects receive more and more trials in which the prime and target are semantically related, they should be more likely to adopt the strategy of using the prime to direct their attention to semantically related logogens.

However, there are other data from the experiment that suggest that the inhibition effect obtained in Condition U may not have been due to misdirected attention. First of all, contrary to what the Posner-Snyder theory predicts, the inhibition effect in Condition U did not increase as the SOA increased, but there may have been a failure to detect this predicted growth in inhibition because of its small magnitude, i.e., 15 msec. A possible reason why the inhibition effect was so small in Condition U is that, unlike the previous lexical decision studies, the present experiment did not require that the subject respond to the priming word. (This was done in order to better control the SOA between the priming word and the target word and to equate the overt-response requirements for the neutral warning signal and the word primes.) Therefore, the subject may not have committed the limited-capacity attentional mechanism to the read out of information from the priming logogen, because the probability that a word prime was semantically related to the target word was only 50%, conditionalized on the presentation of a priming word and a word target, and because the automatic facilitation effects may have been substantial enough by themselves, such that there was no overriding motivation for the subject to focus his attention on logogens semantically related to the priming word.

Notwithstanding this reasonable explanation for the small magnitude of the inhibition effect in Condition U, the problematic fact still remains that the inhibition effect was statistically significant and yet did not increase as the SOA increased. A proponent of the Posner-Snyder theory might maintain that, since the amount of inhibition did not increase with increases in the SOA, the small inhibition effect seen in Condition U should not be attributed to the operation of the limited-capacity attentional mechanism. This argument can be made less tautological by an appeal to the nonword data. If the priming word was depleting some of the subject's limited-capacity conscious attention, according to the Posner-Snyder theory there should have been an inhibition effect for the N targets as well as for the semantically unrelated W targets. However, RTs for the N targets were significantly faster in Condition WP than in Condition NX. Thus, within the framework of the Posner-Snyder theory, the facilitation effect for the nonword targets argues against the limited-capacity attentional explanation of the inhibition effect in Condition U. Equally important is the fact that the facilitation effect for the nonword targets also argues against other one-factor explanations for the inhibition effect obtained in Condition U. For example, it cannot be argued that the act of reading the priming word slowed down RTs in Condition U because it should have had the same effect for the nonwords; nor can it be argued that subjects were slower to respond to the N targets in Condition NX than in Condition WP because they were less aroused following a "boring" X prime than following a more interesting word prime, because the same arousal factor should have been operative for the W targets and should have produced a facilitation effect in Condition U.

Although the present experiment was designed to eliminate the physical-match strategy that Posner and Snyder (1975b) attributed to their subjects, the results of the present experiment nevertheless correspond to their findings. That is, in both the present experiment and Posner and Snyder's experiments, when the Posner-Snyder theory predicted an inhibition in the processing of a target array for which a positive response was correct, the predicted inhibition was obtained; however, when the Posner-Snyder theory predicted an inhibition in the processing of a target array for which a negative response was correct, the predicted inhibition was not obtained, but a statistically significant facilitation effect was obtained instead.

The commonality in the results of these experiments suggests a possible explanation for the inhibition effect in Condition U-W and the facilitation effect in Condition WP-N. Although the design of the present experiment precluded a physical-match strategy, the use of highly stereotyped primary associates may have encouraged the subjects to adopt an associative matching strategy of generating the primary associate of the priming word, matching this self-generated item with the target item and then responding on the basis of a match or mismatch. For example, given CAT as a priming word, the subject would generate "dog" as a candidate for the target; if DOG was indeed the target, he would be fast to respond "word"; if any other letter string appeared as the target, he would have a tendency to respond "nonword." This tendency would speed up (and decrease errors for) a "nonword" response to TARK, but it would slow down (and increase errors for) a "word" response to NURSE. The idea that subjects adopted this strategy becomes more reasonable when one considers the structure of the present experiment. Since a W target was a word semantically unrelated to the word prime on half of the word-prime trials and a W target followed a word prime on only half of the word-prime trials, the subject could have based his response on an associative match, and he would have been correct and benefited on 75% of the word-prime trials (including N-target trials).

Of course, this associative-matching strategy does not explain the failure to find a statistically significant Inhibition by SOA interaction, because an associative-matching strategy depends on a conscious attentional strategy of generating a word associatively related to the priming word; thus, it too should become more fully operative as the SOA increases. Nevertheless, the associative-matching explanation does serve to integrate the results of the Posner and Snyder (1975b) experiments with the present results. It also suggests that the use of a matching strategy is not confined to priming experiments in which the primes and targets are often physically identical, but rather may be used in all kinds of priming experiments, with the match being made at the level appropriate to the particular experiment. If future priming experiments should provide more evidence for some sort of matching strategy, the implication would be that in priming experiments conscious-attention inhibition is not exerting its influence during the stimulus encoding or information read-out stage of processing, as is currently postulated by the Posner-Snyder (1975a) theory, but rather is having its effect in the response-decision stage of processing.

Whatever the ultimate theoretical resolution of the time course and the mechanism of the inhibition effects obtained in the present experiment may be, it would seem that the present experiment furnishes three empirical facts that should be counted among the core set of facts that any theory of semantic priming and the lexical decision process must accommodate if it is to be an adequate theory. The three facts are that, in comparison to a noninformative and semantically neutral warning-signal prime, a word prime (1) facilitates lexical decisions about a subsequently presented semantically related word, (2) inhibits lexical decisions about a subsequently presented semantically unrelated word, and (3) facilitates lexical decisions about a subsequently presented nonword.

REFERENCE NOTE

1. Meyer, D. E., Schvaneveldt, R. W., & Ruddy, M. G. *Activation of lexical memory.* Paper presented at the meeting of the Psychonomic Society, St. Louis, November 1972.

REFERENCES

Collins, A. M., & Loftus, E. F. A spreading-activation theory of semantic processing. *Psychological Review,* 1975, 82, 407–428.

James, C. T. The role of semantic information in lexical decisions. *Journal of Experimental Psychology: Human Perception and Performance,* 1975, 1, 130–136.

Kucera, H., & Francis, W. N. *Computational analysis of present-day American English.* Providence, R.I.: Brown University Press, 1967.

LaBerge, D. Identification of the time to switch attention: A test of a serial and parallel model of attention. In S. Kornblum (Ed.). *Attention and performance IV.* New York: Academic Press, 1973.

Meyer, D. E., & Schvaneveldt, R. W. Facilitation in recognizing pairs of words: Evidence of a dependence between retrieval operations. *Journal of Experimental Psychology,* 1971, 90, 227–234.

Morton, J. A functional model for memory. In D. A. Norman (Ed.), *Models of human memory.* New York: Academic Press, 1970.

Posner, M. I., & Boies, S. W. Components of attention. *Psychological Review,* 1971, 78, 391–408.

Posner, M. I., & Snyder, C. R. R. Attention and cognitive control. In R. L. Solso (Ed.), *Information processing and cognition: The Loyola symposium.* Hillsdale, N.J.: Erlbaum, 1975. (a)

Posner, M. I., & Snyder, C. R. R. Facilitation and inhibition in the processing of signals. In P. M. A. Rabbitt & S. Dornic (Eds.), *Attention and performance V.* New York: Academic Press, 1975. (b)

Schvaneveldt, R. W., & Meyer, D. E. Retrieval and comparison processes in semantic memory. In S. Kornblum (Ed.), *Attention and performance IV.* New York: Academic Press, 1973.

Shapiro, S. I., & Palermo, D. S. An atlas of normative free association data. *Psychonomic Monograph Supplements,* 1968, 2, 219–250.

POSTSCRIPT

Although initially very successful, the two-factor account of priming developed by Neely (see also Neely, 1977) has difficulty accounting for a variety of results observed since (see Neely, 1991, and Neely & Keefe, 1989, for general reviews; see McKoon & Ratcliff, 1992, and McNamara, 1992, for reviews and for data pertaining more specifically to the controversy between spreading-activation-based and nonspreading-activation-based models). One problem discussed in this selection is that the processing of a nonword—which presumably is not represented by a logogen—is facilitated when it is preceded by a word rather than by a series of *X*s (see de Groot, 1984, and Favreau & Segalowitz, 1983, which describe the effects a variety of other variables have on priming). A second problem also hinted at in this selection is that the kind of processing the prime is subjected to also affects degree of priming (Friedrich, Henik, & Tzelgov, 1991; Lorch, Balota, & Stamm, 1986). Perhaps most problematic, however, is evidence that the processing of a word is sometimes affected by words presented subsequently—that is, backward priming can sometimes be observed (Seidenberg, Waters, Sanders, & Langer, 1984).

Neely and Keefe (1989; Neely, Keefe, & Ross, 1989) have proposed a hybrid prospective/retrospective processing theory to account for these results. The hybrid theory suggests that in addition to the two prospective processes discussed in this selection—expectancy and spreading activation—semantic priming involves a retrospective component consisting of processes that operate after both the prime and the target have been identified but before a response is made. Unfortunately, neither the hybrid theory nor other promising alternatives (such as Ratcliff & McKoon, 1988) accounts perfectly for all the available data (Neely & Keefe, 1989; see also Balota, Black, & Cheney, 1992).

Although our discussion so far has focused on priming between visually presented words that are associated with one another in meaning, other kinds of priming are also possible. For example, priming can take place (1) between sentence fragments and words (West & Stanovich, 1982), (2) between words and pictures (Biederman & Cooper, 1992; Schacter, Delaney, & Merikle, 1990), (3) between musical chords (Bharucha & Stoeckig, 1986, 1987), and (4) cross-modally—between words presented auditorily and words presented visually (Swinney, Onifer, Prather, & Hirshkowitz, 1979). Priming also occurs when the same word, picture, or fragment of a word serves as both prime and target. Close examination, however, suggests that the effects observed in the latter case (called repetition, direct, or perceptual priming) differ from those observed with semantic priming (Farah, 1989; Tulving & Schacter, 1990). Some of the implications of this observation are discussed in Reading 15.

FOR FURTHER THOUGHT

1. What should Neely's results have been if spreading activation were the only process involved in priming? What should Neely's results have been if expectancy were the only process involved in priming? What result obtained by Neely is problematic for location-shifting as an explanation of expectancy effects?
2. Neely found that words (as opposed to strings of Xs) will facilitate lexical decisions for nonwords. According to Neely, what one-factor alternative explanations are ruled out by this finding? Why is this result also problematic for the two-factor theory? How does Neely address this problem?
3. Neely argues that the physical-match strategy cannot be applied in this experiment. What is the physical-match strategy, and why can't it be applied here? What extension of this strategy does Neely suggest may be operating instead, and what results lead him to this hypothesis?
4. Why does Neely report his subjects' error rates? How would we interpret the reaction-time results if their error rates were uniformly high?

REFERENCES

Balota, D. A., Black, S. R., & Cheney, M. (1992). Automatic and attentional priming in young and older adults: Reevaluation of the two-process model. *Journal of Experimental Psychology: Human Perception and Performance, 18,* 485–502.

Bharucha, J. J., & Stoeckig, K. (1986). Reaction time and musical expectancy: Priming of chords. *Journal of Experimental Psychology: Human Perception and Performance, 12,* 403–410.

Bharucha, J. J., & Stoeckig, K. (1987). Priming of chords: Spreading activation or overlapping frequency spectra? *Perception & Psychophysics, 41*, 519–524.

Biederman, I., & Cooper, E. E. (1992). Size invariance in visual object priming. *Journal of Experimental Psychology: Human Perception and Performance, 18*, 121–133.

de Groot, A. M. B. (1984). Primed lexical decision: Combined effects of the proportion of related prime-target pairs and the stimulus-onset asynchrony of prime and target. *Quarterly Journal of Experimental Psychology, 36A*, 253–280.

Farah, M. J. (1989). Semantic and perceptual priming: How similar are the underlying mechanisms? *Journal of Experimental Psychology: Human Perception and Performance, 15*, 188–194.

Favreau, M., & Segalowitz, N. (1983). Automatic and controlled processes in the first- and second-language reading of fluent bilinguals. *Memory & Cognition, 11*, 565–574.

Friedrich, F. J., Henik, A., & Tzelgov, J. (1991). Automatic processes in lexical access and spreading activation. *Journal of Experimental Psychology: Human Perception and Performance, 17*, 792–806.

Lorch, R. F., Balota, D., & Stamm, E. (1986). Locus of inhibition effects in the priming of lexical decisions: Pre- or post-lexical access? *Memory & Cognition, 14*, 95–103.

McKoon, G., & Ratcliff, R. (1992). Spreading activation versus compound cue accounts of priming; Mediated priming revisited. *Journal of Experimental Psychology: Learning, Memory, and Cognition, 18*, 1155–1172.

McNamara, T. P. (1992). Theories of priming I: Associative distance and lag. *Journal of Experimental Psychology: Learning, Memory, and Cognition, 18*, 1173–1190.

Neely, J. H. (1977). Semantic priming and retrieval from lexical memory: Roles of inhibitionless spreading activation and limited-capacity attention. *Journal of Experimental Psychology: General, 106*, 226–254.

Neely, J. H. (1991). Semantic priming effects in visual word recognition: A selective review of current findings and theories. In D. Besner & G. Humphreys (Eds.), *Basic processes in reading: Visual word recognition* (pp. 264–336). Hillsdale, NJ: Erlbaum.

Neely, J. H., & Keefe, D. E. (1989). Semantic context effects on visual word processing: A hybrid prospective-retrospective processing theory. In G. H. Bower (Ed.) *The psychology of learning and motivation* (Vol. 24, pp. 207–248). New York: Academic Press.

Neely, J. H., Keefe, D. E., & Ross, K. (1989). Semantic priming in the lexical decision task: Roles of prospective prime-generated expectancies and retrospective semantic matching. *Journal of Experimental Psychology: Learning, Memory, and Cognition, 15*, 1003–1019.

Ratcliff, R., & McKoon, G. (1988). A retrieval theory of priming in memory. *Psychological Review, 95*, 385–408.

Schacter, D. L., Delaney, S. M., & Merikle, E. P. (1990). Priming of nonverbal information and the nature of implicit memory. In G. H. Bower (Ed.), *The psychology of learning and memory*, (Vol. 26, pp. 83–123). New York: Academic Press.

Seidenberg, M. S., Waters, G., Sanders, M., & Langer, P. (1984). Pre- and post-lexical loci of contextual effects on word recognition. *Memory & Cognition, 12,* 315–328.

Swinney, D. A., Onifer, W., Prather, P., & Hirshkowitz, M. (1979). Semantic facilitation across sensory modalities in the processing of individual words and sentences. *Memory & Cognition, 7,* 159–165.

Tipper, S. P. (1992). Selection for action: The role of inhibitory mechanisms. *Current Directions in Psychological Science, 1,* 105–109.

Tulving, E., & Schacter, D. L. (1990). Priming and the human memory system. *Science, 247,* 301–306.

West, R. F., & Stanovich, K. (1982). Source of inhibition in experiments on the effect of sentence context on word recognition. *Journal of Experimental Psychology: Learning, Memory, and Cognition, 8,* 385–399.

INTRODUCTION

In "Priming across Modalities and Priming across Category Levels," Peter Graf, Arthur Shimamura, and Larry Squire study amnesics to investigate the possibility that not all of our knowledge or memories are explicit or conscious, that some of our memories are implicit. Although we may not be able to articulate or even be aware of such implicit memories, they affect certain aspects of our behavior. Specifically, Graf, Shimamura, and Squire try to show that although amnesics may lack the processes that allow them to acquire or access some of the knowledge or memories that are consciously available to most of us, they retain the processes that allow them to acquire and be affected (in certain ways) by implicit memories. (See the Introduction to Reading 23 for a fuller discussion of the use of special populations to understand normal cognitive functioning.)

Graf and his associates test their assumptions by looking at patterns of free recall and repetition priming in amnesic and nonamnesic patients. Repetition priming tasks—also called direct or perceptual priming tasks—contrast with free-recall tasks in that retrieval in the former is typically in response to some cue (free recall is used in Reading 10). For example, both a repetition priming task and a free-recall task may begin with giving a subject a set of words to work with or study without specifically telling the subject to memorize the set. In a free-recall task, subjects are later asked to recall as many words as they can, in any order that they choose. In a repetition priming task, subjects are asked to list the words that begin, for example, with the letters *str;* that is, they are asked to respond to the cue *str.* The assumption here is that repetition priming taps into processes that remain intact in amnesics because these processes deal with implicit memories, whereas recall tasks tap into processes that amnesics lack.

Although Graf, Shimamura, and Squire simply use the term *priming* for the most part to describe their task, repetition priming differs from the semantic, or associative, priming studied by Neely (see Reading 14). In semantic priming, the speed with which a word can be recognized or the likelihood of its being retrieved from memory is affected by the prior presentation of a *related* word (Roediger & Challis, 1992). In repetition priming, the likelihood that a word will be retrieved from memory is affected by prior presentation of the *same* word.

You might notice that Graf and his colleagues never refer to implicit memories by name, only to the processes and memories tapped by repetition priming. However, they mention in passing that priming instructions are implicit because the instructions do not explicitly ask subjects to retrieve certain information. As you read this article, try to imagine what mechanisms could be responsible for repetition priming effects and how those might differ from mechanisms responsible for conscious knowledge. Can you think of instances in your own experience that make the distinction apparent to you?

Priming across Modalities and Priming across Category Levels: Extending the Domain of Preserved Function in Amnesia

Peter Graf

University of Toronto, Toronto, Canada

Arthur P. Shimamura

Department of Psychiatry, University of California School of Medicine, La Jolla

Larry R. Squire

Veterans Administration Medical Center, San Diego, and Department of Psychiatry, University of California School of Medicine, La Jolla

Studies of amnesia have provided significant insights into the organization of normal memory (for reviews, Cermak, 1982; Rozin, 1976; Squire & Butters, 1984; Squire & Cohen, 1984; Talland, 1965). Recently, studies of new learning capacity in amnesic patients have provided compelling evidence for a distinction between two kinds of memory. These studies showed that amnesia patients are severely impaired in learning new facts and episodes—the events of daily life—yet they are entirely normal in learning perceptual–motor and cognitive skills (Brooks & Baddeley, 1976; Cohen, 1984, Cohen & Squire 1980; Corkin, 1968). For example, amnesic patients can acquire at a normal rate the skills involved in reading words from a mirror, reversed display, and they can retain this skill at a normal level for a three-month period, despite failing to recognize the same words on a recognition test and failing to recognize the apparatus that was used for testing (Cohen & Squire, 1980).

In addition to memory for skills, it is now known that amnesia also spares direct or repetition priming—the facilitation in processing an item, such as a

The research was supported in part by Medical Research Service of the Veterans Administration and NIMH Grant MH24600, by a postdoctoral fellowship and research grant U0229 from the Natural Sciences and Engineering Research Council of Canada to Peter Graf, and by NIMH National Research Services Award MH08992 to Arthur P. Shimamura. We thank Joyce Zouzounis, Brian Leonard, Armand Bernheim, and Patty Feldstein for their research assistance.

Request for reprints should be sent to Larry R. Squire Veterans Administration Medical Center (V116A), 3350 La Jolla Village Drive, San Diego, California 92161.

SOURCE: *Journal of Experimental Psychology: Learning, Memory, and Cognition, 11*(2), 1985, pp. 386–396. Copyright 1985 by the American Psychological Association. Reprinted by permission.

written word, that had been presented recently (Cofer, 1967; Cramer, 1966). For example, Graf, Squire, and Mandler (1984) found normal priming on a word completion test that required subjects to complete the first three letters of recently presented words with the first words that came to mind. Both amnesic patients and control subjects produced the recently presented words as completions for the test cues more than 4 times as often as would have been expected if the words had not been presented. In contrast to word completion performance, however, the amnesic patients showed a severe impairment on a free-recall test and a word recognition test. This pattern of findings and the results from related studies (e.g., Diamond & Rozin, 1984; Jacoby & Witherspoon, 1982; Mortensen, 1980; Schacter, in press; Shimamura & Squire, 1984; Squire, Shimamura, & Graf, 1985a; Warrington & Weiskrantz, 1970, 1974, 1978) indicate that amnesia impairs the ability to recall or recognize words, but it spares the capacity for word priming.

These findings from amnesic patients support the view that the nervous system honors a distinction between two forms of memory, one or more that are spared in amnesia and one that is impaired. Skill learning and priming rely on memory systems or processes that are spared in amnesia, whereas the explicit retention of facts and events, as measured by recall and recognition tests, depends on a different and independent memory system, i.e., a brain system, that is damaged in amnesia (Mishkin, Malamut, & Bachevalier, 1984; Squire, 1982a). This distinction has been expressed in terms of procedural and declarative memory (Cohen, 1984; Cohen & Squire, 1980; Squire & Cohen, 1984). The relationship of this distinction to others that have been proposed is discussed elsewhere (Squire & Cohen, 1984).

To the extent that amnesia reveals a biologically important division of memory functions, it will be useful to obtain a precise delineation of what amnesic patients can and cannot do. Toward this end, the present study further examined priming in amnesic patients. Previous studies of amnesic patients have reported normal priming effects, but these studies did not explore a number of factors that are important determinants of priming in normal subjects. For example, in normal subjects the perceptual similarity be-

tween study list items and test cues influences the magnitude of priming (Clarke & Morton, 1983; Graf & Mandler, 1984; Roediger & Blaxton, 1983; Scarborough, Gerard, & Cortese, 1979; Winnick & Daniel, 1970). Specifically, normal subjects show less priming when study words and test cues are presented in different sensory modalities than when they are presented in the same modality (Graf & Mandler, 1984; Kirsner, Milech, & Standen, 1983; Roediger & Blaxton, 1983). This finding indicates that the priming phenomenon depends to some extent on modality-specific sensory and perceptual information (Forster, 1976; Jacoby, 1983; Morton, 1969, 1979; Scarborough et al., 1979). At the same time, the finding that normal subjects show some priming when study and testing are in different sensory modalities suggests that some aspects of priming are not tied to modality.

Priming across sensory modalities might be mediated by different memory processes than priming within a sensory modality (Clarke & Morton, 1983). It is possible, therefore, that only some of these processes are spared in amnesia. Thus, although amnesic patients show normal priming within a modality, they may show no evidence of priming when the study list and test items are presented in different sensory modalities. In contrast, it is possible that priming is mediated by a set of related processes, all of which are spared in amnesia, such that amnesic patients and normal control subjects would show a similar pattern of priming within modality and across sensory modalities.

The study of priming across modalities in amnesic patients can also address questions that have been raised as to whether across-modality priming in normal subjects even reflects true priming. A number of authors have argued that priming is strictly a modality-specific phenomenon (Clarke & Morton, 1983; Scarborough et al., 1979), and they have dismissed priming across sensory modalities as an artifact that arises as a result of subjects' ability to remember the critical study items (see Clarke & Morton, 1983). Because amnesic patients typically fail to recall a list of words after even a short delay, their performance on a priming test is less likely to be confounded by explicit remembering. Thus amnesic patients could provide stronger evidence for across-modality priming than what can be obtained from normal subjects.

The present study explored these issues in two separate experiments. Both experiments varied the sensory and perceptual similarity between study words and test cues and compared the effects of these variations on test performance in amnesic patients and in control subjects. Experiment 1 compared priming for words that were studied and tested in the same sensory modality or in different sensory modalities. Experiment 2 assessed priming for category exemplars (e.g., *avocado, raspberry)* by presenting category labels as test cues (e.g., *fruit)* and then asking subjects to produce the first exemplars that came to mind (see Kihlstrom, 1980). The critical issue addressed by both experiments is whether amnesic patients exhibit normal priming when there is little or no overlap of sensory and perceptual information between study items and test cues.

EXPERIMENT 1

Experiment 1 compared amnesic patients and control subjects under within-modality and across-modality priming conditions. Subjects were presented words, either visually or orally, and then they received both a free-recall and word completion test. On the word completion test, the initial three letters of words were shown as cues, and subjects were asked to complete the cues with the first words that came to mind. The question of interest was whether or not amnesic patients would exhibit normal priming under all study–test conditions.

Method

Subjects

Amnesic patients.   We tested two groups of amnesic patients. One group consisted of 3 women and 5 men with alcoholic Korsakoff syndrome. These patients, who averaged 53.8 years of age (range 39–74 years) and 12.4 years of formal education (range 12–14), were residents of chronic care facilities in San Diego County. Their average full-scale Wechsler Adult Intelligence Scale (WAIS) IQ was 102.6 (range 91–114), and their average Wechsler Memory Scale (WMS) score was 78 (range 64–93). In normal subjects, the WMS score is equivalent to the WAIS IQ. Neuro-

psychological screening and independent neurological examination indicated that memory impairment was the only notable deficit in higher cortical functions. All of these patients could draw a cube and a house in perspective, and none had aphasia or apraxia. The memory impairment shown by this group has been documented in previous studies (Cohen & Squire, 1981; Graf et al., 1984; Squire, 1982b).

We also tested 2 men who had amnesia of relatively recent onset, caused by hypotensive episodes. One (Case 1) became amnesic in 1976 following a cardiac arrest and a period of unconsciousness [age at testing = 45 years; formal education = 20 years (doctorate in clinical psychology); WAIS IQ = 119; WMS = 91]. The second patient (Case 2) became amnesic in 1978 following complications associated with open heart surgery that included a hypotensive episode (age at testing = 56 years; formal education = 10 years; WAIS IQ = 111; WMS = 91).

All the amnesic patients were characterized by a severe impairment in tests of delayed recall and paired-associate learning. Their scores for immediate and delayed recall (12 min) of a short prose passage average 4.5 and 0.5 segments, respectively (21 segments total). Their recall of 10 unrelated noun–noun pairs on each of three successive trials was 0.5, 1.0, and 1.5.

This description of the amnesic patients is intended to facilitate comparisons between this and other studies of amnesia and to emphasize the severe but circumscribed nature of their memory deficit. However, the main interest here is in overall differences between amnesic patients and control subjects, rather than differences between individual subjects. The data analyses and discussion will therefore focus on the overall pattern of performance on each test.

Control groups.   Two control groups were tested in order to assess the performance of the amnesic patients, one group consisting of alcoholic patients, and a second group consisting of medical patients. The alcoholic control group included 8 men who were participating in alcoholic treatment programs in San Diego County. They had been drinking for an average of 18.9 years, they had abstained from alcohol for an average of 6.5 weeks prior to participating in the present study, and they had no history of head injury or liver disease. This group averaged 48.2 years of age (range 40–59), had 13.5 years of formal education (range 12–20), and had a WAIS-R subtest score of 22 for information (18.1 for the amnesic patients) and 49.9 for vocabulary (44.1 for the amnesic patients). Their scores for immediate and delayed recall (12 min) of a short-prose passage averaged 8.7 and 7.1 segments, respectively. Their recall of 10 unrelated noun–noun pairs on each of three successive trials was 3.9, 7.4, and 8.9.

The second control group consisted of 8 men from the medical and surgical wards of the San Diego Veterans Administration Medical Center. None of these subjects had a psychiatric diagnosis, and none had a history of alcoholism. These patients averaged 50.6 years of age (range 46–56) and had an average of 14.2 years of formal education (range 11–18); they had WAIS-R subtest scores that averaged 22.9 for information (18.1 for the amnesic patients) and 52.8 for vocabulary (44.1 for the amnesic patients).

Materials

One hundred and ten words were selected from Webster's Pocket Dictionary (average frequency of occurrence per million = 70, Kucera & Francis, 1967) and hand printed on index cards in 12 mm high capital letters. These words were from four to eight letters long. The initial three letters, the "stem" of each word (e.g., ELE, BAS), appeared only once among the set of selected words. The pocket dictionary listed at least 10 common words that could be used to complete each stem. The 110 selected words were divided into 3 sets: Set 1 included 80 words that were assigned to 8 target lists of 10 words each; Set 2 included 20 words that were used as fillers at the beginning and end of the target lists to prevent primacy and recency effects; and Set 3 included 10 words that were used for instruction and practice.

Procedure

The subjects were tested individually. They were first instructed in a task that required rating their like or dislike of words with the aid of a 5-point scale that was displayed continuously in front of them. The ends of this scale were labeled *like extremely* (1) and *dislike extremely* (5). This rating task required subjects to analyze the semantic features of the study list words. Subjects practiced this task with words that were presented one at a time, first with five words printed on index cards, and then with five words spoken by the experimenter. Subjects recorded their liking ratings on a blank page. Word presentation was self-paced by each subject's speed on the rating task, about 5-s per word; previous work has shown that rates of presentation that vary from 3 to 7 s have little systematic effects on word completion performance (Graf & Mandler, 1984).

Immediately after practice, there were four study–test trials, with each trial consisting of two presentations of a study list followed by tests of free recall and word completion. The study list for a trial was presented in a different random order on each presentation, and subjects rated how much they liked each word. The study lists were presented visually on two trials, and auditorily on the other two trials. The presentation modality alternated from trial to trial, with the order of modality counterbalanced across subjects. The word completion test cues were always presented visually. Thus, word completion performance following a visual presentation of the study list provided a measure of within-modality priming, whereas word completion performance following an oral presentation provided a measure of across-modality priming.

Each study list included one 10-word target list from Set 1 and 5 filler words. Three of the fillers were always presented at the beginning and two at the ending of the study list. Immediately after the second study list presentation, subjects were asked to recall the list words and write them on a blank page in any order. Then they were given a word-completion test that showed 20 word beginnings, 10 from the critical study list of target words, and 10 from a target list that had not been presented to the same subject. Subjects were told that each of the completion-test cues was "the beginning of an English word," and they were asked to write a "few letters to make each into a word. You can write any English word—but please write the first word that comes to mind." We urged subjects to write the first words that came to mind, but not to give proper names as cue completions.

When a proper name was given, an alternative completion was requested. Subjects usually required only a few seconds to complete each word. When all cues were completed, there was a short pause (about 2–3 min) before the next trial was given.

In summary, each subject studied four of the eight target lists, two that were presented in their written form and two in their spoken form. A recall test was always given immediately after the study phase, followed by a completion test that included the initial three letters of the 10 presented target words, as well as the initial letters of 10 words from one of the four target lists that was never presented to the same subject. The probability of producing target words for the latter word stems provided a measure of baseline completion performance. Across subjects, each target list was presented equally often in each modality. Target lists were also used equally often in study lists and for assessing baseline completion performance.

Results and Discussion

A strict criterion was used in scoring both the free recall and the completion protocols: words were counted as correct only if they had appeared in a tar-

get list in exactly the same form (no plurals, changes in tense, adjectival forms, etc.). Alternative scoring methods did not alter the pattern of findings. In addition, subjects performed similarly on the two study–test trials that were given in each modality, and thus, for the analysis described later, we averaged the results across the two trials. The significance level was set at .05 for all statistical tests.

Figure 1 shows the critical data for amnesic patients and control subjects on the free-recall test and on the word completion test, under both visual–visual and auditory–visual study-test conditions. Overall, average free recall of words was lower for amnesic patients (14.8%) than for inpatient controls (37.2%) or for alcoholic controls (36.9%). However, in each subject group, a similar percentage of words was recalled under visual–visual and visual–auditory study–test conditions. An analysis of variance (ANOVA) of the recall data showed a significant main effect for subject groups, $F(2, 23) = 7.36$, $MS_e = 14.8$, with no other effects approaching significance. This pattern of results illustrates the severe memory deficit of the amnesic patients, and it extends to amnesic patients the familiar finding that modality of study list presentation has little or no effect on measures of explicit remembering (Clarke & Morton, 1983; Graf & Mandler, 1984;

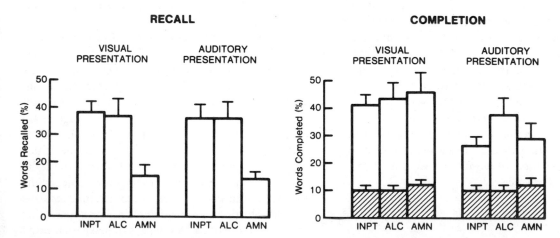

FIGURE 1   Free recall (left) and word completion (right) by amnesic patients (AMN), medical inpatients (INPT), and alcoholic controls (ALC). (Test cues in the word completion test were always presented visually. Thus, test cues were either in the same sensory modality as the study list items (visual presentation) or in a different sensory modality (auditory presentation). The shaded area of each bar shows baseline performance.)

Roediger & Blaxton, 1983; Scarborough et al., 1979; Winnick & Daniel, 1970).

Figure 1 also shows the average level of word completion test performance for words that had appeared on the study list and for words that had not been presented. The latter words provided a measure of baseline completion performance. The three subject groups showed similar levels of baseline completion performance, averaging 10.6%, 10.0%, and 12.8% for the inpatient control group, the alcoholic control group, and the amnesic group, respectively. Figure 1 also indicates that the three groups performed similarly on the critical study list words. In order to obtain a measure of priming from these word completion test scores, each subject's score on the critical study list words was reduced by his or her baseline score on the target words that had not been presented. These difference scores for word completion differed in two important ways from recall test scores. First, the magnitude of priming was similar across the three subject groups (23.4%, 31.4%, and 26.2% for inpatient, alcoholic, and amnesic groups respectively), $F(2, 23) = .5$, thus replicating the finding that amnesic patients can show normal priming on a word completion test despite their profound deficit on tests that require explicit remembering (Diamond & Rozin, 1984; Graf et al., 1984; Jacoby & Witherspoon, 1982; Shimamura & Squire, 1984, Warrington & Weiskrantz, 1974).

Second, modality of study list presentation influenced the magnitude of priming for both amnesic patients and control subjects. Priming was greater for words that had been studied and treated in the same modality (32.9%) than for words that had been studied and tested in different modalities (20.9%), $F(2, 23) = 12.1$, $MS_e = 6.5$. Although within-modality priming was greater than across-modality priming, subjects nevertheless showed significant priming under across-modality conditions (all $ts > 2.92$). The analysis of the completion test data showed no other significant effects. In particular, there was no interaction effect between modality of presentation and subject group.

Finally, we calculated completion performance contingent on recall performance. Averaged over the two types of presentations, word completion performance for words that were correctly recalled was 50%, 56%, and 59% for inpatients, alcoholics, and amnesic patients, respectively. Word completion performance for words not recalled was 25%, 29%, and 31% for these same groups. Thus recalling a word increased the probability that it would be completed, and this increase was similar in the three subject groups.

These findings show that amnesia spares the processes that mediate priming across sensory modalities, as well as the specific sensory and perceptual processes that mediate priming within a modality. All groups exhibited significant priming across modalities, but the magnitude of priming was larger under the within-modality condition. The priming effects found in this study are consistent with the findings of previous studies (Graf & Mandler, 1984; Kirsner et al., 1983; Roediger & Blaxton, 1983).

Others have found no evidence for priming across modalities in normal subjects in studies that revealed substantial priming under within-modality conditions (Clarke & Morton, 1983; Jacoby & Dallas, 1981; Scarborough et al., 1979; Winnick & Daniel, 1970). The absence of a priming effect across sensory modalities in these experiments has been viewed as strong evidence that priming is a modality-specific phenomenon. It has been argued that instances of successful priming across sensory modalities are artifacts, mediated by a subject's tendency to image the written version of words while listening to a study list of spoken words (cf. Jacoby & Witherspoon, 1982). An "imaging" strategy might engage modality-specific visual processes that then mediate priming across modalities. This suggestion was reinforced by the finding that when task instructions focused subjects' attention on visual or written images of spoken words, priming across modalities was sometimes increased (Jacoby & Witherspoon, 1982; but see Graf & Mandler, 1984).

One way to examine this possibility would be to study priming under study–test conditions where the sensory–perceptual overlap between study items and test cues is reduced to a minimum. Instead of cuing with information that had been previously presented (e.g., the initial letters of words), we next cued previously presented words with category labels for those words. Under these conditions, there should be little chance that subjects would image the test cues during presentation of the study list. Thus, this procedure tests whether priming can be semantically or conceptually driven, or whether it is restricted to circumstances where the study items and test cues share the same sensory-perceptual features.

EXPERIMENT 2

Subjects were presented a random list of words belonging to different conceptual categories, and then they were given a priming test. We provided category labels as cues, and subjects were required to generate the first eight exemplars that came to mind (see Kihlstrom, 1980). A free-recall test followed the priming task. This study–test procedure ensured that there was only incidental overlap in sensory and perceptual information between study list items and test cues, because the test cues themselves were never presented in the study list.

Method

Subjects

Amnesic patients.   Two groups of amnesic patients were tested: the 8 patients with Korsakoff syndrome described in Experiment 1, and 2 patients who became amnesic as a result of hypotensive episodes. The latter group included Case 1, described in Experiment 1, and Case 3 who became amnesic in 1983, following a period of reduced blood pressure that occurred during major surgery. Case 3 was 43 years old at the time of testing: he had 13 years of formal education, a WAIS IQ of 104 and a WMS score of 81. His immediate- and delayed- (12 min) recall score for a prose passage was 5 and 0 segments, respectively.

Control groups.   Two groups were used to assess the performance of the amnesic patients; one group consisted of alcoholic patients and the second group consisted of hospital volunteers. The alcoholic control group included 10 men who were participating in alcoholic treatment programs in San Diego County. They had been drinking for an average of 21 years, they had abstained from alcohol for an average of 18 weeks prior to participating in the present study, and they had no history of head injury or liver disease. This group averaged 51.6 years of age (range 37–63),

they had an average of 12.5 years of formal education (range 10–14), and they had an average WAIS-R subtest score of 21.4 for information (18.8 for the amnesic patients) and 52.1 for vocabulary (45.3 for the amnesic patients). Immediate- and delayed- (12 min) recall scores for a prose passage were 6.3 and 4.7 (4.4 and 0.4 for amnesic patients). Their recall of 10 unrelated noun–noun pairs on each of three successive trials was 3.9, 7.4, and 8.9 (0.5, 0.9, and 1.3 for amnesic patients).

The second group consisted of 8 volunteers, 5 men and 3 women, at the San Diego Veterans Administration Medical Center. None of these subjects had a psychiatric diagnosis, and none had a history of alcoholism. This group averaged 39.6 years of age (range 25–61) and 12.2 years of formal education (range 12–14).

Materials

The materials were drawn from the Battig and Montague (1969) norms. From each of 12 categories (e.g., *a piece of furniture, a fruit, a sport, a part of the human body),* we selected five common exemplars (e.g., *bookcase, cabinet, bench, rocker,* and *footstool).* The items selected were not ranked among the 10 most frequently produced exemplars for a category, but each item was listed as an exemplar by at least 10 subjects in the sample of 400 subjects used to collect the normative data. On the basis of overall production frequency, the average rank of the selected category exemplars was 23.9 (range 11–46) in the Battig and Montague norms. These 12 sets of 5 words formed the target lists for Experiment 2.

We used the label from each category as a cue for the priming tests. We changed some of the category labels slightly from those used in collecting the norms, in order to make them more concrete descriptors of the particular items selected for the experiment (e.g., *a kitchen utensil* became *something used in the kitchen).*

Procedure

Subjects were tested individually. They were first instructed in the *liking rating* task described in Experiment 1, and they practiced this task with five unrelated words that were not members of the categories used in the study. Immediately after practice there were two study–test trials. For each trial, a study list of 15 words was read to the subjects twice in succession in a different random order on each presentation, and subjects rated how much they liked each word. The 15-word study list was composed of the five exemplars from each of three different target categories. These words were always arranged randomly in the study list. Word presentation was self-paced by each subject's speed on the liking rating task, about 5-s per word.

Immediately after the second presentation of each study list, subjects were given a priming test, followed by a free-recall test. The priming test instructions advised subjects that "we will now do something different. I'm going to give you a title—the name of a category, and I want you to say eight things that belong to that category as fast as you can." To illustrate this *word production* test, the experimenter provided a label (*a relative*) and some exemplars (*aunt, uncle, sister*), and subjects were asked to produce some further exemplars. For the test itself, subjects were given six category labels, one at a time, and they were asked to produce eight exemplars from each category. Eight exemplars were requested from each category in order to ensure that exemplars other than very common ones would be produced.

Three of the six categories were always the ones from which the study items were drawn, and the other three categories were ones whose exemplars had not been presented to the same subject. The six category labels were presented in a random order. The probability of producing the words from the study list on this word production test provided the measure of interest. The probability of producing target words belonging to the other three categories provided a measure of baseline performance for word production. Across subjects, we counterbalanced the categories that were used for the study list and the categories that were used to assess baseline performance.

Following word production, a free-recall test was given. Subjects were reminded that this test concerned the items that they had heard in the study list, and they were asked to write the words from the study list in any order on a blank page. Then there was a short pause (2–3 min) before the second study–test trial was administered. The second study–test trial was administered in the same way as the first, using a new study list and new category labels. Across the subjects in each group, the exemplars from each category were studied and tested equally often on the first and second trials.

In summary, subjects received two study–test trials, each of which involved the presentation of 15 words followed by a word production test and a free-recall test. The word production test required subjects to produce eight exemplars for each of six category labels. Three of the categories had provided the 15 study words (five from each category), and three of the categories were used to assess baseline word production performance.

Results and Discussion

As in Experiment 1, a strict criterion was used in scoring both the free-recall and the word production test forms. Performance on the first and second study–test trials was virtually identical for both free recall and word completion (F scores less than 1), and thus the results from the two trials were averaged for statistical analyses. Figure 2 shows the average recall performance and word production performance for the three subject groups. The average level of recall was similar for the healthy control group (46.2%) and for the alcoholic group (39.0%), $t = .76$, but recall performance was substantially lower in the amnesic group (1.0%). An ANOVA showed a significant main effect for subject groups, $F(2, 26) = 41.1$, $MS_e = 13.9$.

The three subject groups showed different levels of baseline performance on the word production test, $F(2, 26) = 6.9$, $MS_e = 2.2$ (5.0% for healthy controls, 11.7% for alcoholic controls, and 5.3% for amnesic patients). In order to obtain a measure of priming on the word production test, each subject's score for items for the study list was adjusted by his or her score on the nonpresented items (baseline score). In this way, we obtained a measure of priming that was not influenced by the differences in baseline scores across subject groups. As illustrated in Figure 2, each group showed a significant tendency to generate target words from the study list more often than expected without a study list presentation (12.5% for volunteers, $t(7) = 2.55$, $p < .05$; 11.0% for alcoholic

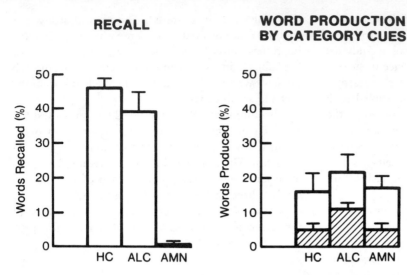

FIGURE 2   Recall (left) and word production (right) by amnesic patients (AMN), healthy controls (HC), and alcoholic controls (ALC). (The study words were exemplars from different categories, and word production was tested by cueing with category labels. The shaded area of each bar shows baseline performance.)

controls, $t(9) = 2.07$, $p = .068$; and 12.3% for amnesic patients, $t(9) = 4.92$, $p < .01$). All groups showed a similar amount of priming, $F(2, 25) = .04$.

An analysis of word production performance contingent on subsequent recall performance was performed for the alcoholic and inpatient control groups (the level of recall for the amnesic group was too low to evaluate). Those items that were produced in the priming task were recalled better than items that were not produced. This effect was seen in Experiment 1 in this article as well as in Tulving, Schacter, and Stark (1982).

This pattern of results strengthens the findings from Experiment 1 by showing priming even under conditions where there was only incidental overlap in sensory and perceptual information between study list items and test cues. Because items from different conceptual categories in the study list were ordered randomly, it was unlikely that during study list presentation subjects would have been able to image the cues that were subsequently used on the word production test. Thus, the present findings indicate that overlap in sensory and perceptual information between study list items and test cues is not essential for priming. Moreover, the finding of similar amounts of

priming in amnesic patients and in 2 control groups is inconsistent with the view that subjects accomplish priming by using a recall strategy to generate words. If that view were correct, one would have expected amnesic patients, who have a severe deficit in free recall, to exhibit poorer performance on the word production test than the control groups.

GENERAL DISCUSSION

The present findings provide a more detailed description of the conditions under which preserved priming can be observed in amnesic patients. In the word completion test of Experiment 1, amnesic patients showed normal priming under both visual–visual and auditory–visual study–test conditions. Both amnesic patients and control subjects showed a larger priming effect under the within-modality condition than they showed under the across-modality condition. The results from Experiment 2 strengthen the evidence for priming across sensory modalities by showing normal and significant priming effects in amnesic patients, even under conditions where there is little or no overlap in sensory and perceptual information between study-list items and test cues. Together, these findings illustrate that amnesia preserves not only modality-specific sensory and perceptual processes, but that it also spares processes that mediate the transfer of information across modalities.

The results from Experiment 1 revealed a significant amount of priming across sensory modalities and an even larger amount of priming within a modality. The larger priming effect found under within-modality conditions suggests that the priming phenomenon is mediated to some extent by the specific sensory and perceptual processes that are engaged when words are presented for study. These modality-specific effects may be similar to what has been found in other priming paradigms such as lexical decision and word identification tasks (Clarke & Morton, 1983; Jacoby, 1983; Jacoby & Dallas, 1981; Scarborough et al., 1979). In lexical decision and word-identification tasks, consistent priming effects that last longer than a second or two occur only when study items and test cues are presented in the same modality. In our experiment, however, and in others (Graf & Mandler, 1985; Roediger & Blaxton, 1983), there was priming across modality boundaries that lasted for at least several minutes. Whether or not priming across modalities is observed may depend on the type of test that is used to measure priming. Lexical decision and word identification tasks assess priming under conditions where speed of processing is the key variable. In contrast, priming on word completion tests does not depend on processing speed because subjects are asked simply to complete test cues with the first words that come to mind. These and other test differences may determine the conditions under which priming across modalities is found (see Graf & Mandler, 1985, for further discussion).

It has been suggested that priming across modalities is an artifact caused by subjects' tendency to invoke visual imagery during the oral presentation of study words (Jacoby & Witherspoon, 1982). To the extent that subjects used imagery while hearing spoken words, priming across modalities could be mediated by processes specific to the visual mode. Although this suggestion provides one possible account for priming across modalities in Experiment 1, it cannot account for the priming effects found in Experiment 2. In Experiment 2, there was essentially no sensory and perceptual overlap between study items and

test cues. In addition, the items from the different categories were ordered randomly in the study list, thus making it unlikely that subjects would discover and image the identity of test cues during study list presentation. Nevertheless, amnesic patients and control groups showed a significant amount of priming. Thus, the finding of priming across sensory modalities is difficult to dismiss as an artifact owing to imaging (Jacoby & Witherspoon, 1982).

The priming of words by category cues found in Experiment 2 is similar to the finding that amnesic patients can be primed with semantic associates in a word association test (Shimamura & Squire, 1984). In this test, subjects were first shown words (e.g., *child)* in an incidental learning task and then asked to free associate to cue words that were semantically related to previously presented words (e.g., *baby).* Amnesic patients and control subjects exhibited priming of words by semantic associates that was about 2 times greater than baseline. This finding provides a particularly strong argument that imaging of study words cannot account for priming, when study and test cues share no sensory or perceptual features. In the present study, 15 words belonging to three categories were presented, and one might suppose that subjects perceived the three relevant categories and imaged them during list presentation. In the word association study (Shimamura & Squire, 1984), 12 different words were presented, and each of them was tested separately by presenting a semantic associate. It is highly unlikely that subjects encoded each of these words by imaging its associate.

In word completion tests and word association tests, the priming effect disappeared in amnesic and normal groups after a 2-hr delay (Graf et al., 1984; Shimamura & Squire, 1984). Some related studies with normal subjects have shown that priming effects can be observed as long as a few days or a week after study list presentation (Jacoby, 1983; Scarborough, Cortese, & Scarborough, 1977; Tulving et al., 1982). Findings from amnesic patients indicate that they do not exhibit such long-lasting effects, thus raising the possibility that the long-lasting effects are qualitatively different from the effects that are present for a few hours (Squire, Shimamura, & Graf, 1985b).

Amnesic patients exhibited normal priming effects despite severe deficits on standard tests of memory such as recall and recognition. We suggest that amnesic patients can activate or prime previously presented materials but they lack the ability to elaborate, organize, and consciously recollect information learned since the onset of amnesia. This impairment prevents the establishment of long-lasting memories. Priming tests assess the activation of previously presented materials without asking subjects explicitly to retrieve from memory. Priming tests are designed to emphasize the effects of automatic activation on performance and to minimize the effects of elaboration, organization, and conscious recollection. When tests prevent these latter effects, amnesic patients perform normally. This view is also consistent with the finding that instructions that emphasize recalling items from a study list improve the performance of normal subjects compared with when implicit or priming test instructions are given. Amnesic patients, however, are not affected by this change in instructions (Graf et al., 1984; Shimamura & Squire, 1984).

The present findings for amnesic patients should not be compared directly with the findings obtained from subjects exhibiting hypnotically induced amnesia (Kihlstrom, 1980). These subjects were presented words during hypnosis and were then instructed that they would be unable to remember the same words until a specific command was given. Upon awakening from hypnosis, free recall of words was impaired, but there was no effect on priming when the same words were cued by category labels or by semantic associates. After the suggestion to forget the study words was lifted by giving the command, the subjects recalled as many words as control subjects. In this case, one must conclude that hypnotically induced amnesia produced a failure to retrieve information rather than a failure to store information during hypnosis. Because no test procedures have ever produced normal free-recall performance in the organic amnesia associated with brain injury or disease, it is difficult to make direct comparisons between hypnotically induced amnesia and organic amnesia.

Recent studies of memory and the brain have developed the perspective that amnesia reflects damage to a specific brain system that is required for information to be elaborated, consolidated, and available to conscious recall (Baddeley, 1982; Mishkin et al., 1984; Moscovitch, 1982; Squire, 1982a). Priming and skill learning are spared in amnesia because they do not depend on this brain system and because in these cases elaboration, consolidation, and conscious recollection are not required for the effects of experience to be expressed. The present findings, together with related findings (Graf et al., 1984; Shimamura & Squire, 1984; Squire et al., 1985a), show that amnesic patients exhibit normal priming across modality boundaries and normal priming when cued by category labels or semantic associates. Moreover, because amnesic patients can exhibit chance performance on recognition memory tests at the same time that priming is intact (Squire et al., 1985a), we suppose that the processes that support priming can be independent of the processes that support performance on conventional memory tests.

REFERENCES

Baddeley, A. (1982). Implications of neuropsychological evidence for theories of normal memory. *Philosophical Transactions of the Royal Society of London, 298,* 59–72.

Battig, W. F., & Montague, W. E. (1969). Category norms of verbal items in 56 categories: A replication and extension of the Connecticut category norms. *Journal of Experimental Psychology Monographs, 80* (3, Pt. 2).

Brooks, D. N., & Baddeley, A. (1976). What can amnesic patients learn? *Neuropsychologia, 14,* 111–122.

Cermak, L. S. (1982). *Human memory and amnesia.* Hillsdale, NJ: Erlbaum.

Clarke, R., & Morton, J. (1983). Cross modality facilitation in tachistoscopic word recognition. *Quarterly Journal of Experimental Psychology, 35A,* 79–96.

Cofer, N. C. (1967). Conditions for the use of verbal associates. *Psychological Bulletin, 68,* 1–12.

Cohen, N. J. (1984). Preserved learning capacity in amnesia: Evidence for multiple memory systems. In L. Squire & N. Butters (Eds.), *The neuropsychology of memory* (pp. 83–103). New York: Guilford Press.

Cohen, N. J., & Squire, L. R. (1980). Preserved learning and retention of pattern analyzing skill in amnesia: Association of knowing how and knowing that. *Science, 210,* 207–209.

Cohen, N. J., & Squire, L. R. (1981). Retrograde amnesia and remote memory impairment. *Neuropsychologia, 19*, 337–356.

Corkin, S. (1968). Acquisition of motor skill after bilateral medial temporal lobe excision. *Neuropsychologia, 6,* 225–265.

Cramer, P. (1966). Mediated priming of associative responses: The effect of time lapse and interpolated activity. *Journal of Verbal Learning and Verbal Behavior 5,* 103–166.

Diamond, R., & Rozin, P. (1984). Activation of existing memories in the amnesic syndromes. *Journal of Abnormal Psychology, 93,* 98–105.

Forster, K. I. (1976). Accessing the mental lexicon. In R. J. Wales & E. Walker (Eds.), *New approaches to language mechanisms.* Amsterdam: North-Holland.

Graf, P., & Mandler, G. (1984). Activation makes words more accessible, but not necessarily more retrievable. *Journal of Verbal Learning and Verbal Behavior, 23,* 553–568.

Graf, P., & Mandler, G. (1985). *Direct priming across sensory modalities and word boundaries.* Manuscript submitted for publication.

Graf, P., Squire, L. R., & Mandler, G. (1984). The information that amnesic patients do not forget. *Journal of Experimental Psychology: Learning, Memory, and Cognition, 10*(1), 164–178.

Jacoby, L. L. (1983). Perceptual enhancement: Persistent effects of an experience. *Journal of Experimental Psychology: Learning, Memory, and Cognition, 9,* 21–38.

Jacoby, L. L., & Dallas, M. (1981). On the relationship between autobiographical memory and perceptual learning. *Journal of Experimental Psychology: General, 110,* 306–340.

Jacoby, L. L., & Witherspoon, D. (1982). Remembering without awareness. *Canadian Journal of Psychology 32,* 300–324.

Kihlstrom, J. F. (1980). Posthypnotic amnesia for recently learned material: Interactions with "episodic" and "semantic" memory. *Cognitive Psychology, 12,* 227–251.

Kirsner, K., Milech, D., & Standen, P. (1983). Common and modality-specific processes in the mental lexicon. *Memory & Cognition, 11,* 621–630.

Kucera, M., & Francis, W. (1967). *Computational analysis of present-day American English.* Providence, RI: Brown University Press.

Mishkin, M., Malamut, B., & Bachevalier, J. (1984). Memories and habits: Two neural systems. In G. Lynch, J. L. McGaugh, & N. M. Weinberger (Eds.) *Neurobiology of learning and memory* (pp. 65-77). New York: Guilford Press.

Mortensen, E. L. (1980). The effects of partial information in amnesic and normal subjects. *Scandinavian Journal of Psychology 21,* 75–82.

Morton, J. (1969). The interaction of information in word recognition. *Psychological Review, 76,* 165–178.

Morton, J. (1979). Facilitation in word recognition: Experiments causing change in the logogen models. In P. A. Kolers, M. E. Wrolstad, & H. Bouma (Eds.), *Processing of visible language* (Vol. 1, pp. 259–268). New York: Plenum.

Moscovitch, M. (1982). Multiple dissociations of function in amnesia. In L. Cermak (Ed.), *Human memory and amnesia* (pp. 337–370). Hillsdale, NJ: Erlbaum.

Roediger III, H., & Blaxton, T. A. (1983, November). *Priming in word fragment completion: Effects of modality and orthography.* Paper presented at the 24th annual meeting of the Psychonomic Society, San Diego, CA.

Rozin, P. (1976). The psychobiological approach to human memory. In M. R. Rosenzweig & E. L. Bennett (Eds.), *Neural mechanisms of learning and memory* (pp. 3–46). Cambridge, MA: MIT Press.

Scarborough, D. L., Cortese, C., & Scarborough, H. (1977). Frequency and repetition effects in lexical memory. *Journal of Experimental Psychology: Human Perception and Performance, 3,* 1–17.

Scarborough, D. L., Gerard, L., & Cortese, C. (1979). Accessing lexical memory: The transfer of word repetition effects across tasks and modality. *Memory & Cognition, 7,* 3–12.

Schacter, D. L. (in press). Priming of old and new knowledge in amnesic patients and normal subjects. In D. Olton, S. Corkin, & E. Gamzu (Eds.), *Conference on memory dysfunctions.* New York: New York Academy of Sciences.

Shimamura, A. P., & Squire, L. R. (1984). Paired-associate learning and priming effects in amnesia: A neuropsychological study. *Journal of Experimental Psychology: General, 113,* 556–570.

Squire, L. R. (1982a). The neuropsychology of human memory. *Annual Review of Neuroscience, 5,* 241–273.

Squire, L. R. (1982b). Comparisons between forms of amnesia: Some deficits are unique to Korsakoff's syndrome. *Journal of Experimental Psychology: Learning, Memory, and Cognition, 8,* 560–571.

Squire, L. R., & Butters, N. (Eds.). (1984). *Neuropsychology of memory.* New York: Guilford Press.

Squire, L. R., & Cohen, N. J. (1984). Human memory and amnesia. In G. Lynch, J. L. McGaugh, & N. M. Weinberger (Eds.), *Neurobiology of learning and memory* (pp. 3–64). New York: Guilford Press.

Squire, L. R., Shimamura, A., & Graf, P. (1985a). Independence of recognition memory and priming effects: A neuropsychological analysis. *Journal of Experimental Psychology: Learning, Memory and Cognition, 11,* 37–44.

Squire, L. R., Shimamura, A. P., & Graf P. (1985b). *The duration of priming effects in normal subjects and amnesic patients.* Manuscript submitted for publication.

Talland, G. A. (1965). *Deranged memory.* New York: Academic Press.

Tulving, E., Schacter, D., & Stark, H. A. (1982). Priming effects in word-fragment completion are independent of recognition memory. *Journal of Experimental Psychology: Learning, Memory and Cognition, 8,* 352–373.

Warrington, E. K., & Weiskrantz, L. (1970). The amnesic syndrome: Consolidation or retrieval? *Nature, 228,* 628–630.

Warrington, E. K., & Weiskrantz, L. (1974). The effect of prior learning on subsequent retention in amnesic patients. *Neuropsychologia, 12,* 419–428.

Warrington, E. K., & Weiskrantz, L. (1978). Further analysis of the prior learning effect in amnesic patients. *Neuropsychologia, 16,* 169–177.

Winnick, W. A., & Daniel, S. A. (1970). Two kinds of response priming in tachistoscopic recognition. *Journal of Experimental Psychology, 84,* 74–81.

POSTSCRIPT

Later in 1985, Graf (Graf & Schacter, 1985) introduced the phrase *implicit memory* to refer to the kinds of information tapped by repetition priming tasks. Since then, there has been an explosion of work in this area (for reviews, see Richardson-Klavehn & Bjork, 1988; Roediger, 1990; Schacter,1987; Tulving & Schacter, 1990). Although this research has yielded interesting insights, particularly about the nature of amnesia (Shimamura, 1986; Squire & McKee, 1992; Weiskrantz, 1987), many controversies remain. Chief among them is whether the differences in implicit and explicit memory tasks emerge from the different memory *systems* for which different parts of the brain are likely responsible (Schacter, 1992; Tulving & Schacter, 1990; Weiskrantz, 1987), or from the different kinds of *processing* or information that the two kinds of tasks tap (Roediger, Weldon, & Challis, 1989), or from some combination of the two (Schacter, 1990).

Those who argue for distinct memory systems generally identify four such systems; two—episodic and semantic—that are generally tapped by explicit memory tasks, and two—procedural and perceptual representational, or PRS—that are generally tapped by implicit memory tasks (Schacter, 1990, 1992; Tulving & Schacter, 1990). In the article reprinted here, Graf, Shimamura, and Squire study PRS (although in the mid-1980s, when it was written, the only implicit memory system clearly identified was that for procedural knowledge, the knowledge we acquire in learning cognitive-perceptual skills; see Tulving, 1985). Those who believe that the implicit/explicit distinction reflects processing differences argue that we don't need distinct memory systems to explain the available evidence (Roediger, Rajaram, & Srinivas, 1990). They argue further that parsimony supports instead the proposal of a single memory system (see Reading 11).

FOR FURTHER THOUGHT

1. What did the baseline completion in the first experiment represent? Why was it important to have such a measure?
2. Why was there a free-recall task in each experiment? How were the results of the free-recall task interpreted?
3. Both experiments try to determine whether priming is modality specific. What alternative hypothesis was the second experiment intended to eliminate that wasn't addressed in the first experiment? In your opinion, did it succeed in doing so? Why or why not?
4. What is the recall strategy explanation of direct priming? On what grounds do Graf, Shimamura, and Squire argue against it?

REFERENCES

Graf, P., & Schacter, D. L. (1985). Implicit and explicit memory for new associations in normal and amnesic patients. *Journal of Experimental Psychology: Learning, Memory, and Cognition, 11,* 501–518.

Richardson-Klavehn, A., & Bjork, R. A. (1988). Measures of memory. *Annual Review of Psychology, 36,* 475–543.

Roediger, H. L., III (1990). Implicit memory: Retention without remembering. *American Psychologist, 45,* 1043–1056.

Roediger, H. L., III, & Challis, B. H. (1992). Effects of exact repetition and conceptual repetition on free recall and primed word-fragment completion. *Journal of Experimental Psychology: Learning, Memory, and Cognition, 18,* 3–14.

Roediger, H. L., III, Rajaram, S., & Srinivas, K. (1990). Specifying criteria for postulating memory systems. *Annals of the New York Academy of Sciences, 608,* 572–595.

Roediger, H. L., III, Weldon, M. S., & Challis, B. H. (1989). Explaining dissociations between implicit and explicit measures of retention: A processing account. In H. L. Roediger & F. I. M. Craik (Eds.), *Varieties of memory and consciousness: Essay in honour of Endel Tulving* (pp. 3–41). Hillsdale, NJ: Erlbaum.

Schacter, D. L. (1987). Implicit memory: History and current status. *Journal of Experimental Psychology: Learning, Memory, and Cognition, 13,* 501–518.

Schacter, D. L. (1990). Perceptual representation systems and implicit memory: Toward a resolution of the multiple memory systems debate. In A. Diamond (Ed.), *The development and neural bases of higher cognitive functions* (pp. 543–567).

Schacter, D. L. (1992). Understanding implicit memory: A cognitive neuroscience approach. *American Psychologist, 47,* 559–569.

Shimamura, A. P. (1986). Priming effects in amnesia: Evidence for a dissociable memory function. *Quarterly Journal of Experimental Psychology, 38A,* 619–644.

Squire, L. R., & McKee, R. (1992). Influence of prior events on cognitive judgments in amnesia. *Journal of Experimental Psychology: Learning, Memory, and Cognition, 18,* 106–115.

Tulving, E. (1985). How many memory systems are there? *American Psychologist, 40,* 385–398.

Tulving, E., & Schacter, D. L. (1990). Priming and human memory systems. *Science, 247,* 301–306.

Weiskrantz, L. (1987). Neuroanatomy of memory and amnesia: A case for multiple memory systems. *Human Neurobiology, 6,* 93–105.

CHAPTER FIVE
Concepts and Imagery

INTRODUCTION

Whereas models of semantic memory (Reading 12; Smith, 1978; Smith, Shoben, & Rips, 1974) usually focus on how the information associated with words is organized, most models of concepts—our mental representations of categories—focus on what kind of information is associated with words.

Traditionally, psychologists have assumed that concepts specify the features of a category that are individually necessary and collectively sufficient for membership (see Bruner, Goodnow, & Austin, 1956). To say that the features are *individually necessary* means that each member of the category must have every specified feature. To say that the features are *collectively sufficient* means that anything that possesses all the specified features must be a member of the category. One consequence of this assumption is that membership in a category is an all-or-none phenomenon or what Rosch and Mervis call *digital*; something either is or is not a member. If it has the necessary and sufficient features, it is a member; if it does not, it is not.

But membership in conceptual categories is rarely all-or-none. Something is not simply either a bird or not; it ranges from being a good example of a bird—as is a robin—to a poor example—a penguin. Furthermore, goodness-of-membership predicts performance on a variety of tasks. For example, people more quickly verify that a robin is a bird than they verify that a penguin is a bird (Rosch, 1975). It is very difficult for the traditional necessary-and-sufficient-features approach to accommodate this goodness-of-example effect (Smith & Medin, 1981).

In an extraordinarily productive period during the early and mid-1970s (summarized in Rosch, 1978), Eleanor Rosch and her colleagues—especially Carolyn Mervis—explored alternatives to this traditional view. Along with Rosch, Mervis, Gray, Johnson, and Boyes-Braem (1976; see the Introduction to Reading 17), this article is perhaps the most influential of the series. For our purposes, we have excluded Experiments 2, 3, 5, and 6 and references to the multidimensional approach to concepts. As you read it, ask yourself what alternative to the traditional assumptions Rosch and her colleagues offer and how these experiments address that alternative.

Family Resemblances: Studies in the Internal Structure of Categories

Eleanor Rosch and Carolyn B. Mervis

University of California, Berkeley

As speakers of our language and members of our culture, we know that a chair is a more reasonable exemplar of the category *furniture* than a radio, and that some chairs fit our idea or image of a chair better than others. However, when describing categories analytically, most traditions of thought have treated category membership as a digital, all-or-none phenomenon. That is, much work in philosophy, psychology, linguistics, and anthropology assumes that categories are logical bounded entities, membership in which is defined by an item's possession of a simple set of criterial features, in which all instances possessing the criterial attributes have a full and equal degree of membership.

In contrast to such a view, it has been recently argued (see Lakoff, 1972; Rosch, 1973; Zadeh, 1965) that some natural categories are analog and must be represented logically in a manner which reflects their analog structure. Rosch (1973, 1975c) has further characterized some natural analog categories as internally structured into a prototype (clearest cases, best examples of the category) and nonprototype members, with nonprototype members tending toward an order from better to poorer examples. While the domain for which such a claim has been demonstrated most unequivocally is that of color (Berlin & Kay, 1969; Heider, 1971, 1972; Mervis, Catlin, & Rosch, 1975; Rosch, 1974, 1975a, 1977), there is also considerable evidence that natural superordinate semantic categories have a prototype structure. Subjects can reliably rate the extent to which a member of a category fits their idea or image of the meaning of the category name (Rosch, 1973, 1975a), and such ratings predict performance in a number of tasks (Rips, Shoben, & Smith, 1973; Rosch, 1973, 1975a, 1975b, 1977; Smith, Rips, & Shoben, 1974; Smith, Shoben, & Rips, 1974).

However, there has, as yet, been little attention given to the problem of how internal structure arises. That is, what principles govern the formation of category prototypes and gradients of category membership? For some categories which probably have a physiological basis, such as colors, forms, and facial expressions of basic human emotions, prototypes may be stimuli which are salient prior to formation of the category, whose salience, at the outset, determines the categorical structuring of those domains (Ekman, 1971; McDaniel, [Reference] Note 1; Rosch, 1974, 1975c). For the artificial categories which have been used in prototype research—such as families of dot patterns (Posner, 1973) and artificial faces (Reed, 1972)—the categories have been intentionally structured and/or the prototypes have been defined so that the prototypes were central tendencies of the categories. For most domains, however, prototypes do not appear to precede the category (Rosch, 1976) and

This research was supported by grants to the first author (under her former name Eleanor Rosch Heider) by the National Science Foundation (GB-38245X), by the Grant Foundation, and by the National Institutes of Mental Health 1 R01 MH24316–01). We wish to thank David Johnson, Joseph Romeo, Ross Quigley, R. Scott Miller, Steve Frank, Alina Furnow, and Louise Jones for help with testing and analysis of the data. We also wish to thank Ed Smith, Ed Shoben, and Lance Rips for permission to refer to the multidimensional scaling study of superordinate categories which was performed jointly with them. Carolyn Mervis is now at Cornell University. She was supported by an NSF Predoctoral Fellowship during the research. Requests for reprints should be sent to Eleanor Rosch, Department of Psychology, University of California at Berkeley, Berkeley, CA 94720.

must be formed through principles of learning and information processing from the items given in the category. The present research was not intended to provide a processing model of the learning of categories or formation of prototypes; rather, our intention was to examine the stimulus relations which underlie such learning. That is, the purpose of the present research was to explore one of the major *structural* principles which, we believe, may govern the formation of the prototype structure of semantic categories.

This principle was first suggested in philosophy; Wittgenstein (1953) argued that the referents of a word need not have common elements in order for the word to be understood and used in the normal functioning of language. He suggested that, rather, a family resemblance might be what linked the various referents of a word. A family resemblance relationship consists of a set of items of the form AB, BC, CD, DE. That is, each item has at least one, and probably several, elements in common with one or more other items, but no, or few, elements are common to all items. The existence of such relationships in actual natural language categories has not previously been investigated empirically.

In the present research, we viewed natural semantic categories as networks of overlapping attributes; the basic hypothesis was that members of a category come to be viewed as prototypical of the category as a whole in proportion to the extent to which they bear a family resemblance to (have attributes which overlap those of) other members of the category. Conversely, items viewed as most prototypical of one category will be those with least family resemblance to or membership in other categories. In natural categories of concrete objects, the two aspects of family resemblance should coincide rather than conflict since it is reasonable that categories tend to become organized in such a way that they reflect the correlational structure of the environment in a manner which renders them maximally discriminable from each other (Rosch, 1976; Rosch, Mervis, Gray, Johnson, & Boyes-Braem, 1976) .

The present structural hypothesis is closely related to a *cue validity* processing model of classification in which the validity of a cue is defined in terms of its total frequency within a category and its proportional frequency in that category relative to contrasting categories. Mathematically, cue validity has been defined as a conditional probability—specifically, the frequency of a cue being associated with the category in question divided by the total frequency of that cue over all relevant categories (Beach, 1964; Reed, 1972). Unfortunately, cue validity has been treated as a model in conflict with a prototype model of category processing where prototypes are operationally defined solely as attribute means (Reed, 1972). If prototypes are defined more broadly—for example, as the abstract representation of a category, or as those category members to which subjects compare items when judging category membership, or as the internal structure of the category defined by subjects' judgments of the degree to which members fit their "idea or image" of the category—then prototypes should coincide rather than conflict with cue validity. That is, if natural categories of concrete objects tend to become organized so as to render the categories maximally discriminable from each other, it follows that the maximum possible cue validity of items within each category will be attained (Rosch *et al.*, 1976). The principle of family resemblance relationships can be restated in terms of cue validity since the attributes most distributed among members of a category and least distributed among members of contrasting categories are, by definition, the most valid cues to membership in the category in question. We use the term *family resemblance* rather than *cue validity* primarily to emphasize that we are dealing with a description of structural principles and not with a processing model. We believe that the principle of family resemblance relationships is a very general one and is applicable to categories regardless of whether or not they have features common to members of the category or formal criteria for category membership.

In all of the studies of the present research, family resemblances were defined in terms of discrete attributes such as *has legs, you drive it,* or *the letter B is a member.* These are the kinds of features of natural semantic categories which can be most readily reported and the features normally used in definitions of categories by means of lists of formal criteria. Insofar as the context in which an attribute occurs as part of a stimulus may always affect perception and understanding of the attribute, discrete attributes of this type may be an analytic myth. However, in one sense, the purpose of the present research was to show that it is not necessary to invoke attribute interactions or higher order gestalt properties of stimuli (such as those used by Posner, 1973; Reed, 1972; Rosch, Simpson, & Miller, [Reference] Note 2) in order to analyze the prototype structure of categories. That is, even at the level of analysis of the type of discrete attributes normally used in definitions of categories by means of criterial features, we believe there is a principle of the structure of stimulus sets, family resemblances, which can be shown to underlie category prototype structure.

The present paper reports studies using three different types of category; superordinate semantic categories such as *furniture* and *vehicle,* basic level semantic categories such as *chair* and *car,* and artificial categories formed from sets of letter strings. For each type of stimulus, both aspects of the family resemblance hypothesis (that the most prototypical members of categories are those with most attributes in common with other members of that category and are those with least attributes in common with other categories) were tested.

Superordinate semantic categories are of particular interest because they are sufficiently abstract that they have few, if any, attributes common to all members (Rosch *et al.,* 1976). Thus, such categories may consist almost entirely of items related to each other by means of family resemblances of overlapping attributes. In addition, superordinate categories have the advantage that their membership consists of a finite number of names of basic level categories which can be adequately sampled. Superordinate categories have the disadvantage that they do not have contrasting categories (operationally defined below); thus, the second half of the family resemblance hypothesis (that prototypical members of categories have least resemblance to other categories) had to be tested indirectly by measuring membership in, rather than attributes in common with, other superordinate categories.

Basic level semantic categories are of great interest because they are the level of abstraction at which the basic category cuts in the world may be made (Rosch, 1976; Rosch *et al.,* 1976). However, basic level categories present a sampling problem since their membership consists of an infinite number of objects.

On the positive side, basic level categories do form contrast sets, thus, making possible a direct test of the second part of the family resemblance hypothesis. . . .

PART 1: SUPERORDINATE SEMANTIC CATEGORIES

Experiment 1

Although it is always possible for an ingenious philosopher or psychologist to invent criterial attributes defining a category, earlier research has shown that actual subjects rate superordinate semantic categories as having few, if any, attributes common to all members (Rosch *et al.,* 1976). Thus, if the "categorical" nature of these categories is to be explained, it appeared most likely to reside in family resemblances between members. Part of the purpose of the present experiment was to obtain portraits of the distribution of attributes of members of a number of superordinate natural language categories. Part of the hypothesis was that category members would prove to bear a family resemblance relationship to each other. The major purpose of the experiment, however, was to observe the relation between degree of relatedness between members of the category and the rated prototypicality of those members. The specific hypothesis was that a measure of the degree to which an item bore a family resemblance to other members of the category would prove significantly correlated with previously obtained prototypicality ratings of the members of the category.

Method

Subjects.   Subjects were 400 students in introductory psychology classes who received this 10 min task as part of their classroom work.

Stimuli.   The categories used were the six most common categories of concrete nouns in English, determined by a measure of word frequency (Kucera & Francis, 1967). All of the categories were ones for which norms for the prototypicality of items had already been obtained for 50–60 category members (Rosch, 1975a). These norms were derived from subjects' ratings of the extent to which each item fit their "idea or image" of the meaning of the category name. (The rating task and instructions were very similar to those used in Experiment 3 of the present research [excluded]. A complete account of the methods for deriving the six superordinate categories and complete norms for all items of the six categories are provided in Rosch, 1975a.) The 20 items from each category used in the present experiment were chosen to represent the full range of goodness-of-example ranks. These items are listed, in their goodness-of-example order, in Table 1.

Procedure.   Each of the 120 items shown in Table 1 was printed at the top of a page, and the pages assembled into packets consisting of six items, one from each superordinate category. Items were chosen randomly within a category such that each subject who received an item received it with different items from the other five categories and received the items representing each category in a different order. Each item was rated by 20 subjects. Each subject rated six items, one from each category.

Subjects were asked to list the attributes possessed by each item. Instructions were:

This is a very simple experiment to find out the characteristics and attributes that people feel are common to and characteristic of different kinds of ordinary everyday objects. For example, for *bicycles* you might think of things they have in common like two wheels, pedals, handlebars, you ride on them, they don't use fuel, etc. For *dogs* you might think of things they have in common like having four legs, barking, having fur, etc.

There are six pages following this one. At the top of each is listed the name of one common object. For each page, you'll have a minute and a half to write down all of the attributes of that object that you can think of. But try not to *just* free associate—for example, if bicycles just happen to remind you of your father, *don't* write down *father*.

Okay—you'll have a minute and a half for each page. When I say turn to the next page, read the name of the object and write down the attributes or characteristics you think are characteristic of that object as fast as you can until you're told to turn the page again.

TABLE 1   Superordinate Categories and Items Used in Experiments 1 and 2

			Category			
Item	Furniture	Vehicle	Fruit	Weapon	Vegetable	Clothing
1	Chair	Car	Orange	Gun	Peas	Pants
2	Sofa	Truck	Apple	Knife	Carrots	Shirt
3	Table	Bus	Banana	Sword	String beans	Dress
4	Dresser	Motorcycle	Peach	Bomb	Spinach	Skirt
5	Desk	Train	Pear	Hand grenade	Broccoli	Jacket
6	Bed	Trolley car	Apricot	Spear	Asparagus	Coat
7	Bookcase	Bicycle	Plum	Cannon	Corn	Sweater
8	Footstool	Airplane	Grapes	Bow and arrow	Cauliflower	Underpants
9	Lamp	Boat	Strawberry	Club	Brussel sprouts	Socks
10	Piano	Tractor	Grapefruit	Tank	Lettuce	Pajamas
11	Cushion	Cart	Pineapple	Teargas	Beets	Bathing suit
12	Mirror	Wheelchair	Blueberry	Whip	Tomato	Shoes
13	Rug	Tank	Lemon	Icepick	Lima beans	Vest
14	Radio	Raft	Watermelon	Fists	Eggplant	Tie
15	Stove	Sled	Honeydew	Rocket	Onion	Mittens
16	Clock	Horse	Pomegranate	Poison	Potato	Hat
17	Picture	Blimp	Date	Scissors	Yam	Apron
18	Closet	Skates	Coconut	Words	Mushroom	Purse
19	Vase	Wheelbarrow	Tomato	Foot	Pumpkin	Wristwatch
20	Telephone	Elevator	Olive	Screwdriver	Rice	Necklace

Measurement of family resemblance.   To derive the basic measure of family resemblance, for each category, all attributes mentioned by subjects were listed and each item, for which an attribute had been listed, was credited with that attribute. Two judges reviewed the resulting table and indicated cases in which an attribute was clearly and obviously false. These attributes were deleted from the tabulation. The judges also indicated any attribute which had been listed for one or more items, but was clearly and obviously true of another item in the category for which it had not happened to be listed by any of the 20 subjects. These items were also credited with the relevant attribute. Judges were not permitted to list new attributes, and no item was credited with an attribute about which judges disagreed or about which either judge was uncertain. The total changes made by the judges were infrequent.

Each attribute received a score, ranging from 1–20, representing the number of items in the category which had been credited with that attribute. By this means, each attribute was weighted in accordance with the number of items in the category possessing it. The basic measure of degree of family resemblance for an item was the sum of the weighted scores of each of the attributes that had been listed for that item.

This basic measure of family resemblance possessed a source of potential distortion, however. In the measure, each additional item with which an attribute was credited added an equal increment of family resemblance. Thus, the measure depended upon the assumption that the numerical frequency of an attribute within a category was an interval measure of the underlying psychological weight of that attribute (e.g., the difference between an attribute which belonged to two items versus one item was equal to the difference between an attribute which belonged to 19 versus 18 items). Such an assumption is not necessarily reasonable; therefore, a second measure of family resemblance was also computed. To derive this measure, each attribute was weighted with the natural logarithm of the raw score representing the number of items in the category which had been credited with that attribute; the second measure, thus, consisted of the sum of the natural logarithms of the scores of each of the attributes that had been listed for an item.

Results and Discussion

The purpose of the study was both to provide a portrait of the structure of the categories and to test the correlation between family resemblance and prototypicality of items. In terms of structure, Figure 1 shows the mean frequency distribution for the number of attributes applied to each number (1–20) of items/category. As had been previously found when subjects listed attributes for superordinate category names (Rosch *et al.*, 1976), in the present study, few attributes were given which were true of all 20 members of the category—for four of the categories, there was only one such item; for two of the categories, none. Furthermore, the single attribute which did apply to all members, in three cases was true of many other items besides those within that superordinate (for example, "you eat it" for fruit). Thus, the salient attribute structure of these categories tended to reside, not in criterial features common to all members of the category which distinguished those members from all others, but in a large number of attributes true of some, but not all, category members.

Those attributes unique to a single member are not of primary interest for the present study since they do not contribute to the structure of the category per se. In actual fact, the number of unique attributes applicable to items was evenly distributed over members of the categories; for none of the six categories was the number of unique attributes significantly correlated with prototypicality. Of the attributes applicable to

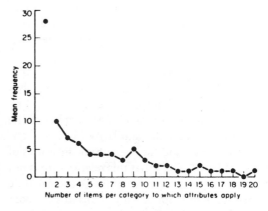

FIGURE 1   Frequency distribution for number of attributes applied to each number of items/category.

two or more members, Figure 1 shows that the number of attributes decreases as the number of items to which the attribute is applicable increases. In summary: the majority of attributes listed for items in the six categories demonstrated a family resemblance relationship; that is, they were common to only some of the category members.

The major hypothesis of the experiment was that this family resemblance structure would prove significantly correlated with the prototypicality of items. Correlations were computed separately for each of the two measures of family resemblance and separately for each category. The measure of prototypicality was the mean rating on a 7-point scale of the extent to which items fit subjects' idea or image of the meaning of the category names (Rosch, 1975a). The basic measure of degree of family resemblance for an item was the sum of the weighted raw scores of each of the attributes listed for the item. The logarithmic measure of family resemblance was the sum of the natural logarithms of the scores of each of the attributes that had been listed for an item. Items in each category were ranked 1–20 on the basis of prototypicality and were ranked 1–20 on the basis of each of the measures of family resemblance. Spearman rank–order correlations between the ranks of items on family resemblance and their ranks on prototypicality were performed separately for each of the measures of family resemblance and for each of the categories. These correlations, for the basic measure of family resemblance, were: furniture, 0.88; vehicle, 0.92; weapon, 0.94; fruit, 0.85; vegetable, 0.84; clothing, 0.91. These correlations for the logarithmic measure of family resemblance were: furniture, 0.84; vehicle, 0.90; weapon, 0.93; fruit, 0.88; vegetable, 0.86; clothing, 0.88. All were significant ($p < .001$).

Such results strongly confirm our hypothesis that the more an item has attributes in common with other members of the category, the more it will be considered a good and representative member of the category. Furthermore, the similarity in results obtained with the basic and the logarithmic measures of family resemblance argues that this relationship is not dependent upon the properties of the particular scale used in measurement. Specifically, items in a category tended to be credited with approximately equal numbers of attributes, but the less prototypical the item,

the fewer other items in the category tended to share each attribute. Thus, the ranks for the basic and logarithmic measures of family resemblance were almost identical, and the correlations between family resemblance and prototypicality were scarcely affected by the change in measure. The relationship between degree of family resemblance and prototypicality for these categories, thus, appears to be a robust one.

A corollary of this finding may account for one of the persistent illusions concerning superordinate categories. Subjects, upon receiving feedback from the experiment, and audiences, upon being told of it, generally argue that they feel positive that there are many attributes common to all members of the category even when they cannot think of any specific attributes for which there are not counterexamples. If the more prototypical members of a category are those which have most attributes common to other members of the category it is probable that they are most likely to have attributes in common with each other. To investigate this possibility, the number of attributes common to the five most and five least prototypical items in each category were compared. The number of attributes are shown in Table 2. It is clear from this count that, while category members as a whole may not have items in common, the five most typical items of each category tend to have many items in common. Thus, if subjects think of the best examples of the category when hearing the category name (Rosch, 1975a), the illusion of common elements is likely to arise and persist—an illusion which may be what makes definition of categories in terms of criterial attributes appear so reasonable. . . .

In summary: The hypotheses of Experiment 1 were confirmed. For six superordinate categories, 20 members of the category were characterized by at-

TABLE 2   Number of Attributes in Common to Five Most and Five Least Prototypical Members of Six Categories

Category	Most Typical Members	Least Typical Members
Furniture	13	2
Vehicle	36	2
Fruit	16	0
Weapon	9	0
Vegetable	3	0
Clothing	21	0

tributes which were common to some, but not all, members. The degree to which a given member possessed attributes in common with other members was highly correlated with the degree to which it was rated prototypical (representative) of the category name. . . .

[Experiment 2 is excluded here.]

PART II: BASIC LEVEL CATEGORIES

It has been previously argued (Rosch, 1976; Rosch *et al.*, 1976) that there is a basic level of abstraction at which the concrete objects of the world are most naturally divided into categories. A working assumption has been that, in the domains of both man-made and biological objects, there occur information-rich bundles of attributes that form natural discontinuities. These bundles are both perceptual and functional. It is proposed that basic cuts are made at this level. Basic objects (for example, *chair, car*) are the most inclusive level of abstraction at which categories can mirror the correlational structure (Garner, 1974) of the environment and the most inclusive level at which there can be many attributes common to all or most members of the categories. The more abstract combinations of basic level objects (e.g., categories such *furniture* and *vehicle* used in Experiments 1 and 2) are superordinates which share only a few attributes; the common attributes are rather abstract ones. Categories below the basic level are subordinates (e.g., *kitchen chair, sports car*). Subordinates are also bundles of predictable attributes and functions, but contain little more information than the basic level object to which they are subordinate. Basic categories are, thus, the categories for which the cue validity of attributes within categories is maximized: Superordinate categories have lower cue validity than basic because they have fewer common attributes within the category; subordinate categories have lower cue validity than basic because they share attributes with contrasting subordinate categories (e.g., *kitchen chair* shares most of its attributes with *living room chair*).

In a converging series of experiments (Rosch *et al.*, 1976), it was confirmed that basic objects are the most inclusive categories in which clusters of attributes occur which subjects agree are possessed by members of the category; sets of common motor movements are made when using or interacting with objects of that type; commonalities in the shape, and, thus, the overall look, of objects occur; it is possible to recognize an averaged shape of an object of that class; and it is possible to form a representation of a typical member of the class which is sufficiently concrete to aid in detection of the object in visual noise. In addition, basic objects were shown to be the first categorizations made by young children, and basic object names the level of abstraction at which objects are first named by children and usually named by adults.

The present research concerned the question of whether the family resemblances of items in basic level categories were related to prototypicality in the way in which it had proved to be in the superordinate categories studied in Experiments 1 and 2. Do subjects agree concerning which members of basic object categories are the more prototypical—do they agree, for example, about which cars more closely fit their idea or image of the meaning of *car*? And, if agreement in prototypicality ratings is obtained, does it hold, as it did in the case of superordinate categories, that the more prototypical category members are those with most resemblance to members of that category and least resemblance to other categories? In Experiment 3, the hypothesis was tested that prototypicality ratings and degree of family resemblance were positively correlated. Experiment 4 tested the converse hypothesis that prototypicality ratings were negatively correlated with the degree to which an item possessed attributes which were also possessed by members of contrasting categories.

[Experiment 3 is excluded here.]

Experiment 4

The purpose of both Experiments 2 and 4 was to provide data complementary to that of Experiments 1 and 3. The basic hypothesis of both experiments was that categories tend to become organized in such a way that they are maximally discriminable from other categories at the same level of contrast; hence, the most prototypical members of a category are those with least resemblance to, or membership in, other categories. For superordinate categories, it had not been possible to obtain contrast sets and, thus, not possible to measure commonality of attributes between contrasting categories directly; instead, the hypothesis had been tested indirectly by means of an item's membership in multiple categories. For members of basic level categories, the hypothesis proved testable directly.

The basic design of the experiment was: (a) to determine which categories were seen in direct contrast to a sample of the basic level categories for which we had obtained prototypicality ratings and attribute lists in Experiment 2, (b) to obtain lists of attributes for pictures representing items in the contrasting categories, and (c) to correlate the number of attributes which items shared with contrasting categories with prototypicality ratings for the items; a negative correlation was predicted.

Method

Subjects.   Subjects were 44 students in psychology classes who performed the task as part of their classroom work; 24 of the subjects served in the contrast set portion of the experiment; 20 subjects listed attributes.

Stimuli and procedure.   The first part of the experimental procedure required obtaining contrast sets of the basic level categories to be used. Subjects were read the following instructions:

> Suppose that you are participating in a communication task experiment. Another person is describing "items" to you, and you have to figure out what kind of "item" he is describing. The person tells you about each item's *physical attributes* (what it looks like, what parts it has, etc.), and about its *functions* (what people do with it), and about its *actions* (what it does). Suppose, also, that you have guessed once for each item, and you have been told that your answer was not correct, but was very close to the correct one. Assume that each word I read was your first answer to one item. After I read each item, write down what your second answer would be. Remember that your first guess was very close to being correct. Think of something that has physical attributes, functions, and actions very similar to the ones your "first answer" had.

Subjects were then given the six names of basic level items used in Experiment 2 and asked to write their first guess as to what the item might be. Thirty seconds per item were allowed.

Subjects' responses were tallied. From the six basic level categories, two were selected for which the most consistent responses had been given. These two, *chair* and *car,* were used for the second part of the experiment.

Stimuli for the attribute listing consisted of pictures of two examples of each of the three most frequently given contrast items for *chair* and *car.* These were: for chair—sofa, stool, and cushion; for car—truck, bus, and motorcycle. The pictures were chosen randomly from the pool of available pictures of these items, with the restriction that all of the pictures chosen had been rated (by two judges) as good examples of their category.

Attribute lists had already been obtained for the chair and car pictures in Experiment 3. Attributes for the six contrast categories were obtained by the same procedures as used in Experiment 3; subjects were read the same instructions as in Experiment 3, were shown slides of the pictures in the contrast categories in random order and were given 1.5 min to list attributes for each picture. Each subject saw six pictures, one of each contrast item. Each picture was seen by 10 subjects.

Results and Discussion

For each of the 15 chair and 15 car pictures, a tally was made of the number of attributes listed for that picture, which had also been listed for at least one of the pictures of one of the three contrast categories. This tally was used as the measure of amount of overlap between the attributes of a given item and the attributes of items in the closest contrasting categories. A Spearman rank–order correlation was performed between the prototypicality and attribute overlap ranks of the 15 chair and 15 car pictures. Results were: chairs, $r = -.67$; cars, $r = -.86$. Both were significant ($p < .01$). In short, it was clearly confirmed for two basic level categories that the more prototypical of the category a picture had been rated, the fewer attributes it shared with categories in direct contrast with that category.

[Part III of this article as first published reported on two experiments using artificial categories, which allowed Rosch and Mervis (1) to completely control patterns of featural overlap—degree of family resemblance—of each item to other items in the same and different categories, and (2) to control subject's exposure to those items. As expected, they found that items that bear great family resemblance to their categories are learned faster and identified as more prototypical than are items that have little family resemblance to their categories.]

GENERAL DISCUSSION

The results of the present study confirmed the hypothesis that the most prototypical members of common superordinate, basic level, and artificial categories are those which bear the greatest family resemblance to other members of their own category and have the least overlap with other categories. In probabilistic language, prototypicality was shown to be a function of the cue validity of the attributes of items. In the particular studies in this paper, we defined and measured family resemblance in terms of discrete attributes; however, previous studies indicate that the principle can be applied, to some extent, to other types of categories, such as dot patterns distorted around a prototype and categories consisting of items composed of continuous attributes which have a metric (Posner, 1973; Reed, 1972: Rosch, Simpson, & Miller, [Reference] Note 2). In such categories, the prototype dot pattern and the pattern with attributes at mean values have more in common with (are more like) the other items in the category than are items further from the prototype or the mean. Family resemblances (even broadly defined) are undoubtedly not the only principle of prototype formation—for example, the frequency of items and the salience of particular attributes or particular members of the categories (perceptual, social, or memorial salience) as well as the as yet undefined gestalt properties of stimuli and stimulus combinations, undoubtedly contribute to prototype formation (Rosch, 1975c)—however, the results of the present study indicate that family resemblance is a major factor.

Such a finding is important in six ways: (a) It suggests a structural basis for the formation of prototypes of categories, (b) It argues that in modeling natural categories, prototypes and cue validity are not conflicting accounts, but, rather, must be incorporated into a single model, (c) It indicates a structural rationale for the use of proximity scaling in the study of categories, even in the absence of definable category dimensionality, (d) It offers a principle by which prototype formation can be understood as part of the general processes through which categories themselves may be formed, (e) It provides a new link between adult and children's modes of categorization, and (f) It offers a concrete alternative to criterial attributes in understanding the logic of categorical structure.

Family resemblance as a structural basis for prototype formation. The origin of prototypes of categories is an issue because, as outlined in the introduction, there is now considerable evidence that the extent to which members are conceived typical of a category appears to be an important variable in the cognitive processing of categories (Rosch, 1975a, 1975b, 1975c, 1976, 1977). From that previous work alone, it could be argued that ratings of prototypicality are only measures of the associative linkage between an item and the category name and that it is such associative strength which determines the effects of typicality on processing tasks such as those used in semantic memory. While in a processing model, associative strength may, by definition, be directly related to typicality effects, associative strength need not be conceived only as the result of the frequency of (arbitrary or accidental) pairings of the item with the category name. The present experiments have attempted to provide a structural principle for the formation of prototypes; family resemblance relationships are not in contradiction to, but, rather, themselves offer a possible structural reason behind associative strength.

The principle of family resemblance is similar but not identical to two recent accounts of prototype effects: the attribute frequency model (Neumann, 1974) and an element tag model (Reitman & Bower, 1973). Both of these models were designed to account, without recourse to an "abstraction process," for the findings of several specific previous experiments—primarily those of Bransford and Franks (1971) and Franks and Bransford (1971). Both models predict memory (particularly the mistaken memory for prototype items which were not actually presented) from the frequency with which elements appear in a learning set.

A family resemblance account of prototypes is of greater generality than these models. In the first place, it accounts for prototypes in terms of distributions of attributes rather than in terms of the simple frequency of attributes (a factor which also distinguishes family resemblances from a narrow definition of cue validity). In the second place, it includes an account of the distribution of attributes over contrasting categories rather than focusing only on the category in question. That it is distribution rather than simple frequency of attributes which is most relevant to prototypes in natural categories is argued by two facts: (a) The measure of distribution used in the present study was highly correlated with ratings of prototypicality for superordinate categories, whereas a measure of the frequency of items (which is necessarily correlated with frequency of attributes) in the category is not correlated with prototypicality (Mervis, Rosch, & Catlin, [Reference] Note 3), and (b) The overlap of attributes with contrasting categories is itself a distributional property, not a property of simple frequency. (In the artificial categories of Experiment 5 of the present paper, distributional and simple frequency were equivalent; however, in the other experiments, they were not—clarification of the relations between distribution and frequency of attributes is an issue which requires further research.) That the distribution of attributes over contrasting categories is as important a principle of prototype formation as distribution of attributes within a category is argued by the results of Experiments 2, 4, and 6.

At this point, it should be reiterated that the principle of family resemblance, as defined in the present research, is a descriptive, not a processing, principle. Family resemblances are related to process models in two ways: (a) Any account of the processes by which humans convert stimulus attributes into mental or behavioral prototypes (such as an attribute tag model) should be able to account for the family resemblance attribute structure of categories outlined by the present research, and (b) Classification by computation of cue validity and classification by matching to a prototype have been treated as alternative process models which are in conflict; however, the principle of family resemblance suggests that, for natural categories, both should be aspects of the same processing model.

Family resemblance as an argument for the compatibility of cue validity and prototype models. Probability models, such as cue validity, and distance models, such as matching to a prototype, have been treated as two fundamentally different forms of categorization model whose conflicting validities must be tested by empirical research (Reed, 1972). However, the present study has shown that empirically defined prototypes of natural categories are just those items with highest cue validity. Such a structure of categories would, in fact, appear to provide the means for maximally efficient processing of categories. Computation and summation of the validities of individual cues is a laborious cognitive process. However, since cue validity appears to be the basis of categories (Rosch *et al.*, 1976), it is ecologically essential that cue validities be taken into account, in some manner, in categorization. If prototypes function cognitively as representatives of the category and if prototypes are items with the highest cue validities, humans can use the efficient processing mechanism of matching to a prototype without sacrificing attention to the validity of cues. (Note that such an account is similar to the compromise model which ultimately proved the most predictive for Reed's 1972 categories of schematic faces—a prototype matching model in which the importance of each feature in the prototype was weighted in accordance with its cue validity.) In short, humans probably incorporate probabilistic analysis of cues and computation of distance from a representation of the category into the same process of categorization; future research on categorization would do well to attempt to model the ways in which that incorporation can occur rather than to treat cue validity and prototypes as conflicting models.

Family resemblance as a basis for proximity scaling. Just as it has been customary to treat categories in terms of logical defining features which were assumed to be common to all members of the category, it is also not uncommon to treat proximity scaling of items in categories only as a means of determining the general dimensions along which items of the category are seen to differ. However, the results of the multidimensional scaling of the items of the superordinate categories in Experiment 1 (performed with Smith, Shoben, and Rips) indicated that family resemblance was predictive of centrality of items in the derived similarity space regardless of interpretability of dimensions or of item clusters. It should, in general, be the case that the more that items have in common with other items in a class (the closer the items are to all other items irrespective of the basis of closeness), the more central those items will be in a space derived from proximity measures. The demonstration of the importance of family resemblances (and of prototypicality) in classification provided by the present research suggests that the dimension of centrality may itself be an important aspect of and deserve to be a focus of attention in the analysis of proximity spaces.

Family resemblance as a part of the general process of category formation.   The concept of family resemblances is also of general use because it characterizes prototype formation as part of the general process by which categories themselves are formed. It has been argued by Rosch *et al.* (1976) that division of the world into categories is not arbitrary. The basic category cuts in the world are those which separate the information-rich bundles of attributes which form natural discontinuities. Basic categories have, in fact, been shown to be the most inclusive categories in which all items in the category possess significant numbers of attributes in common, and, thereby, are used by means of similar sequences of motor movements and are like each other in overall appearance. Basic categories are the categories for which the cue validity of attributes within categories is maximized since superordinate categories have fewer common attributes within the category than do basic categories and subordinate categories share more attributes with contrasting categories than do basic categories. Basic categories are, thus, the categories which mirror the correlational structure of the environment.

The present study has shown that formation of prototypes of categories appears to be likewise non-arbitrary. The more prototypical a category member, the more attributes it has in common with other members of the category and the fewer attributes in common with contrasting categories. Thus, prototypes appear to be just those members of the category which most reflect the redundancy structure of the category as a whole. That is, categories form to maxi-

mize the information-rich clusters of attributes in the environment and, thus, the cue validity of the attributes of categories; when prototypes of categories form by means of the principle of family resemblance, they maximize such clusters and such cue validity still further within categories.

Family resemblance as a link with children's classifications.   The principle of family resemblances in adult categories casts a new perspective on children's classifications. Young children have been shown to classify objects or pictures by means of *complexive classes,* that is, classes in which items are related to each other by attributes not shared by all members of the class (Bruner, Olver, & Greenfield, 1966; Vygotsky, 1962). For example, Vygotsky (1962) speaks of the child in the "phase of thinking in complexes" starting with a small yellow triangle, putting with it a red triangle, then a red circle—in each case matching the new item to one attribute of the old. Bruner *et al.* describe the young child's tendency to classify by means of "complexive structures," for example, "banana and peach are yellow, peach and potato round. . . ." Such complexive classes have been considered logically more primitive than the adult preferred method of grouping taxonomically by "what a thing is"—that is, grouping by superordinate classes and justifying groups by their superordinate names. However, the present research has shown that family resemblances, a form of complexive grouping, appears to be one of the structural principles in the composition of the superordinate classes themselves, and, thus, one of the structural principles in adult classification. Since adult taxonomic classes such as *furniture* or *chair* themselves consist of complexive groupings of attributes, it would appear appropriate to study the development of the integration of complexive into taxonomic categories rather than the replacement of the former by the latter.

Family resemblance as a logical alternative to criterial attributes.   There is a tenacious tradition of thought in philosophy and psychology which assumes that items can bear a categorical relationship to each other only by means of the possession of common criterial attributes. The present study is an empirical confirmation of Wittgenstein's (1953) argument that formal criteria are neither a logical nor psychological necessity; the categorical relationship in categories which do not appear to possess criterial attributes, such as those used in the present study, can be understood in terms of the principle of family resemblance.

REFERENCES

Beach, L. R. Cue probabilism and inference behavior. *Psychological Monographs*, 1964, **78**, 120.

Berlin, B., & Kay, P. *Basic color terms: Their universality and evolution.* Berkeley: University of California Press, 1969.

Bransford, J. D., & Franks, J. J. Abstraction of linguistic ideas. *Cognitive Psychology*, 1971, **2**, 331–350.

Bruner, J. S., Olver, R. R., & Greenfield. P. M. *Studies in cognitive growth.* New York: Wiley, 1966.

Ekman, P. Universals and cultural differences in facial expressions of emotion. In J. K. Cole (Ed.), *Nebraska symposium on motivation.* Lincoln, NE: University of Nebraska Press, 1971.

Frake, C. O. The ethnographic study of cognitive systems. In S. A. Tyler (Ed.), *Cognitive anthropology.* New York: Holt, Rinehart & Winston, 1969.

Franks, J. J., & Bransford, J. D. Abstraction of visual patterns. *Journal of Experimental Psychology*, 1971, **90**, 65–74.

Garner, W. R. *The processing of information and structure.* New York: Halsted Press, 1974.

Heider, E. R. Universals in color naming and memory. *Journal of Experimental Psychology*, 1972, **93**, 10–20.

Henley, N. M. A psychological study of the semantics of animal terms. *Journal of Verbal Learning and Verbal Behavior*, 1969, **8**, 176–184.

Kucera, H. K., & Francis, W. N. *Computational analysis of present-day American English.* Providence, RI: Brown University Press, 1967.

Lakoff, G. Hedges: A study in meaning criteria and the logic of fuzzy concepts. *Papers from the Eighth Regional Meeting, Chicago Linguistics Society.* Chicago: University of Chicago Linguistics Department, 1972.

Loftus, E. F., & Scheff. R. W. Categorization norms for fifty representative instances. *Journal of Experimental Psychology*, 1971, **91**, 355–364.

Mervis, C. B., Catlin. J., & Rosch, E. Development of the structure of color categories. *Developmental Psychology*, 1975, **11**, 54–60.

Neuman, P. G. An attribute frequency model for the abstraction of prototypes. *Memory and Cognition*, 1974, **2**, 241–248.

Posner, M. I. *Cognition: An introduction.* Glencoe, IL: Scott, Foresman, 1973.

Reed, S. K. Pattern recognition and categorization. *Cognitive Psychology*, 1972, **3**, 382–407.

Reitman, J. S., & Bower, C. H. Storage and later recognition of concepts. *Cognitive Psychology*, 1973, **4**, 194–206.

Rips, L. J., Shoben, E. J., & Smith, E. E. Semantic distance and the verification of semantic relations. *Journal of Verbal Learning and Verbal Behavior*, 1973, **12**, 1–20.

Rosch, E. On the internal structure of perceptual and semantic categories. In T. E. Moore (Ed.), *Cognitive development and the acquisition of language.* New York: Academic Press, 1973.

Rosch, E. Linguistic relativity. In A. Silverstein (Ed.), *Human communication: Theoretical perspectives.* New York: Halsted Press, 1974.

Rosch, E. Cognitive representations of semantic categories. *Journal of Experimental Psychology: General*, 1975, **104**, 192–233. (a)

[Rosch, E. (1975). Cognitive reference points. *Cognitive Psychology, 7*, 532–547. (b)]

[Rosch, E. (1975). The nature of mental codes for color categories. *Journal of Experimental Psychology: Human Perception and Performance, 1*, 303–322. (d)]

Rosch, E. Universals and cultural specifics in human categorization. In R. Brislin, S. Bochner, & W. Lonner (Eds.). *Cross-cultural perspectives on learning.* New York: Halsted Press, 1975. (c)

[Rosch, E. (1976). Classifications of objects in the real world: Origins and representations in cognition. *Bulletin de Psychologie*, 242–250.]

[Rosch, E. (1977). Human categorization. In N. Warren (Ed.), *Advances in cross-cultural psychology* (Vol. 1). New York: Academic Press.]

Rosch, E., Mervis, C. B., Gray, W., Johnson, D., & Boyes-Braem, P. Basic objects in natural categories. *Cognitive Psychology*, 1976, **8**, 382–439.

Shepard, R. N. The analysis of proximities: Multidimensional scaling with an unknown distance function. I and II. *Psychometrika*, 1962, **27**, 125–140, 219–246.

Shepard, R. N., Romney. A. K., & Nerlove, S. B. *Multidimensional scaling: Theory and applications in the behavioral sciences.* (Vols I & II). New York: Seminar Press, 1972.

Smith, E. E., Rips, L . J., & Shoben, E. J. Semantic memory and psychological semantics. In G. H. Bower (Ed.), *The psychology of learning and motivation* (Vol. 8). New York: Academic Press, 1974.

Smith, E. E., Shoben, E. J., & Rips, L. J. Structure and process in semantic memory: A featural model for semantic decisions. *Psychological Review*, 1974, **81**, 214–241.

Vygotsky, L. S. *Thought and language.* New York: Wiley, 1962.

Wittgenstein, L. *Philosophical investigations.* New York: Macmillan, 1953.

Zadeh, L. A. Fuzzy sets. *Information and Control*, 1965, **8**, 338–353.

REFERENCE NOTES

1. McDaniel, C. K. *Hue perception and hue naming.* Unpublished B.A. thesis, Harvard College, 1972.
2. Rosch, E., Simpson, C., & Miller, R. S. *Structural bases of typicality effects.* Manuscript submitted for publication, 1975.
3. Mervis, C. B., Rosch, E., & Catlin, J. *Relationships among goodness-of-example, category norms, and word frequency.* Unpublished manuscript, 1975. (Available from the second author.)

POSTSCRIPT

Although Tversky and Hemenway (1984) have pointed out a number of problems with the feature-listing task Rosch and Mervis used, the phenomena described here—and goodness-of-example effects more generally—are very robust. Goodness-of-example effects are found not only with object categories, but also in social situations (Cantor, Mischel, & Schwartz, 1982), with psychiatric categories (Cantor, Smith, French, & Mezzich, 1980; Genero & Cantor, 1987), in emotions (Fehr & Russell, 1984), and in personality traits and types (Cantor & Mischel, 1977). Not surprisingly, the family resemblance view and its very close relative, the prototype view, quickly gained acceptance among psychologists.

The exemplar view is another alternative to the traditional necessary-and-sufficient view that is roughly contemporaneous with the family resemblance view (Smith & Medin, 1981; see also the Introduction to Reading 18). The family resemblance view suggests that people maintain general information about what the instances of a conceptual category are like on average. In contrast, the exemplar view suggests that people maintain specific information (which is imperfect and incomplete) about the individual instances of a conceptual category. The family resemblance and exemplar views are difficult to distinguish empirically (Smith & Medin, 1981), and it is likely that people retain both summary and specific information. This is the position taken by both the so-called schema theory (Cohen & Murphy, 1984; Komatsu, 1992) and the connectionist approaches to concepts (Reading 18).

Recently, a number of psychologists have argued that when people know a concept, in addition to knowing about instances of the concept and the features of those instances, they know about the *relations* among those features (for example, see Carey, 1985; Keil, 1989; Malt, 1990; Medin & Ortony,

1989; Murphy & Medin, 1985; Rips, 1989; Reading 17). For example, rather than knowing simply that dogs share a certain genetic structure and that they share features (such as barking and having fur), people also know that dogs share these features *because* they share a genetic structure. Knowledge of these relationships explains why it is that although people generally consider barking to be an important characteristic of "dogness," people consider it an unimportant feature in a context in which it makes sense that barking is not manifest—as when a dog is asleep. Although relatively underdeveloped so far, this new knowledge-based view has gathered some impressive theoretical and empirical support (see Medin, 1989, for a short review).

FOR FURTHER THOUGHT

1. According to Rosch and Mervis, what predicts how prototypical of its category any given member is?
2. What is cue validity? How is it similar to and different from family resemblance?
3. If the traditional necessary-and-sufficient view were correct, how would the results of Experiment 1 have turned out? How do Rosch and Mervis explain why belief in the necessary-and-sufficient view persisted for so long in the face of the common intuition that most categories are analog?
4. What is a contrast category? Why wasn't it possible to generate contrast categories at the superordinate level? Why should there have been a negative correlation in number of features shared between contrasting categories?
5. Try to think of a few categories that do meet the assumption of necessary-and-sufficient characteristics. Do they have the digital properties Rosch and Mervis imply they ought to have, or are they analog in the same way the categories investigated by Rosch and Mervis are? (For experiments on this problem, see Armstrong, Gleitman, & Gleitman, 1983; Bourne, 1982; and Nosofsky, 1991.)

REFERENCES

Armstrong, Gleitman, & Gleitman (1983). What some concepts might not be. *Cognition, 13,* 263–308.

Bourne, L. E., Jr. (1982). Typicality effects in logically defined categories. *Memory & Cognition, 10,* 3–9.

Bruner, J. S., Goodnow, J. J., & Austin, G. A. (1956). *A study of thinking.* New York: Wiley.

Cantor, N., & Mischel, W. (1977). Traits as prototypes: Effects on recognition memory. *Journal of Personality and Social Psychology, 35,* 38–48.

Cantor, N., Mischel, W., & Schwartz, J. C. (1982). A prototype analysis of psychological situations. *Cognitive Psychology, 14,* 45–77.

Cantor, N., Smith, E. E., French, R. D., & Mezzich, J. (1980). Psychiatric diagnosis as prototype categorization. *Journal of Abnormal Psychology, 89,* 181–193.

Carey, S. (1985). *Conceptual change in childhood.* Cambridge, MA: MIT Press.

Cohen, B., & Murphy, G. L. (1984). Models of concepts. *Cognitive Science, 8,* 27–58.

Fehr, B., & Russell, J. A. (1984). Concept of emotion viewed from a prototype perspective. *Journal of Experimental Psychology: General, 113,* 464–486.

Genero, N., & Cantor, N. (1987). Exemplar prototypes and clinical diagnosis: Toward a cognitive economy. *Journal of Social and Clinical Psychology, 5,* 59–78.

Keil, F. C. (1989). *Concepts, kinds, and cognitive development.* Cambridge, MA: MIT Press.

Komatsu, L. K. (1992). Recent views of conceptual structure. *Psychological Bulletin, 112,* 500–526.

Malt, B. C. (1990). Features and beliefs in the mental representation of categories. *Journal of Memory and Language, 29,* 289–315.

Medin, D. L. (1989). Concepts and conceptual structure. *American Psychologist, 44,* 1469–1481.

Medin, D., & Ortony, A. (1989). Psychological essentialism. In S. Vosniadou & A. Ortony (Eds.), *Similarity and analogical reasoning* (pp. 179–195). New York: Cambridge University Press.

Murphy, G. L., & Medin, D. L. (1985). The role of theories in conceptual coherence. *Psychological Review, 92,* 289–316.

Nosofsky, R. M. (1991). Typicality in logically defined categories: Exemplar-similarity versus rule instantiation. *Memory & Cognition, 19,* 131–150.

Rips, L. J. (1989). Similarity, typicality, and categorization. In S. Vosniadou & A. Ortony (Eds.), *Similarity and analogical reasoning* (pp. 21–59). New York: Cambridge University Press.

Rosch, E. (1975). Cognitive representations of semantic categories. *Journal of Experimental Psychology: General, 104,* 192–233.

Rosch, E. (1978). Principles of categorization. In E. Rosch & B. B. Lloyd (Eds.), *Cognition and categorization* (pp. 27–48). Hillsdale, NJ: Erlbaum.

Rosch, E., Mervis, C. B., Gray, W. D., Johnson, D. M., & Boyes-Braem, P. (1976). Basic objects in natural categories. *Cognitive Psychology, 8,* 382–439.

Smith, E. E. (1978). Theories of semantic memory. In W. K. Estes (Ed.), *Handbook of learning and cognitive processes* (Vol. 6, pp. 1–56). Hillsdale, NJ: Erlbaum.

Smith, E. E., & Medin, D. L. (1981). *Concepts and categorization.* Cambridge, MA: Harvard University Press.

Smith, E. E., Shoben, E. J., & Rips, E. J. (1974). Structure and process in semantic memory: A featural model for semantic decisions. *Psychological Review, 81,* 214–241.

Tversky, B., & Hemenway, K. (1984). Objects, parts and categories. *Journal of Experimental Psychology: General, 113,* 169–193.

INTRODUCTION

Eleanor Rosch and her colleagues (Mervis, Gray, Johnson, & Boyes-Braem, 1976) argued that in many domains there is a most natural, or basic, level of abstraction. For example, the concept of *cat* appears to be at a basic level of abstraction, with both broader, or superordinate, levels (animal) and narrower, or subordinate, levels (Persian) possible. But what makes *cat* basic? In "Object Categories and Expertise: Is the Basic Level in the Eye of the Beholder?" James Tanaka and Marjorie Taylor point out that answering that question requires recognizing that *cat* is basic in two ways: psychologically and perceptually.

Cat is likely to be psychologically basic—that is, basic in terms of our information storage and processing—because it represents the best compromise between informativeness and economy (Rosch, 1978). Categorizing something as *animal* is not very informative (because the average person knows little that is true of all or most animals); *cat* is much more informative (the average person knows much more that is true of all or most cats). Categorizing something as *Persian* is not very economical (the extra information conveyed by *Persian* relative to *cat* is often not necessary, and if all categories were as specific as *Persian,* then the number of categories would be enormous). A possible consequence of this psychological primacy may be that people tend to categorize something as *cat* before they categorize it as *animal* or *Persian.* (See Reading 13, Experiment 2, for further discussion.)

Rosch and her associates (1976) also argued that categorizing at the basic level "carves nature at its [perceptual] joints." That is, given the structure of the physical world and how our perceptual systems respond to it, objects in the same basic- or subordinate-level category appear to us to share many features, whereas objects in the same superordinate-level category appear to share relatively few (Rosch, 1978; Tversky & Hemenway, 1984). For example, different animals share relatively few features, but different cats and different Persians share many. The crucial point, however, is that whereas different cats share many more features than do different animals, different Persians share only a few more features than do different cats. There's an abrupt increase—a discontinuity, or joint—in the number of shared features when we move from the superordinate to the basic level compared to when we move from the basic to the subordinate level.

Rosch and her colleagues (1976) reported a long series of experiments supporting this analysis. In one study, they used a computer to average silhouettes of different objects into a single silhouette. Subjects were not able to identify the averaged silhouette if the objects were taken from the same superordinate category, but they were able to if the objects were taken from the same basic-level category. This indicated that the basic level is the most inclusive level at which subjects can identify an averaged or "generalized" shape. (A second experiment indicated that the basic level is also the most inclusive level at which subjects can imagine a generalized shape.) Similarly, when the researchers asked subjects to act out how they would interact with a particular object, objects in the same basic-level category elicited similar actions (motor programs).

Rosch and her colleagues conducted their experiments within the framework of Rosch's family resemblance theory (see Reading 16). As is probably apparent from the experiments described above, in this framework the psychological properties of "basicness" follow directly from its perceptual properties; the two senses of "basicness" are therefore often conflated in their work.

Since the Rosch group's experiments were conducted, other psychologists have presented both theoretical and empirical arguments against the family resemblance view (see Keil, 1989; Medin, 1989; Murphy & Medin, 1985; see also the Postscript to Reading 16). Their alternative, often called the knowledge- or explanation-based view, suggests that people's knowledge about a particular domain strongly influences how they structure and use categories within that domain. The knowledge-based view suggests that the psychological properties of a category derive not only from the perceptual or functional properties of its instances, but also from people's more general understanding of how the world works. Tanaka and Taylor explore the possibility that different levels of abstraction are basic for people with different amounts or kinds of knowledge and try to separate the perceptual and psychological senses of basicness.

In this selection, Tanaka and Taylor's third experiment has been excluded. As you read, keep in mind the difference between Rosch's original ideas about the basic level and the position Tanaka and Taylor adopt. How do these experiments address that difference?

Object Categories and Expertise: Is the Basic Level in the Eye of the Beholder?

James W. Tanaka and Marjorie Taylor

University of Oregon

In a series of important experiments, Rosch, Mervis, Gray, Johnson, and Boyes-Braem (1976) established that a basic level of abstraction has special significance in human categorization (also see Brown, 1958). The basic level was shown to be the most inclusive level at which a generalized shape of category exemplars is identifiable and imaginable. In addition, basic categories elicit similar motor programs and basic-level category labels are the first names learned by children. Based on their analysis of structure at the basic level, Rosch et al. (1976) predicted that basic-level categories would be the classifications made when objects are first perceived.

Rosch et al. (1976) demonstrated the special status of basic-level categories for object identification in a free-naming and a category-verification task. In the naming task, subjects were presented with a series of pictures in rapid succession and were asked to write down the word which named the object. The main finding was that subjects used basic-level names (e.g., table, bird) more frequently to identify objects than superordinate- (e.g., furniture, animal) or sub-

ordinate-level names (e.g., coffee table, robin). In the category-verification task, subjects heard a category label (superordinate, basic, or subordinate) and then indicated whether a picture shown after a brief delay was an exemplar of the category. The results showed that subjects were faster to categorize objects at the basic level than at the superordinate or subordinate levels. Rosch et al. interpreted subjects' naming preferences and verification times as indicating that people first identify objects at the basic level and then access the superordinate or subordinate categories.

An important issue raised by the research of Rosch and her colleagues is the extent to which the basic level is determined by structure in the world or in the mind of the perceiver. As Rosch et al. (1976) and others (Malt & Smith, 1984; Mervis & Rosch, 1981) have pointed out, attributes are not distributed randomly across objects in the world, but instead typically occur in correlated clusters. For example, feathers and wings occur together more frequently than fur and wings. According to Rosch (1978), "a working assumption of the research on basic objects is that (1) in the perceived world, information-rich bundles of perceptual and functional attributes occur that form natural discontinuities, and that (2) basic cuts in categorization are made at these discontinuities" (p. 31). It is important to note that, although Rosch's research emphasizes structure in the world, she did not view this structure as existing independently of the human perceiver. Rosch (1978) was careful to explain that it is the interaction between the human perceiver and the world that specifies the basic level. Lakoff (1987) also describes basic-level category formation as a consequence of human perceiver and object-world interac-

We would like to thank our subjects for their enthusiastic support of this project, Gregory Murphy for his expert advice, Robert Mauro for the use of his lab, and Steve Jones, Keith Millis, Lisa Arnold, Todd Bennett, and Athena Wang for their assistance with Experiment 1. We would also like to thank Fred Attneave, Asher Cohen, Oliver John, Peter Jusczyk, and Mick Rothbart for comments on an earlier draft of this paper. We are also grateful to Douglas Medin and two anonymous reviewers for their helpful reviews of the manuscript. Correspondence concerning this article should be addressed to James Tanaka who is now at the Department of Psychology, Severance Laboratory, Oberlin College, Oberlin, OH 44074.

tions. "Perhaps the best way of thinking about basic-level categories is that they are 'human-sized.' They depend not on the objects themselves, independent of people, but on the way people interact with objects: the way they perceive them, image them, organize information about them and behave toward them with their bodies" (p. 51).

In addition to the general role of the human perceiver, Rosch et al. (1976) speculated that individual differences in domain-specific knowledge could also be important in determining the basic level. For example, they found that one of their subjects who was an airplane mechanic answered questions about airplanes quite differently from the other subjects. Based on this observation, Rosch et al. (1976) suggested that the contribution of the perceiver to the categorization process could be examined by research which systematically varied subjects' level of expertise with respect to the objects being categorized.

Although a number of studies have examined differences between experts and novices in pattern recognition (Biederman & Shiffrar, 1988; Chase & Simon, 1973) and conceptual organization (e.g., Chi, Feltovich, & Glaser, 1981; Murphy & Wright, 1984; Schvaneveldt, Durso, Goldsmith, Breen, & Cooke, 1985), the issue of whether there is a change in the structure of classification hierarchies in object categorization with expertise has not been addressed. This question has become particularly important given the recent interest in how a person's knowledge in a given domain affects their conceptual structure (Carey, 1985; Medin & Ortony, 1989; Murphy & Medin, 1985). Neisser (1987) describes the emphasis of categorization research as shifting from the role of objective characteristics of objects to the role of people's theories and knowledge about those objects. According to Neisser, research based solely on the characteristics of objects will never provide an adequate account of categorization.

In the present experiments, we examined the performance of subjects in expert and novice knowledge domains on three tasks: feature listing, object naming, and category verification. Previously, subjects' feature lists have been used to identify the basic level (Rosch et al., 1976). Subjects list many more attributes for basic-level categories than for superordinate-level categories and do not add many new attributes for subordinate-level categories. However, experts and novices differ in their knowledge about subordinate category attributes, and this difference should be reflected in their feature lists. Thus, in Experiment 1, we examined subjects' feature lists for categories in expert and novice domains. We hypothesized that the usual patterns in feature lists reported by Rosch et al. (1976) might be altered when subjects are experts in the domain. More specifically, we expected that experts would list at least as many new features for subordinate-level categories as for basic-level categories.

In Experiment 2 . . ., we tested the effects of expertise on object categorization. As mentioned above, subjects tend to supply basic-level labels when asked to name objects, and they are fastest to verify category membership at the basic level. The primacy of the basic level in naming and category-verification tasks has been interpreted as a consequence of the differentiation of basic-level categories (i.e., the structure to be found in subjects' attribute lists). However, if experts know many attributes that distinguish objects at the subordinate level, they might be more apt than novices to identify objects at the subordinate level, rather than at the basic level. For example, a bird expert might spontaneously identify a bird with its subordinate-level name (e.g., "robin") instead of its basic-level name (e.g. "bird"). . . .

EXPERIMENT 1

Feature Listing

Most operational definitions of the basic level refer to the attribute structure in classification hierarchies. Rosch et al. (1976) found that subjects listed significantly more attributes for basic-level categories (e.g., hammer, chair, car) than for superordinate categories (e.g., tool, furniture, vehicle). In addition, the number of new attributes added for subordinate-level categories (e.g., ball peen hammer, kitchen chair, sedan) were significantly fewer than the number added for the basic-level categories. Rosch et al. (1976) noted that the effect of expertise was not examined in their research, and they speculated about its possible effect on the location of the basic level. "Would, for example, an ichthyologist, whether presented with an actual example of a category or with a fish name, be able to list sufficient attributes specific to *trout, bass,* and *salmon* that the basic level for fish would have been placed at that level of abstraction?" (p. 393).

Rosch et al.'s speculation suggests that the number of features added at the subordinate level should increase as a consequence of expertise in a domain. Note, however, that one might not expect similar increases in the number of attributes listed at the basic or superordinate level as a function of expertise. Presumably, much of the knowledge that makes a person an expert concerns the subordinate categories in the domain. For example, the expert birdwatcher knows more than the novice with respect to the characteristics of specific kinds of birds (e.g., robins, sparrows) and in fact, may not necessarily be more knowledgeable about the general characteristics that distinguish birds from other kinds of animals. Thus, we predicted that an expert's knowledge would be demonstrated by an increase in the number of attributes listed for subordinate-level categories rather than by an increase in attributes distributed equally throughout the hierarchy.

To test this hypothesis, we asked bird and dog experts to list features for superordinate, basic, and subordinate categories. We describe a feature as new for a particular level if it is not listed at a more inclusive level of abstraction. For example, the property "has wings" is a new feature for the basic category "bird" because it is not a feature for the more general superordinate category "animal." However, the same feature "has wings" is not new for the subordinate category "robin" because it is also true of the more inclusive category "bird."[1] If expert knowledge is added primarily at the subordinate level of categorization, experts should list as many new features for subordinate-level categories as for basic-level categories. In the novice domain, however, subjects should

list more new features for the basic-level category than for subordinate-level categories. Thus, we predicted an interaction between knowledge domain (expert and novice) and category level (basic and subordinate) for the number of new features listed by dog and bird experts.

Method

Subjects.   Twelve dog and 12 bird experts participated in the experiment. Subjects were selected on the basis of their membership and participation in local dog and birdwatching organizations and on the basis of personal recommendations from other organization members. All subjects had a minimum of 10 years experience in their area of expertise with the majority of experts having over 20 years of experience. The group of dog experts consisted of nine women and three men ranging in age from 40 to 70 years with a mean age of 50 years. The group of bird experts consisted of five women and seven men ranging in age from 32 to 76 years whose mean age was also 50 years. Subjects were paid for their participation.

Prior to the feature-listing task, subjects filled out a general questionnaire concerning their past experience with dog and bird animals, membership in related professional organizations, and subscriptions to professional journals and magazines. Analysis of the questionnaire responses indicated that the two groups of experts met the criteria of expertise for either the dog or bird domains. None of the subjects had extensive experience in both domains.

Stimuli.   The subordinate-level bird categories selected for the feature-listing experiment were "robin," "crow," "jay," and "cardinal." The subordinate-level dog categories were "beagle," "Doberman pinscher," "collie," and "poodle." The four bird exemplars were among the 10 most frequently mentioned birds in Battig and Montague's (1969) category study. The four dog exemplars were among the 20 most frequently occurring dogs as determined by the American Kennel Club's list of registered dogs for 1984. (The category of dog was not included in the Battig and Montague study.) Subjects also completed feature listings for the superordinate category "animal" and basic categories "dog" and "bird." Additional cat-

---

[1]The new feature index is equivalent to the method employed by Rosch et al. (1976). In their feature-listing study, they found that subjects listed slightly more features for subordinate-level categories than for basic-level categories. However, the number of new features added at the basic level were significantly more than the number of new features added at the subordinate level. Thus, by Rosch et al.'s definition, the basic-level category is determined by the amount of information gained when moving from a more general level of abstraction to a more specific level.

egories were used as fillers: "fruit," "musical instrument," and "furniture" (superordinate level); "chair" and "table" (basic level); "easy chair," "desk chair," "coffee table," and "kitchen table" (subordinate level). In total, there were 20 categories: 11 categories from the two expert domains and 9 filler categories. Category names were printed at the top of separate sheets of $8\frac{1}{2} \times 11"$ paper and randomly assembled into test booklets with the restriction that categories sharing the same superordinate could not appear in consecutive presentations.

Procedure. At the beginning of the experiment, subjects were given the following written instructions: "At the top of each attached sheet of paper is the name of a familiar object. In the spaces provided, list as many characteristics or attributes that you can think of which describe the object. For example, for the common object 'fish,' you might list the characteristics of 'swims,' 'lives in water,' 'has gills,' etc. The same characteristic can be listed for more than one item. You will have two minutes for each item. The experimenter will signal when it is time to turn the page and go on to the next item. Remember to list only those things that are characteristic of the object and avoid listing simple free associations (e.g., 'salt' and 'pepper')." Subjects were tested individually.

Results and Discussion

Differentiation of subordinate-level categories. The number of features added at the basic and subordinate levels was determined for each individual subject based on his or her own feature list. Features that were semantically equivalent (e.g., "big" and "large") were collapsed and scored as a single feature as decided by a panel of three judges. To obtain the number of new features added at each level of abstraction, features were deleted from the more specific level of abstraction if the subject listed the same feature at a more inclusive level. For example, if a subject listed the attribute "has wings" for the basic level of "bird" and for the subordinate-level category "robin," it was deleted from the subordinate-level category. A single new features value for the subordinate-level categories was obtained by averaging the number of new features for the four subordinate categories (e.g.,

"cardinal," "crow," "jay," "robin"). Thus, after removing any repeated or synonymous features from the feature lists, the number of new features for the superordinate-, basic-, and subordinate-level categories was obtained for each individual subject.

For categories outside the domain of expertise (e.g., bird categories for dog experts), we expected to replicate the finding that subjects list more new features for basic-level categories than for subordinate-level categories. However, we predicted that representations of subordinate categories in the domain of expertise would contain as many new features as their basic-level equivalents. To test this prediction, an ANOVA was performed with expert type (bird expert and dog expert) as a between-group factor and category level (basic and subordinate) and knowledge domain (expert and novice) as within-subject factors. The main effect for expert type was not significant, $F(1,22) = .75$, $MS_e = 22.28$, *ns*. However, experts listed more features in their knowledge domain of expertise, $F(1,23) = 6.45$, $MS_e = 17.72$, $p < .05$, and the number of features was affected by category level, $F(1,23) = 27.59$, $MS_e = 207.83$, $p < .001$. As predicted, the interaction between category level and knowledge domain was significant, $F(1,23) = 19.82$, $MS_e = 68.77$, $p < .001$. As shown in Figure 1, the source of the interaction can be attributed to the increased number of attributes listed at the subordinate level in the domain of expertise. That is, in the expert knowledge domain, subjects added almost the same number of attributes at the subordinate level as at the basic level. Hence, the bird expert knows as much about the distinguishing properties of "robin" and "crow" as he or she knows about the distinguishing properties of "bird." However, consistent with the original Rosch et al. result, in the novice knowledge domain, subjects were able to list substantially *more* attributes at the basic level than at the subordinate level.

The findings reported above suggest that expert knowledge is primarily organized at the subordinate level of abstraction rather than at the basic level. In addition to the interaction between knowledge domain and category level with respect to new features, we were interested in (a) the extent that features listed for one subordinate category overlapped with features listed for the other subordinate level categories, and (b) the possibility that experts and novices differed in

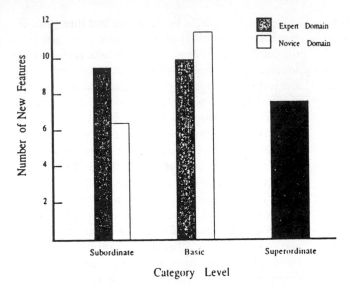

FIGURE 1   Mean number of new features listed by subjects as a function of knowledge domain (expert and novice) and category level (subordinate, basic, and superordinate). Note that the basic-level categories "bird" and "dog" share the same superordinate category "animal."

the kinds of attributes they listed at the basic and subordinate levels.

Degree of feature overlap at the subordinate level.   By calculating the number of nonoverlapping subordinate features, it was possible to determine if subjects simply described subordinates at a finer level of detail or if they added information that was distinctive to particular subordinate-level categories. Two independent judges scored each feature listed by each subject as "nonoverlapping" if it was listed for only one of the subordinate-level categories or as "overlapping" if it was listed for more than one category. For example, if a subject listed the feature "red breast" for the subordinate-level category "robin" and not for any other subordinate-level category, then "red breast" would be considered a nonoverlapping feature of "robin." The data from the two judges agreed 98% of the time. The small number of discrepancies was resolved by discussion. The amount of nonoverlapping subordinate-level features was 75 and 74% for the expert and novice categories, respectively. The relatively high percentage of nonoverlapping features indicated that subjects listed features with respect to some implicit

contrast set, which appeared to be objects that shared the same level of abstraction (Tversky & Hemenway, 1984).[2]

Classification of features.   Further analyses of the feature lists were performed to assess whether there were interesting differences in the types of features listed by experts and novices at the basic and subordinate levels. Booklets were made by listing in random order all the features generated for each category on separate sheets, with the name of the category at the top of each page. Four judges independently classified in-

---

[2]Murphy and Wright (1984) found that the categories of expert clinical psychologists were in fact *less* distinctive than the categories of intermediate and novice psychologists (child counselors and undergraduate students). There are several explanations that could account for the discrepancy between our result and Murphy and Wright's. Perhaps, the subordinate-level categories selected for our study happened to be more distinctive than the psychological categories used in the Murphy and Wright experiment. Alternatively, as mentioned by Murphy and Wright (1984), there may be important differences between the structure of abstract categories, such as those used in psychological assessment, and the structure of object categories (Barsalou, 1985) as well as differences in how experts organize abstract categories versus object categories.

dividual features as belonging to one of four categories: (1) behaviors—either an action (e.g., barks) or habitat (e.g., lives in trees) of the animal, (2) parts—a segment or portion of the animal (e.g., eyes, beak), (3) dimension—the color or size of the animal, and (4) none of the above. For part features, judges were told to indicate whether the part was simply named (e.g., ears) or contained additional information (e.g., floppy ears). If three of the four judges agreed on the classification of the feature, it was added to a final master list. To find the number of behaviors, parts, and dimensions listed by each subject, the original feature lists were scored according to the master list. Thus, for each subject, the number of behaviors, parts, and dimensions mentioned for the basic- and subordinate-level categories was obtained. For the subordinate level, a single value was calculated by averaging the number of features of each type across the four subordinate-level categories. Three separate ANOVAs were performed for the three feature categories, with expert type (bird expert or dog expert) as a between-groups factor, and category level (basic or subordinate) and knowledge domain (expert or novice) as within-subjects factors.

Behaviors. This analysis yielded main effects for knowledge domain, $F(1, 22) = 4.23$, $MS_e = 7.09$, $p < .05$, and category level $F(1, 22) = 14.01$, $MS_e = 48.76$, $p < .01$, as well as a significant interaction between these two factors, $F(1, 22) = 5.60$, $MS_e = 10.72$, $p < .05$. However, these effects should

be interpreted in light of the significant three-way interaction between expert type, knowledge domain, and category level, $F(1, 1, 22) = 17.96$, $MS_e = 34.34$, $p < .01$. As shown in Table 1, in the category of dog, significantly more behaviors were listed at the basic level than at the subordinate level by both dog experts, $t(12) = 2.87$, $p < .05$, and novices, $t(12) = 2.40$, $p < .05$. However, in the bird category, experts listed slightly more behaviors at the subordinate level than at the basic level. Bird novices, on the other hand, listed significantly more behavioral features at the basic level than at the subordinate level, $t(12) = 9.62$, $p < .01$. These results indicate that novices list behaviors primarily at the basic level. Moreover, behavioral features do not distinguish dog experts and novices, but do distinguish bird experts and novices. This finding suggests that attending to behavioral cues (e.g., habitat, feeding activity) is a particularly important aspect of bird expertise.

Parts. There was a significant main effect for category level, $F(1, 22) = 6.86$, $MS_e = 31.80$, $p < .05$, showing that subjects listed more parts for basic-level categories than for subordinate-level categories, as Tversky and Hemenway (1984) found in their research. However, as shown in Table 1, there was a significant three-way interaction between expert type, knowledge domain, and category level, $F(1, 1, 22) = 4.82$, $MS_e = 13.69$, $p < .05$. In the bird category, both experts, $t(12) = 3.42$, $p < .01$, and novices, $t(12) = 2.21$, $p < .05$, listed significantly more parts at the

Table 1 Means and Standard Deviations (in Parentheses) of New Features Listed as a Function of Object Category, Expertise, Feature Type, and Category Level

	Dog Category		Bird Category	
	Experts	Novices	Experts	Novices
Behavioral features				
Subordinate	2.50 (.84)	2.00 (1.47)	5.06 (1.99)	3.15 (1.00)
Basic	4.91 (2.81)	4.83 (3.75)	4.17 (2.12)	4.50 (1.98)
Part features				
Subordinate	2.96 (1.34)	2.25 (1.07)	1.44 (.92)	1.33 (.91)
Basic	2.50 (3.43)	3.50 (1.88)	3.41 (1.93)	3.17 (2.76)
Dimensional features				
Subordinate	2.29 (.87)	1.38 (.53)	1.54 (.66)	1.40 (.67)
Basic	.25 (.45)	.42 (.67)	.42 (.67)	.50 (.67)

basic level than at the subordinate level. However, in the dog category, novices listed significantly more parts at the basic level., $t(12) = 3.16$, $p < .01$, but experts listed slightly more parts at the subordinate level. Thus, the amount of part information listed at the basic and subordinate levels distinguished dog experts and novices, but not bird experts and novices.

Part features were further analyzed in terms of the number of modified part features. At the basic level, only 14% of the parts were modified whereas at the subordinate level, 78% were modified. This finding is consistent with Tversky and Hemenway's (1984) result showing that unmodified parts are most frequently listed at the basic level and modified parts at the subordinate level. With respect to expertise, in the dog category the mean number of modified parts listed by experts and novices was not significantly different, 2.5 and 2.2, respectively. However, in the bird category, there was a significant difference, $t(12) = 2.35$, $p < .05$, between the mean number of modified parts listed by bird experts, 1.25, and novices, .58. Bird experts listed the same number of subordinate level parts as the novices, but significantly more of these were modified parts.

Dimensions.   Overall, experts listed more dimensional features than novices, $F(1, 22) = 4.50$, $MS_e = .99$, $p < .05$, and more dimensional features were listed at the subordinate level than at the basic level, $F(1, 22) = 68.18$, $MS_e = 37.81$, $p < .001$. The main effect for expert type was not significant, $F(1, 22) = 1.58$, $MS_e = .77$, ns, and expert type was not involved in any significant interactions. There was a significant interaction between knowledge domain and category level, $F(1, 22) = 5.10$, $MS_e = 2.58$, $p < .05$. As shown in Table 1, both experts and novices listed very few dimensions at the basic level. At the subordinate level, more dimensions were listed and at this level, experts listed more dimensional features than novices, $t(23) = 2.73$, $p < .05$.

Summary

According to Rosch et al. (1976), a defining characteristic of a basic-level category is that it contains a larger number of new features than either its superordinate- or subordinate-level categories. We found that in their domain of expertise, subjects listed almost as many new features for subordinate-level categories as the basic-level category. Thus, our results show that the distinctiveness of subordinate-level categories changes as a function of expertise.

The above analyses also clarified the type of knowledge that distinguishes experts from novices. The exact nature of expertise varies across domains, and thus, the object attributes that experts select as most salient will depend on the goals and demands of the task domain. For example, we would expect that because the goals of expert ichthyologists and expert sport fishermen are different, their knowledge of fish would also differ in certain ways. Similarly, we found that differences exist between what bird experts and dog experts list as the salient features of the animals in their domain. Dog experts differed from novices in listing more part features, whereas bird experts differed from novices in listing more modified part features. Bird experts listed more behavioral features than novices. Both dog and bird experts listed more dimensional features than novices. With respect to the more general issue of expertise and category structure, it was found that in both these domains, the experts' knowledge was added at the subordinate level of abstraction. One implication of this information increase at the subordinate level is that subordinate-level categories may play a more central role in the processes of object categorization in an expert domain. In the next two experiments, the effect of expertise on object categorization is more closely examined.

EXPERIMENT 2

Free Naming Study

Previous researchers (Jolicoeur, Gluck, & Kosslyn, 1984; Rosch et al., 1976; Segui & Fraisse, 1968) have shown that subjects use basic-level names (e.g., bird, dog, chair, hammer) when asked to spontaneously identify pictures of common objects. This finding has been used as evidence that the most accessible level of abstraction for categorizing objects is the basic level. However, given the increased differentiation of the experts' subordinate categories found in Experiment 1, it is possible that a shift in object naming might occur with expertise. Experts may tend to categorize objects in the domain of expertise at a more specific level of abstraction and subsequently, experts should use subordinate-level names more often than novices for identification. For example, the expert bird-watcher might use the subordinate-level name "robin" rather than the basic-level name "bird" when identifying this animal. For object classifications outside the domain of expertise, subjects should use basic-level names for identification (e.g., the expert birder should use the name "dog" when shown a picture of a beagle). To test this hypothesis, dog and bird experts were asked to name pictures of four dog and bird exemplars as quickly as possible.

Method

Subjects.   The subjects were 12 dog experts recruited from a local dog organization and 12 bird experts who were members of a local birdwatching association. Nine of the dog experts and eight of the bird experts participated in Experiment 1. All subjects had a minimum of 10 years of experience in their area of expertise. The group of dog experts consisted of nine women and three men ranging in age from 39 to 70 years with a mean age of 53 years. The group of bird experts consisted of four women and eight men ranging in age from 38 to 76 years with a mean age of 53 years. None of the subjects had expertise in both the dog and bird domains. Subjects were paid for their participation.

Stimuli.   Picture stimuli consisted of 86 black-and-white drawings and photographs of common objects mounted on 15.4 × 12.6 cm white index cards. To minimize response bias, the target dog and bird pictures were embedded in a larger set of 78 filler pictures drawn from artifactual and natural kind categories. The artifactual categories were musical instrument, sports equipment, vehicle, food, furniture, tool, clothing, foot gear, jewelry, office equipment, cooking utensil, kitchen appliance, and home electronics. The natural categories were dog, bird, fish, insect, tree, flower, vegetable, fruit, four-legged animal, and famous person. The pictures of the four bird exemplars (robin, sparrow, jay, and cardinal) were taken from a book on bird identification (Zim, 1949). Robin, sparrow, jay, and cardinal were among the 10 most frequently mentioned birds in the Battig and Montague (1969) category norms. The pictures of the four dog exemplars (German shepherd, Doberman pinscher, beagle, cocker spaniel) were taken from an encyclopedia. German shepherd, Doberman pinscher, beagle, and cocker spaniel were among the 20 most frequently occurring dogs as determined by the American Kennel Club's list of registered dogs for 1984.

Procedure.   The subject was seated at a table directly across from the experimenter. Subjects were instructed that they would see a series of pictures depicting common everyday objects. Their task was "to say the word that names the object as quickly as possible." The experimenter presented each picture one at a time and recorded the category level (i.e. superordinate, basic, or subordinate) of each response. For the target pictures in the domain of expertise, the experimenter also noted the order of appearance (i.e. first, second, third, or fourth position). Pictures were presented at a rate of approximately one picture every 2 s. The order of presentation was randomized across subjects with the restriction that consecutive pictures were drawn from different superordinate categories.

According to Rosch et al., novices use basic-level names when identifying objects because this is the most useful level of abstraction for referring to objects. However, the use of basic-level names could also be due to lack of knowledge about subordinate-level categories. For example, dog experts might use the label "bird" rather than "sparrow" because they do not know the features that distinguish sparrows from other birds. To assess the possibility that novices were unfamiliar with the subordinate-level categories after the naming portion of the experiment. subjects were asked to identify the four pictures from the novice knowledge domain using their subordinate names. Any picture that could not be identified at the subordinate level was excluded from the main analysis.

Results and Discussion

None of the pictures was identified with a superordinate term. The comparison of primary interest was the percentage of trials in which basic versus subordinate level names were used to identify objects in the domain of expertise. On 57% of the trials, pictures of objects from the expert domain were identified with subordinate-level names and on 43% of the trials, they were identified with basic-level names. The difference in proportions between the basic-level and subordinate-level names was not significant, $\chi^2(1) =$ 2.04. *ns.* Rather than consistently applying the basic-level name, expert subjects frequently used subordinate-level names. The likelihood of using a subordinate-level name was not affected by the target picture's order of appearance, $\chi^2(3) = 2.76$, *ns.*

For identifying pictures of objects in the novice domain, subjects used basic-level names on 76% of the trials and subordinate-level names on 21% of the trials (3% of the trials were omitted from the analysis because pictures could not be identified with the appropriate subordinate-level names). The difference between the occurrence of basic-level and subordinate-level names was significant, $\chi^2(1) = 26.50$, $p <$ .001. Thus, our results for the novice domain replicate past research showing that subjects tend to use basic-level names for identifying objects (Jolicoeur et al., 1984; Rosch et al., 1976; Segui & Fraisse, 1968).

Separate analyses performed on the dog and bird experts revealed a difference in the naming patterns between the two types of experts. As shown in Figure 2, bird experts identified bird pictures with subordinate-level names on 74% of the trials and on 26% of

the trials, they choose basic-level names, $\chi^2(1) =$ 12.00, $p < .001$. Thus, for identifying objects from their domain of expertise, bird experts preferred subordinate-level names over basic-level names. On the other hand, although dog experts used subordinate category labels more frequently than novices, they did not show a distinct preference for either basic- or subordinate-level labels. On 60% of the trials they used the basic-level label and on 40% of the trials they used the subordinate-level label, $\chi^2(1) = 2.08$, *ns.* This difference between dog and bird experts in naming performance may be due to the different skills that are emphasized for acquiring expertise in these two fields. Almost by definition, an expert birdwatcher is a person who can make fast and accurate perceptual identifications at specific levels of abstraction. In contrast, dog expertise tends to take the form of experience in the handling, training, grooming, and breeding of one or two particular breeds. In their study of dog experts, Diamond and Carey (1986) found that subjects showed effects of expertise only for those breeds of dog in which they specialized. As it turned out, only one of our experts had prior direct contact with the breeds used in the naming experiment. Our point is not that dog experts know about only one or two breeds of dogs (the results of Experiment 1 indicate that they know more than novices about the breeds used in this research), but that identifying spe-

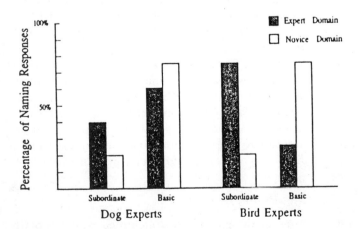

FIGURE 2   Percentage of pictures identified with subordinate-level and basic-level names as a function of knowledge domain (expert and novice) and expert type (dog experts and bird experts).

cific breeds of dogs is less central to the activities of dog experts than identifying specific species of birds is to the activities of bird experts.

In summary, the results from the naming study demonstrate that expert subjects frequently use subordinate-level names for identifying objects in their domain of expertise. This result can be contrasted to the primary use of basic-level names by novices (Jolicoeur et al., 1984; Rosch et al., 1976; Segui & Fraisse, 1968). Taken together with the findings from Experiment 1, these results show that experts are more informed about the specific features that distinguish exemplars at the subordinate level, and they have ready access to this information for the purpose of object naming. . . .

[In their third experiment, Tanaka and Taylor measured the amount of time it took bird and dog experts to verify that a picture depicted an instance of a particular category, either at the superordinate, basic, or subordinate level. For example, a subject would be presented with a category label, such as *beagle, dog,* or *animal.* As expected, within their domain of expertise, experts verified membership in the subordinate-level category as quickly as they verified membership in the basic-level category, and they did both more quickly than they verified membership in the superordinate-level category. Also as expected, outside their domain of expertise, novices and experts verified membership in the basic-level category more quickly than they did in either the subordinate- or the superordinate-level categories.]

GENERAL DISCUSSION

While Rosch et al. (1976) claimed that the privileged status of the basic-level category is a reflection of the general characteristics of the human perceiver and inherent structure of objects in the world, they also acknowledged the possible contribution of individual differences in knowledge to the organization of human categories: "Different amounts of knowledge about objects can change the classification scheme. Thus, experts in some domain of knowledge can make use of attributes that are ignored by the average person" (p. 430). The present experiments were designed to address this speculation. In the first experiment, it was found that in novice domains, subjects listed the greatest number of new features for basic-level categories, but, in their domain of expertise, they listed equivalent numbers of new features for subordinate-level and basic-level categories. The implications of increased knowledge at the subordinate level were demonstrated in Experiments 2 and 3. In Experiment 2, subjects used the subordinate-level name as frequently as the basic-level name for identifying objects in their domain of expertise. . . .

Implications for What Is Meant by the "Basic Level"

Discussions of conceptual hierarchies often suggest that the basic level can be defined as the level which is the most psychologically fundamental. For example, the basic level is claimed to be the first level of categorization for object recognition, objects are typically identified at the basic level, and names for basic categories are the first words acquired by children. According to this view, it is possible to describe basic-level categories at a more specific level of abstraction for one group of individuals and at a more inclusive level for another. In other words, one might hypothesize a downward shift in the basic level or the creation of a second more specific basic level in a classification hierarchy as a function of expertise. The downward shift hypothesis is implicit in Rosch et al.'s (1976) speculation that the basic level for a fish expert would be the level of trout, bass, and salmon; categories generally considered to be at the subordinate level for novice populations. Rosch et al. (1976) also considered the possibility of experts having hierarchies with two or more basic levels, and discussed which types of hierarchies would allow the creation of multiple basic levels.

Although a definition of the basic level in terms of psychological preference has some advantages (e.g., the notion of basic level is not limited to concrete objects like dogs and chairs, but can be extended to other types of categories such as emotions and personality traits (John, Hampson, & Goldberg, 1990; Shaver, Schwartz, Kirson, & O'Connor, 1987)), the basic level is often conceptualized quite differently (Jolicoeur et al., 1984; Mervis, 1987; Mervis & Crisafi, 1982; Murphy & Smith, 1982; Rosch, 1978). Rosch et al. originally used four converging operational definitions of the basic level: (1) the level which maximizes information gain as indexed by subjects' attribute lists; (2) the most inclusive level at which objects elicit highly similar sequences of motor movements; (3) the most inclusive level at which the shapes of object are very similar as indexed by the ratio of overlapping to nonoverlapping areas for normalized pictures of category exemplars; and (4) the most inclusive level at which an averaged shape of an object is identifiable. Because of the emphasis on "most inclusive" in these definitions, we interpret them collectively as based primarily on perceived structure in the world and as inconsistent with the idea of a downward shift in the location of the basic level as a function of expertise. Definitions based on perceived structure in the world make the location of the basic level relatively independent of the effects of the domain-specific expertise. Although the subordinate-level categories of the experts are more differentiated than the novices', the basic level remains the *most inclusive* at which objects look alike. For example, even though the characteristics that distinguish breeds of dogs are better known to dog experts, for experts (and for novices as well), the level of "dog" would still be the most general level at which these animals would share similar overall shapes.

Our work with experts indicates that it is important not to assume that the psychological definition and the "perceived structure" definition of the basic-level category always converge on the same level of abstraction. Past research has demonstrated such a convergence because the subjects have been selected from novice populations in a single culture. However, our experiments with experts show that extensive knowledge in a domain may result in categories at the level of "collie" and "robin" sharing some of the psychological advantages usually attributed solely to categories at the level of "dog" and "bird." In keeping with Rosch et al.'s operational definition of the basic level, we interpret our results not as the construction of a second basic level, but as an increase in the accessibility of the subordinate level as a function of expertise.

Implications for the Process of Categorization

According to Rosch et al. (1976), objects are first identified at the basic level. Subsequent categorizations at the superordinate level involve retrieval of semantic information and categorizations at the subordinate level require additional perceptual analysis (Jolicoeur et al., 1984). The *basic first hypothesis* requires that basic-level categorizations are always faster than superordinate-level or subordinate-level categorizations because perceptual input accesses semantic memory initially at the basic level. However, counter to the predictions of the basic first hypothesis, we found in Experiment 3 that expert subjects made subordinate-level categorizations as quickly as basic-level categorizations, suggesting that basic-level and subordinate-level categorizations can be performed independently of each other. Other studies have challenged the basic first hypothesis by showing that atypical exemplars of a basic-level category (e.g., racing car) are categorized faster at the subordinate level than at the basic level (Murphy & Brownell, 1985; Jolicoeur et al., 1984). Recently, Murphy and Wisniewski (1989) have also shown that superordinate-level categorizations can be as fast as basic-level categorizations when objects are placed in the appropriate contextual scene. Thus, the converging evidence shows that, contrary to the basic first hypothesis, people do not automatically identify objects at the basic level before making categorizations at the other levels of abstraction.

Murphy and Brownell's (1985) *differentiation hypothesis* seems to provide a more parsimonious account of the empirical findings. The differentiation hypothesis maintains that the accessibility of a category is a function of specificity and distinctiveness, taken together as the degree of category differentiation. The more differentiated the category, the more easily it can be accessed. This hypothesis is consistent with the general finding that objects are usually categorized fastest at the basic level (Rosch et al., 1976), and with the exceptions to the basic-level finding: (1) when an object is an atypical exemplar of a basic-level category (i.e., its subordinate is more distinctive than most subordinates from the same basic level), it is categorized *faster* at the subordinate level than at the basic level, and (2) when people are particularly knowledgeable about the features that distinguish subordinate categories in a domain (i.e., they become experts), their subordinate-level categorizations are as fast as their basic-level categorizations.

Variability in Expertise across Individuals and across Cultures

The exact nature of the difference between an expert and a novice is bound to be affected by characteristics of the expert domain (e.g., the type of activity that the expert participates in, the goals or reasons for the expert knowledge, important aspects of the objects in the domain). The domain of birds is quite similar to the domain of dogs when one considers the wide range of topics on which one could become an expert (e.g., chess, automechanics, stamps, flowers, etc.), yet dog experts and bird experts differed in some respects. For example, bird experts showed a clear preference for naming birds at the subordinate level while dog experts used both subordinate- and basic-level names for identifying dogs. The differences between experts in diverse domains are interesting topics for research, but the main point of the present investigation was to demonstrate the increased psychological importance of more specific categories as a function of expert knowledge. We believe this is a general finding with broad applications. For example, research on social stereotypes indicates that when a person is well-known, their membership in a social category (e.g., Asian, black) tends not to be invoked because they are encoded at a more specific level of abstraction (see Rothbart & John, 1985).

We also think that our results on the effects of expertise are not limited to people who, like our subjects, have devoted many years of their life to gaining knowledge and experience in a particular domain. Expertise does not have to span an entire domain. Instead, it could be quite narrow in scope, perhaps limited to a single subordinate category. For example, a person who owns a collie and spends a lot of time with the dog could be considered a "collie expert." Such a person might be aware of the distinguishing features of collies, but know very little about distinctive properties of other breeds of dogs. Presumably, this person would refer to collies by their subordinate-level name, but refer to other breeds of dogs simply as "dogs." We suspect such specificity in the level of categorization is commonplace, and consequently, there may be considerable unevenness in the way an individual categorizes objects in a single domain. Rosch et al. (1976) considered this possibility,

giving the example of an antique furniture dealer "for whom Chippendale and Hepplewhite chairs are the basic level objects, but for whom kitchen and living room chairs, in the average house, are as undifferentiated as for our subjects" (p. 432).[3]

In addition to individual differences in the way particular objects are categorized as a function of idiosyncratic life experiences, it is also possible to suggest that differences in the way objects are categorized would exist between members of different population groups. Within a given culture, there may be a typical level of expertise with respect to a particular domain, determined by the relative importance of the domain for the culture. However, the importance of a given domain may vary cross-culturally, with more specific levels of categorization being associated with cultures in which the domain is more important. Evidence drawn from cross-cultural studies is consistent with this idea. The basic level, as defined by the most inclusive level at which objects share perceptual features, is not necessarily the level at which objects are usually categorized in nonwestern societies. For example, Dougherty (1978) found that the Tzeltal Mayan people identify common plants and animals at the folk-genera level (e.g., oak) rather than at the life-form level (e.g., tree). In a related study, Stross (1973) found that Tzeltal children first learn the names of plants corresponding to our subordinate-level categories and later on, acquire the more inclusive basic-level names. Presumably, the pragmatic concerns of an agrarian society make the more specific categorization of plants and animals desirable (Cruse, 1975).

In conclusion, this research emphasizes diversity in conceptual structure as a function of expertise and is consistent with the views of many researchers (Jolicoeur et al., 1984; Murphy & Medin, 1985; Murphy & Smith, 1982; Rosch et al., 1976) concerning the role that world knowledge plays in shaping object categorization. By emphasizing the importance of world knowledge, we do not mean to suggest that stimulus structure plays no role in the categorization

---

[3]In this example. Rosch et al. (1976) use the psychological definition of the basic level rather than the definition based upon perceived structure in the world.

process. However, while the external environment and the human perceptual system impose certain constraints, human categorization appears to be continually reshaped and altered by learning and experience.

REFERENCES

Barsalou, L. W. (1985). Ideals, central tendency, and frequency of instantiation as determinants of graded structure in categories. *Journal of Experimental Psychology: Learning, Memory, and Cognition,* 11, 629–653.

Batlig, W. F., & Montague, W. E. (1969). Category norms for verbal items in 56 categories: A replication and extension of the Connecticut category norms. *Journal of Experimental Psychology Monograph,* 80, 1–46.

Biederman, I. (1987). Recognition-by-components: A theory of human image understanding. *Psychological Review,* 94, 115–147.

Biederman, I., & Ju, G. (1988). Surface versus edge-based determinants of visual recognition. *Cognitive Psychology,* 20, 38–64.

Biederman, I., & Shiffrar. M. (1988). Sexing day-old chicks: A case study and expert systems analysis of a difficult perceptual-learning task. *Journal of Experimental Psychology: Learning, Memory and Cognition,* 13, 640–645.

Brown, R. (1958). How should a thing be called? *Psychological Review,* 65, 14–21.

Carey, S. (1985). *Conceptual change in childhood.* Cambridge, MA: MIT Press.

Chase, W. G., & Simon, H. A. (1973). Perception in chess. *Cognitive Psychology,* 4, 55–81.

Chi, M. T. H., Feltovich, P. J., & Glaser, R. (1981). Categorization and representation of physics problems by experts and novices. *Cognitive Science,* 5, 121–152.

Cruse, D. A. (1975). The pragmatics of lexical specificity. *Journal of Linguistics,* 13, 153–164.

Diamond, R., & Carey, S. (1986). Why faces are and are not special: An effect of expertise. *Journal of Experimental Psychology: General,* 115, 107–117.

Dougherty, J. W. D. (1978). Salience and relativity in classification. *American Ethnologist,* 5, 66–80.

Glover, H. (1976). *Spotter's guide to dogs.* New York: Smith Publishers.

John, O. P., Hampson, S. E., & Goldberg, L. R. (1990). The basic level in personality-trait hierarchies: Studies of trait use and accessibility in different contexts. *Journal of Personality and Social Psychology,* 60, 348–361.

Jolicoeur, P., Gluck, M. A., & Kosslyn, S. M. (1984). Picture and names: Making the connection. *Cognitive Psychology,* 16, 243–275.

Lakoff, G. (1987). *Women, fire and dangerous things: What categories tell us about the nature of thought.* Chicago: University of Chicago Press.

Mall, B. C., & Smith, E. E. (1984). Correlated properties in natural categories. *Journal of Verbal Learning and Verbal Behavior,* 23, 250–269.

Medin, D. L., & Ortony, A. (1989). Psychological essentialism. In S. Vosniadou & A. Ortony (Eds.), *Similarity and analogical reasoning* (pp. 179–195). New York: Cambridge University Press.

Mervis, C. B. (1987). Child-basic object categories and early lexical development. In U. Neisser (Ed.). *Concepts and conceptual development: Ecological and intellectual factors in categorization* (pp. 201–233). Cambridge: Cambridge University Press.

Mervis, C. B., & Crisafi, M. A. (1982). Order of acquisition of subordinate-, basic-, and superordinate-level categories. *Child Development,* 53, 258–266.

Mervis, C. B., & Rosch, E. (1981). Categorization of natural objects. *Annual Review of Psychology,* 32, 89–115.

Murphy, G. L., & Brownell, H. H. (1985). Category differentiation in object recognition: Typicality constraints on the basic category advantage. *Journal of Experimental Psychology: Learning, Memory, and Cognition,* 11, 70–84.

Murphy, G. L., & Medin, D. L. (1985). The role of theories in conceptual coherence. *Psychological Review,* 92, 289–316.

Murphy, G. L., & Smith, E. E. (1982). Basic level superiority in picture categorization. *Journal of Verbal Learning and Verbal Behavior,* 21, 1–20.

Murphy, G. L., & Wisniewski, E. J. (1989). Categorizing objects in isolation and in scenes: What a superordinate is good for. *Journal of Experimental Psychology: Learning, Memory, and Cognition,* 15, 572–586.

Murphy, G. L., & Wright, J. C. (1984). Changes in conceptual structure with expertise: Differences between real-world experts and novices. *Journal of Experimental Psychology: Learning, Memory, and Cognition,* 10, 141–155.

Neisser, U. (1987). Introduction: The ecological and intellectual bases of categorization. In U. Neisser (Ed.), *Concepts and conceptual development: Ecological and intellectual factors in categorization* (pp. 1–10). Cambridge: Cambridge University Press.

Peterson, R. T. (1985). *First field guide to birds.* Boston: Houghton Mifflin.

Rosch, E. (1978). Principles of categorization. In E. Rosch & B. B. Lloyd (Eds.), *Cognition and categorization* (pp. 27–48). Hillsdale, NJ: Erlbaum.

Rosch, E., Mervis, C. B., Gray, W., Johnson, D., & Boyes-Braem, P. (1976). Basic objects in natural categories. *Cognitive Psychology, 8,* 382–439.

Rothbart, M., & John, O. P. (1985). Social categories and behavioral episodes: A cognitive analysis of the effects of intergroup contact. *Journal of Social Issues, 41,* 81–104.

Schvaneveldt, R. W., Durso, F. T., Goldsmith, T. E., Breen, T. J., & Cooke, N. J. (1985). Measuring the structure of expertise. *International Journal of Man-Machine Studies, 23,* 699–728.

Segui, J., & Fraisse, P. (1968). Le temps de reaction verbale. III Responses specifiques et responses icategorielles a des stimulus objects. *L'Annee psychologique, 68,* 69–82.

Shaver, P., Schwartz, J., Kirson, D., & O'Connor, C. (1987). Emotion knowledge: Further explanation of a prototype approach. *Journal of Personality and Social Psychology, 52,* 1061–1086.

Stross, B. (1973). Acquisition of botanical terminology by Tzeltal children. In M. Edmonson (Ed.), *Meaning in Mayan language* (pp. 109–141). The Hague: Mouton.

Tversky, B., & Hemenway, K. (1984). Objects, parts and categories. *Journal of Experimental Psychology: General, 113,* 169–193.

Zim, H. (1949). *Birds.* New York: Simon & Schuster.

POSTSCRIPT

A "basic level" of abstraction has been reported for categories other than the simple object categories studied by Rosch and her associates (1976) and Tanaka and Taylor, including: event categories (Morris & Murphy, 1990; Rifkin, 1985); musical instrument categories (Palmer, Jones, Hennessy, Unze, & Pick, 1989); and the emotion and personality trait categories mentioned by Tanaka and Taylor.

It is worth noting that there are considerable methodological problems involved in the feature-listing task used by Rosch and her colleagues and in Tanaka and Taylor's first experiment. Tversky and Hemenway (1984) present a thorough discussion of those problems as well as a number of interesting insights into the nature of the basic level. Tversky and Hemenway also support a slightly different conception of the basic level than the one taken in this reading and shared by Neisser (1987). In Tversky and Hemenway's view, at the basic level of categorization, distinctions among categories rest heavily on information about parts (for debate on this claim, see Murphy, 1991a, 1991b; and Tversky & Hemenway, 1991). Corter and Gluck (1992) argue for yet another characterization of the basic level that is based on feature predictability.

FOR FURTHER THOUGHT

1. By listing out features for vehicles, cars, and Honda Civics, give your own examples of what Rosch and her colleagues would call "discontinuities in the information richness" of different levels of abstraction.

2. Why do Tanaka and Taylor argue that the effect of expertise on category structure and processes takes place at the subordinate level rather than at either the basic or superordinate level?

3. What kinds of general (domain independent) statements about the effects of expertise on category structure and use do Tanaka and Taylor make? Are there any effects of expertise that are particular to one or another domain that do not carry over to all other domains? If so, explain what they are, and discuss whether this is a weakness in Tanaka and Taylor's argument.

4. How do Tanaka and Taylor demonstrate that their results reflect the effects of expertise within a particular domain and not the idiosyncrasies of a somewhat odd group of subjects?

5. Describe the results with naming by dog experts that Tanaka and Taylor received in Experiment 2. Do these pose a problem for the arguments Tanaka and Taylor want to make?

6. The kinds of expertise studied by Tanaka and Taylor involve visual identification. Think of an area of expertise that does not involve visual identification. How would these experiments have to be adapted to accommodate that kind of expertise? Would you expect the same kind of results? Why or why not?

REFERENCES

Corter, J. E., & Gluck, M. A. (1992). Explaining basic categories: Feature predictability and information. *Psychological Bulletin, 111,* 291–303.

Keil, F. C. (1989). *Concepts, kinds, and cognitive development.* Cambridge, MA: MIT Press.

Medin, D. L. (1989). Concepts and conceptual structure. *American Psychologist, 44,* 1469–1481.

Morris, M. W., & Murphy, G. L. (1990). Converging operations on a basic level in event taxonomies. *Memory & Cognition, 18,* 407–418.

Murphy, G. L. (1991a). More on parts in object concepts: Response to Tversky and Hemenway. *Memory & Cognition, 19,* 443–447.

Murphy, G. L. (1991b). Parts in object concepts: Experiments with artificial categories. *Memory & Cognition, 19,* 423–438.

Murphy, G. L., & Medin, D. L. (1985). The role of theories in conceptual coherence. *Psychological Review, 92,* 289–316.

Neisser, U. (1987). From direct perception to conceptual structure. In U. Neisser (Ed.), *Concepts and conceptual development* (pp. 11–24). New York: Cambridge University Press.

Palmer, C. F., Jones, R. K., Hennessy, B. L., Unze, M. G., & Pick, A. D. (1989). How is a trumpet known? The "basic object level" concept and perception of musical instruments. *American Journal of Psychology, 102,* 17–37.

Rifkin, A. (1985). Evidence for a basic level in event taxonomies. *Memory & Cognition, 13,* 538–556.

Rosch, E. (1978). Principles of categorization. In E. Rosch & B. B. Lloyd (Eds.), *Cognition and categorization* (pp. 27–48). Hillsdale, NJ: Erlbaum.

Rosch, E., Mervis, C. B., Gray, W. D., Johnson, D. M., & Boyes-Braem, P. (1976). Basic objects in natural categories. *Cognitive Psychology, 8,* 382–439.

Tversky, B., & Hemenway, K. (1984). Objects, parts and categories. *Journal of Experimental Psychology: General, 113,* 169–193.

Tversky, B., & Hemenway, K. (1991). Parts and the basic level in natural categories and artificial stimuli: Comments on Murphy (1991). *Memory & Cognition, 19,* 439–442.

INTRODUCTION

Psychologists generally agree that a concept is a mental representation of a category. But what does a concept specify about a category? Does it specify information common to all or most members, or exemplars, of the category? Or does a concept specify unique information for every member of the category? Although most early views of concepts have argued that they consist of one or the other kind of information (Komatsu, 1992), in "Distributed Memory and the Representation of General and Specific Information," James McClelland and David Rumelhart propose a model of concepts that integrates both kinds of information.

Early evidence for the availability of information abstracted or averaged across category members came from an experiment in which subjects classified various dot patterns (Posner & Keele, 1968). Posner and Keele created the members of a given category of dot patterns by taking a single pattern (the prototype) and making a few well-defined changes; a different prototype was used for each category. Subjects learned a category by viewing a number of its members but *not* its prototype; subjects were later tested for their ability to sort dot patterns into one or another category. The crucial result was that subjects sometimes categorized the never-before-viewed prototype more accurately than they categorized the previously viewed members. This outcome is consistent with the view that subjects represent a category in terms of the information that *summarizes* its members. These summaries, or abstractions, of general tendencies are sometimes called prototypes or logogens (see Reading 16 for a discussion of prototypes, and see the Introduction to Reading 14 for a discussion of logogens).

As McClelland and Rumelhart point out, certain results pose difficulties for an abstractive view. These results suggest that people retain information about specific members of the category. In this enumeration or exemplar-based view, a concept is a collection of individual representations of the different members of a category, not a representation of a single summarization. When we are asked to classify some object, we decide which item or set of items the object in question is most similar to and then conclude that it belongs to the same category as that item or set of items. By assuming that our representations of members are incomplete and that certain biases exist in which member representations we retrieve, enumeration models can also account for the Posner and Keele results (Hintzman & Ludlam, 1980; Nosofsky, 1988).

Unfortunately, as McClelland and Rumelhart point out in their article, such exemplar-based models have certain logical difficulties. McClelland and Rumelhart therefore argue instead for a distributed memory, or connectionist, model (see the Introduction and Postscript to Reading 6 for a discussion of connectionist models). Very briefly, a connectionist model is a network of simple, interconnected units that can be activated to a greater or lesser degree by incoming information and by each other. (See the Introduction to Reading 12 for a more detailed description of networks.) Different concepts are represented by different patterns of activation among these units. Information about a particular item to be categorized is input to the network by activating certain units, which in turn raise and lower the other units' activation levels until the levels stabilize. That stable pattern of activations among units represents a particular categorization decision.

What we want is a network with units connected in such a way that they stabilize into the pattern of activation that represents the category *dog* whenever we input information about dogs (that is, whenever we start out by imposing a pattern of activation among the units that corresponds to "barks," "has a tail," and so on). What's important is that a network that stabilizes into the pattern that represents *dog* whenever we input dog information may also stabilize into a pattern that represents *cat* when we input cat information. Thus, one network can represent many categories. Individual units in such a network do not represent anything; *patterns of activation* do. For this reason, representations are said to be *distributed* over the units of the network.

Much of the discussion in McClelland and Rumelhart's paper results from the fact that networks must be trained to represent certain categories. When a network is first given an input, its output (that is, its final, stable activation pattern) will not match the desired pattern. Using a formula called the delta rule, the weights of the connections between the units of the network are adjusted so that the output is closer to the desired pattern. (The weights affect how much units raise or lower the activations of the units to which they are connected.) The sequence of presenting an example and adjusting the connection weights is called a training cycle. After many such training cycles, the network gives the desired output in response to all the relevant inputs without adjustment. A fully trained network is achieved by superimposing the effect of each example (that is, the adjustment in connection weights caused by an input) on the effects of all previous examples; the final connection weights are derived through an accretion of specific instances. McClelland and Rumelhart argue that a connectionist network in this way captures both abstracted and specific instance data, but it is neither an abstractive nor an enumeration model.

It is extremely difficult in a brief introduction to adequately describe the components of a connectionist model and explain how it works. Without such background, many of the technical details McClelland and Rumelhart discuss in their article are quite opaque and so have been excluded. Several relatively nontechnical treatments are available and are useful for developing that background (for example, see Bechtel & Abrahamsen, 1991; Clark, 1989; Martindale, 1991).

In these excerpts, McClelland and Rumelhart describe how a connectionist network can simulate the results of certain experiments on people. This is an interesting case in which a theory of human cognition is tested first by programming a computer to behave according to the theory and then by comparing the "behavior" of the computer to that of people. As you read this selection, ask yourself how this connectionist approach is different from the kinds of approaches adopted in other studies in this book.

Distributed Memory and the Representation of General and Specific Information

James L. McClelland and David E. Rumelhart

University of California, San Diego

In the late 1960s and early 1970s a number of experimenters, using a variety of different tasks, demonstrated that subjects could learn through experience with exemplars of a category to respond better —more accurately, or more rapidly—to the prototype than to any of the particular exemplars. The

Preparation of this article was supported in part by a grant from the Systems Development Foundation and in part by a National Science Foundation Grant BNS-79-24062. The first author is a recipient of a Career Development Award from the National Institute of Mental Health (5-K01-MH00385).

This article was originally presented at a conference organized by Lee Brooks and Larry Jacoby on "The Priority of the Specific." We would like to thank the organizers, as well as several of the participants, particularly Doug Medin and Rich Shiffrin, for stimulating discussion and for empirical input to the development of this article.

Requests for reprints should be sent to James L. McClelland, Department of Psychology, Carnegie-Mellon University, Pittsburgh, Pennsylvania 15213 or to David E. Rumelhart, Institute for Cognitive Science, C-015, University of California—San Diego, La Jolla, California 92093.

seminal demonstration of this basic point comes from the work of Posner and Keele (1968, 1970). Using a categorization task, they found that there were some conditions in which subjects categorized the prototype of a category more accurately than the particular exemplars of the category that they had previously seen. This work, and many other related experiments, supported the development of the view that memory by its basic nature somehow abstracts the central tendency of a set of disparate experiences, and gives relatively little weight to the specific experiences that gave rise to these abstractions.

Recently, however, some have come to question this "abstractive" point of view, for two reasons. First, specific events and experiences clearly play a prominent role in memory and learning. Experimental demonstrations of the importance of specific stimulus events even in tasks which have been thought to involve abstraction of a concept or rule are now legion. Responses in categorization tasks (Brooks, 1978; Medin & Shaffer, 1978), perceptual identification tasks (Jacoby, 1983a, 1983b; Whittlesea, 1983), and pronunciation tasks (Glushko, 1979) all seem to be quite sensitive to the congruity between particular training stimuli and particular test stimuli in ways which most abstraction models would not expect.

At the same time, a number of models have been proposed in which behavior which has often been characterized as *rule-based* or *concept-based* is attributed to a process that makes use of stored traces of specific events or specific exemplars of the concepts or rules. According to this class of models, the apparently rule-based or concept-based behavior emerges from what might be called a conspiracy of individual memory traces or from a sampling of one from the set of such traces. Models of this class include the Medin and Shaffer (1978) context model, Hintzman's (1983) multiple trace model, and Whittlesea's (1983) episode model. This trend is also exemplified by our interactive activation model of word perception (McClelland & Rumelhart, 1981; Rumelhart & McClelland, 1981, 1982), and an extension of the interactive activation model to generalization from exemplars (McClelland, 1981).

One feature of some of these exemplar-based models troubles us. Many of them are internally inconsistent with respect to the issue of abstraction. Thus, though our word perception model assumes that linguistic rules emerge from a conspiracy of partial activations of detectors for particular words, thereby eliminating the need for abstraction of rules, the assumption that there is a single detector for each word implicitly assumes that there is an abstraction process that lumps each occurrence of the same word into the same single detector unit. Thus, the model has its abstraction and creates it too, though at slightly different levels.

One logically coherent response to this inconsistency is to simply say that each word or other representational object is itself a conspiracy of the entire ensemble of memory traces of the different individual experiences we have had with that unit. We will call this view the *enumeration of specific experiences* view. It is exemplified most clearly by Jacoby (1983a, 1983b), Hintzman (1983), and Whittlesea (1983).

As the papers just mentioned demonstrate, enumeration of specific experiences can work quite well as an account of quite a number of empirical findings. However, there still seems to be one drawback. Such models seem to require an unlimited amount of storage capacity, as well as mechanisms for searching an almost unlimited mass of data. This is especially true when we consider that the primitives out of which we normally assume one experience is built are themselves abstractions. For example, a word is a sequence of letters, or a sentence is a sequence of words. Are we to believe that all of these abstractions are mere notational conveniences for the theorist, and that every event is stored as an extremely rich (obviously structured) representation of the event, with no abstraction?

In this article, we consider an alternative conceptualization: a distributed, superpositional approach to memory. This view is similar to the separate enumeration of experiences view in some respects, but not in all. On both views, memory consists of traces resulting from specific experiences; and on both views, generalizations emerge from the superposition of these specific memory traces. Our model differs, though, from the enumeration of specific experiences in assuming that the superposition of traces occurs at the time of storage. We do not keep each trace in a separate place, but rather we superimpose them so that what the memory contains is a composite.

Our theme will be to show that distributed models provide a way to resolve the abstraction–representation of specifics dilemma. With a distributed model, the superposition of traces automatically results in abstraction, though it can still preserve to some extent the idiosyncrasies of specific events and experiences, or of specific recurring subclasses of events and experiences.

We will begin by introducing a specific version of a distributed model of memory. We will show how it works and describe some of its basic properties. We will show how our model can account for several recent findings (Salasoo, Shiffrin, & Feustel, 1985; Whittlesea, 1983) on the effects of specific experiences on later performance, and the conditions under which functional equivalents of abstract representations such as prototypes or logogens emerge. . . .

Our distributed model is not a complete theory of human information processing and memory. It is a model of the internal structure of some components of information processing, in particular those concerned with the retrieval and use of prior experience. The model does not specify in and of itself how these acts of retrieval and use are planned, sequenced, and organized into coherent patterns of behavior.

A DISTRIBUTED MODEL OF MEMORY

General Properties

Our model adheres to the following general assumptions, some of which are shared with several other distributed models of processing and memory.

Simple, highly interconnected units. The processing system consists of a collection of simple processing units, each interconnected with many other units. The units take on activation values, and communicate with other units by sending signals modulated by weights associated with the connections between the units. Sometimes, we may think of the units as corresponding to particular representational primitives, but they need not. For example, even what we might consider to be a primitive feature of something, like having a particular color, might be a pattern of activation over a collection of units.

Modular structure. We assume that the units are organized into modules. Each module receives inputs from other modules, the units within the module are richly interconnected with each other, and they send outputs to other modules. Figure 1 illustrates the internal structure of a very simple module, and Figure 2 illustrates some hypothetical interconnections between a number of modules. Both figures grossly underrepresent our view of the numbers of units per module and the number of modules. We would imagine that there would be thousands to millions of units per module and many hundreds or perhaps

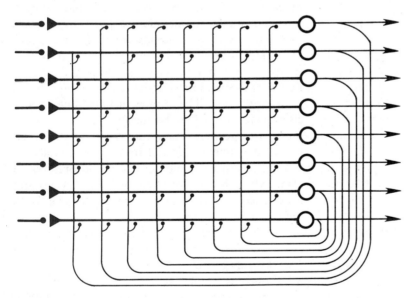

FIGURE 1   A simple information processing module, consisting of a small ensemble of eight processing units. [Each unit receives inputs from other modules (indicated by the single input impinging on the input line of the node from the left; this can stand for a number of converging input signals from several nodes outside the module) and sends outputs to other modules (indicated by the output line proceeding to the right from each unit). Each unit also has a modifiable connection to all the other units in the same module, as indicated by the branches of the output lines that loop back onto the input lines leading into each unit. All connections, which may be positive or negative, are represented by dots.]

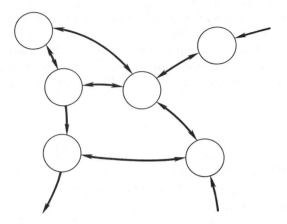

FIGURE 2 An illustrative diagram showing several modules and interconnections among them. (Arrows between modules simply indicate that some of the nodes in one module send inputs to some of the nodes in the other. The exact number and organization of modules is of course unknown; the figure is simply intended to be suggestive.)

many thousands of partially redundant modules in anything close to a complete memory system.

The state of each module represents a synthesis of the states of all of the modules it receives inputs from. Some of the inputs will be from relatively more sensory modules, closer to the sensory end-organs of one modality or another. Others will come from relatively more abstract modules, which themselves receive inputs from and send outputs to other modules placed at the abstract end of several different modalities. Thus, each module combines a number of different sources of information.

Mental state as pattern of activation. In a distributed memory system, a mental state is a pattern of activation over the units in some subset of the modules. The patterns in the different modules capture different aspects of the content of the mental states in a partially overlapping fashion. Alternative mental states are simply alternative patterns of activation over the modules. Information processing is the process of evolution in time of mental states. . . .

Memory traces as changes in the weights. Patterns of activation come and go, leaving traces behind when they have passed. What are the traces? They are changes in the strengths or *weights* of the connections between the units in the modules.

This view of the nature of the memory trace clearly sets these kinds of models apart from traditional models of memory in which some copy of the "active" pattern is generally thought of as being stored directly. Instead of this, what is actually stored in our model is changes in the connection strengths. These changes are derived from the presented pattern, and are arranged in such a way that, when a part of a known pattern is presented for processing, the interconnection strengths cause the rest of the pattern to be reinstated. Thus, although the memory trace is not a copy of the learned pattern, it is something from which a replica of that pattern can be recreated. As we already said, each memory trace is distributed over many different connections, and each connection participates in many different memory traces. The traces of different mental states are therefore superimposed in the same set of weights. Surprisingly enough, as we will see in several examples, the connections between the units in a single module can store the information needed to complete many different familiar patterns.

Retrieval as reinstatement of prior pattern of activation. Retrieval amounts to partial reinstatement of a mental state, using a cue which is a fragment of the original state. For any given module, we can see the cues as originating from outside of it. Some cues could arise ultimately from sensory input. Others would arise from the results of previous retrieval operations fed back to the memory system under the control of a search or retrieval plan. It would be premature to speculate on how such schemes would be implemented in this kind of a model, but it is clear that they must exist.

Detailed Assumptions

In the rest of our presentation, we will be focusing on operations that take place within a single module. This obviously oversimplifies the behavior of a complete memory system because the modules are assumed to be in continuous interaction. The simplification is justified, however, in that it allows us to focus on some of the basic properties of distributed memory that are visible even without these interactions with other modules.

Let us look, therefore, at the internal structure of one very simple module, as shown in Figure 1. Again, our image is that in a real system there would be much larger numbers of units. We have restricted our analysis to small numbers simply to illustrate basic principles as clearly as possible; this also helps to keep the running time of simulations in bounds.

Activation values.   The units take on activation values which range from −1 to +1. Zero represents in this case a neutral resting value, toward which the activations of the units tend to decay.

Inputs, outputs, and internal connections.   Each unit receives input from other modules and sends output to other modules. For the present, we assume that the inputs from other modules occur at connections whose weights are fixed. . . . In addition to extra-modular connections, each unit is connected to all other units in the module via a weighted connection. The weights on these connections are modifiable, as described later. The weights can take on any real values, positive, negative, or 0. There is no connection from a unit onto itself.

The processing cycle.   Processing within a module takes place as follows. Time is divided into discrete ticks. An input pattern is presented at some point in time over some or all of the input lines to the module and is then left on for several ticks, until the pattern of activation it produces settles down and stops changing.

Each tick is divided into two phases. In the first phase, each unit determines its net input, based on the external input to the unit and activations of all of the units at the end of the preceding tick modulated by the weight coefficients which determine the strength and direction of each unit's effect on every other.

For mathematical precision, consider two units in our module, and call one of them unit *i*, and the other unit *j*. The input to unit *i* from unit *j*, written i_{ij} is just

$$i_{ij} = a_j w_{ij},$$

where a_j is the activation of unit *j*, and w_{ij} is the weight constant modulating the effect of unit *j* on unit *i*. The total input to unit *i* from all other units internal to the module i_p is then just the sum of all of these separate inputs:

$$i_i = \sum_j i_{ij}.$$

Here, *j* ranges over all units in the module other than *i*. This sum is then added to the *external* input to the unit, arising from outside the module, to obtain the net input to unit *i*, n_i:

$$n_i = i_i + e_i,$$

where e_i is just the lumped external input to unit *i*.

In the second phase, the activations of the units are updated. If the net input is positive, the activation of the unit is incremented. . . . If the net input is negative, the activation is decremented. . . . There is also a decay factor which tends to pull the activation of the unit back toward the resting level of 0. . . .

Given a fixed set of inputs to a particular unit, its activation level will be driven up or down in response until the activation reaches the point where the incremental effects of the input are balanced by the decay. In practice, of course, the situation is complicated by the fact that as each units' activation is changing it alters the input to the others. Thus, it is necessary to run the simulation to see how the system will behave for any given set of inputs and any given set of weights. In all the simulations reported here, the model is allowed to run for 50 cycles, which is considerably more than enough for it to achieve a stable pattern of activation over all the units.

Memory traces.   The memory trace of a particular pattern of activation is a set of changes in the entire set of weights in the module. We call the whole set of changes an *increment* to the weights. After a stable pattern of activation is achieved, weight adjustment takes place. This is thought of as occurring simultaneously for all of the connections in the module.

The delta rule.   The rule that determines the size and direction (up or down) of the change at each connection is the crux of the model. The idea is often difficult to grasp on first reading, but once it is understood it seems very simple, and it directly captures the goal of facilitating the completion of the pattern, given some part of the pattern as a retrieval or completion cue.

To allow each part of a pattern to reconstruct the rest of the pattern, we simply want to set up the internal connections among the units in the module so that when part of the pattern is presented, activating some of the units in the module, the internal connections will lead the active units to tend to reproduce the rest. To do this, we want to make the internal input to each unit have the same effect on the unit that the external input has on the unit. That is, given a particular pattern to be stored, we want to find a set of connections such that the internal input to each unit from all of the other units matches the external input to that unit. The connection change procedure we will describe has the effect of moving the weights of all the connections in the direction of achieving this goal.

The first step in weight adjustment is to see how well the module is already doing. If the network is already matching the external input to each unit with the internal input from the other units, the weights do not need to be changed. To get an index of how well the network is already doing at matching its excitatory input, we assume that each unit i computes the difference Δ_i between its external input and the net internal input to the unit from the other units in the module:

$$\Delta_i = e_i - i_i.$$

In determining the activation value of the unit, we added the external input together with the internal input. Now, in adjusting the weights, we are taking the difference between these two terms. This implies that the unit must be able to aggregate all inputs for purposes of determining its activation, but it must be able to distinguish between external and internal inputs for purposes of adjusting its weights.

Let us consider the term Δ_i for a moment. If it is positive, the internal input is not activating the unit enough to match the external input to the unit. If negative, it is activating the unit too much. If zero, everything is fine and we do not want to change any-

thing. Thus, Δ_i determines the magnitude and direction of the overall change that needs to be made in the internal input to unit i. To achieve this overall effect, the individual weights are then adjusted according to the following formula:

$$\dot{w}_{ij} = S\Delta_i a_j.$$

The parameter S is just a global strength parameter which regulates the overall magnitude of the adjustments of the weights; $\dot{w}_{ij}$ is the change in the weight to i from j.

We call this weight modification rule the *delta rule*. It has all the intended consequences; that is, it tends to drive the weights in the direction of the right values to make the internal inputs to a unit match the external inputs. For example, consider the case in which Δ_i is positive and a_j is positive. In this case, the value of Δ_i tells us that unit i is not receiving enough excitatory input, and the value of a_j tells us that unit j has positive activation. In this case, the delta rule will increase the weight from j to i. The result will be that the next time unit j has a positive activation, its excitatory effect on unit i will be increased, thereby reducing Δ_i.

Similar reasoning applies to cases where Δ_i is negative, a_j is negative, or both are negative. Of course, when either Δ_i or a_j is 0, w_{ij} is not changed. In the first case, there is no error to compensate for; in the second case, a change in the weight will have no effect the next time unit j has the same activation value. . . .

Illustrative Examples

In this section, we describe a few illustrative examples to give the reader a feel for how we use the model, and to illustrate key aspects of its behavior.

Storage and retrieval of several patterns in a single memory module. First, we consider the storage and retrieval of two patterns in a single module of 8 units. Our basic aim is to show how several distinct patterns of activation can all be stored in the same set of weights, by what Lashley (1950) called a kind of algebraic summation, and not interfere with each other.

Before the first presentation of either pattern, we start out with all the weights set to 0. The first pattern

TABLE 1   Behavior of an 8-Unit Distributed Memory Module

Case	Input or Response for Each Unit							
Pattern 1								
The Pattern:	+	−	+	−	+	+	−	−
Response to Pattern before learning	+.5	−.5	+.5	−.5	+.5	+.5	−.5	−.5
Response to Pattern after 10 learning trials	+.7	−.7	+.7	−.7	+.7	+.7	−.7	−.7
Test Input (Incomplete version of Pattern)	+	−	+	−				
Response	+.6	−.6	+.6	−.6	+.4	+.4	−.4	−.4
Test Input (Distortion of Pattern)	+	−	+	−	+	+	−	+
Response	+.6	−.6	+.6	−.6	+.6	+.6	−.6	+.1
Pattern 2								
The Pattern:	+	+	−	−	−	+	−	+
Response to Pattern with weights learned for Pattern 1	+.5	+.5	−.5	−.5	−.5	+.5	−.5	+.5
Response to Pattern after 10 learning trials	+.7	+.7	−.7	−.7	−.7	+.7	−.7	+.7
Retest of response to Pattern 1	+.7	−.7	+.7	−.7	+.7	+.7	−.7	−.7

is given at the top of Table 1. It is an arrangement of +1 and −1 inputs to the eight units in the module. (In Table 1, the 1s are suppressed in the inputs for clarity.) When we present the first pattern to this module, the resulting activation values simply reflect the effects of the inputs themselves because none of the units are yet influencing any of the others.

Then, we teach the module this pattern by presenting it to the module 10 times. Each time, after the pattern of activation has had plenty of time to settle down, we adjust the weights. The next time we present the complete pattern after the 10 learning trials, the module's response is enhanced, compared with the earlier situation. That is, the activation values are increased in magnitude, owing to the combined effects of the external and internal inputs to each of the units. If we present an incomplete part of the pattern, the module can complete it; if we distort the pattern, the module tends to drive the activation back in the direction it thinks it ought to have. . . .

Figure 3 shows the weights our learning procedure has assigned. Actual numerical values have been suppressed to emphasize the basic pattern of excitatory and inhibitory influences. In this example, all the numerical values are identical. The pattern of + and − signs simply gives the pattern of pairwise correlations of the elements. This is as it should be to allow pattern enhancement, completion, and noise elimina-

tion. Units which have the same activation in the pattern have positive weights, so that when one is activated it will tend to activate the other, and when one is inhibited it will tend to inhibit the other. Units which have different activations in the pattern have negative weights, so that when one is activated it will inhibit the other and vice versa.

What happens when we present a new pattern, dissimilar to the first? This is illustrated in the lower portion of Table 1. At first, the network responds to it just as though it knew nothing at all: The activations simply reflect the direct effects of the input, as they would in a module with all 0 weights. The reason is simply that the effects of the weights already in the network cancel each other out. This is a result of the fact that the two patterns are maximally dissimilar from each other. If the patterns had been more similar, there would not have been this complete cancellation of effects.

Now we learn the new pattern, presenting it 10 times and adjusting the weights each time. The resulting weights (Figure 3) represent the sum of the weights for Patterns 1 and 2. The response to the new pattern is enhanced, as shown in Table 1. The response to the old, previously learned pattern is not affected. The module will now show enhancement, completion, and noise elimination for both patterns though these properties are not illustrated in Table 1.

```
     Pattern 1              Pattern 2
  + - + - + + - -        + + - - - + - +

  Weights for Pattern 1   Weights for Pattern 2    Composite Weights
                                                    for Both Patterns

  1 2 3 4 5 6 7 8         1 2 3 4 5 6 7 8          1 2 3 4 5 6 7 8
1    - + - + + - -          + - - + - +               --   ++--
2  - - + - + + +          + - - + - + +             --   --    ++
3  + -   - + + -          - -   + + - + -           --      ++
4  - + -   - + + +        - - + - + - +             --         --++
5  + - + -   + -          - - + +   - + -             --++        --
6  + - + - +   -          + + - - -   +             ++     --
7  - + - + -     +        - + - + + -   -           --     ++   --
8  - + - + - +            + + - - + -               ++-- --
```

FIGURE 3   Weights acquired in learning Pattern 1 and Pattern 2 separately, and the composite weights resulting from learning both. (The weight in a given cell reflects the strength of the connection from the corresponding column unit to the corresponding row unit. Only the sign and relative magnitude of the weights are indicated. A blank indicates a weight of 0; + and − signify positive and negative, with a double symbol, ++ or − −, representing a value twice as large as a single symbol, + or −.)

Thus, we see that more than one pattern can co-exist in the same set of weights. There is an effect of storing multiple patterns, of course. When only one pattern is stored, the whole pattern (or at least, a pale copy of it) can be retrieved by driving the activation of any single unit in the appropriate direction. As more patterns are stored, larger subpatterns are generally needed to specify the pattern to be retrieved uniquely.

Learning a Prototype from Exemplars

In the preceding section, we considered the learning of particular patterns and showed that the delta rule was capable of learning multiple patterns, in the same set of connections. In this section, we consider what happens when distributed models using the delta rule are presented with an ensemble of patterns that have some common structure. The examples described in this section illustrate how the delta rule can be used to extract the structure from an ensemble of inputs, and throw away random variability.

Let us consider the following hypothetical situation. A little boy sees many different dogs, each only once, and each with a different name. All the dogs are a little different from each other, but in general there is a pattern which represents the typical dog: each one is just a different distortion of this prototype. (We are not claiming that the dogs in the world have no more structure than this; we make this assumption for purposes of illustration only.) For now we will assume that the names of the dogs are all completely different. Given this experience, we would expect that the boy would learn the prototype of the category, even without ever seeing any particular dog which matches the prototype directly (Posner & Keele, 1968, 1970; Anderson, 1977, applies an earlier version of a distributed model to this case). That is, the prototype will seem as familiar as any of the exemplars, and he will be able to complete the pattern corresponding to the prototype from any part of it. He will not, however, be very likely to remember the names of each of the individual dogs though he may remember the most recent ones.

We model this situation with a module consisting of 24 units. We assume that the presentation of a dog produces a visual pattern of activation over 16 of the units in the hypothetical module (the 9th through 24th, counting from left to right). The name of the dog produces a pattern of activation over the other 8 units (Units 1 to 8, counting from left to right).

Each visual pattern, by assumption, is a distortion of a single prototype. The prototype used for the simulation simply had a random series of +1 and −1 values. Each distortion of the prototype was made by probabilistically flipping the sign of randomly selected elements of the prototype pattern. For each new distorted pattern, each element has an independent chance of being flipped, with a probability of .2. Each name pattern was simply a random sequence of +1s and −1s for the eight name units. Each encounter with a new dog is modeled as a presentation of a new name pattern with a new distortion of the prototype visual pattern. Fifty different trials were run, each with a new name pattern–visual pattern pair.

For each presentation, the pattern of activation is allowed to stabilize, and then the weights are adjusted as before. The increment to the weights is then allowed to decay considerably before the next input is presented. For simplicity, we assume that before the next pattern is presented, the last increment decays to a fixed small proportion of its initial value, and thereafter undergoes no further decay.

What does the module learn? The module acquires a set of weights which is continually buffeted about by the latest dog exemplar, but which captures

Prototype pattern:

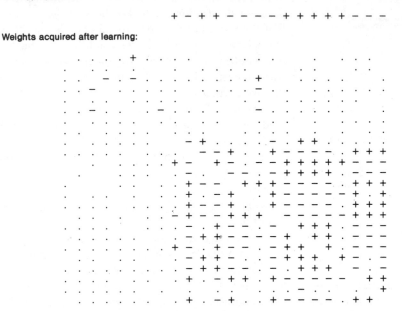

Weights acquired after learning:

FIGURE 4   Weights acquired in learning from distorted exemplars of a prototype. (The prototype pattern is shown above the weight matrix. Blank entries correspond to weights with absolute values less than .01; dots correspond to absolute values less than .06; pluses or minuses are used for weights with larger absolute values.)

the prototype dog quite well. Waiting for the last increment to decay to the fixed residual yields the weights shown in Figure 4.

These weights capture the correlations among the values in the prototype dog pattern quite well. The lack of exact uniformity is due to the more recent distortions presented, whose effects have not been corrected by subsequent distortions. This is one way in which the model gives priority to specific exemplars, especially recent ones. The effects of recent exemplars are particularly strong, of course, before they have had a chance to decay. The module can complete the prototype quite well, and it will respond more strongly to the prototype than to any distortion of it. It has, however, learned no particular relation between this prototype and any name pattern, because a totally different random association was presented on each trial. If the pattern of activation on the name units had been the same in every case (say, each dog was just called *dog),* or even in just a reasonable

fraction of the cases, then the module would have been able to retrieve this shared name pattern from the prototype of the visual pattern and the prototype pattern from the name.

Multiple, nonorthogonal prototypes.   In the preceding simulation we have seen how the distributed model acts as a sort of signal averager, finding the central tendency of a set of related patterns. In and of itself this is an important property of the model, but the importance of this property increases when we realize that the model can average several different patterns in the same composite memory trace. Thus, several different prototypes can be stored in the same set of weights. This is important, because it means that the model does not fall into the trap of needing to decide which category to put a pattern in before knowing which prototype to average it with. The acquisition of the different prototypes proceeds without any sort of explicit categorization. If the patterns are sufficiently dissimilar, there is no interference among them at all. Increasing similarity leads to increased confusability during learning, but eventually the delta rule finds a set of connection strengths that minimizes the confusability of similar patterns.

To illustrate these points, we created a simulation analog of the following hypothetical situation. Let us say that our little boy sees, in the course of his daily experience, different dogs, different cats, and different bagels. First, let's consider the case in which each experience with a dog, a cat, or a bagel is accompanied by someone saying *dog, cat,* or *bagel,* as appropriate.

The simulation analog of this situation involved forming three *visual* prototype patterns of 16 elements, two of them (the one for dog and the one for cat) somewhat similar to each other (r = .5), and the third (for the bagel) orthogonal to both of the other two. Paired with each visual pattern was a name pattern of eight elements. Each name pattern was orthogonal to both of the others. Thus, the prototype visual pattern for cat and the prototype visual pattern for dog were similar to each other, but their names were not related.

Stimulus presentations involved presentations of distorted exemplars of the name–visual pattern pairs to a module of 24 elements like the one used in the previous simulation. This time, both the name pattern and the visual pattern were distorted, with each element having its sign flipped with an independent probability of .1 on each presentation. Fifty different distortions of each name–visual pattern pair were presented in groups of three consisting of one distortion of the dog pair, one distortion of the cat pair, and one distortion of the bagel pair. Weight adjustment occurred after each presentation, with decay to a fixed residual before each new presentation.

At the end of training, the module was tested by presenting each name pattern and observing the resulting pattern of activation over the visual nodes, and by presenting each visual pattern and observing the pattern of activation over the name nodes. The results are shown in Table 2. In each case, the model reproduces the correct completion for the probe, and there is no apparent contamination of the cat pattern by the dog pattern, even though the visual patterns are similar to each other. . . .

Thus far we have seen that several prototypes, not necessarily orthogonal, can be stored in the same module without difficulty. It is true, though we do not illustrate it, that the model has more trouble with the cat and dog visual patterns earlier on in training, before learning has essentially reached asymptotic levels as it has by the end of 50 cycles through the full set of patterns. And, of course, even at the end of learning, if we present as a probe a part of the visual pattern, if it does not differentiate between the dog and the cat, the model will produce a blended response. Both these aspects of the model seem generally consistent with what we should expect from human subjects.

Category learning without labels.   An important further fact about the model is that it can learn several different visual patterns, even without the benefit of distinct identifying name patterns during learning. To demonstrate this we repeated the previous simulation, simply replacing the name patterns with 0s. The model still learns about the internal structure of the visual patterns, so that, after 50 cycles through the stimuli, any unique subpart of any one of the patterns is sufficient to reinstate to the rest of the corresponding pattern correctly. This aspect of the model's behavior is illustrated in Table 3. Thus, we have a model that can, in effect, acquire a number of distinct categories, simply through a process of incrementing connection strengths in response to each new stimulus presentation. Noise, in the form of distortions in the patterns, is filtered out. The model does not require a name or other guide to distinguish the patterns belonging to different categories.

Coexistence of the prototype and repeated exemplars. One aspect of our discussion up to this point may have been slightly misleading. We may have given the impression that the model is simply a prototype extraction device. It is more than this, however; it is a device that captures whatever structure is present in a set of patterns. When the set of patterns has a prototype structure, the model will act as though it is extracting prototypes; but when it has a different structure, the model will do its best to accommodate this as well. For example, the model permits the coexistence of

TABLE 2 Results of Tests after Learning the Dog, Cat, and Bagel Patterns

| | Input or Response for Each Unit | | | | | | | | | | | | | | | | | | | | | | |
| | Name Units | | | | | | | | Visual Pattern Units | | | | | | | | | | | | | | |
Case																							
Pattern for dog prototype	+	−	+	−	+				+	−	+	+	−	−	−	−	−	+	+	+	+	+	−
Response to dog name	+	+	−	+	−				+3	−4	+4	−4	−4	−4	−4	−4	+4	+4	+4	+3	+4	−4	−3
Response to dog visual pattern	+5	−4	+4	−5	+5	−4	−4		+	−	+	+	−	−	−	−	−	+	+	+	+	+	−
Pattern for cat prototype	+	+	−	−	+				+	−	+	−	−	−	−	−	−	+	+	+	+	+	+
Response to cat name	+	+	−	−	+				+4	−3	+4	−4	−4	−3	−3	−4	+4	+4	+4	+4	+4	−4	+4
Response to cat visual pattern	+5	+4	−4	−5	+4	+4	−4	−4	+	−	+	−	−	−	−	−	−	+	+	+	+	+	+
Pattern for bagel prototype	+	−	−	+	+				+	−	−	+	−	−	+	+	+	−	+	+	+	+	−
Response to bagel name	+	−	−	+	+				+3	+4	−4	+4	−4	−4	−4	−4	+4	+4	+4	+3	+4	+4	−4
Response to bagel visual pattern	+4	−4	−4	+4	+4	−4	−4	+4	+	−	−	+	−	−	+	+	+	−	+	+	+	+	−

Note. Decimal points have been suppressed for clarity; thus, an entry of +.4 represents an activation value of +.4.

TABLE 3   Results of Tests after Learning the Dog, Cat, and Bagel Patterns without Names

Case	Input or Response for Each Visual Unit															
Dog visual pattern	+	−	+	+	−	−	−	−	+	+	+	+	+	−	−	−
Probe									+	+	+	+				
Response	+3	−3	+3	+3	−3	−4	−3	−3	+6	+5	+6	+5	+3	−2	−3	−2
Cat visual pattern	+	−	+	+	−	−	−	−	+	−	+	−	+	+	−	+
Probe									+	−	+	−				
Response	+3	−3	+3	+3	−3	−3	−3	−3	+6	−5	+6	−5	+3	+2	−3	+2
Bagel visual pattern	+	+	−	+	−	+	+	−	+	−	−	+	+	+	+	−
Probe									+	−	−	+				
Response	+2	+3	−4	+3	−3	+3	+3	−3	+6	−6	−6	+6	+3	+3	+3	−3

representations of prototypes with representations of particular, repeated exemplars.

Consider the following situation. Let us say that our little boy knows a dog next door named Rover and a dog at his grandma's house named Fido. And let's say that the little boy goes to the park from time to time and sees dogs, each of which his father tells him is a dog.

The simulation-analog of this involved three different eight-element name patterns, one for Rover, one for Fido, and one for Dog. The visual pattern for Rover was a particular randomly generated distortion of the dog prototype pattern, as was the visual pattern for Fido. For the dogs seen in the park, each one was simply a new random distortion of the prototype. The probability of flipping the sign of each element was again .2. The learning regime was otherwise the same as in the dog–cat–bagel example.

At the end of 50 learning cycles, the model was able to retrieve the visual pattern corresponding to either repeated exemplar (see Table 4) given the associated name as input. When given the Dog name pattern as input, it retrieves the prototype visual pattern for dog. It can also retrieve the appropriate name from each of the three visual patterns. This is true, even though the visual pattern for Rover differs from the visual pattern for dog by only a single element. Because of the special importance of this particular element, the weights from this element to the units that distinguish Rover's name pattern from the prototype name pattern are quite strong. Given part of a visual pattern, the model will complete it; if the part corresponds to the prototype, then that is what is completed, but if it corresponds to one of the repeated exemplars, that exemplar is completed. The model, then, knows both the prototype and the repeated exemplars quite well. Several other sets of prototypes and their repeated exemplars could also be stored in the same module, as long as its capacity is not exceeded; given large numbers of units per module, a lot of different patterns can be stored.

Let us summarize the observations we have made in these several illustrative simulations. First, our distributed model is capable of storing not just one but a number of different patterns. It can pull the central tendency of a number of different patterns out of the noisy inputs; it can create the functional equivalent of perceptual categories with or without the benefit of labels; and it can allow representations of repeated exemplars to coexist with the representation of the prototype of the categories they exemplify in the same composite memory trace. The model is not simply a categorizer or a prototyping device; rather, it captures the structure inherent in a set of patterns, whether it be characterizable by description in terms of prototypes or not.

The ability to retrieve accurate completions of similar patterns is a property of the model which depends on the use of the delta learning rule. This allows both the storage of different prototypes that are not completely orthogonal and the coexistence of prototype representations and repeated exemplars.

TABLE 4 Results of Tests with Prototype and Specific Exemplar Patterns

	Input or Response for Each Unit																	
	Name Units						Visual Pattern Units											
Case																		
Pattern for dog prototype	+	−	+	+	−	+	+	−	+	+	−	−	+	+	+	+	−	−
Response to prototype name							+4	−5	+3	+3	−3	−3	+3	+4	+3	+4	−3	−4
Response to prototype visual pattern	+5	−4	+4	+5	−4	−4												
Pattern for "Fido" exemplar	+	−	−	+		+	+	−	(−)	+	−	−	+	+	+	+	−	−
Response to Fido name							+4	−4	−4	+4	−4	−4	+4	+4	+4	+4	−4	−4
Response to Fido visual pattern	+5	−3	−5	+4	−5	−3	−5											
Pattern for "Rover" exemplar	+	(+)	+	+	−	+	−	−	+	+	+	+	+	+	+	+	−	−
Response to Rover name							+4	+5	+4	+4	−4	−4	+4	+4	+4	+4	−4	−4
Response to Rover visual pattern	+4	−4	−2	+4	+4	−2	+4											

SIMULATIONS OF EXPERIMENTAL RESULTS

Up to this point, we have discussed our distributed model in general terms and have outlined how it can accommodate both abstraction and representation of specific information in the same network. We will now consider, in the next two sections, how well the model does in accounting for some recent evidence about the details of the influence of specific experiences on performance.

Repetition and Familiarity Effects

When we perceive an item—say a word, for example—this experience has effects on our later performance. If the word is presented again, within a reasonable interval of time, the prior presentation makes it possible for us to recognize the word more quickly, or from a briefer presentation.

Traditionally, this effect has been interpreted in terms of units that represent the presented items in memory. In the case of word perception, these units are called *word detectors* or *logogens,* and a model of repetition effects for words has been constructed around the logogen concept (Morton, 1979). The idea is that the threshold for the logogen is reduced every time it *fires* (that is, every time the word is recognized), thereby making it easier to fire the logogen at a later time. There is supposed to be a decay of this priming effect, with time, so that eventually the effect of the first presentation wears off.

This traditional interpretation has come under serious question of late, for a number of reasons. Perhaps paramount among the reasons is the fact that the exact relation between the specific context in which the priming event occurs and the context in which the test event occurs makes a huge difference (Jacoby, 1983a, 1983b). Generally speaking, nearly any change in the stimulus—from spoken to printed, from male speaker to female speaker, and so forth—tends to reduce the magnitude of the priming effect.

These facts might easily be taken to support the enumeration of specific experiences view, in which the logogen is replaced by the entire ensemble of experiences with the word, with each experience capturing aspects of the specific context in which it oc-

curred. Such a view has been championed most strongly by Jacoby (1983a, 1983b).

Our distributed model offers an alternative interpretation. We see the traces laid down by the processing of each input as contributing to the composite, superimposed memory representation. Each time a stimulus is processed, it gives rise to a slightly different memory trace: either because the item itself is different or because it occurs in a different context that conditions its representation. The logogen is replaced by the set of specific traces, but the traces are not kept separate. Each trace contributes to the composite, but the characteristics of particular experiences tend nevertheless to be preserved, at least until they are overridden by canceling characteristics of other traces. And the traces of one stimulus pattern can coexist with the traces of other stimuli, within the same composite memory trace.

It should be noted that we are not faulting either the logogen model or models based on the enumeration of specific experiences for their physiological implausibility here, because these models are generally not stated in physiological terms, and their authors might reasonably argue that nothing in their models precludes distributed storage at a physiological level. What we are suggesting is that a model which proposes explicitly distributed, superpositional storage can account for the kinds of findings that logogen models have been proposed to account for, as well as other findings which strain the utility of the concept of the logogen as a psychological construct. In the discussion section we will consider ways in which our distributed model differs from enumeration models as well.

To illustrate the distributed model's account of repetition priming effects, we carried out the following simulation experiment. We made up a set of eight random vectors, each 24 elements long, each one to be thought of as the prototype of a different recurring stimulus pattern. Through a series of 10 training cycles using the set of eight vectors, we constructed a composite memory trace. During training, the model did not actually see the prototypes, however. On each training presentation it saw a new random distortion of one of the eight prototypes. In each of the distortions, each of the 24 elements had its value flipped with a probability of .1. Weights were adjusted after every presentation, and then allowed to decay to a fixed residual before the presentation of the next pattern.

The composite memory trace formed as a result of the experience just described plays the same role in our model that the set of logogens or detectors play in a model like Morton's or, indeed, the interactive activation model of word perception. That is, the trace contains information which allows the model to enhance perception of familiar patterns, relative to unfamiliar ones. We demonstrate this by comparing the activations resulting from the processing of subsequent presentations of new distortions of our eight familiar patterns with other random patterns with which the model is not familiar. The pattern of activation that is the model's response to the input is stronger, and grows to a particular level more quickly, if the stimulus is a new distortion of an old pattern than if it is a new pattern. We already observed this general enhanced response to exact repetitions of familiar patterns in our first example (see Table 1). Figure 5 illustrates that the effect also applies to new distortions of old patterns, as compared with new patterns, and illustrates how the activation process proceeds over successive time cycles of processing. . . .

But what about priming and the role of congruity between the prime event and the test event? To examine this issue, we carried out a second experiment. Following learning of eight patterns as in the previous experiment, new distortions of half of the random vectors previously learned by the model were presented as primes. For each of these primes, the pattern of activation was allowed to stabilize, and changes in the strengths of the connections in the model were then made. We then tested the model's response to (a) the same four distortions; (b) four new distortions of the same patterns; and (c) distortions of the four previously learned patterns that had not been presented as primes. There was no decay in the weights over the course of the priming experi-

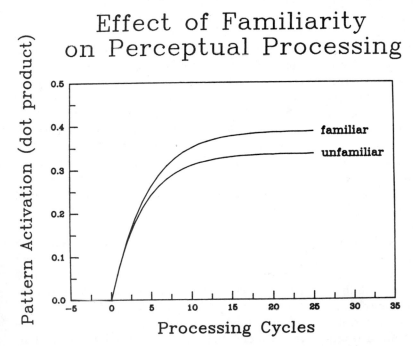

FIGURE 5   Growth of the pattern of activation for new distortions of familiar and unfamiliar patterns. (The measure of the strength of the pattern of activation is the dot product of the response pattern with the input vector. See text for an explanation.)

ment; if decay had been included, its main effect would have been to reduce the magnitude of the priming effects.

The results of the experiment are shown in Figure 6. The response of the model is greatest for the patterns preceded by identical primes, intermediate for patterns preceded by similar primes, and weakest for patterns not preceded by any related prime.

Our model, then, appears to provide an account, not only for the basic existence of priming effects, but also for the graded nature of priming effects as a function of congruity between prime event and test event. It avoids the problem of multiplication of context-specific detectors which logogen theories fall prey to, while at the same time avoiding enumeration of specific experiences. Congruity effects are captured in the composite memory trace.

The model also has another advantage over the logogen view. It accounts for repetition priming effects for unfamiliar as well as familiar stimuli. When

a pattern is presented for the first time, a trace is produced just as it would be for stimuli that had previously been presented. The result is that, on a second presentation of the same pattern, or a new distortion of it, processing is facilitated. The functional equivalent of a logogen begins to be established from the very first presentation.

To illustrate the repetition priming of unfamiliar patterns and to compare the results with the repetition priming we have already observed for familiar patterns, we carried out a third experiment. This time, after learning eight patterns as before, a priming session was run in which new distortions of four of the familiar patterns and distortions of four new patterns were presented. Then, in the test phase, 16 stimuli were presented: New distortions of the primed, familiar patterns; new distortions of the unprimed, familiar patterns; new distortions of the primed, previously unfamiliar patterns; and finally, new distortions of four patterns that were neither

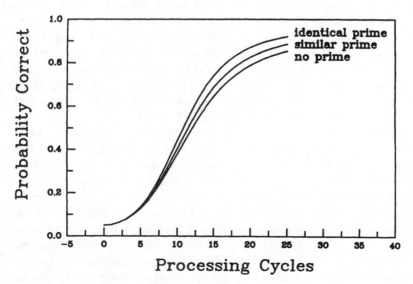

FIGURE 6 Response probability as a function of exposure time for patterns preceded by identical primes, similar primes, or no related prime.

Priming of Familiar
and Unfamiliar Patterns

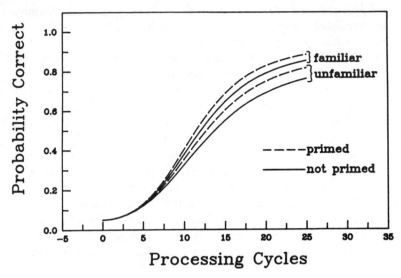

FIGURE 7   Response to new distortions of primed, familiar patterns, unprimed, familiar patterns, primed, unfamiliar patterns, and unprimed, unfamiliar patterns.

primed nor familiar. The results are shown in Figure 7. What we find is that long-term familiarity and recent priming have approximately additive effects on the asymptotes of the time-accuracy curves. The time to reach any given activation level shows a mild interaction, with priming having slightly more of an effect for unfamiliar than for familiar stimuli.

These results are consistent with the bulk of the findings concerning the effects of preexperimental familiarity and repetition in the recent series of experiments by Feustel, Shiffrin, and Salasoo (1983) and Salasoo et al. (1985). They found that preexperimental familiarity of an item (word vs. nonword) and prior exposure had this very kind of interactive effect on exposure time required for accurate identification of all the letters of a string, at least when words and nonwords were mixed together in the same lists of materials.

A further aspect of the results reported by Salasoo, Shiffrin, and Feustel is also consistent with our approach. In one of their experiments, they examined threshold for accurate identification as a function of number of prior presentations, for both words and pseudowords. Although thresholds were initially elevated for pseudowords, relative to words, there was a rather rapid convergence of the thresholds over repeated presentations, with the point of convergence coming at about the same place on the curve for two different versions of their perceptual identification task. (Salasoo et al., 1985, Figure 7.) Our model, likewise, shows this kind of convergence effect, as illustrated in Figure 8.

The Feustel et al. (1983) and Salasoo et al. (1985) experiments provide very rich and detailed data that go beyond the points we have extracted from them here. We do not claim to have provided a detailed account of all aspects of their data. However, we simply wish to note that the general form of their basic findings is consistent with a model of the distributed type. In particular, we see no reason to assume that the process by which unfamiliar patterns become familiar involves the formation of an abstract, logogenlike unit separate from the episodic traces responsible for repetition priming effects. . . .

Repetition Effects for Familiar & Unfamiliar Patterns

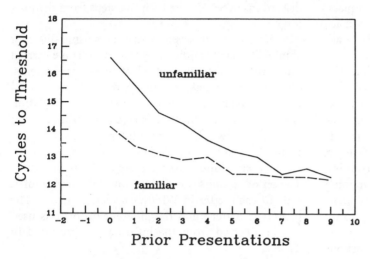

FIGURE 8   Time to reach a fixed-accuracy criterion (60% correct) for previously familiar and unfamiliar patterns, as a function of repetitions.

Representation of General and Specific Information

In the previous section, we cast our distributed model as an alternative to the view that familiar patterns are represented in memory either by separate detectors or by an enumeration of specific experiences. In this section, we show that the model provides alternatives to both abstraction and enumeration models of learning from exemplars of prototypes.

Abstraction models were originally motivated by the finding that subjects occasionally appeared to have learned better how to categorize the prototype of a set of distorted exemplars than the specific exemplars they experienced during learning (Posner & Keele, 1968). However, pure abstraction models have never fared very well, because there is nearly always evidence of some superiority of the particular training stimuli over other stimuli equally far removed from the prototype. A favored model, then, is one in which there is both abstraction and memory for particular training stimuli.

Recently, proponents of models involving only enumeration of specific experiences have noted that such models can account for the basic fact that abstraction models are primarily designed to account for—enhanced response to the prototype, relative to particular previously seen exemplars, under some conditions—as well as failures to obtain such effects under other conditions (Hintzman, 1983; Medin & Shaffer, 1978). In evaluating distributed models, it is important to see if they can do as well. Anderson (1977) has made important steps in this direction, and Knapp and Anderson (1984) have shown how their distributed model can account for many of the details of the Posner–Keele experiments. Recently, however, two sets of findings have been put forward which appear to strongly favor the enumeration of specific experiences view, at least relative to pure abstraction models. It is important, therefore, to see how well our distributed model can do in accounting for these kinds of effects.

The first set of findings comes from a set of studies by Whittlesea (1983). In a large number of studies,

Whittlesea demonstrated a role for specific exemplars in guiding performance on a perceptual identification task. We wanted to see whether our model would demonstrate a similar sensitivity to specific exemplars. We also wanted to see whether our model would account for the conditions under which such effects are not obtained.

Whittlesea used letter strings as stimuli. The learning experiences subjects received involved simply looking at the stimuli one at a time on a visual display and writing down the sequence of letters presented. Subjects were subsequently tested for the effect of this training on their ability to identify letter strings bearing various relations to the training stimuli and to the prototypes from which the training stimuli were derived. The test was a perceptual identification task; the subject was simply required to try to identify the letters from a brief flash.

The stimuli Whittlesea used were all distortions of one of two prototype letter strings. Table 5 illustrates the essential properties of the sets of training and test stimuli he used. The stimuli in Set Ia were each one step away from the prototype. The Ib items were also one step from the prototype and one step from one of the Ia distortions. The Set IIa stimuli were each two steps from the prototype, and one step from a particular Ia distortion. The Set IIb items were also two steps from the prototype, and each was one step from one of the IIa distortions. The Set IIc distortions were two steps from the prototype also, and each was two steps from the closest IIa distortion. Over the set of five IIc distortions, the A and B subpatterns each occurred once in each position, as

they did in the case of the IIa distortions. The distortions in Set III were three steps from the prototype, and one step from the closest member of Set IIa. The distortions in Set V were each five steps from the prototype.

Whittlesea ran seven experiments using different combinations of training and test stimuli. We carried out simulation analogs of all of these experiments, plus one additional experiment that Whittlesea did not run. The main difference between the simulation experiments and Whittlesea's actual experiments was that he used two different prototypes in each experiment, whereas we only used one.

The simulation used a simple 20-unit module. The set of 20 units was divided into five submodules, one for each letter in Whittlesea's letter strings. The prototype pattern and the different distortions used can be derived from the information provided in Table 5.

Each simulation experiment began with null connections between the units. The training phase involved presenting the set or sets of training stimuli analogous to those Whittlesea used, for the same number of presentations. To avoid idiosyncratic effects of particular orders of training stimuli, each experiment was run six times, each with a different random order of training stimuli. On each trial, activations were allowed to settle down through 50 processing cycles, and then connection strengths were adjusted. There was no decay of the increments to the weights over the course of an experiment.

In the test phase, the model was tested with the sets of test items analogous to the sets Whittlesea

TABLE 5   Schematic Description of Stimulus Sets Used in Simulations of Whittlesea's Experiments

	Stimulus Set						
Prototype	Ia	Ib	IIa	IIb	IIc	III	V
PPPPP	APPPP	BPPPP	ABPPP	ACPPP	APCPP	ABCPP	CCCCC
	PAPPP	PBPPP	PABPP	PACPP	PAPCP	PABCP	CBCBC
	PPAPP	PPBPP	PPABP	PPACP	PPAPC	PPABC	BCACB
	PPPAP	PPPBP	PPPAB	PPPAC	CPPAP	CPPAB	ABCBA
	PPPPA	PPPPB	BPPPA	CPPPA	PCPPA	BCPPA	CACAC

Note. The actual stimuli used can be filled in by replacing P with + − + −; A with + + − −; B with + − − +; and C with + + + +. The model is not sensitive to the fact the same subpattern was used in each of the five slots.

used. As a precaution against effects of prior test items on performance, we simply turned off the adjustment of weights during the test phase.

A summary of the training and test stimuli used in each of the experiments, of Whittlesea's findings, and of the simulation results are shown in Table 6. The numbers represent relative amounts of enhancement in performance as a result of the training experience, relative to a pretest baseline. For Whittlesea's data, this is the per letter increase in letter identification probability between a pre- and posttest. For the simulation, it is the increase in the size of the dot product for a pretest with null weights and a posttest after training. For comparability to the data, the dot product difference scores have been doubled. This is simply a scaling operation to facilitate qualitative comparison of experimental and simulation results.

A comparison of the experimental and simulation results shows that wherever there is a within-experiment difference in Whittlesea's data, the simulation produced a difference in the same direction. (Between experiment comparisons are not considered because of subject and material differences which renders such differences unreliable.) The next several paragraphs review some of the major findings in detail.

Some of the comparisons bring out the importance of congruity between particular test and training experiences. Experiments 1, 2, and 3 show that when distance of test stimuli from the prototype is controlled, similarity to particular training exemplars makes a difference both for the human subject and in the model. In Experiment 1, the relevant contrast was between Ia and Ib items. In Experiment 2, it was between IIa and IIc items. Experiment 3 shows that the subjects and the model both show a gradient in performance with increasing distance of the test items from the nearest old exemplar.

Experiments 4, 4', and 5 examine the status of the prototype and other test stimuli closer to the prototype than any stimuli actually shown during training. In Experiment 4, the training stimuli were fairly far away from the prototype, and there were only five different training stimuli (the members of the IIa set). In this case, controlling for distance from the nearest training stimuli, test stimuli closer to the prototype showed more enhancement than those farther away (Ia versus III comparison). However, the actual train-

TABLE 6   Summary of Perceptual Identification Experiments with Experimental and Simulation Results

Whittlesea's Experiment	Training Stimulus Set(s)	Test Stimulus Sets	Experimental Results	Simulation Results
1	Ia	Ia	.27	.24
		Ib	.16	.15
		V	.03	−.05
2	IIa	IIa	.30	.29
		IIc	.15	.12
		V	.03	−.08
3	IIa	IIa	.21	.29
		IIb	.16	.14
		IIc	.10	.12
4	IIa	P	—	.24
		Ia	.19	.21
		IIa	.23	.29
		III	.15	.15
4'	Ia	P	—	.28
		Ia	—	.24
		IIa	—	.12
5	IIa, b, c	P	—	.25
		Ia	.16	.21
		IIa	.16	.18
		III	.10	.09
6	III	Ia	.16	.14
		IIa	.16	.19
		III	.19	.30
7	IIa	IIa	.24	.29
		IIc	.13	.12
		III	.17	.15

ing stimuli nevertheless had an advantage over both other sets of test stimuli, including those that were closer to the prototype than the training stimuli themselves (IIa versus Ia comparison).

In Experiment 4' (not run by Whittlesea) the same number of training stimuli were used as in Experiment 4, but these were closer to the prototype. The result is that the simulation shows an advantage for the prototype over the old exemplars. The specific training stimuli used even in this experiment do influence performance, however, as Whittlesea's first experiment (which used the same training set) shows (Ia–Ib contrast). This effect holds both for the subjects and for the simulation. The pattern of results is similar to the findings of Posner and Keele (1968), in the condition where subjects learned six exemplars which were rather close to the prototype. In this condition, their subjects' categorization performance was most accurate for the prototype, but more accurate for old than for new distortions, just as in this simulation experiment.

In Experiment 5, Whittlesea demonstrated that a slight advantage for stimuli closer to the prototype than the training stimuli would emerge, even with high-level distortions, when a large number of different distortions were used once each in training, instead of a smaller number of distortions presented three times each. The effect was rather small in Whittlesea's case (falling in the third decimal place in the per letter enhancement effect measure) but other experiments have produced similar results, and so does the simulation. In fact, because the prototype was tested in the simulation, we were able to demonstrate a monotonic drop in performance with distance from the prototype in this experiment.

Experiments 6 and 7 examine in different ways the relative influence of similarity to the prototype and similarity to the set of training exemplars, using small numbers of training exemplars rather far from the prototype. Both in the data and in the model, similarity to particular training stimuli is more important than similarity to the prototype, given the sets of training stimuli used in these experiments.

Taken together with other findings, Whittlesea's results show clearly that similarity of test items to particular stored exemplars is of paramount importance in predicting perceptual performance. Other experiments show the relevance of these same factors in other tasks, such as recognition memory, classification learning, and so forth. It is interesting to note that performance does not honor the specific exemplars so strongly when the training items are closer to the prototype. Under such conditions, performance is superior on the prototype or stimuli closer to the prototype than the training stimuli. Even when the training stimuli are rather distant from the prototype, they produce a benefit for stimuli closer to the prototype, if there are a large number of distinct training stimuli each shown only once. Thus, the dominance of specific training experiences is honored only when the training experiences are few and far between. Otherwise, an apparent advantage for the prototype,

though with some residual benefit for particular training stimuli, is the result.

The congruity of the results of these simulations with experimental findings underscores the applicability of distributed models to the question of the nature of the representation of general and specific information. In fact, we were somewhat surprised by the ability of the model to account for Whittlesea's results, given the fact that we did not rely on context-sensitive encoding of the letter string stimuli. That is, the distributed representation we assigned to each letter was independent of the other letters in the string. However, a context sensitive encoding would prove necessary to capture a larger ensemble of stimuli.

Whether a context-sensitive encoding would produce the same or slightly different results depends on the exact encoding. The exact degree of overlap of the patterns of activation produced by different distortions of the same prototype determines the extent to which the model will tend to favor the prototype relative to particular old exemplars. The degree of overlap, in turn, depends on the specific assumptions made about the encoding of the stimuli. However, the general form of the results of the simulation would be unchanged: When all the distortions are close to the prototype, or when there is a very large number of different distortions, the central tendency will produce the strongest response; but when the distortions are fewer, and farther from the prototype, the training exemplars themselves will produce the strongest activations. What the encoding would effect is the similarity metric. . . .

DISCUSSION

Until very recently, the exploration of distributed models was restricted to a few workers, mostly coming from fields other than cognitive psychology. Although in some cases, particularly in the work of Anderson (1977; Anderson et al., 1977; Knapp & Anderson, 1984), some implications of these models for our understanding of memory and learning have been pointed out, they have only begun to be applied by researchers primarily concerned with understanding cognitive processes per se. The present article, along with those of Murdock (1982) and Eich (1982), represents what we hope will be the beginning of a more serious examination of these kinds of models by cognitive psychologists. For they provide, we believe, important alternatives to traditional conceptions of representation and memory.

We have tried to illustrate this point here by showing how the distributed approach circumvents the dilemma of specific trace models. Distributed memories abstract even while they preserve the details of recent, or frequently repeated, experiences. Abstraction and preservation of information about specific stimuli are simply different reflections of the operation of the same basic learning mechanism.

The basic points we have been making can of course be generalized in several different directions. Here we will mention two: The relation between episodic and semantic memory (Tulving, 1972) and the representations underlying the use of language.

With regard to episodic and semantic memory, our distributed model leads naturally to the suggestion that semantic memory may be just the residue of the superposition of episodic traces. Consider, for example, representation of a proposition encountered in several different contexts, and assume for the moment that the context and content are represented in separate parts of the same module. Over repeated experience with the same proposition in different contexts, the proposition will remain in the interconnections of the units in the proposition submodule, but the particular associations to particular contexts will wash out. However, material that is only encountered in one particular context will tend to be somewhat contextually bound. So we may not be able to retrieve what we learn in one context when we need it in other situations. Other authors (e.g., Anderson & Ross, 1980) have recently argued against a distinction between episodic and semantic memory, pointing out interactions between traditionally episodic and semantic memory tasks. Such findings are generally consistent with the view we have taken here.

Distributed models also influence our thinking about how human behavior might come to exhibit the kind of regularity that often leads linguists to postulate systems of rules. We have recently developed a distributed model of a system that can learn the past tense system of English, given as inputs pairs of patterns, corresponding to the phonological structure of the present and past tense forms of actual English

verbs (Rumelhart & McClelland, 1986). Given plausible assumptions about the learning experiences to which a child is exposed, the model provides a fairly accurate account of the time course of acquisition of the past tense (Brown, 1973; Ervin, 1964; Kuczaj, 1977).

In general distributed models appear to provide alternatives to a variety of different kinds of models that postulate abstract, summary representations such as prototypes, logogens, semantic memory representations, or even linguistic rules.

Why Prefer a Distributed Model?

The fact that distributed models provide alternatives to other sorts of accounts is important, but the fact that they are sometimes linked rather closely to the physiology often makes them seem irrelevant to the basic enterprise of cognitive psychology. It may be conceded that distributed models describe the *physiological substrate* of memory better than other models, but why should we assume that they help us to characterize human information processing at a more abstract level of description? There are two parts to the answer to this question. First, though distributed models may be approximated by other models, on close inspection they differ from them in ways that should have testable consequences. If tests of these consequences turn out to favor distributed models— and there are indications that in certain cases they will—it would seem plausible to argue that distributed models provide an importantly different description of cognition, even if it does take the phenomena somewhat closer to the physiological level of analysis. Second, distributed models alter our thinking about a number of aspects of cognition at the same time. They give us a whole new constellation of assumptions about the structure of cognitive processes. They can change the way we think about the learning process, for example, and can even help shed some light on why and how human behavior comes to be as regular (as bound by rules and concepts) as it seems to be. In this section we consider these two points in turn.

A different level, or a different description? Are distributed models at a different level of analysis than cognitive models, or do they provide a different description of cognition? We think the answer is some of both. Here we focus primarily on underscoring the differences between distributed and other models.

Consider, first, the class of models which state that concepts are represented by prototypes. Distributed models approximate prototype models, and under some conditions their predictions converge, but under other conditions their predictions diverge. In particular, distributed models account both for conditions under which the prototype dominates and conditions under which particular exemplars dominate performance. Thus, they clearly have an advantage over such models, and should be preferred as accounts of empirical phenomena.

Perhaps distributed models are to be preferred over some cognitive level models, but one might argue that they are not to be preferred to the correct cognitive level model. For example, in most of the simulations discussed in this article, the predictions of enumeration models are not different from the predictions of our distributed model. Perhaps we should see our distributed model as representing a physiologically plausible implementation of enumeration models.

Even here, there are differences, however. Though both models superimpose traces of different experiences, distributed models do so at the time of storage, while enumeration models do so at the time of retrieval. But there is no evidence to support the separate storage assumption of enumeration models. Indeed, most such models assume that performance is always based on a superimposition of the specific experiences. Now, our distributed model could be rejected if convincing evidence of separate storage could be provided, for example, by some kind of experiment in which a way was found to separate the effects of different memory experiences. But the trend in a number of recent approaches to memory has been to emphasize the ubiquity of interactions between memory traces. Distributed models are essentially constructed around the assumption that memory traces interact by virtue of the nature of the manner in which they are stored, and they provide an explanation for these interactions. Enumeration models, on the other hand, simply assume interac-

tions occur and postulate separate storage without providing any evidence that storage is in fact separate.

There is another difference between our distributed model and the enumeration models, at least existing ones. Our distributed model assumes that learning is an *error-correcting* process, whereas enumeration models do not. This difference leads to empirical consequences which put great strain on existing enumeration models. In existing enumeration models, what is stored in memory is simply a copy of features of the stimulus event, independent of the prior knowledge already stored in the memory system. But there are a number of indications that what is learned depends on the current state of knowledge. For example, the fact that learning is better after distributed practice appears to suggest that more learning occurs on later learning trials, if subjects have had a chance to forget what they learned on the first trial. We would expect such effects to occur in an error-correcting model such as ours.

The main point of the foregoing discussion has been to emphasize that our distributed model is not simply a plausible physiological implementation of existing models of cognitive processes. Rather, the model is an alternative to most, if not all, existing models, as we have tried to emphasize by pointing out differences between our distributed model and other models which have been proposed. Of course this does not mean that our distributed model will not turn out to be an exact notational variant of some particular other model. What it does mean is that our distributed model must be treated as an alternative to—rather than simply an implementation of—existing models of learning and memory.

Interdependence of theoretical assumptions. There is another reason for taking distributed models seriously as psychological models. Even in cases where our distributed model may not be testably distinct from existing models, it does provide an entire constellation of assumptions which go together as a package. . . .

Similar contrasts exist between our distributed model and other models; in general, our model differs from most abstractive models (that is, those that postulate the formation of abstract rules or other abstract representations) in doing away with complex acquisition mechanisms in favor of a very simple connection strength modulation scheme. Indeed, to us, much of the appeal of distributed models is that they do not already have to be intelligent in order to learn, like some models do. Doubtless, sophisticated hypothesis testing models of learning such as those which have grown out of the early concept identification work of Bruner, Goodnow, and Austin (1956) or out of the artificial intelligence learning tradition established by Winston (1975) have their place, but for many phenomena, particularly those that do not seem to require explicit hypothesis formation and testing, the kind of learning mechanism incorporated in our distributed model may be more appropriate.

Two final reasons for preferring a distributed representation are that it leads us to understand some of the reasons why human behavior tends to exhibit such strong regularities. Some of the regularity is due to the structure of the world, of course, but much of it is a result of the way in which our cultures structure it; certainly the regularity of languages is a fact about the way humans communicate that psychological theory can be asked to explain. Distributed models provide some insight both into why it is beneficial for behavior to be regular, and how it comes to be that way.

It is beneficial for behavior to be regular, because regularity allows us to economize on the size of the networks that must be devoted to processing in a particular environment. If all experiences were completely random and unrelated to each other, a distributed model would buy us very little—in fact it would cost us a bit—relative to separate enumeration of experiences. An illuminating analysis of this situation is given by Willshaw (1981). Where a distributed model pays off, though, is in the fact that it can capture generalizations economically, given that there are generalizations. Enumeration models lack this feature. There are of course limits on how much can be stored in a distributed memory system, but the fact that it can abstract extends those limits far beyond the capacity of any system relying on the separate enumeration of experiences, whenever abstraction is warranted by the ensemble of inputs.

We have just explained how distributed models can help us understand why it is a good thing for be-

havior to exhibit regularity, but we have not yet indicated how they help us understand how it comes to be regular. But it is easy to see how distributed models tend to impose regularity. When a new pattern is presented, the model will impose regularity by dealing with it as it has learned to deal with similar patterns in the past; the model automatically generalizes. In our analysis of past tense learning (Rumelhart & McClelland, 1986), it is just this property of distributed models which leads them to produce the kinds of over-regularizations we see in language development; the same property, operating in all of the members of a culture at the same time, will tend to produce regularizations in the entire language.

CONCLUSION

The distributed approach is in its infancy, and we do not wish to convey the impression that we have solved all the problems of learning and memory simply by invoking it. Considerable effort is needed on several fronts. We will mention four that seem of paramount importance: (a) Distributed models must be integrated with models of the overall organization of information processing, and their relation to models of extended retrieval processes and other temporally extended mental activities must be made clear. (b) Models must be formulated which adequately capture the structural relations of the components of complex stimuli. Existing models do not do this in a sufficiently flexible and open-ended way to capture arbitrarily complex propositional structures. (c) Ways must be found to take the assignment of patterns of activation to stimuli out of the hands of the modeler, and place them in the structure of the model itself. (d) Further analysis is required to determine which of the assumptions of our particular distributed model are essential and which are unimportant details. The second and third of these problems are under intensive study. Some developments along these lines are reported in a number of recent papers (Ackley, Hinton, & Sejnowski, 1985; McClelland, 1985; Rumelhart & Zipser, 1985).

Although much remains to be done, we hope we have demonstrated that distributed models provide distinct, conceptually attractive alternatives to models involving the explicit formation of abstractions or the enumeration of specific experiences. Just how far distributed models can take us toward an understanding of learning and memory remains to be seen.

REFERENCES

Ackley, D., Hinton, G. E., & Sejnowski, T. J. (1985). Boltzmann machines: Constraint satisfaction networks that learn. *Cognitive Science, 9,* 147–169.

Anderson, J. A. (1977). Neural models with cognitive implications. In D. LaBerge & S. J. Samuels (Eds.), *Basic processes in reading: Perception and comprehension.* Hillsdale, NJ: Erlbaum.

Anderson, J. A. (1983). Cognitive and psychological computation with neural models. *IEEE Transactions on Systems, Man, and Cybernetics, SMC-13,* 799–815.

Anderson, J. A., & Hinton, G. E. (1981). Models of information processing in the brain. In G. E. Hinton & J. A. Anderson (Eds.), *Parallel models of associative memory.* Hillsdale, NJ: Erlbaum.

Anderson, J. A., Silverstein, J. W., Ritz, S. A., & Jones, R. S. (1977). Distinctive features, categorical perception, and probability learning: Some applications of a neural model. *Psychological Review, 84,* 413–451.

Anderson, J. R. (1983). *The architecture of cognition.* Cambridge, MA: Harvard.

Anderson, J. R., & Ross, B. H. (1980). Evidence against a semantic-episodic distinction. *Journal of Experimental Psychology: Human Learning and Memory, 6,* 441–465.

Brooks, L. R. (1978). Nonanalytic concept formation and memory for instances. In E. Rosch & B. B. Lloyd (Eds.), *Cognition and categorization.* Hillsdale, NJ: Erlbaum.

Brown, R. (1973). A *first language.* Cambridge, MA: Harvard University Press.

Bruner, J. S., Goodnow, J. J., & Austin, G. A. (1956). A *study of thinking.* New York: Wiley.

Eich, J. M. (1982). A composite holographic associative retrieval model. *Psychological Review, 89,* 627–661.

Ervin, S. (1964). Imitation and structural change in children's language. In E. Lenneberg (Ed.), *New directions in the study of language.* Cambridge, MA: MIT Press.

Feustel, T. C., Shiffrin, R. M., & Salasoo, A. (1983). Episodic and lexical contributions to the repetition effect in word identification. *Journal of Experimental Psychology: General, 112,* 309–346.

Glushko, R. J. (1979). The organization and activation of orthographic knowledge in reading aloud. *Journal of Experimental Psychology: Human Perception and Performance, 5,* 674–691.

Hinton, G. E. (1981a). Implementing semantic networks in parallel hardware. In G. E. Hinton & J. A. Anderson (Eds.), *Parallel models of associative memory.* Hillsdale, NJ: Erlbaum.

Hinton, G. E. (1981b). A parallel computation that assigns canonical object-based frames of reference. *Proceedings of the Seventh International Joint Conference in Artificial Intelligence* (pp. 683–685). Vancouver, British Columbia, Canada.

Hinton, G. E., & Anderson, J. A. (Eds.). (1981) *Parallel models of associative memory.* Hillsdale, NJ: Erlbaum.

Hinton, G E., McClelland, J. L., & Rumelhart, D. E. (in press). Distributed representations. In D. E. Rumelhart & J. L. McClelland (Eds.), *Parallel distributed processing: Explorations in the microstructure of cognition. Volume 1: Foundations.* Cambridge, MA: Bradford Books.

Hintzman, D. (1983). *Schema abstraction in a multiple trace memory model.* Paper presented at conference on "The priority of the specific." Elora, Ontario, Canada.

Jacoby, L. L. (1983a). Perceptual enhancement: Persistent effects of an experience. *Journal of Experimental Psychology: Learning, Memory, and Cognition, 9,* 21–38.

Jacoby, L. L. (1983b). Remembering the data: Analyzing interaction processes in reading. *Journal of Verbal Learning and Verbal Behavior, 22,* 485–508.

Knapp, A., & Anderson, J. A. (1984). A signal averaging model for concept formation. *Journal of Experimental Psychology: Learning, Memory, and Cognition, 10,* 616–637.

Kohonen, T. (1977). *Associative memory: A system theoretical approach.* Berlin: Springer-Verlag.

Kohonen, T., Oja, E., & Lehtio, P. (1981). Storage and processing of information in distributed associative memory systems. In G. E. Hinton & J. A. Anderson (Eds.), *Parallel models of associative memory.* Hillsdale, NJ: Erlbaum.

Kuczaj, S. A., II. (1977). The acquisition of regular and irregular past tense forms. *Journal of Verbal Learning and Verbal Behavior, 16,* 589–600.

Lashley, K. S. (1950). In search of the engram. *Society for Experimental Biology Symposium No. 4: Physiological*

Mechanisms in Animal Behavior (pp. 478–505). London: Cambridge University Press.

Luce, R. D. (1963) Detection and recognition. In R. D. Luce, R. R. Bush, & E. Galanter (Eds.), *Handbook of Mathematical Psychology: Vol. 1.* New York: Wiley.

McClelland, J. L. (1979). On the time-relations of mental processes: An examination of systems of processes in cascade. *Psychological Review, 86,* 287–330.

McClelland, J. L. (1981). Retrieving general and specific information from stored knowledge of specifics. *Proceedings of the Third Annual Meeting of the Cognitive Science Society* (pp. 170–72). Berkeley, CA.

McClelland, J. L. (1985) Putting knowledge in its place: A framework for programming parallel processing structures on the fly. *Cognitive Science, 9,* 113–146.

McClelland, J. L., & Rumelhart, D. E. (1981). An interactive activation model of the effect of context in perception, Part 1. An account of basic findings. *Psychological Review, 88,* 375–407.

Medin, D., & Schwanenflugel, P. J (1981). Linear separability in classification learning. *Journal of Experimental Psychology: Human Learning and Memory, 7,* 355–368.

Medin, D. L., & Shaffer, M. M. (1978). Context theory of classification learning. *Psychological Review, 85,* 207–238.

Morton, J. (1979). Facilitation in word recognition: Experiments causing change in the logogen model. In P. A. Kohlers, M, E. Wrolstal, & H. Bouma (Eds.) *Processing visible language I.* New York: Plenum.

Murdock, B. B. (1982). A theory for the storage and retrieval of item and associative information. *Psychological Review, 89,* 609–626.

Posner, M. I., & Keele, S. W. (1968). On the genesis of abstract ideas. *Journal of Experimental Psychology, 77,* 353–363.

Posner, M. I., & Keele, S. W. (1970). Retention of abstract ideas. *Journal of Experimental Psychology, 83,* 304–308.

Rosenblatt, F. (1962). *Principles of neurodynamics.* Washington, DC: Spartan.

Rumelhart, D. E., & McClelland, J. L. (1981). Interactive processing through spreading activation. In A. M. Lesgold & C. A. Perfetti (Eds.), *Interactive Processes in Reading.* Hillsdale, NJ: Erlbaum.

Rumelhart, D. E., & McClelland, J. L. (1982). An interactive activation model of the effect of context in perception Part II. The contextual enhancement effect and some tests and extensions of the model. *Psychological Review, 89,* 60–94.

Rumelhart, D. E., & McClelland, J. L. (1986). On learning the past tenses of English verbs. In J. L. McClelland & D. E. Rumelhart (Eds.), *Parallel distributed processing Explorations in the microstructure of cognition. Volume II: Applications.* Cambridge, MA: Bradford Books.

Rumelhart, D. E., & Zipser, D. (1985). Competitive learning. *Cognitive Science, 9,* 75–112.

Salasoo, A., Shiffrin, R. M, & Feustel, T. C. (1985). Building permanent memory codes: Codification and repetition effects in word identification. *Journal of Experimental Psychology: General, 114,* 50–77.

Stone, G. (1985). *An analysis of the delta rule.* Manuscript in preparation.

Sutton, R. S., & Barto, A. G. (1981). Toward a modern theory of adaptive networks: Expectation and prediction. *Psychological Review, 88,* 135–170.

Tulving, E. (1972) Episodic and semantic memory. In E. Tulving & W. Donaldson (Eds.), *Organization of Memory.* New York: Academic Press.

Whittlesea, B. W. A. (1983). *Representation and generalization of concepts: The abstractive and episodic perspectives evaluated.* Unpublished doctoral dissertation, MacMaster University.

Wickelgren, W. A. (1979). Chunking and consolidation: A theoretical synthesis of semantic networks, configuring in conditioning, S-R versus cognitive learning, normal forgetting, the amnesic syndrome, and the hippocampal arousal system. *Psychological Review, 86,* 44–60.

Willshaw, D. (1981). Holography, associative memory, and inductive generalization. In G. E. Hinton & J. A. Anderson (Eds.), *Parallel models of associative memory.* Hillsdale, NJ: Erlbaum.

Winston, P. H. (1975). Learning structural descriptions from examples. In P. H. Winston (Ed.), *The psychology of computer vision.* Cambridge, MA: Harvard.

POSTSCRIPT

Although the terms *connectionism* and *parallel distributed processing* (PDP) are not used in this article, the work reported here is clearly part of such an approach (see Reading 6, and the Postscript to that reading). Many of the technical issues raised in this article are explored more fully in the two-volume *Parallel Distributed Processing* (McClelland, Rumelhart, & the PDP Research Group, 1986; Rumelhart, McClelland, & the PDP Research Group, 1986—other, less technical, sources are cited in the Postscript to Reading 6).

Since this article was originally published, a number of other researchers have developed connectionist or distributed array models of concepts (Estes, 1986a, 1986b; Gluck, 1991; Gluck & Bower, 1988; Kruschke, 1992; Schyns, 1991; Shanks, 1990, 1991). These models generally have been very successful in modeling many of the properties of human conceptual representation and use that first led to the development of the abstractive and exemplar-based views. However, it remains unclear whether they are able to illuminate results that suggest that much of what we think of as conceptual knowledge implies an understanding of causal relationships among the different characteristics of the instances of a concept (see the Postscript to Reading 16 or the Introduction to Reading 17).

When "Distributed Memory and the Representation of General and Specific Information" was published, it was immediately followed by a response suggesting that the McClelland and Rumelhart model is not really different from an exemplar-based model (Broadbent, 1985). That argument, however, hinges on whether exemplar-based models should be distinguished from the view that concepts involve the explicit representation of both abstracted and specific information. McClelland and Rumelhart argue that the two views should be distinguished, as do supporters of the schema view (Komatsu, 1992). (For a discussion of the relationship between schema and connectionist models, see Rumelhart, Smolensky, McClelland, & Hinton, 1986.) More broadly, however, it is important to note that the usefulness of connectionist models for understanding cognition *in general* is a point of considerable debate (see the Postscript to Reading 6).

FOR FURTHER THOUGHT

1. In what way is McClelland and Rumelhart's distributed memory model like an exemplar-based model? Describe the problems with exemplar-based models that McClelland and Rumelhart identify. Why don't these problems occur with a distributed memory model?

2. What is the significance of the fact that a single network can represent several categories at once?
3. What is context-sensitive encoding? Give an example of how the Whittlesea stimuli might be coded in a context-sensitive manner.
4. What evidence do McClelland and Rumelhart present to suggest that their model is not simply a kind of prototype model?
5. What reasons do McClelland and Rumelhart give for preferring distributed memory models over other cognitive models of memory processes? What does it mean to say that two explanations are at "different levels"?

REFERENCES

Bechtel, W., & Abrahamsen, L. (1991). *Connectionism and the mind: An introduction to parallel processing in networks.* Cambridge, MA: Basil Blackwell.

Broadbent, D. (1985). A question of levels: Comment on McClelland and Rumelhart. *Journal of Experimental Psychology: General, 114,* 189–192.

Clark, A. (1989). *Microcognition: Philosophy, cognitive science, and parallel distributed processing.* Cambridge, MA: MIT Press.

Estes, W. K. (1986a). Array models for category learning. *Cognitive Psychology, 18,* 500–549.

Estes, W. K. (1986b). Memory storage and retrieval processes in category learning. *Journal of Experimental Psychology: General, 115,* 155–174.

Gluck, M. A. (1991). Stimulus generalization and representation in adaptive network models of category learning. *Psychological Science, 2,* 50–55.

Gluck, M. A., & Bower, G. H. (1988). From conditioning to category learning: An adaptive network model. *Journal of Experimental Psychology: General, 117,* 227–247.

Hintzman, D. L., & Ludlam, G. (1980). Differential forgetting of prototypes and old instances: Simulation by an exemplar-based classification model. *Memory & Cognition, 8,* 378–382.

Komatsu, L. K. (1992). Recent views of conceptual structure. *Psychological Bulletin, 112,* 500–526.

Kruschke, J. K. (1992). ALCOVE: An exemplar-based connectionist model of category learning. *Psychological Review, 99,* 22–44.

Martindale, C. (1991). *Cognitive psychology: A neural-network approach.* Pacific Grove, CA: Brooks/Cole Publishing Co.

McClelland, J. L., Rumelhart, D. E., & the PDP Research Group (1986). *Parallel Distributed Processing: Explorations in the microstructure of cognition (Vol. 2): Psychological and biological models.* Cambridge, MA: MIT Press.

Nosfosky, R. M. (1988). Exemplar-based accounts of relations between classification, recognition, and typicality. *Journal of Experimental Psychology: Learning, Memory, and Cognition, 14,* 700–708.

Posner, M. I., & Keele, S. W. (1968). On the genesis of abstract ideas. *Journal of Experimental Psychology, 77,* 353–363.

Rumelhart, D. E., McClelland, J. L., & the PDP Research Group (1986). *Parallel Distributed Processing: Explorations in the microstructure of cognition (Vol. 1): Foundations.* Cambridge, MA: MIT Press.

Rumelhart, D. E., Smolensky, P., McClelland, J. L., & Hinton, G. E. (1986). Schemata and sequential thought processes in PDP models. In J. L. McClelland & D. E. Rumelhart (Eds.), *Parallel Distributed Processing: Explorations in the microstructure of cognition (Vol. 2): Psychological and biological models* (pp. 7–57). Cambridge, MA: MIT Press.

Schyns, P. G. (1991). A modular neural network model of concept acquisition. *Cognitive Science, 15,* 461–508.

Shanks, D. R. (1990). Connectionism and the learning of probabilistic concepts. *Quarterly Journal of Experimental Psychology, 42A,* 209–237.

Shanks, D. R. (1991). Categorization by a connectionist network. *Journal of Experimental Psychology: Learning, Memory, and Cognition, 17,* 433–443.

INTRODUCTION

Most research in cognitive psychology assumes that certain general properties of cognition are shared by pretty much all people (see Chapter 10 for exceptions to this assumption). Given this assumption, it doesn't make too much difference whom you test your theories on: if the theories apply correctly to one person, they should apply to others. That is why theories of cognition are often tested by measuring the performance of ordinary college students who have no special characteristics. But it is often useful to test theories of cognition on special populations; in fact, sometimes, the performance of special individuals can help us address questions that are difficult to answer otherwise. In "Visual and Spatial Mental Imagery: Dissociable Systems of Representation," Martha Farah, Katherine Hammond, David Levine, and Ronald Calvanio observe the breakdown of mental imagery in a person with brain damage to test their analysis of how certain mental imagery tasks are performed. (See the Introduction to Reading 23 for further discussion of the use of special populations to understand normal cognition.)

Although there has been some controversy over exactly what mental images are (Block, 1981; Tye, 1991), most psychologists agree it is reasonable to conclude that people represent at least some information about visual characteristics and spatial relationships in a picture-like rather than verbal-descriptive ("propositional") form (Anderson, 1978). Over the last 20 years, psychologists have studied how people use visual images as an aid to memory (Einstein, McDaniel, & Lackey, 1989; Kroll, Schepler, & Angin, 1986) and how they generate and manipulate mental images (for summaries of research on imagery, see Kosslyn, 1980, 1983; Finke, 1989; Reisberg, 1992; and Shepard & Cooper, 1982).

One influential view of imagery, sometimes called the levels of perceptual equivalence view, suggests that many of the anatomical structures that are involved in visual imagery are also involved in visual perception (Finke, 1985, 1986). Thus, we expect (1) that certain visual and imaginal processes would interact with one another (see Finke, 1989), and (2) that many of the phenomena observed with vision will be observed with imagery and vice versa.

Recently, it has been discovered that the anatomical structures responsible for our ability to *recognize* objects visually appear to be distinct from those responsible for our ability to *locate* objects visually (Rueckl, Cave, & Kosslyn, 1989; Ungerleider & Mishkin, 1982). As Farah and her colleagues point out, this leads to the expectation that a similar distinction may apply in visual imagery. In fact, the "what" versus "where" distinction in visual perception is closely related to an ongoing debate in imagery research over whether visual imagery involves the representation and manipulation of *visual* information or *spatial* information. The assumption Farah and her associates make is that the "what" system deals with more purely visual information, whereas the information processed by the "where" system is more spatial in nature.

Farah and her colleagues argue that some imagery tasks depend on purely visual information, which makes them difficult for a person with an impaired "what" visual system. Imagery tasks that depend on spatial information pose no problem for a person with an impaired "what" system as long as the "where" system is intact. The first step in testing this claim is to identify imagery tasks as being either visual or spatial. Farah and her colleagues suggest that we should classify as visual only those tasks that involve information that either can *only* be described visually or is *almost certainly* acquired visually (such as the shape of a state). All other tasks are classified as spatial. If this analysis is borne out, the answer to the visual versus spatial debate in imagery is that *both* are actually involved, but in differing degrees with different imagery tasks.

As you read this article, ask yourself whether there are possible alternative explanations of either the pattern of results obtained or the classifications of the tasks. How might those alternatives be tested, and what would the implications be if those alternatives could not be eliminated?

Visual and Spatial Mental Imagery: Dissociable Systems of Representation

Martha J. Farah and Katherine M. Hammond

Carnegie-Mellon University

David N. Levine and Ronald Calvanio

Departments of Neurology
Massachusetts General Hospital and Spaulding Rehabilitation Hospital

Much of the early history of research on mental imagery was concerned with the format of mental images. The principal issue was whether images are "analog" or "array format" representations or whether they are "propositional" or "descriptive" in format (see Pinker, 1985, for a recent discussion of the format of mental images). Currently, there is fairly widespread agreement that the images represent some of the spatial properties of visual stimuli in an analog format (although dissenters certainly exist; see Pylyshyn, 1984). This view of imagery, while clearly a contrast to the propositional view, is sufficiently general that several more specific positions can be accommodated within it. One issue that divides researchers who hold the "analog" view of imagery is whether images are best characterized as visual or spatial representations. For example, in a recent introduction to imagery research, Kosslyn (1983, p. 77) states that "It seems clear that some of the same mechanisms are involved in both vision and visual imagery," whereas Anderson's cognitive psychology text (1985, p. 95) states that

"[Images] are not tied to the visual modality, but seem to be part of a more general system for representing spatial and continuously varying information." In this paper we address the issue of visual and spatial representation in imagery using neuropsychological data.

"Visual" and "Spatial" Representation

To understand what is meant by visual and spatial representation in the context of this debate it is helpful to review the kinds of evidence that have been taken to be relevant to the issue. Several different types of research strategies have been used in arguing for either visual or spatial representation in imagery, and from these research strategies one can reconstruct operational definitions of visual and spatial representation. One way of distinguishing between visual and spatial representations is in terms of modality specificity. Visual representations are by definition specific to the visual modality, whereas spatial representations are not. This distinction has given rise to a line of experimentation using selective interference paradigms. Segal and Fusella's (1970) experiment on visual and auditory imagery is one of the best known examples of a selective interference experiment in imagery research. They asked subjects to form and hold either visual images or auditory images while the subjects were engaged in visual and auditory signal detection. Imaging interfered more with same-modality

This research was supported by ONR Contract N0014-86-0094, NIH Grant NS23458, the Alfred P. Sloan Foundation, and NIH Program Project Grant NS06209-21 to the Aphasia Research Center of the Boston University School of Medicine. The authors thank Margaret Jean Intons-Peterson, Michael McCloskey, Lynne Robertson, and an anonymous reviewer for their many helpful comments on an earlier draft of this manuscript. We also thank L.H. for his help in this project.

SOURCE: *Cognitive Psychology, 20,* 1988, pp. 439–462. Copyright © 1988 by Academic Press, Inc. Reprinted by permission.

signal detection than other modality signal detection, and this was taken to imply that, in the case of visual imagery, visual perceptual representations were being engaged. However, a different conclusion about the nature of imagery came from Baddeley and Lieberman's (1980) selective interference experiment. They had subjects perform an imagery task with two different secondary tasks: one which was visual but not spatial (discriminating the brightness of two lights) and one which was spatial but not visual (tracking a moving sound source with hand movements). Their imagery task involved constructing and maintaining an image of a path through a two-dimensional matrix, given a starting position in the matrix and instructions to move left, right, up, or down. Baddeley and Lieberman found that the nonvisual spatial task interfered with the imagery task, whereas the nonspatial visual task did not, implying that imagery engages amodal spatial representations.

A second experimental strategy that has been used to address the modality specificity of imagery has been to compare the imagery processes of sighted and congenitally blind subjects. Congenitally blind subjects would be expected to have spatial representations from their tactile interactions with the world, but would not be expected to have visual representations, having never seen. The logic of this research is that, if congenitally blind subjects perform normally on imagery tasks, then imagery tasks must engage spatial representations, not visual representations. Among the imagery tasks that have been used with congenitally blind subjects are mental rotation tasks (Carpenter & Eisenberg, 1978; Marmor & Zabeck, 1976), mental scanning tasks (Kerr, 1983), imagery mnemonic tasks (Jonides, Kahn, & Rozin, 1975; Kerr, 1983; Zimler & Keenan, 1983), and semantic information retrieval under imagery instructions (Kerr, 1983). For imagery tasks that normally require visual stimuli these researchers devised tactile analogs, such as mental rotation of palpated block letters or mental scanning of a palpated relief map. The general finding that emerges from these studies is that congenitally blind subjects are able to perform these mental imagery tasks and, furthermore, their patterns of response time are qualitatively similar to those of sighted subjects, suggesting that both groups of sub-

jects are using the same types of representations to perform the tasks. This implies that visual information per se is not an essential aspect of imagery.

Another way of distinguishing visual from spatial representations is based on the inclusion of intrinsically visual information, of which color is the prime example. Finke and Schmidt (1977, 1978) found perceptual aftereffects of imagined line orientation but not imagined color, consistent with the idea that images are spatial and not visual. In contrast, Intons-Peterson (1987) has found that the color of an image has functional consequences: With eyes open, subjects require less time to form an image when the color of the image matches the color of the perceptual surface on which the image is projected. This implies that imagery is visual, in the sense of encoding intrinsically visual information in a form in which it interacts with perceived visual stimuli.

In addition to properties such as color that can be encoded only visually, some researchers have identified properties that are unlikely to have been encoded through any modality other than vision and have used these to address the issue of whether imagery is visual. For example, knowledge of the precise shapes and sizes of objects that one has seen but never touched is presumably represented visually. Many of Kosslyn's experiments (e.g., 1975) involve the retrieval of visual form information that is unlikely to have been encoded through other modalities, for example, the sizes and shapes of zoo animals' body parts. Indeed, Kerr (1983) was unable to use animal body-part imagery questions with her congenitally blind subjects and attributed this to the subjects' lack of familiarity with this type of information, as it is unlikely to have been encoded any way other than visually (p. 269).

Visual representations have also been distinguished from spatial representations based on their perspective properties, such as foreshortening and occlusion. Several studies have addressed the issue of visual versus spatial representation in imagery by determining whether or not images have perspective properties, that is, contain just the information about spatial relations available in the surface appearance of an object or scene. The alternative possibility is that images contain more abstract information about the spatial relations among the elements of the image, including information not available from any single vantage point. Thus, the finding that subjects can mentally rotate objects in depth as quickly and accurately as in the picture plane (Shepard & Metzler, 1971), even though the appearance of an object undergoing a depth rotation changes in much more complex ways than the appearance of an object undergoing a picture-plane rotation, is taken as evidence for the spatial nature of imagery. As Hinton (1979) has pointed out, if subjects were rotating visual representations, they would have to carry out additional foreshortening and hidden line removal operations in depth rotation that would not be required during picture plane rotation. Image scanning is another type of mental image operation which seems to involve perspectiveless spatial representations: Pinker (1980) has shown that subjects scan mental images of three-dimensional scenes equally quickly in all three dimensions and that the time to scan between two objects is linearly related to their three-dimensional separation rather than their separation in a two-dimensional picture-plane projection.

The role of perspective properties in imagery has also been explored in the context of imagery mnemonics in paired associate learning. Neisser and Kerr (1973) and Kerr and Neisser (1983) have found that the mnemonic effectiveness of images in paired associate learning is undiminished when one of the two associates is present in the image but occluded by the other associate. For example, an image of a harp sitting inside the Statue of Liberty's torch was as effective in facilitating the later association of harp and torch as an image of the harp on top of the torch. They interpret this as supporting the idea that images represent the "layout" of objects in space, rather than the projective view of those objects that meets the eye.

In sum, visual representations are taken to be modality-specific representations that encode the literal appearance of objects, including perspective properties, color information, and aspects of form not available through touch or other modalities. Spatial representations are taken to be relatively abstract, amodal, or multimodal representations of the layout of objects in space with respect to the viewer and each other.

Both Visual and Spatial Imagery?

A basic assumption in the debate over whether imagery is visual or spatial is that it is either visual *or* spatial. That is, the intent of most of the research reviewed above is not to demonstrate that imagery has some visual properties or some spatial properties and that different tasks call upon one component of the imagery system or the other. Rather, the general aim of research in this area has been to demonstrate an apparently more parsimonious conclusion, that imagery is either just visual or just spatial. Accordingly, researchers on each side of the issue have tried to give alternative accounts for the other side's demonstrations. For example, Kosslyn (1980, Chapter 2) presents a lengthy methodological critique of Neisser and Kerr's (1973) study of the mnemonic effectiveness of occluded images. He also attempts to account for three-dimensional mental rotation phenomena using a two-dimensional "visual buffer" representation (Kosslyn, Pinker, Smith, & Shwartz, 1979). Similarly, Neisser (1976, Chapter 7) has offered alternative interpretations of many demonstrations of visual properties of images (e.g., Kosslyn, 1975; Segal & Fusella, 1970) in terms of visual expectations engendered in the subject by imaging, rather than the existence of an internally generated representation of visual appearance.

In this paper it is argued that different mental imagery tasks call upon different kinds of imagery representations, some of which are visual and some of which are spatial, in the senses of "visual" and "spatial" discussed above. In effect, imagery researchers have been misled by the use of a common term, "imagery," to label what are in fact two distinct types of representation. Although this would certainly resolve the apparently conflicting results obtained by the "visual" and "spatial" camps, at first glance the idea seems unparsimonious. However, there is neurophysiological evidence that normal vision involves parallel, independent systems of visual and spatial representation. Given this evidence for the existence of both visual and spatial representations, the claim that imagery might also involve these two types of representations seems less extravagant. In fact, in the context of a "levels of perceptual equivalence" view of imagery (Finke, 1980), it seems quite natural that the structure of imagery would parallel this two-component structure of vision.

Before presenting the results of our neuropsychological case study, which provides evidence for the existence of distinct visual and spatial imagery systems, we briefly review the neurophysiological and neuropsychological evidence for a distinction between visual and spatial representations of visual stimuli in perception.

The Concept of "Two Cortical Visual Systems"

Ungerleider and Mishkin (1982) coined the term "two cortical visual systems" to capture a distinction between two functionally and anatomically distinct systems of visual representation, one concerned with the appearance of individual objects and the other with the location of objects in space. They and other researchers (e.g., Pohl, 1973; Iwai & Mishkin, 1968; Brody & Pribram, 1978) have observed a marked contrast between the effects of parietal and temporal lesions in visual discrimination tasks: Monkeys with lesions in the parietal cortex are unimpaired in tasks that require visual discriminations on the basis of objects' appearances, but are grossly impaired in tasks that require assessing objects' spatial relations, such as reaching for objects or judging which of two objects is closer to a landmark. Lesions of certain regions of the parietal lobe also lead to a "neglect" of stimuli occurring in certain regions of space, whether the stimuli be visual or tactile (Rizzolatti, Gentilucci, & Matelli, 1985). In contrast, monkeys with lesions in inferior temporal cortex are unimpaired on the spatial tasks that the parietal-lesioned monkeys fail, but are grossly impaired at learning to discriminate between different forms, patterns, and objects. Ungerleider and Mishkin called the system that represents visual appearance, located in the temporal lobes, the "what" system and the system that represents spatial layout, located in the parietal lobes, the "where" system.

Data from single neuron recordings also support the distinction between representations of appearance in the temporal lobe and representations of spatial location in the parietal lobe: Temporal recordings have revealed neurons that respond to the shape and color of stimuli, including the three-dimensional perspective from which an object is viewed (e.g.,

Desimone, Albright, Gross, & Bruce, 1984), whereas parietal recordings have not revealed such sensitivities (Robinson, Goldberg, & Stanton, 1978). In contrast, parietal recordings reveal more sensitivity to the motion of a stimulus and its position relative to eye fixation than do temporal recordings (Lynch, Mountcastle, Talbot, & Yin, 1977; Mountcastle, Anderson, & Motter, 1981; Robinson et al., 1978; Sakata, Shibutani, & Kawano, 1983).

There is clinical evidence that this rather counterintuitive division of labor in the monkey visual system also holds for the human visual system. Neurologists studying patients with bilateral posterior brain lesions recognized early in this century that impairments in the identification of visual stimuli (the visual agnosias) could occur independently of impairments in their spatial localization (Potzl, 1928; Lange, 1936). Patients with a rare combination of bilateral inferior temporal and occipital lobe damage and intact parietal lobes may be unable to recognize visually presented objects, despite adequate elementary visual abilities (e.g., light sensitivity, acuity). These "agnosic" patients, like temporal-lesioned monkeys, have lost their internal representations of the visual appearances of objects and thus cannot name or in other ways indicate their recognition of visually presented objects. Also like temporal-lesioned monkeys, these patients are able to represent the positions in space of visually presented objects; they can point to objects, describe their positions with respect to one another in three dimensions, and draw accurate maps representing the layout of objects in space (see, e.g., Bauer & Rubens, 1985). Patients with bilateral parietal disease, like parietal-lesioned monkeys, are able to recognize visually presented objects, but are unable to localize stimuli, even the same stimuli that they are able to recognize. That is, such patients would be able to name a wristwatch or paper clip held by an examiner at some location in their visual field, but when asked to point to or describe the location of this stimulus they would be grossly inaccurate (DeRenzi, 1982; Ratcliff, 1982). A dissociation between relatively milder visual and spatial impairments has also been observed in unilateral right-hemisphere-damaged patients, with visual impairments associated with right temporal damage and spatial impairments associated with right parietal damage (Newcombe & Russell, 1969; Newcombe, Ratcliff, & Damasio, 1987).

In summary, there exists evidence that in animals and in humans the representation of the visual appearance of stimuli and the spatial location of stimuli are subserved by distinct, independent systems. For present purposes, the anatomical separateness of these two systems is of less importance than their functional independence—the fact that each one can continue to function in the absence of the other. It is a fact about the functional architecture of vision that the visual appearances of objects and their spatial relations are represented separately and independently by two different perceptual systems.

On the basis of our clinical observations of two patients and a review of the neurological literature for similar cases, we have argued that the same distinction between the representation of visual appearance and spatial relations exists in mental imagery as well as in perception (Levine, Warach, & Farah, 1985). That is, patients who are impaired in the recognition but not the localization of visual stimuli do poorly at describing and drawing objects' appearances from memory, but can describe and draw the spatial layouts of objects and scenes from memory. Similarly, patients who are impaired in the localization but not the recognition of visual stimuli do poorly at describing and drawing the spatial layout of objects and scenes from memory, but can describe and draw objects' appearances from memory. In the present paper we relate these clinical observations more directly to the debate in cognitive psychology over whether imagery is best characterized as visual or spatial, by presenting the performance of a patient with impaired visual object recognition and intact object localization on a set of imagery tasks adapted from the cognitive psychology literature. The dissociation between this patient's performance on imagery tasks borrowed from the "visual imagery" camp and imagery tasks borrowed from the "spatial imagery" camp supports a direct correspondence between the visual versus spatial distinction in visual neurophysiology and the visual versus spatial distinction in the cognitive psychology debate about mental imagery. It is argued that the dissociation in this patient's visual and spatial imagery abilities implies that imagistic representation, like perceptual representation, is not an undifferentiated faculty, but rather consists of at least the two independent sets of representational abilities, visual and spatial. Thus, the argument over whether imagery is visual or spatial is based on the false premise that it is one or the other; in fact, each type of representation exists and is necessary for a different subset of imagery tasks.

METHODS

Subject Information

The brain-damaged subject, L.H., is a 36-year-old minister currently working toward a second Master's degree. When he was 18 years old, he sustained a severe closed head injury in an automobile accident. Brain damage from the accident and subsequent surgery involved both temporo-occipital regions, the right temporal lobe, and the right inferior frontal lobe, as demonstrated by CT scan, neurological examination, and surgical records. Figure 1 shows the locations of cortical damage projected onto lateral views of the two hemispheres. The bilateral posterior inferior temporal injury, with relative sparing of the parietal regions, constitutes a rare configuration of brain damage that is generally associated with visual

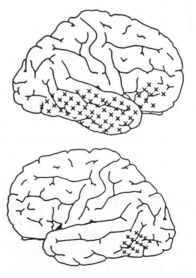

FIGURE 1   Reconstruction of areas of damage from CT scan and surgical records displayed on lateral views of the two hemispheres.

agnosia. Details of L.H.'s medical history are published elsewhere (Levine, Calvanio, & Wolf, 1980; Levine et al., 1985).

L.H. made a remarkable recovery from his accident, eventually returning to the ivy-league college in which he was enrolled to complete his Bachelor's degree and going on to earn a Master's degree. When tested on the Wechsler Adult Intelligence Scale 7 years after his accident, his verbal IQ was 132 and his performance IQ was 93. His memory quotient on the Wechsler Memory Scale was 121. He had no detectable language or motor skill deficits. His spatial localization of visual stimuli was normal, and his elementary visual capabilities were basically intact: Acuity was 20/50 in the left eye and 20/70 in the right, with blindness in the peripheral visual field, particularly in the upper left and lower right quadrants of the visual field. Despite his general intellectual and elementary visual capabilities, L.H. was and still is profoundly impaired in visual recognition. He cannot reliably recognize his wife or children unless they are wearing distinctive articles of clothing. He is also impaired at recognizing animals, plants, foods, drawings, and some common objects. For example, when shown the 260 line drawings published by Snodgrass and Vanderwart (1986), for 4 s each, he was able to identify only 191 or 73%. Figure 2 shows three drawings of common objects (not from the Snodgrass and Vanderwart set) that L.H. was unable to recognize, along with copies he drew of these drawings. The copies demonstrate his good elementary visual capabilities.

In the tasks described below, L.H.'s performance is compared with that of a control group of 12 men in their mid-30s with Master's degrees (mean age 35, range 33–38) who volunteered to participate for pay.

Visual and Spatial Imagery Tasks

Subjects were given a variety of tasks tapping visual and spatial information in imagery. Our strategy was to administer imagery tasks from the cognitive psychology literature that are either similar or identical to the tasks that have been used by researchers on one side or the other of the "visual versus spatial" issue, in order to make contact as directly as possible with that issue as it has been studied in cognitive psychology.

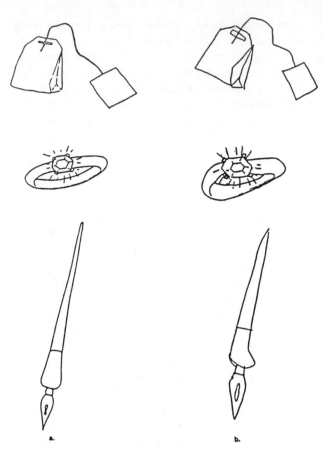

FIGURE 2   (a) Examples of drawings that L.H. could not recognize given unlimited time: a teabag, a ring, and a pen. (b) L.H.'s copies of these drawings, made without knowing their identity.

In general, the spatial imagery tasks have been more thoroughly validated than the visual imagery tasks: That is, researchers who have used the spatial tasks have shown, empirically, that these tasks involve spatial representations per se, by the criteria discussed in the introduction. In contrast, researchers using the visual tasks have generally relied on the logical inference that if a task involves representing information that could only be visually encoded (e.g., color, and the precise sizes and shapes of objects familiar by sight but not normally touched) then the task must involve visual imagery. We have not attempted to provide more thorough validation of these tasks than already exists. We selected four visual imagery tasks involving information about object appearance, such as relative size, shape, and color, and seven spatial imagery tasks, three involving information about the relative locations of objects and four involving spatial transformations of objects. The only task that has figured prominently in the "visual versus spatial" imagery debate that we have not used here is paired-associate learning with imagery mnemonics, because of mixed findings implicating both visual and spatial components (e.g., Baddeley, Grant, Wight, & Thomson, 1975; Byrne, 1974; Kerr & Neisser, 1983; Neisser & Kerr, 1973; and Zimler & Keenan, 1983, have found evidence of spatial representation; Atwood, 1971; Janssen, 1976; Keenan & Moore, 1979; and Paivio & Okovita, 1971, have found evidence of visual representation; and Beech, 1984, has found evidence of both visual and spatial representation).

Visual Imagery Tasks

Color.   Color is an intrinsically visual property and questions about the colors of objects often occur in experiments on visual imagery (Eddy & Glass, 1981; Kosslyn & Jolicoeur, 1980; Hever, Fischman, & Reisberg, 1986). We selected 20 common items that have characteristic colors but are nevertheless not verbally associated with their colors, for example, a football. These objects were read to the subject and his task was to name the characteristic color of each one.

Size comparison.   Another type of question used by researchers in the "visual" camp involves comparing the sizes of similar-sized objects (e.g., Kosslyn, Murphy, Bemesderfer, & Feinstein, 1977; Holyoak, 1977). It is claimed that subjects must use visual imagery when the sizes are similar, although imagery is not necessary when they compare the sizes of different-sized objects. The present task involved judging which of two similar-sized items was bigger, e.g., a popsicle and a pack of cigarettes. Sixteen pairs of common, inanimate household items were selected, and their names were read aloud to subjects, one pair at a time.

Animal tails.   Judging or classifying the shapes of objects and parts of objects is a common visual imagery task. Animals and their body parts are often used in

these tasks (e.g., Kosslyn, 1975) because one generally does not have nonvisual experience that would tell one whether, for example, a kangaroo has a long tail, and such facts are rarely explicitly encoded in verbal memory (cf. Kerr, 1983). We selected 20 animal names that were not verbally associated with tails (e.g., we did not use rats, beavers, or peacocks) and asked subjects to respond whether or not the animals had long tails, proportional to their body size. As a control task to verify that subjects were familiar with the animals in the task and had general/nonvisual knowledge of these animals, we also asked them to judge whether the animals were native to the state in which the subject resided (which for L.H. was Massachusetts and for the control subjects was Pennsylvania).

State shapes.   Shepard & Chipman (1970) found that subjects' ratings of the shape similarity between pairs of imagined states were highly similar to their ratings of shape similarity between pairs of visually presented states. They concluded from this that the representations accessed by subjects when recalling shape information from memory were "second-order isomorphic" to the representations of shape engendered by seeing the same shapes. In the present task, subjects were given 20 triads of state names and were instructed to circle the two in each triad which were most similar in their outline shape. A related task, testing spatial imagery in the same knowledge domain, consists of circling the pair of states within a triad that are closest. This is described more fully in the next section.

Spatial Imagery Tasks— Image Transformations

Letter rotation.   Cooper and Shepard (1973) found that subjects must mentally rotate letter forms to an upright position before they are able to judge whether the letters have been printed normally or as mirror images. Mental rotation has been claimed to involve spatial representations, and indeed Cooper and Shepard (1973, p. 84) have said of the representations involved in the present task that "to classify these representations as purely visual images would be misleading. We should rather refer to them, more abstractly, as spatial images . . ." Five asymmetrical capital letters (F, G, J, K, and R) were presented four times each, twice normally and twice mirror-reversed, for a total of 20 trials. The letters were oriented at roughly 45, 90, 135, and 180 degrees of angular displacement from the upright. Subjects' task was to say whether each letter was normal or mirror-reversed.

Three-dimensional form rotation. Shepard and Metzler's (1971) demonstration that the rate of rotation of three-dimensional forms was the same whether the forms were rotated in the picture plane or in depth is one of the most compelling pieces of evidence in favor of abstract spatial representations in imagery. In this task, 34 pairs of Shepard and Metzler forms were to be judged the same or different (mirror image). Half of the pairs required 30, 60, or 90 degrees of rotation, and half required 120, 150, or 180 degrees of rotation. Half of the required rotations were in the picture plane and half were in depth. Amount of rotation was somewhat confounded with dimensionality of rotation, such that only 6 of the 17 shorter rotations (30, 60, or 90 degrees) were in depth.

Mental scanning. In mental image scanning experiments, subjects focus their attention on one part of an image and then move it continuously from that starting position to another part of the image. Kosslyn, Ball, and Keiser (1978) first developed the mental image scanning paradigm as a way of showing that mental images preserve metric spatial information in an analog or array format. This finding is neutral with respect to the issue of whether images are visual or spatial, because both Kosslyn's "visual buffer" and more abstract spatial representations are considered to have an analog or array format. However, Pinker's (1980) finding that subjects' scanning times depended on the distance scanned in three dimensions rather than in a two-dimensional projection and Kerr's (1983) finding that congenitally blind subjects show similar linear scanning times for memory images of tactile scenes imply that the representations involved in image scanning are primarily spatial. The present scanning task was based on Finke and Pinker's (1982) paradigm, which they found evoked spontaneous mental image scanning, whether or not subjects were instructed to scan. In the version used here, two dots were placed pseudo-randomly on either the left half

or right half of a 3 × 5-inch index card, along with an arrow 3 to 4 inches away from the dot to which it points or comes closest to pointing. Thirty-two such trials were constructed. The subjects' task was to say whether or not the arrow pointed to one of the dots. Note that this task differs from Finke and Pinker's task in that the dots and arrow are presented simultaneously. This was necessary because L.H. was unable to maintain an accurate image of the dot pattern after it was removed. However, Thorndike's (1981) finding that subjects' patterns of reaction times did not differ as a function of whether they were scanning perceived or imagined displays implies that this change in procedure should not affect the process of interest.

Size-scaling. The process of comparing the shapes of two stimuli presented simultaneously but at different sizes involved scaling the stimulus representations using a process that Larsen and Bundesen describe as "essentially *position-wise:* The [short-term] memory representation specifies a spatial arrangement of pattern elements (points or subpatterns), and the comparison is made with respect to particular positions in the field of view" (p. 1, emphasis theirs). Our task was based on the work of Larsen and Bundesen. Random 10-point polygons, like those of Larsen (1985), were presented in pairs, one above the other. The polygons in a pair were either identical or differed by being mirror images of one another. One polygon was large (4.5 inches average width) and the other was small (1.75 inches average width). There were 32 such pairs of polygons. The subjects' task was to say whether the pair of figures had the same shape, disregarding size differences.

Spatial Imagery Tasks—Imagery for Spatial Locations

Matrix memory. One of the clearest demonstrations of the spatial nature of imagery is Baddeley and Leiberman's (1980) finding, described earlier, that subjects' performance on an imagery task was significantly impaired by a nonvisual spatial secondary task but not by a nonspatial visual secondary task. In the imagery task used by Baddeley and Leiberman, the subject hears the numbers 1 through 8, accompanied by instructions about where each of these numbers should be placed in an imaginary four-by-four matrix. The starting cell of the matrix is always the leftmost cell in the second row down from the top. A typical trial would consist of "In the starting square put a 1; in the square to the right put a 2; in the square below put a 3; in the square below put a 4 . . ." and so on. After hearing a sequence of eight such instructions, the subject must recall the path, using the same verbal format, e.g., "In the starting square put a 1 . . ." Subjects in the present study were given 20 such eight-step sequences, which had been prerecorded on tape. Approximately 3 s elapsed between the beginning of each instruction in each sequence. The tape was stopped at the end of each sequence and the subject recalled the sequence at his own pace.

Letter corner classification. In this task, a block letter with an asterisk next to the lower left corner is shown to the subject and then removed. The subject's task is to maintain an image of the letter and, beginning with the asterisked corner and traveling in a clockwise direction, classify the corners of the letter according to whether they are on the top or bottom of the letter (in which case the response is "yes") or whether they are from neither the top nor the bottom (in which case the response is "no"). After the letters F, G, M, N, W, and Z have each been classified in this way, they are then presented again, with instructions to say "yes" for corners on the extreme right or left and "no" for the other corners. Brooks (1968) and Baddeley, Grant, Wight, and Thompson (1975) have demonstrated that this task is susceptible to interference from concurrent visual/spatial tasks, that is, tasks with both visual and spatial components. Brooks (1968, Experiment 7) addressed the question of whether the interference was specifically visual, or more generally spatial, by assessing the interference from a secondary tactile/spatial task. The latter task interfered significantly with the letter corner classification task, leading Brooks to conclude that this imagery task involves representations that are spatial but not specifically visual.

State locations. The final spatial imagery task does not come directly from the cognitive psychology literature, but is included as a contrast with the state shape task in the visual imagery section. Subjects were given 20 triads of state names and were asked to circle the two states in each triad that were closest to one another. Triads that could be correctly grouped on the basis of verbal associations to regions (e.g., two "southern" states and a "northern" state) were not used.

Procedural details. With the exception of the matrix memory task, stimulus presentation in all tasks was paced by the subject. In tasks for which the stimulus words were spoken by the experimenter, subjects were free to request that a word be repeated. In tasks with visual stimuli, subjects viewed the printed words or the drawn figures on xeroxed sheets of paper (or, in the case of the scanning task, index cards) for as long as they wished.[1]

The tasks were administered to L.H. on three separate days, the first and third of which included two separate testing sessions. The order of tasks in each session was first (Day 1, session 1), Animal Tails and Color; second (Day 1, session 2), Size Comparison, Mental Scanning, and Size Scaling; third (Day 2), Letter Rotation and Matrix Memory; fourth (Day 3, session 1), Three-Dimensional Form Rotation, Letter Corners; and fifth (Day 3, session 2), State Shape and State Location. Normal control subjects were also tested individually. Seven subjects received all the tasks in one session (lasting about 2½ h with a 5-min break in the middle), three subjects received the tasks in two sessions on different days, one subject received the tasks in three sessions on 3 different days, and one subject received the tasks in four sessions on 4 different days. The tasks were given in the following order to all normal control subjects: Animal Tails, Color, Mental Scanning, Size Scaling, Letter Rotation, Matrix Memory, Size Comparison, Three-Dimensional Form Rotation, State Shape, State Location, and Letter Corners.

RESULTS

The performance of L.H. and the 12 control subjects on each of the 11 tasks is shown in Figures 3 and 4. These figures show a clear dissociation between L.H.'s performance on the visual imagery tasks, which is below normal (Figure 3), and his performance on the

---

[1] Further information about the stimulus materials can be obtained by writing to the first author.

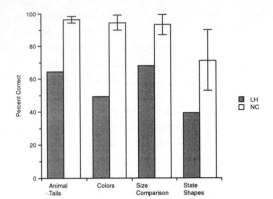

FIGURE 3   Performance of L.H. (gray bars) and normal control subjects (white bars) on four visual imagery tasks. See text for descriptions of tasks. Error bars show one standard deviation above and below the normal subjects' means.

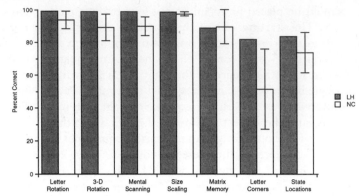

FIGURE 4   Performance of L.H. (gray bars) and normal control subjects (white bars) on seven spatial imagery tasks. See text for descriptions of tasks. Error bars show one standard deviation above and below the normal subjects' means.

spatial imagery tasks, which is normal (Figure 4). We have quantified the extent to which L.H.'s performance may be considered abnormal in each of the imagery tasks by considering all 13 subjects together and asking whether, on each task, L.H. is a statistical outlier.

In the tasks which require specifically visual imagery, L.H. was impaired. On the Colors task, L.H. was correct on only 10 of the 20 items. The average performance of the control subjects was 18.9 out of 20 items correct, with a standard deviation of .9. Considering the 13 subjects together, L.H. is an outlier, with a z-score of –3.14, $p < .001$. On the Size Comparison task, L.H. was correct on 11 out of 16 items. The average performance of the control subjects was 14.9 out of 16, with a standard deviation of 1.0. Again, when all 13 subjects are considered together, L.H. is an outlier, $z = –2.50$, $p < .01$. On the Animal Tails task, L.H. was correct on 13 out of 20 items. The average performance of the normal control subjects was 19.25 out of 20, with a standard deviation of .45. L.H. is an outlier, $z = –3.22$, $p < .001$. On the control task for Animal Tails, judging whether the same animals were native to the subject's home state, L.H. was correct on 20 out of 20, and the average performance of the control subjects was 19.9 out of 20, with a standard deviation of .29. L.H. is not an outlier on this task, $z = +.28$. This supports the claim that L.H.'s

poor performance on the Animal Tails task is due to an inability to visualize the animals, and not a general lack of knowledge about the animals. On the State Shape task, L.H. was correct on 8 out of 20 items. The average performance of the control subjects was 14.4 out of 20, with a standard deviation of 3.65. L.H. is a borderline outlier here, $z = –1.51$, $p < .07$.

In contrast to his low performance on the visual imagery tasks, L.H.'s performance on the spatial imagery tasks is well within the range of the normal subjects' performance. For the image transformation tasks, L.H. performs better than the average normal control subject, although these differences are all nonsignificant. On the Letter Rotation task, L.H. was correct on 20 out of 20 items. The average performance of control subjects was 19 out of 20, with a standard deviation of 1.13. On the Three-Dimensional Form Rotation task, L.H. was correct on 34 out of 34 items. The average performance of control subjects was 30.5 out of 34 with a standard deviation of 2.84. On the Scanning task, L.H. was correct on 32 out of 32 items. The average performance of control subjects was 29 out of 32, with a standard deviation of 1.95. The Size-Scaling task was evidently too easy and produced ceiling effects, which prevent a meaningful comparison of L.H. and the control subjects. However, we can at least conclude that L.H. can perform size scaling, without being able to compare his proficiency to that of normal control subjects. L.H. was correct on 32 out of 32 items. The average performance of control subjects was 31.8 with a standard deviation of .39.

In the tasks requiring imagery for spatial locations, L.H. was again well within the range of normal performance. On the Letter Corner Classification task L.H. was correct on 10 out of 12 items. The average performance of control subjects was 6.25 out of 12 with a standard deviation of 3.0. On the Matrix Path Memory task, L.H. was correct on 18 out of 20 items. The average performance of control subjects was 18.17 with a standard deviation of 2.17. L.H. is not an outlier, $z = -.12$. On the State Location task, L.H. was correct on 17 out of 20 items. The average performance of control subjects was 15 out of 20 with a standard deviation of 2.59.

The only visual and spatial imagery tasks that permit a direct comparison are the state shape and state location tasks, as these two tasks were identical in format and in the general knowledge domain that they tested. For normal subjects, performances on the two tasks were similar: The average normal subject's performance on state locations was 1.23 points higher than his performance on state shapes. In contrast, L.H. showed a spread of 9 points between these two tasks. Applying the same statistical analysis to the spreads between state location performance and state shape performance as was applied to the individual task performances, L.H. is again an outlier: $z = 2.69$, $p < .001$.

DISCUSSION

L.H. shows a profound imagery deficit on certain imagery tasks and yet does well on other imagery tasks. If we divide the imagery tasks into two groups according to whether L.H. can or cannot perform them, the resultant groups are exactly co-extensive with two groups of tasks used by researchers who have maintained that imagery is either spatial or visual, respectively. Furthermore, this coincidence of the two ways of grouping imagery tasks was predicted by neurophysiological considerations of the brain substrates of spatial and visual representation. We first consider some alternative explanations of these results and then discuss the broader implications of the findings for the nature of mental imagery.

Is it possible that the spatial imagery tasks, on which L.H. performs well, are simply easier than the visual imagery tasks? If we had simply compared the absolute performance of L.H. on visual and spatial imagery tasks, this would indeed be a possibility. However, by comparing his performance on each task to that of a group of normal control subjects, the intrinsic difficulty of the tasks does not affect our conclusions. Easier or harder tasks will produce higher or lower levels of performance for both L.H. and the normal control subjects; what we have examined here is the performance of L.H. relative to that of the control subjects.

A related possibility is that ceiling effects in the spatial tasks may have obscured a true difference between the capabilities of L.H. and the normal control subjects. Fortunately, this hypothesis cannot account for the data from the letter corners and state locations tasks. It should also be noted that normal subjects' performance was, if anything, slightly higher in visual tasks, for which a difference between normal subjects' and L.H.'s performance was found.

Another possible source of artifact is that the visual/spatial distinction could be confounded with some other distinction in our tasks, and the other distinction could be the true cause of the dissociation observed here. One candidate for such a confounding factor is the degree to which the two types of imagery tasks require image generation.[2] All of the visual imagery tasks require image generation, compared with only two of the spatial imagery tasks. Furthermore, recent research with brain-damaged patients has shown that the ability to generate images from memory can be lost after posterior left hemisphere damage (Farah, 1984; Farah, Levine, & Calvanio, 1988), a quadrant of the brain in which L.H. sustained damage. In order to argue against this alternative explanation we must delineate the different ways in which imagery ability may be impaired after brain damage, in terms of the components of normal imagery ability, and present evidence regarding the nature of L.H.'s deficit.

---

[2]We thank Lynne Robertson for pointing out this alternative explanation.

Farah (1984) analyzed published neurological case reports of loss of imagery in terms of the theoretical framework of Kosslyn (1980). The ability to form mental images from memory requires two major components of processing: *long-term memories* of the visual and spatial characteristics of the objects and scenes to be imaged, and an *image generation process* by which long-term visual memory information is transformed into the consciously experienced short-term mental image. If a brain-damaged patient were to lose either of these abilities, he or she would lose the ability to use mental imagery. Therefore, in order to distinguish between patients with long-term memory deficits and patients with image generation process deficits, the patients' perceptual visual–spatial abilities were assessed. If a patient has normal perceptual functioning, including normal recognition of visual stimuli and their spatial relations, then the loss of imagery cannot be due to loss of long-term visual–spatial memories. By a process of elimination, the underlying deficit must be in the image generation process. In general, these patients have damage to the left posterior regions of the brain.

The most parsimonious interpretation of imagery deficits in patients with deficits of higher perceptual functioning is that the long-term visual or spatial memories, required for both higher perceptual functioning and mental imagery, have been damaged. If long-term visual memory has been damaged, then the patient will be unable either to recognize objects or to image them. In Farah's (1984) review, several such cases were found, generally with bilateral posterior damage. Further support for the idea that joint deficits in imagery and perception result from damage to shared long-term memory representations comes from cases of content-specific imagery and perceptual deficits. For example, visual agnosias do not always affect visual recognition across the board, but may disproportionately impair the recognition of certain stimulus categories (most commonly faces and animals). In these cases, the imagery deficit parallels the perceptual deficit, just as would be expected if the same malfunctioning component were being used in both cases. Farah (1988) reviews other parallels between perceptual and imagery impairments that imply the existence of shared long-term memories for imagery and perceptual systems.

In the case of L.H., we have two main reasons for believing that the underlying locus of impairment in his mental imagery system is the long-term visual memory rather than the image generation process. First, like the other cases of long-term visual memory deficit identified by Farah (1984), L.H. has an associative visual agnosia. His recognition abilities parallel his poor imagery abilities. As an informal demonstration of this, we measured his performance on perceptual analogs of the visual imagery tasks just described. Each of these tasks was designed to tap the same long-term visual memory knowledge as the visual imagery tasks, without requiring the generation of images. For the Animal Tails task, we had him name line drawings of the animals, drawn by a professional artist. We also presented him with a special set of these drawings in which the tail lengths of half of the animals had been changed and asked him to judge whether each animal had the right or wrong tail. He was able to name 7 out of 20 of the animals, and, when incorrect, tended to be far off: For example, he called an owl "a dog," a tiger "a zebra," and a horse "a lion." He correctly classified 10 out of 20 animal pictures according to whether their tails had been drawn the correct length. For the Color task, we presented him with three differently colored drawings of each of 16 of the 20 items used in the Color task.[3] He chose the correct version, after prolonged scrutiny of each drawing, 13 out of 16 times, erring by selecting the red carrot, the blue ladybug, and a grey tiger. For the Size Comparison task, we had each of the items drawn, for naming, and we also paired the objects for size comparison with the larger item depicted either larger or smaller. On naming, he correctly identified 24 out of 32 of the drawings. The three drawings in Figure 2 were copies of items from this task which he was unable to identify, even after copying them. He correctly classified 11 of the 16 pairs in terms of whether the depicted size relationship was right or wrong. For the State Shapes task, we presented him with outline shapes of the states that had been used in the imagery task for naming. He cor-

---

[3]Four of the original 20 items were accidentally omitted. It is worth noting that he made errors on all 4 of these items in the imagery task, so that their omission would only be likely to improve his performance on the perceptual task.

rectly named 7 out of 39 state outlines. However, some of these outlines were presented multiple times (as they had occurred in multiple triads), and even his correct responses were seen to be inconsistent: For example, he correctly identified all three occurrences of Oklahoma, but also called Colorado "Oklahoma," and he correctly identified Iowa once and once called it "Rhode Island." We did not ask him to judge shape similarity of the outline drawings as this task would not be expected to require long-term visual memory. In sum, L.H. does poorly on the perceptual versions of the visual imagery tasks, as one would expect if his imagery impairment is due to damaged long-term visual memories.

Our second reason for believing that L.H. does not have an image generation deficit is that he does well on the two spatial imagery tasks that require image generation: Matrix Memory and State Locations. In both of these tasks, subjects must generate a mental image based on verbal cues and then "read off" the relative locations of parts of the image, and in both of these tasks L.H. performs normally. We therefore conclude that the dissociation between visual and spatial imagery tasks observed with L.H. is not due to the differential image generation demands of two types of task coupled with an image generation deficit in this patient. Rather, the present data suggest an impairment in the long-term visual memories from which images are generated.

A related alternative explanation of the dissociation is based on amount of *general* long-term memory knowledge demanded in each of the tasks. The visual imagery tasks all draw upon long-term memory knowledge, whereas most of the spatial imagery tasks do not. However, this alternative explanation is inconsistent with several aspects of the present results. First, there is a spatial imagery task whose demands on long-term memory knowledge are as great as the visual imagery tasks, namely, the State Location task. On this task, L.H. did better than the average normal control subject. In contrast, on a visual imagery task with the identical format, namely the State Shape task, L.H. was impaired relative to the normal control subjects. This same dissociation is evident in the clinical assessments of L.H.'s visual and spatial *memory* imagery (Levine et al., 1985): He is able to draw maps and describe the spatial layouts of cities, neighborhoods, and rooms from memory, but is unable to draw or describe the appearances of most objects from memory. Second, on a control task for one of the visual imagery tasks, which tested general long-term memory knowledge of the test items, L.H. was unimpaired: For the same animals whose tail lengths he could not recall, he was able to recall whether they were native to Massachusetts. Third, extensive neuropsychological testing of L.H. has failed to reveal any impairments in retrieving general knowledge or semantic memory, and only mild impairments in the acquisition of new memories. These considerations argue against the possibility that the apparent visual imagery deficit in L.H. is actually a memory deficit. In examining the relation between memory retrieval and visual and spatial imagery tasks it is clear that, in general, the spatial imagery tasks do weight image maintenance and manipulation more than visual imagery tasks, whereas visual imagery tasks weight information retrieval and image generation more than spatial imagery tasks. This is a generalization about the kinds of tasks that typically evoke the use of visual and spatial imagery in cognitive psychology experiments.

In considering alternative explanations of these results, we should also discuss the ways in which the single case study method might limit or distort our conclusions. The use of single cases, rather than groups of subjects, has recently come into favor in cognitive neuropsychology (Caramazza, 1984; Schwartz, 1984; Shallice, 1979). It is argued that if we view brain damage as an "experiment of nature," each subject in any group will have undergone a different "experimental manipulation," and we risk basing our conclusions on average performance profiles which are in a sense artifactual as they do not exist in any one case. In contrast to the cognitive psychology approach of testing a *group* of subjects on *one* task, it is therefore preferable to study *single* cases across a *variety* of converging tasks. This approach is nowhere more called for than in the study of subjects with visual object agnosia, a condition that is both extremely rare and somewhat variable from case to case. The logic of single case study is that, if we can observe a dissociation between two abilities, tested in multiple ways in the same subject, then we can conclude that these two abilities do not rely on the same underlying cognitive system. The sense in which such conclusions are limited, by virtue of coming from a single case study rather than a group study, is that it is logically possible that the single case was anomalous before sustaining brain damage. In the present case, the danger is that L.H. might have an abnormally organized mental imagery system and that other subjects perform both visual and spatial imagery tasks with the same cognitive system. Although this remains a logically correct possibility, it violates a basic assumption of cognitive science, which is that the large-scale architecture of cognition is fixed from one member of the species to another. Even the study of individual differences in cognition is based on the idea that individuals differ in the capacities of specific components of a common cognitive architecture or in their strategic or habitual choice of which components to use for performing a particular task, not that the architecture itself differs from person to person. In the present case, L.H. was for all appearances psychologically and neurologically normal prior to his accident at age 18, and there is therefore no reason to suspect that he has an anomalous cognitive architecture.

In answer to the question "Is mental imagery visual or spatial?" the results of the present study say "both." Each side of the visual versus spatial debate has been correct, in that mental imagery does involve both visual and spatial representations, but each side of the debate has also been wrong, in that imagery is not exclusively visual or exclusively spatial. The fable of the blind men standing around an elephant and trying to describe it seems relevant here: They all disagree, one maintaining that an elephant is a long, dangling, snakelike beast, another saying that an elephant is a stout cylindrical creature planted firmly on the ground like a tree trunk, another saying that elephants are big, floppy, roughly circular sheets of rough skin, and so on. Like the different positions of the blind men next to the elephant, the different sets of experimental tasks used by the two sides of the debate have each revealed only a limited aspect of the imagery system. This initial source of bias has been compounded by a desire for parsimony, leading us to assume that only one type of representation could underlie the range of abilities that we call imagery. However, whereas the difference in parsimony seems large when one considers the imagery system in isolation and asks whether it includes just one type of representation or two, the difference becomes much smaller when one considers the array of representations already known to exist in our cognitive architecture and asks whether the imagery system engages just one of the available representations or two. Neurophysiological evidence suggests that our cognitive architecture includes both representations of the visual appearance of objects in terms of their form, color, and perspective and of the spatial structure of objects in terms of their three-dimensional layout in space. The fact that an impairment of the visual appearance representations due to brain damage affects performance on just the imagery tasks used to argue for visual representation in imagery, and spares performance on the imagery tasks used to argue for spatial representation in imagery, implies that these two groups of tasks tap independent components of imagery representation, shared with visual and spatial perception, respectively.

REFERENCES

Anderson, J. R. (1985). *Cognitive psychology and its implications.* (2nd ed.). New York: Freeman.

Atwood, G. E. (1971). An experimental study of visual imagination and memory. *Cognitive Psychology, 2,* 290–299.

Baddeley, A. D., Grant, S., Wight, E., & Thomson, N. (1975). Imagery and visual working memory. In P. M. A. Rabbitt & S. Domic (Eds.), *Attention and Performance V.* London: Academic Press.

Baddeley, A. D., & Lieberman, K. (1980). Spatial working memory. In *Attention and performance* (Vol. 8). Hillsdale, NJ: Erlbaum.

Bauer, R. M., & Rubens, A. B. (1985). Agnosia. In K. M. Heilman & E. Valenstein (Eds.), *Clinical neuropsychology* (2nd ed.). New York: Oxford University Press.

Beech, J. R. (1984). The effects of visual and spatial interference on spatial working memory. *The Journal of General Psychology, 110,* 141–149.

Brody, B. A., & Pribram, K. H. (1978). The role of frontal and parietal cortex in cognitive processing. *Brain, 101,* 607–633.

Brooks, L. R. (1968). Spatial and verbal components in the act of recall. *Canadian Journal of Psychology, 22,* 349–368.

Byrne, B. (1974). Item concreteness versus spatial organization as predictors of visual imagery. *Memory & Cognition, 2*, 53–59.

Caramazza, A. (1984). The logic of neuropsychological research and the problem of patient classification in aphasia. *Brain and Language, 21*, 9–20.

Carpenter, P. A., & Eisenberg, P. (1978). Mental rotation and the frame of reference in blind and sighted individuals. *Perception & Psychophysics, 23*, 117–124.

Cooper, L. A., & Shepard, R. N. (1973). Chronometric studies of the rotation of mental images. In W. G. Chase (Ed.), *Visual information processing*. New York: Academic Press.

DeRenzi, E. (1982). *Disorders of space exploration and cognition*. New York: Wiley.

Desimone, R., Albright, T. D., Gross, C. G., and Bruce, C. (1984). Stimulus selective properties of inferior temporal neurons in the macaque. *Journal of Neuroscience, 4*, 2051–2062.

Eddy, P., & Glass, A. (1981). Reading and listening to high and low imagery sentences. *Journal of Verbal Learning and Verbal Behavior, 20*, 333–345.

Farah, M. J. (1984). The neurological basis of mental imagery: A componential analysis. *Cognition, 18*, 245–272.

Farah, M. J. (1988). Is visual imagery really visual? Overlooked evidence from neuropsychology. *Psychological Review, 95*, 307–317.

Farah, M. J., Levine, D. N., & Calvanio, R. (1988). A case study of mental imagery deficit. *Brain and Cognition, 8*, 147–164.

Finke, R. A. (1980). Levels of equivalence in imagery and perception. *Psychological Review, 87*, 113–132.

Finke, R. A., & Pinker, S. (1982). Spontaneous imagery scanning in mental extrapolation. *Journal of Experimental Psychology: Learning, Memory, and Cognition, 8*, 142–147.

Finke, R. A., & Schmidt, M. J. (1977). Orientation-specific color aftereffects following imagination. *Journal of Experimental Psychology: Human Perception and Performance, 3*, 599–606.

Finke, R. A., & Schmidt, M. J. (1978). The quantitative measure of pattern representation in images using orientation-specific aftereffects. *Perception & Psychophysics, 23*, 515–520.

Hever, F., Fischman, D., & Reisberg, D. (1986). Why does vivid imagery hurt color memory? *Canadian Journal of Psychology, 40*.

Hinton, G. E. (1979). Imagery without arrays. *Behavioral and Brain Sciences, 2*, 555–556.

Holyoak, K. J. (1977). The forms of analog size information in memory. *Cognitive Psychology, 9*, 31–51 .

Intons-Peterson, M. J. (1987). Unpublished experiment, University of Indiana at Bloomington.

Iwai, E., & Mishkin, M. (1968). Two visual foci in the temporal lobe of monkeys. In Yoshii, N., & Buchwald, N. A. (Eds.), *Neurophysiological Basis of Learning and Behavior*. Osaka, Japan: Osaka University Press.

Janssen, W. H. (1976). Selective interference during the retrieval of visual images. *Quarterly Journal of Experimental Psychology, 28*, 535–539.

Jonides, J., Kahn, R., & Rozin, P. (1975). Imagery instructions improve memory in blind subjects. *Bulletin of the Psychonomic Society, 5*, 424–426.

Keenan, J. M., & Moore, R. G. (1979). Memory for images of concealed objects: A reexamination of Neisser and Kerr. *Journal of Experimental Psychology: Human Learning and Memory, 5*, 374–385.

Kerr, N. H. (1983). The role of vision in visual imagery experiments: Evidence from the congenitally blind. *Journal of Experimental Psychology: General, 112*, 265–277.

Kerr, N. H., & Neisser, U. (1983). Mental images of concealed objects: New evidence. *Journal of Experimental Psychology: Learning, Memory, and Cognition, 9*, 212–221.

Kosslyn, S. M. (1975). Information representation in visual images. *Cognitive Psychology, 7*, 341–370.

Kosslyn, S. M. (1980). *Images and mind*. Cambridge: Harvard University Press.

Kosslyn, S. M. (1983). *Ghosts in the mind's machine*. New York: Norton.

Kosslyn, S. M., Ball, T. M., & Reiser, B. J. (1978). Visual images preserve metric spatial information: Evidence from studies of image scanning. *Journal of Experimental Psychology: Human Perception and Performance, 4*, 47–60.

Kosslyn, S. M., & Jolicoeur, P. (1980). A theory-based approach to the study of individual differences in mental imagery. In R. E. Snow, P. A. Federico, & W. E. Montague (Eds.), *Aptitude, learning, and instruction: Cognitive processes analysis of aptitude*. Hillsdale, NJ: Erlbaum.

Kosslyn, S. M., Murphy, G. L., Bemesderfer, M. E., & Feinstein, K. J. (1977). Category and continuum in mental comparisons. *Journal of Experimental Psychology: General,* **106,** 341–376.

Kosslyn, S. M., Pinker, S., Smith, G. E., & Shwartz, S. P. (1979). On the demystification of mental imagery. *Behavioral and Brain Sciences,* **2,** 535–548.

Lange, J. (1936). Agrosien und Apraxien. In O. Bunke & O. Foerster (Eds.), *Handbuch der Neurologie.* Berlin: Springer.

Larsen, A. (1985). Pattern matching: Effects of size ratio, angular difference in orientation, and familiarity. *Perception & Psychophysics,* **38,** 63–68.

Levine, D., Calvanio, R., & Wolf, E. (1980). Disorders of visual behavior following bilateral posterior cerebral lesions. *Psychological Research,* **41,** 217–234.

Levine, D. N., Warach, J., & Farah, M. J. (1985). Two visual systems in mental imagery: Dissociation of 'What' and 'Where' in imagery disorders due to bilateral posterior cerebral lesions. *Neurology,* **35,** 1010–1018.

Lynch, J. C., Mountcastle, V. B., Talbot, W. H., & Yin, T. C. T. (1977). Parietal lobe mechanisms for directed visual attention. *Journal of Neurophysiology,* **40,** 362–389.

Marmor, C. S., & Zabeck, L. A. (1976). Mental rotation by the blind: Does mental rotation depend on visual imagery? *Journal of Experimental Psychology: Human Perception and Performance,* **2,** 515–521.

Mountcastle, V. B., Andersen, R. A., & Motter, B. C. (1981). The influence of attentive fixation upon the excitability of the light-sensitive neurons of the posterior parietal cortex. *Journal of Neuroscience,* **1,** 1218–1235.

Neisser, U. (1976). *Cognition and reality.* San Francisco: Freeman.

Neisser, U., & Kerr, N. (1973). Spatial and mnemonic properties of visual images. *Cognitive Psychology,* **5,** 138–150.

Newcombe, F., Ratcliff, G., & Damasio, H. (1987). Dissociable visual and spatial impairments following right posterior cerebral lesions: Clinical, neuropsychological and anatomical evidence. *Neuropsychologia,* **25,** 149–161.

Newcombe, F., & Russell, W. R. (1969). Dissociated visual perceptual and spatial deficits in focal lesions of the right hemisphere. *Journal of Neurology, Neurosurgery, and Psychiatry,* **32,** 73–81.

Paivio, A., & Okovita, H. W. (1971). Word imagery modalities and associative learning in blind and sighted subjects. *Journal of Verbal Learning and Verbal Behavior,* **10,** 506–510.

Pinker, S. (1980). Mental imagery and the third dimension. *Journal of Experimental Psychology: General,* **109,** 354–371.

Pinker, S. (1985). Visual cognition: An introduction. In S. Pinker (Ed.), *Visual Cognition.* Cambridge: MIT Press.

Pohl, W. (1973). Dissociation of spatial discrimination deficits following frontal and parietal lesions in monkeys. *Journal of Comparative and Physiological Psychology,* **82,** 227–239.

Potzl, O. (1928). *Die Aphasielehre vom Standpunkte der Kliniscen Psychitrie.* Leipzig: FranzDeudicte.

Pylyshyn, Z. W. (1984). *Computation and cognition.* Cambridge, MA: MIT Press.

Ratcliff, G. (1982). Disturbances of spatial orientation associated with cerebral lesions. In M. Potegal (Ed.), *Spatial abilities: Development and physiological foundations.* New York: Academic Press.

Rizzolatti, G., Gentilucci, M., & Matelli, M. (1985). Selective spatial attention: One center, one circuit, or many circuits? In M. Posner and O. Mann (Eds.), *Attention and performance X.* Hillsdale, NJ: Erlbaum.

Robinson, D. L., Goldberg, M. E., & Stanton, G. B. (1978). Parietal association cortex in the primate: Sensory mechanisms and behavioral modulations. *Journal of Neurophysiology,* **41,** 910–932.

Sakata, H., Shibutani, H., & Kawano, K. (1983). Functional properties of visual tracking neurons in posterior parietal association cortex of the monkey. *Journal of Neurophysiology,* **49,** 1364–1380.

Schwartz, M. F. (1984). What the classical aphasia categories can't do for us, and why. *Brain and Language,* **21,** 3–8.

Segal, S. J., & Fusella, V. (1970). Influences of imaged pictures and sounds on detection of visual and auditory signals. *Journal of Experimental Psychology,* **83,** 458–464.

Shallice, T. (1979). Case study approach in neuropsychological research. *Journal of Clinical Neuropsychology,* **1,** 183–211.

Shepard, R. N., & Chipman, S. (1970). Second-order isomorphism of internal representations: Shapes of states. *Cognitive Psychology,* **1,** 1–17.

Shepard, R. N., & Metzler, J. (1971). Mental rotation of three-dimensional objects. *Science,* **171,** 701–703.

Snodgrass, J. G., & Vanderwart, M. (1986). Norms for pictures. *Journal of Experimental Psychology: Human Learning and Memory,* **6,** 174–215.

Thorndike, P. (1981). Distance estimation from cognitive maps. *Cognitive Psychology, 13,* 526–550.

Ungerleider, L. G., & Mishkin, M. (1982). Two cortical visual systems. In D. J. Ingle, M. A. Goodale, and R. J. W. Mansfield (Eds.), *Analysis of visual behavior.* Cambridge, MA: MIT Press.

Zimler, J., & Keenan, J. M. (1983). Imagery in the congenitally blind: How visual are visual images? *Journal of Experimental Psychology: Learning, Memory, & Cognition, 9,* 269–282.

POSTSCRIPT

Recently a number of studies have employed subjects with certain kinds of brain damage to further our understanding of the nature of visual imagery and its relationship to visual perception (see Kosslyn, 1987, for a general review; Tippett, 1992, reviews the neurophysiological evidence specifically with respect to the generation of mental images). Farah and her colleagues (Farah, Péronnet, Gonon, & Girard, 1988) have used measurements of electrical activity in the brains of nonimpaired subjects to argue that visual images are represented somewhere in the visual system. Other researchers have looked at the manipulation of visual images and the use of visual images as mnemonics by those who are blind (Carpenter & Eisenberg, 1978; Jonides, Kahn, & Rozin, 1975; Kerr, 1983; Marmor & Zaback, 1976). Farah (1988) and Schacter (1992) describe arguments for the usefulness of neuropsychological evidence for testing not just theories of imagery, but cognitive theory in general.

In the article reprinted here, Farah and her associates use a single subject with some special characteristics. Although the value of single-subject or small-*n* (small sample) designs under particular circumstances is generally accepted (Kazdin & Tuma, 1982), there is currently some debate about the range of circumstances for which such studies are suited and the extent to which results from special populations can be generalized to the general population (Caplan, 1988; Caramazza & McCloskey, 1988; McCloskey & Caramazza, 1988; Newcombe & Marshall, 1988).

FOR FURTHER THOUGHT

1. In this article, what is the authors' conclusion about the controversy over whether mental imagery involves visual information or spatial information? What is their evidence?
2. The authors describe an experiment by Baddeley and Lieberman (1980) that tested whether mental images involve spatial or visual information by using an interference paradigm. The idea behind such selective interference experiments is that if mental imagery interferes more, say, with a concurrent nonvisual spatial task than with a concurrent nonspatial

visual task, then it is likely that mental imagery involves spatial rather than visual information. What is the reasoning behind this prediction?

3. What does it mean to say that the two-cortical visual systems are "functionally and anatomically distinct systems of visual representation"? How does that argument fit with the authors' conclusions about mental imagery?

4. We assume that L.H.'s particular pattern of visual abilities is the result of the pattern of brain damage that he suffered. We assume further that L.H.'s particular pattern of imagery abilities stems from the same source. What does this imply about the relationship between visual abilities and imagery abilities?

5. Notice that this study involved only one subject with brain damage. What are the strengths and weaknesses of using only one such subject? Would it have made sense to compare L. H.'s performance to just one other, nonimpaired subject? Why or why not?

REFERENCES

Anderson, J. R. (1978). Arguments concerning representations for mental imagery. *Psychological Review, 85,* 249–277.

Block, N. (Ed.). (1981). *Imagery.* Cambridge, MA: MIT Press.

Caplan, D. (1988). On the role of group studies in neuropsychological and pathopsychological research. *Cognitive Neuropsychology, 5,* 535–547.

Caramazza, A., & McCloskey, M. (1988). The case for single-patient studies. *Cognitive Neuropsychology, 5,* 517–527.

Carpenter, P. A., & Eisenberg, P. (1978). Mental rotation and the frame of reference in blind and sighted individuals. *Perception & Psychophysics, 23,* 117–124.

Einstein, G. O., McDaniel, M. A., & Lackey, S. (1989). Bizarre images, interference, and distinctiveness. *Journal of Experimental Psychology: Learning, Memory, and Cognition, 15,* 137–146.

Farah, M. J. (1988). Is visual imagery really visual? Overlooked evidence from neuropsychology. *Psychological Review, 95,* 307–317.

Farah, M. J., Péronnet, F., Gonon, M. A., & Girard, M. H. (1988). Electrophysiological evidence for a shared representational medium for visual images and visual percepts. *Journal of Experimental Psychology: General, 117,* 248–257.

Finke, R. A. (1985). Theories relating mental imagery to perception. *Psychological Bulletin, 98,* 236–259.

Finke, R. A. (1986). Mental imagery and the visual system. *Scientific American, 254,* 88–95.

Finke, R. A. (1989). *Principle of mental imagery.* Cambridge, MA: MIT Press.

Jonides, J., Kahn, R., & Rozin, P. (1975). Imagery instructions improve memory in blind subjects. *Bulletin of the Psychonomic Society, 5,* 424–426.

Kazdin, A. E., & Tuma, A. H. (Eds.). (1982). *Single-case research designs.* San Francisco: Jossey-Bass.

Kerr, N. H. (1983). The role of vision in "visual imagery" experiments: Evidence from the congenitally blind. *Journal of Experimental Psychology: General, 112,* 265–277.

Kosslyn, S. M. (1980). *Image and mind.* Cambridge, MA: Harvard University Press.

Kosslyn, S. M. (1983). *Ghosts in the mind's machines: Creating and using images in the brain.* New York: Norton.

Kosslyn, S. M. (1987). Seeing and imagining in the cerebral hemispheres: A computational approach. *Psychological Review, 94,* 148–175.

Kosslyn, S. M. (1988). Aspects of a cognitive neuroscience of mental imagery. *Science, 240,* 1621–1626.

Kroll, N. E., Schepler, E. M., & Angin, K. T. (1986). Bizarre imagery: The misremembered mnemonic. *Journal of Experimental Psychology: Learning, Memory, and Cognition, 12,* 42–53.

Marmor, G. S., & Zaback, L. A. (1976). Mental rotation by the blind: Does mental rotation depend on visual imagery? *Journal of Experimental Psychology: Human Perception and Performance, 2,* 515–521.

McCloskey, M., & Caramazza, A. (1988). Theory and methodology in cognitive neuropsychology: A response to our critics. *Cognitive Neuropsychology, 5,* 583–623.

Newcombe, F., & Marshall, J. C. (1988). Idealization meets psychometrics: The case for the right groups and the right individuals. *Cognitive Neuropsychology, 5,* 549–564.

Reisberg, D. (Ed). (1992). *Auditory imagery.* Hillsdale, NJ: Erlbaum.

Rueckl, J. G., Cave, K. R., & Kosslyn, S. M. (1989). Why are "what" and "where" processed by separate cortical visual systems? A computational investigation. *Journal of Cognitive Neuroscience, 1,* 171–186.

Schacter, D. L. (1992). Understanding implicit memory: A cognitive neuroscience approach. *American Psychologist, 47,* 559–569.

Shepard, R. N., & Cooper, L. A. (1982). *Mental images and their transformations.* Cambridge, MA: MIT Press.

Tippett, L. J. (1992). The generation of visual images: A review of neuropsychological research and theory. *Psychological Bulletin, 112,* 415–432.

Tye, M. (1991). *The imagery debate.* Cambridge, MA: MIT Press.

Ungerleider, L. G., & Mishkin, M. (1982). Two-cortical visual systems. In D. J. Ingle, M. A. Goodale, & R. J. W. Mansfield (Eds.), *Analysis of visual behavior.* Cambridge, MA: MIT Press.

Part III

Higher-Order Processing of Knowledge

The three chapters in this part deal with what are often called higher cognitive processes. Because these processes apparently involve the abstract manipulation of internally represented information, we often regard them as characteristic of the intelligence that perhaps distinguishes humans from other animals.

Although the first reading (Reading 20) in Chapter Six (Language and Comprehension) appears at first to deal simply with the special case of bilingualism, it in fact has general implications for lexical representation (the storage of words) and lexical retrieval (the recovery of word meanings). Language is not solely concerned with words, however. Understanding a sentence involves understanding not only the meaning of the individual words but also the role each word plays in the overall structure of the sentence; contrast the phrases "dog bites person" and "person bites dog." Reading 21 examines the processes involved in determining the structure of a sentence. Reading 22 focuses specifically on the factors that contribute to meaningful coherence among sentences. Finally, Reading 23 looks at a case of language breakdown, or aphasia. Through studies such as this, we gain insight not only into the neurophysiological characteristics of language but also into the normal operation of language. A reading on the relationship between language and thought can be found in Part IV (Reading 32).

The articles in Chapter Seven (Reasoning and Judgment) describe psychologists' investigations of the cognitive structures and processes responsible for human reasoning and judgment. Reading 24 reports on studies that require people without special training to do a task that involves formal deductive reasoning. Reading 25 describes a series of studies in which people who have not had special training are asked to make judgments regarding the likelihood of certain outcomes. A theme that runs through both of these articles is that people do not behave as the rules of logic and statistics dictate they should. People generally do behave rationally, however, and these experiments show certain consistent patterns in their behavior.

The two readings in Chapter Eight (Problem Solving) examine different aspects of human problem solving. Reading 26 examines the reasons for the difficulty people have solving problems even when, at some level, they have the knowledge necessary to do so. Reading 27 examines insight and people's intuitions about how they solve problems.

INTRODUCTION

The distinction between concepts and their labels—words—is subtle and sometimes difficult to maintain (see Chapter 5 on concepts). But the usefulness of this distinction is particularly clear when we look at people who speak more than one language and therefore have more than one set of labels for their concepts. These are the people that Malcolm Preston and Wallace Lambert study in "Interlingual Interference in a Bilingual Version of the Stroop Color-Word Task."

Consider the problems posed by having two sets of labels for concepts. On the one hand, the two sets must be kept distinct; people rarely accidentally place a Spanish word in the middle of an English sentence (however, there are systematic conditions under which people will deliberately do so, a phenomenon called code-switching; see Grosjean, 1982). On the other hand, it must be possible to bridge the two sets; people often translate between languages easily, and accidental intrusions do occur sometimes, particularly when a language is not well learned. To reconcile these two requirements, Preston and Lambert explore the possibility that the words that label the same or similar concepts in different languages are somehow (perhaps indirectly) linked, and when a bilingual person uses one language, her or his other language is somehow shut down or inhibited.

Most of the studies in previous readings used relatively straightforward tasks such as recognition or recall to investigate various phenomena. The Stroop procedure that Preston and Lambert used to study interference is somewhat more elaborate. There are many aspects to and variants of the Stroop procedure (see MacLeod, 1991). Basically, the procedure involves measuring how long it takes subjects to name the color of the ink used in various printed stimuli. Preston and Lambert mention three possible kinds of stimuli, although they actually use only the latter two: names of colors (color-words) printed in black, shapes or strings of symbols printed in color, and names of colors printed in incompatible colors (such as the word *RED* printed in blue ink). The main outcome of this procedure is that subjects experience interference in naming the ink color of a word that is the name of a different color.

Preston and Lambert also added two interesting wrinkles to the basic procedure. First, half the time the color-words were in English, and half the time they were in the subject's second language. Second, the subjects were asked to name the color of the ink in English half the time, and in their second language half the time. Because each of the three kinds of stimuli—symbol strings, English color-words, and non-English color-words—was named in two languages, there were six conditions altogether; Preston and Lambert call these conditions "tasks." It's important to keep in mind what the different tasks represent. Tasks 3 and 6 were control conditions, naming the color of the symbol strings in English and the second language. The other four conditions involved the color-words. Tasks 2 and 4 were between- or cross-language conditions (sometimes called interlingual conditions) because the language of the color-word and the language the subject responded in were different. Tasks 1 and 5 were within-language conditions (sometimes called intralingual conditions) because the language of the color word and the response language were the same.

In the two experiments reprinted here, Preston and Lambert dealt specifically with balanced bilinguals—people who are approximately equally proficient in two languages. In the original report, Preston and Lambert conducted a third experiment that looked at nonbalanced bilinguals, but it is not reprinted here. As you read this selection, ask yourself what the relative amounts of interference should be for Tasks 3 and 6, compared to the amounts observed for Tasks 2 and 4 and for Tasks 1 and 5, if use of one language "shuts down" the other. What should be the amounts of interference for Tasks 2 and 4, compared to Tasks 1 and 5?

Interlingual Interference in a Bilingual Version of the Stroop Color-Word Task

Malcolm S. Preston and Wallace E. Lambert

McGill University, Montreal

The fully bilingual person is usually able to function in one of his languages with a minimum of disruptive interference from the other. However, occasional interference suggests that the two language systems may come in contact or overlap in some fashion. The degree to which the two language systems overlap and the points at which the overlap occurs have interested several researchers (Ervin and Osgood, 1954; Lambert, 1962; Kolers, 1963). The present set of experiments examines more closely the functional relations between the bilingual's two languages. The question of interest centers around the following problem: Does the activation of one language system make the other language system inoperative? To explore this problem on a behavioral level, a search was made for a situation that would present the bilingual with a conflict by bringing processes in both language systems into play simultaneously.

A procedure very likely to put two sets of processes (color naming vs. word reading) in competition is the color-word task, first reported in this country by Stroop (1935). In this procedure, S is presented with several cards one at a time and asked to perform three tasks: (1) Card A, reading the names of color-words all printed in black, (2) Card B, naming the colors of patches or blocks of color, and (3) Card C, naming the ink colors of printed color-words. On Card C, for instance, the word *RED* might be printed in blue, green, or brown ink but never in red ink. The time taken to complete each card invariably increases in the above order (Rand, Wapner, Werner, and McFarland, 1963).

The fact that Card C always takes the most time to complete suggests that word reading interferes in some fashion with color naming. For our purposes, the color-word task was modified so that both intralanguage and interlanguage interference could be examined in bilinguals. The basic design of these experiments employed Cards B and C. Two forms of Card C were used, one for each language. Words in corresponding positions on these cards were translations. During the course of the experiment, Ss named the colors of words or shapes on all three cards (Card B and the two forms of Card C) for a total of six tasks. The primary aim of these experiments was to determine to what extent and under what conditions interlingual interference could be produced in this bilingual version of the color-word task. The results were analyzed for both time scores and errors.

The experiments reported here were presented as part of a Ph.D. dissertation (Preston, 1965) submitted to the graduate faculty of McGill University. This research was supported by grants from the Defense Research Board of Canada and the Carnegie Corporation of New York to Wallace E. Lambert. The Center for Advanced Study in the Behavioral Sciences made it possible for us to conduct Exp. III, while the second author was a Fellow in 1964–65, and to have Mr. David Nyberg help in collecting data. The authors are indebted to Howard Blanchette, Gisele Stahlberg, Rosanne Baetz, and Kenneth Williamson for their assistance in gathering the data and to Elizabeth Shannon, Richard Tucker, and Grace Yeni-Komshian for their suggestions and criticisms.

[Malcolm S. Preston is] now at The Johns Hopkins University School of Medicine and The Haskins Laboratories.

SOURCE: *Journal of Verbal Learning and Verbal Behavior, 8,* 1969, pp. 295–301. Copyright © 1969 by Academic Press, Inc. Reprinted by permission.

EXPERIMENT I

Method

Subjects. Experiment I examined the performance of bilinguals who were presumed to be equally skilled in both languages. Eight English-French (E-F) and eight English-Hungarian (E-H) bilinguals served as *Ss*. All were fluent in both languages and reported that their reading abilities were equal in their two languages. Therefore, it was assumed that if a group showed no difference in the time taken to name the colors on Card B in the two languages, then the group as a whole could be considered balanced. The mean difference on these two tasks was 0.5 sec for E-H *Ss* and 1.0 sec for E-F *Ss*; neither comparison differed significantly from zero. All *Ss* responded normally to a standard test for color blindness.

Materials. Three forms of Card C were prepared, one each in English, French, and Hungarian. Each card had ten rows of ten words. The colors and words used on the English card were *red, blue, green,* and *brown.* The French equivalents were *rouge, bleu, vert,* and *brun;* the Hungarian equivalents were *piros, kék, zöld,* and *barna.* Each word and color appeared 25 times on each card in a random arrangement except that no word or color ever appeared twice in succession. Three forms of Card B were prepared. On these cards an asterisk of the appropriate color was entered for each letter of the corresponding Card C.

Design and Procedure. Each *S* performed the following six tasks: (1) Named the colors of English color-words in English, (2) named the colors of French or Hungarian color-words in English, (3) named the colors of asterisks in English, (4) named the colors of English color-words in French or Hungarian, (5) named the colors of French or Hungarian color-words in French or Hungarian, (6) named the colors of asterisks in French or Hungarian. Each *S* worked through a different random order of these six tasks; however, all *Ss* worked with the asterisk cards before going on to the color-word cards. The *Ss* were instructed to correct any mistakes and to avoid squinting, looking out of the corner of the eye, or pointing a finger while performing each task.

Results and Discussion

Time Scores. The time scores were taken directly from tape recordings made of each session. Mean time scores on the six tasks for both groups were calculated and are presented in Table l. Since comparisons between almost all the means for each group are of interest, a one-way analysis of variance model with repeated measures was chosen (Winer, 1962, p. 111). In this model the six means in each group are treated as one dimension (Tasks). For both groups, the Task effect was significant, $F(5, 35) = 24.43$, $p < .01$ for E-H *Ss* and $F(5, 35) = 34.99$, $p < .01$ for E-F *Ss*. Following the analyses of variance, the Newman-Keuls multiple comparison procedure for the .05 level of significance was applied (Winer, 1962, p. 114).

The following points summarize the results of the Newman-Keuls test for E-H *Ss*. (a) There was no difference between the two languages in time to name

TABLE 1   Mean Time Scores (Sec) for E-H And E-F Bilinguals on the Six Numbered Tasks

	English-Hungarian Bilinguals (N= 8)			English-French Bilinguals (N= 8)		
	English Color-Words	Hungarian Color-Words	Asterisks	English Color-Words	French Color-Words	Asterisks
English Response	1 111.5	2 103.9	3 76.6	l 99.2	2 94.2	3 67.5
Hungarian or French Response	4 98.3	5 113.1	6 77.1	4 102.2	5 100.1	6 68.5

the colors on the asterisk cards (Tasks 3 and 6). (b) The usual intralanguage interference in color naming with words as the color-bearing stimuli occurred; that is, significant differences were obtained between Tasks 1 and 3, and Tasks 5 and 6. In addition, there was strong evidence that interference occurred even when response and interfering languages were different (significant differences between Tasks 2 and 3, and Tasks 4 and 6). (c) In general there was less interference when response and interfering languages were different compared to the case when they were the same. Thus, the means for Tasks 2 and 4 were both lower than the means for Tasks 1 and 5. The Newman-Keuls procedure indicated that Tasks 1 and 4, and Tasks 4 and 5 differed significantly. The differences between Tasks 1 and 2, and 2 and 5 were very close to significance. Also, Task 2 did not differ significantly from Task 4.

For E-F *Ss* the multiple comparison test revealed: (a) There was no significant difference between the two asterisk cards (Tasks 3 and 6). (b) Tasks 1 and 2 differed from Task 3, and Tasks 4 and 5 differed from Task 6. (c) In contrast to the E-H *Ss*, no significant differences between Tasks 1, 2, 4, and 5 were found.

Errors. In the error analysis, the complete testing session for each S was transcribed and all utterances other than correct responses were examined. Of particular interest were the errors found on Tasks 1, 2, 4, and 5. In general, the most frequent kind of error in both groups were hesitations such as "uh" or "um." On Tasks 2 and 4, the cross-language conditions, the second most frequent error consisted of the translation of the printed word. For example, during Task 2, if the word was *brun* printed in red ink, a translation error would occur if an E-F S said "brown." For Tasks 1 and 5, the second most frequent error consisted of reading the printed word instead of naming its color. The least frequent kinds of errors consisted of color-words that were neither translation nor reading errors, repeating a correct response or making a comment. With the exception of "uh" and "um," all errors occurred in the correct response language.

The results make it clear that for balanced bilinguals, interference in color naming occurs even when the response language differs from the language of the color-words. On the other hand, only E-H Ss showed a tendency for word reading to cause less interference in color naming in the cross-language conditions. The error data suggest that one possible way word reading may interfere with color naming in the cross-language conditions is via a translation process. Following this reasoning, one difference between E-H and E-F Ss that might account for their different patterns of time scores is that three of the four French translations of the English color-words had similar stimulus characteristics (*bleu-blue, rouge-red,* and *brun-brown*) while three of the four Hungarian translations had different stimulus characteristics (*kék-blue, zöld-green,* and *piros-red*). Interference in color naming on Tasks 2 and 4 may be less when the color-words employed have translations with different stimulus characteristics. Experiment II examined this possibility.

EXPERIMENT II

Method

Subjects. Sixteen English-German bilinguals with normal color vision served as Ss. All used German at home and English at McGill University where they were studying as undergraduates.

Materials. Two sets of C Cards were prepared following the method and restrictions employed in Exp. I. In Set 1 the English color-words were *green, red, blue,* and *brown*; the German color-words were *grün, rot, blau,* and *braun.* In Set 2 the color-words were *black, yellow, pink,* and *purple* in English and *schwarz, gelb, rosa,* and *lila* in German. Translated equivalents look and sound more similar in Set 1 than Set 2. Wavy lines were used in preparing the B Cards.

Design and Procedure. The 16 Ss were divided equally into two groups. Group 1 was tested with Set 1 cards, Group 2 was given Set 2 cards. Each S performed the six tasks described in the first experiment with the exception that German was substituted for French or Hungarian.

TABLE 2   Mean Time Scores (Sec) for Groups 1 And 2 on the Six Numbered Tasks

| | Group 1 (N = 8) | | | Group 2 (N = 8) | | |
	English Color-Words	German Color-Words	Wavy Lines	English Color-Words	German Color-Words	Wavy Lines
English Response	1 100.8	2 101.6	3 65.5	1 94.8	2 82.3	3 67.6
German Response	4 105.2	5 99.7	6 66.6	4 85.6	5 93.9	6 66.0

Results and Discussion

Time Scores.   The mean time scores for both groups on the six tasks are presented in Table 2. On the B Cards, all of the Ss in both groups had time scores for responding in English and German that were lower than any of the time scores for the other four tasks on the C Cards, suggesting as in the first experiment that interference in color naming takes place even when response and interfering languages are different. Furthermore, on the B Cards, there were no differences between English and German responses for either group. Thus the two groups as a whole could be considered balanced on color naming. Since the differences between the B Cards and the C Cards were so marked, a three-way analysis of variance (Winer, 1962, p. 319) was carried out for the C Cards alone. The three main variables were Groups, word language, and response language. The only significant effects found were for the triple interaction, $F(1, 14) = 23.67$, $p < .01$, and the Word Language × Response Language interaction, $F(1, 14) = 6.81$, $p < .05$. To explore these interactions, the Newman-Keuls procedure for the .05 level was applied to the four means of each group separately.

The following points summarize the results of the multiple-comparison tests for both groups. (a) In Group 1, Tasks 1, 2, 4, and 5 did not differ from each other, which suggests that the amount of interference experienced by this group is the same under the four conditions. (b) In Group 2, interference tended to be less when response and interfering languages were different; that is, Tasks 2 and 4 showed lower time scores than Tasks 1 and 5. The Newman-Keuls procedure indicated that Tasks 1 and 2, and Tasks 2 and 5 differed significantly. Differences between Tasks 1 and 4, and Tasks 4 and 5 were close to significance. The difference between Tasks 2 and 4 was not significant.

Errors.   The results of the error analysis are consistent with the findings for time scores. Significantly fewer translation errors on the average occurred on Tasks 2 and 4 combined for Group 2 compared with Group 1, $t(14) = 2.16$, $p < .05$. For reading errors combined on Tasks 1 and 5, the means of the two groups did not differ significantly. As in Exp. I, no particular pattern emerged for the other types of errors.

The results of both experiments clearly demonstrate that balanced bilinguals suffer interlingual interference in the bilingual version of the Stroop color-word task. The fact that translations of the printed word are a frequent type of error suggests that the interference in the cross-language condition results, in part, from a tendency to translate and pronounce the printed word. The time-score and error data of Exp. II suggest that the tendency to translate is slightly less when the translations of the color-words have different stimulus characteristics. . . .

The results of these . . . studies clearly suggest that in comparisons between any two tasks in the bilingual version of the Stroop color-word task, at least three factors may operate. In some comparisons, these factors may work in the same direction and in others they may work in opposition. Of the two factors related to bilingual dominance [examined in an experiment not reprinted here], encoding efficiency is apparently more important than decoding efficiency for the *Ss* tested. A third factor depends on the similarity of the stimulus characteristics of the translated equivalents. Interlingual interference still occurs, however, when the stimulus characteristics of the translated equivalents are different. It seems, then, at least as far as the color-word task is concerned, that activation of a set of processes in one language does not make the other language system totally inoperative.

REFERENCES

Ervin, S. M., & Osgood, C. E. Second language learning and bilingualism. *J. abnorm. soc. Psychol. Suppl.,* 1954, **49**, 139–146.

Kolers, P. Interlingual word associations. *J. Verb. Learn. verb. Behav.,* 1963, 2, 291–300.

Lambert, W. E. Behavioral evidence for contrasting forms of bilingualism. Paper read at Georgetown University Symposium, Washington, D.C., 1962.

Rand, G., Wapner, S., Werner, H., & McFarland, J. H. Age differences in performance on the Stroop color-word test. *J. Pers.,* 1963, **31**, 534–558.

Stroop, J. R. Studies of interference in serial verbal reactions. *J. exp. Psychol.,* 1935, **18**, 643–661.

Winer, B. J. *Statistical principles in experimental design.* New York: McGraw-Hill, 1962.

POSTSCRIPT

In Experiment 2, Preston and Lambert suggest that the cause of the similarity effect—greater interference for color-words like *green* and *grün* than for *black* and *schwarz*—is an increased tendency to translate similar over unsimilar words. However, Dyer (1971) found that English speakers who had no knowledge of German showed the same similarity effect (crucially, however, the overall level of interference was very low). This suggests that it is not the tendency to translate per se that causes the increased interference, but rather the tendency for a foreign word to activate the corresponding English word if the two are similar in sound or appearance.

Two hypotheses about lexical organization in bilinguals have been supported by subsequent work, both using the Stroop procedure (Chen & Ho, 1986; Mägiste, 1984, 1985; Tzelgov, Henik, & Leiser, 1990; see MacLeod, 1991, for review) and other tasks (such as intra- and interlingual priming; Chen & Ng, 1989; Kirsner, Smith, Lockhart, & King, 1984). The word-association hypothesis (Potter, So, von Eckardt, & Feldman, 1984) suggests that words in a second language are directly linked to and understood in terms of their corresponding forms in the first language. The concept-mediation hypothesis suggests that words in the two languages are not directly linked to one another but instead are each directly linked to abstract conceptual representations (which can also be accessed with pictures; Potter et al., 1984). Some evidence suggests that the word-association hypothesis may more accurately describe the early stages of second language acquisition, whereas the concept-mediation hypothesis better describes later stages (see Chen & Ho, 1986; Chen & Leung, 1989; Tzelgov, Henik, & Leiser, 1990). This suggests that proficiency in the two languages is perhaps more important than stimulus characteristics are in determining the pattern of inter- and intralingual interference found with the Stroop task (Mägiste, 1984, 1985). However, not all researchers have found a proficiency effect (see Potter, So, von Eckardt, & Feldman, 1984).

Some researchers (such as Mägiste, 1985) have suggested that because the interlingual condition of the Stroop task requires the simultaneous use of two languages, it is limited in its applicability. Although it can probe for degree of association between languages, it cannot be used to test the idea that using one language typically causes the other to shut down, as Preston and Lambert originally intended. Furthermore, it is somewhat difficult to interpret any study that uses the Stroop procedure to probe some other cognitive phenomenon, because we are not terribly sure at exactly which point or points in our processing the observed Stroop interference occurs. Although some psychologists have suggested that the interference occurs in recognizing the ink color, most have argued that the interference occurs in selecting the proper response (MacLeod, 1991). One version of the selection-interference account suggests that interference occurs because people are faster at reading a word than at naming a color. A second suggests that interference occurs because reading a word is automatic: it requires very little attention and people find it difficult to avoid (see Reading 4 for a discussion of automaticity).

The retrieval of word meanings also appears to be automatic. Research on the processing of ambiguous words (for example, *bank*) suggests that people automatically retrieve multiple meanings for ambiguous words, although multiple meanings may be available only very briefly (for less than a second) and people may not be consciously aware of them (Swinney, 1979; Onifer & Swinney, 1981). The commonly (but not universally) accepted conclusion is that even a strongly biasing prior context does not constrain retrieval (see Forster, 1990, and various readings in Small, Cottrell, & Tanenhaus, 1988, and particularly Prather & Swinney, 1988, for reviews). Thus, even in the sentence "The James-Younger Gang rode to Northfield to rob the bank," both "financial institution" and "side of a river" meanings are retrieved for *bank*. Some psychologists have recently examined the effects, if any, that different kinds of context can have on lexical retrieval (for example, syntactic structure, as opposed to overall meaning; see Tabossi, 1988; Tanenhaus & Lucas, 1987). Others have explored the possibility that context affects the degree to which particular meanings are activated, so that even if all meanings are retrieved, they are not activated to an equivalent extent (Paul, Kellas, Martin, & Clark, 1992).

The rapidity with which lexical retrieval occurs and the fact that it operates autonomously, unaffected by other knowledge we consciously may have at the time, suggests that lexical retrieval may be achieved through the operation of what is called a cognitive module (Fodor, 1983; Tanenhaus & Lucas,

1987). Modularity theory asserts that in addition to general-purpose components such as memory, the mind consists of special-purpose components that operate quickly, automatically, and in isolation from one another. Other possible cognitive modules include those processes responsible for speech perception, those responsible for figuring out the grammatical structure (syntax) of a sentence (see Reading 21), and some of the initial stages of visual perception. Modularity is an extremely influential idea in modern cognitive psychology, but many particulars remain to be worked out (see Fodor, 1983, 1985—the latter is followed by extensive commentary by others in the field—and various readings in Garfield, 1987, particularly Tanenhaus, Dell, & Carlson, 1987, who try to reconcile modularity and connectionism in the context of lexical processing, and Marslen-Wilson & Tyler, 1987, who argue against a modularity interpretation).

FOR FURTHER THOUGHT

1. Suppose we carried out the Preston and Lambert experiments with a new set of balanced bilinguals. Give a possible interpretation for each of the following pattern of results: (a) fastest reading times on Tasks 3 and 6, faster reading times on Tasks 2 and 4 compared to Tasks 1 and 5 (fastest on the control conditions, faster on the between-language conditions than on the within-language conditions); (b) equal reading times on Tasks 3 and 6 as on Tasks 2 and 4, both being faster than Tasks 1 and 5 (equal on control and between-language conditions, slowest on within-language condition); (c) fastest reading times on Tasks 3 and 6, equal reading times on Tasks 1 and 5 and on Tasks 2 and 4 (fastest on the control conditions, equal on the within- and between-language conditions).

2. Which particular results obtained by Preston and Lambert led them to suggest the translation hypothesis, and what does the translation hypothesis propose? Does it provide an explanation for all of Preston and Lambert's results? If so, explain how it deals with each major result. If not, specify which results are not addressed by or are inconsistent with the translation hypothesis, and explain the problem(s).

3. Why do Preston and Lambert conclude that using one language does not shut down the other? Why does Mägiste argue that the Stroop task cannot test that claim?

4. As mentioned in the postscript, Dyer (1971) used monolingual subjects and found the same similarity effect reported by Preston and Dyer. Why is this finding problematic for the translation hypothesis? The postscript states that "crucially, however, the overall level of interference was very low." Why was it crucial that Dyer find that monolinguals showed very low interlingual interference overall?

REFERENCES

Chen, H.-C., & Ho, C. (1986). Development of Stroop interference in Chinese-English bilinguals. *Journal of Experimental Psychology: Learning, Memory, and Cognition, 12,* 397–401.

Chen, H.-C., & Leung, Y. S. (1989). Patterns of lexical processing in non-native language. *Journal of Experimental Psychology: Learning, Memory, and Cognition, 15,* 316–325.

Chen, H.-C., & Ng, M. -L. (1989). Semantic facilitation and translation priming effects in Chinese-English bilinguals. *Memory & Cognition, 17,* 454–462.

Dyer, F. N. (1971). Color-naming interference in monolinguals and bilinguals. *Journal of Verbal Learning and Verbal Behavior, 10,* 297–302.

Fodor, J. A. (1983). *The modularity of mind.* Cambridge, MA: MIT Press.

Fodor, J. A. (1985). Précis of *The modularity of mind. Behavioral and Brain Sciences, 8,* 1–42.

Forster, K. I. (1990). Lexical processing. In D. N. Osherson & H. Lasnik (Eds.), *An invitation to cognitive science: Vol. 1. Language* (pp. 95–131). Cambridge, MA: MIT Press.

Garfield, J. (Ed.). (1987). *Modularity in knowledge representation and natural-language understanding.* Cambridge, MA: MIT Press.

Grosjean, F. (1982). *Life with two languages: An introduction to bilingualism.* Cambridge, MA: Harvard University Press.

Kirsner, K., Smith, M. C., Lockhart, R. S., & King, M. L. (1984). The bilingual lexicon: Language-specific units in an integrated network. *Journal of Verbal Learning and Verbal Behavior, 23,* 519–539.

MacLeod, C. M. (1991). Half a century of research on the Stroop effect: An integrative review. *Psychological Bulletin, 109,* 163–203.

Mägiste, E. (1984). Stroop tasks and dichotic translation: The development of interference patterns in bilinguals. *Journal of Experimental Psychology: Learning, Memory, and Cognition, 10,* 304–315.

Mägiste, E. (1985). Development of intra- and interlingual interference in bilinguals. *Journal of Psycholinguistic Research, 14,* 137–154.

Marslen-Wilson, W., & Tyler, L. K. (1987). Against modularity. In J. Garfield (Ed.), *Modularity in knowledge representation and natural-language understanding* (pp. 37–62). Cambridge, MA: MIT Press.

Onifer, W., & Swinney, D. A. (1981). Accessing lexical ambiguities during sentence comprehension: Effects of frequency of meaning and contextual bias. *Memory & Cognition, 9,* 225–236.

Paul, S. T., Kellas, L., Martin, M., & Clark, M. B. (1992). Influence of contextual features on the activation of ambiguous word meanings. *Journal of Experimental Psychology: Learning, Memory, and Cognition, 18,* 703–717.

Potter, M. C., So, K.-F., von Eckardt, B., & Feldman, L. B. (1984). Lexical and conceptual representation in beginning and proficient bilinguals. *Journal of Verbal Learning and Verbal Behavior, 23,* 23–38.

Prather, P. A., & Swinney, D. A. (1988). Lexical processing and ambiguity resolution: An autonomous process in an interactive box. In S. I. Small, G. W. Cottrell, & M. K. Tanenhaus (Eds.), *Lexical ambiguity resolution: Perspectives from psycholinguistics, neuropsychology, & artificial intelligence* (pp. 289–310). San Mateo, CA: Morgan Kaufmann.

Small, S. I., Cottrell, G. W., & Tanenhaus, M. K. (Eds.). (1988). *Lexical ambiguity resolution: Perspectives from psycholinguistics, neuropsychology, & artificial intelligence.* San Mateo. CA: Morgan Kaufmann.

Swinney, D. A. (1979). Lexical access during sentence comprehension: (Re)consideration of context effects. *Journal of Verbal Learning and Verbal Behavior, 18,* 645–659.

Tabossi, P. (1988). Sentential context and lexical access. In S. I. Small, G. W. Cottrell, & M. K. Tanenhaus (Eds.), *Lexical ambiguity resolution: Perspectives from psycholinguistics, neuropsychology, & artificial intelligence* (pp. 331–342). San Mateo, CA: Morgan Kaufmann.

Tanenhaus, M. K., Dell, G. S., & Carlson, G. (1987). Context effects in lexical processing: A connectionist approach to modularity. In J. Garfield (Ed.), *Modularity in knowledge representation and natural-language understanding* (pp. 83–108). Cambridge, MA: MIT Press.

Tanenhaus, M. K., & Lucas, M. M. (1987). Context effects in lexical processing. *Cognition, 25,* 213–234.

Tzelgov, J., Henik, A., & Leiser, D. (1990). Controlling Stroop interference: Evidence from a bilingual task. *Journal of Experimental Psychology: Learning, Memory, and Cognition, 16,* 760–771.

INTRODUCTION

To understand most sentences, we must determine not only what the individual words or phrases in the sentence mean but also the syntax, or structure, of the sentence. Furthermore, our final interpretation of a sentence reflects the integration of lexical (word-level) meaning, syntactic structure, and pragmatic knowledge (roughly, knowledge about the world). But does this integration of different kinds of information take place from the very start of the sentence comprehension process or only after the individual kinds of information have all been made available? Perhaps the syntactic processor (sometimes called the parser) yields an initial parse, or structural description, of the sentence that does not take other kinds of information into account. That initial description may be integrated with lexical (word meaning) and pragmatic knowledge only during subsequent processing. If so, does the syntactic processor initially generate all, or at least many, possible parsings of the sentence or just one? These are questions addressed by Keith Rayner, Marcia Carlson, and Lyn Frazier in "The Interaction of Syntax and Semantics during Sentence Processing: Eye Movements in the Analysis of Semantically Biased Sentences."

Consider the structure of the sentence "The student passed the note." As do all active sentences, this sentence consists of a noun phrase (NP) followed by a verb (V) followed by another NP. Together, the V and the second NP make up the verb phrase (VP) *passed the note.* Because active sentences are so common and are structurally very simple, it might be efficient for a syntactic parser to adopt a strategy that says: "As soon as you find an NP-V-NP sequence, parse it as a simple active in which the first NP is the subject and the second (postverbal) NP is the object." (In the study of syntax, sequences of words or phrases are often called strings. Grammatical sequences or sentences are sometimes described as being well-formed strings.)

This is basically the approach described by the minimal attachment principle, which suggests that people are biased toward parsing a sentence into the simplest structure possible. Ironically, much of the complexity of this principle lies in defining what it means for a structure to be simple. For our purposes, we consider an active sentence the simplest structure possible; therefore the parser is biased toward analyzing NP-V-NP sequences as active sentences. The minimal attachment principle also argues that people generate only one (initial) parse of the sentence, and that parse does not integrate different kinds of information.

Unfortunately, an NP-V-NP sequence might be not a complete active sentence at all but just the start of a more complex sentence. Consider the sentence "The student passed the note read it quickly." This is a reduced (or shortened) form of the sentence "The student who was passed the note read it quickly." Our simple strategy doesn't apply to the reduced form because the sequence is now NP-*who was*-V-NP; the sentence contains the relative clause "who was passed the note," for which the first NP (the student) is actually the indirect object. However, in the reduced form the relative pronoun *who* and the verb element *was* are missing: a V-NP sequence immediately follows the first NP, which triggers the simple strategy. This leads to the erroneous structural description of the NP-V-NP sequence as an active sentence rather than as a reduced relative (the colorful phrase used in these cases is that the parser is "led down the garden path").

One way to prevent the syntactic processor from being "garden-pathed" would be to have it consider and generate many possible structures simultaneously, rather than being biased toward any particular one. As long as one of the alternatives is the actual structure of the string, the parser will never be garden-pathed. But that strategy would probably often cause a lot of extra processing.

Another approach that would reduce but not eliminate garden-pathing would be to combine syntactic information with semantic, thematic, or pragmatic information to begin with. Part of what we know about a verb is what can be called its thematic structure. For example, we expect that a grammatical sentence with the verb *passed* in it will have a direct object—the thing passed—and may have an indirect object as recipient, and/or a subject—the passer. We also have some pragmatic knowledge, related to the verb *passed*, about what sorts of things in the world are likely to be passed, are likely to be passed to, or are likely to do the passing. Although integrating such knowledge with the structural information available in generating the initial parse would not prevent garden-pathing in our note-passing example—students are likely both to pass notes and to receive notes—it may be useful with other sentences. For example, Rayner, Carlson, and Frazier point out that most people believe that performers are more likely in general to receive flowers than to send them. Having the syntactic parser take such knowledge into account may increase the likelihood of parsing "The performer sent the flowers" as a reduced form of "The performer who was sent the flowers," thus reducing the likelihood of being garden-pathed.

To determine whether and at what point people are garden-pathed, Rayner and his associates examined people's eye movements while reading particular sentences. The sentences were presented on a computer screen with the brightness (luminance) adjusted to a comfortable level for each subject. Because the instrument used to track people's eyes was extremely sensitive (it had a resolution of 10 minutes of arc, which means its measurements were accurate down to 10/60 of one degree of rotation of the eye), subjects used their teeth to hold on to a mounted bite bar to keep their heads still. (Incidentally, the visual angle referred to in the article is a measurement of field of vision; 360° of visual angle would be a complete circle around one's head.) Although subjects read with both eyes open, only one eye was tracked.

If you watch someone's eyes while she or he reads a sentence, you find that they do not move smoothly over individual letters or words. Instead, the eyes will focus (or fixate) on one part of the sentence for a fraction of a second and then move with a jerk over several words to the next fixation point. Although we can be sure that people will fixate several times in a sentence of any appreciable length, we cannot guarantee that everyone will fixate at exactly the same points. So, in analyzing their results, Rayner and his associates discuss the serial order of the fixations—first, second, third, and so on—rather than specific fixation locations. In this method, lengthened fixations and movements back to earlier parts of the sentence (regressive movements) are regarded as indications of garden-pathing. To determine how subjects ultimately interpreted the sentences, the researchers occasionally asked subjects to paraphrase the sentences in their own words.

The original article also included a brief discussion on regressions and appendixes listing all of the stimuli, but these are not reprinted here. As you read this article, ask yourself what characteristics you would give a sentence processor that you were building to make it as efficient as possible. What considerations enter into an evaluation of a sentence processor as efficient?

The Interaction of Syntax and Semantics during Sentence Processing: Eye Movements in the Analysis of Semantically Biased Sentences

Keith Rayner, Marcia Carlson, and Lyn Frazier

University of Massachusetts

One major concern of recent psycholinguistic investigation is whether syntactic and semantic information contribute independently to sentence understanding or whether they interact in the comprehension process. Some investigators (Forster & Ryder, 1972; Forster & Olbrei, 1973; Forster, 1979) have argued that syntactic processing is autonomous and is not affected by semantic information available from higher level semantic processing operations. According to Forster's (1979) model, the autonomy of syntactic processing is attributed to the basic organization of the processing system. This organization reflects the structure of the grammar in which the rules which characterize the well-formed strings of the language are organized into distinct rule systems. The autonomy constraint is a direct result of the separation of the syntactic and semantic components of the processing system and absolute restrictions on communication between distinct components of that system. For example, the semantic or message-level processor may not provide any feedback to the lower level lexical or syntactic processors concerning the semantic analysis that is being considered; it has access only to the output of these lower level processors and may not otherwise interact with them.

A view that is conceptually opposed to an autonomous syntactic processor is taken by Marslen-Wilson (1975), who proposed an unstructured, fully interactive model of comprehension. In such a model all different categories of information interact in an ongoing fashion to constrain the processing of a sentence. Numerous studies have demonstrated the effects of context on the immediate processing of linguistic material (e.g., Marslen-Wilson & Welsh, 1978; Marslen-Wilson & Taylor, 1980; Ehrlich & Rayner, 1981). However, as Forster (1979) pointed out, demonstrating that contextual constraints facilitate the comprehension of material does *not* indicate what stage of comprehension has been facilitated.

The central issue in the debate between autonomy and interaction in processing is not whether all the relevant types of information can be exploited at some point in the comprehension of a linguistically conveyed message. Rather, it concerns how the distinct types of information are utilized. Of particular interest are the constraints, both inherent and arising from efficiency considerations, on the processor's use of information, and what these constraints tell us about the structure of the language processing system and about the mental representation and use of grammatical and world knowledge.

Given the constraints on immediate memory capacity, it seems reasonable to assume that there is a pressure for items occurring early in the linear sequence of a message to be structured quickly, pre-

This work represents a totally collaborate arrangement and the order of authors is arbitrary. The research was supported by Grant BNS79-17600 from the National Science Foundation. We thank Patrick Carroll, David Balota, Marcel Just, and two anonymous reviewers for their helpful comments. We are especially grateful to Chuck Clifton for his help throughout this project. Requests for reprints should be addressed to Keith Rayner, Department of Psychology, University of Massachusetts, Amherst, Mass. 01003.

SOURCE: *Journal of Verbal Learning and Verbal Behavior, 22,* 1983, pp. 358–374. Copyright © 1983 by Academic Press, Inc. Reprinted by permission.

sumably at all levels of linguistic structure—phonological, lexical, syntactic, and semantic. This pressure would seem to require some integration across different levels of linguistic structure before a complete representation of the entire input sequence could be computed within any one level of structure. If assignment of structure within each level occurred as the words of a sentence were encountered but without integration between the different levels of structure, much needless processing effort would be expended. Integration across different levels of linguistic structure might eliminate or drastically reduce the need for multiple representations and/or reduce the extent to which the garden-path phenomenon occurs.

Early integration of real world knowledge might be helpful because people use natural language to communicate information about the world and some real world situations are more likely to occur than others. Thus, there are probabilistic correlations between the real world properties of the referents of phrases and the linguistic relations of those phrases. The indirect object of a dative verb is most *likely* to be an animate object. The agents of verbs in particular semantic classes are likely to share certain real world properties. This sort of probabilistic correlation is certainly not contained in the grammar; yet it is potentially helpful information that might be exploited before all grammatical processing of an input has been completed. Thus, there are potential computational savings to be derived from early integration across levels of structure and early use of real world information; the actual computational savings will depend on the processing cost of integration unless the integration must, in any case, occur at some point during the analysis of the sentence.

The grammar provides some hints about what processing decisions would not be facilitated by early integration across different levels of structure. For example, to know that the first word of a sentence begins with "p" is not relevant to a decision about the syntactic structure of the sentence; it does not directly bear on the question of whether the word is a noun or a verb or whether the sentence is an imperative or a declarative. Examples like this suggest that a processing system which organizes itself into subsystems reflecting the nature of the information that it processes would very likely exhibit a certain amount of

autonomy due to basic constraints on that information. A subsystem concerned with the syntactic structure of a sentence would simply expend needless effort trying to determine the segmental composition of words and morphemes.

The potential advantages of early integration of information types in certain instances and the lack of computational advantages in others suggests that hypotheses falling somewhere in between completely autonomous models and completely interactive models of comprehension should be explored. The two experiments reported here explore intermediate positions between extreme autonomy and extreme interaction. The first experiment demonstrates the independence of the initial structural analysis of sentences from a certain type of pragmatic constraint. The second explores the effect of lexical, semantic, and pragmatic preferences on the ultimate structural analysis of ambiguous sentences.[1] When the results of the experiments are considered together, they support a model in which independent mechanisms are responsible for structural parsing preferences on the one hand, and lexical, semantic, and pragmatic preferences on the other.

EXPERIMENT 1

There are numerous intermediate positions on the interaction of syntactic and semantic information intervening between the two extremes defined by rigid autonomy and complete interaction. Frazier (1978) argued for a Weak Semantic Principle which specifies that the processor's initial syntactic decisions are immediately checked to make sure that they lead to a semantically coherent analysis of the sentence. A

---

[1]We will use "pragmatic information" to refer to knowledge of the real world properties of objects and events and the likely or expected relations between them. We reserve the term "semantic information" for referring to readers' linguistic knowledge of the meaning of the expressions of their language. In the absence of a specific detailed theory of the semantics of a language, it is impossible to draw a sharp distinction between semantic and pragmatic information. This may lead to some confusion, especially in terms of the biasing information for the sentences in Experiment 2. In fact, we do not intend to make any claim about the exact nature of the biases in these sentences. Most likely, these biases implicate both semantic and pragmatic information.

syntactic decision which would give rise to a local anomaly is rejected; in such circumstances, the processor is claimed to immediately search for some alternative analysis which would not result in semantic anomaly. Crain and Coker (Note 1) correctly observed that Frazier's evidence for the Weak Semantic Principle would not distinguish this principle from one which specified that semantic or pragmatic plausibility—not semantic anomaly—constrains the processor's initial syntactic decisions. Crain and Coker argued that people are garden-pathed only in semantically unbiased sentences.

In sentence fragments like those in (1), the structural preference is for the simple active sentence analysis, not the reduced relative clause analysis where the subject noun phrase is the recipient of *the flowers* (cf. Bever, 1970). Frazier (1978) attributed this preference to the *minimal attachment strategy* which predicts that perceivers structure linguistic material using the fewest syntactic nodes possible. Thus, the minimal attachment strategy predicts that the simple active sentence reading should be initially computed in (1a) and (1b). In sentence (1b), however, the *non*minimal (reduced relative) analysis of the sentence involves the most plausible assignment of thematic relations on pragmatic grounds. Crain and Coker argued that people will tend to compute the reduced relative reading of (1b), due to the presence of biasing pragmatic information.

(1)   a. The florist sent the flowers.
      b. The performer sent the flowers.

Using a paraphrase verification task, they showed that subjects interpreted sentence fragments like (1a) as a reduced relative clause (i.e., corresponding to *the florist who was sent the flowers*) only 16% of the time, whereas they assigned the reduced relative reading to (1b) 42% of the time. In short, the pragmatic constraints in (1b) almost tripled the number of (nonminimal) reduced relative readings.

In the absence of evidence concerning the online processing of these sentence fragments, it is impossible to determine whether pragmatic plausibility considerations influenced the initial (first pass) analyses of the fragments, or whether they only affected some later stage of processing after an initial analysis had already been computed.

To determine whether pragmatic constraints concerning the relative likelihood of two possible real word events influence the processor's choice of an initial structural analysis of an ambiguous string, we recorded eye movements as subjects read sentences like those in (2).

(2)   a. The florist sent the flowers was very pleased. (reduced implausible)
      b. The performer sent the flowers was very pleased. (reduced plausible)
      c. The performer who was sent the flowers was very pleased. (unreduced plausible)
      d. The performer sent the flowers and was very pleased with herself. (active implausible)

In (2a), the fact that florists are expected senders of flowers renders the correct reduced relative analysis of the sentence relatively implausible. In (2b), the fact that performers are likely recipients of flowers renders the correct reduced relative analysis plausible. The control sentence (2c) is structurally unambiguous and does not permit the simple active analysis of the initial portion of the sentence which is available in the other versions of the sentence. In (2d), the correct analysis of the first portion of the sentence is the simple active analysis; however, this analysis is less plausible on pragmatic grounds than the reduced relative analysis.

If the language processor initially adopts the pragmatically most plausible analysis of a string, then readers should be garden-pathed in the implausible sentences (2a) and (2d), but not in the plausible sentences (2b) and (2c). By contrast, if the processor initially follows its structural preference for assigning the minimal necessary syntactic structure to a string (cf. Frazier, 1978; Frazier & Rayner, 1982) without regard for the relative pragmatic plausibility of this analysis, then readers should be garden-pathed in sentences (2a) and (2b), but not in (2c) or (2d). If the reader is garden-pathed in these sentences, then the words following the ambiguous clause cannot be incorporated into a grammatical analysis of the sentences. Hence, we would expect longer reading times and longer fixation durations on these words. In addition, we would expect an increase in the number of regressive eye movements initiated from this (disambiguating) region of the sentence. Note that neither of the above hypotheses predicts difficulty or garden-path effects in the active plausible form of the above sentences or in the unambiguous implausible form of the relative clause sentences; thus they were not included in the experiment.[2]

Method

Subjects.   Twenty members of the University of Massachusetts community were paid to participate in the experiment. All of the subjects had normal uncorrected vision and they were all naive with respect to the purpose of the experiment.

Apparatus and Materials.   Eye movements were recorded via a Stanford Research Institute Dual Purkinje Eyetracker. The eyetracker, which has a resolution of 10 minutes of arc, was interfaced with a Hewlett-Packard 2100 computer that controlled the experiment. The signal from the eyetracker was sampled every millisecond and the position of the eye was determined every 4 milliseconds. A complete record of the sequence of eye movements and the location and duration of the eye fixations were stored on the computer disk for later analysis. Sentences were presented on a Hewlett-Packard 1300A Cathode Ray Tube (CRT). In the experiment, the subject's eye was 46 cm from the CRT and three characters equaled one degree of visual angle.

Eye movements were monitored from the right eye and viewing was binocular. Luminance on the CRT was adjusted to a comfortable level for each subject and held constant throughtout the experiment. The letters making up the sentences were presented in lower case (except for the first letter of the sentence) on the CRT. A black theater gel covered the CRT so that the letters appeared clear and sharp to the subjects. The room was dark, except for a dim indirect light source that enabled the experimenter to record the subjects' responses in a paraphrase task.

Twelve sentences like those in (2) were constructed. There were four versions of each sentence as described above. The experimental sentences were divided into four sets with an equal number of each of the four versions; more than one version of the same sentence never appeared within a given set. The experimental sentences were embedded in 80 filler sentences, which consisted of a wide variety of sentence types. . . .

Procedure.   When a subject arrived for the experiment, a bite bar was prepared that eliminated head movement during the experiment. Then the eye tracking system was calibrated for each subject. Since most of the subjects were experienced in experiments of this type, the initial calibration was accomplished within 15 minutes. Prior to reading each sentence, the experimenter checked the calibration of the eye movement system to insure that accurate records were being obtained. Each subject read ten warm-up sentences and then the set of 92 experimental and filler sentences. The experimenter explained to the subjects that the purpose of the experiment was to understand what people look at when they read and that they should read the sentences as they normally do to comprehend them. They were further instructed that the experimenter would check their comprehension on approximately every fifth sentence by asking them to paraphrase it. Subjects were not told in advance of a particular sentence if they would have to paraphrase it or not. When the experimenter requested the subject to paraphrase a sentence, the subject released the bite bar and reported the paraphrase of the previously read sentence. So that subjects would not adopt specific strategies for dealing with the set of experimental sentences, the experimenter only asked the subjects to paraphrase half of the experimental sentences.

Results

The primary results of the experiment will be presented via analyses of (1) the paraphrase data, (2) the total reading time per character, (3) the total reading time per character in different regions of the sentence, (4) mean fixation durations, and (5) the pattern of eye movements. Following Frazier and Rayner (1982), we have divided the total reading time by the number of character spaces (including spaces between words)

---

[2]If there are large effects of plausibility in the ambiguous sentences, then the unambiguous implausible form of the relative clause sentence could be of theoretical interest in addressing the question of whether or under what circumstances pragmatic constraints can override syntactic well-formedness.

to minimize any differences due to sentence length. We have also separated the *first pass* reading time from the *total* reading time. The first pass reading time only includes fixations that were made in a left-to-right direction that were the first fixations in the region. Regressive fixations (i.e., an eye movement back into some part of the sentence that had previously been read) were not included in the first pass analysis. In our prior work (Frazier & Rayner, 1982) we compared first pass reading times with second pass (including regressions) reading times. However, in the present experiment, subjects did not consistently make regressions and there was too much missing data to meaningfully compare first and second pass reading times. However, the total reading time measure does include regressions and the second pass reading, and any difference between the pattern of results for the first pass reading and the total reading time would be due to second pass reading time. Both subjects (F_1) and sentences (F_2) were treated as random effects in separate analyses of total reading time.

Table 1 shows the paraphrase data collected during the experiment. Each subject was asked to paraphrase at least one reduced plausible and one reduced implausible sentence. For the reduced plausible sentences 70% of the paraphrases were correct. In the reduced implausible sentences only 50% of the paraphrases were correct. Many of the inaccurate paraphrases were due to four subjects who invariably gave active readings for the reduced relative sentences. (This is not surprising given that there is known to be a dialect difference with respect to the movement of indirect objects of dative verbs, cf. Langendoen, Kalish-Landon, & Dore, 1974). If the paraphrases from these four subjects are removed, the reduced plausible sentence paraphrases were accurate 88% of the time; the reduced implausible paraphrases were accurate 64% of the time. Thus, the manipulation of pragmatics was effective in determining the final reading assigned to sentences. The reading data presented below includes data from all subjects. However, when the data were excluded from the four subjects whose paraphrases were inaccurate the same pattern of results emerged as reported below.

Table 2 shows the total reading time per character for each of the four sentence types. As seen in Table 2, reading time differed as a function of sentence type, F_1

TABLE 1   Percent Correct Paraphrase for the Reduced Relative Clauses (Values in parentheses excluded the data from four subjects who never gave correct "relative clause" paraphrases for reduced relative clauses)

| | Sentence Presented | |
Interpretation of Sentence	Reduced Plausible	Reduced Implausible
Relative clause	70% (88%)	50% (64%)
Active	30% (12%)	44% (29%)
Confused	0%	6% (7%)

$(3, 57) = 5.96, p < .002$ and $F_2 (3, 33) = 5.85, p < .01$. A Newman–Keuls test ($p < .05$) revealed that the reduced implausible and reduced plausible sentence types (which did not differ from each other) required longer reading times than did the unreduced plausible and the active implausible sentence types. In turn, the unreduced plausible required longer reading times than did the active implausible. Hence, consistent with the hypothesis that the processor initially follows its structural preference for assigning the minimal necessary structure without regard for the relative pragmatic plausibility of this analysis, subjects appear to have been garden-pathed in both the reduced implausible and reduced plausible sentences to a greater extent than in the other two types of sentences.

The crucial prediction, however, concerns the reading time per character for the disambiguating region of the reduced relative clauses versus reading time in this region for the control sentences with the unreduced relative and the simple active version of the sentence. Reading times were computed for the initial portion of the sentence (up to and including the head of the relative clause), the relative clause itself (excluding the head of the relative clause), and the disambiguating region (the two words immediately following the relative clause). In sentence (2), *sent the flowers* represents the relative clause and the next two words (*was very*) the disambiguating region. Reading times for these local regions of the sentence are presented in Table 3 for first pass fixations; total reading times per character (including first pass and all later fixations) for these regions are also presented in Table 3. It is clear that the reading times associated with the disambiguating region of the reduced rela-

TABLE 2   Reading Time per Character (msec) and Average Reading Rate (wpm) for Each Sentence Type in Experiment 1

	Reduced Plausible	Reduced Implausible	Unreduced Plausible	Active Implausible
Reading time (character)	44.6	45.4	39.6	33.5
Reading rate (wpm)	260	254	283	310

tive clause sentences were much longer than for the nongarden-path sentences in an analysis of first pass reading times. The difference between sentence types was not significant, $F (3, 57) = 2.01$, $p > .10$, and the difference between different regions only approached significance, $F (2, 38) = 3.10$, $p < .055$. However, the theoretically crucial interaction between region and sentence type was significant, $F (6, 114) = 3.70$, $p < .003$. In the analysis of total reading time per character for the different regions, the differences between sentence types were significant, $F (3, 57) = 6.40$, $p < .002$; the differences between the regions of the sentence were also significant, $F (2, 38) = 5.15$, $p < .02$, as was the interaction of the two, $F (6, 114) = 2.28$, $p < .05$.

Table 4 presents the average fixation duration on each of the three fixations immediately preceding and immediately following the point of disambiguation. The main effects of sentence type, $F (3, 57) = 5.20$, $p < .01$, and serial order of fixation, $F (5, 95) = 5.87$, $p < .001$, were both significant. However, the interaction of the two failed to reach significance ($p > .10$). In examining the data, it was apparent that for the two reduced relative sentence types the average fixation duration increased upon reaching the disambiguating word, while it was not the case for the other two sentence types as the average fixation durations remained about the same between the third and fourth fixation. The failure of the interaction to reach significance seemed to be due to variability in the fixation durations, which is not surprising given that fixation location cannot be controlled for when serial order of fixation is examined. Two subsequent analyses confirmed the contention that fixation duration rose significantly upon encountering the disambiguating material for the reduced relative sentences but not for the control sentences. First, an analysis of variance comparing the mean of the three fixations prior to the disambiguation to the means of the three fixations after reaching the disambiguation yielded significant main effects of sentence type, $F (3, 57) = 4.17$, $p < .05$, and serial order, $F (1, 19) = 16.66$, $p < .001$, and a significant interaction, $F (3, 57) = 4.33$, $p < .01$. Second, a comparison of the average duration of the last fixation prior to the disambiguation and the first fixation in the disambiguating region yielded significant differences for the two reduced relative sentences, $t (19) = 3.67$ and 4.12, $p < .05$, but not for the other two sentence types, $t < 1$. Hence, we conclude that for the reduced relative sentences, fixation duration increased significantly on the first fixation in the disambiguating region.

The number of regressive eye movements extending beyond a word boundary that were initiated from some region of the sentence in or following the ambiguous phrase is presented in Table 5. As expected,

TABLE 3   Reading Time per Character (msec) for Each Sentence Type in Different Regions for First Pass and Total (in Parentheses) Reading Time

	Region		
	Initial	Relative Clause	Disambiguating
Reduced plausible	28.2 (38.5)	27.5 (43.7)	36.6 (51.8)
Reduced implausible	30.6 (41.1)	28.2 (49.7)	35.4 (54.9)
Unreduced plausible	30.8 (35.0)	29.4 (45.0)	25.6 (38.7)
Active implausible	29.7 (34.5)	27.6 (34.3)	29.8 (35.9)

TABLE 4   Mean Fixation Duration (msec) for the Fixation prior to and after Disambiguation (Columns on the right of the table represent the means of the three fixations before and the three fixations after disambiguation)

| | Serial Order | | | | | | | |
| | Prior to Disambiguation | | | Disambiguation | | | | |
	1	2	3	4	5	6	Before	After
Reduced plausible	209	213	222	243	245	254	215	247
Reduced implausible	198	208	209	240	256	264	205	253
Unreduced plausible	197	220	234	208	214	232	217	218
Active implausible	195	207	209	197	200	229	204	209

there were more regressions in the reduced relatives than in the other versions of the sentence. This was due to regressions initiated from within or after the disambiguating region of the sentence. By contrast, regressions initiated from the very end of the sentence were distributed roughly evenly across the different sentence types. . . .

Discussion

The result of Experiment 1 clearly indicated that subjects were garden-pathed in both types of reduced relatives as predicted by the hypothesis that the processor initially adopts its structurally preferred analysis of a sentence (Frazier, 1978; Frazier & Rayner,

1982), even if the analysis is less plausible on pragmatic grounds than some alternative analysis. The complexity associated with the reduced relative sentences was reflected in longer reading times per character in the disambiguating region of the reduced relatives and by longer average fixation durations following the point of disambiguation in these sentences (but not in the unreduced relatives or the simple active sentences). There was also an increase in the number of regressions initiated after the ambiguous string in the reduced relative sentences. Further, there was no evidence of subjects having been garden-pathed in the simple active sentences, counter to the predictions of the hypothesis that the processor initially pursues the pragmatically most plausible analysis of a sentence.

TABLE 5   Number of Regressions for Each Sentence Type
(Based on 188 regressions; values in parentheses represent percentages)

	Reduced Plausible	Reduced Implausible	Unreduced Plausible	Active Implausible
Regressions from in or after disambiguating region to an earlier region in or before disambiguating region	26 (14)	33 (18)	13 (7)	8 (4)
Regressions from end of sentence to the region in or before disambiguating region	21 (11)	22 (11)	16 (8)	23 (12)
Total regressions initiated after ambiguous region ending in or before disambiguating region	47 (25)	55 (29)	29 (15)	31 (16)
Regressions within relative clause	3 (2)	5 (3)	15 (8)	3 (2)
Total	50 (27)	60 (32)	44 (23)	34 (18)

In short, the results provide rather clear confirmation of the hypothesis that the relative plausibility of two analyses of an ambiguous string does not govern the selection of an initial syntactic analysis of the string. The range of plausibility constraints tested here has been shown to affect the interpretation assigned to sentences as indicated both by the paraphrase data for the present experiment and by the outcome of the Crain and Coker experiment discussed above. Nevertheless, more extreme plausibility differences based on real world knowledge (which still fall short of producing semantic anomaly) might have different effects from those observed here. It will take further investigation to determine whether the pragmatic constraints derived from extremely implausible real world relations behave like the constraints tested here or whether they behave more like the constraints from semantic anomaly and thus prevent the processor from pursuing an implausible syntactic analysis of a sentence.

The results of Experiment 1 raise an interesting question concerning the interaction of syntactic analysis and pragmatic plausibility in the processing of fully ambiguous sentences. It is intuitively clear that plausibility factors of the level tested here do influence the ultimately preferred analysis of fully ambiguous sentences. The question is precisely how plausibility factors exert this influence on the particular interpretation that is eventually assigned to an ambiguous sentence. Experiment 1 seems to show that all syntactic analyses of a sentence are not initially computed (otherwise subjects should not have been garden-pathed in the reduced relative clause sentences) and that the selection of an initial syntactic analysis of a sentence is not guided by pragmatic constraints of the type we tested. Thus, in fully ambiguous sentences we cannot claim that pragmatic plausibility factors are simply used to select the pragmatically most plausible syntactic analysis of the sentence since this presupposes that all potential syntactic analyses of the sentence have been computed. But, if a single (structurally determined) syntactic analysis of a sentence is initially computed and, further, if it is not anomalous or wildly implausible, how could the language processor determine that a pragmatically more plausible analysis of the sentence exists? Perhaps the language processor considers the pragmatic plausibility of all logically conceivable relations between each of the major phrases (i.e., noun phrases, prepositional phrases, adjective phrases, verb phrases) of the sentence to determine which set of relations is most plausible on pragmatic grounds. Then we need only assume that pragmatic constraints take a long time to use, relative to the time it takes to compute the structurally preferred syntactic analysis of the sentence. Reanalysis of the chosen syntactic analysis of the sentence would then occur if a pragmatically more plausible set of relations had been identified on the basis of real world knowledge.

There are two problems with this view. First, it would complicate the processing of unambiguous sentences enormously and needlessly, since by definition only one set of relations will be permissible in an unambiguous sentence, namely those corresponding to the syntactic analysis of the sentence. Secondly, even in ambiguous sentences there would often be much needless effort expended since the number of logically conceivable relations between some sets of phrases can be quite large if the sets of relations considered are not limited to those which correspond to some potentially grammatical or well-formed analysis of the sentence.

One way to circumvent these problems would be to appeal to information about the possible thematic structures associated with verbs and other heads of phrases. The verb *see*, for example, is associated with (at least) two thematic structures which presumably must be listed in its lexical entry. The verb may occur with an *experiencer* and a *theme* (as in *John saw the lunar eclipse*) or it may occur with an *experiencer*, a *theme*, and an *instrument* (as in *John saw the lunar eclipse with a telescope*). These thematic structures could be used to delimit the set of relations whose pragmatic plausibility will be considered. Given the phrases *John, the lunar eclipse*, and *with a telescope*, the processor could consider whether the set of relations including just an experiencer and a theme, or the set of relations including an experiencer, a theme, and an instrument is more plausible on the basis of pragmatic factors concerning real world knowledge and knowledge of the preceding discourse. We will call this the *thematic selection hypothesis*, though in fact it subsumes a whole family of hypotheses that differ in detail. The essence of the hypothesis, however, is that pragmatic plausibility influences the processing of sentences in the following manner: using the initial syntactic analysis of an input string to identify (minimal) major phrases, the language processor then calls on real world knowledge and information about the current discourse to compare the pragmatic plausibility of whatever sets of relations between phrases are listed in the thematic structures associated with the head of a phrase. If the thematic selection process turns up a set of relations which is incompatible with the chosen syntactic analysis of the input string, then revision of that analysis will be attempted.

In a structurally ambiguous sentence, the thematic selection hypothesis predicts that the processor should ultimately arrive at the pragmatically most plausible analysis of sentence. However, this should involve reanalysis of the syntactic structure of the sentence if the ultimately preferred analysis does not correspond to the structurally preferred analysis of the sentence. Assuming that this reanalysis requires extra computations which will contribute to the processing complexity of the sentence, such sentences should take longer to read than sentences where the structurally preferred analysis is also preferred on pragmatic grounds.

The ambiguous sentences in [Figure 1] provide a test of this prediction. In [Figure 1a] the structurally preferred ("minimal attachment") analysis of the sentence would be preferred on pragmatic grounds, whereas in [Figure 1b] it is the structurally nonpreferred ("nonminimal attachment") analysis which is pragmatically most plausible (as indicated in [Figure 1]). Thus, the thematic selection hypothesis predicts that it should take longer to read [Figure 1b] than [Figure 1a] because arriving at the most plausible analysis of [Figure 1b] will involve reanalysis of the syntactic structure initially assigned to the sentence.

By contrast, if pragmatic plausibility governs the initial syntactic analysis assigned to fully ambiguous sentences, then there is no reason to expect a difference in the complexity of [Figure 1a] and [Figure 1b]. Similarly, if all syntactic analyses of ambiguous sentences were developed (contrary to the evidence obtained in Experiment 1) and pragmatic factors simple governed the selection of the most plausible analysis from this set, then again there is no reason to expect a difference in the complexity of [Figure 1a] and [Figure 1b].

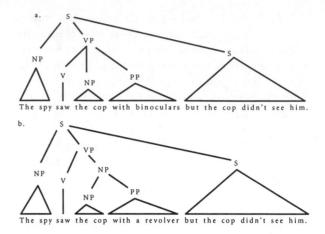

FIGURE 1

One final possibility is that the most frequently used thematic structure of a verb governs the selection of the initial syntactic analysis assigned to a sentence (see Ford, Bresnan, & Kaplan, 1982, for one hypothesis of this general type). According to this hypothesis the relative complexity of the minimal attachment and nonminimal attachment versions of a sentence should differ from sentence to sentence depending on the relative frequency of occurrence of the alternative thematic structures of the verb. Unfortunately, there are no frequency counts of this type available, making it impossible at present to test the detailed predictions of the hypothesis. It should be noted, however, that the predictions of this hypothesis could coincide with the predictions of the thematic selection hypothesis only if each of the verbs in the experimental sentences happened to occur most frequently with the thematic structure that is compatible with the minimal attachment analysis of the sentence.

EXPERIMENT 2

To test the predictions of the hypotheses, twelve sentence pairs like those in [Figure 1] were constructed. In one member of each sentence pair, the minimal attachment analysis of the sentence was designed to be the most plausible pragmatically; in the other member, the nonminimal attachment analysis was the most plausible. The sentences were presented to subjects and we again recorded eye movements during reading.

Method

Subjects.   Twenty members of the University of Massachusetts community were paid to participate in the experiment. All of the subjects had normal uncorrected vision and were naive with respect to the purpose of the experiment.

Apparatus and materials.   The apparatus was identical to Experiment 1. Twelve sets of sentences like those in [Figure 1] were constructed. There were four versions of each sentence. In two of the sentences, the minimal attachment analysis of the sentence was designed to be the most plausible pragmatically, as in [Figure 1a]; in the other two sentences, the nonminimal attachment analysis was the most plausible, as in [Figure 1b]. The length of the noun phrase in the ambiguous prepositional phrase was varied within both the minimal attachment and nonminimal attachment sentences, yielding a long and short version of each. The experimental sentences are presented in Appendix 2 [not reprinted here]. The experimental sentences were divided into four sets with an equal number of each of the four versions; more than one version of the same sentence never appeared within a given set. The experimental sentences were embedded in 80 filler sentences and presented to the subjects on the CRT. The sequence of events in the experiment was identical to Experiment 1 and subjects were told that their comprehension would be checked by asking them to paraphrase about 25% of the sentences.

Results

Analyses similar to those reported in Experiment 1 were carried out on the data. Table 6 shows the paraphrase data for Experiment 2. Again, each subject was asked to paraphrase at least one minimal attachment and one nonminimal attachment sentence. Seventy-eight percent of the paraphrases for the minimal attachment sentences indicated the minimal attachment reading. Eighty-four percent of the paraphrases for the nonminimal attachment sentences indicated nonminimal attachment reading. (If subjects' initial paraphrases did not distinguish between a minimal attachment and nonminimal attachment interpretation, subjects were questioned further about their interpretation of the sentence.) Thus, these paraphrase

TABLE 6   Percent Correct Paraphrase for the Sentences in Experiment 2 (Values in parentheses include final paraphrases for cases where subjects changed their initial paraphrase)

	Sentence Presented	
Paraphrase	*Minimal Attachment*	*Nonminimal Attachment*
Minimal attachment	78%	16% (5%)
Nonminimal attachment	22%	84% (95%)

data indicate that the pragmatic biases were by and large effective.

Table 7 shows the total reading time per character for each sentence type. Separate analyses treating subjects (F_1) and sentences (F_2) as random effects were performed for the total reading time data. Nonminimal attachment sentences resulted in longer reading times than minimal attachment sentences, $F_1(1, 19) = 8.27$, $p < .01$, and $F_2(1, 11) = 4.95$, $p < .05$, but there was no effect of the length of the ambiguous phrase and the interaction was nonsignificant. These results are consistent with the thematic selection hypothesis and with prior results reported by Frazier and Rayner (1982).

TABLE 7   Reading Time per Character (msec) and Average Reading Rate (wpm) for Sentence Types in Experiment 2

	Nonminimal Attachment	*Minimal Attachment*
Reading time/character	40.0	34.0
Reading rate (wpm)	280	306

Table 8 shows the reading time per character broken down by region of the sentence: the initial region of the sentence was defined as all words preceding the postverbal noun phrase; the ambiguous region was defined as the postverbal noun phrase, together with any subsequent words that were identical for the different versions of a sentence; the biased region included the first biasing word and all subsequent words. In [Figure 1], *the cop with* represents the ambiguous region and the biasing region begins with *binoculars* (or *a revolver*).

TABLE 8   Reading Time per Character (msec) for Each Sentence Type in Different
Regions for First Pass and Total (in Parentheses) Reading Time

	Region		
	Initial	Ambiguous	Biased
Nonminimal attachment	27.5 (40.1)	25.9 (34.6)	30.3 (40.0)
Minimal attachment	27.4 (35.1)	25.3 (31.8)	23.7 (30.9)

The first pass analysis also yielded a significant main effect of region, $F(2, 38) = 5.25$, $p < .01$, and an interaction of Sentence Type × Region, $F(2, 38) = 4.17$, $p < .03$. An examination of Table 8 reveals that the interaction was due to the fact that there were no differences between the two sentence types in the initial portion of the sentence or in the ambiguous region, but that reading times were somewhat longer for the nonminimal attachment sentences than for the minimal attachment sentences in the biased region. The two sentence types were identical up to the beginning of the biased region, so we should not expect differences between the sentence types except in the biased region following the ambiguous phrase. The results indicate that on their first pass through the sentence, subjects took longer to process the biased region when reading the nonminimal attachment version of the sentence. The results of the analysis performed on the total reading time measure yielded results that were consistent with the first pass analysis. The main effects of sentence type and region were both significant, $F(1, 19) = 7.59$, $p < .02$, and $F(2, 38) = 3.85$, $p < .03$, respectively. However, the interaction of Sentence Type × Region which was clearly significant in the first pass analysis was only marginally significant, $F(2, 38) = 2.37$, $p < .10$.

An analysis of variance comparing the mean of the three fixations prior to the biased region to the means of the three fixations after reading the biased region yielded a marginally significant effect of sentence type, $F(1, 19) = 4.18$, $p < .06$. The main effect of length did not approach significance ($F < 1$), but there was a highly significant effect of region, $F(1, 19) = 10.44$, $p < .01$. The Sentence Type × Region interaction was significant, $F(1, 19) = 4.31$, $p < .05$, and is shown in Table 9. It should be noted that an analysis of the three fixations prior to the biased

region in comparison to the three fixations after reaching the biased region (as opposed to the means of each set of three fixations as just reported) yielded only a significant effect of serial order of fixation. Furthermore, we did not analyze the type of regressive eye movements due to the rather small number of regressions in the data. (There was a small, and comparable, number of regressions in each sentence type.) Experiment 2 contrasts with Experiment 1 (and with Frazier and Rayner, 1982) both with respect to the number of regressions made by subjects and with respect to the absolute size of the reading time differences (and average fixation durations observed, as might be expected given that, unlike Experiment 1, the misanalysis of the ambiguous phrases in Experiment 2 does not interact with the structural analysis of subsequent items in the sentence.

Discussion

It is clear from these results that sentences in which the minimal attachment version of the sentence was the most plausible took less time for subjects to read than did sentences in which the nonminimal attachment version was the most plausible. This asymmetry was indicated by both the first pass and total reading time per character measures. Further, first pass reading times in the biased region of the sentence were longer than in preceding regions for the nonminimal

TABLE 9   Mean Fixation Duration (msec) for the Three Fixations prior to and after the Biased Region

	Prior	After
Nonminimal attachment	208	234
Minimal attachment	207	210

attachment sentences, but not for the minimal attachment sentences (as indicated by a significant interaction of sentence type and region). These differences in the relative complexity of different forms of the experimental sentences are consistent with the thematic selection hypothesis, but were not predicted by the alternative hypotheses (with the caveat noted above concerning the relative frequency of a verb's thematic structures).

GENERAL DISCUSSION

Taken together, Experiments 1 and 2 help delimit the interaction of syntactic and semantic information during sentence processing. Experiment 1 shows that probabilistic semantic and pragmatic information does not influence the processor's initial choice of a syntactic analysis. Although semantic and pragmatic plausibility information does influence the ultimately preferred analysis of a sentence, Experiment 2 provides evidence that reading times are longer when the most plausible analysis does not correspond to the analysis selected by the processor's structural preferences. This set of results can be explained by the hypothesis that there exist two largely independent processors that are operative during sentence comprehension: a syntactic processor that initially computes only the structurally preferred analysis of a sentence, and a *thematic processor* that examines the alternative thematic structures of a word (to compare the relative plausibility of each) and selects the semantically and pragmatically most plausible one. Given this assumption, we may account both for the evidence that readers initially pursue just one syntactic analysis of a sentence (and hence can explain the considerable evidence for the existence of garden paths in sentence comprehension) and for the fact that readers do eventually arrive at the semantically and pragmatically most plausible analysis of a sen-

tence even when that analysis is not the one preferred on purely structural grounds.

Alternatively, one might assume that just a single processor is responsible for constructing an initial syntactic analysis of the sentence and then later for evaluating the relative pragmatic plausibility of different sets of thematic relations using real world and discourse knowledge. But this processor would then no longer have a single set of coherent properties. In performing the syntactic analysis of the sentence, it would consider only a single analysis at a time and would not consult information about real world plausibility. Later, in evaluating thematic structure, it would no longer exhibit these properties, since it must compare more than one analysis at a time to determine the *relative* plausibility of analyses and must use real word information to do so.[3] Hence, to the extent that it is important to identify the clustering of distinct properties of the processor at different stages in the processing of a sentence with the existence of distinct processors (rather than a single chameleon-like processor that changes its characteristics depending on the task it is executing and the representations it is manipulating), the results of our experiments provide evidence for distinct processors during language comprehension. . . .

REFERENCES

Bever, T. G. The cognitive basis for linguistic structures. In J. R. Hayes (Ed.). *Cognition and the development of language.* New York: Wiley, 1970.

Ehrlich, S. F., & Rayner, K. Contextual effects on word perception and eye movements during reading. *Journal of Verbal Learning and Verbal Behavior,* 1981, 20, 641–655.

Ford, M., Bresnan, J., & Kaplan, R. A competence-based theory of syntactic closure. In J. Bresnan (Ed.), *The mental representation of grammatical relations.* Cambridge, Mass.: MIT Press, 1982.

Forster, K., & Olbrei, I. Semantic heuristics and syntactic analysis. *Cognition,* 1973, 2, 319–347.

Forster, K., & Ryder, L. S. Perceiving the structure and meaning of sentences. *Journal of Verbal Learning and Verbal Behavior,* 1971, 10, 285–296.

Forster, K. Levels of processing and the structure of the language processor. In W. E. Cooper and E. C. T. Walker

---

[3]For those who would opt for the distinct processors view, it should be noted that the properties of the processor responsible for selecting thematic structures are congruent with the properties governing the selection of one meaning of an ambiguous lexical item, since this latter process also involves consideration of more than one analysis at a time and implicates the use of real world knowledge.

(Eds.), *Sentence processing*. Hillsdale, N.J.: Erlbaum, 1979.

Frauenfelder, U., Segui, J., & Mehler, J. Monitoring around the relative clause. *Journal of Verbal Learning and Verbal Behavior*, 1980, **19**, 328–337.

Frazier, L. On comprehending sentences: Syntactic parsing strategies. Doctoral dissertation, University of Connecticut, 1978. Available from Indiana University Linguistics Club.

Frazier, L., & Fodor, J. D. The sausage machine: A new two-stage parsing model. *Cognition*, 1978, **6**, 291–325.

Frazier, L., & Rayner, K. Making and correcting errors during sentence comprehension: Eye movements in the analysis of structurally ambiguous sentences. *Cognitive Psychology*, 1982, **1**, 178–210.

Holmes, V. M., & O'Regan, J. K. Eye fixation patterns during the reading of relative clause sentences. *Journal of Verbal Learning and Verbal Behavior*, 1981, **20**, 417–430.

Langendoen, D. T., Kalish-Landon, N., & Dore, J. Dative questions: A study in the relation of acceptability to grammaticality of an English sentence type. *Cognition*, 1974, **2**, 451–478.

Marslen-Wilson, W. D. The limited compatibility of linguistic and perceptual explanations. *Paper from the Parasession on Functionalism*. University of Chicago, 1975.

Marslen-Wilson, W. D., & Tyler, L. K. The temporal structure of spoken language understanding. *Cognition*, 1980, **8**, 1–71.

Marslen-Wilson, W. D., & Welsh, A. Processing interactions and lexical access during word recognition in continuous speech. *Cognitive Psychology*, 1978, **10**, 29–63.

REFERENCE NOTE

1. Crain, S., & Coker, P. A semantic constraint on syntactic parsing. Paper presented at the Annual Meeting of the Linguistic Society of America, December, 1979.

POSTSCRIPT

Although the conclusion that an initial structural description of a sentence is constructed by a syntactic processor that operates independently of pragmatic knowledge is still somewhat controversial (compare Crain & Steedman, 1985; Marslen-Wilson & Tyler, 1980, 1987), many other researchers report evidence supporting that conclusion (for example, Ferreira & Clifton, 1986; see Frazier, 1987 and Garrett, 1990, for reviews and Linebarger, 1990, for neuropsychological evidence). The central role of thematic structure in helping avoid or recover from being garden-pathed has also been pursued by other researchers (Tannenhaus & Carlson, 1989; Taraban & McClelland, 1988), although there is also controversy regarding the extent to which lexical information is used in initially parsing a sentence (Clifton, Frazier, & Connine, 1984; Frazier, 1989).

To fully understand sentence processing, and language more generally, it is clear that we need to combine insights from a variety of disciplines, including linguistics, computer science, neuroscience, philosophy, and psychology. Such a multidisciplinary approach is being applied to a variety of problems in cognition, and it usually goes by the label *cognitive science*. Several sources are available that can give you a good sense of cognitive science (Osherson, 1990, particularly *Volume 1: Language*; Posner, 1989; and Stillings et al., 1987).

The multidisciplinary approach to language yields many insights. But it also means that understanding research on language often requires a great deal of technical knowledge from a variety of disciplines. Furthermore, several relatively distinct approaches can be identified within the study of language: the formal, the human information-processing, the neuropsychological, and the computational. An example may help clarify the differences among these approaches.

Consider the game tic-tac-toe. We can give a formal description of tic-tac-toe, in which we would specify what's involved in such a game—the moves allowed and how the game ends. Alternatively, we can try to explain how people actually play tic-tac-toe—that is, how people process tic-tac-toe information. Through a series of experiments, we might determine, for example, what visual processes are involved in scanning a grid to figure out what squares are available, what strategies people use to decide where to place an O or an X, what movements are used to draw the symbols, and how people learn tic-tac-toe. By observing people with brain damage or by taking certain measurements of people's brains as they play tic-tac-toe, we may identify the parts of the brain that are involved in the relevant visual, strategic, or motor processes. Finally, we could try to program a computer to play tic-tac-toe.

The formal, or competence, model would tell us exactly what would and would not constitute a legal game of tic-tac-toe, but it would not tell us how to actually go about playing tic-tac-toe. An information-processing, or performance, model would tell us how people play. It may or may not make direct reference to the description specified by the formal model, just as the computational model may or may not use the same procedures that people actually use when playing the game. For example, computers may play tic-tac-toe without ever directly checking the spatial relationships among the various squares. Thus, although the four different approaches can study the same phenomenon, they have different goals and—with the probable exception of the information-processing and neuropsychological approaches—it is unclear exactly how they should feed into one another (Berwick & Weinberg, 1983). Furthermore, it is often not entirely clear exactly what range of data or theoretical questions each kind of model must explain. This is one reason for the widespread controversy in the area of sentence processing.

Much of the work on language by linguists and philosophers is in the form of formal descriptions of language structure. Computer scientists, not surprisingly, tend to work on computational models and are often more concerned with getting computers to do a certain task than with getting the computer to do a task the way humans do. Psychologists and neuroscientists usually try to produce (human) performance models, but they frequently borrow heavily from linguists and computer scientists. This article is an example of how psychologists borrow from linguists; see Reading 23 for an example of how neuroscientists borrow from linguists.

FOR FURTHER THOUGHT

1. What arguments do Rayner and his colleagues give for rejecting extreme integration (in which every kind of information affects the initial interpretation)? What arguments do they give against extreme independence (autonomy) of processing components?

2. What is the Weak Semantic Principle? How does it differ from extreme autonomy? from extreme integration? Explain Crain and Coker's criticisms of Frazier's original statement of the Weak Semantic Principle.

3. What is meant by on-line processing? Why does the Crain and Coker result not provide direct evidence about on-line processing?

4. According to the authors (see the introduction to Experiment 1), what position predicts that subjects would be garden-pathed by sentences (2a) and (2d), but not by (2b) and (2c)? Why? What position predicts garden-path effects with sentences (2a) and (2b) but not with (2c) and (2d)? Why? Which position do the authors' data support? At the very end of that section, the authors point out that certain sentence forms were not included in the experiment. Elaborate on their reasoning for the exclusion.

5. Rayner and his colleagues presented 80 filler sentences in addition to the critical sentences. Why?

6. In their results, the authors present analyses of five different measures. For each kind of measurement, describe the outcome that would indicate garden-path effects. Why did they separate first pass timing results from total timing results?

7. What problem motivates Experiment 2?

8. Rayner and his colleagues argue that the results of their experiments provide evidence for what two kinds of processors? On what grounds do they argue that two distinct processors are involved rather than a single processor with two functions?

REFERENCES

Berwick, R. C., & Weinberg, A. S. (1983). The role of grammars in models of language use. *Cognition, 13,* 1–62.

Clifton, C., Frazier, L., & Connine, C. (1984). Lexical expectations in sentence comprehension. *Journal of Verbal Learning and Verbal Behavior, 23,* 696–708.

Crain, S., & Steedman, M. (1985). On not being led up the garden path: The use of context by the psychological parser. In D. Dowty, L. Karttunen, & A. Zwicky (Eds.), *Natural language parsing* (pp. 320–358). Cambridge, MA: Cambridge University Press.

Ferreira, F., & Clifton, C. (1986). The independence of syntactic processing. *Journal of Memory and Language, 25,* 348–368.

Frazier, L. (1987). Theories of sentence processing. In J. L. Garfield (Ed.), *Modularity in knowledge representation and natural-language understanding* (pp. 291–307). Cambridge, MA: MIT Press.

Frazier, L. (1989). Against lexical generation of syntax. In W. Marslen-Wilson (Ed.), *Lexical representation and process* (pp. 505–528). Cambridge, MA: MIT Press.

Garrett, M. F. (1990). Sentence processing. In D. N. Osherson & H. Lasnik (Eds.), *An invitation to cognitive science: Vol. 1. Language* (pp. 133–175). Cambridge, MA: MIT Press.

Linebarger, M. C. (1990). Neuropsychology of sentence parsing. In A. Caramazza (Ed.), *Cognitive neuropsychology and neurolinguistics* (pp. 55–122). Hillsdale, NJ: Erlbaum.

Marslen-Wilson, W. & Tyler, L. K. (1980). The temporal structure of spoken language understanding. *Cognition, 8,* 1–71.

Marslen-Wilson, W. & Tyler, L. K. (1987). Against modularity. In J. L. Garfield (Ed.), *Modularity in knowledge representation and natural-language understanding* (pp. 37–62). Cambridge, MA: MIT Press.

Osherson, D. N. (Ed.). (1990). *An invitation to cognitive science. Vols. 1–3.* Cambridge, MA: MIT Press.

Posner, M. I. (Ed.). (1989). *Foundations of cognitive science.* Cambridge, MA: MIT Press.

Stillings, N. A., Feinstein, M. H., Garfield, J. L., Rissland, E. L., Rosenbaum, D. A., Weisler, S. E., & Baker-Ward, L. (1987). *Cognitive science: An introduction.* Cambridge, MA: MIT Press.

Tannenhaus, M. K., & Carlson, G. N. (1989). Lexical structure and language comprehension. In W. Marslen-Wilson (Ed.), *Lexical representation and process* (pp. 529–561). Cambridge, MA: MIT Press.

Taraban, R., & McClelland, J. L. (1988). Constituent attachment and thematic role assignment in sentence processing: Influences of content-based expectations. *Journal of Memory and Language, 27,* 597–632.

INTRODUCTION

When we use language, we rarely deal in isolated sentences. Instead, language use typically involves producing or comprehending sequences of related sentences. Susan Haviland and Herbert Clark address the issue of sentence-to-sentence integration of information in their article "What's New? Acquiring New Information as a Process in Comprehension."

Although this article is unusually thorough and clear, readers need to be familiar with a number of linguistic concepts. *Syntax* refers to the structure of a sentence; syntactic rules therefore govern the structure of a sentence (they are often called grammatical rules; see also Reading 21). *Restrictive relative clauses* are defining clauses introduced with a relative pronoun, such as *who* or *that*; but sometimes the pronoun is only implicit, as in "the dog I fed" versus "the dog that I fed." *Pronominalization* is the process by which simple expressions such as pronouns replace complicated ones (Clark & Clark, 1977). For example, once the phrase "the woman with the three Bernese Mountain Dogs" is used in a conversation or paragraph, the rules of pronominalization allow *she* or *her* to replace the phrase in subsequent references. *Propositions* are somewhat more difficult to explain, but for our purposes we can just regard them as basic idea units. Haviland and Clark assume that knowledge is represented by a rich network of propositions, or interconnected basic idea units. Clark and Clark (1977) give a thorough but nontechnical description of propositional knowledge.

Given the current dominance of computers in our lives and laboratories, many readers also may be unfamiliar with elite type and tachistoscopes. Typewriters generally produce type with either 10 or 12 characters per inch; type of the latter sort is called elite. Tachistoscopes are devices for presenting visual stimuli for precisely controlled periods of time. Through elaborate arrangements of mirrors, a tachistoscope allows a subject to see, one at a time, anywhere between 2 and 4 presentation fields in which the experimenter has placed different stimuli. (See the Introduction to Reading 1 for a fuller description of tachistoscopes.)

We have excluded Haviland and Clark's third experiment involving sentences that marked presupposed knowledge with adverbs, such as *again* or *too*, and that included negatives, such as "Stephen can't dance the rumba either." As you read this article, see whether you can draw from lectures you have heard or conversations you have had to find examples that violate and examples that obey the strategies Haviland and Clark describe. Do their predictions work for your examples?

What's New? Acquiring New Information as a Process in Comprehension

Susan E. Haviland and Herbert H. Clark

Stanford University

As we are all aware, linguistic and factual contexts have a powerful effect on how we understand language. We all know that the same sentence can mean vastly different things when uttered by different people in different situations. For example, it does not take too much imagination to come up with situations in which *Are you going to cut your hair?* serves as a simple question, a polite request, or a thinly veiled threat, independent of intonation pattern (Gordon & Lakoff, 1971). And we all know that sentences taken out of context often lose their original meaning. Some even lose all meaning entirely. *George thinks vanilla* is rather schizophrenic by itself. But as an answer to *What kind of ice cream does Vivien like?*, it is perfectly sensible. In paragraphs, such context effects have a tendency to snowball. Dooling and Lachman (1971) and Bransford and Johnson (1973), for example, have constructed paragraphs that seem arrant nonsense by themselves, but which become quite understandable when a contextual theme is provided. In the real world, of course, the presence of context is the normal case. We very rarely process sentences in isolation, and although we can understand such sentences this is not what we normally mean by "understanding" or "comprehension" at all. In ordinary language, these words refer to the way we take in the meaning of a sentence and integrate it with information we already know—from context and from past memory. In fact, we often say, "I don't understand," or something to that effect, when we have understood a sentence by itself but do not see how it fits into the conversational situation. Such fitting in is obviously necessary for full understanding, and a natural model of comprehension will have to account for how this integration takes place.

In Clark and Haviland (1974) we have proposed a comprehension strategy, called the Given–New Strategy, that expressly deals with just such integration of information. It rests on the unsurprising assumption that language is primarily used for imparting new information. The speaker's purpose is to provide new information to his audience, and the listener's is to extract the new information and integrate it with old information already in memory. Indeed, communication is a cooperative effort between the speaker and listener. The speaker syntactically identifies what he thinks his audience already knows, what we will call the *Given information,* and he similarly identifies what he thinks his audience does not already know, what we will call the *New information.*

This research was supported in part by MH-20021, a grant from the National Institute of Mental Health. We thank Eve V. Clark, Lance Rips, and Edward E. Smith for their helpful suggestions on the manuscript.

[Susan E. Haviland is] now at University of California, Irvine.

The listener, for his part, assumes that the speaker is cooperative and has good judgment about what he, the listener, does and does not know. The listener's strategy, therefore, is to identify the syntactically marked Given and New information, treat the Given information as an address to information already in memory, and then integrate the New information into memory at that point (see also Clark, 1973b).

The syntactic devices the speaker has available for the marking of Given and New information are numerous (Halliday, 1967). The sentence in (1), for example, has roughly the following Given–New structure.

(1) The jokes Horace tells are awful.
     Given: Horace tells jokes.
     New: Those jokes are awful.

As this analysis indicates, (1) conveys two pieces of information, that Horace tells jokes and that they are awful. But (1) distinguishes syntactically between these two pieces of information. It presupposes the first and asserts the second. The speaker who chooses this sentence, therefore, assumes that his audience already knows that Horace tells jokes. The new information he wants to get across is that the jokes are awful. Restrictive relative clauses in an initial part of the sentence (here, *that Horace tells*) are a common device for conveying Given information. Sentences (2), (3), and (4) have similar analyses:

(2) Elizabeth tells awful jokes too.
     Given: Someone else tells awful jokes.
     New: Elizabeth tells awful jokes.
(3) It was Einstein who searched in vain for the unified field.
     Given: Someone searched in vain for the unified field.
     New: That someone was Einstein.
(4) The morning star is the evening star.
     Given: There is a morning star (just one).
             There is an evening star (just one).
     New: The first is identified as the second.

Sentence (2) uses the adverbial *too* to distinguish Given and New information; (3) makes use of the so-called cleft construction in which the New information is introduced by *it is;* and (4) uses the definite article *the* to presuppose existence. These are only a few of the possible devices for distinguishing Given from New.

The listener's success with the Given–New Strategy depends critically on whether the Given information, as so marked by the speaker, actually does match information already in memory. To borrow a term normally associated with pronominalization, the Given information must have an *Antecedent* in memory. If there is no Antecedent, the listener must construct one by elaborating information he already has, or he must construct one from scratch. It is only when the listener finds (or constructs) the Antecedent in memory that he can attach the New information to it, thereby integrating the New information with what he already knows. To illustrate, assume that the listener already knows that Horace tells jokes. This knowledge is coded, along with all sorts of information from both linguistic and other sources, in a complex of interrelated, primitive propositions similar in nature to those posited by Clark and Chase (1972), Kintsch (1972), Rumelhart, Lindsay, and Norman (1972), and others. When told *The jokes Horace tells are awful,* the listener will extract the Given information (*Horace tells jokes*), search his memory structure for the matching Antecedent (*Horace tells jokes*), and on finding it, attach the New information (*the jokes are awful*) to this Antecedent. The result is a revised memory structure now containing the New information.

This model leads to several important predictions about the time it takes a listener, or reader, to understand sentences in experimentally manipulated contexts. The basic notion is that the listener will not feel he has fully comprehended a sentence until he has integrated its novel information in memory. So, if the Given information matches something in context, that is, if it has an Antecedent, the listener should be very quick to claim he comprehends the sentence. But if it does not, if there is no suitable Antecedent for the Given information, the listener should be very slow to claim he comprehends the sentence. In such cases the listener will search long and hard and, upon failure, will try another strategy. He may find that the Given information is semantically similar to something in context, so he can construct an Antecedent based on an inferential bridge; or he may find he has to set up a new, separate Antecedent. In any case, these additional steps will take time.

To illustrate such a prediction, imagine that a subject is presented with a sentence like (5) and is asked to indicate when he thinks he fully understands the sentence.

(5) The alligator was his favorite present.

This sentence, of course, presupposes the existence of a particular alligator (see sentence (4)). Our prediction is that the subject will be relatively fast in understanding (5) in such a sequence as (6),

(6) Ed was given an alligator for his birthday. The alligator was his favorite present.

but relatively slow for such a sequence as (7).

(7) Ed was given lots of things for his birthday. The alligator was his favorite present.

The context sentence in (6) makes the existence of a specific alligator clear, and so *an alligator* can serve as Antecedent to the Given information in the target sentence (5). The context sentence in (7), on the other hand, although still appropriate to the situation, does not mention that there is a specific alligator about. With no direct Antecedent for the Given information in the target sentence, the connection between the two sentences requires an extra inferential step, something like, "Ah, one of those 'things' must have been an alligator," and this should require time.

EXPERIMENT I

This prediction was tested in Experiment I, in which subjects were presented pairs of context and target sentences, where the target sentence always contained a definite noun phrase (as in (5)). Half the time the context sentence preceding the target sentence explicitly mentioned the existence of the referent of the noun phrase (as in (6)), and half the time it did not (as in (7)). The context and target sentences of each pair were presented sequentially, and comprehension time was measured by having the subjects press a button when they felt they understood the target sentence. According to the Given–New Strategy, comprehension time of the target sentence should be faster when preceded by a context sentence of the first type (to be called Direct Antecedent pairs) than when preceded by one of the second type (to be called Indirect Antecedent pairs).

Method

Experiment I made use of 68 context-target pairs, 34 Direct Antecedent pairs and 34 Indirect Antecedent pairs. Each Direct Antecedent pair, such as

(8) We got some beer out of the trunk. The beer was warm.

was matched with an Indirect Antecedent pair containing the same target sentence and a slightly changed context sentence, such as:

(9) We checked the picnic supplies. The beer was warm.

These context-target pairs were made up to be as natural as possible, and they covered a large number of different topics. The 68 pairs were then divided up into two lists of 34 pairs. Each list contained half Direct and half Indirect Antecedent pairs, with the added constraint that if a Direct Antecedent pair occurred on one list, its matched Indirect Antecedent pair occurred on the other. Half the subjects received one list, and half the other. It was therefore possible to compare the comprehension time of the same target sentence (for example, *The beer was warm*) in both a Direct Antecedent and Indirect Antecedent context.

The context and target sentences were presented to the subject sequentially in a modified tachistoscope which had two 13 x 7 cm presentation fields, one 1 cm above the other. The context sentence appeared in the upper presentation field and the target sentence in the lower one. When the subject pressed a (black) button, the context sentence appeared in the upper field. Another press of the same button then caused the context sentence to disappear, the target sentence to appear in the lower field, and a clock to start. A press of a second (red) button removed the target sentence from view and stopped the clock. The sentences, typed in elite type, were viewed at a distance of 51 cm and were centered in their respective fields.

Each subject was given 57 such trials, 23 practice trials followed by 34 test trials. He was told that he would be reading pairs of sentences. He was to be sure to read and pay attention to the first sentence in each pair since it would be related to the second. But, he was told, it was the second sentence that we were interested in, and he was to be sure to press the red button as soon as he understood what it meant. Although the instruction, "Press the red button as soon as you understand what the second sentence means," was left deliberately vague (for example, subjects were not specifically told to understand the target sentence in the context of the first) no subject had any difficulty following it.

In this and the two subsequent experiments, the subjects were Stanford University students either paid $2.00 for their services or given credit towards a course requirement in introductory psychology. There were 16 subjects, seven women and nine men, in Experiment I.

Results and Discussion

As predicted, comprehension time of the target sentences was faster in the Direct Antecedent pairs than in the Indirect Antecedent pairs, 835 msec to 1016 msec, a difference of 181 msec. This difference was significant in an analysis of variance that treated both target sentences and subjects as random effects, min $F'(1,36) = 6.47$, $p < .025$ (see Clark, 1973a). There were no reliable differences between the two lists nor were there any interactions.

Although the results of Experiment I conformed to our predictions, there is one obvious alternative explanation of these results. All of the Direct Antecedent pairs contained the repetition of a noun, while none of the Indirect Antecedent pairs did. Our results might therefore have arisen because of the simple facilitating effect of repetition (Smith, Chase, & Smith, 1973). To test for this possibility we performed Experiment II, in which both Direct and Indirect Antecedent pairs involved repetition.

EXPERIMENT II

In discourse, after a noun has been mentioned once, it is usually necessary to definitize it when it is mentioned a second time. So if we speak of an alligator once, we will thereafter refer to it as the alligator.

There are, however, important exceptions to this general rule (see Chafe, 1972), as illustrated in (10).

(10)   Ed wanted an alligator for his birthday.

Whereas in most sentences the phrase an alligator posits the existence of the beast, the phrase in (10) does not. The fact that Ed wants one does not mean that the speaker had a particular one in mind (except in a rather rare reading). For this reason, the target sentence in (11)

(11)   Ed wanted an alligator for his birthday. The alligator was his favorite present.

has nothing for the alligator to match up to; there is no Antecedent for the alligator in memory. So even though the word alligator was mentioned in the context sentence, the connection will require an extra inferential step, something like, "Oh, he must have actually been given an alligator," and therefore (11) should take a relatively long time to comprehend.

In Experiment II, therefore, we altered each Indirect Antecedent pair used in Experiment I along the lines of (11). If the difference between Direct and Indirect Antecedent pairs in Experiment I is attributable to repetition, that difference should disappear. If, on the other hand, it is attributable to the Given–New Strategy, it should remain.

Method

Experiment II was identical to Experiment I except for two features. Each context sentence in the 34 Indirect Antecedent pairs was altered, along the lines of (11), so that each contained a repetition of the critical noun of the target sentence, but did not posit the existence of the object referred to by the critical noun. The Indirect Antecedent pair replacing (9), for example, was:

(12)   Andrew was especially fond of beer. The beer was warm.

There were 10 subjects, seven women and three men.

Results

Again as predicted, comprehension time for target sentences was faster for the Direct Antecedent pairs than for the Indirect Antecedent pairs, 1031 to 1168 msec, a difference of 137 msec, *min F'*(1,23)= 15.7, *p* < .001. There were no reliable differences between the two lists of sentences, nor were there any interactions. These results, therefore, argue that mere repetition of the critical noun is not enough to account for the results of Experiment I. . . .

[Experiment III is excluded.]

GENERAL DISCUSSION

As we have argued, sentences are normally comprehended within some larger framework, represented internally by a complex network of interrelated propositions. Employing the Given–New Strategy, the listener takes in a sentence, breaks it into its syntactically defined Given and New information, and then attempts to add the New information to memory. This he does by treating the Given information as a pointer or address to some Antecedent already in memory. That is, he searches memory for a matching Antecedent to this Given information, and on finding it, attaches the New information to the Antecedent. If he cannot find a matching Antecedent, then he must (*a*) build some sort of bridging structure, (*b*) treat all information in the sentence as new and begin construction of a new separate structure, or (*c*) attempt to recompute what is Given and what is New in the sentence.

This model leads to important predictions about the comprehension of pairs of sentences in a laboratory setting. The subject, we assume, will treat the first sentence of such a pair as completely new information and set up a separate structure in memory. But when processing the second, he will try to comprehend it with respect to the information contained in the first. So he will take the Given information of the second and try to find a matching Antecedent in the information provided by the first. If the Antecedent is available directly, then he will comprehend the second (target) sentence quickly; if not, he will require more time, since he will have to construct a bridging structure. Consistent with the predictions, Experiment I showed that comprehension of a sentence containing a definite noun phrase, say, *the beer*, took less time when the context sentence had explicitly posited the existence of some beer than when it had not. Experiments II and III showed that this re-

sult could not simply be a result of repetition of the critical noun. . . .

In testing the Given–New Strategy here, we have relied on a subjective criterion of comprehension, how long it takes the subject to feel he has understood a sentence. But as several psychologists have argued (for example, Dooling, 1972; Mistler-Lachman, 1972; Schwartz, Sparkman, & Deese, 1970; Wang, 1970a, b), there may be several different levels of comprehension. At a shallow level we may be able to judge how comprehensible a sentence is without actually comprehending it fully; at a deeper level we may be able to comprehend a sentence without relating it to context; and at a still deeper level we comprehend sentences with respect to context. Obviously, the interest here is in the third and deepest level. The present evidence is consistent with the assumption that most subjects were indeed using this criterion for their judgments on most sentences. If they had used either of the first two criteria, there should have been no reliable differences between conditions, since all conditions contained the identical target sentences. The differences actually found must therefore be attributed to the subject comprehending the sentences at the deepest level. Nevertheless, there may have been some instances of "incomplete" contextual comprehension, and so the absolute differences between conditions cannot be taken very seriously.

The Given–New Strategy is an attempt to formalize part of what people do in integrating new information with what they already know. It therefore ought to apply to previous studies where the main interest was in how subjects went about integrating new information. Consider the study by Bransford and Franks (1971) in which subjects were presented with a number of sentences derived from sets of four propositions (for example, *The rock rolled down the mountain; The hut was tiny; The rock crushed the hut;* and *The hut was at the edge of the woods*). The presented sentences contained either one, two, or three of these four propositions in various combinations, but subjects were never presented with a sentence containing all four. Later, however, when subjects were given a recognition task, they were found to claim, with the highest confidence, that the sentence containing all four propositions (for example, *The rock which rolled down the mountain crushed the tiny hut at the edge of the woods*) was old, even though they had never seen it. According to Bransford and Franks, the subjects had built up information structures which eventually contained the same information as the four-proposition distractor sentences, and this is what led them to make their judgments. Rumelhart, Lindsay, and Norman (1972) illustrated this process more explicitly with the use of graph structure notation. Although these are plausible accounts for why the subjects erred on the four-proposition sentences, they nevertheless say little about how the subjects went about building up this information structure.

According to the present view, one important aspect of the Bransford and Franks sentences was that they contained definite noun phrases. As we have argued, *the* makes specific existential and uniqueness presuppositions and induces the subjects to believe that there is only one hut, rock, mountain, and so on. By the Given–New Strategy, the subject is therefore encouraged to treat each combination sentence as relevant to all others and to attach all instances of the same noun phrase to a common Antecedent. In the Bransford and Franks study, this strategy could have been especially important since four different sets of four propositions were mixed together on the same list. But if Bransford and Franks had replaced every definite article by an indefinite article, the result might have been somewhat different. The subjects should not have been quite so compelled to build up a single structure for every set of four propositions, and they should have found it a little easier to keep each instance of a noun phrase separate. This is not to say that Bransford and Franks' results were due entirely to the fact that the sentences they used contained definite noun phrases, but rather that definiteness may have been an important contributing factor.

To consider another example, Bransford and Johnson (1973) found that subjects rated the following paragraph as rather incomprehensible:

> The procedure is actually quite simple. First you arrange things into different groups depending on their makeup. Of course, one pile may be sufficient depending on how much there is to do. If you have to go somewhere else due to lack of facilities that is the next step, otherwise you are pretty well set. It is important not to overdo any particular endeavor. That is, it is better to do too few things at once than too many. . . .

In addition, subjects found this paragraph very difficult to recall. But when told beforehand that the paragraph was about washing clothes, other subjects found the paragraph quite comprehensible and much easier to remember. Bransford and Johnson argued, rightly, that the topic "washing clothes" helps the subjects to build up some sort of semantic product, but they did not specify how this might be done.

Without the topic "washing clothes," we would argue, someone reading this paragraph simply has no way of constructing the intended Antecedents of each sentence. For example, *the procedure* in the first sentence presupposes that the subject already knows about some particular procedure. Without the topic, he does not, but with the topic, he does. The second sentence requires the subject to know what things are to be arranged; the third sentence requires him to know what one pile is sufficient for and what there is to do. Each of these involves Given information and requires an Antecedent in memory for proper integration. Without the topic, there is no way of computing the intended Antecedents, but with the topic there is, though some will be indirect. The Given–New Strategy provides a relatively natural account for why subjects only found the paragraph comprehensible when they were given the topic beforehand.

The Given–New Strategy also provides us with a clue about the role of redundancy in language. At first it seems rather odd that sentences should contain so much information that both the listener and speaker already accept as true. Language is a medium for communication, and an efficient speaker ought never to say things his listener already knows. But in light of the Given–New Strategy this redundant information actually becomes a prerequisite for communication. As Given information, it serves as an address directing the listener to where New information should be stored. And as such, of course, it is not really redundant at all. It simply serves a different purpose.

REFERENCES

Bransford, J. D., & Franks, J. J. The abstraction of linguistic ideas. *Cognitive Psychology,* 1971, **2,** 330–350.

Bransford, J. D., & Johnson, M. K. Considerations of some problems of comprehension. In W. G. Chase (Ed.), *Visual information processing.* New York: Academic Press, 1973.

Chafe, W. L. Discourse structure and human knowledge. In J. B. Carroll & R. O. Freedle (Eds.), *Language comprehension and the acquisition of knowledge.* Washington, D.C.: V. H. Winston, 1972.

Clark, H. H. The language-as-fixed-effect fallacy: A critique of language statistics in psychological research. *Journal of Verbal Learning and Verbal Behavior,* 1973, **12,** 335–359. (a)

Clark, H. H. Comprehension and the given–new contract. Paper presented at conference on "The role of grammar in interdisciplinary linguistic research," University of Bielefeld, Bielefeld, Germany, December 11–15, 1973. (b)

Clark, H. H., & Chase, W. G. On the process of comparing sentences against pictures. *Cognitive Psychology,* 1972, **3,** 472–517.

Clark, H. H., & Haviland, S. E. Psychological processes as linguistic explanation. Paper presented at UWM Symposium: The nature of explanation in linguistics. University of Wisconsin, Milwaukee, May 1973. In D. Cohen (Ed.), *Explaining linguistic phenomena.* Washington: V. H. Winston, 1974.

Dooling, D. J. Some context effects in the speeded comprehension of sentences. *Journal of Experimental Psychology,* 1972, **93,** 56–62.

Dooling, D. J., & Lachman, R. Effects of comprehension on retention of prose. *Journal of Experimental Psychology,* 1971, **88,** 216–222.

Gordon, D., & Lakoff, G. Conversational postulates. *Papers from the Seventh Regional Meeting, Chicago Linguistic Society,* 1971.

Halliday, M. A. K. Notes on transitivity and theme in English: II. *Journal of Linguistics,* 1967, **3,** 199–244.

Kintsch, W. Notes on the structure of semantic memory. In E. Tulving & W. Donaldson (Eds.), *Organization of memory.* New York: Academic Press, 1972.

Mistler-Lachman, J. Levels of comprehension in processing of normal and ambiguous sentences. *Journal of Verbal Learning and Verbal Behavior,* 1972, **5,** 614–623.

Rumelhart, D. E., Lindsay, P. H., & Norman, D. A. A process model for long-term memory. In E. Tulving & W. Donaldson (Eds.), *Organization of memory.* New York: Academic Press, 1972.

Schwartz, D., Sparkman, J. P., & Deese, J. The process of understanding and judgments of comprehensibility. *Journal of Verbal Learning and Verbal Behavior,* 1970, **9,** 87–95.

Smith, E. E., Chase W., & Smith, P. Stimulus and response repetition effects in retrieval from short-term memory: Trace decay and memory search. *Journal of Experimental Psychology,* 1973, **98,** 413–422.

Wang, M. D. Influence of linguistic structure on comprehensibility and recognition. *Journal of Experimental Psychology,* 1970, **85,** 83–89. (a)

Wand, M. D. The role of syntactic complexity as a determiner of comprehensibility. *Journal of Verbal Learning and Verbal Behavior,* 1970, **9,** 398–404. (b)

POSTSCRIPT

In a subsequent article (Clark & Haviland, 1977), Haviland and Clark suggest that speakers and listeners (or writers and readers) maintain a Given–New contract with one another, stipulating that most sentences will provide explicit or implicit clues as to how new information ties in with previously attained information. Thus, for listeners or readers, there are three steps to comprehending a sentence within a certain context: (1) identifying the given and new information in a sentence, (2) finding the relevant information (the Antecedent) in memory, and (3) integrating the new information into that memory representation. Most subsequent research on discourse processes has assumed that the conventions of the Given–New contract are routinely observed and has focused on how people identify the relevant given information in memory and integrate the new information into it.

A large part of identifying the proper Antecedent involves identifying just what the given information in a sentence refers to. For example, in order to understand the sentence "Bussey was upset because Eskie and Tandy barked at him," we must determine the proper Antecedent for *him*. This usually requires that we make an inference about the proper referent: does *him* refer to Bussey or to some other male specified earlier? Just and Carpenter (1987) and Rayner and Pollatsek (1989) provide accessible accounts of recent work on referential inferences.

In addition to studying how relevant information in memory is identified, psychologists have studied how people integrate incoming information with existing knowledge. This has led to several models of what is usually called text comprehension. Perhaps the most influential of these is that developed by Kintsch and van Dijk (Kintsch & van Dijk, 1978; van Dijk & Kintsch, 1983). Others include Thorndyke's story grammar model (Thorndyke, 1977) and Trabasso's recursive transition network representation (Trabasso & van den Broek, 1985; see also Fletcher & Bloom, 1988). Some "general purpose" models of knowledge representation have also been applied to the understanding of connected discourse (for example, Johnson-Laird's 1983 mental models approach; see also Bower & Morrow, 1990). All of these alternatives are thoroughly described by Rayner and Pollatsek (1989) and Singer (1990).

FOR FURTHER THOUGHT

1. What are the four syntactic devices described by Haviland and Clark for marking Given information? Give an example using each, and identify the Given and New information in each example.
2. What is an Antecedent, as used by Haviland and Clark?
3. According to Haviland and Clark, if an Antecedent to some information marked as Given cannot be found in memory, a listener may be required to form an inferential bridge. What is an inferential bridge? Aside from forming an inferential bridge, what two other possible courses of action are open to a listener in such a situation?
4. Why were the stimulus lists set up so that each consisted of half direct Antecedent and half indirect Antecedent sentence pairs, with the constraint that if a direct Antecedent pair was used on one list the matching indirect Antecedent pair was used on a different list?
5. What problem led Haviland and Clark to conduct Experiment II?
6. What is Haviland and Clark's argument for concluding that a subject will be able to find an Antecedent in memory for their example sentence 8 but not for their example sentence 11?

7. Why do Haviland and Clark *not* conclude that the difference in time it takes to comprehend sentences with indirect and direct Antecedents is due to the time it takes to infer or build an Antecedent?

8. How would Haviland and Clark explain why so much time in ordinary conversations is spent stating information that both participants already know?

REFERENCES

Bower, G. H., & Morrow, D. G. (1990). Mental models in narrative comprehension. *Science, 247,* 44–48.

Clark, H. H., & Clark, E. V. (1977). *Psychology and language.* New York: Harcourt Brace Jovanovich.

Clark, H. H., & Haviland, S. E. (1977). Comprehension and the Given-New contract. In R. O. Freedle (Ed.), *Discourse production and comprehension* (pp. 1–40). Norwood: Ablex.

Fletcher, C. R., & Bloom, C. P. (1988). Causal reasoning in the comprehension of simple narrative texts. *Journal of Memory and Language, 27,* 235–244.

Johnson-Laird, P. N. (1983). *Mental models.* Cambridge, MA: Harvard University Press.

Just, M. A., & Carpenter, P. A. (1987). *The psychology of reading and language comprehension.* Newton, MA: Allyn & Bacon.

Kintsch, W., & van Dijk, T. A. (1978). Toward a model of text comprehension and production. *Psychological Review, 85,* 363–394.

Rayner, K., & Pollatsek, A. (1989). *The psychology of reading.* Englewood Cliffs, NJ: Prentice-Hall.

Singer, M. (1990). *Psychology of language: An introduction to sentence and discourse processes.* Hillsdale, NJ: Erlbaum.

Thorndyke, P. W. (1977). Cognitive structures in comprehension and memory of narrative discourse. *Cognitive Psychology, 9,* 135–147.

Trabasso, T., & van den Broek, P. (1985). Causal thinking and the representation of narrative events. *Journal of Memory and Language, 24,* 612–630.

van Dijk, T. A., & Kintsch, W. (1983). *Strategies of discourse comprehension.* New York: Academic Press.

INTRODUCTION

Linguists and cognitive psychologists have developed a number of theories of language structure and everyday use. Generally, the data for these theories are provided by systematic observations of the intuitions people have about language, of their production and understanding of language, and of children learning language for the first time. A different approach is to test these theories against the language deficits of people with brain damage. This is the approach taken by Andrew Ellis, Diane Miller, and Gillian Sin in "Wernicke's Aphasia and Normal Language Processing: A Case Study in Cognitive Neuropsychology."

Examining special populations often helps us understand "normal" cognitive processes. For example, suppose our theory suggests that two tasks differ in that the first requires a certain cognitive process A and the second doesn't. In that case, we would predict that someone who happens to lack process A, perhaps as a result of damage to a certain portion of his or her brain, might be able to do the second task but not the first. If such an outcome is observed, three possible conclusions are supported (although alternative interpretations are still possible): (1) people generally use something like process A to accomplish the first task but not the second; (2) the person with brain damage lacks process A; (3) the portion of the brain damaged in that person is directly or indirectly involved in process A. In fact, observations of task breakdown in special populations can sometimes help settle issues that are difficult or impossible to establish with traditional experiments on "normal" populations (Farah, 1988).

The approach called cognitive neuropsychology studies cognitive structure and processes by observing the patterns of cognitive deficits in people with brain damage (see Tyler, 1992, for discussion). One way of characterizing this approach is that it tries to link different levels of description or explanation (Putnam, 1973). Most complex systems can be described in a number of ways. For example, we could describe the pieces of an engine of a car either in purely physical terms (such as the upper-left cubic inch) or in functional terms (such as the fuel system; Stillings et al., 1987). There is no guarantee that these two kinds of descriptions will overlap neatly, so that a single physical piece will uniquely constitute the entirety of a single functional piece. Similarly, there is no guarantee that each cognitive structure and process described by linguists and cognitive psychologists will directly correspond to distinct physical structures in the brain. However, cognitive neuropsychologists such as Ellis, Miller, and Sin assume that the brain, like the mind, is organized for the most part into modules that are functionally distinct; they operate on, or represent, specific kinds of information (such as particular steps in the production or perception of language; Fodor 1983, 1985; see also Reading 21). Furthermore, they also assume that these brain modules are, for the most part, materially distinct; the portion of the brain that serves a particular function is a distinct physical piece of the brain. This leads Ellis, Miller, and Sin and others to predict that, when a particular physical piece of the brain is damaged, a particular functional piece of the brain is also damaged, which often results in the loss of a specific cognitive structure or process.

The theoretical framework within which Ellis and his associates place their work stems largely from Garrett's (1980, 1990) model of sentence production. Understanding the details of that work requires a great deal of technical background that is beyond our scope, but a few points can be mentioned. Garrett suggests that there are several steps in the production of a sentence. The first is the formulation of an intended message at a purely conceptual level, not a linguistic one. We can describe this stage as knowing what to say but not how to say it. The second step is the formulation of a syntactic framework for the message. In this step, decisions are made about the structure of the sentence to be used, such as active versus passive. In very simplified terms, the formulation of this syntactic framework requires the selection of various function words like articles and prepositions that don't in themselves make a substantial contribution to the sense of a sentence but that help define its structure. These function words define a skeletal sentence structure. The third step involves the selection of the content words like adjectives and nouns that make the major contribution to the sense of the sentence. These content words are then inserted into their proper positions, or syntactic slots, within the skeletal sentence. Garrett believes that this results in a representation that contains the conceptual and gross structural properties of the words. We could say that at this point that we know what the sentence is but not what it sounds like. It is only in a fourth step that we retrieve the phonological representations of the words (roughly, more specific information about what the words sound like).

Notice that in Garrett's model, people with problems in the insertion of content words might produce syntactically well-formed sentences in which some of the content words are semantically anomalous, such as "The hair spun by pianos." Errors of this sort are called semantic or verbal paraphrasias. Garrett's model also predicts that problems in the fourth step would result in sentences in which the pronunciation of certain words is distorted, as in "the gog darked" instead of "the dog barked." Errors of this sort are called neologisms, or phonemic (or literal) paraphasias. Ellis and his colleagues studied someone who makes errors of the latter kind, implying that he has a problem with Garrett's fourth step.

When studying neologisms, we often need to communicate exactly how a patient pronounces her or his words. A common practice, followed by Ellis and his colleagues, is to use a phonetic alphabet to represent the patient's utterances. Tables explaining phonetic alphabets can be found in any introductory linguistics text (for example, Fromkin & Rodman, 1978). In this article Ellis and his associates generally provide enough clarification so that a reader not familiar with such alphabets can understand the pattern and implications of their results.

A particularly interesting aspect of this article is the authors' comparison of the subject's comprehension and production of written words with his comprehension and production of spoken words. It is intuitively plausible that understanding a written word or spelling a word involves first retrieving information about how it sounds (its phonological representation) and then either retrieving its meaning or deciding on its spelling. In so-called regularly spelled words, spelling is predictable from sound (for example, *take, bake*). But it is also possible that deciding whether a string of letters forms a real word in the language (which is what subjects do in the lexical decision task) or going from a written word to its meaning and vice versa involves the use of special orthographic representations; these representations give information about how the word is spelled or what it looks like rather than how it sounds. Orthographic representations are probably necessary for irregularly spelled words, in which spelling is not predictable from sound (for example, *wand, wood*).

Various tests that Ellis, Miller, and Sin performed on their subject and some of their theoretical discussions have been excluded in this selection. As you read this article, ask yourself what sorts of results we would expect with this patient if the comprehension and production of written and spoken language make use of the same phonological representations. What sorts of results would we expect if they did not?

Wernicke's Aphasia and Normal Language Processing: A Case Study in Cognitive Neuropsychology

Andrew W. Ellis, Diane Miller, and Gillian Sin
University of Lancaster

INTRODUCTION

This paper is about how some of the psychological systems which mediate human language performance are organized, how they work, and how they are interrelated. By the end of the paper we hope to be able to make some sensible statements about normal speech production, writing, reading and (to a lesser extent) speech perception. The primary empirical content of the paper records the performance of a single language-disordered (aphasic) patient on a variety of tasks which we asked him to carry out for us, but many of the theoretical conclusions we draw are conclusions about the structure and function of language systems in normal, intact human beings. We identify ourselves therefore with a growing band of cognitive psychologists and psycholinguists who seek to supplement standard experimental methods of investigating cognitive processes in normals with analyses of how those same cognitive processes may be neurologically impaired (cf., Ellis, 1982). We feel, however, that this approach is still sufficiently new (in modern times at least) and perhaps controversial to require a brief attempt at justification.

In a persuasive (to us) exposition of the rationale behind the resurgence of interest in which might be called "cognitive neuropsychology," Shallice (1981) begins by drawing attention to Marr's (1976) discussion of the "principle of modularity." Marr's work is concerned first and foremost with the interpretation by computers of visual scenes, but in a passage cited by Shallice (1981), Marr draws a general moral about how the information-processing architecture of both machines and people *should* be organized. Marr (1976) writes:

> Any large computation should be split up and implemented as a collection of small sub-parts that are as nearly independent of one another as the overall task allows. If a process is not designed in this way, a small change in one place will have consequences in many other places. This means that the process as a whole becomes extremely difficult to debug or to improve, whether by a human designer or in the course of natural evolution, because a small change to improve one part has to be accompanied by many simultaneous compensating changes elsewhere.

Developing this theme, Shallice (1981, p. 187) adds:

> if, in addition, one makes the plausible assumption that computational independence is made easier by separability of physical processes in the brain then one would predict that the cognitive processes are implemented by functional subsystems that are in some way materially distinct. On this extended principle of modularity occasionally a lesion might well damage any particular subsystem selectively. . . . Moreover, the nature of the selective deficits observed may well speak to theories of the overall functional architecture.

We should like to thank the consultant medical staff of Lancaster Health District, Dr. J. V. Dyer, District Medical Officer, Mr. H. Carr, District Administrator, and the District Management Team for permission to work with R. D. We should also like to thank the Speech Therapists at the Lancaster Moor Hospital, Maureen Millar, Garry Withnell, and Shan Williams for their cheerful cooperation and many helpful comments. Diane Miller's research was supported by a postgraduate award from the Social Science Research Council. Finally we should like to thank Mrs. D. for making us so welcome on our weekly visits.

Reprint requests should be sent to Dr. A. W. Ellis, Psychology Department, University of Lancaster, Lancaster LA1 4 YF, U.K.

SOURCE: *Cognition, 15,* 1983, pp. 111–144. Copyright 1983 by Elsevier Sequoia. Reprinted by permission.

The notion that the human cognitive apparatus is best described as a set of independent and distributed, but interacting content-specific devices is also advocated by Allport (1980) who notes the compatibility of this view with the wide range of highly selective cognitive deficits documented by neuropsychologists (see also Allport and Funnell, 1981).

Specificity and dissociability of functions, then, tell us something about which cognitive subsystems are independent from which others, and also possibly something about how those subsystems might interconnect. This, of course, was exactly the position espoused by those late nineteenth century neurologists who pioneered the study of aphasia, but who were later scorned by Henry Head as (mere) "diagram makers" (e.g., Bastian, 1897; Broadbent, 1872; Lichtheim, 1885; Wernicke, 1874). In fact it turns out that modular cognitive systems are well captured by information-flow diagrams (Morton, 1981).

In a discussion of possible reasons for the decline and fall of the earlier school of diagram makers, Marshall (1974) observes that while they developed elegant and, by the standards of their day, sophisticated cognitive models, they could make few suggestions regarding the internal structure of their postulated "centers" (= distributed content-specific computational devices). Hopefully we are in a better position today. First, computer metaphors help us think about how our centers *might* work. Second, accumulated data from normal cognitive psychology and psycholinguistics place more constraints on our models of how they *do* work. Third, cognitive neuropsychologists have developed another, complementary approach to neurological patients where, in addition to cataloguing dissociations and deficits, the opportunities which these patients afford to examine cognitive subsystems operating at something less than their normal efficiency are also exploited. Inefficient systems make errors, and errors we know from many areas of cognitive psychology to be highly revealing of underlying mechanisms. If dissociations and selective deficits allow us to lay out the cognitive boxes in appropriate positions, then by studying deficient subsystems we can take the lids off those boxes and peer inside.

Another charge which may be laid at the door of the diagram makers is that they often displayed excessive zeal in attempting to localize their centers in particular areas of the cortex on the basis of what, it

must be admitted, was fairly scanty evidence. A view now widely held (though that is no guarantee of its ultimate truth or validity) is that neurological impairments to cognitive functions can be adequately captured (at one level of explanation anyway) in the terminology of cognitive, information-processing psychology, and that the nature of the neural bases of any hypothesized subsystems is an interesting, but separate, question (e.g., Marshall, 1982; Morton, 1981; Shallice, 1981). That is also a view to which we should like to subscribe.

A final point in our preamble: the growth of cognitive neuropsychology is being marked by a return to detailed case studies, as favored by the diagram makers, in preference to studies which compare groups of patients either with groups of patients manifesting a different syndrome or with groups of normals. As Shallice (1981, p. 187) says, "the 'sharpness' of particular dissociations is liable to be lost with group data through averaging over different functional deficits" (see also Kinsbourne, 1971; Shallice, 1979). We agree with Marin *et al.* (1976, p. 871) when they write that:

> . . . at this stage in the endeavour, more useful insights into normal language function will be provided by the detailed consideration of privileged cases, cases where there is still sufficient language to study language behaviour, and where there are rather clear dissociations of function.

The detailed examination of just such a privileged case makes up the bulk of this paper. The case study is fairly lengthy, though we have tried to break it up into coherent and digestible chunks. The patient we describe (R.D.) is a Wernicke's (fluent) aphasic whose spontaneous speech contained many distorted attempts at words (neologisms or phonemic paraphasias). Following the basic case history we document the preservation of reading comprehension in R.D. which is independent of his ability or inability to read a word aloud correctly. We then show how R.D.'s written spelling is better than his oral naming of words. The determinants of R.D.'s ability to say a word correctly rather than produce a neologism are then examined, particularly the relevance of the distinction between content and function words (alias open *versus* closed class words or major *versus* minor lexical categories). Finally we analyze something of the nature of R.D.'s neologisms and spelling errors. Our conclusions pertain to the characterization of the nature of the deficits in Wernicke's (neologistic jargon) aphasia, to the independence or otherwise of the mechanisms for the recognition and production of spoken and written words, and to the procedures by which lexical entries are retrieved and outputted in speech and writing.

THE SYNDROME AND THE PATIENT

Aphasia, occurring as a consequence of brain injury, takes different forms in different patients. Whilst there is not universal agreement about the categories that should be recognized, certain syndromes are acknowledged in virtually all classificatory systems (see Kertesz, 1979). The particular syndrome with which we shall be predominantly concerned was first described in detail by Wernicke (1874) after whom it is often known as Wernicke's aphasia. Proliferation of terminology is, however, characteristic of this area, and what we shall call Wernicke's aphasia (following Goodglass and Kaplan, 1972; Kertesz, 1979) has also been called sensory aphasia (by Wernicke himself, and also by Bay, 1964; Luria, 1964), receptive aphasia (Weisenburg and McBride, 1935) and many other things (Kertesz, 1979, pp. 4–5).

The patient with Wernicke's aphasia shows poor comprehension of speech, allied with fluent but distorted speech production. The spontaneous speech of a Wernicke's aphasic may contain incorrectly used words, termed verbal or semantic paraphasias, or distorted but recognizable words variously referred to as literal paraphasias, phonemic paraphasias, or (as we shall call them) neologisms. The particular patient (R.D.) whom we shall shortly be discussing made few verbal paraphasias but a substantial number of neologisms. R.D.'s variety of Wernicke's aphasia is what Kertesz and Benson (1970), Buckingham and Kertesz (1976) and others would call "neologistic jargonaphasia."

Case History

R.D., a right-handed man, was born in April 1908, received a grammar school education, and worked for most of his adult life as a quantity surveyor. He suffered a heart attack in December 1978 at the age of 69, followed by a stroke in February 1979. On recovery he experienced a slight loss of sensation from and control of his right arm and leg, but was left with a moderately severe loss of auditory speech comprehension and a fluent, neologistic Wernicke's aphasia.

In October 1980 R.D. was given a shortened form of the Minnesota Test for the Differential Diagnosis of Aphasia (Schuell, 1965). He showed severe auditory disturbances, being at chance level on matching spoken words to pictures and matching spoken to printed letters. He was unable to answer questions based on a heard paragraph, unable to repeat sentences spoken by the examiner, unable to answer simple yes/no questions, and unable to point to items named from a picture. In marked contrast, he performed without error on tests of matching written words to shapes or to pictures, and he was able to answer written questions requiring yes/no answers, including questions based on a read paragraph. His attempts to read aloud were, however, replete with verbal paraphasias and neologisms, as were all his attempts at expressive speech. R.D. was able to copy Greek letters correctly, reproduce Roman letters, write numbers to twenty, and write short sentences incorporating a word shown to him (though these contained spelling errors of the sort described later in this paper).

Table 1 gives an extended sample of R.D.'s spontaneous speech produced on 20 November 1980 when asked to describe the goings-on in a detailed picture of activities around a scout camp. Words printed in italicized capital letters within brackets are our attempts at guessing R.D.'s targets whenever he produced a neologism.

R.D. lived at home with his wife and attended weekly Speech Therapy Clinics at the Lancaster Moor Hospital. He was tested by us once or twice a week, both at the clinic and in his own home between October 1980 and June 1981, when he was aged 70-71. He was fully aware of his language problems (showing no signs of "anosognosia" or denial of illness) and was naturally frustrated and sometimes annoyed with his difficulties. Nevertheless he remained remarkably cheerful, and willingly undertook the assortment of tasks we set him, however bizarre. Sadly, R.D. died in June 1981 following a heart attack. We have no information on the precise locus of R.D.'s lesion. Although such data might have been desirable

TABLE 1 R.D.'s Description of a Picture of Activities around a Scout Camp. R.D.'s neologisms are shown in phonemic notation. Upper-case italicized words in parentheses are the authors' guesses at R.D.'s target words.

1. A / bʌn bʌn / (*BULL*) a / bʌk / (*BULL*) is er . . .
2. / tʃɜtʃɪŋ / (*CHASING*) a boy or / ş̊kɜt / (*SCOUT*). A
3. / ş̊k / . . . boy / skʌt / (*SCOUT*) is by a / bəʊn
4. pəʊ / (*POST*) of pine. A . . . post . . . / pəʊn / (*POST*)
5. with a er /təʊn təʊ / (*LINE?*) with / wɒʃɪŋt/
6. (*WASHING*) hanging on including his socks / saɪz /
7. (?). A . . . a / nek / (*TENT*) is by the
8. washing. A b-boy is / swɪʔɪŋ / (*SWINGING*) on
9. the bank with his hand (*FEET*) in the
10. / strɪŋt / (*STREAM*). A table with / ɔstrəm
11. (*SAUCEPAN?*) and . . . I don't know . . . and a
12. three-legged / strəʊ / (*STOOL*) and a / streɪn /
13. (*PAIL*) table, table [E: *It's a bucket*] near
14. the water. A er / trəʊlvɒt / (*TRIVET*) three-
15. legged er er means for hanging a / tɒŋ tɒŋ /
16. (*PAN?*) on the / faɪəst / (*FIRE*) which is
17. blowed by a boy-boy. A boy / skrʌt / (*SCOUT*)
18. is up a tree and looking at . . . through . . .
19. / həʊ / (?) glasses. A man is knocking a
20. paper . . . paper with a / nəʊtɪst / (*NOTICE*) by
21. the er . . . / tɜ / tent, tent er / tet / er tent. A boy is
22. / pləʊɪŋ / (*BLOWING*) a . . . no, I beg your pardon, by a
23. bull (*BOWL?*) and a . . . in his right hand, and
24. his left hand is a bottle. Another boy has
25. a arm full of bottles to put on the
26. bottle (?) by the fire. The other boy / sk / . . .
27. boy is putting the er / bɒks / (*BLOCKS*) of
28. bottles (?) of / wʊdəʊ / (*WOOD*) which has
29. been / hɒpt / (*CHOPPED*) in small pieces.

from some points of view, our interest lies in the cognitive rather than the anatomical localization of R.D.'s deficits.

DISSOCIATIONS OF FUNCTION AND SELECTIVITY OF DEFICITS

R.D. showed a number of interesting dissociations of function and selective deficits. In this section we shall concentrate upon the discrepancy between R.D.'s poor speech comprehension and his very good reading comprehension, and also upon the superiority of his written spelling over his spoken naming.

1. Comprehension of Speech and Writing

Clinically R.D.'s speech comprehension was very poor. He had the greatest difficulty understanding speech addressed to him, and when he did respond appropriately it appeared to be through use of the nonverbal context. He also appeared on occasions to use lipreading cues though we have no documentary proof of the efficacy of this strategy. Unfortunately we were not able to carry out any more systematic investigations of R.D.'s comprehension problems so we cannot say whether his difficulty was a peripheral, auditory one or of a more central linguistic nature.

Early on the course of our investigation of R.D. it became apparent to us that not only was R.D.'s reading comprehension far better than his speech comprehension, but also his ability to understand a written word was independent of whether or not he could pronounce the word correctly. When R.D. was given single words to read aloud he would often spontaneously follow his incorrect attempt to say the word with a definition or paraphrase. For example, when shown *grief* written on a card, R.D. said "/ prɪvd / . . . one is sad." Other examples include *depth*— "/ seft / . . . it's very deep down"; *chaos* — "/kwɒst/ . . . people all muddled up . . . out of order . . . /čɒst/"; and *quilt* — "/ kwɪst / . . . on top of you on the bed . . . / kwɪt . . . kwɪtst /."

In order to corroborate our belief that R.D. understood the vast majority of written words we showed him, Studies 1 to 5 were carried out.

Study 1. Sorting written words into countries and parts of the body (15 January 1981). Fifteen names of countries and 15 parts of the body were printed individually on cards in capital (upper-case) letters and presented to R.D. who was required to read each word aloud and, after reading each word, place its card on one pile for countries and another for parts of the body. He read correctly one country and 13 body parts but sorted all 30 words correctly. These results are reasonably convincing, but it could be argued that R.D. might have sorted correctly on the basis of the assumption that if he could read it correctly the word was a body part and if not it was a country. To eliminate this possibility Study 2 was carried out.

Study 2. Sorting written words into animals and musical instruments (29 January 1981). Study 2 required R.D. once again to read aloud then sort words presented singly on cards, the two categories in this instance being animals and musical instruments. R.D. read correctly 6 of 12 animal names and 2 of 12 musical instruments, but sorted all 24 words correctly.

Study 3. Delayed word–picture matching (15 March 1981). Study 3 examined R.D.'s ability to read aloud an object name then, with the name removed, point to the appropriate picture in a set of four alternatives. Twenty pictures which reliably elicit a particular name were selected from the set provided by Snodgrass and Vanderwart (1980). The twenty names were then written on cards in capital letters. The cards were shown to R.D. one at a time. As each card was presented, R.D. was required to read aloud the object name written on it. When he had attempted to read the word the card was removed and a sheet of A4 paper[1] with four pictures (the picture corresponding to the word just shown plus three distractors) was shown. The correct picture occurred equally often at each of the four positions. R.D. was required to point to the picture whose name he had just attempted to read.

R.D. read correctly 11/20 written object names, but pointed correctly to the appropriate picture on all 20 trials, providing further evidence that he understood words he could not read aloud correctly, and also corroborating the clinical impression that he had no difficulty in identifying and understanding pictures (i.e., he did not have a visual agnosia). R.D.'s reading errors on Study 3, as on all reading aloud tasks, were neologisms very similar to those he produced in spontaneous speech and in picture naming. Examples of reading and naming errors from Study 3 are *flag* read as / flækt / and named (on a separate occasion) as / flæt /, *pipe* read as / pɪptə / and named as / penz /, and *candle* read as / krætəlz / and named as / bækʌnz /.

---

[1]Editor's note: A4 paper is paper of a common size in Europe, slightly larger than 8½ × 11 inches.

Study 4. Judging the similarity of meaning of pairs of written words (7 May 1981). In Study 4 R.D. was required to read aloud two words written on a card then place the card on one pile if the words had "similar meanings" and on another pile if the words had "different meanings." There were 15 pairs with similar meanings and 15 pairs with different meanings, generated by rearranging the similar-meaning pairs. Examples of similar-meaning pairs are *corner–angle, abode–residence,* and *exhaustion–fatigue;* examples of different-meaning pairs are *hurricane–troops, oven–ghost* and *cottage–mate.*

The results are presented in Table 2, which shows that R.D. sorted all 30 cards correctly despite only twice being able to read both words correctly and failing to read either word correctly on 16 occasions.

TABLE 2 Reading Aloud Pairs of Words Then Sorting into "Similar Meaning" or "Different Meaning" (Study 4)

	Similar Meaning	Different Meaning
Read both words aloud correctly	2	0
Read one word aloud correctly	5	7
Read neither word aloud correctly	8	8
Sorted correctly	15/15	15/15

Study 5. Reading aloud then sorting sentences into "sense" and "nonsense" (19 March 1981, 26 March 1981 and 2 April 1981). Hécaen and Albert (1978) claim that some patients, whom they call "sentence dyslexics," can understand the meanings of individual words but often fail to understand the meanings of full sentences. Study 5 examined R.D.'s appreciations of sentence meanings by requiring him over the course of three sessions to read aloud 36 sentences then sort them into those which made "sense" and those which were "nonsense."

The stimuli were adapted from Morton (1967, Reference Note 2) who gave incomplete sentences to normal individuals and asked them to provide one word for each sentence making a plausible completion. Eighteen incomplete sentences were selected along with 18 frequently-given completion words; these formed the sentences which "made sense." The 18 completion words were then reassigned to the incomplete sentence contexts so as to form sentences which in our view were "nonsense" (though syntactically correct). Examples of "sense" sentences include *He sat reading a paper* and *Thoughtfully he chewed a pencil*. Examples of "nonsense" sentences include *She played her favorite window* and *Passing overhead was a kitchen*. R.D. was given six "sense" and six "nonsense" sentences in each of three sessions such that no sentence context or completion word occurred twice in any session. R.D. read only 4/36 entire sentences correctly and only 9/36 completion words (five "sense," 4 "nonsense"). Nevertheless he correctly classified all 18 "sense" sentences and 16/18 "nonsense" sentences. (Two low probability sentences were classified as "sense"; these were *The cat jumped on the station* and *She watched him blow up the music*). Given that we have no data from normal 70-year-olds on this task, and given the fact that we always gave written instruction for all our tasks which he never failed to understand (however bizarre), we are not inclined to impute to R.D. *any* deficit in written sentence comprehension.

Although there are a few reports of good reading comprehension in Wernicke's aphasics (e.g., Kertesz and Benson, 1970, Case 4; Heilman, *et al.*, 1979, Case 2), the majority of Wernicke's aphasics show poor reading comprehension (Kertesz, 1979). This somewhat unusual aspect of R.D.'s deficits meant that we could use word naming alongside other tasks like picture naming and description to investigate his lexical retrieval for speech.

2. Spelling versus Spoken Naming

When R.D. was unable to pronounce a word correctly he would not uncommonly reach for pen and paper and try to write the word. His written attempts were often correct when his pronunciation was not. Studies 6–8 were carried out to confirm or disconfirm our impression that R.D. could spell many words he could not say.

Study 6. Saying then writing picture names with one, two, or three syllables (11 December 1980).   Thirty pictures were selected from Snodgrass and Vanderwart (1980) with name frequencies of 1–11 occurrences per million written words (Kucera and Francis, 1967). There were 10 one-syllable, 10 two-syllable and 10 three-syllable words. R.D. was shown the pictures individually and was asked to attempt first to say the name of the depicted object then to spell the name. The results are shown in Table 3.

Thus, R.D. correctly named 5/30 pictures and also spelled those names correctly. In addition, 12 pictures which he was unable to name correctly were nevertheless spelled correctly. On no occasion did he say correctly a picture name he was unable to spell. Interestingly, there is no evidence that the length of the name in syllables affected R.D.'s ability to spell a word—he made as many errors spelling one-syllable as three-syllable names.

TABLE 3   Naming Then Spelling Pictures with One-, Two-, or Three-Syllable Names (Study 6)

	Number of Syllables in Picture Name			
	One	*Two*	*Three*	*Total*
Named correctly, spelled correctly	2/10	3/10	0/10	5/30
Named wrongly, spelled correctly	4/10	2/10	6/10	12/30
Named correctly, spelled wrongly	0/10	0/10	0/10	0/30
Named wrongly, spelled wrongly	4/10	5/10	4/10	13/30
Total named correctly	2/10	3/10	0/10	5/30
Total spelled correctly	6/10	5/10	6/10	17/30

Study 7. Naming then spelling pictures with regularly or irregularly spelled names (22 May 1981).   Twenty-eight pictures were selected from the Snodgrass and Vanderwart (1980) set. Fourteen of the objects depicted had regularly spelled names, and 14 had irregularly spelled names. As with Study 6, R.D. was

TABLE 4 Naming Then Spelling Pictures with Regularly or Irregularly Spelled Names (Study 7)

	Regular Words	Irregular Words	Total
Named correctly, spelled correctly	4/14	7/14	11/28
Named wrongly, spelled correctly	7/14	3/14	10/28
Named correctly, spelled wrongly	0/14	1/14	1/28
Named wrongly, spelled wrongly	3/14	3/14	6/28
Named correctly	4/14	8/14	12/28
Spelled correctly	11/14	10/14	21/28

asked to name the pictures then spell their names. Table 4 shows the results. Once again, R.D.'s spelling is better than his naming, though here we have an instance of R.D. naming a picture (of a door) correctly but misspelling it (as BOOR—an error which he corrected when it was pointed out that the letter B was wrong). If anything, R.D. performed better on both naming and spelling pictures with irregularly spelled names than on those with regularly spelled names.

Study 8. Naming pictures, spelling picture names and reading picture names (May–June 1981). In Study 8 R.D. was asked either to name a picture then spell the name, or to read aloud a written object name then select the appropriate picture from a set of six. Forty-two pictures were selected from Snodgrass and Vanderwart (1980). Half had high frequency names (15–80 occurrences per million words; Kucera and Francis, 1967) and half had low frequency names (0–4 occurrences per million words). The high and low frequency names were matched on syllable length (1 to 3 syllables). The study was carried out over the course of four sessions. In session 1 R.D. named-then-spelled half the pictures. In sessions 2 and 3 he read written picture names of the same set of words then selected the appropriate picture from a set of 6. In session 4 he named-then-spelled the remaining pictures.

Once again, R.D.'s spelling (33/42 correct) was better than his spoken naming (12/42). There was one picture (of a basket) which he named correctly and then misspelled (as BASHEL), but 21 pictures which he spelled correctly after having been unable to name them correctly. Of importance for later studies is the finding that there was no appreciable difference between R.D.'s naming from pictures (12/42) and his reading aloud (16/42). In the reading aloud task, R.D. pointed to the correct picture on every single occasion, irrespective of whether his attempt at reading had been correct or not. The effects of word frequency will be dealt with later.

This section has been concerned with dissociations and selective deficits. We have established dissociations between good reading comprehension and poor speech comprehension and between moderately impaired written naming and more severely impaired spoken naming. We argued earlier that the study of partially impaired subsystems could throw light on the normal operation of those subsystems. In the next section we shall attempt to justify that claim with respect to the process of lexical retrieval in speech. We begin with data on R.D.'s spontaneous speech, followed by an illustration of the effect of word frequency on his lexical retrieval. We then consider the relevance (or, as we believe, the irrelevance) of the content-function word distinction to the characterization of R.D.'s deficit before finally discussing similarities between R.D.'s neologistic attempts and their real-word targets.

LEXICAL RETRIEVAL FOR SPEECH AND WRITING

1. Aspects of R.D.'s Spontaneous Speech

Inspection of the corpus of R.D.'s speech reproduced in Table 1 reveals a number of noteworthy features. First, the speech is manifestly directed at the subject matter of the picture and contains readily identifiable sentences. There are a few clear verbal paraphasias (e.g., "hand" for FEET on line 9). Verbal paraphasias are, however, greatly outnumbered by neologisms. Sometimes these are only slight deviations from the apparent target word (e.g., / wɒʃɪŋt / for WASHING on line 5, or / wʊdəʊ / for WOOD on line 28); sometimes the neologism deviates considerably from any plausible target (e.g., / ɔstrəm / for the presumed target *SAUCEPAN* on line 11). With these latter cases we are obviously less confident of our proposal regarding R.D.'s target. The investigator's knowledge and ingenuity play perhaps too much of a role here. Thus, for a long time we dismissed / trɔulvɒt / (line 14) as grossly deviant until a colleague of ours—himself an ex-scout—pointed out that a "trivet" is a three-legged stand for holding a vessel over a fire. Because of these uncertainties we confined our study of similarities between target words and R.D.'s neologisms to the situations of reading aloud and picture naming.

That said, there are certain things one *can* usefully do with spontaneous speech samples. We took as our model Butterworth's (1979) insightful analysis of the spontaneous speech of a 72-year-old neologistic Wernicke's aphasic patient (K.C.). Using the immediate speech context as a guide, Butterworth was able to ascribe 138 of K.C.'s 164 neologisms to particular grammatical classes. Sixty-one percent of neologisms were nouns, 20% verbs and 14% adjectives, the remainder being adverbs, conjunctions, prepositions or demonstratives. That is, 95% of K.C.'s neologisms fell into the broad category of "content" or "open-class" words (i.e., nouns, verbs and adjectives) and only 5% into the category of "function" or "closed-class" words. In R.D.'s case, by our estimation, 24 of the neologisms in the scout picture passage occupy noun slots, and 4 occupy verb slots. None of the neologisms appears to occupy the positions of function words. (We anticipate that some readers will disagree with us over these precise numbers: all that matters is that they should agree on the general trend.)

We have followed Butterworth (1979) in electing to classify as neologisms certain items which are, in fact, real words in English. Examples include / bʌn / and / bʌk / for *BULL* (line 1), / streɪn / for *PAIL* (line 12) and / bɒks / for (*BLOCKS*) (line 27). Although *bun, book, strain* and *box* are all familiar words in English, we believe that these errors are "jargon homophones" (that is, approximations to a target word which, by chance, happen themselves to be real words) rather than phonologically based verbal paraphasias (cf., Butterworth, 1979). It should be said,

however, that none of our theoretical conclusions stands or falls on this decision.

Another point to note is the *inconsistency* of R.D.'s neologisms. For example, *SCOUT* is variously pronounced / sk3t / (line 2), / skʌt / (line 3) and / skrʌt / (line 17). Thus it is not the case that R.D.'s stroke has in some way replaced the correct pronunciations of words in his internal lexicon by deviant ones; rather each neologism seems to be a fresh attempt at a target word. Further, although we were not able to document this formally, R.D. was by no means certain when he pronounced a word correctly and when he made an error (witness the string of attempts at *TENT* on line 21). He would sometimes continue to generate attempts at a target word despite having already said it correctly, and he would sometimes say, "Got that right, didn't I?" when, in fact, he had not. R.D. knew he had a speech problem—there was no suggestion of anosognosia (in the sense of a denial of symptoms)—but we assume that difficulties with speech perception prevented him from accurately monitoring his own output.

Following Butterworth (1979) we conducted an analysis of the pauses in the scout passage. The voice signal from the tape was fed into a pen recorder, providing a trace of phonation and silence against time. Any period of silence longer than 250 ms was treated as a pause. The mean duration of pauses preceding neologisms was 1460 ms whilst the mean duration of pauses before correctly produced words was 808 ms. This difference is significant (t (175) = 3.38, $p < 0.01$, one-tailed) and is in line with Butterworth's own finding.

2. The Effect of Word Frequency on R.D.'s Spoken Naming

In Study 8 which we discussed earlier, R.D. was asked to name 42 pictures with high or low frequency names. On 14 May 1981 a further 25 pictures with low frequency names and 25 with high frequency names were presented. R.D. correctly named 22/25 high frequency pictures and 10/25 low frequency pictures. Combining these results with those of Study 8, R.D. named correctly 33/46 high frequency pictures and 11/46 low frequency pictures, this difference being significant (chi-square = 19.2, df = 1, $p < 0.01$).

That is, the probability of R.D. being able to pronounce a word correctly depends on its frequency of usage.

3. Parts of Speech and the Content-Function Word Distinction

A distinction which has enjoyed a measure of popularity in recent psycho- and neurolinguistics is that between *content words* and *function words*. Content words (alias "major lexical categories" or "open class" words) comprise the nouns, main verbs, adjectives and (in some accounts) some of the adverbs. They form a large set, of varying length and frequency, which is continuously being added to as new words enter the language (hence the designation "open class" words). Function words (alias "minor lexical categories" or "closed class" words) comprise pronouns (*this, your, he,* etc.), determiners (*the, a(n), every,* etc.), prepositions (*of, at, without,* etc.), conjunctions (*and, that, although,* etc.), auxiliary verbs (*can, should, will,* etc.), and, in some accounts, some adverbs like *too, maybe* and *perhaps.*

Bradley (1978, Reference Note 1) and Bradley *et al.* (1980) claimed that normal subjects show an effect of word frequency on speed of responding to written content words in a lexical decision task, but no effect of word frequency on speed of responding to function words. Gordon and Caramazza (1982) have, however, presented evidence which casts doubt on this claim. Gordon and Caramazza showed that both content and function words show similar sensitivity to word frequency for frequencies less than around 316 per million. Above that value, function words are unaffected by word frequency and there are probably too few content words for a meaningful analysis to be carried out. That is, Bradley's results may be an artifact of the typical frequency ranges of content and function words.

In his analyses of slips of the tongue, Garrett (1975; 1982) has shown that exchanges of phonemes and words in spontaneous speech errors have a strong tendency to involve pairs of content words, with function words (or phonemes in function words) only rarely being involved in these particular types of error.

In addition to having possible relevance for explaining aspects of normal performance, the content/function word distinction has been held to be pertinent to the description and explanation of certain (acquired) dyslexic and aphasic syndromes. Thus, brain injury appears selectively to impair the reading of function words in acquired phonological dyslexia (Patterson, 1982) and deep dyslexia (Morton and Patterson, 1980). Marin *et al.* (1976) applied the same distinction to the syndrome of Broca's aphasia. Broca's aphasics produce short, halting phrases containing a high proportion of concrete nouns and main verbs (e.g., when asked to describe a picture, patient H. T. described by Marin *et al.* says, "Like the door . . . crash . . . like, pants . . . shirt . . . shoes . . . the boy . . . the dress . . . I dunno"). Marin *et al.* propose that the normal internal lexicon embodies a distinction between, on the one hand, content words used for naming or making reference and, on the other hand, function words and bound, inflectional morphemes (which are also lost in Broca's aphasia) used to express sentence *structure* and accessed via the "syntactic machinery." For Marin *et al.* (see also Saffran *et al.,* 1980) Broca's aphasia is "lexicon without syntax," being the result of a syntactic deficit which prevents the expression of function words and bound morphemes (see Berndt and Caramazza (1980) for a comprehensive review of this and alternative explanations).

The question then arises: Can the content/function word distinction profitably be applied to the explanation of Wernicke's (neologistic jargon) aphasia? Several investigators believe it can. As was reported earlier, the neologisms of patients like R.D. and Butterworth's (1979) patient K.C. undoubtedly occupy syntactic slots where one would expect to find content words. To take another example, patient B.F. reported by Buckingham and Kertesz (1976) produced in a sample of spontaneous speech 182 neologisms whose "grammatical class" could be inferred from the sentential context. Of these, 134 (73.6%) were "nouns" and 43 (23.6%) "verbs." Green (1969) and O'Connell (1981) likewise document the tendency of neologisms to occur in the place of content words. Marin *et al.* (1976) and Friederici and Schoenle (1980) have both compared Wernicke's aphasics' reading of pairs of homophones, one of which is a content word and the other a function word (e.g., *sum–some, bee–be, wood–would*). Both studies found better reading of the function words than their homophonic content word partners, and both studies report the opposite pattern of results for Broca's aphasics.

Marin *et al.* (1976) propose that whereas Broca's aphasia represents "lexicon without syntax," Wernicke's aphasia represents "syntax without lexicon," the idea being that Wernicke's aphasics retain command over syntax—hence their utterances are syntactically structured and contain function words (and inflectional morphemes) in correct positions—but content words are absent (in anomia), or replaced in neologistic Wernicke's aphasia by neologisms which act as fillers to mask lexical gaps (cf., Buckingham, 1979; Buckingham and Kertesz, 1976). Garrett (1982) holds a similar view regarding the appropriateness of the content/function word distinction to the characterization and explanation of Wernicke's aphasia. Such a view is coherent and plausible but, we believe, wrong.

Function words are known to be, on average, both shorter and of far higher frequency than content words (Miller *et al.,* 1958). This is illustrated by the observation that the hundred most frequent words in the language (Kucera and Francis, 1967) contain only three nouns—*time, man* and *year*—at rank orders 67, 81 and 95 respectively (Marshall, 1977). Now, we know from the work of Howes (1964; 1967*a,b*; Howes and Geschwind, 1964) and Oldfield (1966) that many aphasics, but most especially Wernicke's aphasics, show a marked bias towards high frequency words in their spontaneous utterances. It is possible, therefore, that a deficit in production of all but the commoner words with no distinction as to grammatical class might *look* like a selective deficit in the production of content words.

To test the rival hypotheses of R.D.'s lexical retrieval difficulties (a content word deficit *versus* a low-frequency word deficit) we conducted two studies (9 and 10 below) in which R.D. was asked to read aloud content and function words matched on frequency. We would argue that reading aloud can be used to tap lexical retrieval processes in R.D. because a) there was no question of failure on R.D.'s part to recognize or understand the words shown, his problems relat-

ing to the production of the spoken response; b) as Study 8 has shown, his reading aloud is comparable to his picture naming in terms of percent correct; and c) his errors when reading aloud are indistinguishable from his errors in spontaneous speech or his picture naming errors.

Study 9. Nouns versus *function words I (18 December 1980).* In our first investigation of R.D.'s performance on content and function words, R.D. was presented with 20 imageable nouns and 20 function words matched on letter length and Kucera and Francis (1967) frequency. As before, the words were shown singly on cards in a random order to be read aloud. Because there is no universal consent as to what precisely counts as a function word, the words used, together with R.D.'s responses, are shown in Table 5, where it can be seen that there was effectively no difference between R.D.'s scores on nouns and function words. Of note is the fact that it is the less common function words that R.D. tends to get wrong.

Study 10. Nouns versus *function words II (5 February 1981).* Because of the theoretical importance of the comparison of content and function words, we prepared a fresh set of 24 nouns, verbs and adjectives, and 24 function words matched on length and frequency. Inevitably there is some overlap in words used with Study 9. The words were presented singly on cards in a random order for R.D. to read aloud. The results are shown in Table 6. Again there is no trace of a difference between content and function words once word frequency is controlled.

We conclude from the results of Studies 9 and 10 that the apparent sparing of function words in neologistic Wernicke's aphasia is an artifact of the higher average frequency of function words as compared with content words. Once word frequency is controlled no differences remain in R.D.'s performance on these two classes of word. . . .

GENERAL DISCUSSION

Our discussion will be divided into two main parts. First we shall consider how the speech production aspects of R.D.'s neologistic jargonaphasia and other varieties of Wernicke's aphasia might be explained

TABLE 5 R. D.'s Performance on Reading Aloud Single Nouns and Function Words (Study 12)

	Nouns		Function Words	
	Word Presented	R.D.'s Response	Word Presented	R.D.'s Response
1.	Men	+	Off	+
2	Car	+	Yet	+
3.	Boy	+	Why	+
4.	Bed	/ beg . . . peg /	Nor	+
5.	Hand	+	Once	+
6.	Head	+	Away	+
7.	City	+	Ever	+
8.	Door	+	Thus	+
9.	Girl	+	Else	/ elʃə . . . gelst /
10.	Wall	+	Whom	+
11.	Beach	/ bist /	Apart	+
12.	Father	+	Except	+
13.	Doctor	+	Hardly	+
14.	Sister	+	Rarely	/ beɪvlɪ . . . bevlɪ /
15.	Jacket	+	Seldom	/ sevɪtɒn . . . seldɒn /
16.	Tennis	+	Lately	/ teleɪyɒn /
17.	Morning	+	Instead	+
18.	Station	+	Despite	/ redijvɪst /
19.	Balloon	/ bəlɒns /	Beneath	/ brɪnʌst /
20.	Biscuit	/ bɪskyʌt /	Whither	+
Total correct		16/20		14/20

+ indicates a correct response.

within the framework of Garrett's (1982) theory of normal speech production. We shall argue that R.D.'s primary deficit is one of *lexical retrieval* and discuss what his deficit might tell us about normal lexical retrieval for speech. We shall also consider the role played by the characteristic speech comprehension disorder in jargonaphasia. In the second part of this discussion we shall argue that the pattern of deficits shown by R.D. and other aphasics requires us to postulate not one mental lexicon but at least two and possibly four. . . .

Neologistic Jargon and Normal Lexical Retrieval

In this section we wish briefly to make some claims about the normal language processing which we believe follow from studies of neologistic jargonaphasia. These claims receive converging support from ortho-dox psycholinguistic studies: we regard this provision of converging evidence as one of the strengths of the cognitive neuropsychological approach.

1. Reading and spelling familiar words do not require obligatory phonological mediation. R.D. could understand written words he was unable to pronounce correctly. This implies some more direct visual access to semantics from print mediated by some device such as the visual input logogens of Morton (1979a, b) or the orthographic lexicon of Allport and Funnell (1981). This aspect of R.D.'s abilities therefore lends weight to the conclusion for which there is already substantial experimental and neuropsychological evidence (Patterson, 1982) that there is not an obligatory stage of phonological encoding in the comprehension of familiar written words. R.D. could also spell many words he could not pronounce correctly, reinforcing the conclusion that the spellings of familiar words are

TABLE 6   R. D.'s Performance on a Second Task Involving Reading Aloud
Content and Function Words Matched on Word Frequency (Study 10)

Content Words			
Word Presented	R. D.'s Response	Word Presumed	R. D.'s Response
People	+	Family	/ fɑmɪ /
Little	+	Country	+
Good	+	Problem	/ pretən /
See	+	Door	/ bə /
Number	/ mʌndə /	Help	/ hept /
War	+	Million	+
Public	/ pʌbək /	Book	+
Hand	+	Fire	+
Head	+	Father	+
Better	+	Hope	+
Nothing	+	Feeling	/ switɪŋ /
End	+	Wall	+
		Total correct = 17/24	

Function Words			
Should	/ sud /	Ever	+
How	+	Thus	+
Own	+	Perhaps	/ pəhɑst /
Between	+	Finally	/ finæst fizəltɪ /
Once	+	Whether	/ geɪʃtə /
Always	+	Soon	/ pun /
Away	+	Nor	+
Enough	+	Except	/ eksaɪt sekst /
Yet	+	Else	+
Nothing	+	Instead	+
Why	+	Higher	/ haɪtə /
Toward	/ tɒwʊd /	Whom	+
		Total correct = 16/24	

not assembled from their phonological forms but are retrieved from some form of orthographic lexicon (Morton, 1980; Ellis, 1982).

2. The phonological and orthographic lexicons are distinct cognitive components. We have characterized the problems experienced by neologistic jargon-aphasics in speech and writing as problems in retrieving full phonological and orthographic specifications of words. The most commonly observed pattern is for spelling to be more impaired in such patients than speech (Kertesz, 1979). If this were the only known

pattern then one could argue that we are seeing the effects of damage to a single lexicon used in both speech and writing, and that the reason speech is better preserved is because that is the more practiced skill. However, in R.D. and in patients reported by Hier and Mohr (1977) and Ulatowska *et al.* (1979) spelling was better preserved than speech. When contrasted with the more commonly observed pattern these patients provide us with a double dissociation between lexical retrieval for speech and writing, implying separate lexicons capable of being separately impaired.

Morton's (1979b; 1980) latest version of the logogen model includes four separate lexicons or logogen systems for the recognition and production of spoken and written words. Within this framework R.D.'s deficits would be explicable in terms of a moderate impairment to the speech output logogen system, a lesser impairment to the graphic output logogen system, little or no impairment to the visual input logogen system, and a severe but unspecified deficit afflicting the auditory word recognition pathway. However, Allport and Funnell (1981) have argued that the available data are compatible with the existence of just two lexicons—a phonological lexicon mediating speech perception and production and an orthographic lexicon mediating the recognition and production of written words. Within this alternative framework R.D. would be construed as having lost input to the phonological lexicon with moderate problems of retrieval from it, and as having intact access to the orthographic lexicon with milder problems of retrieval. . . .

3. *Lexical retrieval is frequency-biased.* It is well established that the frequency with which we use a word affects how rapidly and efficiently we will be able to process it in a wide variety of tasks (e.g., Morton, 1979a). However, most of the tasks used incorporate a perceptual component (e.g., word naming or object naming, both of which show an effect of frequency), and it is difficult to devise a task for use with normal subjects which would directly implicate word frequency in the process of converting semantic codes into phonological representations.

When R.D. attempted to name a word or picture there was no time pressure and no question of his failing to comprehend the stimulus, yet the likelihood of his being able to say the name correctly was affected by how common the name was—presumably by how often he had used that word himself in the past. Something about the organization of R.D.'s speech output lexicon rendered commonly used words less susceptible to the influence of a stroke than less commonly used words. This frequency effect could be due to varying strengths of associations between meanings and phonemic forms, or different resting levels of activation or thresholds in speech output logogens (cf., Morton, 1979b), or perhaps due

to the greater discriminability of high than low frequency signals against an increased level of background noise. At present we would prefer not to make a choice between these alternatives and simply note that in our view the data from R.D. provide the cleanest evidence that lexical retrieval for speech is frequency-biased.

Of course, as we have said, there is supportive evidence from work on normals. For example, Beattie and Butterworth (1980) report that in those slips of the tongue which result in the substitution of an error word for an intended word (e.g., "He got hot under the belt (collar)"), the error word tends to be of higher frequency than the intended word (whereas in blends such as the blend of *shout* and yell in "Don't shell so loud," the two words involved tend to be of similar frequencies).

4. *Lexical retrieval is not all-or-nothing.* Most of R.D.'s neologisms showed obvious phonological affinities to the target word (in Butterworth's (1979) terminology they were predominantly "target-related," and in many schemes they would have been classed as literal or phonemic paraphasias). In particular, syllabic information seemed to be less fragile than segmental information. In this respect R.D.'s neologisms are reminiscent of the tip-of-the-tongue (TOT) state in normals where people often know the number of syllables in a word whose full phonological form temporarily eludes them. This comparison might seem to fall foul of the finding of Goodglass et al. (1976) that Wernicke's aphasics are unable reliably to provide the number of syllables for pictures they cannot name correctly. We would speculate that these patients were predominantly "high level" Wernicke's aphasics, and we would not at this stage like to exclude the possibility that neologistic jargonaphasics like R.D. (whom we were unfortunately unable to test on such tasks) could not perform this sort of task reasonably well.

Although these have not to our knowledge been documented before, normal individuals will sometimes produce attempts at target words which look like neologisms when caught in a tip-of-the-tongue state. Widlöf (1983, Reference Note 3) read definitions of relatively uncommon words to normal subjects aged between 16 and 19 years. If they felt that the word was on the tip of their tongue they were encouraged to "try to say the word you are looking for aloud." Many of the errors were real words similar in either sound or meaning to the target word, but subjects also produced quasi-neologistic attempts. For example, one subject after hearing the definition *A platform for public speaking* said, "/ pæst . . . pestəl . . . pedæ / . . . pedestal" whilst another said, "/ strəu . . . strum / . . . rostrum." Other examples of this phenomenon were "/ belfrum / . . . belfry" for *The part of a steeple where bells are hung,* and "/ fleksɪ . . . pleksɪ . . . pleksɪæ / . . . dyslexia" for *word-blindness; difficulty in learning to read or spell.*

These attempts at a target prior to pronouncing it correctly seem to be based on partial information about the word's pronunciation, and are very like R.D.'s target-related neologisms, the difference being that R.D. often got no further than this stage. We have argued that R.D.'s spelling errors were also based on partial retrieval of information from the orthographic lexicon. Again there are parallels with normal performance—in this case with spelling errors of normal children and adults which show partial but incomplete knowledge of a target word's spelling (Ellis, 1982). The similarity between R.D.'s neologisms and normal tip-of-the-tongue errors, and between R.D.'s spelling errors and certain normal errors encourages us in the belief that in neologistic jargon-aphasia we are seeing an impaired version of the normal system in operation rather than processes or strategies created *de novo* after the brain injury.

REFERENCES

Allport, D. A. (1980) Patterns and actions: cognitive mechanisms are content-specific. In G. Claxton (ed.), *Cognitive psychology: New Directions.* London, Routledge and Kegan Paul.

Allport D. A. and Funnell, E. (1981) Components of the mental lexicon. *Phil. Trans. R. Soc. Lond. B, 295,* 397–410.

Bastian, H. C. (1897) Some problems in connection with aphasia and other speech defects. *Lancet, 75,* 933–942.

Bay, E. (1964) Principles of classification and their influence on our concepts of aphasia. In A. V. S. DeReuck and M. O'Connor (eds.), *Disorders of Language.* London, Churchill.

Beattie, G. W. and Butterworth, B. (1980) Contextual probability and word frequency as determinants of pauses and errors in spontaneous speech. *Lang. Sp., 22,* 201–211.

Berndt, R. S. and Caramazza, A. (1980) A re-definition of the syndrome of Broca's aphasia: Implications for a neuropsychological model of language. *Appl. Psycholing., 1,* 225–278.

Bradley, D. C., Garrett, M. F. and Zurif, E. B. (1980) Syntactic deficits in Broca's aphasia. In D. Caplan (ed.). *Biological studies of mental processes.* Cambridge, Mass., MIT Press.

Broadbent, W. H. (1872) On the cerebral mechanisms of speech and thought. *Medico-Chirurgical Trans., 55,* 144–194.

Browman, C. P. (1978) Tip of the tongue and slip of the ear: implications for language processing. *U.C.L.A. Working Papers in Phonetics No. 42.*

Brown, J. W. (1972) *Aphasia, Apraxia and Agnosia: Clinical and Theoretical Aspects.* Springfield, Ill., C. C. Thomas.

Brown, J. W. (1981) Case reports of semantic jargon. In J. W. Brown (ed.), *Jargonaphasia.* New York, Academic Press.

Brown, R. and McNeill, D. (1966) The "tip of the tongue" phenomenon. *J. verb. Learn. verb. Behav., 5,* 325–337.

Buckingham, H. W. (1979) Linguistic aspects of lexical retrieval disturbances in the posterior fluent aphasias. In H. Whitaker and H. A. Whitiker (eds.), *Studies in Neurolinguistics, Vol. 4.* New York, Academic Press .

Buckingham, H. W. and Kertesz, A. (1976) *Neologistic jargon aphasia.* Amsterdam, Swets and Zeitlinger.

Buckingham, H. W., Whitaker, H. and Whitaker, H. A. (1978) Alliteration and assonance in neologistic jargon aphasia. *Cortex, 14,* 365–380.

Buckingham, H. W., Whitaker, H. and Whitaker, H. A. (1979) On linguistic perseveration. In H. Whitaker and H. A. Whitaker (eds.), *Studies in Neurolinguistics, Vol. 4.* New York, Academic Press.

Butterworth, B. (1979) Hesitation and the production of verbal paraphasias and neologisms in jargon aphasia. *Br. Lang., 8,* 133–161.

Cappa, S., Cavalloti, G. and Vignolo, L. A. (1981) Phonemic and lexical errors in fluent aphasia: correlation with lesion site. *Neuropsychol., 19,* 171–177.

Caramazza, A. and Berndt, R. S. (1978) Semantic and syntactic processes in aphasia. *Psychol. Bull., 85,* 898–918.

Ellis, A. W. (1982) Spelling and writing (and reading and speaking). In A. W. Ellis (ed.), *Normality and Pathology in Cognitive Functions.* London, Academic Press.

Friederici, A. D. and Schoenle, P. W. (1980) Computational dissociation of two vocabulary types. *Neuropsychol., 18,* 11–20.

Garrett, M. F. (1975) The analysis of sentence production. In G. H. Bower (ed.), *The Psychology of Learning and Motivation Vol. 9.* New York, Academic Press.

Garrett, M. F. (1976) Syntactic processes in sentence production. In R. Wales and E. Walker (eds.), *New Approaches to Language Mechanisms.* Amsterdam, North-Holland.

Garrett. M. F. (1980a) Levels of processing in sentence production. In B. Butterworth (ed.), *Language Production, Vol. 1: Speech and Talk.* London. Academic Press.

Garrett. M. F. (1980b) The limits of accommodation. In V. A. Fromkin (ed.), *Errors in Linguistic Performance.* New York, Academic Press.

Garrett, M. F. (1982) Production of speech: Observations from normal and pathological language use. In A. W. Ellis (ed.), *Normality and Pathology in Cognitive Functions.* London, Academic Press.

Goodglass, H. and Kaplan, E. (1972) *Assessment of Aphasia and Related Disorders.* Philadelphia, Lea and Febinger.

Goodglass, H ., Kaplan, E., Weintraub, S. and Ackerman, N. (1976) The "tip-of-the-tongue" phenomenon in aphasia. *Cortex, 12,* 145–153.

Gordon, B. and Caramazza, A. (1982) Lexical decision for open- and closed-class words: Failure to replicate differential frequency sensitivity. *Br. Lang., 15,* 143–160.

Green, E. (1969) Phonological and grammatical aspects of jargon in an aphasic patient: A case study. *Lang. Sp., 12,* 103–118.

Grossman, M. (1981) A bird is a bird is a bird: making reference within and without superordinate categories. *Br. Lang., 12,* 313–331.

Hécaen, H. and Albert, M. L. (1978) *Human Neuropsychology.* New York, Wiley.

Heilman, K. M., Rothi, L., Campanella, D. and Wolfson, S. (1979) Wernicke's and global aphasia without alexia. *Arch. Neurol., 36,* 129–133.

Hier, D. B. and Mohr, J. P. (1977) Incongruous oral and written naming: evidence for a subdivision of the syndrome of Wernicke's aphasia. *Br. Lang., 4,* 115–126.

Howes. D. (1964) Application of the word frequency concept to aphasia. In A. V. S. DeReuck and M. O'Connor (eds.), *Disorders of Language.* London, Churchill.

Howes, D. (1967a) Some experimental investigations of language in aphasia. In K. Salzinger and S. Salzinger (eds.), *Research in Verbal Behaviour and Some Neurophysiological Implications.* New York, Academic Press .

Howes, D. (1967b) Hypotheses concerning the functions of the language mechanism. In K. Salzinger and S. Salzinger (eds.), *Research in Verbal Behaviour and Some Neurophysiological Implications.* New York, Academic Press.

Howes, D. and Geschwind, N. (1964) Quantitative studies of aphasic language. In D. M. Rioch and E. A. Weinstein (eds.), *Disorders of Communication.* Baltimore, Williams and Wilkins.

Joanette, Y., Keller, E. and Lecours, A. R. (1980) Sequences of phonemic approximations in aphasia. *Br. Lang., 11,* 30–44.

Kertesz, A. (1979) *Aphasia and Associated Disorders: Taxonomy, Localization and Recovery.* New York, Grune and Stratton.

Kertesz, A. and Benson, D. F. (1970) Neologistic jargon: a clinicopathological study. *Cortex, 6,* 362–368.

Kinsbourne, M. (1971) Cognitive deficit: experimental analysis. In J. L. McGauge (ed.), *Psychobiology.* New York, Academic Press.

Kucera, H. and Francis, W. N. (1967) *Computational Analysis of Present-day American English.* Providence, RI, Brown University Press.

Lecours, A. R., Osborn, E., Travis, L., Rouillon, F. and Lavallee-Huynh, G. (1981) Jargons. In J. W. Brown (ed.), *Jargonaphasia.* New York, Academic Press.

Lichtheim, L. (1885) On aphasia. *Brain, 7,* 433–484.

Luria, A. R. (1964) Factors and forms of aphasia. In A. V. S. DeReuck and M. O'Connor (eds.), *Disorders of Language.* London, Churchill.

Marin, O. S. M., Saffran, E. M. and Schwartz, M. F. (1976) Dissociations of language in aphasia: Implications for normal function. In S. R. Harnad, H. D. Steklis and J. Lancaster (eds.), *Origins and Evolution of Language and Speech.* (*Ann. N. Y. Acad. Sc., 280,* (1976) 868–884). New York, New York Academy of Sciences.

Marr, D. (1976) Early processing of visual information. *Phil. Trans. R. Soc. Lond., B, 275,* 483–524.

Marshall, J. C. (1974) Freud's psychology of language. In R. Wollheim (ed.), *Freud: A Collection of Critical Essays.* New York, Anchor Books.

Marshall, J. C. (1977) Disorders in the expression of language. In J. Morton and J. C. Marshall (eds.), *Psycholinguistics Series Vol. 1.* London, Elek Science.

Marshall, J. C. (1982) Models of the mind in health and disease. In A. W. Ellis, (ed.), *Normality and Pathology in Cognitive Functions.* London, Academic Press.

Miller, G. A., Newman, E. B. and Friedman, E. A. (1958) Length-frequency statistics for written English. *Info. Contr., 1,* 370–389.

Morton, J. (1979a) Word recognition. In J. Morton and J. C. Marshall (eds.), *Psycholinguistics Series, Vol. 2.* London, Elek Science.

Morton, J. (1979b) Facilitation in word recognition: Experiments causing change in the logogen model. In P. A. Kolers, M. Wrolstad and H. Bouma (eds.), *Processing of Visible Language, Vol. 1.* New York, Plenum.

Morton, J. (1980) The logogen model and orthographic structure. In U. Frith. (ed.), *Cognitive Processes in Spelling.* London, Academic Press.

Morton, J. (1981) The status of information processing models of language. *Phil. Trans. R. Soc. Lond., B, 295,* 387-396.

Morton, J. and Patterson, K. E. (1980) Little words—No! In M. Coltheart, K. E. Patterson and J. C. Marshall (eds.), *Deep Dyslexia.* London, Routledge and Kegan Paul.

O'Connell, P. F. (1981) Neologistic jargon aphasia: a case report. *Br. Lang., 12,* 292–302.

Oldfield, R. C. (1966) Things, words and the brain. *Q. J. exper. Psychol., 18,* 340–353.

Patterson, K. E. (1982) The relation between reading and phonological encoding: Further neuropsychological observations. In A. W. Ellis (ed.), *Normality and Pathology in Cognitive Functions.* London, Academic Press.

Perecman, E. and Brown, J. W. (1981) Semantic jargon: A case report. In J. W. Brown (ed.), *Jargonaphasia.* New York, Academic Press.

Saffran, E. M., M. F. and Mann, O. S. M. (1980) Evidence from aphasia: Isolating the components of a production model. In B. Butterworth (ed.), *Language Production, Vol. 1: Speech and Talk.* London, Academic Press.

Schuell, H. (1965) *The Minnesota Test for Differential Diagnosis of Aphasia.* Minneapolis, University of Minnesota Press.

Shallice, T. (1979) Case study approach in neuropsychological research. *J. Clin. Neuropsychol., 1,* 183–211.

Shallice, T. (1981) Neurological impairment of cognitive processes. *Br. med. Bul., 37,* 187–192.

Snodgrass, J. G. and Vanderwart, M. (1980) A standardized set of 260 pictures: Norms for name agreement, image agreement, familiarity and visual complexity. *J. exper. Psychol.: Hum. Percep. Perf., 6,* 174–215.

Thorndike, E. L. and Lorge, I. (1944) *The Teacher's Word Book of 30,000 Words.* New York, Teachers College.

Ulatowska, H. K., Baker, T. and Stern, R. F. (1979) Disruption of written language in aphasia. In H. Whitaker and H. A. Whitaker (eds.), *Studies in Neurolinguistics, Vol. 4.* New York, Academic Press.

Weinstein, E. A. (1981) Behavioral aspects of jargonaphasia. In J. W. Brown (ed.), *Jargonaphasia.* New York, Academic Press.

Weisenburg, T. and McBride, K. (1935) *Aphasia.* New York, Commonwealth Fund.

Wernicke, C. (1874) *Der aphasische symptomencomplex.* Breslau, Cohn and Weigart. Translated in G. H. Eggert. *Wernicke's Works on Aphasia.* The Hague, Mouton, 1977.

REFERENCE NOTES

1. Bradley, D. C. (1978) *Computational distinctions of vocabulary type.* Unpublished Ph.D. thesis, Massachusetts Institute of Technology.

2. Morton, J. (1967) Population norms for sentence completion. Unpublished paper, MRC Applied Psychology Unit, Cambridge.

3. Widlöf, I. (1983) Lexical access: Evidence from the TOT phenomenon. Undergraduate project dissertation, Department of Psychology, University of Lancaster, 1983.

POSTSCRIPT

A great deal of research, both preceding and subsequent to this article (such as Hawkins, Reicher, Rogers, & Peterson, 1976; Just & Carpenter, 1987) has supported the conclusion that fluent readers can use both graphemic (letter) and phonological representations for words (but see Van Orden, Johnston, & Hale, 1988). Crowder and Wagner (1992) provide an extensive and accessible discussion of the conditions under which people tend to use one or the other in reading (see also Rayner & Pollatsek, 1989). Similarly, Garrett's model of sentence production has been supported and added to by a number of authors (for example, Lapointe & Dell, 1989; Levelt, 1989) However, somewhat more controversial is the conclusion that differences in the accessing of content and function words stem entirely from differences in their frequency of occurrence (Zurif, Swinney, & Garrett, 1990).

Garrett's model of speech production suggests that content and function words are retrieved in separate steps. It's possible that the same retrieval procedure is used for both steps (which is Ellis, Miller, and Sin's conclusion); it's also possible that the two steps involve different kinds of procedures. Garrett (1990) points out that in normal speakers, certain errors of pronunciation common in content words rarely occur with function words, which supports the latter possibility. Furthermore, if a subject is asked to understand a sequence of words and simultaneously monitor for the occurrence of a certain letter in the words of that sequence, he or she will miss an occurrence much more often if the letter is embedded in a function word than if the target is embedded in a content word. This also supports the conclusion that different processes are involved in retrieving content versus function words. Interestingly, this pattern is observed in Wernicke's aphasics whether the sequence of words is meaningful or not, but it is observed in normal subjects only if the sequence of words is meaningful (assuming that the words are not of extremely high frequency; Healy, 1976), and is not observed under either condition in Broca's aphasics (Friederici, 1983, 1985; Rosenberg, Zurif, Brownell, Garrett, & Bradley, 1985).

Wernicke's aphasics and Broca's aphasics are distinguished by the primary locus of their brain damage and by a variety of functional losses. The general rule of thumb is that the speech of Wernicke's aphasics is often fluent but riddled with semantic or phonological paraphasias, and their comprehension is generally deficient; the speech of Broca's aphasics is often halting but meaningful, consisting almost entirely of content words, and their comprehension is generally intact (Zurif, 1990). Actually, the patterns of language loss due to brain damage are much more complicated than these rules of thumb imply and are the subject of intense research (see Caplan, 1992;

Damasio & Damasio, 1992; Kean, 1988; and Zurif et al., 1990, for relatively accessible reviews; Caplan, 1987, and Grodzinsky, 1990, for more technical treatments). There has also been considerable controversy about using a single patient when studying aphasia (see Reading 19 or Caramazza & McCloskey, 1988, and various responses that follow in the same issue).

FOR FURTHER THOUGHT

1. Give an example of a neologism in R. D.'s speech. What makes this a neologism or phonemic paraphasia and not a verbal or semantic paraphasia? Make up an example of the latter.
2. Studies 1 and 2 used essentially the same task and addressed essentially the same issue. Why was Study 2 conducted?
3. What evidence supports the authors' contention that R. D.'s reading comprehension was better than his speech comprehension? What evidence supports their contention that his ability to understand a written word was independent of his ability to pronounce it?
4. Give some examples of function words and content words. How are function and content words distinguished from one another? How is the function/content distinction related to the issues of word length and frequency of occurrence? According to the authors, what is the significance of the function/content distinction in Wernicke's aphasics?
5. Why did Ellis and his colleagues use a reading task in Studies 9 and 10 rather than spontaneous production or picture-naming tasks? Note that some of the authors' studies involved picture-naming; why is it important with Wernicke's aphasics to conduct picture-naming as well as reading tests?

REFERENCES

Caplan, D. (1987). *Neurolinguistics and linguistic aphasiology: An introduction.* Cambridge: Cambridge University Press.

Caplan, D. (1992). *Language: Structure, processing, and disorders.* Cambridge, MA: MIT Press.

Caramazza, A., & McCloskey, M. (1988). The case for single-patient studies. *Cognitive Neuropsychology, 5,* 517–527.

Crowder, R. G., & Wagner, R. K. (1992). *The psychology of reading* (2nd ed.). New York: Oxford University Press.

Damasio, A. R., & Damasio, H. (1992, September). Brain and language. *Scientific American,* pp. 88–95.

Farah, M. J. (1988). Is visual imagery really visual? Overlooked evidence from neuropsychology. *Psychological Review, 95,* 307–317.

Fodor, J. A. (1983). *The modularity of mind.* Cambridge, MA: MIT Press.

Fodor, J. A. (1985). Précis of *The modularity of mind. The Behavioral and Brain Sciences, 8,* 1–42.

Friederici, A. D. (1983). Aphasics' perception of words in sentential context: Some real-time processing evidence. *Neuropsychologia, 21,* 351–358.

Friederici, A. D. (1985). Levels of processing and vocabulary types: Evidence from on-line comprehension in normals and agrammatics. *Cognition, 19,* 133–166.

Fromkin, V. & Rodman, R. (1978). *An introduction to language* (2nd ed.). New York : Holt, Rinehart & Winston.

Garrett, M. F. (1980). Levels of processing in sentence production. In B. Butterworth (Ed.), *Language production: Vol. 1. Speech and talk* (pp. 177–220). London: Academic Press.

Garrett, M. F. (1990). Sentence processing. In D. N. Osherson & H. Lasnik (Eds.), *An invitation to cognitive science: Vol. 1. Language* (pp. 133–175). Cambridge, MA: MIT Press.

Grodzinsky, Y. (1990). *Theoretical perspectives on language deficits.* Cambridge, MA: MIT Press.

Hawkins, H. L., Reicher, G. M., Rogers, M., & Peterson, L. (1976). Flexible coding in word recognition. *Journal of Experimental Psychology: Human Perception and Performance, 2,* 380–385.

Healy, A. F. (1976). Detection errors on the word *the:* Evidence for reading units larger than letters. *Journal of Experimental Psychology: Human Perception and Performance, 2,* 235–242.

Just, M. A., & Carpenter, P. A. (1987). *The psychology of reading and language comprehension.* Newton, MA: Allyn & Bacon.

Kean, M.-L. (1988). Brain structures and linguistic capacity. In F. J. Newmeyer (Ed.), *Linguistics: The Cambridge survey II. Linguistic theory: Extensions and implications* (pp. 74–95). New York: Cambridge University Press.

Lapointe, S. G., & Dell, G. S. (1989). A synthesis of some recent work in sentence production. In G. N. Carlson & M. K. Tannenhaus (Eds.), *Linguistic structure in language processing* (pp. 107–156). Dordrecht: Kluwer Academic Publishers.

Levelt, W. J. M. (1989). *Speaking: From intention to articulation.* Cambridge, MA: MIT Press.

Putnam, H. (1973). Reductionism and the nature of psychology. *Cognition, 2,* 131–146.

Rayner, K., & Pollatsek, A. (1989). *The psychology of reading.* Englewood Cliffs, NJ: Prentice-Hall.

Rosenberg, B., Zurif, E., Brownell, H., Garrett, M., & Bradley, D. (1985). Grammatical class effects in relation to normal and aphasic sentence processing. *Brain and Language, 26,* 287–303.

Stillings, N. A., Feinstein, M. H., Garfield, J. L., Rissland, E. L., Rosenbaum, D. A., Weisler, S. E., & Baker-Ward, L. (1987). *Cognitive science: An introduction.* Cambridge, MA: MIT Press.

Tyler, L. K. (1992). *Spoken language comprehension: An experiment approach to disordered and normal processing.* Cambridge, MA: MIT Press.

Van Orden, G. C., Johnston, J. C., & Hale, B. L. (1988). Word identification in reading proceeds from spelling to sound to meaning. *Journal of Experimental Psychology: Learning, Memory, and Cognition, 14,* 371–386.

Zurif, E. B. (1990). Language and the brain. In D. N. Osherson & H. Lasnik (Eds.), *An invitation to cognitive science: Vol. 1. Language* (pp. 177–198). Cambridge, MA: MIT Press.

Zurif, E., Swinney, D., & Garrett, M. (1990). Lexical processing and sentence comprehension in aphasia. In A. A. Caramazza (Ed.), *Cognitive neuropsychology and neurolinguistics* (pp. 123–136). Hillsdale, NJ: Erlbaum.

CHAPTER SEVEN
Reasoning and Judgment

INTRODUCTION

Over the centuries, logicians have developed (or perhaps discovered) various systems of rules for making logical deductions. Every day, people encounter situations that require them to reason: if I find that one of my books has been chewed and my wife, son, and one of our three dogs has had access to the book, I conclude that the culprit is the dog with access. But do people with little or no formal training reason in accordance with the rules of logic? This is the issue examined by Peter Wason and Diana Shapiro in "Natural and Contrived Experience in a Reasoning Problem."

The kind of reasoning investigated in this article is called conditional reasoning. In a conditional reasoning task, the subject decides what conclusion, if any, logically follows certain given conditions. These conditions include a rule of the form "If p, then q," called a conditional rule. This rule must be distinguished from an equivalence rule, which is of the form "If and only if p, then q"; conditional rules allow some conclusions that equivalence rules do not. The p part of the rule is called the antecedent and the q is called the consequent. A second condition is specified by a statement that either affirms or denies (negates) the antecedent or consequent. Thus the second condition can take one of four forms: p; not p; q; or not q. Typically in a conditional reasoning task, the subject is also given a possible conclusion, a statement that affirms or denies that part of the rule not mentioned in the second condition. The subject then must judge whether the conclusion follows logically, whether it must be true given the two conditions.

One common observation is that people find some conditional arguments easier to evaluate than others. For example, we might give a subject the conditional rule "If it rains, then people use umbrellas" (although it might sound more natural to say, "Every time it rains, people use umbrellas") and then a condition, "It's raining." We might then ask the subject to judge the validity of the conclusion "People are using umbrellas." The conclusion is valid in this case, and subjects generally find this argument easy to evaluate. This argument has the structure "if p then q; p $\therefore$ q"; the symbol $\therefore$ is generally read as "therefore" or "it follows that." Also valid but harder to evaluate is the structure "if p, then q; not q $\therefore$ not p": "If it rains, people use umbrellas. People are not using umbrellas. It's not raining."

A much more difficult example is "If it rains, then people use umbrellas. People are using umbrellas. It's raining" (which has the structure "if p then q;

$q \therefore p$"). Most people are tempted to accept the validity of this argument, but the rules of logic dictate that no conclusion logically follows because no one conclusion *must* be true. Specifically, p *may* be true, but need not be; not p may also be true. It's possible—that is, it's not a violation of the conditions specified—to say "If it rains, then people use umbrellas. People are using umbrellas. It's not raining (but the sun is so intense it's nice to have some shade)." Although somewhat awkward, the second sentence shows that both p and not p are consistent with the two conditions given: "if p, then q" and "q." If the second condition affirms the consequent of the conditional rule, neither conclusion *must* be true, so nothing logically follows. It's important to keep in mind that, as far as formal logic is concerned, the validity of the conclusion depends only on the structure of the argument and has nothing to do with the real world. Furthermore, to say that a conclusion logically follows means that it *must* be true given the conditions specified. Therefore, if the conditions are consistent with more than one conclusion, then neither one *must* be true, and so no conclusion logically follows.

Wason and his colleagues developed a simple procedure called the selection task for testing whether people actually follow the rules of logic when reasoning with conditionals. In this task, the subject is given a rule and is then presented with four cards; Wason and Shapiro use the rule "If a card has a D on one side, then it has a 3 on the other side." On one side of each card is a number and on the other side, a letter. Two of the cards are placed letter-side up—one showing a D, the other a letter other than D—and two are placed number-side up—one showing a 3, the other a number other than 3 (Wason and Shapiro use the term *uppermost* instead of *side up*). The subject's task is to select all and only those cards that would test the truth of the rule. The simplicity of the task is deceptive; few get it right.

Note that the rule to be tested is a conditional rule; think of the exposed side of each card as the second condition of a conditional argument and of the hidden side of each card as the conclusion. Choosing the card that denies the consequent (in this example, a card showing a number other than 3) is like constructing an argument that begins "if p then q; not q." The conclusion to such an argument must be not p; in this example, the hidden side must be a letter other than D. If the hidden side has a D, the rule is falsified. Choosing the cards that affirm the antecedent, D, or the consequent, 3, is called seeking verification of the rule. But the card showing 3 should not be chosen; if the second condition affirms the consequent, either conclusion will be consistent with the rule and the rule is not tested. (A complete understanding of why the correct choices in the Wason selection task are p and not q isn't necessary to follow the arguments in this article, but such an understanding is very helpful.)

Some additional analyses of subjects' performance in Experiment I and some elaboration of an alternative hypothesis presented in the original article have been excluded in this reading. Wason's selection task is very deceptive. Although it appears to be very simple, even intelligent, well-educated subjects don't behave in the way that logic predicts. As you read this selection, ask yourself why it is so difficult to behave in accordance with the rules of logic on this task. Under what conditions does it become easier to do so? Why?

Natural and Contrived Experience in a Reasoning Problem

Peter C. Wason and Diana Shapiro
University College London

INTRODUCTION

This study is about the effects of two kinds of experience on a deceptive reasoning problem. In the first experiment the experience is introduced as part of the procedure, and in the second it is inherent in the material used.

Previous experiments (Wason, 1968, 1969a) have established that it is very difficult to decide what information is required to test the truth of an abstract conditional sentence. For example, given the sentence: *Every card which has a D on one side has a 3 on the other side* (and knowledge that each card has a letter on one side and a number on the other side), together with four cards showing respectively D, K, 3, 7, hardly any individuals make the correct choice of cards to turn over (D and 7) in order to determine the truth of the sentence. This problem is called the "selection task" and the conditional sentence is called "the rule."

The rule has the logical form, "if p then q," where p refers to the stimulus mentioned in the antecedent (D); $\bar{p}$, i.e. not p, refers to the stimulus which negates it (K); q refers to the stimulus mentioned in the consequent (3); and $\bar{q}$, i.e. not q, refers to the stimulus which negates it (7). In order to solve the problem it is necessary and sufficient to choose p and $\bar{q}$, since if these stimuli were to occur on the same card the rule would be false but otherwise true.

The combined results of four experiments (see Table 1) show that the subjects (students) are dominated by *verification* rather than *falsification*. On the whole, they failed to select $\bar{q}$, which could have falsified the rule, and they did select q, which could not have falsified it although this latter error is much less prevalent.

EXPERIMENT I

The previous experiments have been concerned with the stability of the errors and their resistance to correction by "remedial procedures." After the subjects had performed the selection task they had to evaluate the cards independently, i.e. turn them over and say whether the rule was true or false in relation to each. The present experiment is concerned with the pre-

The experiments in this paper form part of research to be reported in a thesis to be submitted for the degree of Ph.D. of London University by the second author, under the supervision of the first author. We are most indebted to our colleague, Dr. P. N. Johnson-Laird, for invaluable critical comments and suggestions, and also to the Medical Research Council for a grant for scientific assistance.

SOURCE: *Quarterly Journal of Experimental Psychology*, 23, 1971, pp. 63–71. Copyright 1971 by the Experimental Psychology Society. Reprinted by permission.

TABLE 1   Frequency of the Selection of Cards in Four Previous Experiments ($n = 128$)

p and q	59
p	42
p, q and $\bar{q}$	9
p and $\bar{q}$	5
others	13

vention of error. The subjects are made familiar with the other side of the cards before the selection task is performed.

This prior experience is introduced by two methods. The "construction" method requires the subject to imagine, or project, a value on the other side of a card which would make the rule true, or make it false, in relation to it. In effect, positive and negative instances of the rule are constructed. The "evaluation" method simply requires the subject to turn over the card and say whether the rule is true, or false, in relation to it. The construction method clearly involves an imaginative act, and hence a greater degree of involvement than the evaluation method. It was accordingly predicted that it would be associated with superior performance in the subsequent selection task.

Design

Two independent groups were used: the construction group and the evaluation group. Both carried out their respective tasks on 24 cards in relation to a given conditional rule. They then performed the *initial selection task* with four more cards in relation to the *same* rule. A new conditional rule was then presented together with a further four cards. This *transfer selection task* was designed to assess the extent to which specific knowledge, gained in the prior experience, would be generalized.

Subjects

Twenty-four undergraduates (paid volunteers) of University College London were allocated alternately to the groups and tested individually. They had no previous experience with tasks of this type.

Procedure

Before presenting the rule all the subjects were first handed 28 cards, and instructed to inspect them to ensure that each had a letter of the alphabet on one side and a number on the other side.

They were then presented with the following rule: *Every card which has a vowel on one side has an even number on the other side.* Twenty-four of the 28 cards were then presented, one at a time, the remaining four being reserved for the transfer selection task. In the construction group they were instructed to name a value on the other side of each card which would make the rule true (or make it false). They were, however, told that it would be in order to say that no value on the other side would make the rule either true or false. In the evaluation group they turned over each card and said that it made the rule true (or false). Similarly, they were told that it would be in order to say that a card was irrelevant to the truth or falsity of the rule.

The eight possible ways of permuting the logical values were each represented three times in the series of 24. They were presented successively in the following pairs, where the value given first refers to the symbol uppermost: $(pq, p\bar{q})$ $(\bar{p}\,\bar{q}, \bar{p}q)$ $(qp, q\bar{p})$ $(\bar{q}\bar{p}, \bar{q}p)$. All the subjects received the cards in the same order, and within a pair the order of presenting the two cards was constant, but the pairs themselves were randomized in a different order within each of the three blocks of eight cards. In the construction group, where only the uppermost symbol was presented, the instruction for the first card within a pair was to name a symbol to make a verifying instance, and for the second card to name a symbol to make a falsifying instance.

In both groups the subjects were told they were wrong if they failed to evaluate (construct) $p\bar{q}$ and $\bar{q}p$ as falsifying, and if they did evaluate (construct) $\bar{p}q$ and $q\bar{p}$ as falsifying. This was to ensure that they did appreciate the falsifying instances of a conditional rule, but did not confuse them with the falsifying instances of an equivalence rule. The $\bar{p}q$ and $q\bar{p}$ instances do falsify an equivalence rule in the form: "if, and only if p then q."

For the initial selection task four cards (E, Z, 6, 7), taken from the 24 used in the prior experience, were placed on the table in a random order. The subjects were instructed that the rule now applied to these four cards taken as a whole, i.e. no longer independently. They were told "to select those cards, and only those cards, that would need to be turned over in order to discover whether the rule was true or false." No comments were made about these selections, and the subjects were not allowed to turn over any of the cards.

For the transfer selection task the following rule was presented: *Every card which has a D on one side has a 3 on the other side,* together with the four cards (D, K, 3, 5) which had not occurred in the series of 24, but had been included in the 28 originally inspected. The instructions were similar to those given for the initial selection task.

Results

Table 2 shows the frequency of correct and incorrect solutions, the first number in each cell referring to the initial selection task and the second to the transfer selection task.

As predicted, there is a trend in favor of the construction group, but it falls short of statistical significance. The performance overall is unimpressive, particularly in the evaluation group. It will also be noted that the difference between the two selection tasks is negligible: knowledge is generalized to the extent that it has been gained. The two types of error, i.e. the selection of q and the omission of $\bar{q}$ are examined separately in Tables 3 and 4.

Table 3 shows that both groups do better in omitting q than in getting the solution correct. But the frequency of this particular error also increases the difference between the groups in the predicted direction. On the transfer selection task it is significant ($P = 0.05$, one-tailed, Fisher-Yates exact test).

It may be inferred from Table 4 that the proportion of subjects in both groups who select $\bar{q}$ is greater

TABLE 2   Frequency of Correct and Incorrect Solutions

	Correct	Incorrect	N
Construction	5 (6)	7 (6)	12
Evaluation	2 (2)	10 (10)	12
Totals	7 (8)	17 (16)	24

TABLE 3   Frequency of Selecting q

	q Selected	q Omitted	N
Construction	2 (3)	10 (9)	12
Evaluation	7 (8)	5 (4)	12
Totals	9 (11)	15 (13)	24

than ever obtained initially in previous experiments. But it is also evident that none of the frequencies differ from chance expectancy. However, it may be inferred that the trend, showing the construction group superior on the correct solution, is entirely due to a greater tendency to omit q rather than one to select $\bar{q}$....

It may be concluded that the putative experience of logical structure, introduced procedurally, is relatively ineffective in enabling insight to be gained into the problem. It is reasonable to inquire whether "natural" experience, inherent in the subjects' everyday knowledge, may be more successful in inducing insight. It was predicted that when the material is realistic ("thematic"), as opposed to abstract, the selection task will be significantly easier.

TABLE 4   Frequency of Omitting $\bar{q}$

	q̄ Omitted	q̄ Selected	N
Construction	7 (5)	5 (7)	12
Evaluation	6 (6)	6 (6)	12
Totals	13 (11)	11 (13)	24

EXPERIMENT II

Design

Two independent groups were used: the "thematic group" and the "abstract group" which differed solely in the terms in which the problem was presented.

Subjects

Thirty-two first year psychology undergraduates of University College London were allocated alternately to the groups and tested individually. They had no previous experience with tasks of this type.

Procedure

The thematic material represented a journey made on 4 different days of the week. Before presenting the rule about these journeys the subjects were given 16 cards which they inspected to ensure that each had the name of a town on one side and a mode of transport on the other side.

They were then presented with the four selection task cards, taken from the 16 originally presented, and arranged in random order on the table. They were instructed that they would now only be concerned with these cards. On two of them a different destination was written, i.e. "Manchester" and "Leeds," and on the other two a different mode of transport, i.e. "Car" and "Train." In addition each had a different day of the week in smaller type at the top.

The rule was then presented as a claim made by the experimenter about four journeys she had made on the four different days indicated on the cards. One variant of this rule was: *Every time I go to Manchester I travel by car.* Three other variants, derived from permuting the items on the cards, were also used. The presentation of all four was systematically rotated between the subjects to control for any possible preconceptions about the relation between destinations and modes of transport.

It was explained to the subjects that for each journey the destination appeared on one side of the card and the transport used on the other side. They were then instructed to say which cards they would need to turn over to decide whether the experimenter's claim was true or false. They were encouraged to take their time before answering.

A similar procedure was followed in the abstract group. Sixteen cards with a letter of the alphabet on one side and a number on the other side were first inspected. Four of these, D, K, 3, 7, were used for the selection task. The rule: *Every card which has a D on one side has a 3 on the other side,* was then presented as a claim made by the experimenter about the arrangement of letters and numbers on the cards. The subjects were instructed that this rule applied only to the four cards, and that they were to say which they would need to turn over to decide whether the claim was true or false.

Results

Table 5 shows the frequency of correct and incorrect solutions.

The prediction that the thematic group would perform better than the abstract group is clearly confirmed by the distribution of the frequencies in Table 5 ($P = 0.004$, one-tailed, Fisher-Yates exact test). It is evident that representing the problem in the form of a realistic situation had a dramatic effect on the subjects' ability to gain insight into it. There may, however, be several reasons for this result.

TABLE 5   *Frequency of Correct and Incorrect Solutions*

	Correct	Incorrect	N
Thematic	10	6	16
Abstract	2	14	16
Totals	12	20	32

DISCUSSION

The results of the two experiments show the relative failure of procedurally introduced experience and the relative success of realistic material in allowing insight to be gained into the problem.

It could, of course, be argued that if the experience, introduced in Experiment I, had been more intensive, or if only the falsifying contingencies had been used, then performance would have been improved. But the purpose of the experience was only to acquaint the subjects with the logical structure of the problem, and not to train them to make particular responses. Previous results (Johnson-Laird and Wason, 1970b) have shown that various factors, such as cognitive load, may affect the appreciation of the task, and over-learning of the contingencies might be one more variable affecting performance. The point is that understanding the contingencies did not allow this knowledge to be used with maximum efficiency in the selection tasks. This result may seem incredible to anyone unacquainted with the difficulty of the problem. The reasons for it will not be discussed until the effects of thematic material on the task have been considered because these help to explain it.

Three hypotheses about different aspects of the thematic material used in Experiment II could account for its beneficial effects. First, the terms used in the thematic material, the towns and modes of transport, are concrete as opposed to the abstract terms which consisted of letters and numbers. It is well known that concrete material is better remembered than abstract material, and that in syllogistic reasoning familiar terms inhibit fallacious inferences (Wilkins, 1929). Thus in Experiment II the concrete terms may have been symbolically manipulated more readily and more appropriately than the abstract terms. This hypothesis might be tested by using concrete terms with an arbitrary connection, e.g. "Every card which has *iron* on one side has *apple* on the other side," where metals and fruits are known to occur on either side of the cards.

Second, it may be the concrete relation between the terms, rather than the terms themselves, which is beneficial. In the thematic material the relation which connects the terms is "traveling," as opposed to "the other side of the card" which connects the abstract material. This hypothesis could be tested by using abstract terms with a concrete relation between them, e.g. "Every time I go to K I travel by 3," where letters and numbers are known to stand for towns and transport respectively.

Third, the thematic material, unlike the abstract material, forms a coherent, unified whole: a claim about journeys supposed to have been made on four different days. Hence the subjects may have been more inclined to distribute their attention equally on its components, i.e. the four cards. They would thus be liberated from fixations on those cards which correspond to items mentioned in the rule. Cyril Burt (personal communication) has even suggested that thematic material enables the subjects to concentrate on the situation depicted, unfettered by the presence of the cards. This does not, in itself, explain why thematic material is helpful. But if it is assumed that knowledge about such material is represented in the brain in schemata, which may be activated by appropriate cues, then the solution to the problem may be simply "read off" by reference to this stored information.

The abstract material has no unifying link: each card is distinct and separate rather than being parts of a whole. The subjects are instructed that the rule refers only to the four cards, but in spite of this they may have construed it merely as a formula. They may, in fact, have regarded the cards as items in a sample from a larger universe, and reasoned about them inductively rather than deductively. In doing this they may have implicitly followed the Bayesian rule which assumes that the probability of a generalization is increased by repetition of confirming instances. Hence they might not have been disposed to consider the potential relevance of $\bar{q}$. There was some introspective support for probabilistic reasoning of this kind. It would follow, of course, that the experience of the problem's logical structure, introduced in Experiment I, would not have disabused the subjects of this particular misconception.

In fact, the difficulty of the abstract selection task may be due, not to the failure to recognize the correct solution, but to the failure to generate alternatives in order to derive the correct solution. In other words, abstract material may inhibit the realization of the necessity of combinatorial analysis rather than hindering the performance of such an analysis. The meaninglessness of the rule may tempt the subjects to interpret it, not as a rule, but as a sentence to be matched against instances. With thematic material it is gratuitous to talk about combinatorial analysis: the activation of stored knowledge spontaneously generates "real" alternatives. This hypothesis might be tested by comparing thematic and abstract material, but presenting all the possible solutions in a list from which one has to be selected, thus obviating the need for a combinatorial analysis. It would then be predicted only that the correct solution would be located more quickly with thematic material than with abstract material without a difference in its relative frequency.

Finally, the present results support the suggestion (Wason, 1969b) that it is not so much the logical structure which makes the abstract problem difficult, as the structure which the subjects impose upon the problem. Its difficulty does not lie in the fact that inferences of the kind demanded "hardly ever occur in real life"—a criticism sometimes voiced of the early experiments. On the contrary, when the task is made realistic it becomes appreciably easier. What makes the abstract task difficult is the arbitrariness of material which seems to defy the reasoning process. A more precise definition of the impediments involved must await further investigation.

REFERENCES

Johnson-Laird, P. N. and Tagart, J. (1969). How implication is understood. *American Journal of Psychology*, **82**, 367–73.

Johnson-Laird, P. N. and Wason, P. C. (1970*a*). A theoretical analysis of insight into a reasoning task. *Cognitive Psychology* **1**, 134–148 .

Johnson-Laird, P. N. and Wason, P. C. (1970*b*). Insight into a logical relation. *Quarterly Journal of Experimental Psychology*, **22**, 49–61.

Wason, P. C. (1968). Reasoning about a rule. *Quarterly Journal of Experimental Psychology*, **20**, 273–81.

Wason, P. C. (1969*a*). Regression in reasoning? *British Journal of Psychology*, **60**, 471–80.

Wason, P. C. (1969*b*). Structural simplicity and psychological complexity. *Bulletin of the British Psychological Society*, **22**, 281–84.

Wilkins, M. C. (1929). The effect of changed material on ability to do formal syllogistic reasoning. *Archives of Psychology*, No. 102.

POSTSCRIPT

An enormous amount of research has been done on the Wason selection task (see Evans, 1982, for an excellent summary). In this particular article, two observations stand out. First, even people with some training find it difficult to behave in the fashion prescribed by logical rules. Second, giving realistic content to the task can make it easier to reason logically.

Subsequent research has indicated that the content effect is quite complicated. Although some researchers have found that couching the argument in terms that describe a possible situation in the real world helps the reasoning process (see Gilhooly & Falconer, 1974; Johnson-Laird, Legrenzi, & Legrenzi, 1972), others have failed to find an advantage with real-world content (for example, Manktelow & Evans, 1979). It appears that what helps subjects is not the meaningfulness of the materials per se but rather subjects' familiarity with the real-world situations described (Griggs & Cox, 1982).

Research on reasoning with syllogisms (problems of the form "All A are B, No B are C, therefore No A are C") has confirmed the difficulty people have in giving the answers prescribed by formal logic and the effect that the contents of an argument sometimes have. These observations suggest that it is unlikely that people use formal rules of logic when they reason, at least with the Wason selection task or when dealing with syllogisms. How then do people reason? Some psychologists propose that people reason by using "natural" deduction principles that are closely related to the rules of formal logic but modified to account for actual human reasoning behavior (for example, Braine, 1978; Rips, 1983, 1989). For instance, unlike standard formal logic, people's natural logic may include a principle that yields the conclusion "p" when given the conditions "if p then q; q" (Rips, 1988).

Cheng and Holyoak (1985) argue that instead of following natural logic rules, people develop pragmatic reasoning schemas through life experiences (see the Introduction to Reading 32 for a description of schemas). These schemas specify the inferences that can be made in certain kinds of situations. For example, the permission schema specifies the conditions under which certain actions must be taken, must not be taken, or may be taken. People use the permission schema to decide when to cross the street or which card to pick in the Wason selection task (but see Jackson & Griggs, 1990).

Johnson-Laird and his colleagues, on the other hand, believe that people reason by constructing a mental representation (called a mental model) that instantiates or makes concrete the situation described by the argument. That representation is then manipulated, and the results are interpreted (Johnson-Laird & Bara, 1984; Johnson-Laird & Byrne, 1991, 1992). The mental model approach has been applied to a wide variety of cognitive tasks, not just to reasoning (see Gentner & Stevens, 1983; Johnson-Laird, 1983, 1989; Rouse & Morris, 1986). However, the mental models approach has been criticized (see some of the comments that are part of Johnson-Laird & Byrne, 1993; the appendix to Chapter 2 in Macnamara, 1986; or Rips, 1986).

Braine (1990, 1993) suggests that all three explanations (natural logic rules, pragmatic reasoning schemas, mental models), either singly or in combination, are needed to account for people's reasoning in different situations (see also Galotti, Baron, & Sabini, 1985). A lively debate among proponents of these different views can be found in Johnson-Laird and Byrne (1993). An interesting alternative to all of these approaches is social exchange theory (Cosmides, 1989; Gigerenzer & Hug, 1992). This theory sees the selection task as tapping into a very specific cognitive ability that evolution has selected for in humans.

For a discussion of the relevance of the study of deductive reasoning to the kinds of reasoning people do outside the laboratory, see Galotti (1989).

FOR FURTHER THOUGHT

1. Describe the two procedures used in Experiment I to train subjects to solve selection problems in accordance with the predictions of standard formal logic. Although subjects in this experiment did somewhat better than subjects in previous experiments using the selection task, Wason and Shapiro conclude that these manipulations are "relatively ineffective." Why?

2. Wason and Shapiro defend the training procedures used in Experiment I against the argument that only falsifying contingencies should have been used in training. What is the basis for arguing that only falsifying contingencies be used? On what grounds do Wason and Shapiro defend their

approach? How do they explain the limited success experienced by subjects in this experiment?

3. What "training" is at issue in Experiment II?

4. Wason and Shapiro mention three ways in which the task differs when thematic rather than abstract material is used. For this question, focus on the first two differences; they lead to two alternative hypotheses about subjects' greater success when thematic material is used. Explain why the data from Experiment II are consistent with each of these hypotheses. How might each hypothesis be tested? (Wason and Shapiro give suggestions.) Based on your introspection, how would you expect each hypothesis to fare?

5. Explain Wason and Shapiro's suggestion that, if knowledge is represented as schemas, then it helps to be able to concentrate on the overall situation described by the conditional sentence rather than on the individual cards. (See the Introduction to Reading 32 if you are unfamiliar with schemas.)

6. For testing their final (third) alternative hypothesis, Wason and Shapiro suggest giving all possible solutions to subjects and asking them to pick the correct one. What is the third hypothesis, and how would this procedure test it?

REFERENCES

Braine, M. D. S. (1978). On the relation between the natural logic of reasoning and standard logic. *Psychological Review, 85,* 1–21.

Braine, M. D. S. (1990). The "natural logic" approach to reasoning. In W. F. Overton (Ed.), *Reasoning, necessity, and logic: Developmental perspectives* (pp. 133–157). Hillsdale, NJ: Erlbaum.

Braine, M. D. S. (1993). Mental models cannot exclude mental logic and make little sense without it. *Behavioral and Brain Sciences, 16,* 338–339.

Cheng, P. W., & Holyoak, K. J. (1985). Pragmatic reasoning schemas. *Cognitive Psychology, 17,* 391–416.

Cosmides, L. (1989). The logic of social exchange: Has natural selection shaped how humans reason? Studies with the Wason selection task. *Cognition, 31,* 187–276.

Evans, J. St. B. T. (1982). *The psychology of deductive reasoning.* Boston: Routledge & Kegan Paul.

Galotti, K. M. (1989). Approaches to studying formal and everyday reasoning. *Psychological Bulletin, 105,* 331–351.

Galotti, K. M., Baron, J., & Sabini, J. P. (1985). Individual differences in syllogistic reasoning: Deduction rules or mental models? *Journal of Experimental Psychology: General, 115,* 16–25.

Gentner, D., & Stevens, A. L. (Eds.). (1983). *Mental models.* Hillsdale, NJ: Erlbaum.

Gigerenzer, G., & Hug, K. (1992). Domain-specific reasoning: Social contracts, cheating, and perspective change. *Cognition, 43,* 127–171.

Gilhooly, K. J., & Falconer, W. A. (1974). Concrete and abstract terms and relations in testing a rule. *Quarterly Journal of Experimental Psychology, 26,* 355–359.

Griggs, R. A., & Cox, J. R. (1982). The elusive thematic-materials effect in Wason's selection task. *British Journal of Psychology, 73,* 407–420.

Jackson, S. L., & Griggs, R. A. (1990). The elusive pragmatic reasoning schema effect. *Quarterly Journal of Experimental Psychology, 42A,* 353–373.

Johnson-Laird, P. N. (1983). *Mental models: Towards a cognitive science of language, inference, and consciousness.* New York: Cambridge University Press.

Johnson-Laird, P. N. (1989). Mental models. In M. I. Posner (Ed.), *Foundations of cognitive science* (pp. 469–499). Cambridge, MA: MIT Press.

Johnson-Laird, P. N., & Bara, B. G. (1984). Syllogistic inference. *Cognition, 16,* 1–61.

Johnson-Laird, P. N., & Byrne, R. M. J. (1991). *Deduction.* East Sussex: Erlbaum.

Johnson-Laird, P. N., & Byrne, R. M. J. (1992). Modal reasoning, models, and Manktelow and Over. *Cognition, 43,* 173–182.

Johnson-Laird, P. N., & Byrne, R. M. J. (1993). Précis of *Deduction. Behavioral and Brain Sciences, 16,* 323–380.

Johnson-Laird, P. N., Legrenzi, P., & Legrenzi, M. S. (1972). Reasoning and a sense of reality. *British Journal of Psychology, 63,* 395–400.

Macnamara, J. (1986). *A border dispute: The place of logic in psychology.* Cambridge, MA: MIT Press.

Manktelow, K. I., & Evans, J. St. B. T. (1979). Facilitation of reasoning by realism: Effect or non-effect? *British Journal of Psychology, 70,* 477–488.

Rips, L. J. (1983). Cognitive processes in propositional reasoning. *Psychological Review, 90,* 38–71.

Rips, L. J. (1986). Mental muddles. In M. Brand and R. M. Harnish (Eds.), *Problems in the representation of knowledge and belief* (pp. 258–286). Tucson: University of Arizona Press.

Rips, L. J. (1988). Deduction. In R. J. Sternberg & E. E. Smith (Eds.), *The psychology of human thought* (pp. 116–152). New York: Cambridge University Press.

Rips, L. J. (1989). The psychology of knights and knaves. *Cognition, 31,* 85–116.

Rouse, W. B., & Morris, N. M. (1986). On looking into the black box: Prospects and limits in the search for mental models. *Psychological Bulletin, 100,* 349–363.

INTRODUCTION

Many of the decisions we make are based on our judgments about the likelihood or probabilities of certain events or outcomes. We make these judgments by applying certain heuristics (rules of thumb) to the information we have. In "On the Psychology of Prediction," Daniel Kahneman and Amos Tversky examine one of these heuristics, which they call representativeness.

Much as logicians have developed rules for reasoning (see Reading 24), statisticians have developed a variety of rules that give the correct or normative answers to questions about probabilities. For example, suppose a friend describes her dog to you; what's the likelihood that her dog is a Berner (Bernese Mountain Dog)? In this case, the relevant rule is Bayes' theorem or Bayes' rule, which states that the likelihood that your friend's dog is a Berner depends on three factors. The first factor is called the *prior odds,* or *probability*. In our example, this is a measure of the likelihood that a dog selected at random from the relevant population (in this case, the population of pet dogs) would be a particular breed. The prior odds of your friend's dog being a Berner would depend on the proportion of Berners among the overall population of pet dogs: its base-rate or its distribution in the population. Because Berners are relatively uncommon, those prior odds are relatively low.

The second factor that, according to Bayes' rule, must be considered in determining your final prediction about the likelihood of your friend's dog being a Berner (the posterior probability of its being a Berner) is the informativeness or *diagnosticity* of the information you have about the specific case, the *individuating information*. In this case, the specific information you have is your friend's description of her dog. Individuating information becomes more informative as its descriptiveness of the specific choice increases and its descriptiveness of the alternatives decreases. Thus a description such as "He has four legs" is not informative because it's no more or less descriptive of Berners than it is of other dogs. Such a description should not influence your final prediction much. On the other hand "He's got thick fur that's predominantly black but white on the feet with white blazes down his face, muzzle, and chest and a rust color separating the black and white areas" is typically descriptive of Berners but not of most other breeds. Such a description is highly informative and should greatly influence your final prediction.

A third factor that a normative calculation of posterior probability takes into account is the accuracy or *reliability* of the individuating information. If your friend is well known for giving poor descriptions or being unreliable in her descriptions, you should not allow the individuating information to influence your judgment too much. This assessment is described as lowering the weight of the specific information, or as making your prediction more regressive—more influenced by the prior probabilities. If your friend's descriptions are consistently accurate, you would increase its weight and make your prediction less regressive.

One, perhaps counterintuitive, consequence of these considerations is that the more accurate the available individuating information, the more predictions will vary from case to case, because the different specific information for each case would heavily influence the final prediction. The less accurate or reliable the individuating information, the less it should influence predictions; thus from case to case, predictions will be more similar and closer to the prior probabilities.

Kahneman and Tversky present evidence that people do not behave normatively—that is, in accordance with Bayes' rule. Instead, they seem to follow a rule of thumb (a heuristic) that weights specific information on the basis of representativeness (how closely it matches a stereotype) rather than on accuracy, and that tends to ignore prior probabilities whenever specific information is available.

In this selection from the original article, some of the more technical statistical discussions have been excluded, as have discussions of confidence in predictions and people's intuitions about regression. A further study showing lack of regression effects with numerical prediction has also been excluded. As you read this article, ask yourself why people would use a representativeness heuristic rather than something like Bayes' rule, particularly given that it can be shown statistically that the representativeness heuristic often gives the wrong prediction.

On the Psychology of Prediction

Daniel Kahneman and Amos Tversky

Hebrew University of Jerusalem and Oregon Research Institute

In this paper, we explore the rules that determine intuitive predictions and judgments of confidence and contrast these rules to the normative principles of statistical prediction. Two classes of prediction are discussed: category prediction and numerical prediction. In a categorical case, the prediction is given in nominal form, for example, the winner in an election, the diagnosis of a patient, or a person's future occupation. In a numerical case, the prediction is given in numerical form, for example, the future value of a particular stock or of a student's grade point average.

In making predictions and judgments under uncertainty, people do not appear to follow the calculus of chance or the statistical theory of prediction. Instead, they rely on a limited number of heuristics which sometimes yield reasonable judgments and sometimes lead to severe and systematic errors (Kahneman & Tversky, 1972; Tversky & Kahneman, 1971, 1973). The present paper is concerned with the role of one of these heuristics—representativeness—in intuitive predictions.

Given specific evidence (e.g., a personality sketch), the outcomes under consideration (e.g., oc-cupations or levels of achievement) can be ordered by the degree to which they are representative of that evidence. The thesis of this paper is that people predict by representativeness, that is, they select or order outcomes by the degree to which the outcomes represent the essential features of the evidence. In many situations, representative outcomes are indeed more likely than others. However, this is not always the case, because there are factors (e.g., the prior probabilities of outcomes and the reliability of the evidence) which affect the likelihood of outcomes but not their representativeness. Because these factors are ignored, intuitive predictions violate the statistical rules of prediction in systematic and fundamental ways. To confirm this hypothesis, we show that the ordering of outcomes by perceived likelihood coincides with their ordering by representativeness and that intuitive predictions are essentially unaffected by considerations of prior probability and expected predictive accuracy.

In the first section, we investigate category predictions and show that they conform to an independent assessment of representativeness and that they are essentially independent of the prior probabilities of outcomes. In the next section, we investigate numerical predictions and show that they are not properly regressive and are essentially unaffected by considerations of reliability. . . .

Research for this study was supported by the following grants: Grants MH 12972 and MH 21216 from the National Institute of Mental Health and Grant RR 05612 from the National Institute of Health, U. S. Public Health Service, Grant GS 3250 from the National Science Foundation. Computing assistance was obtained from the Health Services Computing Facility, University of California at Los Angeles, sponsored by Grant MH 10822 from the U.S. Public Health Service.

The authors thank Robyn Dawes, Lewis Goldberg, and Paul Slovic for their comments. Sundra Gregory and Richard Kleinknecht assisted in the preparation of the test material and the collection of data.

Requests for reprints should be sent to Daniel Kahneman, Department of Psychology, Hebrew University, Jerusalem, Israel.

CATEGORICAL PREDICTION

Base Rate, Similarity, and Likelihood

The following experimental example illustrates prediction by representativeness and the fallacies associated with this mode of intuitive prediction. A group

SOURCE: *Psychological Review, 80*(4), July 1973, pp. 237–251. Copyright 1973 by the American Psychological Association. Reprinted by permission.

TABLE 1 Estimated Base Rates of the Nine Areas of Graduate Specialization and Summary of Similarity and Prediction Data for Tom W.

Graduate Specialization Area	Mean Judged Base Rate (in %)	Mean Similarity Rank	Mean Likelihood Rank
Business Administration	15	3.9	4.3
Computer Science	7	2.1	2.5
Engineering	9	2.9	2.6
Humanities and Education	20	7.2	7.6
Law	9	5.9	5.2
Library Science	3	4.2	4.7
Medicine	8	5.9	5.8
Physical and Life Sciences	12	4.5	4.3
Social Science and Social Work	17	8.2	8.0

of 69 subjects[1] (the *base-rate* group) was asked the following question: "Consider all first-year graduate students in the U. S. today. Please write down your best guesses about the percentage of these students who are now enrolled in each of the following nine fields of specialization." The nine fields are listed in Table 1. The first column of this table presents the mean estimates of base rate for the various fields.

A second group of 65 subjects (the *similarity* group) was presented with the following personality sketch:

Tom W. is of high intelligence, although lacking in true creativity. He has a need for order and clarity, and for neat and tidy systems in which every detail finds its appropriate place. His writing is rather dull and mechanical, occasionally enlivened by somewhat corny puns and by flashes of imagination of the sci-fi type. He has a strong drive for competence. He seems to have little feel and little sympathy for other people and does not enjoy interacting with others. Self-centered, he nonetheless has a deep moral sense.

The subjects were asked to rank the nine areas in terms of "how similar is Tom W. to the typical graduate student in each of the following nine fields of graduate specialization?" The second column in Table 1 presents the mean similarity ranks assigned to the various fields.

Finally, a *prediction* group, consisting of 114 graduate students in psychology at three major universities in the United States, was given the personality sketch of Tom W., with the following additional information:

The preceding personality sketch of Tom W. was written during Tom's senior year in high school by a psychologist, on the basis of projective tests. Tom W. is currently a graduate student. Please rank the following nine fields of graduate specialization in order of the likelihood that Tom W. is now a graduate student in each of these fields.

The third column in Table 1 presents the means of the ranks assigned to the outcomes by the subjects in the prediction group.

The product-moment correlations between the columns of Table 1 were computed. The correlation between judged likelihood and similarity is .91, while the correlation between judged likelihood and estimated base rate[2] is −.65. Evidently, judgments of likelihood essentially coincide with judgments of similarity and are quite unlike the estimates of base rates.

---

[1]Unless otherwise specified, the subjects in the studies reported in this paper were paid volunteers recruited through a student paper at the University of Oregon. Data were collected in group settings.

[2]In computing this correlation, the ranks were inverted so that a high judged likelihood was assigned a high value.

This result provides a direct confirmation of the hypothesis that people predict by representativeness, or similarity.

The judgments of likelihood by the psychology graduate students drastically violate the normative rules of prediction. More than 95% of those respondents judged that Tom W. is more likely to study computer science than humanities or education, although they were surely aware of the fact that there are many more graduate students in the latter field. According to the base-rate estimates shown in Table 1, the prior odds for humanities or education against computer science are about 3 to 1. (The actual odds are considerably higher.)

According to Bayes' rule, it is possible to overcome the prior odds against Tom W. being in computer science rather than in humanities or education, if the description of his personality is both accurate and diagnostic. The graduate students in our study, however, did not believe that these conditions were met. Following the prediction task, the respondents were asked to estimate the percentage of hits (i.e., correct first choices among the nine areas) which could be achieved with several types of information. The median estimate of hits was 23% for predictions based on projective tests, which compares to 53%, for example, for predictions based on high school seniors' reports of their interests and plans. Evidently, projective tests were held in low esteem. Nevertheless, the graduate students relied on a description derived from such tests and ignored the base rates.

In general, three types of information are relevant to statistical prediction: (a) prior or background information (e.g., base rates of fields of graduate specialization); (b) specific evidence concerning the individual case (e.g., the description of Tom W.); (c) the expected accuracy of prediction (e.g., the estimated probability of hits). A fundamental rule of statistical prediction is that expected accuracy controls the relative weights assigned to specific evidence and to prior information. When expected accuracy decreases, predictions should become more regressive, that is, closer to the expectations based on prior information. In the case of Tom W., expected accuracy was low, and prior probabilities should have been weighted heavily. Instead, our subjects predicted by representativeness, that is, they ordered outcomes by their similarity to the specific evidence, with no regard for prior probabilities.

In their exclusive reliance on the personality sketch, the subjects in the prediction group apparently ignored the following considerations. First, given the notorious invalidity of projective personality tests, it is very likely that Tom W. was never in fact as compulsive and as aloof as his description suggests. Second, even if the description was valid when Tom W. was in high school, it may no longer be valid now that he is in graduate school. Finally, even if the description is still valid, there are probably more people who fit that description among students of humanities and education than among students of computer science, simply because there are so many more students in the former than in the latter field.

Manipulation of Expected Accuracy

An additional study tests the hypothesis that, contrary to the statistical model, a manipulation of expected accuracy does not affect the pattern of predictions. The experimental material consisted of five thumbnail personality sketches of ninth-grade boys, allegedly written by a counselor on the basis of an interview in the context of a longitudinal study. The design was the same as in the Tom W. study. For each description, subjects in one group ($N = 69$) ranked the nine fields of graduate specialization (see Table 1) in terms of the similarity of the boy described to their "image of the typical first-year graduate student in that field." Following the similarity judgments, they estimated the base-rate frequency of the nine areas of graduate specialization. These estimates were shown in Table 1. The remaining subjects were told that the five cases had been randomly selected from among the participants in the original study who are now first-year graduate students. One group, the high-accuracy group ($N = 55$), was told that "on the basis of such descriptions, students like yourself make correct predictions in about 55% of the cases." The low-accuracy group ($N = 50$) was told that students' predictions in this task are correct in about 27% of the cases. For each description, the subjects ranked the nine fields according to "the likelihood that the person described is now a graduate student in that field."

For each description, they also estimated the probability that their first choice was correct.

The manipulation of expected accuracy had a significant effect on these probability judgments. The mean estimates were .70 and .56, respectively, for the high- and low-accuracy group ($t = 3.72$, $p < .001$). However, the orderings of the nine outcomes produced under the low-accuracy instructions were not significantly closer to the base-rate distribution than the orderings produced under the high-accuracy instructions. . . . This pattern of judgments violates the normative theory of prediction, according to which any decrease in expected accuracy should be accompanied by a shift of predictions toward the base rate.

Since the manipulation of expected accuracy had no effect on predictions, the two prediction groups were pooled. Subsequent analyses were the same as in the Tom W. study. For each description, two correlations were computed: (a) between mean likelihood rank and mean similarity rank and (b) between mean likelihood rank and mean base rate. These correlations are shown in Table 2, with the outcome judged most likely for each description. The correlations between prediction and similarity are consistently high. In contrast, there is no systematic relation between prediction and base rate: the correlations vary widely depending on whether the most representative outcomes for each description happen to be frequent or rare.

Here again, considerations of base rate were neglected. In the statistical theory, one is allowed to ignore the base rate only when one expects to be infallible. In all other cases, an appropriate compromise must be found between the ordering suggested by the description and the ordering of the base rates. It is hardly believable that a cursory description of a fourteen-year-old child based on a single interview could justify the degree of infallibility implied by the predictions of our subjects.

Following the five personality descriptions, the subjects were given an additional problem:

> About Don you will be told nothing except that he participated in the original study and is now a first-year graduate student. Please indicate your ordering and report your confidence for this case as well.

For Don the correlation between mean likelihood rank and estimated base rate was .74. Thus, the knowledge of base rates, which was not applied when a description was given, was utilized when no specific evidence was available.

Prior versus Individuating Evidence

The next study provides a more stringent test of the hypothesis that intuitive predictions are dominated by representativeness and are relatively insensitive to prior probabilities. In this study, the prior probabilities were made exceptionally salient and compatible with the response mode. Subjects were presented with the following cover story:

> A panel of psychologists have interviewed and administered personality tests to 30 engineers and 70 lawyers, all successful in their respective fields. On the basis of this information, thumbnail descriptions of the 30 engineers and 70 lawyers have been written. You will find on your forms five descriptions, chosen at random from the 100 available descriptions. For each description, please indicate your probability that the person described is an engineer, on a scale from 0 to 100.
>
> The same task has been performed by a panel of experts, who were highly accurate in assigning probabilities to the various descriptions. You will be paid a bonus to the extent that your estimates come close to those of the expert panel.

These instructions were given to a group of 85 subjects (the low-engineer, or L group). Subjects in

TABLE 2   Product-Moment Correlations of Mean Likelihood Rank with Mean Similarity Rank and with Base Rate

	Modal First Prediction				
	Law	Computer Science	Medicine	Library Science	Business Administration
With mean similarity rank	.93	.96	.92	.88	.88
With base rate	.33	−.35	.27	−.03	.62

another group (the high-engineer, H group; $N = 86$) were given identical instructions except for the prior probabilities: they were told that the set from which the descriptions had been drawn consisted of 70 engineers and 30 lawyers. All subjects were presented with the same five descriptions. One of the descriptions follows:

> Jack is a 45-year-old man. He is married and has four children. He is generally conservative, careful, and ambitious. He shows no interest in political and social issues and spends most of his free time on his many hobbies which include home carpentry, sailing, and mathematical puzzles.
>
>   The probability that Jack is one of the 30 engineers in the sample of 100 is ___%.

Following the five descriptions, the subjects encountered the *null* description:

> Suppose now that you are given no information whatsoever about an individual chosen at random from the sample.
>
>   The probability that this man is one of the 30 engineers in the sample of 100 is ___%.

In both the high-engineer and low-engineer groups, half of the subjects were asked to evaluate, for each description, the probability that the person described was an engineer (as in the example above), while the other subjects evaluated, for each description, the probability that the person described was a lawyer. This manipulation had no effect. The median probabilities assigned to the outcomes *engineer* and *lawyer* in the two different forms added to about 100% for each description. Consequently, the data for the two forms were pooled, and the results are presented in terms of the outcome *engineer*. . . . [Here Kahneman and Tversky explain how Bayes' rule is used to derive the curved line in Figure 1.]

Figure 1 presents the median probability estimates for each description, under the two conditions of prior odds. For each description, the median estimate of probability when the prior is high ($Q_H = 70/30$) is plotted against the median estimate when the prior is low ($Q_L = 30/70$). According to the normative equation developed in the preceding paragraph, all points should lie on the curved (Bayesian) line. In fact, only the empty square which corresponds to the

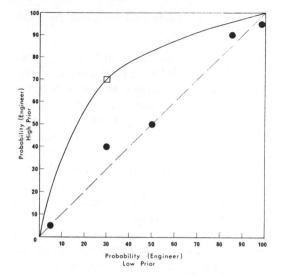

FIGURE 1   Median judged probability (engineer) for five descriptions and for the null description (square symbol) under high and low prior probabilities. (The curved line displays the correct relation according to Bayes' rule.)

null description falls on this line: when given no description, subjects judged the probability to be 70% under Q_H and 30% under Q_L. In the other five cases, the points fall close to the identity line.

The effect of prior probability, although slight, is statistically significant. For each subject the mean probability estimate was computed over all cases except the null. The average of these values was 50% for the low-engineer group and 55% for the high-engineer group ($t = 3.23$, $df = 169$, $p < .01$). Nevertheless, as can be seen from Figure 1, every point is closer to the identity line than to the Bayesian line. It is fair to conclude that explicit manipulation of the prior distribution had a minimal effect on subjective probability. As in the preceding experiment, subjects applied their knowledge of the prior only when they were given no specific evidence. As entailed by the representativeness hypothesis, prior probabilities were largely ignored when individuating information was made available.

The strength of this effect is demonstrated by the responses to the following description:

> Dick is a 30-year-old man. He is married with no children. A man of high ability and high motivation, he

promises to be quite successful in his field. He is well liked by his colleagues.

This description was constructed to be totally uninformative with regard to Dick's profession. Our subjects agreed: median estimates were 50% in both the low- and high-engineer groups (see Figure 1). The contrast between the responses to this description and to the null description is illuminating. Evidently, people respond differently when given no specific evidence and when given worthless evidence. When no specific evidence is given, the prior probabilities are properly utilized; when worthless specific evidence is given, prior probabilities are ignored.

There are situations in which prior probabilities are likely to play a more substantial role. In all the examples discussed so far, distinct stereotypes were associated with the alternative outcomes, and judgments were controlled, we suggest, by the degree to which the descriptions appeared representative of these stereotypes. In other problems, . . . there are no well-delineated stereotypes. . . . Consequently, they are not likely to be ignored. In addition, we would expect extreme prior probabilities to have some effect even in the presence of clear stereotypes of the outcomes. A precise delineation of the conditions under which prior information is used or discarded awaits further investigation.

One of the basic principles of statistical prediction is that prior probability, which summarizes what we knew about the problem before receiving independent specific evidence, remains relevant even after such evidence is obtained. Bayes' rule translates this qualitative principle into a multiplicative relation between prior odds and the likelihood ratio. Our subjects, however, failed to integrate prior probability with specific evidence. When exposed to a description, however scanty or suspect, of Tom W. or of Dick (the engineer/lawyer), they apparently felt that the distribution of occupations in his group was no longer relevant. The failure to appreciate the relevance of prior probability in the presence of specific evidence is perhaps one of the most significant departures of intuition from the normative theory of prediction.

NUMERICAL PREDICTION

A fundamental rule of the normative theory of prediction is that the variability of predictions, over a set of cases, should reflect predictive accuracy. When predictive accuracy is perfect, one predicts the criterion value that will actually occur. When uncertainty is maximal, a fixed value is predicted in all cases. (In category prediction, one predicts the most frequent category. In numerical prediction, one predicts the mean, the mode, the median, or some other value depending on the loss function.) Thus, the variability of predictions is equal to the variability of the criterion when predictive accuracy is perfect, and the variability of predictions is zero when predictive accuracy is zero. With intermediate predictive accuracy, the variability of predictions takes an intermediate value, that is, predictions are regressive with respect to the criterion. Thus, the greater the uncertainty, the smaller the variability of predictions. Predictions by representativeness do not follow this rule. It was shown in the previous section that people did not regress toward more frequent categories when expected accuracy of predictions was reduced. The present section demonstrates an analogous failure in the context of numerical prediction.

Prediction of Outcomes versus Evaluation of Inputs

Suppose one is told that a college freshman has been described by a counselor as intelligent, self-confident, well-read, hard-working, and inquisitive. Consider two types of questions that might be asked about this description:

> (a) *Evaluation:* How does this description impress you with respect to academic ability? What percentage of descriptions of freshmen do you believe would impress you more? (b) *Prediction:* What is your estimate of the grade point average that this student will obtain? What is the percentage of freshmen who obtain a higher grade point average?

There is an important difference between the two questions. In the first, you evaluate the input; in the second, you predict an outcome. Since there is surely greater uncertainty about the second question than about the first, your prediction should be more regressive than your evaluation. That is, the percentage you give as a prediction should be closer to 50% than the percentage you give as an evaluation. To highlight the difference between the two questions, consider the possibility that the description is inaccurate. This should have no effect on your evaluation: the ordering of descriptions with respect to the impressions they make on you is independent of their accuracy. In predicting, on the other hand, you should be regressive to the extent that you suspect the description to be inaccurate or your prediction to be invalid.

The representativeness hypothesis, however, entails that prediction and evaluation should coincide. In evaluating a given description, people select a score which, presumably, is most representative of the description. If people predict by representativeness, they will also select the most representative score as their prediction. Consequently, the evaluation and the prediction will be essentially identical. Several studies were conducted to test this hypothesis. In each of these studies the subjects were given descriptive information concerning a set of cases. An *evaluation* group evaluated the quality of each description relative to a stated population, and a *prediction* group predicted future performance. The judgments of the two groups were compared to test whether predictions are more regressive than evaluations.

In two studies, subjects were given descriptions of college freshmen, allegedly written by a counselor on the basis of an interview administered to the entering class. In the first study, each description consisted of five adjectives, referring to intellectual qualities and to character, as in the example cited above. In the second study, the descriptions were paragraph-length reports, including details of the student's background and of his current adjustment to college. In both studies the evaluation groups were asked to evaluate each one of the descriptions by estimating "the percentage of students in the entire class whose descriptions indicate a higher academic ability." The prediction groups were given the same descriptions and were asked to predict the grade point average achieved by each student at the end of his freshman year and his class standing in percentiles.

The results of both studies are shown in Figure 2, which plots, for each description, the mean prediction of percentile grade point average against the mean evaluation. The only systematic discrepancy between predictions and evaluations is observed in the adjectives study where predictions were consistently higher than the corresponding evaluations. The standard deviation of predictions or evaluations was com-

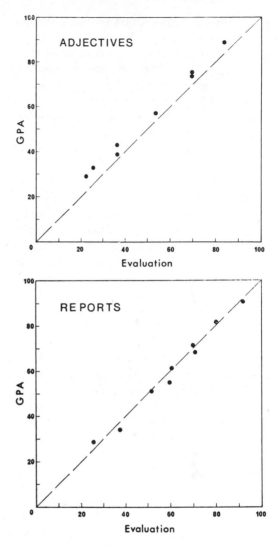

FIGURE 2   Predicted percentile grade point average as a function of percentile evaluation for adjectives (A) and reports (B).

puted within the data of each subject. A comparison of these values indicated no significant differences in variability between the evaluation and the prediction groups, within the range of values under study. In the adjectives study, the average standard deviation was 25.7 for the evaluation group ($N = 38$) and 24.0 for the prediction group ($N = 36$) ($t = 1.25$, $df = 72$, ns). In the reports study, the average standard deviation was 22.2 for the evaluation group ($N = 37$) and 21.4 for the prediction group ($N = 63$) ($t = .75$, $df = 98$, ns). In both studies the prediction and the evaluation groups produced equally extreme judgments, although the former predicted a remote objective criterion on the basis of sketchy interview information, while the latter merely evaluated the impression obtained from each description. In the statistical theory of prediction, the observed equivalence between prediction and evaluation would be justified only if predictive accuracy were perfect, a condition which could not conceivably be met in these studies.

Further evidence for the equivalence of evaluation and prediction was obtained in a master's thesis by Beyth (1972). She presented three groups of subjects with seven paragraphs, each describing the performance of a student-teacher during a particular practice lesson. The subjects were students in a statistics course at the Hebrew University. They were told that the descriptions had been drawn from among the files of 100 elementary school teachers who, five years earlier, had completed their teacher training program. Subjects in an evaluation group were asked to evaluate the quality of the lesson described in the paragraph, in percentile scores relative to the stated population. Subjects in a prediction group were asked to predict in percentile scores the current standing of each teacher, that is, his overall competence five years after the description was written. An evaluation–prediction group performed both tasks. As in the studies described above, the differences between evaluation and prediction were not significant. This result held in both the between-subjects and within-subject comparisons. Although the judges were undoubtedly aware of the multitude of factors that intervene between a single trial lesson and teaching competence five years later, this knowledge did not cause their predictions to be more regressive than their evaluations. . . .

METHODOLOGICAL CONSIDERATIONS

The representativeness hypothesis states that predictions do not differ from . . . assessments of similarity, although the normative statistical theory entails that predictions should be less extreme than these judgments. The test of the representativeness hypothesis therefore requires a design in which predictions are compared to another type of judgment. Variants of two comparative designs were used in the studies reported in this paper.

In one design, labeled A-XY, different groups of subjects judged two variables (X and Y) on the basis of the same input information (A). In the case of Tom W., for example, two different groups were given the same input information (A), that is, a personality description. One group ranked the outcomes in terms of similarity (X), while the other ranked the outcomes in terms of likelihood (Y). Similarly, in several studies of numerical prediction, different groups were given the same information (A), for example, a list of five adjectives describing a student. One group provided an evaluation (X) and the other a prediction (Y).

In another design, labeled AB-X, two different groups of subjects judged the same outcome variable (X) on the basis of different information inputs (A and B). In the engineer/lawyer study, for example, two different groups made the same judgment (X) of the likelihood that a particular individual is an engineer. They were given a brief description of his personality and different information (A and B) concerning the base-rate frequencies of engineers and lawyers. . . .

The representativeness hypothesis was supported in these comparative designs by showing that contrary to the normative model, predictions are no more regressive than . . . judgments of similarity. It is also possible to ask whether intuitive predictions are regressive when compared to the actual outcomes; . . . we expect [predictions] to be slightly regressive when compared to . . . outcomes, because of the well-known central-tendency error (Johnson, 1972; Woodworth, 1938). In a wide variety of judgment tasks, . . . subjects tend to avoid extreme responses and to constrict the variability of their judgments (Stevens & Greenbaum, 1966). Because of this response bias, judgments will be regressive, when compared . . . to outcomes. The designs employed in the present paper neutralize this effect by comparing two judgments, both of which are subject to the same bias.

The present set of studies was concerned with situations in which people make predictions on the basis of information that is available to them prior to the experiment, in the form of stereotypes (e.g., of an engineer) and expectations concerning relationships between variables. Outcome feedback was not provided, and the number of judgments required of each subject was small. In contrast, most previous studies of prediction have dealt with the learning of functional or statistical relations among variables with which the subjects had no prior acquaintance. These studies typically involve a large number of trials and various forms of outcome feedback. (Some of this literature has been reviewed in Slovic and Lichtenstein, 1971.) In studies of repetitive predictions with feedback, subjects generally predict by selecting outcomes so that the entire sequence or pattern of predictions is highly representative of the distribution of outcomes. For example, subjects in probability-learning studies generate sequences of predictions which roughly match the statistical characteristics of the sequence of outcomes. Similarly, subjects in numerical prediction tasks approximately reproduce the scatterplot, that is, the joint distribution of inputs and outcomes (see, e.g., Gray, 1968). To do so, subjects resort to a mixed strategy: for any given input they generate a distribution of different predictions. These predictions reflect the fact that any one input is followed by different outcomes on different trials. Evidently, the rules of prediction are different in the two paradigms, although representativeness is involved in both. In the feedback paradigm, subjects produce response sequences which represent the entire pattern of association between inputs and outcomes. In the situations explored in the present paper, subjects select the prediction which best represents their impressions of each individual case. The two approaches lead to different violations of the normative rule: the representation of uncertainty through a mixed strategy in the feedback paradigm and the discarding of uncertainty through prediction by evaluation in the present paradigm. . . .

REFERENCES

Beyth, R. Man as an intuitive statistician: On erroneous intuitions concerning the description and prediction of events. Unpublished master's thesis (in Hebrew). The Hebrew University, Jerusalem, 1972.

Campbell, D. T. Reforms as experiments. *American Psychologist,* 1969, **24**, 409–429.

Gray, C. W. Predicting with intuitive correlations. *Psychonomic Science,* 1968, **11**, 41–42.

Guilford, J. P. *Psychometric methods.* New York: McGraw-Hill, 1954.

Johnson, D. M. *Systematic introduction to the psychology of thinking.* New York: Harper & Row, 1972.

Kahneman, D., & Tversky, A. Subjective probability: A judgment of representativeness. *Cognitive Psychology,* 1972, **3**, 430–454.

Mischel, W. *Personality and assessment.* New York: Wiley, 1968.

Slovic, P. Cue consistency and cue utilization in judgment. *American Journal of Psychology,* 1966, **79**, 427–434.

Slovic, P., & Lichtenstein, S. Comparison of Bayesian and regression approaches to the study of information processing in judgment. *Organizational Behavior and Human Performance,* 1971, **6**, 649–744.

Stevens, S. S., & Greenbaum, H. B. Regression effect in psychophysical judgment. *Perception & Psychophysics,* 1966, **1**, 439–446.

Tversky, A., & Kahneman, D. Belief in the law of small numbers. *Psychological Bulletin,* 1971, **76**, 105–110.

Tversky, A., & Kahneman, D. Availability: A heuristic for judging frequency and probability. *Cognitive Psychology,* 1973, **4**, 207–232.

Wallis, W. A., & Roberts, H. V. *Statistics: A new approach.* New York: The Free Press, 1956.

Woodworth, R. S. *Experimental psychology.* New York: Holt, 1938.

POSTSCRIPT

Kahneman and Tversky (and others) have conducted extensive studies on how people make judgments that involve the estimation of probabilities, often referred to as judgments under uncertainty. They have found that to make such judgments, people often use a heuristic of availability in addition to one of representativeness. The availability heuristic leads people to judge the frequency of occurrence of some outcome or event, and therefore its probability, by the ease with which they can bring examples to mind (see Reading 31). Other heuristics that people use include anchoring and adjustment (Tversky & Kahneman, 1974). Kahneman, Slovic, and Tversky (1982) have edited an excellent collection of articles on judgment under uncertainty. Psychologists have also studied other kinds of judgments and decision-making situations, two of which are described below. (For reviews, see Baron, 1988; Fischhoff, 1988; Osherson, 1990; and Slovic, 1990; for a collection of articles examining decision making in a variety of specific settings, see Arkes & Hammond, 1986.)

Sometimes, the alternatives from which we must choose are laid out before us; no uncertainties are involved, or the uncertainties do not play a major role in the choice. For example, suppose you were trying to decide what kind of car to buy. Your decision would probably be based on considerations of safety, purchase cost, maintenance cost, transportation needs, status conferred, styling, and so forth. The alternatives available differ from one another in these attributes; one car may be low in cost but also low in safety features or status conferred, whereas another may be high in safety and styling, but also high in cost.

Psychologists have identified two main approaches to making decisions of this kind (Reed, 1992). In the compensatory approach, the attractive attributes of an alternative compensate for its unattractive ones; the choice depends on how much weight different attributes are given and how the attribute weights are combined (whether they are simply added up or combined in a more elaborate fashion to allow attributes to interact). In the noncompensatory approach, if an alternative has an attribute that falls below some level of attractiveness, it is eliminated from further consideration. The noncompensatory approach does not require the potentially complicated computations of weighting and combining weights that the compensation approach depends on, but it may not be as sensitive under most circumstances. There is some evidence that people often use a mixed approach, employing a noncompensatory method when there are many alternatives to reduce the number to choose from, and then switching to a compensatory method once there are fewer alternatives to compare (Payne, 1976).

Another kind of decision-making situation is one in which the choice is among differently valued alternatives but the alternatives differ in probability. This represents an extension of judgment under uncertainty, sometimes referred to as decision making under risk. For example, would you prefer a bet that offers you a sure gain of $50 or one that offers a 25% chance of a $200 gain and a 75% chance of no gain at all? Prospect theory, derived from a normative model called expected utility theory, is a psychological model that describes people's behavior when given this kind of choice (Kahneman & Tversky, 1979, 1984). A description of prospect theory would be too lengthy to go into here. However, it is an interesting example of how relatively small changes in a normative model can yield a psychological model that systematically explains what might otherwise appear to be irrational behavior (an example would be the "framing" effect, wherein people's choices are strongly affected when probabilities and values are not changed but the wording of a problem is; Tversky & Kahneman, 1981).

FOR FURTHER THOUGHT

1. Why did Kahneman and Tversky collect base-rate data from subjects in the first two studies of categorical prediction instead of using the actual percentages of people in each field? Why did they collect similarity data?
2. In their second study of categorical prediction, Kahneman and Tversky report a significant effect of accuracy manipulation, but they conclude that accuracy does not affect subjects' predictions in the relevant manner. How should accuracy have affected their predictions? How would you characterize the way subjects use accuracy information?
3. In the second study, why does the pattern of high correlations between predictions and similarity judgments support the claim that subjects used the representativeness hypothesis? What determines the pattern of correlations between predictions and base rates?
4. In the third study of categorical prediction, subjects given the null description behaved in accordance with Bayes' rule, using only prior probabilities in making their judgments. But subjects given the uninformative description ("Dick is a 30-year-old man . . .") ignored prior probabilities. What does this demonstrate? How did Kahneman and Tversky determine that their uninformative description was objectively worthless?
5. In the study on numerical prediction, Kahneman and Tversky state that "the percentage you give as a prediction should be closer to 50% than the percentage you give as an evaluation" (p. 414). Why is that? Why does the representativeness hypothesis argue that prediction and evaluation should give the same results?

REFERENCES

Arkes, H. R., & Hammond, K. R. (Eds.). (1986). *Judgment and decision making*. New York: Cambridge University Press.

Baron, J. (1988). *Thinking and deciding*. New York: Cambridge University Press.

Fischhoff, B. (1988). Judgment and decision making. In R. J. Sternberg & E. E. Smith (Eds.), *The psychology of human thought* (pp. 153–187). New York: Cambridge University Press.

Kahneman, D., Slovic, P. & Tversky, A. (Eds.). (1982). *Judgment under uncertainty: Heuristics and biases.* New York: Cambridge University Press.

Kahneman, D., & Tversky, A. (1979). Prospect theory: An analysis of decisions under risk. *Econometrica, 47,* 263–291.

Kahneman, D., & Tversky, A. (1984). Choices, values, and frames. *American Psychologist, 39,* 341–350.

Osherson, D. N. (1990). Judgment. In D. N. Osherson & E. E. Smith (Eds.), *An invitation to cognitive science: Vol. 3. Thinking* (pp. 55–87). Cambridge, MA: MIT.

Payne, J. W. (1976). Task complexity and contingent processing in decision making: An information search and protocol analysis. *Organizational Behavior and Human Performance, 16,* 366–387.

Reed, S. K. (1992). *Cognition* (3rd ed.). Pacific Grove, CA: Brooks/Cole.

Slovic, P. (1990). Choice. In D. N. Osherson & E. E. Smith (Eds.), *An invitation to cognitive science: Vol. 3. Thinking* (pp. 89–116). Cambridge, MA: MIT.

Tversky, A., & Kahneman,, D. (1974). Judgment under uncertainty: Heuristics and biases. *Science, 185,* 1124–1131.

Tversky, A., & Kahneman, D. (1981). The framing of decisions and the psychology of choice. *Science, 211,* 453–458.

CHAPTER EIGHT
Problem Solving

INTRODUCTION

As most students know, being able to do all of the exercise problems in a textbook does not necessarily imply being able to do all of the problems on an exam, even if the professor swears that the exam problems are no more difficult. Greg Perfetto, John Bransford, and Jeffery Franks explore this failure-of-transfer phenomenon in "Constraints on Access in a Problem Solving Context."

The authors begin by entertaining two possible explanations for this failure of transfer. The first is that people retrieve the relevant information but fail to notice its relevance. But Perfetto and his colleagues argue that, if that is the case, then transfer should take place if the relevance of the information is made obvious enough. The second explanation is that people simply fail to retrieve the relevant information. If that is the case, the obviousness of the relevance would not matter.

As a first step to testing these ideas, Perfetto and his associates ran a pilot experiment, a preliminary study that is typically rather informal but is quite useful for either working out the kinks in an experiment or gathering information needed for completing the design of the experiment. For example, a pilot experiment may test some of the assumptions the experiment depends on, or it may gather normative data—information about how subjects can be expected to respond.

Two experiments reported in the original article are excluded in our presentation. Those experiments developed and tested some alternate explanations of the results obtained in the first two experiments. As you read this selection, ask yourself what makes the relevance of certain information for solving a particular problem obvious.

Constraints on Access in a Problem Solving Context

Greg A. Perfetto, John D. Bransford, and Jeffery J. Franks

Vanderbilt University

Effective comprehension and problem solving require more than the availability of potentially relevant information; people must access this information when it is needed (e.g., Bransford & Johnson, 1972, Experiment 2). One method for investigating the processes involved in accessing information is to first present subjects with potentially relevant information and to then explore the conditions necessary for them to utilize this information in problem solving tasks (e.g., Weisberg, DiCamillo, & Phillips, 1978).

Weisberg et al. (1978) had subjects learn a list of paired associates, one of which was candle-box. It was expected that this association would later cue a solution to the "candle problem" (Dunker, 1945). The candle problem involves attaching a candle to the wall so that it will burn properly. The available materials are a box of nails, a book of matches, a hammer, and the candle. The solution sought by Weisberg et al. was to attach the box to the wall using the hammer and nails, and to then put the candle on top of or in the box. The critical manipulation was whether subjects were informed that one of the paired associates acquired previously (i.e., candle-box) was relevant to the candle problem.

Weisberg et al.'s (1978) results indicate that the candle-box association was effective in cuing the expected solution only when subjects were explicitly informed that previously acquired information was relevant to the candle problem. Weisberg et al. interpreted their results as evidence that transfer is a non-automatic process. However, the failure of uninformed subjects to solve the candle problem can be accounted for by two distinct hypotheses. First, subjects may have spontaneously retrieved the appropriate cue when working on the candle problem but discarded it as irrelevant (note that the cue "candle-box" does not communicate much specific information). Alternately, subjects may have failed to retrieve the appropriate cue. Although both of the hypotheses provide plausible explanations for the failure of uninformed subjects to utilize prior information, they do so in very different ways.

The first hypothesis argues that subjects may have spontaneously retrieved "candle-box," but that this information may have been insufficient to facilitate problem solving because subjects did not perceive the information to be relevant. Since the information conveyed by the clue "candle-box" is not very explicit, it would not be surprising if subjects who were not informed that this information was useful failed to use it to solve the candle problem. In contrast, subjects who were informed of the connection between the tasks would expect the clue to provide relevant information and hence might be more likely to realize the significance of this information. This hypothesis implies that if clues were constructed that were highly related to problems (i.e., that provided obvious solutions), subjects should be able to utilize this information to solve problems even if the connection between the tasks was not explicitly pointed out. The second hypothesis noted above suggests that subjects actually fail to retrieve the relevant information in the absence of explicit instructions to do so. If

This research was supported in part by the National Institute of Education (Grant NIE-G-79-0017). The authors wish to thank Jonathan Doner, Karen Mezynski, and Pam Auble for their helpful comments throughout the course of this research. Requests for reprints should be addressed to Greg A. Perfetto, Department of Psychology, Vanderbilt University, 134 Wesley Hall, Nashville, Tennessee 37240.

SOURCE: *Memory and Cognition, 11*(1), 1983, pp. 24–31. Reprinted by permission of the Psychonomic Society, Inc.

this is the case, then increases in the relevance of the clues may still be insufficient to facilitate problem solving by uninformed subjects.

The first experiment was designed to investigate the former hypothesis by constructing obvious clues that were relevant to problem solving. The problems chosen for this experiment were 12 "insight" problems adapted from Gardner (1978). For each problem, a sentence clue was constructed that blatantly suggested the solution to the problem. For example, one problem was "A man who lived in a small town in the U.S. married 20 different women of the same town. All are still living and he has never divorced one of them. Yet, he has broken no law. Can you explain?" The sentence constructed as a clue to this problem's solutions was "A minister marries several people each week." The relevance of the sentence clues to the problems was verified by presenting 15 pilot subjects with each problem and its respective clue sentence. In addition, the candle problem was presented to subjects with the association "candle-box." The pilot subjects were given approximately 40 sec to solve each problem.

Overall, subjects solved an average of 96% of the insight problems. The candle problem was solved by only 46% of the subjects. Subjects were also asked to rate the clues according to the obviousness with which they pointed to a solution. The sentence clues had an average rating of 1.6 (1 being extremely obvious to 5 being not at all obvious), whereas the candle-box association had an average rating of 2.5. An additional analysis indicated that each of the 12 problem-sentence clue pairs was solved by more subjects than was the candle problem. Furthermore, each of the sentence clues was rated as providing a more obvious solution than the "candle-box" clue. Thus, the sentence clues constructed for the present study appear to meet the requirement of indicating an obvious solution to their corresponding problems.

EXPERIMENT 1

In Experiment 1, all experimental subjects were exposed to the sentence clues. The initial task required subjects to rate the clues on a scale of general truthfulness; this constituted an incidental acquisition. Subjects then received the set of problems. One group of subjects was explicitly told that the sentences they had rated would help them solve the problems they were about to receive. No mention of this connection was made to a second group. A control group did not receive the acquisition sentence clues prior to their problem solving attempts.

Method

Subjects.   Subjects were 60 undergraduate students enrolled in an introductory psychology class at Vanderbilt University. They received course credit for their participation in the experiment.

Materials and Procedure.   Materials for this experiment included the 12 problem-sentence clue pairs described previously. Subjects were introduced to the experiment by the experimenter, who told them that they would be given several tasks to complete. The subjects were told that the purpose of these tasks was to gather normative data for future experiments,

Subjects were first asked to rate 14 statements on a 5-point scale of truthfulness (e.g., never true, sometimes true, always true). Twelve of the 14 statements were the sentences constructed to clue solutions to the experimental problems. The first and last statements were fillers that were similar in form to the other statements but unrelated to the experimental problems. Subjects were allowed 20 sec to read and rate each statement. This rating task constituted an incidental acquisition for the subsequent problem solving task.

Following the acquisition task, a delay of 3 min was provided by collecting the rating sheet and directing subjects to fill out their attendance forms. All subjects were then told that they were going to receive some problems to solve. Subjects in the first group were told that the sentences they had just rated would help them to answer most of the problems (informed group). A second group was not made aware of the connection between the tasks (uninformed group). Both groups were then given problem booklets and answer sheets. The problem booklets contained one of four randomized orders of the experimental problems. In addition, prior to the 12 experimental problems, all of the problem booklets included 3 additional problems taken from Gardner (1978). These three initial filler problems were included to reinforce the separation of the acquisition and problem solving tasks, and to provide an additional delay (for a total of 5 min) between the end of the acquisition task and the first clue-related problem. Subjects were allowed 40 sec to read each problem and write down a solution. They were not allowed to turn the page to the next problem until the full 40 sec had expired. A third group (baseline) did not receive the acquisition (clue) sentences. Instead, these subjects were immediately given the problems to solve.

After the problem solving task, all subjects were asked to fill out a questionnaire. One purpose of the questionnaire was to assess the degree to which informed and uninformed subjects were aware that a relationship existed between the acquisition task and the problem solving task. Subjects were also asked to indicate which, if any, problems they had seen prior to the experiment and to answer questions about the processes they used during their problem solving attempts.

Results

Subjects who had previously seen more than two of the experimental problems were dropped from the study. By this criterion, data from three subjects in each of the experimental groups (informed and uninformed) and from four subjects in the baseline group were not used in the analyses. In addition, four subjects in the uninformed condition reported that they were aware of the purpose of the experiment before they received any of the problems. Because they were not actually uninformed, data from these subjects were not used in the analyses. Additional subjects were tested to attain 20 subjects in each condition.

The primary data involved subjects' answers to the 12 problems. A preliminary analysis revealed that all subjects generated some sort of answer to each problem, but that many answers were inadequate. For example, the problem "Uriah Fuller, the famous Israeli superpsychic, can tell you the score of any baseball game before the game starts. What is his secret?" was often answered by "He is a superpsychic." (The sentence clue was "Before any game is played, there is no score.") Similarly, the problem "Why are 1977 dollar bills worth more than 1976 dollar bills?" was

often answered by a reference to inflation, whereas the actual clue was "1,966 dollar bills are worth more than a 1967 dollar bill."

The mean proportion of solutions that were congruent with the clue sentences (these clues suggest the only appropriate answers that we have found for our problems, i.e., those that do not violate constraints on the problem) were .19 (SD = .118), .29 (SD = .216), and .54 (SD = .231) for subjects in the baseline, uninformed, and informed groups, respectively. A one-way ANOVA revealed a significant main effect [$F(2,57)= 16.80$, $p < .001$] . Pairwise comparisons using Dunn's procedure (Kirk, 1968) were performed to investigate the relative performance of each group. Subjects in the uninformed group were not superior to those in the baseline condition [$t'D(3,57) = 1.57$, $p > .05$]. In contrast, subjects in the informed condition produced more correct solutions than both baseline subjects [$t'D(3,57) = 5.62$, $p < .01$] and uninformed subjects [$t'D(3,57) = 4.06$, $p < .01$].

An item analysis of the number of correct responses made by each group to each problem was also performed in order to determine if the observed data were consistent across the different problems or if the results might be due to the effects of only a few problems. For each of the 12 problems, subjects in the informed group produced more solutions than did subjects in either the uninformed or baseline groups ($N = 12$, $P = 12$, $Q = 0$; $p < .001$). A comparison of the uninformed and baseline groups revealed that uninformed subjects produced more solutions to only 8 of the 12 problems; this was not significant by a sign test.

Subjects' responses to the questionnaire revealed two main results. First, subjects in the uninformed group reported that it did not occur to them to try to use the clues presented during acquisition when attempting to solve the problems. They therefore did not appear to spontaneously access these clues and then reject them because the clues seemed to be irrelevant to the problems they were trying to solve. Second, the comments of subjects in the informed group seemed to indicate that problems tended either to cue the appropriate acquisition clue or to cue no specific acquisition information. None of the subjects in the informed group indicated that they attempted to free recall the acquisition clues until they found one that helped them solve a particular problem. Instead, the problems frequently acted as retrieval cues that permitted access to the relevant clue.

Discussion

The results of the first experiment replicate those reported by Weisberg et al. (1978). In the present study, subjects who were not explicitly told that the sentences they had rated were useful problem solving clues did not use this information when presented with the experimental problems. In contrast, the identical clues were used by subjects in the informed group. Due to the nature of the sentence clues, it is unlikely that subjects would have failed to solve a problem had they retrieved the relevant clue. Furthermore, subjects' reports indicated that they did not attempt to recall the clue information while uninformed. Thus, the uninformed subjects' problem solving failure does not appear to be due to their actually retrieving the appropriate clues but then failing to recognize the relevance of these clues to problem solutions.

Our initial belief before conducting Experiment 1 was that even subjects in our uninformed condition would spontaneously access the relevant acquisition clues because the latter seemed so obviously relevant to the problems that the subjects were asked to solve. However, the results of Experiment 1 indicate that subjects in fact failed to spontaneously access obviously relevant information unless they were explicitly informed of the relationship between the acquisition task and the problem solving task. The use of informed and uninformed conditions therefore seems to be an important manipulation for exploring the conditions necessary for access to occur.

The results of Experiment 1 provide an additional opportunity to explore possible constraints on the processes involved in accessing relevant information. As we noted earlier, subjects in all conditions (baseline, uninformed, informed) generated some sort of answer to the problems they were asked to solve. The present design therefore allows us to explore the consequences of producing an inappropriate answer to a problem. In particular, what if subjects who are initially uninformed are given a second

trial in which they are informed that their acquisition experiences are relevant to the problems they are trying to solve? Will they now be able to access relevant information or will they be hurt by the fact that they initially generated answers that were incorrect? This issue is explored in Experiment 2.

EXPERIMENT 2

Method

Subjects. Subjects were 60 undergraduate students enrolled in an introductory psychology class at Vanderbilt University. They received course credit for their participation in the experiment.

Materials and Procedure. Materials for Experiment 2 were the same as those used in Experiment 1. However, unlike Experiment 1, subjects were given two attempts to solve the problems (Trial 1 and Trial 2). The procedures for the first trial were the same as those described in the first experiment. That is, informed and uninformed groups were first given the acquisition rating sheet. After completion of the acquisition task, the relationship between the rated clues and the problems was pointed out to subjects in the informed condition. Uninformed subjects did not receive these instructions. Both groups were then given the problems to solve. Subjects in the baseline condition solved the problems without having seen the acquisition items. All subjects then completed a questionnaire. These procedures constituted a replication of Experiment 1. Following this, both informed and uninformed subjects were told of the connection between the acquisition items and the problems.

In order to make the connection between acquisition and problem solving clear, subjects were given an example. This example consisted of the experimenter reading the marriage problem and its corresponding clue from the rating sheet. This illustration problem was the same for all subjects and was not included in the Trial 2 analyses conducted on the remaining 11 problems. Subjects were then administered a second trial on all problems. This was done in the same manner as Trial 1, with subjects being given 40 sec to answer each problem.

Results

Subjects who had previously seen more than two of the experimental problems were dropped from the study. By this criterion, data from four subjects in each of the experimental groups (informed and uninformed) and three subjects in the baseline group were not included in the analyses. In addition, three subjects in the uninformed condition reported that they were aware of the purpose of the experiment before they received any of the problems. Because they were not actually uninformed, data from these subjects were not used in the analyses. Additional subjects were tested to attain 20 subjects in each condition.

Since one of the problems and clues was used as an example prior to Trial 2, data from Experiment 2 were transformed into proportions prior to being analyzed. The mean percentage of correct solutions for each of the six conditions is presented in Table 1.

The data were analyzed in a 2 (trials) by 3 (time of informed) ANOVA. There were significant main effects for both trials $[F(1,57) = 23.8, p < .001]$ and when subjects were informed $[F(2,57) = 30.6, p < .001]$. The interaction was also significant $[F(2,57) = 5.1, p < .01]$. Tests of simple main effects were conducted by means of Dunn's procedure in order to investigate the relative performance of subjects on Trials 1 and 2. The Trial 1 data replicated Experiment 1. Uninformed subjects did not solve a significantly greater proportion of problems than did baseline subjects $[t'D(4,57) = 1.29, p > .05]$. However, the informed subjects produced a greater proportion of correct solutions than did those in the uninformed condition $[t'D(4,57) = 4.67, p < .01]$.

The pattern of results for Trial 2 was similar. Informed subjects produced a significantly greater proportion of solutions than did subjects in the uninformed condition $[t'D(4,57) = 2.62, p < .05]$. The difference between the uninformed and the baseline groups approached but did not reach significance $[t'D(4,57) = 2.25, p > .05]$.

Discussion

The results for the first trial of Experiment 2 replicate those found in Experiment 1. That is, subjects in the informed group were more likely to produce correct solutions to the problems than were subjects in the uninformed or baseline groups.

The major purpose of Experiment 2 was to explore an additional question: What would happen if subjects in the uninformed group were told that their initial acquisition experiences provided information that was relevant to each problem's solution and were then given a second chance to solve the problems? The results for the second trial of Experiment 2 indicate that these subjects still perform at a level that is inferior to that of subjects in the group informed at Trial 1.

There are several possible reasons for the inferior performance of subjects who were not informed until Trial 2. One is that they may have forgotten much of the information that was presented during acquisition. Note that subjects who were initially informed on Trial 1 had the chance to activate previously experienced clues on Trial 1. This activation of relevant information could retard the forgetting process. Some sort of differential forgetting hypothesis may therefore account for the Trial 2 results found in Experiment 2.

There is a second possible reason for the inferior Trial 2 performance of subjects who were not informed until Trial 2. We noted in Experiment 1 that subjects in all groups generated some answer to each problem. The same was true in Experiment 2. It is possible that subjects who were uninformed on Trial 1 felt that most of their Trial 1 answers were correct. They may therefore have decided to provide the same answers on Trial 2. We will refer to this hypothesis as the "my answer is better than yours" hypothesis. . . .

[The two experiments excluded here were similar to Experiment 2, involving the use of two trials. In these experiments, the authors found that poor Trial

TABLE 1 Mean Percentage and Standard Deviations of Problems Solved in Experiment 2

	Trial 1		Trial 2	
	Mean	SD	Mean	SD
Baseline	17.9	10.6	26.3	14.1
Uninformed	26.2	14.6	40.9	19.2
Informed	56.3	17.1	57.7	17.5

2 performance was limited to those problems that subjects had worked on in Trial 1 while uninformed. The reasons for this restriction were unclear, although one possibility raised by the authors was that the incorrect answers generated by uninformed subjects in Trial 1 interfered with their ability to find the correct answer (see also Perfetto, Yearwood, Franks, & Bransford, 1987). It does indicate, however, that uninformed subjects' poor performance on Trial 2 is not because they could not remember the initial clues in general.]

GENERAL DISCUSSION

Two major findings emerged from the present experiments. First, the results of all four experiments indicate that subjects did not spontaneously utilize previously acquired information to solve problems unless they were explicitly informed about the relationship between initial acquisition and the later problem solving. These results replicate those found by Weisberg et al. (1978). Weisberg et al. had subjects learn associations such as "candle-box" and demonstrated that this did not help them solve Dunker's (1945) candle problem unless they were explicitly informed about the relationship between acquisition and test. We argued that the clue "candle-box" was not particularly informative and hence devised materials in which the clues provided information that was more likely to lead to problem solution (see the initial assessment of clue effectiveness described prior to Experiment 1). Even under these conditions, the present results show that subjects who were informed about the acquisition-test relationship were much more likely to utilize the acquisition information than were subjects who were not informed about this relationship. Furthermore, uninformed subjects did not solve a significantly greater number of problems than did subjects in the baseline groups.

The results discussed above are also consistent with investigations by Gick and Holyoak (1980) of the ability to transfer solutions between analogical problems. Gick and Holyoak found that subjects typically failed to transfer a solution read in conjunction with one problem to an analogous problem (Dunker's 1945 "radiation problem") unless they were given a hint to use the prior story to help them solve the problem. However, Gick and Holyoak's task required an abstract matching of the target problem and solution to the analogous problem. The direct nature of the materials in the present experiment demonstrates that this phenomenon is not the result of subjects' inability to "see the analogy" but is of a more general nature. Furthermore, neither Weisberg et al. (1978) nor Gick and Holyoak consider the effects attributable to the initial spontaneous transfer failure. These effects are discussed below.

A second major result of the present experiments involves the consequences of initial failures to access potentially relevant information. In Experiment 2, for example, uninformed subjects were not told that their acquisition experiences were relevant to the problems they were about to solve on Trial 1 and hence performed more poorly than informed subjects. However, even when uninformed subjects were informed on Trial 2, they were still less likely to use relevant acquisition information to generate solutions than were subjects in the informed group. The results of Experiments 3 and 4 indicated that this decrement was not due to the general act of attempting to solve problems during Trial 1. Instead, the decrement occurred only for Trial 2 problems that had actually been attempted during Trial 1. Thus, initial failures to access relevant information can lead to problem-specific deficits in later problem solving performance. . . .

The present results are similar to findings of research conducted in an educational setting. For example, Howe (1970) found that the contents of weekly attempts at written reproduction were very closely related to previous recall attempts. The contents of a given recall attempt, even when incorrect, were more likely to recur in the succeeding weeks than were correct but nonrecalled items. This was true despite an intervening presentation of the correct material.

The importance of the present findings can be seen when one notes that many, if not most, ordinary problem solving situations involve cases in which the problem solver is essentially uninformed and is engaged in self-generation of potential answers to the problem. To have any chance of solving such problems, one must presume that the problem solver has previously acquired information that is relevant to the problem solution. A major aspect of problem solving involves accessing this relevant information. However, usually the problem solver does not have someone telling him what information is relevant or when it was acquired (i.e., the problem solver is uninformed). The present work indicates that this uninformed state can lead to serious difficulties in accessing previously acquired, relevant information. Furthermore, in attempting to solve problems in this uninformed state, the problem solver will probably generate at least partial answers, which are inadequate solutions to the problem. The present work indicates that these inadequate self-generated answers may lead to even greater deficits in accessing relevant information and problem solving in any future attempts to solve the same or similar problems. Given such possible difficulties, one important area for future research involves investigations of types of acquisition experiences (and/or kinds of access or retrieval strategies) that can be engaged during problem solving. Specifically, researchers might investigate the types of experiences that are effective in overcoming deficits that stem from being uninformed as to when the relevant information was acquired. . . .

Finally, the finding that access to relevant information is strongly influenced by whether one is informed or uninformed has important implications for educational practice. Many classroom tests designed to assess learning seem to be episodic in nature. That is, students know that the correct answers to problems were provided by a particular professor, set of readings, and so forth. They are therefore informed about possible sources of information that are relevant to the test question they receive. Imagine that a student performs very well on a test such as this yet, when leaving the classroom, confronts everyday problems in which information from the course would be useful. Will the student spontaneously utilize this information? The results of the present experiments suggest that the answer may well be no. It seems clear that theories of learning and instruction must address the question of how information can become accessible under conditions in which students are not explicitly informed about the particular acquisition context that is relevant to the problems they confront.

REFERENCES

Auble, P. M., Frank, J. J., & Soraci, S. A. Effort toward comprehension: Elaboration or "aha!"? *Memory & Cognition,* 1979, 7, 426–434.

Bobrow, S. A., & Bower, G. H. Comprehension and recall of sentences. *Journal of Experimental Psychology,* 1969, 80, 455–461.

Bransford, J. D., & Johnson, M. K. Contextual prerequisites for understanding: Some investigations of comprehension and recall. *Journal of Verbal Learning and Verbal Behavior,* 1972, 11, 717–726.

Dunker, K. On problem-solving. *Psychological Monographs,* 1945, 58, No. 270.

Gardner, M. *Aha! Insight.* New York: W. H. Freeman, 1978.

Gick, M. L., & Holyoak, K. J. Analogical problem solving. *Cognitive Psychology,* 1980, 12, 306–355.

Howe, J. A. Repeated presentation and recall of meaningful prose. *Journal of Educational Psychology,* 1970, 61, 214–219.

Kirk, R. E. *Experimental design: Procedures for the behavioral sciences.* Belmont, Calif: Wadsworth, 1968.

Slamecka, N. J., & Graf, P. The generation effect: Delineation of a phenomenon. *Journal of Experimental Psychology: Human Learning and Memory,* 1978, 4, 592–604.

Thomson, D. M., & Tulving, E. Associative encoding and retrieval: Weak and strong cues. *Journal of Experimental Psychology,* 1970, 86, 255–262.

Tulving, E., & Thomson, D. M. Encoding specificity and retrieval processes in episodic memory. *Psychological Review,* 1973, 80, 352–373.

Weisberg, R., DiCamillo, M., & Phillips, D. Transferring old associations to new situations: A nonautomatic process. *Journal of Verbal Learning and Verbal Behavior,* 1978, 17, 219–228.

POSTSCRIPT

In a subsequent study, Bowden (1985) found that increasing the amount of time subjects were given increased the use of clues by uninformed subjects. However, Ross, Ryan, and Tenpenny (1989) argued that this could be accounted for by uninformed subjects' "catching on" to the relevance of the prior information, making them, in essence, delayed-informed subjects.

When the prior information relevant for solving a problem is the solution to a similar problem, we are dealing with analogical reasoning, or transfer (learning). Studies of analogical reasoning have confirmed the finding that subjects often fail to spontaneously retrieve and/or apply relevant information (see Gick & Holyoak, 1980, 1983). Much of the recent research in this area has focused on the factors that affect the likelihood of subjects' noticing and applying the appropriate source problems, or analogs, to the target problem. (The descriptions that follow apply to novices, people who are not extremely familiar with the subject matter the problems are drawn from; experts behave differently; see Reading 35. Gick, 1986, provides a good overview with an emphasis on educational implications; Holyoak, 1990, and VanLehn, 1990, provide more recent coverage. Several excellent, somewhat technical, articles on analogical reasoning can be found in Vosniadou & Ortony, 1989.)

Factors that increase the likelihood of subjects' spontaneously noticing the relevance of earlier problems include the following: (1) the surface similarity of the problems—both problems are about the same thing (Ross, 1984); (2) the wording of source and target problems to emphasize shared concepts (Stein, Way, Benningfield, & Hedgecough, 1986); (3) the placement of the problems in similar contexts—for instance, as part of the same experiment, rather than as two separate tasks (Spencer & Weisberg, 1986); and (4) the processing of source and target problems in a similar fashion (Adams, Kasserman, Yearwood, Perfetto, Bransford, & Franks, 1988). Simply noticing surface similarities or knowing that a previous problem is relevant to the current problem does not guarantee successful transfer, however (Reed, 1987; Reed, Dempster, & Ettinger, 1985). Successful transfer requires that subjects represent the problems in a fashion that makes their shared underlying structure clear (Kotovsky & Fallside, 1989). The distinction between surface similarity and shared underlying structure can be made clear with an example.

Consider a game in which there are two players who take turns selecting cards numbered from 1 through 9. Once a card has been selected by one player, it cannot be selected by the other. The goal is to have three cards that add up to 15. Newell and Simon (1972) call this game number scrabble. On the surface, this game is very different from tic-tac-toe. Tic-tac-toe is about Xs and Os being placed on a grid rather than adding up numbers between 1 and 9. But tic-tac-toe and number scrabble are structurally identical, or isomorphic, to each other. This becomes apparent if we think about the cards in number scrabble as arranged like this:

```
6   1   8
7   5   3
2   9   4
```

Methods that tend to draw subjects' attention to underlying structural characteristics include (1) giving hints (Holyoak & Koh, 1987); (2) forcing explicit comparisons of analogous problems (Catrambone & Holyoak, 1989); (3) having subjects experience some initial failure with source problems (Gick & McGarry, 1992; Lockhart, Lamon, & Gick, 1988); or (4) requiring subjects to explain why an example instantiates a general principle (Brown & Kane, 1988).

FOR FURTHER THOUGHT

1. Exactly why was it necessary for Perfetto and his associates to do a pilot study? What did they learn from that pilot?
2. Why were three different groups needed for these experiments (informed, uninformed, and control)? What is the proper interpretation of any difference in performance for each pair-wise comparison of groups—informed versus uninformed, informed versus control, uninformed versus control?
3. Why were subjects in Experiment 1 only given 40 seconds to solve the problem, rather than as much time as they needed to solve the problem? Why was it important to give the subjects a questionnaire *after* they had done the experiment? Why were people who were familiar with two or more problems dropped from these experiments?
4. In Experiment 2, why wasn't it a silly redundancy to give informed subjects an example of the connection between acquisition and problem solving before doing Trial 2?
5. In none of the conditions in this article did problem solution accuracy average 100%, even with those subjects who were informed and given a chance to solve the problems. What are some possible reasons for this? How would you test those possibilities?

REFERENCES

Adams, L. T., Kasserman, J. E., Yearwood, A. A., Perfetto, G. A., Bransford, J. D., & Franks, J. J. (1988). Memory access: The effects of fact-oriented versus problem-oriented acquisition. *Memory & Cognition, 16,* 167–175.

Bowden, E. M. (1985). Accessing relevant information during problem solving: Time constraints on search in the problem space. *Memory & Cognition, 13,* 280–286.

Brown, A. L., & Kane, M. J. (1988). Preschool children can learn to transfer: Learning to learn and learning from example. *Cognitive Psychology, 20,* 493–523.

Catrambone, R., & Holyoak, K. J. (1989). Overcoming contextual limitations on problem-solving transfer. *Journal of Experimental Psychology: Learning, Memory, and Cognition, 15,* 1147–1156.

Gick, M. L. (1986). Problem-solving strategies. *Educational Psychologist, 21,* 99–120.

Gick, M. L., & Holyoak, K. J. (1980). Analogical problem solving. *Cognitive Psychology, 12,* 306–355.

Gick, M. L., & Holyoak, K. J. (1983). Schema induction and analogical transfer. *Cognitive Psychology, 15,* 1–38.

Gick, M. L., & McGarry, S. J. (1992). Learning from mistakes: Inducing analogous solution failures to a source problem produces later successes in analogical transfer. *Journal of Experimental Psychology: Learning, Memory, and Cognition, 18,* 623–639.

Holyoak, K. J. (1990). Problem solving. In D. N. Osherson & E. E. Smith (Eds.), *An invitation to cognitive science: Vol. 3. Thinking* (pp. 117–146). Cambridge, MA: MIT Press.

Holyoak, K. J., & Koh, K. (1987). Surface and structural similarity in analogical transfer. *Memory & Cognition, 15,* 332–340.

Kotovsky, K., & Fallside, D. (1989). Representation and transfer in problem solving. In D. Klahr & K. Kotovsky (Eds.), *Complex information processing: The impact of Herbert A. Simon* (pp. 69–108). Hillsdale, NJ: Erlbaum.

Lockhart, R. S., Lamon, M., & Gick, M. L. (1988). Conceptual transfer in simple insight problems. *Memory & Cognition, 16,* 36–44.

Newell, A., & Simon, H. A. (1972). *Human problem solving.* Englewood Cliffs, NJ: Prentice-Hall.

Perfetto, G. A., Yearwood, A. A., Franks, J. J., & Bransford, J. D. (1987). Effects of generation on memory access. *Bulletin of the Psychonomic Society, 25,* 151–154.

Reed, S. K. (1987). A structure-mapping model for word problems. *Journal of Experimental Psychology: Learning, Memory, and Cognition, 13,* 124–139.

Reed, S. K., Dempster, A., & Ettinger, M. (1985). Usefulness of analogous solutions for solving algebra word problems. *Journal of Experimental Psychology: Learning, Memory, and Cognition, 11,* 106–125.

Ross, B. H. (1984). Remindings and their effects in learning a cognitive skill. *Cognitive Psychology, 16,* 371–416.

Ross, B. H., Ryan, W. J., & Tenpenny, P. L. (1989). The access of relevant information for solving problems. *Memory & Cognition, 17,* 639–651.

Spencer, R. M., & Weisberg, R. W. (1986). Context-dependent effects on analogical transfer. *Memory & Cognition, 14,* 442–449.

Stein, B. S., Way, K. R., Benningfield, S. E., & Hedgecough, C. A. (1986). Constraints on spontaneous transfer in problem-solving tasks. *Memory & Cognition, 14,* 432–441.

VanLehn, K. (1989). Problem solving and cognitive skill acquisition. In M. I. Posner (Ed.), *Foundations of cognitive science* (pp. 527–579). Cambridge, MA: MIT Press.

Vosniadou, S., & Ortony, A. (Eds.). (1989). *Similarity and analogical reasoning.* New York: Cambridge University Press.

INTRODUCTION

Psychologists (and nonpsychologists) have traditionally recognized a distinction between problems that require insight to solve and those that do not. One aspect of that distinction rests on a subjective response: insight problems are solved in a sudden flash of understanding, or what's sometimes called the "Aha!" experience. But how do you study this kind of subjectively defined phenomenon scientifically? This is the issue addressed by Janet Metcalfe and David Wiebe in "Intuition in Insight and Noninsight Problem Solving."

To study insight, Metcalfe and Wiebe examine people's metacognitions about insight and noninsight problems. *Metacognition* refers to both the knowledge we have about how our thinking works and our ability to control or regulate our thinking (Brown, Bransford, Ferrara, & Campione, 1983). Among our metacognitions are the intuitions we have about whether we'll be able to solve a problem or about how close we are to solving a problem. How accurate are such intuitions?

Metcalfe and Wiebe used two kinds of problems: those that earlier researchers have traditionally assumed require insight and those that can be solved through a relatively straightforward sequence of steps. Presumably, people solve the latter kind of problems by using a heuristic that says "identify the difference between the goal (the solution) and where you are, and then take a step that reduces that difference." Metcalfe and Wiebe's description of such problems is based on the problem-solving-as-search approach. In this approach, all of the possible steps (also called moves or "problem states") in solving the problem are depicted as points called nodes. If it is possible to go from one step to another, a line or path is drawn between the respective nodes. The result is a diagram of nodes and paths that represents all the possible states and all the legal ways of getting from one state to another. This diagram defines the problem space. Solving a problem involves finding your way through the problem space to your goal state, a proper solution.

Although it is not typically thought of as a problem to be solved, consider the game of tic-tac-toe. The rules, which define the possible moves or paths between problem states, are: (1) there are two players, *X* and *O*, who alternate; (2) each player puts a symbol in an unoccupied cell on each turn; (3) *X* goes first; and (4) the goal is for a player to have his or her symbol in three adjoining cells. We start with a blank grid of three rows and three columns. This is our initial state, and it is depicted in our problem space diagram by a single node. There are nine possible moves that X can make, so we must have nine additional nodes representing each of these possibilities. Because it is legal to move from the initial state node to any of these nine other nodes, our diagram has paths connecting the initial state node to each of these other nodes. Each of these nine nodes in turn must have paths leading to eight other nodes, representing the eight possible moves for O, given an initial move by X. For example, suppose X takes the leftmost cell of the top row. This leaves O with eight possible moves, to any cell except the leftmost cell of the top row. So, from the node representing X's choice, the diagram must have eight paths, leading to the eight nodes representing the eight possible moves for O. Next we consider the case if X's first move is to the middle cell of the top row; the diagram again has eight paths, but this time one leads to a node representing O's move to the leftmost cell in the top row, and none leads to the middle cell in the top row because that is not a legal move for O. We do this for every possible combination of alternating moves by X and O, and we end up with a diagram depicting the entire problem space for tic-tac-toe.

A few aspects of Metcalfe and Wiebe's method and analyses may be unfamiliar. One is their measure of angular warmth. To understand this measure, construct two response sheets of the sort Metcalfe and Wiebe gave to their subjects (see the procedure subsection of Experiment 1 for a description), and fill them out as described in the angular warmth example they give in the results section. On each of your answer sheets, draw a line from the first response to the last. The angles of the lines you draw give the angular warmth values for those two answer sheets.

The problem posed by a restricted range raised in the analysis of personal and normative predictions may also be unfamiliar. If, when you correlate two variables, the range of values that one (or both) of the variables takes is very narrow, then the correlation between them will be very low regardless of the extent of the relationship between them. For example, in a large introductory psychology class, the correlation between grade on an exam and amount of studying is typically pretty high because a relationship exists between those two variables. But if the exam were extremely easy (one might say that it had no difficulty structure) and everyone scored 95% or above (which means that the range of test scores was very narrow, or restricted), the correlation would be low or poor—people who studied a lot and those who studied very little would have about the same score.

Finally, some terms that Metcalfe and Wiebe use may be unfamiliar. A *normative value* is a value that we are led to expect given the behavior of a large group of people. A *step-function* is a graph that shows one or more sudden jumps rather than a smooth rise.

The appendixes included in the original article and references to those appendixes have been deleted here. As you read this article, ask yourself what leads to insight. Why do some problems require insight to solve?

Intuition in Insight and Noninsight Problem Solving

Janet Metcalfe

Indiana University

David Wiebe

University of British Columbia

The rewarding quality of the experience of insight may be one reason why scientists and artists alike are willing to spend long periods of time thinking about unsolved problems. Indeed, creative individuals often actively seek out weaknesses in theoretical structures, areas of unresolved conflict, and flaws in conceptual systems. This tolerance and even questing for problems carries the risk that a particular problem may have no solution or that the investigator may be unable to uncover it. For instance, it was thought for many years that Euclid's fifth postulate might be derivable even though no one was able to derive it (see Hofstadter, 1980). The payoff for success, however, is the often noted "discovery" experience for the individual and (perhaps) new knowledge structures for the culture. This special mode of discovery may be qualitatively different from more routine analytical thinking.

Bergson (1902) differentiated between an intuitive mode of inquiry and an analytical mode. Many other theorists have similarly emphasized the importance of a method of direct apperception, variously called restructuring, intuition, illumination, or insight (Adams, 1979; Bruner, 1966; Davidson & Sternberg, 1984; Dominowski, 1981; Duncker, 1945; Ellen, 1982; Gardner, 1978; Koestler, 1977; Levine, 1986;

Maier, 1931; Mayer, 1983; Polya, 1957; Sternberg, 1986; Sternberg & Davidson, 1982; Wallas, 1926). Polanyi (1958) noted:

> We may describe the obstacle to be overcome in solving a problem as a "logical gap," and speak of the width of the logical gap as the measure of the ingenuity required for solving the problem. "Illumination" is then the leap by which the logical gap is crossed. It is the plunge by which we gain a foothold at another shore of reality. (p. 123)

Sternberg (1985) said that "significant and exceptional intellectual accomplishment—for example, major scientific discoveries, new and important inventions, and new and significant understandings of major literary, philosophical, and similar work—almost always involve [sic] major intellectual insights" (p. 282). Arieti (1976) stated that "the experience of aesthetic insight—that is, of creating an aesthetic unity—is a strong emotional experience. . . . The artist feels almost as if he had touched the universal" (p. 186). Although these major insights are of crucial importance both to the person and to the culture, their unpredictable and subjective nature presents difficulties for rigorous investigation. Sternberg and Davidson (1982) suggested that solving small insight puzzles may serve as a model for scientific insight. We shall adopt this approach in the present paper.

Despite the importance attributed to the process of insight, there is little empirical evidence for it. In fact, Weisberg and Alba (1981a) claimed correctly that there was no evidence whatsoever (see also Weisberg & Alba, 1981b, 1982). Since that time, two

This research was supported by Natural Sciences and Engineering Research Council of Canada Grant A-0505 to the first author. Thanks go to Judith Goldberg and Leslie Kiss for experimental assistance. Thanks also go to W. J. Jacobs. Please send correspondence about this article to Janet Metcalfe, Department of Psychology, Indiana University, Bloomington, IN 47405.

SOURCE: *Memory & Cognition, 15*(3), 1987, pp. 238–246. Reprinted by permission of the Psychonomic Society, Inc.

studies investigating the metacognitions that precede and accompany insight problem solving have provided some data favoring the construct. In the first study (Metcalfe, 1986a), feeling-of-knowing performance was compared on classical insight problems and on general information memory questions (Nelson & Narens, 1980). In the problem-solving phase of the study, subjects were given insight problems to rank order in terms of the likelihood of solution. On the memory half of the study, trivia questions that subjects could not answer immediately (e.g., "What is the name of the villainous people who lived underground in H. G. Wells's book *The Time Machine*?") were ordered in terms of the likelihood of remembering the answers on the second test. The memory part of the study was much like previous feeling-of knowing experiments on memory (e.g., Gruneberg & Monks, 1974; Hart, 1967; Lovelace, 1984; Nelson, Leonesio, Landwehr, & Narens, 1986; Nelson, Leonesio, Shimamura, Landwehr, & Narens, 1982; Schacter, 1983). Metcalfe found that the correlation between predicted solution and actual solution was not different from zero for the insight problems, although this correlation, as in other research, was substantial for the memory questions. Metcalfe interpreted these data as indicating that insightful solutions could not be predicted in advance, which would be expected if insight problems were solved by a sudden "flash of illumination." However, the data may have resulted from a difference between problem solving in general and memory retrieval, rather than a difference between insight and noninsight problem-solving processes.

In a second study (Metcalfe, 1986b), subjects were instructed to provide estimates of how close they were to the solutions to problems every 10 sec during the problem-solving interval. These estimates are called feeling-of-warmth (Simon, Newell, & Shaw, 1979) ratings. If the problems were solved by what subjectively is a sudden flash of insight, one would expect that the warmth ratings would be fairly low and constant until solution, at which point they would jump to a high value. This is what was found in the experiment. On 78% of the problems and anagrams for which subjects provided the correct solution, the progress estimates increased by no more than 1 point, on a 10-point scale, over the entire solution interval.

On those problems for which the wrong answer was given, however, the warmth protocols showed a more incremental pattern. Thus, it did not appear to be the case that there were no circumstances at all under which an incremental pattern would appear. It appeared with incorrect solutions. However, in that study, the incremental pattern may have been attributable to a special decision-making strategy, rather than to an incremental problem-solving process. Thus, whether noninsight problems show a warmth pattern different from that of insight problems is still unclear.

A straightforward comparison of the warmth ratings produced during solution of insight and noninsight problems is, therefore, important and has not been attempted previously. Simon (1977, 1979) provided several models that apply to incremental problems such as algebra, chess, and logic problems. Basically, Simon et al. (1979) proposed that people are able to use a directed-search strategy in problem solving (as opposed to an exhaustive search through all possibilities, which in many cases would be impossible) because they are able to compare their present state with the goal state. If a move makes the present state more like a goal state (i.e., if the person gets "warmer"), that move is taken. Simon et al. (1979) provided several think aloud protocols that suggest that this "functional" or "means-end" analysis of reducing differences can be applied to a wide range of analytical problems. They noted that the Logic Theorist (a computer program that uses this heuristic) "can almost certainly transfer without modification to problem solving in trigonometry, algebra, and probably other subjects such as geometry and chess" (p. 157). If this monitoring process is guiding human problem solving, then the warmth ratings should increase to reflect subjects' increasing nearness to the solutions. Of course, if insight problems are solved by some nonanalytical, sudden process, as previous research suggests, we would expect to find a difference, depending on problem type, in the warmth protocols.

The experiments described below explored the metacognitions exhibited by subjects on insight and on noninsight problems. Experiment 1 compared warmth ratings during the solution of insight problems with those produced during the solution of noninsight problems. The noninsight problems were the type that have been analyzed and modeled by programs that use a functional analysis. Thus, we expected to find that subjects' warmth ratings would increment gradually over the course of the problem-solving interval. We expected that warmth ratings on the insight problems would, in contrast, increase rapidly only when the solution was given. Experiment 2 used algebra problems rather than the multistep problems that have been modeled with search-style programs. Algebra problems may be more characteristic of the sorts of problems people solve daily than are (at least some of) the multistep problems used in Experiment 1. As noted above, however, because the means-end search strategy should be applicable to algebra problems, incremental warmth protocols were expected. For these reasons, as well as their availability, algebra problems were worth investigating. In addition to examining warmth ratings during the course of problem solving, Experiment 2 also investigated other predictors of performance: subjects' feeling-of-knowing rankings, normative predictors of performance, and subjective estimations of the likelihood of success. We expected that noninsight problems would show more incremental warmth protocols than would insight problems. We also expected that people would have more accurate metacognitions (about how well they would be able to solve problems and which problems they would be able to solve) for the noninsight than for the insight problems.

EXPERIMENT 1

Method

Subjects.   Twenty-six volunteers were paid $4 for a 1-h session of problem solving. Seven of these subjects either produced no correct answers on one of the insight or the noninsight problems or produced correct answers immediately, so that no warmth protocols could be obtained for the solution interval. Thus, 19 subjects produced usable data.

Materials.   Ten problems, provided on 3 × 5 in. cards, were given in random order to the subjects for solution one at a time. Half of these problems were noninsight problems, and half were insight problems.

The noninsight problems were designated as such because past literature had labeled them as multistep problems or because they had been analyzed by incremental or search models such as those of Karat (1982) or Simon (1977, 1979). . . . The insight problems were chosen because they had been considered to be insight problems by other authors or by the sources from which they were taken. However, we felt free to eliminate problems that in our previous experiments (Metcalfe, 1986a, 1986b) had been designated by subjects as "grind-out-the-solution" problems rather than insight problems. Our criterion for calling a problem an insight problem was not well defined. This lack of definition may well be one reason that research on insight has progressed so slowly. We shall return to this point in our conclusion. . . .

Procedure.   The subjects were told that they would be asked to solve a number of problems, one at a time. Once they had the answer, they were to write it down so that the experimenter could ascertain whether it was right or wrong. If the experimenter had any doubt about the correctness of the answer, she asked the subject for clarification before proceeding to the next problem. During the course of solving, the subjects were asked to provide warmth ratings to indicate their perceived nearness to the solution. These ratings were marked by the subject with a slash on a 3-cm visual analogue scale on which the far left end was "cold," the far right end was "hot," and intermediate degrees of warmth were to be indicated by slashes in the middle range. Altogether, there were 40 lines that could be slashed for each problem (to allow for the maximum amount of time that a subject was permitted to work on a given problem); these lines were arranged vertically on an answer sheet. The subjects were told to put their first rating at the far left end of the visual analogue scale. They then worked their way down the sheet marking warmth ratings at 15-sec intervals, which were indicated by a click given by the experimenter. Because it requires less attention on the part of the subject, is nonsymbolic, and apparently is less distracting and intrusive, this visual-analogue-scale technique for assessing warmth is superior to the Metcalfe (1986b) technique of writing down numerals.

Results

The probability level of $p \leq .05$ was chosen for significance. The increments in the warmth ratings were assessed in two ways. First, the angle subtended from the first rating to the last rating before the rating given with the answer in a particular protocol for a particular problem was measured. (We refer to this henceforth as the "angular warmth.") Second, the difference between the first slash or rating and the last rating before the rating given with the answer was measured. (We refer to this as the "differential warmth.") These two methods can yield different results because angular warmth, unlike differential warmth, varies according to the total time spent solving the problem. For example, consider two protocols, both of which start at the far left end of the scale and both of which have the warmth immediately before the answer given as a slash in the exact center of the scale. Let the first protocol have a total time of 1 min and the second a total time of 2 min. When these two are ranked according to differential warmth, they will be tied, or be considered to be equally incremental. When they are ranked according to angular warmth, however, the first protocol will be said to be more incremental than the second. Thus, the differential warmth measure considers the total solving time (whatever it is) to be the unit of analysis, whereas the angular warmth measure gives an indication of the increment in warmth per unit of real time. We could not decide which method was more appropriate, so we used both.

The correctly solved problems were separately rank ordered from greatest to least on each of the angular warmth and the differential warmth measures, for each subject. Then a Goodman and Kruskal gamma correlation (see Nelson, 1984, 1986), comparing the rank orderings of the increment in warmth (going from most incremental to least) and problem type was computed. These gammas were treated as summary data scores for each subject. A positive correlation (which is what was expected) indicates that the noninsight problems tended to have more incremental warmth protocols than did the insight problems. The overall correlation on the angular warmth measure was .26, which is significantly different from zero [$t(18) = 2.02$, $MSe = .32$]. The overall correlation on the differential warmth measure was .23, which was also significantly different from zero [$t(18) = 1.63$, $MSe = .37$, by a one-tailed test].

Thus, the warmth protocols of the insight problems in Experiment 1 showed a more sudden achievement of solution than did those of the noninsight problems. This is precisely what was expected given that the insight problems involved sudden illumination and the noninsight problems did not.

EXPERIMENT 2

Method

Subjects. Seventy-three University of British Columbia students in introductory psychology participated in exchange for a small bonus course credit. To allow assessment of performance on the feeling-of-knowing tasks detailed below, it was necessary that the subjects correctly solve at least one insight and one algebra problem, and that they miss at least one insight and one algebra problem. Twenty-one subjects failed to get at least one algebra or one insight problem correct, and so were dropped from the analyses. Four subjects got all the algebra problems correct and were dropped. This left 48 subjects who provided usable feeling-of-knowing data.

For warmth-rating data to be usable, it was necessary that the subjects get at least one insight and one algebra problem correct with at least three warmth ratings. Thirty-nine subjects provided usable data for this analysis.

Materials. The materials were classical insight problems . . . and algebra problems selected from a high school algebra textbook. . . . The insight problems were selected, insofar as possible, to require little cognitive work other than the critical insight. Weisberg and Alba (1981b) argued against the idea of insight because they found that providing the clue or "insight" considered necessary to solve a problem did not ensure problem solution. Sternberg and Davidson (1982) pointed out that this failure of the clue to result in immediate problem solution may have occurred not because there was no process of insight, but rather because there were a number of additional processes involved in solving the problem as well as insight. In an attempt to circumvent such additional processes, we tried to use problems that were minimal.

Procedure and Design.   The subjects were shown a series of insight or algebra problems, one at a time, randomly ordered within insight or algebra problem-set block. If they knew the answer to the problem, either from previous experience or by figuring it out immediately, the problem was eliminated from the test set. Once five unsolved problems (either insight or algebra, depending on order of presentation condition) had been accumulated, the experimenter arranged in a circle the 3 × 5 in. index cards on which the problems were typed and asked the subjects to rearrange them into a line going from the problem they thought they were most likely to be able to solve in a 4-min interval to that which they were least likely to be able to solve. This ranking represents the subjects' feelings that they will know (or feeling-of-knowing) ordering. The five cards were reshuffled, and the subjects were asked to assess the probability that they could solve each problem. The cards were shuffled again and then presented one at a time for solution. Every 15 sec during the course of solving, the subjects were told to indicate their feeling of warmth (i.e., their perceived closeness to solution) by putting a slash through a line that was 3 cm long, as in Experiment 1. The subjects were not told explicitly to anchor the first slash at the far left of the scale, but they tended to do so. Altogether, there were 17 lines that could be slashed for each problem. The subjects continued through the set of five test problems until they had either written a solution or exhausted the time on each. Then the procedure was repeated with the other set of problems (either insight or algebra). The order of problem set (insight or algebra) was counterbalanced across subjects. The subjects were tested individually in 1-h sessions.

Results

Warmth ratings.   The gammas computed on the angular warmth measures indicated that the insight problems showed a less incremental slope than did the algebra problems: Mean $G = .35$, which is significantly greater than zero [$t(37) = 3.10$, $MSe = .49$]. Gammas computed on the differential warmth measure showed the same pattern: Mean $G = .32$, which is also significantly greater than zero [$t(37) = 2.56$, $MSe = .58$].

Figure 1 provides a graphical representation of the subjects' warmth values for insight and algebra problems during the minute before the correct solution was given. The histograms in Figure 1 contain data from all subjects who had ratings in the specified intervals. To convert the visual analogue scale to a numerical scale, the 3-cm rating lines were divided into seven equal regions, and a slash occurring anywhere within one of these regions was given the appropriate numerical warmth value. Thus, ratings of 7 could occur before a solution was given because the subjects could, and did, provide ratings that were almost, but not quite, at the far right end of the scale. The trends of the distributions, over the last minute of solving time, going from the bottom to the top panel in Figure 1, tell the same story as the angular and differential warmth measures: There was a gradual increment in warmth with algebra problems but little increasing warmth with the insight problems.

Feeling of knowing on ranks.   A Goodman and Kruskal gamma correlation was computed between the rank ordering given by the subject and the response (correct or incorrect) on each problem, for each of the two sets of problems. Then an analysis of variance was performed on these scores; the factors were order of presentation of problem block (either algebra first or insight first—between subjects) and problem type (algebra or insight—within subjects). There was a significant difference in gamma between the algebra problems (mean $G = .40$) and the insight problems (mean $G = .08$) [$F(1,46) = 6.46$, $MSe = .77$]. The correlation on the algebra problems was greater than zero [$t(46) = 4.6$, $MSe = .36$], whereas the correlation for the insight problems was not [$t(46) = .8$, $MSe = .47$]. This latter result replicates Metcalfe (1986a). Thus, it appears that the subjects fairly accurately predicted which algebra problems they would be able to solve later, but were unable to predict which insight problems they would solve.

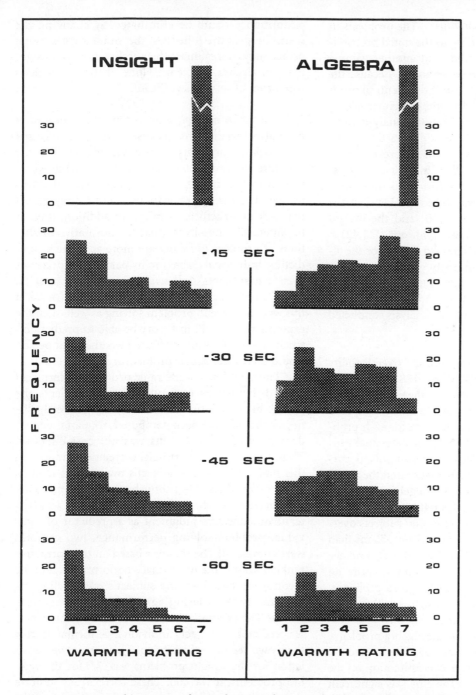

FIGURE 1   Frequency histograms of warmth ratings for correctly solved insight and algebra problems in Experiment 2. The panels, from bottom to top, give the ratings 60, 45, 30, and 15 sec before solution. As shown in the top panel, a 7 rating was always given at the time of solution.

Feeling of knowing on probabilities. The problems in each set were ranked according to the stated probability that they would be solved, and another gamma was computed on the data so arranged. Because the correlation cannot be computed if the identical probabilities are given for all problems (in either set), 4 subjects had to be eliminated from this analysis, leaving 44 subjects. Because there could be ties in the probability estimates, and because there could be some inconsistency between the rankings and the estimates, the results are not identical to those presented above. As before, the difference between the algebra problems (mean $G = .40$) and the insight problems (mean $G = .15$) was significant [$F(1,42) = 2.8$, $MSe = .99$ one-tailed]. The correlation for the algebra problems was significantly greater than zero [$t(42) = 3.82$, $MSe = .48$], whereas the correlation for the insight problems was not [$t(42) = 1.2$, $MSe = .65$]. This analysis is consistent with the analysis conducted on the ranks.

Calibration. To compare the subjects' overall ability (Lichtenstein, Fischoff, & Phillips, 1982) to predict how well they would perform on the insight versus the algebra problems, the mean value was computed for the five probability estimates (one for each problem). This mean was compared with the actual proportion of problems that each subject solved correctly. Both the predicted performance and the actual performance were better on the algebra problems than on the insight problems [$F(1,46) = 54.67$, $MSe = .11$]. Previous research had shown that subjects overestimated their ability more on insight problems than on memory questions (Metcalfe, 1986a), and we thought they would perhaps overestimate more on the insight problems than on the algebra problems. Predicted performance on the insight problems was .59, whereas actual performance was only .34. Predicted performance was .73 on the algebra problems, whereas actual performance was .55. The interaction showing that there was greater overestimation on the insight than on the algebra problems was significant [$F(1,46) = 3.18$, $MSe = .08$, one-tailed]. This result is fairly weak. Not only is the interaction significant only by a one-tailed test, but also, insofar as the actual performance differed between the insight and algebra problems, the interaction involving predicted

performance could be eliminated by changing the scale. Despite these hedges, the result suggests that people may overestimate their ability more on insight than on algebra problems. None of the interactions with order of set was significant.

Personal versus normative predictions. We looked at normative predictions because it was possible that there was no, or a very diffuse, underlying difficulty structure (or a restricted range in the probability correct) with the insight problems, and hence the zero feeling-of-knowing correlations could simply reflect that lack of structure, or range. In addition, there is the interesting possibility that the normative predictions of problem difficulty are more accurate at predicting individual behavior in particular situations than are subjects' self-evaluations. Nelson et al. (1986) found such an effect with memory retrieval. If this were the case in problem solving as well, then the experimenter would in theory be able to predict better than a person him- or herself whether that person would solve a particular problem.

The problems were rank ordered in terms of their difficulty by computing across subjects the probability of solution for each. Although ideally difficulty should have been computed from an independent pool of subjects, this was not cost effective. Thus, there is a small artificial correlation induced in this ranking because a subject's own results made a 2.1%, rather than a 0%, contribution to the difficulty ranking. To see whether normative ranking was better than subjective judgment as a predictor of individual problem-solving performance, two gammas were compared. The first was based on the normative ranking against the individual's performance, and the second was based on the subject's own feeling-of-knowing rank ordering against his or her performance. The normative probabilities were a much better predictor of subjects' individual performance than their own feelings of knowing. The normative correlation for the insight problems was .77; for the algebra problems, it was .60. These correlations indicate that there was sufficient range in the difficulty of the problems (both insight and algebra) that overall frequency correct was a good predictor of individual performance. The zero feeling-of-knowing correlation, discussed earlier, is therefore probably not at-

TABLE 1   Mean Gamma Correlations between Personal and Normative Predictions and Actual Performance for Insight and Algebra Problems in Experiment 2

	Type of Prediction	
	Personal	Normative
Insight	.08	.77
Algebra	.40	.60

tributable to a restricted range of insight-problem difficulty. The interaction between own versus normative gammas as a function of problem type was significant [$F(1, 46) = 10.13$, $MSe = 1.13$]. Table 1 gives the means. The idea that subjects may have privileged access to idiosyncratic information that makes them especially able to predict their own performance was overwhelmingly wrong in this experiment.

DISCUSSION

This study shows that there is an empirically demonstrable distinction between problems that people have thought were insight problems and those that are generally considered not to require insight, such as algebra or multistep problems. The above experiments showed that people's subjective metacognitions were predictive of performance on the noninsight problems, but not on the insight problems. In addition, the warmth ratings that people produced during noninsight problem solving showed a more incremental pattern, in both experiments, than did those problems that were preexperimentally designated as involving insight. These findings indicate in a straightforward manner that insight problems are, at least subjectively, solved by a sudden flash of illumination; noninsight problems are solved more incrementally.

A persistent problem has blocked the study of the process of insight: How can we ascertain when we are dealing with an insight problem? Let us now propose a solution. Given that the warmth protocols differentiate between problems that seem to be insight problems and those that do not, we may use the warmth protocols themselves in a diagnostic manner. If we find problems (or indeed problems for particular in-

dividuals) that are accompanied by step-function warmth protocols during the solution interval, we may define those problems as being insight problems for those people. Thus, we propose that insight be defined in terms of the antecedent phenomenology that may be monitored by metacognitive assessments by the subject. Adopting this solution may have interesting (although as yet unexplored) consequences. Perhaps the underlying processes involved in solving an insight problem are qualitatively different from those involved in solving a noninsight problem. It may (or may not) be that contextual or structural novelty is essential for insight. Perhaps there is a class of problems that provoke insights for all people. But perhaps insight varies with the level of skill within a particular problem-solving domain. If so, we might be able to use the class of problems that provoke insight for an individual to denote the individual's conceptual development in the domain in question. Perhaps this person-problem interaction will provide some optimal difficulty level for motivating a person and therefore have pedagogical consequences. Insight problems may be especially challenging to people, and their solution distinctly pleasurable. Of course, many other possibilities present themselves for future consideration. The process of insight has heretofore been virtually opaque to scientific scrutiny. Differentiating insight problems from other problems by the phenomenology that precedes solution may facilitate illumination of the process of insight.

REFERENCES

Adams, J. L. (1979). *Conceptual blockbusting*. New York: Norton.

Arieti, S. (1976). *Creativity: The magic synthesis*. New York: Basic Books.

Bergson, H. (1902). *An introduction to metaphysics*. New York: Putnam.

Bruner, J. (1966). *On knowing: Essays for the left hand*. Cambridge: Harvard University Press.

Davidson, J. E., & Sternberg, R. J. (1984). The role of insight in intellectual giftedness. *Gifted Child Quarterly*, 28, 58–64.

deBono, E. (1967). *The use of lateral thinking*. New York: Penguin.

deBono, E. (1969). *The mechanism of mind.* New York: Penguin.

Dominowski, R. L. (1981). Comment on an examination of the alleged role of 'fixation' in the solution of 'insight' problems. *Journal of Experimental Psychology: General,* 110, 199–203.

Duncker, K. (1945). On problem solving. *Psychological Monographs,* 58(5, Whole No. 270).

Ellen, P. (1982). Direction, past experience, and hints in creative problem solving: Reply to Weisberg and Alba. *Journal of Experimental Psychology: General,* 111, 316–325.

Fixx, J. F. (1972). *More games for the superintelligent.* New York: Popular Library.

Gardner, M. (1978). *Aha! Insight.* New York: Freeman.

Gruneberg, M. M., & Monks, J. (1974). Feeling of knowing in cued recall. *Acta Psychologica,* 38, 257–265.

Hart, J. T. (1967). Memory and the memory-monitoring process. *Journal of Verbal Learning & Verbal Behavior,* 6, 685–691.

Hofstadter, D. R. (1980). *Gödel, Escher, Bach: An eternal golden braid.* New York: Vintage Books.

Karat, J. (1982). A model of problem solving with incomplete constraint knowledge. *Cognitive Psychology,* 14, 538–559.

Koestler, A. (1977). *The act of creation.* London: Picadoo.

Levine, M. (1986). *Principles of effective problem solving.* Unpublished manuscript, State University of New York at Stonybrook.

Lichtenstein, S., Fischoff, B., & Phillips, L. D. (1982). Calibration of probabilities: The state to the art to 1980. In D. Kahneman, P. Slovic, & A. Tversky (Eds.), *Judgment under uncertainty: Heuristics and biases.* Cambridge: Cambridge University Press.

Lovelace, E. A. (1984). Metamemory: Monitoring future recallability during study. *Journal of Experimental Psychology: Learning, Memory, & Cognition,* 10, 756–766.

Luchins, A. S. (1942). Mechanization in problem solving. *Psychological Monographs,* 54(6, Whole No. 248).

Maier, N. R. F. (1931). Reasoning in humans: II. The solution of a problem and its appearance in consciousness. *Journal of Comparative Psychology,* 12, 181–194.

Mayer, R. E. (1983). *Thinking, problem solving, cognition.* New York: Freeman.

Metcalfe, J. (1986a). Feeling of knowing in memory and problem solving. *Journal of Experimental Psychology: Learning, Memory, & Cognition,* 12, 288–294.

Metcalfe, J. (1986b). Premonitions of insight predict impending error. *Journal of Experimental Psychology: Learning, Memory, & Cognition,* 12, 623–634.

Nelson, T. O. (1984). A comparison of current measures of the accuracy of feeling of knowing prediction. *Psychological Bulletin,* 95, 109–133.

Nelson, T. O. (1986). ROC curves and measures of discrimination accuracy: A reply to Swets. *Psychological Bulletin,* 100, 128–132.

Nelson, T. O., Leonesio, R. J., Landwehr, R. S., & Narens, L. (1986). A comparison of three predictors of an individual's memory performance: The individual's feeling of knowing vs. the normative feeling of knowing vs. base-rate item difficulty. *Journal of Experimental Psychology: Learning, Memory, & Cognition,* 12, 279–287.

Nelson, T. O., Leonesio, R. J., Shimamura, A. P., Landwehr, R. F., & Narens, L. (1982). Overlearning and the feeling of knowing. *Journal of Experimental Psychology: Learning, Memory, & Cognition,* 8, 279–288.

Nelson, T. O., & Narens, L. (1980). Norms of 300 general-information questions: Accuracy of recall, latency of recall, and feeling-of-knowing ratings. *Journal of Verbal Learning & Verbal Behavior,* 19, 338–368.

Polanyi, M. (1958). *Personal knowledge: Towards a post-critical philosophy.* Chicago: University of Chicago Press.

Polya, G. (1957). *How to solve it.* Princeton, NJ: Princeton University Press.

Restle, F., & Davis, J. H. (1962). Success and speed of problem solving by individuals and groups. *Psychological Review,* 69, 520–536.

Schacter, D. L. (1983). Feeling of knowing in episodic memory. *Journal of Experimental Psychology: Learning, Memory, & Cognition,* 9, 39–54.

Simon, H. (1977). *Models of discovery.* Dordrecht, The Netherlands: Reidel.

Simon, H. (1979). *Models of thought.* New Haven: Yale University Press.

Simon, H., Newell, A., & Shaw, J. C. (1979). The process of creative thinking. In H. Simon (Ed.), *Models of thought* (pp. 144–174). New Haven: Yale University Press.

Sternberg, R. J. (1985). *Beyond IQ.* Cambridge, MA: Cambridge University Press.

Sternberg, R. J. (1986). *Intelligence applied.* San Diego: Harcourt, Brace, Jovanovich.

Sternberg, R. J., & Davidson, J. E. (1982, June). The mind of the puzzler. *Psychology Today,* 16, 37–44.

Travers, K. J., Dalton, L. C., Bruner, V. F., & Taylor, A. R. (1976). *Using advanced algebra.* Toronto: Doubleday.

Wallas, G. (1926). *The art of thought.* New York: Harcourt.

Weisberg, R. W., & Alba, J. W. (1981a). An examination of the alleged role of "fixation" in the solution of several "insight" problems. *Journal of Experimental Psychology: General,* 110, 169–192.

Weisberg, R. W., & Alba, J. W. (1981b). Gestalt theory, insight and past experience: Reply to Dominowski. *Journal of Experimental Psychology: General,* 110, 193–198.

Weisberg, R. W., & Alba, J. W. (1982). Problem solving is not like perception: More on gestalt theory. *Journal of Experimental Psychology: General,* 111, 326–330.

POSTSCRIPT

Weisberg (1992) argues that subjects' inability to predict their success or experience a clear pattern of increasing feeling of warmth with certain problems does *not* necessarily mean that those problems are solved in a flash of insight rather than step-by-step (see also Bowers, Regehr, Balthazard, & Parker, 1990). He suggests that problems should not simply be classified as either insight or noninsight. Instead, Weisberg proposes that problems lie on a continuum, from those that require many relatively laborious steps and yield clear feeling-of-warmth data to those that take few or very fast steps and feel instantaneous. Furthermore, it may be difficult in principle to interpret feeling-of-warmth data that subjects generate: a subject may shift attention to the relevant aspect of the problem without realizing that it is the relevant aspect. In fact, most studies of feeling of knowing have examined subjects' intuition that they will be able to recall some information rather than that they will be able to solve a problem (see Costermans, Lories, & Ansay, 1992; Nelson & Narens, 1990; Reder & Ritter, 1992).

Feelings of knowing are just one aspect of metacognition. Other metacognitive abilities, which enable us to plan and effectively use our cognitive capacities, play a crucial role in many of our intelligent behaviors, including reasoning and problem solving (Sternberg, 1985, 1988b; Swanson, 1990). Having an awareness of how thinking works and using that awareness to guide thinking represent an important difference between children and adults (Yussen, 1985). The distinction between such metacognitive abilities as metamemory—an awareness of how memory works and using that awareness to remember better—and such object-level capacities as memory retrieval goes beyond function and time of development, however (Nelson & Narens, 1990). Nelson, McSpadden, Fromme, and Marlatt (1986) found that alcohol intoxication impairs memory retrieval but not metamemory, whereas Nelson, Dunlosky, White, Steinberg, Townes, and Anderson (1990) found that at extreme altitude (such as atop Mount Everest) metamemory is impaired but memory retrieval is not.

In a number of recent studies, the focus has been on insight and the related concept of incubation—the phenomenon wherein better performance is achieved by "taking a break" from a problem (Smith & Blankenship, 1991). Using a somewhat different approach from Metcalfe and Wiebe, Kaplan and Simon (1990) found evidence that to attain insight is to change the way one thinks about or represents a problem so as to make the proper solution more apparent (for useful discussions of problem representation, see Greeno & Simon, 1988, or Hayes, 1989). Kaplan and Simon argue that finding the best representation involves a search, much as solving a problem does. Furthermore, they found that such a search is more likely to be successful if the subject's attention is drawn to the underlying structure of the problem to be solved (see the Postscript to Reading 26). In contrast, Yaniv and Meyer (1987) suggest that priming of previously inaccessible information through spreading activation (see Reading 14) may at least be partially responsible for insight and incubation effects as well as intuition (see also Bowers et al., 1990; Bastick, 1982 provides a different view of intuition).

Creativity is another topic related to insight. What is it about creative people that enables them to consistently come up with solutions that are original and relevant? There are many different views of creativity (Perkins, 1988, gives a short, readable introduction to some of the issues; see Runco & Albert, 1990, and Sternberg, 1988a, for samplings of different positions). One basic difference among these views is the relative emphasis given to general processes (Finke, Ward, & Smith, 1992) and to domain-specific knowledge, or expertise (Perkins, 1981), in enabling or encouraging creativity. Many popular books for improving creativity are available; Bransford and Stein (1984) is much better grounded in the psychological literature than most.

FOR FURTHER THOUGHT

1. What does it mean for problems to have "more incremental warmth protocols"? Why do Metcalfe and Wiebe expect that noninsight problems will have more incremental warmth protocols?
2. Why did Metcalfe and Wiebe ask subjects both to rank cards from most likely to be solved to least likely to be solved and to give a probability-of-solving rating to each card? Why did the authors predict that successful solution of noninsight problems would correlate better with both these measures of feeling of knowing than successful solution of insight problems would?
3. How did Metcalfe and Wiebe derive their normative measure of problem difficulty? Why is it that, in the ideal case, a different pool of subjects would have been used to derive that measure? What is implied by the finding that, with insight problems but not with noninsight prob-

lems, successful solution correlated with normative difficulty better than personal feeling of knowing did?

4. What is Metcalfe and Wiebe's final suggestion regarding categorizing problems as insight or noninsight? Why do they qualify their conclusion with "insight problems are, *at least subjectively,* solved by a sudden flash of illumination" (p. 443; emphasis added)? What does this imply about the possibility of objectively studying insight?

5. Many experiments of problem solving use talk-aloud protocols, in which subjects verbalize their thinking as they solve problems. What do Metcalfe and Wiebe's findings imply about the use of talk-aloud protocols?

REFERENCES

Bastick, T. (1982). *Intuition: How we think and act.* New York: Wiley.

Bowers, K. S., Regehr, G., Balthazard, C., & Parker, K. (1990). Intuition in the context of discovery. *Cognitive Psychology, 22,* 72–110.

Bransford, J. D., & Stein, B. S. (1984). *The ideal problem solver.* New York: W. H. Freeman.

Brown, A. L., Bransford, J. D., Ferrara, R. A., & Campione, J. C. (1983). Learning, remembering, and understanding. In J. H. Flavell & E. M. Markman (Eds.), *Handbook of child psychology: Vol. 3. Cognitive development* (4th ed.; pp. 77–166). New York: Wiley.

Costermans, J., Lories, G., & Ansay, C. (1992). Confidence level and feeling of knowing in question answering: The weight of inferential processes. *Journal of Experimental Psychology: Learning, Memory, and Cognition, 18,* 142–150.

Finke, R. A., Ward, T. B., & Smith, S. M. (1992). *Creative cognition: Theory, research, and applications.* Cambridge, MA: MIT Press.

Greeno, J. G., & Simon, H. A. (1988). Problem solving and reasoning. In R. C. Atkinson, R. H. Herrnstein, G. Lindzey, & R. D. Luce (Eds.), *Stevens' handbook of experimental psychology: Vol. 2. Learning and cognition* (2nd ed.; pp. 589–672). New York: Wiley.

Hayes, J. R. (1989). *The complete problem solver* (2nd ed.). Hillsdale, NJ: Erlbaum.

Kaplan, C. A., & Simon, H. A. (1990). In search of insight. *Cognitive Psychology, 22,* 374–419.

Nelson, T. O., Dunlosky, J., White, D. M., Steinberg, J., Townes, B. D., & Anderson, D. (1990). Cognition and metacognition at extreme altitudes on Mount Everest. *Journal of Experimental Psychology: General, 119,* 367–374.

Nelson, T. O., McSpadden, M., Fromme, K., & Marlatt, G. A. (1986). Effects of alcohol intoxication on metamemory and on retrieval from long-term memory. *Journal of Experimental Psychology: General, 115,* 247–254.

Nelson, T. O., & Narens, L. (1990). Metamemory: A theoretical framework and new findings. In G. H. Bower (Ed.), *The psychology of learning and motivation, Vol. 26* (pp. 125–173). San Diego: Academic Press.

Perkins, D. N. (1981). *The mind's best work*. Cambridge, MA: Harvard University Press.

Perkins, D. N. (1988). Creativity and the quest for mechanism. In R. J. Sternberg & E. E. Smith (Eds.), *The psychology of human thought* (pp. 309–336). New York: Cambridge University Press.

Reder, L. M., & Ritter, F. E. (1992). What determines initial feeling of knowing? Familiarity with question terms, not with the answer. *Journal of Experimental Psychology: Learning, Memory, and Cognition, 18,* 435–451.

Runco, M. A., & Albert, R. S. (Eds.). (1990). *Theories of creativity*. Newbury Park, CA: Sage.

Smith, S. M., & Blankenship, S. E. (1991). Incubation and the persistence of fixation in problem solving. *American Journal of Psychology, 104,* 61–87.

Sternberg, R. J. (1985). *Beyond IQ: A theory of human intelligence*. Cambridge: Cambridge University Press.

Sternberg, R. J. (Ed.). (1988a). *The nature of creativity: Contemporary psychological perspectives*. New York: Cambridge University Press.

Sternberg, R. J. (1988b). *The triarchic mind*. New York: Penguin Books.

Swanson, H. L. (1990). Influence of metacognitive knowledge and aptitude on problem solving. *Journal of Educational Psychology, 82,* 306–314.

Weisberg, R. W. (1992). Metacognition and insight during problem solving: Comment on Metcalfe. *Journal of Experimental Psychology: Learning, Memory, and Cognition, 18,* 426–431.

Yaniv, I., & Meyer, D. E. (1987). Activation and metacognition of inaccessible stored information: Potential bases for incubation effects in problem solving. *Journal of Experimental Psychology: Learning, Memory, and Cognition, 13,* 187–205.

Yussen, S. R. (1985). The role of metacognition in theories of cognitive development. In D. L. Forrest-Pressley, G. E. MacKinnon, & T. G. Waller (Eds.), *Metacognition, cognition, and human performance: Vol. 1. Theoretical perspectives* (pp. 253–283). Orlando: Academic Press.

Part IV

Everyday Cognitive Experiences

The readings in the first three parts of this book provided broad coverage of the topics relevant to a general theory of human cognition. The readings in this final section provide a sampling of topics whose roles in a general theory of cognition are sometimes less clear but whose roles in our everyday lives are substantial.

The readings in Chapter Nine (Everyday Memory and Judgment) focus on cognition outside the laboratory. Although somewhat controversial methodologically (see Banaji & Crowder, 1989; Ceci & Bronfenbrenner, 1991; Roediger, 1991; Tulving, 1991), much of the research on everyday cognition has been on spontaneously formed memories. Reading 28 examines a very common kind of memory—for the names and faces of classmates—but tracks it over very uncommon lengths of time (up to 50 years!). Reading 29, in contrast, looks at memories for very uncommon events—in this case, the explosion of the space shuttle *Challenger*—which often are reported to be unusually vivid and detailed, at least subjectively. On the other hand, when the memories are of crimes or accidents, it is objective accuracy, regardless of vividness or apparent level of detail, that is important. The experiments reported in Reading 30, although conducted in a laboratory setting, have relevance for understanding the accuracy of eyewitness testimony. Reading 31 deals not with memory directly but instead with a phenomenon familiar to anyone who has witnessed or participated with others in some event or situation: egocentric bias in judgments and reporting.

The universal applicability of many of the principles of human cognition discussed in earlier parts of this book is clear. But a striking everyday observation is the diversity in people's performance on different cognitive tasks. There are many dimensions along which people may differ from one another cognitively; it's possible here to give only a brief sampling. The readings in Chapter Ten (Group and Individual Differences in Cognition) focus on differences among cultural groups and among individuals (see Craik & Salthouse, 1992; Halpern, 1992; Sternberg & Berg, 1992, for some areas in which differences or changes in cognitive ability can be observed that are not covered here).

One dimension along which cultural groups clearly vary is language. Reading 32 reports on the impact language differences appear to have on how Chinese and Americans think about people. Cultural groups are also often located in diverse environments, which encourages differences in the ways people in those groups interact with their surroundings. Reading 33 focuses on the cognitive strategies adopted by people from desert Aboriginal and suburban Australian cultures when asked to remember the locations of objects.

Individuals' performances on cognitive tasks differ for a variety of reasons, but two of the most common are differences in ability and in experience in a particular area. Reading 34 identifies some of the things that set apart people who are high in verbal ability from those who are not. Reading 35 does the same for people who are experts in some area and people who are novices.

REFERENCES

Banaji, M. R., & Crowder, R. G. (1989). The bankruptcy of everyday memory. *American Psychologist, 44,* 1185–1193.

Ceci, S. J., & Bronfenbrenner, U. (1991). On the demise of everyday memory: "The rumors of my death are much exaggerated" (Mark Twain). *American Psychologist, 46,* 27–31.

Craik, F. I. M., & Salthouse, T. A. (Eds.). (1992). *The handbook of aging and cognition.* Hillsdale, NJ: Erlbaum.

Halpern, D. F. (1992). *Sex differences in cognitive abilities* (2nd ed.). Hillsdale, NJ: Erlbaum.

Roediger, H. L., III. (1991). They read an article? A commentary on the everyday memory controversy. *American Psychologist, 46,* 37–40.

Sternberg, R. J., & Berg, C. A. (Eds.). (1992). *Intellectual development.* New York: Cambridge University Press.

Tulving, E. (1991). Memory research is not a zero-sum game. *American Psychologist, 46,* 41–42.

CHAPTER NINE
Everyday Memory and Judgment

INTRODUCTION

Most laboratory studies of memory can be summarized as follows: (1) a subject is given some information; (2) a certain amount of time goes by; (3) then the subject is tested on the information. As Harry Bahrick, Phyllis Bahrick, and Roy Wittlinger point out in their article "Fifty Years of Memory for Names and Faces: A Cross-Sectional Approach," this is very unlike the way memory is used in everyday life.

First, most of the information we retain is not practiced intensively for a short period of time (so-called massed practice), as in most experiments; rather, it is acquired over a period of time (so-called distributed practice). Although not all experiments use the massed practice approach, even those that use distributed practice do not distribute that practice over as much time as is common in real life. Furthermore, in real life, we don't usually stop using or practicing what we've learned once we've learned it. Although some experiments have investigated the effects of overlearning on memory, clearly the effects of years of overlearning cannot be duplicated in the laboratory. For similar reasons, the long-term memories psychologists study are usually at most a few days or weeks old: it's rarely possible to follow a group of subjects for years.

Bahrick and his colleagues argue that the solution to studying real-life long-term memories is to use a cross-sectional approach. In this approach, rather than following the same group of subjects over a long period of time as in the longitudinal approach, researchers study subjects of different ages and interpret (cautiously) the differences among them as reflecting the sorts of changes that would take place over time. In this cross-sectional study, Bahrick and his associates studied how well subjects remembered the names and faces of their high school classmates (as well as which names went with which faces) from 3 months to more than 50 years after graduation, using pictures (referred to as *portraits*) from their graduation yearbooks.

Most of the long introduction that was originally part of this article but is excluded here discusses in detail the problems with the cross-sectional approach. For example, psychologists try to make sure that subjects in the different groups of an experiment are alike in all ways except for the variable of interest—in this case, the length of time since their memories for their classmates were formed. But as Bahrick and his colleagues point out, it was less common for people to attend and graduate from high school in the 1920s than it was in the 1970s, which means that the older subjects were from a more select group. Furthermore, when studying memory, psychologists try to make sure that the means by which information is acquired and maintained, or encoded and rehearsed, either is held the same or is varied systematically among subjects. In a cross-sectional study like this reading's, such control is not possible: subjects came from high schools of different sizes, spent differing amounts of time with various classmates, differed in the recency with which they consulted their yearbooks or had contact with their classmates, and so on.

Bahrick, Bahrick, and Wittlinger's solution was to take into account the effects of these other, uncontrolled, factors statistically. All subjects were given a questionnaire that measured factors that are likely to have affected subjects' memory for classmates. We expect that those subjects who consulted their yearbooks recently would be able to correctly recognize more classmates' faces than would subjects who have not consulted their yearbooks for a long time. Because recent graduates, on average, are likely to have consulted their yearbooks more recently than are older graduates (that is, recency-of-yearbook-consultation and time since graduation covary), their superior face recognition is probably due in part to having recently consulted their yearbooks. To adjust for differences in recency-of-yearbook-consultation, we first measure the correlation between subjects' recency-of-yearbook-consultation and recognition of faces for each cohort, or class-year group. Then, using the technique of multiple regression, we statistically adjust face recognition scores for every group to be what we would expect if all groups were, on average, the same in recency-of-yearbook-consultation. We end up with an adjusted face recognition score with the effects of recency-of-yearbook-consultation removed. The process is repeated for all other variables that Bahrick and his colleagues found to be correlated with recognition scores. Most of the technical details of this procedure have been excluded from this selection.

Two concepts that Bahrick and his associates use that may not be familiar to you are those of foils and conditional probability. In a recognition test, the subject must identify the correct answer from several choices; the wrong choices are called foils, or distractors. The conditional probability of some outcome is the likelihood of that outcome given some other event, outcome, or state of affairs. For example, the conditional probability of snow is much higher when given that it's winter in Minnesota than when given that it's summer in Hawaii. Here, Bahrick and his associates show that the conditional probability of remembering a classmate depends in part on the particular relationship the subject had with that classmate.

As you read this selection, see whether you can think of other factors that might have affected subjects' memory for their classmates. Do you think that there is something special about memory for one's classmates that might not apply to other long-term memories?

Fifty Years of Memory for Names and Faces: A Cross-Sectional Approach

Harry P. Bahrick, Phyllis O. Bahrick, and Roy P. Wittlinger

Ohio Wesleyan University

THE CONTENT INQUIRY

Apart from the primary question regarding the loss of information during a 50-year time span, a major content objective of the present study is a comparison of the retention functions for various types of information. One comparison of interest involves visual information vs. verbal information vs. visual–verbal associative information. Previous findings (e.g., Shepard, 1967) indicate superior recognition for pictures over words, but systematic comparisons are lacking for the associative visual–verbal information vs. the visual or verbal information examined individually. The present study gives an opportunity to examine these aspects in a common context.

A further comparison involves free recall, cued recall, and recognition performance related to the same information. Previous findings (Luh, 1922; Postman & Rau, 1957) based on short time spans generally show that recall performance declines more rapidly than recognition performance. This generalization is to be reexamined over the 50-year period with a view to ascertaining factors that limit each type of performance. This information is important for a more general understanding of the relation between recall and recognition. Previous findings comparing free recall and cued recall vary considerably (Bahrick, 1971; Tulving & Pearlstone, 1966) as a function of the availability and accessibility of the cues used. The relationship between free recall and cued recall will also be reexamined with the aim of finding out more about the types of cues used in the organization of free recall of names.

METHOD

General Design of the Study

Three hundred ninety-two subjects were divided into nine groups according to the elapsed time since their high school graduation. Table 1 gives means and standard deviations in months since graduation, along with group size. All subjects took six retention tests in succession, and then filled out a questionnaire that dealt with interaction with members of their high school graduating class and with the perusal of material in the high school yearbook during the retention interval. The questionnaire is reproduced in Table 2. The following retention tests were administered: free recall of names, recognition of names, recognition of portraits, matching of portraits with names and of names with portraits, and cuing of names by means of portraits. . . . Group means were determined for the nine groups on each of the six retention tests, and these group means were adjusted by a multiple regression procedure to reflect constant levels of the variables assessed by the questionnaire.

Subjects

Subjects were 162 male and 230 female high school graduates ranging in age from 17 to 74. Further requirements were that the subject be a member of a class with a minimum of 90 graduates and that a yearbook of his graduating class be available. In most instances yearbooks were supplied by the individual subjects, but some were obtained directly from high schools or from other subjects who were members of

SOURCE: *Journal of Experimental Psychology: General, 104*(1), 1975, pp. 54–75. Copyright 1975 by the American Psychological Association. Reprinted by permission.

TABLE 1   Characteristics of Nine Time Groups

| Group | N | Months since Graduation | |
		M	SD
1	50	3.26	1.82
2	50	9.30	1.37
3	50	23.18	8.19
4	50	45.50	6.11
5	26	89.08	19.59
6	50	173.56	33.47
7	41	309.61	32.19
8	35	408.89	30.42
9	40	570.73	46.96

the same class. Subjects were recruited with the help of educational, charitable, religious, and social organizations in Franklin and Delaware counties of Ohio, and data collection continued over a period of 40 mo. . . . [The authors go on here to detail the methods by which they recruited subjects.] Socioeconomic characteristics of subjects were not determined, but a large percentage had attended college and came from middle and upper-middle income classes. Older subjects may represent a somewhat more selective group than younger ones; they were more difficult to recruit and a larger percentage of those contacted refused to serve. The extent to which intellectual, motivational, and maturational group differences may affect the data has been discussed earlier [not reprinted here].

Procedure

The subjects who agreed to serve and who supplied their own yearbooks were requested not to look at their annuals between the time they made a commitment and the actual time of testing. In most instances the experimenter kept the annuals for several weeks while the individual tests were prepared. This interval, during which subjects had no access to the annual, limited opportunities for rehearsals close to the time of testing.

Test construction. Each test consisted of five subtests in addition to the free-recall test. To assemble these

subtests a total of 130 portrait–name combinations of graduates was needed from each yearbook, in addition to certain foils selected from other yearbooks. These 130 portraits and corresponding names were randomly selected from among portraits of seniors shown in each annual. This meant that in a graduating class of 130 every member was included in the test material, but in a class of 650 only 1 out of 5 members was included. When the class was smaller than 130 (18% of cases), some names and portraits were used more than once. Such repeated use of names or portraits occurred only for foils on test items, so that a particular name or portrait was never used more than once as a correct answer. The assignment of the name–portrait combinations to the various subtests was random, with the constraints that individuals of the appropriate sex were selected as required by certain subtests, and that repeated use of a name or a portrait was limited to use as foils.

To prepare the visual material, photocopies were made of pages in the yearbook portraying the faces of the graduating class. Although these photocopies yielded a somewhat degraded reproduction of the original portrait, this degradation was fairly constant for all visual test material, and actually considerably improved comparability of photographic fidelity for yearbooks of different ages. The very high performance of subjects on visual recognition tests suggests that the effect of this diminished fidelity of photographic reproduction on recognition performance was minor.

In connection with all test responses, except the free-recall responses, subjects indicated their degree of confidence in the selection on a 3-point scale, 3 being a certain response, 2 a probable response, and 1 a guess.

The free-recall test was administered first, and the remaining five subtests were administered in one of five random orders, with 1/5 of the subjects arbitrarily assigned to each order. At the conclusion of the last subtest subjects were shown the names of those 50 graduates whose portraits or names had appeared as correct choices in the five subtests, and were required to indicate the type of association they had had during their school years with each of these individuals. The categories provided are shown in

TABLE 2   Inventory of Conditions Affecting Original Learning and Rehearsal of Material

1. Number of years since your high school graduation: _____.

2. Number of years spent with the majority of your class (i.e., your whole senior class as opposed to the group that came up from grade school with you): (less than 1) (1–2) (3–4) (5–8) (more than 8)

3. Maximum number of years spent with any sizable group in class (i.e., the class from grade school or junior high school into the high school as a group): (less than 1) (1–2) (3–4) (5–8) (more than 8)

4. Number of reunions attended: (0) (1) (2–3) (4–6) (more)

5. Most recent reunion attended: (within last month) (within last 6 months) (within last year) (within last 1–3 years) (within last 4–9 years) (within last 10 or more years)

6. How often do you review the yearbook? (once a week) (once a month) (once a year) (once every several years) (rarely)

7. How recently did you last review the book? (within the last month) (within the last year) (within the last 2 years) (within the last 5 years) (within the last 10 years)

8. Average amount of time spent with it: (several minutes) (half an hour) (1 hour) (2 hours) (4+ hours)

9. Evaluate the most recent contact with classmates that you have had by listing the number who fall into each of the following three time categories (this includes letters and Christmas cards, etc.):

    Number of people   Most recent contact
                        Within last month
                        Within last year
                        Within last 5 years

10. Evaluate your relationship with each person you encountered in this test by marking beside the name the letter or letters of the descriptions below which are most appropriate for each individual:

    (A) One or more classes in common
    (B) Shared in extra-curricular activities
    (C) Friend or acquaintance
    (D) Close friend
    (E) Romantic interest
    (F) Recognized, but did not know
    (G) Never knew or recognized
    (H) Cannot recall true relationship

Table 2. The subjects were instructed to check multiple categories if several categories described their relationship to a particular individual. The questionnaire reproduced in Table 2 was administered after all tests were completed.

Free-recall test.   The subjects were asked to list all the names (first and last) of members of their graduating class that they could remember. A time limit of 8 min was imposed. Pilot data indicated that the rate of additional responses was quite low after 8 min, and thus the obtained data constitute a large fraction of the easily retrievable information for all groups.

Picture recognition test.   Ten portraits were randomly selected from the 130 previously chosen name–portrait pairs which constituted the source material for the entire test. Each of these 10 pictures was placed on a separate $2\frac{1}{2}'' \times 8''$ (6 cm $\times$ 20 cm) card. 4 foil pictures were also placed on each card, with the correct picture randomly positioned in a single row among the 4 foils. The foils were selected from other yearbooks in such a way that there were no distinguishing group characteristics among the 5 pictures. Thus the 5 pictures on each card were homogeneous with regard to picture size, hair style, etc. If the individual graduated from a racially integrated school, members of minority groups were included among the foils in approximately the same proportion as their representation in the graduating class. Thus the visual recognition test consisted of 10 cards of 5 pictures. The subjects were asked to identify on each card the picture taken from their own yearbook. A time limit of 8 sec was imposed, and subjects were forced to guess if they were uncertain. Pilot data had indicated that prolonging the maximum time for recognition responses had no significant effect on the number of correct responses.

Name recognition tests. Ten names (first and last) were randomly selected from among the 130 portrait–name combinations previously chosen as source material. Each name was typed on a 3" × 5" (8 cm × 13 cm) card, and was randomly positioned among 4 foil names. The foils were selected from other yearbooks. No foils were used that had both first names identical to and last names similar to any of the names of graduates of the class. Test administration procedure was comparable to the procedure used in the picture recognition test. A forced guess was solicited after an 8-sec exposure of each card.

Matching tests. Two versions of this test were used: picture matching and name matching. The picture matching test consisted of 10 cards, each with the name of a graduate typed across the top, and 5 portraits of the appropriate sex, among them the matching portrait. All 5 portraits were selected from the subject's own yearbook and were arrayed in a row along the bottom of the card. The subject was instructed to select the portrait that matched the name. A forced guess was required after 5 sec. The name matching test was presented on 10 3" × 5" (8 cm × 13 cm) cards, each with a single portrait of a graduate centered near the top of the card, and 5 names of graduates, among them the correct name randomly positioned, typed in a column near the bottom of the card. The subject was required to select the name which matched the portrait within a 5-sec limit, or guess at the end of that time.

Picture cuing test. The subjects were presented with 10 portraits of the graduating class, each mounted on a 3" × 5" (8 cm × 13 cm) card. The cards were presented one at a time and the subject was asked to write the name of the individual portrayed within a 15-sec time limit. Guessing was encouraged. Answers were scored as correct only if the first and last names given were correct.

RESULTS AND ANALYSIS

Uncontrolled Variables

The responses to Questions 1–7 on the inventory (Table 2) were coded into ordinal scales with high values of the scale designating greater or more recent rehearsal. The means for each group for each question are shown in Table 3. The overall means are shown in the penultimate row of that table. Blank spaces in the table indicate that a given variable is not applicable to a particular group, e.g., recency or frequency of class reunions for those who graduated less than a year ago. In the latter cases the overall mean is based upon the remaining number of subjects. The table is arranged in such a way that the variables in Columns 1–3 reflect conditions related to the original learning situation, and those in Columns 4–9 relate to conditions governing rehearsal during the retention interval. The table also shows the average size of the graduating class for each group and the correlation between the number of months elapsed since graduation and the mean values of each variable. Inspection of these correlations and the mean values within each column indicates that, in general, subjects who graduated long ago were more likely to come from smaller classes; they looked at their annuals less frequently and less recently, and they remained in recent contact with fewer classmates. Since these uncontrolled conditions change systematically with time and are potentially related to retention performance, it is necessary to treat them as covariates for purposes of obtaining unbiased estimates of retention for each age group. Average retention performance for each group must be adjusted for any effects of the uncontrolled conditions. Briefly, this adjustment is accomplished by determining, via individual group regression equations, what the average retention of the group would be if all subjects had been measured at the grand average of each of the uncontrolled conditions.

TABLE 3   Mean Scores on Uncontrolled Variables for All Groups

Group	Class Size	Years with Class	Years with Smaller Group	Frequency of Reunions	Recency of Reunions	Frequency of Review of Yearbook	Recency of Review of Yearbook	Time with Yearbook	Number of Classmate Contacts
1	360.90	3.56	4.14			2.84	4.04	1.60	
2	350.16	3.66	4.00			3.02	4.12	1.80	
3	377.80	3.46	4.26	1.06	.24	2.40	3.70	1.90	32.96
4	284.52	3.60	4.24	1.08	.24	1.88	3.24	1.76	23.86
5	279.65	2.92	3.85	1.15	.54	1.81	3.15	1.81	12.62
6	223.34	3.24	3.88	1.76	1.50	1.40	2.10	1.50	12.44
7	202.12	3.39	4.02	1.80	1.05	1.44	2.49	1.63	6.15
8	203.50	3.67	4.25	1.61	.58	1.17	2.08	1.72	4.36
9	314.54	2.95	3.69	2.03	1.82	1.26	2.03	1.77	7.41
$\overline{X}$	294.20	3.41	4.05	1.50	.86	1.97	3.06	1.71	15.37
r	−.61	−.34	−.39	.89	.69	−.84	−.89	−.19	−.84

Unadjusted Retention Scores

Table 4 shows the mean performance of the nine groups on each of six retention tasks. The scores on five subtests (excluding free recall) are reported as percentages. . . .

Several problems arose in scoring the free-recall responses. The problems relate to defining and identifying intrusion errors, i.e., names of individuals appearing on the free-recall protocol who are not members of the graduating class. The identification of such errors is difficult because yearbooks in some instances fail to list all members of the graduating class. Problems of definition arise because some high schools graduate separate classes at midyear and these classes publish separate yearbooks, whereas other high schools may graduate only a few individuals at midyear, and these individuals are not separately identified.

In order to assess intrusion errors a sample of 30 subjects from Groups 1, 2, and 9, chosen randomly from among those whose yearbooks gave complete lists of names, was scored for all such errors. The mean number of errors was 2.2 ($SD = 2.6$). The great majority of the errors were names of graduates of classes preceding or succeeding the graduating class. Although the absolute number of intrusion errors is small, the number increases significantly ($p < .01$) with the retention interval. The implications of this finding will be discussed in a later section. The ob-

tained means shown in Table 4 are calculated on the basis of lenient rather than strict scoring; i.e., they include intrusion errors. The decision to include them was based upon the fact that the exact number of intrusion errors could not always be established, and that the definition of such errors is somewhat arbitrary.

Although tested on the average 3.26 mo after graduation, the performance of Group 1 is regarded as an indicator of original learning. The validity of this approximation is supported by the near zero correlations between performance measures and time since graduation for the subjects of Group 1. When expressed as a fraction of the total acquisition period of approximately 4 yr, the time lapse between graduation and testing is roughly comparable to time lapses customary for assessing initial performance levels in the laboratory.

Adjustments of Group Means

The general approach to the adjustments was discussed earlier. Basically, the group means are adjusted to reflect the retention performance that would be obtained if the uncontrolled variables pertaining to original learning and rehearsal opportunities had in fact been held constant for all groups. The adjustments are made on the basis of the overall means for each uncontrolled variable. Thus the adjusted scores

TABLE 4 Observed and Adjusted Means on Each of Six Retention Tasks

Group	Obs. Mean	Adj. Mean	Obs. Mean	Adj. Mean	Obs. Mean	Adj. Mean
	Free Recall		Name Recognition		Picture Recognition	
1	52.7	47.0	91	91	90	89
2	46.3	39.2	91	91	88	91
3	41.9	37.2	85	79	84	78
4	41.4	41.6	92	93	92	94
5	37.7	39.6	85	87	92	92
6	28.0	34.5	87	93	91	92
7	26.3	29.3	81	78	91	93
8	24.0	27.8	82	74	90	90
9	21.2	19.5	69	77	71	73
	Picture Matching		Name Matching		Picture Cuing	
1	94	88	89	90	67	68
2	91	90	93	96	57	59
3	87	82	87	90	45	36
4	96	97	93	92	58	64
5	85	86	85	85	51	57
6	83	87	83	91	37	41
7	82	87	78	79	37	53
8	79	89	83	74	33	47
9	58	69	56	59	18	18

are based upon a graduating class of 294 etc., as listed in Row 10 of Table 3. . . . [Here the authors give technical details on how they did the multiple regression.]

The multiple regression equations, when evaluated for the overall means of the uncontrolled variables, yield predicted mean retention performance for each group. These values are plotted on a log scale in Figure 1 and are also presented along with the observed means in Table 4. Comparison of the observed with the adjusted means indicates that the adjustments are generally minor and that the two sets of means show essentially the same trends. . . . [Here the authors give technical details on the results of their multiple regression analysis.] Thus, it appears that the observed means are relatively free of the effects of the uncontrolled variables and primarily reflect memory loss over time.

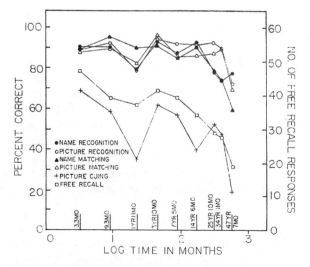

FIGURE 1 Adjusted mean retention scores on six tests.

Cognitive Losses for Six Types of Performance

Comparison of the retention of names and faces.   Since the material on each test represents a random selection of names and faces from the entire graduating class, the percentage scores reported for each test may be viewed as an unbiased estimate of the percentage of the total graduating class correctly identifiable if the test were expanded to include the entire class. Inspection of Table 4 indicates that on a recognition level subjects are able to identify about 90% of the names and faces of the members of their class at the time of graduation. The visual information is retained virtually unimpaired for at least 35 yr. Verbal information declines somewhat after 15 yr. The final loss of information after many years of stability is suggestive of degenerative processes, but the data do not permit this inference to be made with high confidence.

The ability to match names with faces is acquired and retained at nearly the same high level as the ability to identify faces and names separately, and it makes little difference whether subjects select among names to match a portrait or whether they select among portraits to match a name. In both cases almost 90% of the selections are correct at or near graduation, and this performance level is maintained with very little decline for at least 15 yr. The 48-yr group shows a loss suggestive of degenerative changes. In making these comparisons, no correction for chance success has been made in the recognition and matching scores. A variety of corrections are possible; however, all of them would have equal effects on these four subtests, since the uncorrected performance is comparable, forced guessing was used on all tests, and four foils are included on each of the subtests. The most common correction (number right − 1/4 number wrong) produces only slight change as long as performance remains nearly 90% correct, but enhances the decline in performance of the 48-yr group. . . .

[Excluded here are a discussion of some previous findings and a discussion of overlearning.]

Free recall and picture-cued recall.   Initial performance levels for both of these tasks are far below the performance level for identification and matching tasks. Free-recall performance is by far the poorest; when recall performance is expressed as a percentage of the graduating class only about 15% of the names of classmates are recalled at the beginning of the retention period. Although these differences are in the direction expected from previous findings, e.g., Clark (1934), the magnitude of the differences between free recall and recognition performance is much greater than previously reported. This finding will be discussed in more detail below.

Picture-cued recall performance is superior to free-recall performance when both scores are expressed as a percentage of the graduating class. As was previously stated, relative performance on these two tasks depends upon the strength of the cue–response association compared to the accessibility and availability of the covert cues subjects use to organize the free-recall protocol. It is clear that in the present situation the portrait cues presented by the experimenter are strongly associated with the names of the respective individuals. However, portrait cues are less effective in free recall than in cued recall because of their low accessibility (Bahrick, 1974; Frost, 1972). If subjects cannot generate portrait cues on their own, they must rely primarily on other more accessible cues to generate the free-recall sequence. The availability and accessibility of these other cues will determine whether free- or cued-recall performance is superior. The opposite relation between free- and cued-recall performance would probably be obtained if the task involved recalling the names of past United States presidents. The names of presidents may be strongly associated with nonpictorial cues, e.g., historical events or chronological sequences, and these cues would lead to high performance on free recall of names because they are likely to be organized and therefore accessible. Portrait cues in many instances would be only weakly associated with the names of many presidents so that the percentage of names retrievable with portrait cues would probably be below the free-recall level.

The decline of recall performance in time.   Both free and cued recall decline significantly with time. After 48 yr free recall has declined by about 60% of the initial level, and cued-recall performance has declined more than 70%. It is important to note that the decline of performance in these tasks over many years involves only retrieval of names; the ability to identify names, faces, and their associations remains unimpaired, although both recall tasks show significant decline. This lack of correlation between performance on the identification and matching tasks and performance on the recall tasks supports models of memory in which recall depends upon generative processes which are independent of the information content required for recognition.

The retention curves reported here all differ from those reported in the psychological literature for laboratory-learned material in that they show much slower forgetting, i.e. less decline per unit of time. This difference has already been explained for recognition subtests on the basis of overlearning of much of the material in relation to the criterion defining correct performance on these tasks. This interpretation seems less plausible for the recall tasks, since the initial performance level is far below recognition performance, and the discrepancy suggests that much of the material is marginally learned rather than overlearned. Overlearning is generally defined as practice beyond the point at which all responses are correct, but this criterion of overlearning is more applicable to laboratory situations in which a particular task is defined by the experimenter and the subject continues to practice all responses until they have been mastered at a specified criterion level. Even in this traditional situation some responses will be overlearned in relation to others, but the degree of overlearning is likely to be limited as long as the subject is required to respond to that portion of the material which has not yet been mastered. The present study involves no formal practice and no task defined for the subject. The degree of overlearning of individual names therefore stands in no necessary relationship to the number of unlearned remaining names, and high degrees of overlearning of certain names are not inconsistent with a low percentage of free recall based on the entire graduating class. Perhaps even more important than the degree of overlearning per se as an explanation of the slow forgetting observed in the present study is a reinterpretation of the traditional concept of distributed practice. It has been stated previously that all acquisition functions represent net acquisition functions which reflect the balance of gains and losses, and that this is true even during short formal practice sessions in laboratory learning (Melton, 1963). When the acquisition process extends over a period of several years, as in the present situation, the effects of these successive phases of acquisition and loss are enormously magnified. Although contact with certain individuals in the graduating class is likely to be daily, contacts with others are certainly more intermittent and interspersed at irregular intervals. When such successive long periods of acquisition, loss, and reacquisition, arbitrarily designated as the trace formation period, are followed by the retention interval, it is very likely that the rate of decline of performance during the retention interval will be much slower than for material acquired in time-compressed laboratory learning sessions. By comparison, the latter all represent massed-practice conditions. In other words, the very slow decline of free-recall performance observed in the present study (60% loss during 48 yr) is attributed not only to overlearning, but also to an enormous expansion of the retention-enhancing effects of distributed practice observed in the laboratory (Keppel, 1964; Underwood, Keppel, & Schulz, 1962). Such wide distribution of practice is quite common in many real-life learning situations, but has not been investigated in the laboratory because of time constraints.

Despite the very slow rate of forgetting characteristic of the functions shown in Figure 1, it is significant to note that the free-recall and cued-recall functions follow a negatively accelerated pattern. Percentage decline of performance per year clearly diminished during the course of the 48 yr under investigation, and this type of function can thus not be regarded as an artifact of the massed-practice conditions of the laboratory.

The decline of confidence.   The confidence ratings obtained from subjects in regard to their responses on five subtests were scored separately for correct and incorrect answers, and the results are shown in Table 5. On this confidence scale a rating of 3 represents certainty and a rating of 1 represents a guess. It can be seen that subjects had high confidence in their correct responses; picture cuing yielded the highest values, and the other four subtests were approximately equal. Confidence does not seem to decline substantially during the retention interval for at least 35 yr;

TABLE 5   Confidence Ratings for Correct and Wrong Responses

Group	Name Recognition		Picture Recognition		Picture Matching		Name Matching		Picture Cuing	
	Correct Response	Wrong Response	Correct Response	Wrong Response	Correct Response	Wrong Response	Correct Response	Wrong Response	Correct Response	Wrong Response
1	2.86	1.14	2.86	1.30	2.84	1.24	2.85	1.32	2.98	1.72
2	2.83	1.29	2.89	1.45	2.85	1.28	2.87	1.13	2.92	1.24
3	2.75	1.26	2.78	1.33	2.72	1.37	2.79	1.20	2.83	1.77
4	2.85	1.42	2.84	1.34	2.86	1.29	2.87	1.29	2.96	1.60
5	2.79	1.38	2.72	1.50	2.69	1.22	2.81	1.38	2.81	1.57
6	2.69	1.48	2.79	1.51	2.68	1.51	2.72	1.44	2.84	1.72
7	2.67	1.33	2.67	1.29	2.61	1.46	2.73	1.40	2.81	1.78
8	2.76	1.69	2.72	1.33	2.58	1.70	2.62	1.53	2.84	1.70
9	2.42	1.55	2.18	1.43	2.27	1.25	2.53	1.44	2.90	1.61

subjects in Group 9 do show a decline in confidence which affects all tasks except picture cuing. On this task they show a substantial decline in performance (see Figure 1), but discrimination between correct and incorrect responses remains unimpaired. Although most wrong responses are designated as guesses, there is evidence that confidence in wrong responses increases over time, particularly in regard to name recognition.

Social and Individual Difference Variables

The variable of group size. The size of graduating classes is a variable in the present investigation, and the effect of this variable on acquisition and retention of the information called for on each test was examined separately for each group. For this purpose the scores on each of five subtests (excluding free recall) were multiplied by class size separately for each subject. As stated earlier, the products provide an estimate of the total number of individuals in the class that could be correctly identified if each subtest had been extended over the entire graduating class. . . .

The correlations in Table 6 are close to .90 for the four identification and matching tasks except for the 48-yr group. This shows that subjects are able to identify the great majority of individuals in their class by name and by face, and that this is *equally true* for subjects graduating from small and large classes within the range of variation of class size examined in this study. . . . It is apparent that learning and retain-

ing information about names and faces of several hundred individuals does not overtax the capacity of the memory store of most individuals, given the conditions of acquisition typical of the present study. Only for the 48-yr group is there an indication of a decline in the uniform pattern of very high correlations. An examination of the scattergram of this group suggests that graduates from the largest classes identify no more individuals than graduates from classes of intermediate size, and thus, if very large classes are involved, there appears to be some loss of information for this group, particularly on the matching tasks.

Results for the free-recall task are strikingly different from those obtained for the identification and matching tests. The highest correlation of free recall with class size is .31, and several values are negative. This implies that acquisition and retention of free recall of names is not only independent of the size of the group, but is also unaffected by the amount of information the subject has acquired in regard to identification of names and faces of the group. In other words, it does not matter how large the group is, or how many names and faces of group members can be correctly identified and matched. The number of names which can be recalled is independent of these variables. This conclusion can be confirmed more directly by inspecting the correlations between free recall and each of the tests shown in Table 7. Most of these correlations are very low except for those related to the cued-recall task.

TABLE 6   Partial Correlation of Class Size with Performance on Each Subtest

Group	Free Recall	Name Recognition	Picture Recognition	Picture Matching	Name Matching	Picture Cuing
1	−.05	.91	.93	.95	.81	.28
2	−.13	.94	.90	.91	.95	.12
3	.24	.88	.92	.88	.92	.40
4	.31	.96	.88	.97	.94	.61
5	.07	.97	.94	.88	.95	−.28
6	.30	.93	.93	.85	.91	.44
7	.07	.83	.92	.86	.79	.45
8	.10	.89	.95	.91	.92	−.26
9	−.15	.68	.62	.31	.50	−.27

Although previous studies have shown some in-dependence of recall and recognition performance, the present findings show this independence more dramatically for both the acquisition and the retention process. The subjects are not only able to identify and match the great majority of up to 800 names and faces correctly, but they maintain this information practically unimpaired for many years. At the same time they initially recall only about 50 of the names, and fewer than half of these are recalled 48 yr later. This finding is relatively constant whether the class size is 90 or 800. This independence of recall and recognition performance during acquisition is ob-scured in all laboratory situations in which the experimenter defines the task in such a way that the subject rehearses retrieval during the encoding process. Such rehearsals introduce a task-specific correla-tion between recall and recognition performance, a correlation which apparently is not intrinsic to the functioning of the memory system, and which is not observed in real-life acquisition processes of the sort examined here. Laboratory findings comparable to the present ones are likely to be found in incidental learning situations in which subjects are not in-structed to memorize material and are therefore un-likely to develop and rehearse schemes facilitating re-trieval of the material. Only a small portion of the material which can be recognized can also be recalled under these conditions (Craik & Lockhart, 1972; Schulman, 1974).

Sex differences.   The average performance of female subjects is somewhat superior to the performance of male subjects. This is true for all six subtests when the

TABLE 7   Correlations of Free-Recall Performance with Performance on Recognition and Matching Tests

Group	Name Recognition	Picture Recognition	Picture Matching	Name Matching	Picture Cuing
1	.22	.15	.19	.32	.39
2	−.01	−.09	.04	.03	.37
3	.42	.29	.38	.30	.62
4	.32	.40	.31	.37	.57
5	−.09	−.20	−.13	−.12	.72
6	.36	.24	.40	.43	.73
7	.09	.00	.06	−.03	.18
8	.11	.17	.12	.20	.20
9	−.02	−.09	.01	.05	.35

data from all time groups are combined. The superior performance of the female subjects appears to be a function of superior acquisition, rather than superior retention, and this is evident when the comparison is made separately for each group. Table 8 gives the unadjusted percentages of correct responses separately for male and female subjects for each time group, and for all subjects combined. It can be seen that early during the retention interval the performance of female subjects equals or exceeds the performance of male subjects on each task, but after 48 yr male subjects retain more on all tests except free recall. The overall sex differences favoring females are in accord with earlier findings by Kaess and Witryol (1955) and Gates (1917), and the reversal of these differences for older subjects agrees with a report by Van Zooneveld (1958), who found visual memory of older male subjects superior to that of females. No attempt was made to calculate separate adjustments of male and female scores based upon differential rehearsal or trace formation conditions, since the number of subjects was small in some of the groups and the observed differences were minor.

The performance of male and female subjects was also compared in regard to memory for classmates of their own sex vs. those of the opposite sex. Sex differences are very striking on the recall test, but less noticeable on the other subtests. These results are summarized in Figure 2. It can be seen that the free-recall protocols of male subjects contain nearly twice as many male names as female names, and this difference remains stable over the 50-yr retention span. Female subjects recall more female names than male names, but the difference is much smaller. Since these differences are much more pronounced on the free-recall task it is apparent that they reflect primarily organization used for the retrieval of names, rather than available information about names and faces or about the association of names with faces. To explore this inference further, the sequence of names produced by individual subjects in their free-recall protocols was examined to determine the extent of "clustering" of names of the same sex. Specifically, it was assumed that the absence of any organization of the recall sequence by sex would produce a random sequence in which male and female names would alternate with a frequency corresponding to their respective proportions Thus, in a protocol which contains 70% male names and 30% female names, and which is organized randomly with respect to sex, 21% of digram sequences would be female names followed by male names, 21% male names followed by female names, 49% male names followed by male names, and 9% female names followed by female

TABLE 8   Performance of Male and Female Subjects on Each Subtest

	Mean Responses		Percentage Correct									
	Free Recall		Name Recognition		Picture Recognition		Picture Matching		Name Matching		Picture Cuing	
Group	M	F	M	F	M	F	M	F	M	F	M	F
1	43.8	56.5	84	94	87	92	91	95	89	89	66	67
2	45.4	47.2	91	91	86	90	90	92	95	91	55	58
3	38.5	44.8	80	89	80	87	85	89	83	89	38	51
4	42.2	40.4	90	94	88	97	95	97	93	96	60	56
5	37.0	37.9	78	87	82	94	74	88	80	86	40	54
6	25.2	31.0	86	90	93	90	85	83	79	87	37	39
7	20.3	27.7	74	82	88	92	79	83	68	81	25	41
8	21.3	24.5	86	79	86	92	68	79	77	85	33	30
9	19.2	22.4	77	63	72	70	62	52	57	55	19	18
$\bar{X}$[a]	32.6	37.0	85	86	85	89	84	85	83	84	44	47

[a]Weighted mean.

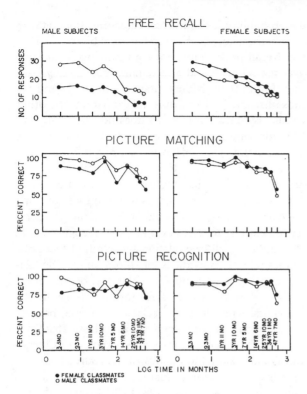

FREE RECALL

MALE SUBJECTS   FEMALE SUBJECTS

PICTURE MATCHING

PICTURE RECOGNITION

LOG TIME IN MONTHS

● FEMALE CLASSMATES
○ MALE CLASSMATES

FIGURE 2 Memory of male and female subjects for male and female classmates.

names. The observed frequency of sex alternation (male followed by female and female followed by male) for 40 subjects, 10 each selected randomly from male and female subjects of Groups 1 and 9, was compared to the chance expected frequency by a chi-square test. The differences were found to be highly significant ($p < .001$). To determine whether organization by sex of the free-recall sequence was more characteristic of male or female subjects and whether or not it diminished in time, chi-square comparisons examining alternation frequency were made between the records of the 20 male vs. the 20 female subjects, the 20 subjects of Group 1 vs. those of Group 9, and of the interaction among the four subgroups. None of these comparisons yielded a significant effect ($p > .05$). It would thus appear that the retrieval sequence in free recall is based upon organization in which sex is a significant variable, and that this is approximately equally true over the entire re-

tention span. These results do not directly reveal whether the clustering by sex reflects a primary or secondary organizational effect, i.e., whether male and female graduates are grouped together on the basis of sex, or whether the grouping occurs on the basis of membership in organizations that are largely sex segregated, e.g., athletic teams or clubs. The latter interpretation is more plausible, since the records of both sexes show equal amounts of relative clustering by sex, but male subjects produce a much greater imbalance in the number of names of each sex that are retrieved. Retrieval on the basis of organizational membership would produce this result if the groups used by male subjects were characterized by more sex segregation than the groups used by female subjects.

Race membership. The number of nonwhite subjects was too small to permit reliable comparisons of racial groups in regard to acquisition and retention. It was possible, however, to compare the performance of white subjects in regard to recall and recognition of white vs. black classmates on the various subtests. Results indicate that picture recognition, picture matching, and name matching were slightly but not significantly better for black classmates than for white classmates, but the reverse results (also nonsignificant) were obtained for picture cuing and free recall. Malpass and Kravitz (1969) found that white faces were more discriminable, and that subjects generally score higher in recognizing members of their own race. The discrepancy between their findings and the ones presented here may be a function of an isolation phenomenon, i.e., the small number of minority group members in the present investigation. The yearbooks used had very few black graduates, and this increased their distinctiveness. As a result, identification and matching performance in relation to black classmates may be much better than in a situation where blacks constitute a larger proportion of the graduating class. The paucity also precluded a reliable comparison of the rate of forgetting of black vs. white classmate portraits.

Interpersonal relationships. Subjects classified the nature of the relationship they had with every classmate whose name or portrait appeared in one of the five subtests (excluding free recall). The subjects were also instructed to classify the same individual in more than one relationship category, if appropriate. The categories used in this classification are listed in Table 2. The conditional probability that the names of individuals who had been assigned to a single category were included in the free-recall protocol was determined separately for each category for each time group. The obtained probability values for Categories A through F are shown in Table 9, together with the overall probability value obtained for all individuals assigned to any one of these categories. A comparable determination was made for all those classmates assigned to two or more categories, and the overall conditional probability of free recall for these classmates is also shown in Table 9.

Inspection of Table 9 shows free-recall probability varies as a function of the nature of the interpersonal relationship. As might be expected, the names most likely to be included in free recall are those of close friends and romantic interests (categories D and E), which appear with nearly 100% probability. The conditional recall probability for those assigned to two or more categories is much higher than the combined probability for those assigned to single categories, but the single categories of romantic interest and close friendship yield higher recall probabilities than the overall probability for multiple relationships.

The most striking aspect of the data is the stability in time of the overall recall probability. Although the probability for individual categories fluctuates in time, particularly if the number of subjects is small, the overall probability shows no evidence of decline over the 50-yr period and remains remarkably constant both for individuals assigned to single and for those assigned to multiple relationships. In other words, free-recall probability does not diminish over 50 yr for names of classmates assigned to one or more of the Relationship Categories A through F. But it has already been demonstrated that the overall number of names recalled declines by 60% during this time span. This apparent inconsistency is resolved by examining the data for Categories G and H. These categories refer respectively to: (G) never knew or recognized and (H) cannot recall true relationship. Both of these categories refer to individuals for whom no specific relationship can be remembered, either (H) because it existed and is reported as forgotten, although the individual is recognized as a classmate, or (G) because the individual is not recognized as a classmate. Table 10 gives the percent of responses assigned to Categories G and H for the various time groups. It can be seen from inspection of that table that the combined percentage increases from 12% to 36% during the 50-yr retention span, and of course this reflects a corresponding decrease in the percentage of individuals assigned to Categories A through F and to those assigned to multiple categories. This shift of individuals from single and multiple categories of specific re-

TABLE 9   Conditional Free-Recall Probability for Classmates Placed in Various Relationship Categories

			Relationship Category					
Group	A	B	C	D	E	F	A–F Combined	All Multiple Relationships Combined
1	.08	.10	.14	.42	.63	.02	.11	.24
2	.07	.02	.09	.33	.40	.02	.08	.25
3	.10	.16	.12	.25	.33	.05	.10	.25
4	.13	.16	.12	.53	.50	.01	.11	.29
5	.08	.27	.17	.56	.67	.04	.12	.28
6	.10	.04	.09	.60	.20	.02	.09	.29
7	.15	.07	.13	.56	.33	.02	.13	.27
8	.06	.16	.11	.39	.36	.00	.11	.27
9	.07	.00	.10	.41	.13	.01	.09	.26
$\bar{X}$[a]	.10	.09	.12	.41	.35	.02	.10	.27

[a]Weighted mean.

TABLE 10   Percentage of Classmates Placed in Categories G and H

Group	Category G	Category H
1	10.2	2.2
2	11.3	2.7
3	16.5	5.1
4	6.1	4.5
5	14.3	7.6
6	12.5	8.5
7	13.4	7.5
8	9.5	9.3
9	21.5	14.6

lationships to a forgotten or unacknowledged relationship is responsible in a large measure for the decline of free recall during the 50-yr retention period. The probability of free recall of names assigned to Categories G and H is close to zero. Thus the data in Tables 9 and 10 show that forgetting in free recall is associated with loss of the nature of the association between the subject and the classmate to be recalled, and not with diminution in the probability of recall of those whose relationship can still be identified.

The increased percentage of names assigned respectively to Categories G and H during the retention period is also revealing of the extent to which information loss is confused with failure to have acquired the information during the acquisition period. Assignment to Category H indicates that the subject is aware of the fact that he had some type of relation-

ship with the individual, and that he has forgotten what that relationship was. Assignment to Category G denies that a relationship existed. The percentage of individuals assigned to Category G increases from 10% to 21% during the retention period, but most of this increase occurs during the last 13 yr of the retention interval (between Groups 8 and 9). There is every reason to believe that the percentage of classmates recognized at the time of graduation was comparable for Groups 1 through 9, and thus the increase in percent of responses assigned to Category G can be interpreted as an index of the subjects' inability to discriminate information that has been lost from information that was never acquired. It would thus appear that for 35 yr or longer, subjects generally discriminate accurately the nature of information they had acquired but lost from information that was never acquired. During the final 13 yr of the retention interval this capacity is impaired. This decline appears to be closely tied to the loss of recognition memory which occurs during that same interval. Further examination of the data from Category H supports this conclusion. Table 11 shows performance on each of six subtests for classmates who are assigned to Category H. It is clear that the loss of social context of the relationship virtually precludes free recall of the name, but that it has a much smaller effect on the other tasks. It can be seen that picture and name identification are least affected by the loss of context, and that name and face matching are more affected, but that performance remains substantially above the

TABLE 11   Percentage of Correct Responses on Six Subtests for Classmates Placed in Category H

Group	Free Recall	Name Recognition	Picture Recognition	Picture Matching	Name Matching	Picture Cuing
1	4	100	82	90	62	44
2	2	71	77	63	83	29
3	0	70	92	73	69	16
4	0	64	74	64	64	0
5	1	65	40	59	56	25
6	0	66	84	59	50	6
7	0	62	70	49	46	2
8	0	63	83	61	61	0
9	1	60	66	39	34	0
$\overline{X}$[a]	1	64	76	56	62	8

[a]Weighted mean.

chance level. Cued recall is severely impaired, particularly after the first year. Thus the knowledge of context appears to be a crucial mediator for independent retrieval of names, but not for recognition of either the name or the face or for the association of the name with the face on a matching level.

Another aspect of the loss of context is reflected in the increase of intrusion errors in free recall during the 48-yr time span. These errors, as previously reported, involve primarily names of individuals belonging to earlier or later graduating classes. Although the absolute number of intrusion errors is small, they constitute approximately 2% of free-recall responses for Groups 1 and 2, but 19% for Group 9. The increase reflects declining ability to differentiate temporal context, and consequent confounding of originally differentiated subgroups used as retrieval mediators.

General Significance of Findings

The principal issue raised in the present investigation is the appropriateness of supplementing laboratory-based investigations of learning and memory with cross-sectional investigations in which statistical adjustments are used to compensate for the lack of experimental control during the acquisition and retention period. It is demonstrated that this approach permits investigators to deal with very long acquisition periods and retention periods. These long time spans are not generally amenable to laboratory exploration but are quite typical of information acquisition in many real-life situations. Because they were moderate, adjustments in the present study did not drastically alter the conclusions based upon unadjusted data. Of course, the ultimate viability of the adjustment approach depends upon the reliability of the functional relationships among variables found in a study and not upon the magnitude and direction of the adjustments themselves.

It has been shown here that under conditions of prolonged acquisition, information is preserved much longer than is usually demonstrated in laboratory investigations, and this is attributed to a very great expansion of distribution of practice and overlearning effects.

This article also argues that laboratory-defined tasks generally impose a greater interdependence upon free recall and recognition performance than is inherent in the functioning of the memory system. The present investigation dramatically demonstrates this independence in a real-life learning situation in which subjects can recognize and match names and faces for several hundred classmates but recall the names of only a small number. Recall is uncorrelated with class size or recognition performance; this supports models of memory in which generative and retrieval processes are independent of storage processes.

Social context is shown to be a very important determinant of recall performance, and a much less important determinant of recognition performance. Apparently the context serves as a mediator for retrieval of information; once the association of mediator and target item is lost, the item can no longer be retrieved for recall but can still be identified on recognition tasks.

REFERENCES

Bahrick, H. P. Retention curves: Facts or artifacts? *Psychological Bulletin*, 1964, *61*, 188–194.

Bahrick, H. P. Discriminative and associative aspects of pictorial paired-associate learning. *Journal of Experimental Psychology*, 1969, *80*, 113–119.

Bahrick, H. P. Accessibility and availability of retrieval cues in the retention of a categorized list. *Journal of Experimental Psychology*, 1971, *89*, 117–125.

Bahrick, H. P. The anatomy of free recall. *Memory & Cognition*, 1974, *2*, 484–490.

Clark, H. M. Recall and recognition for faces and names. *Journal of Applied Psychology*, 1934, *18*, 757–763.

Cofer, C. N. Recall of verbal materials after a four-year interval. *Journal of General Psychology*, 1943, *29*, 155–156.

Craik, F. I. M. Age differences in recognition memory. *Quarterly Journal of Experimental Psychology*, 1971, *23*, 316–323.

Craik, F. I. M., & Lockhart, R. S. Levels of processing: A framework for memory research. *Journal of Verbal Learning and Verbal Behavior*, 1972, *11*, 671–684.

Dixon, W. J. (Ed.). *Biomedical Computer Programs*. Berkeley and Los Angeles: University of California Press, 1967.

Frost, N. Encoding and retrieval in visual memory tasks. *Journal of Experimental Psychology*, 1972, *45*, 317–326.

Gates, A. I. Experiment on the relative efficiency of men and women in memory and reasoning. *Psychological Review*, 1917, *24*, 139–146.

Hanawalt, N. G. Memory traces for figures in recall and recognition. *Archives of Psychology*, 1937, *31*, No. 216.

Kaess, W. A., & Witryol, S. L. Memory for names and faces: A characteristic of social intelligence? *Journal of Applied Psychology*, 1955, *39*, 457–462.

Keppel, G. Facilitation in short- and long-term retention of paired associates following distributed practice in learning. *Journal of Verbal Learning and Verbal Behavior*, 1964, *3*, 91–111.

Krueger, W. C. F. The effect of overlearning on retention. *Journal of Experimental Psychology*, 1929, *12*, 71–81.

Luh, C. W. The conditions of retention. *Psychological Monographs*, 1922, *31* (3, Whole No. 142) .

Malpass, R. S., & Kravitz, J. Recognition for faces of own and other race. *Journal of Personality and Social Psychology*, 1969, *13*, 330–334.

McGuire, W. J. A multiprocess model for paired-associate learning. *Journal of Experimental Psychology*, 1961, *62*, 335–347.

Melton, A. W. Implications of short-term memory for a general theory of memory. *Journal of Verbal Learning and Verbal Behavior*, 1963, *2*, 1–21.

Postman, L., & Rau, L. Retention as a function of the method of measurement. *University of California Publications in Psychology*, 1957, *8*, 217–270.

Schonfield, D., & Robertson, G. Memory storage and aging. *Canadian Journal of Psychology*, 1966, *20*, 228–236.

Schulman, A. I. Memory for words recently classified. *Memory & Cognition*, 1974, *2*, 47–52.

Shepard, R. N. Recognition memory for words, sentences and pictures. *Journal of Verbal Learning and Verbal Behavior*, 1967, *6*, 156–163.

Smith, M. E. Delayed recall of previously memorized material after forty years. *Journal of Genetic Psychology*, 1951, *79*, 337–338.

Terman, L. M., & Oden, M. H. *The gifted child grows up.* Stanford, Calif.: Stanford University Press, 1947.

Titchener, E. B. Relearning after 48 years. *American Journal of Psychology*, 1923, *34*, 468–469.

Tulving, E., & Pearlstone, Z. Availability versus accessibility of information in memory for words. *Journal of Verbal Learning and Verbal Behavior*, 1966, *5*, 381–391.

Underwood, B. J. Degree of learning and the measurement of forgetting. *Journal of Verbal Learning and Verbal Behavior*, 1964, *3*, 112–129.

Underwood, B. J., Keppel, G., & Schulz, R. W. Studies of distributed practice: XXII. Some conditions which enhance retention. *Journal of Experimental Psychology*, 1962, *64*, 355–363.

Underwood, B. J., & Schulz, R. W. *Meaningfulness and verbal learning.* Philadelphia: Lippincott, 1960.

Van Zooneveld, R. J. An orientation study of the memory of old people. *Geriatrics*, 1958, *13*, 532–534.

Woodrow, H. Interrelations of measures of learning. *Journal of Psychology*, 1940, *10*, 49–73.

Worcester, D. A. Learning ability and retention after long periods. *Journal of Educational Psychology*, 1957, *48*, 505–509.

POSTSCRIPT

As is appropriate for a study in a relatively unexplored area, this article is basically descriptive. Rather than proposing and testing an explicit theory of cognitive processes or structure, it explores the application of a methodology—the cross-sectional approach—to an area that we know little about, very long-term memory. Since this article was written, Bahrick and his colleagues have examined very long-term memories for the layout of a city (Bahrick,

1983), a language learned in high school (Bahrick, 1984c), and high school algebra and geometry (Bahrick & Hall, 1991). Because schooling in a language or math is a matter of deliberate instruction and frequent assessment, it is possible to identify (within broad limits) the knowledge subjects had at the end of the acquisition period—this isn't the case with the informal learning of names and faces. Thus Bahrick (1984c) was able to determine that there is considerable loss during the first 3 to 6 years after acquisition, but that what information remains at the end of that period tends to remain stable for at least the next 25 to 50 years, even if it is rarely rehearsed during that interval.

Bahrick (1984c) suggests using the term *permastore* to refer to such semi-permanent memories. He found that the amount of information in permastore is a function of level of initial learning: those who earn higher grades and/or who take more courses retain a greater proportion of their original learning. This means that people who learn something better and/or over a longer period not only have more to remember, they remember more of what they have to remember (Bahrick & Hall, 1991). This probably explains why, in a study of college professors' memory for their students' names and faces, Bahrick (1984b) found that after eight years professors do *not* remember students as well as students remember classmates. The students whose names and faces professors tried to remember had taken only one 3-times-a-week, 10-week course from the professor being tested, and the kinds of interactions that students and professors have are much more limited than those students have with one another. However, this latter study allowed Bahrick to separate the effects of the age of the memory and the age of the rememberer. At least among the 36- to 75-year-olds that he investigated, age of the rememberer did not much matter.

In his comments on Bahrick's work, Neisser (1984) stressed that although we may talk about information being "in" permastore, we need to be careful not to regard permastore as a separate memory structure; it is simply a description of the fact that certain memories are not forgotten for a long time. Furthermore, Neisser claimed that the reason such memories survive is not because they are unusually persistent in their original form. Instead, Neisser argued that we are more likely to be able to reconstruct those memories because, when we learn a lot of information over a period of time, we build up a rich, interconnected network of knowledge called a schema (see the Introduction to Reading 32). Isolated pieces of information tend to be difficult to reconstruct. Although Bahrick agrees that reconstruction from a rich network takes place, he suggests that the strength of individual associations is also likely to play a role in achieving permastore status (Bahrick, 1984a; Bahrick & Hall, 1991). However, the contributions of different factors to very long-term remembering remain to be specified.

FOR FURTHER THOUGHT

1. Why did Bahrick and his colleagues give all subjects the free-recall test first and the questionnaire last and mix up the order of presentation of the other five tests in between?

2. In constructing the stimulus sets for the picture recognition test, Bahrick and his colleagues were careful that people in minority groups appeared among the foils in the same proportions as they did in the subject's class. Why was this important?

3. In the recognition and matching tests, Bahrick and his associates had subjects make a guess if they had not answered by the end of a predetermined time period. What are the advantages and disadvantages of this technique? What other measurements did the authors take to mitigate some of its disadvantages?

4. In scoring their free recall results, Bahrick and his colleagues did not eliminate intrusion errors. What are intrusion errors, and on what grounds do the authors justify their inclusion? The authors also say that the definition of intrusion errors in this case would be somewhat arbitrary. What makes it so?

5. Explain the authors' argument for treating the performance of Group 1 as a measure of original learning, given that Group 1 averaged 3.26 months since graduation.

6. On what grounds do Bahrick and his colleagues conclude that people must be able to recognize the faces of about 90% of their high school graduating classmates?

7. In general, performance on all tests remains relatively constant for all groups except Group 9. What specific impairment might there be for this group?

8. Unlike most memory experiments, Bahrick and his associates' study showed a wide discrepancy between recognition and recall performance. How do these researchers explain this difference?

9. What evidence might suggest that subjects' memory of classmates is, at least to a certain extent, organized by the sex of those classmates? What alternative to organization by sex might also and perhaps more plausibly explain this evidence?

REFERENCES

Bahrick, H. P. (1983). The cognitive map of a city: Fifty years of learning and memory. In G. H. Bower (Ed.), *The psychology of learning and motivation, Vol. 17* (pp. 125–164). New York: Academic Press.

Bahrick, H. P. (1984a). Associations and organization in cognitive psychology: A reply to Neisser. *Journal of Experimental Psychology: General, 113,* 36–37.

Bahrick, H. P. (1984b). Memory for people. In J. E. Harris & P. E. Morris (Eds.), *Everyday memory, actions, and absent-mindedness* (pp. 19–34). New York: Academic Press.

Bahrick, H. P. (1984c). Semantic memory content in permastore: Fifty years of memory for Spanish learned in school. *Journal of Experimental Psychology: General, 113,* 1–29.

Bahrick, H. P., & Hall, L. K. (1991). Lifetime maintenance of high school mathematics content. *Journal of Experimental Psychology: General, 120,* 20–33.

Neisser, U. (1984). Interpreting Harry Bahrick's discovery: What confers immunity against forgetting? *Journal of Experimental Psychology: General, 113,* 32–35.

INTRODUCTION

A striking and common experience is having a vivid memory of some surprising, emotion-laden, or consequential event such as the civil unrest in Los Angeles following the acquittal of the defendants in the original Rodney King trial. This experience has been called a flashbulb memory. Continuing the metaphor, some researchers have suggested that it's almost as if a special memory mechanism exists to take a snapshot of the contents of our awareness when such events occur. This possibility is examined in Michael McCloskey, Cynthia Wible, and Neal Cohen's article "Is There a Special Flashbulb-Memory Mechanism?" (A short discussion of a possible conceptual problem with the notion of flashbulb memories has been excluded in this reading.)

Do you remember the circumstances under which you heard about some surprising and consequential event? Would you say that, compared to memories of ordinary everyday events, it is especially complete, accurate, vivid, and resistant to forgetting? As you read this article, ask yourself how you could go about deciding whether such memories are more like snapshots than ordinary memories.

Is There a Special Flashbulb-Memory Mechanism?

Michael McCloskey, Cynthia G. Wible, and Neal J. Cohen

Johns Hopkins University

Where were you when you learned of the assassination of John F. Kennedy, the shooting of Ronald Reagan, or the explosion of the space shuttle *Challenger*? How did you hear about the event? What were you doing at the time? What were your first thoughts upon hearing the news? Many people report that they can remember vividly the circumstances in which they learned of certain major public or personal events, a feat of memory that has intrigued researchers since at least the turn of the century (e.g., Brewer, 1986; Brown & Kulik, 1977; Colegrove, 1899; Linton, 1975; Neisser, 1982, 1986a, 1986b; Pillemer, 1984; Rubin & Kozin, 1984; Thompson & Cowan, 1986; Winograd & Killinger, 1983; Yarmey & Bull, 1978).

Brown and Kulik (1977) suggested that this phenomenon, which they labeled *flashbulb memory*, implies the existence of a special memory mechanism. They argued that the special mechanism, when triggered by an event exceeding criterial levels of surprise and "consequentiality," creates a permanent record of the contents of awareness for the period immediately surrounding the shocking experience. The special-mechanism hypothesis has been the subject of considerable discussion in recent years, with some authors endorsing the hypothesis and others noting potential problems. Pillemer (1984), for example, argued in favor of the hypothesis on the basis of data concerning subjects' recollections of the circumstances in which they learned about the assassination attempt on President Reagan. In contrast, Neisser (1982) raised doubts about the accuracy of flashbulb memories, and also pointed out problems with several other aspects of the Brown and Kulik hypothesis. Furthermore, Rubin and Kozin (1984) questioned whether the characteristics of flashbulb memories clearly set these memories apart from other autobiographical memories.

Although a number of important issues have been raised, it remains unclear whether the flashbulb-memory phenomenon warrants the postulation of a special flashbulb-memory mechanism. One reason is that no detailed, coherent formulation of a special-mechanism hypothesis has been set forth. The hypothesis as stated by Brown and Kulik (1977) and discussed in subsequent articles is underdeveloped in several crucial respects, and there is also considerable variation between and even within articles in what is claimed about the mechanism and the memories it produces. A related problem is that discussions of the special-mechanism hypothesis have often failed to engage the critical issue of what would constitute a sufficient basis for positing a special flashbulb-memory mechanism.

As a consequence of these problems, the implications of the evidence and arguments presented in studies of flashbulb memory have not always been clear. For example, Neisser (1982) reported two examples of inaccurate flashbulb memories in support of his argument that these memories are not necessarily veridical. Thompson and Cowan (1986), how-

We thank Roberta Goodman-Schulman, Kathi Hirsh, Brenda Rapp, Scott Sokol, and Molly Treadway for their helpful comments. We also thank the Cognitive Lunch group for an illuminating discussion.

Correspondence concerning this article should be addressed to Michael McCloskey, Cognitive Science Center, Johns Hopkins University, Baltimore, Maryland 21218.

SOURCE: *Journal of Experimental Psychology: General, 117*(2), 1988, pp. 171–181. Copyright 1988 by the American Psychological Association. Reprinted by permission.

ever, presented evidence that for one of Neisser's examples the inaccuracy is relatively minor, and concluded that this example does not challenge the "basic accuracy of flashbulb memories" (p. 200). Neisser (1986b), in a reply to Thompson and Cowan, disagreed with their conclusions. Unfortunately, the exchange fails to clarify what implications any particular degree of inaccuracy has for the special-mechanism hypothesis. Do a few examples of minor inaccuracy call the hypothesis into serious question? Or does the hypothesis remain unchallenged if the accounts are usually "basically accurate"?

In this article we attempt to evaluate the special-mechanism hypothesis systematically and, more generally, to assess the implications of the flashbulb-memory phenomenon for theories of memory. On the basis of data and arguments, we conclude that the postulation of a special flashbulb-memory mechanism is unwarranted. Instead, we suggest, flashbulb memories[1] should be viewed as products of "ordinary" autobiographical memory mechanisms, and hence as phenomena that may offer insights into the nature of these mechanisms.

THE SPECIAL-MECHANISM HYPOTHESIS

Underlying the hypothesis of a special flashbulb-memory mechanism is the following implicit argument: Flashbulb memories have special characteristics, that is, characteristics different from those the memories would have if they were produced by "ordinary" memory mechanisms. These special characteristics imply that the memories are products of a special memory mechanism.

Thus, in evaluating the special-mechanism hypothesis, we must consider the following questions: What claims does the hypothesis make about the

characteristics of flashbulb memories? To what extent are these claims warranted by the available evidence? And, if these claims are accepted, do they clearly distinguish flashbulb memories from "ordinary" memories and therefore warrant the postulation of a special flashbulb-memory mechanism?

CHARACTERISTICS OF FLASHBULB MEMORIES

Statements of the special-mechanism hypothesis are not entirely clear with regard to the characteristics of flashbulb memories, at times pressing strong claims while at other times qualifying these claims. As a starting point for discussion, we will consider one particular interpretation of the Brown and Kulik (1977) hypothesis, an interpretation that makes strong claims about the characteristics of flashbulb memories. On this rendering the special flashbulb-memory mechanism, when triggered by criterial levels of surprise and consequentiality, creates in memory a detailed and permanent record of the individual's experience immediately before, during, and immediately after learning of the shocking event. (Brown and Kulik, 1977, p. 87, stated that the mechanism records all "brain events above some level of organization," apparently meaning something like the contents of awareness, including such information as where the individual was, what he or she was doing, etc.) The representations created by the special mechanism are complete, accurate, vivid, and immune to forgetting (i.e., the stored information, in its original veridical form, remains permanently accessible).

One could certainly formulate weaker interpretations of Brown and Kulik's (1977) position (e.g., flashbulb memories are impressively, although not perfectly, complete, accurate, vivid, and resistant to forgetting). However, we consider the strong claims first because these claims, if supportable, would make the most convincing case for the position that flashbulb memories are so remarkable that a special memory mechanism must be posited to account for them. If the strong claims prove untenable, we can then consider whether weaker claims

---

[1]We will use the term *flashbulb memory* in a theoretically neutral sense, to refer to individuals' recollections of the circumstances in which they learned about surprising and consequential events. It should be understood that our use of this term does not imply anything about the memory processes underlying the recollections.

motivate the postulation of a special flashbulb-memory mechanism.[2]

We begin our evaluation of the strong claims about characteristics of flashbulb memories by reporting a study aimed at evaluating these claims.

FLASHBULB MEMORIES FOR THE EXPLOSION OF THE SPACE SHUTTLE

With one exception (Pillemer, 1984), studies of flashbulb memories (Brown & Kulik, 1977; Colegrove, 1899; Winograd & Killinger, 1983; Yarmey & Bull, 1978) have probed subjects' memories for the circumstances in which they learned of an event only once, long after the event. Yet, as Neisser (1982) has pointed out, this procedure does not permit the accuracy of the subjects' reports to be assessed. Moreover, it is difficult to determine whether the amount of remembered information remains constant over time, as it should if flashbulb memories are immune to forgetting, or whether subjects' memories instead become less detailed and complete as time passes.

Potentially more informative is a procedure in which subjects are questioned twice, once shortly after a surprising, consequential event, and again some time later, as in Pillemer's (1984) study concerning the Reagan assassination attempt. The two sets of responses may then be compared with regard to amount and consistency of information reported on the two occasions. The explosion of the space shuttle

Challenger on January 28, 1986, tragically provided the opportunity to carry out a study of this sort. The flight of *Challenger* was highly publicized because the crew included the teacher Christa McAuliffe. Furthermore, the explosion was completely unexpected and had important consequences for the space program and, more generally, for public confidence in government, science, and technology. Thus, with regard to surprise and consequentiality, the presumed triggering conditions for the special flashbulb-memory mechanism, the shuttle explosion appears comparable to the events used in previous studies of flashbulb memory (e.g., the Reagan assassination attempt, assassinations of other political leaders). Indeed, the disaster was widely described in the media as one of those events for which people remember where they were and what they were doing when they learned of it. In the present study we probed subjects' memory for circumstances of learning about the shuttle explosion a few days after the explosion, and again 9 months later.

Method

Questionnaire.   The questionnaire presented to subjects included four questions about the circumstances under which the respondent learned of the explosion of the space shuttle *Challenger:*

1. Where were you when you first learned of the explosion?
2. What were you doing when you first learned of the explosion?
3. Did you see the event at the time it was actually happening, or did you learn about it later? If later, how did you learn about it?
4. What were your first thoughts upon hearing the news?

We will refer to these items collectively as the circumstances questions, and individually as the location, activity, source, and reaction questions, respectively. For each question subjects were asked to rate their confidence in the correctness of their answers on a scale from 1 *(low confidence)* to 7 *(high confidence).*

The four circumstances questions were intended to probe categories of information that should be included in memories generated by a mechanism that

---

[2]It might be suggested that the strong claims we have formulated about characteristics of flashbulb memories are stronger than Brown and Kulik (1977) intended. For example, whereas the strong claims characterize flashbulb memories as complete records of the individual's experience around the time of learning about a surprising, consequential event, Brown and Kulik (1977, pp. 74–75, 85) stated that flashbulb memories vary in "elaboration," suggesting that under some circumstances these memories could be less than complete. However, Brown and Kulik also repeatedly assert (e.g., see Brown & Kulik, 1977, pp. 76, 95–96) that the flashbulb-memory mechanism records all recent brain events. Thus, potential conflicts between the strong claims we have formulated and statements made by Brown and Kulik reflect ambiguities in their claims. In any event, regardless of what Brown and Kulik intended, it is important to consider strong claims about characteristics of flashbulb memories because, as stated earlier, these claims would provide the firmest basis for asserting that flashbulb memories are very different from ordinary memories.

records the contents of awareness for the period immediately surrounding the learning about a surprising, consequential event. Previous studies have focused on six "canonical categories" of information: place, ongoing event, information, own affect, affect in others, and aftermath (see, e.g., Brown & Kulik, 1977; Pillemer, 1984). Our location, activity, and source questions closely correspond to the first three of these categories, respectively, and our reaction question corresponds roughly to the own affect category. We did not probe affect in others or aftermath, because information in these categories may not always be available to be recorded, at least within the span of time over which a special flashbulb-memory mechanism would operate. For example, a person who heard a radio announcement about the shuttle explosion while alone might have no experience of affect in others to remember.

The questionnaire also included a single question about the respondent's memory for his or her whereabouts at the time of the assassination attempt on President Reagan.

These five critical questions (the four shuttle circumstances questions and the single question about the Reagan assassination attempt) occurred in identical form on both the initial and 9-month questionnaires. Instructions on both questionnaires stressed that answers should be as specific as possible.

Both questionnaires also included several additional questions, most of which concerned the sources from which the respondent obtained information about the shuttle disaster subsequent to initially learning about it, and the details of the shuttle flight itself. The results for these questions are not relevant for our purposes and therefore will not be discussed.

Design and procedure. On January 31, 1986, three days after the explosion, questionnaires were distributed to 50 faculty, postdoctoral fellows, graduate students, undergraduate students, and support staff associated with the Psychology Department of Johns Hopkins University. Forty-five of these "immediate" questionnaires (90%) were returned within 1 week of the shuttle disaster.

On October 21, 1986, approximately 9 months after the explosion, follow-up questionnaires were distributed to the 29 subjects who (a) had returned the immediate questionnaire within 1 week of the explosion and (b) were still available at the time of the follow-up. Twenty-seven subjects (93%) completed the 9-month questionnaire. These subjects will be referred to as the *repeated testing* group.

To assess effects of completing the immediate questionnaire on responses given at 9 months, the 9-month questionnaire was also distributed to 35 individuals who had not received the immediate questionnaire. Thirty-one (89%) completed the questionnaire. These subjects will be referred to as the *9-month-only* group.

Results

Answers to the location, activity, source, and reaction questions were first scored simply as substantive or "don't remember" responses. A response was scored as substantive if it provided an answer to the question, even if the response was not highly specific. For example, "at work" as well as "Levering Hall next to the news stand" was scored as a substantive answer to the location question. This scoring criterion appears to be consistent with those used in previous studies (e.g., Brown & Kulik, 1977; Pillemer, 1984) to assess whether a subject provided information in a canonical category. Because some subjects reported information relevant to one of the circumstances questions in an answer to another of these questions, the scoring for each question took account of any relevant information the subject provided in answers to other questions.

Nine-month responses. Table 1 presents, for the repeated testing subjects on the immediate and 9-month questionnaires, and for the 9-month-only subjects on the 9-month questionnaire, the proportion of subjects who offered substantive responses to each of the circumstances questions. From the 9-month results, it is clear that the explosion of *Challenger* is an event for which the flashbulb-memory phenomenon occurs: 9 months after the shuttle explosion most subjects could provide reports concerning where they were, what they were doing, how they heard, and how they reacted when they learned of the disaster.

TABLE 1   Proportion of Repeated Testing and 9-Month-Only Subjects Providing Substantive Responses to the Circumstances Questions on the Immediate and 9-Month Questionnaires

| | Repeated Testing | | 9-Month Only |
Question	Immediate Questionnaire	9-Month Questionnaire	9-Month Questionnaire
Location	1.00	.96	.94
Activity	1.00	.89	.87
Source	1.00	1.00	1.00
Reaction	.96	.89	.97
M	.99	.94	.94

All subjects in both groups gave substantive answers to at least two of the four questions; 22 of the 27 repeated-testing subjects (81%) and 26 of the 31 9-month-only subjects (84%) gave substantive responses to all four questions. Subjects were also highly confident about their responses. Across the four circumstances questions, mean confidence for substantive answers was 6.13 (on a scale with 7 as the highest confidence level) for the repeated-testing group, and 6.16 for the 9-month-only group.

Brown and Kulik (1977) scored a subject as having a flashbulb memory for an event if the subject (a) answered "yes" to the question, "Do you recall the circumstances in which you first heard that [event]?", and (b) provided information in at least one of the six canonical information categories in reporting these circumstances. Assuming that any subject who gave a substantive response to one or more of our circumstances questions would have given a "yes" answer to a question of the form "Do you recall the circumstances in which you first heard that the space shuttle *Challenger* had exploded?", then by the Brown and Kulik criteria all of our repeated-testing and 9-month-only subjects have flashbulb memories for the space shuttle explosion.

Comparison of the 9-month results for the repeated-testing group and the 9-month-only group suggests that completing the immediate questionnaire had little if any effect on the 9-month responses of the repeated-testing group. The mean number of questions answered substantively was 3.74 (out of 4)

for the repeated-testing group and 3.77 for the 9-month-only group, $t < 1$. Furthermore, confidence did not differ across groups (see earlier results on confidence levels).

Comparison of immediate and 9-month responses. The 9-month results paint a seemingly impressive picture of subjects' ability to remember the circumstances in which they learned of the shuttle explosion. However, comparison of the 9-month responses with those given shortly after the explosion reveals that the amount of stored information subjects could access decreased over the retention interval, and further that the immediate and 9-month responses were not always consistent.

For each of the 107 circumstances questions answered substantively on the immediate questionnaire (27 subjects times 4 circumstances questions, minus a single reaction question answered "don't remember"), two independent judges compared the immediate response with the corresponding 9-month response.

A 9-month response was scored as the *same* as the corresponding immediate response if it provided basically the same information (although not necessarily in the same wording). A relatively lax criterion was applied, so that, for example, the responses "reading" and "studying" to the activity question were scored as the same.

A 9-month response was scored as *more specific* than the immediate response if it was not inconsistent with the immediate response, but answered the question at a finer level of detail, or included particular pieces of information not reported on the immediate questionnaire. For example, the 9-month response "eating lunch (actually, drinking coffee) with S_____ S_____, S_____ D_____, and M_____ M_____" to the activity question was scored as more specific than the immediate response "eating lunch with some friends."

Similarly, a 9-month response was scored as *more general* than the corresponding immediate response if it was not inconsistent with the immediate response, but was less specific, or omitted particular details. For example, the 9-month response "word of mouth" was scored as more general than the immediate response "heard C_____ talking about it."

A 9-month response was scored as *inconsistent* if it contradicted the corresponding immediate response in some (although not necessarily all) respects. For example, the 9-month response "at my desk" to the location question was scored as inconsistent with the immediate response "walking out of the door toward B_____'s office."

Finally, a 9-month response was scored as *don't remember* if the question was answered substantively on the immediate questionnaire but given a "don't remember" response on the 9-month questionnaire.

The two judges agreed on 86% of the initial classification decisions. Disagreements were resolved through discussion. For some ambiguous responses, the subject was consulted for clarification. For example, one subject indicated that the 9-month response "examining some data for an experiment" did not refer to the same activity as the immediate response "designing an experiment." Table 2 presents for each of the four circumstances questions the number of responses falling into each of the scoring categories.

Although there is considerable consistency over the 9-month retention interval, there is also substantial evidence of forgetting and inaccuracy. First, the data for "don't remember" responses clearly reveal forgetting over the retention interval. On the immediate questionnaire, 26 of the 27 repeated-testing subjects provided a substantive answer to all four circumstances questions, and the remaining subject gave a substantive response to three of the four questions. On the 9-month questionnaire, however, 4 of the 27 subjects (15.4%) gave "don't remember" responses to a total of 6 questions they had answered substantively on the immediate questionnaire.

Further evidence of forgetting may be found by comparing the frequency of more specific and more general responses. If the accessible information remains constant over time, there should be no systematic difference between the immediate and 9-month questionnaires in specificity of responses. That is, although corresponding immediate and 9-month responses may occasionally vary in specificity due to variation in subjects' decisions about how much of the accessible information to report, we would expect the number of responses that became more specific at 9 months to be approximately the same as the number that became more general. On the other hand, if the amount of accessible information decreased over the interval between questionnaires, we might expect a systematic shift toward more general responses on the 9-month questionnaire. This is just what we found. Whereas only 7 responses became more specific, 20 became more general ($p < .01$ by binomial test).

Finally, subjects' confidence ratings provide additional suggestive, although by no means definitive, evidence of forgetting: Confidence in substantive answers declined over the retention interval, with a mean across the four circumstances questions of 6.84 on the immediate questionnaire, and 6.13 on the 9-month questionnaire, $t(26) = 2.84, p < .01$.

The comparison of immediate and 9-month responses also revealed a number of inconsistencies. On the 9-month questionnaire, 7 of the 27 repeated-testing subjects (25.9%) gave a total of 9 responses (8.4% of the 107 total responses) that were inconsistent with the corresponding immediate responses. For example, one subject reported on the immediate questionnaire that she learned of the explosion when "my

TABLE 2   Comparison of Immediate and 9-Month Responses for Repeated-Testing Subjects

| | Relationship of 9-Month Response to Immediate Response | | | | |
Question	Same	More Specific	More General	Inconsistent	Don't Remember
Location	21	1	2	2	1
Activity	15	1	4	4	3
Source	16	3	7	1	0
Reaction	13	2	7	2	2
Total	65	7	20	9	6

husband telephoned me to ask if I saw it," but stated on the 9-month questionnaire that "I did not see the actual launch but a little while after the explosion the TV news made a statement concerning the shuttle." (See the discussion of scoring for two other examples of inconsistency.)

Subjects were often quite confident about their inconsistent 9-month responses; these responses clearly were not offered as guesses. Three of the 9 inconsistent responses were given with confidence ratings of 7, and the mean over the 9 responses was 5.22. Confidence in incorrect recollections was also apparent when we interviewed subjects to determine whether apparently inconsistent responses were in fact inconsistent. For example, the subject who reported his ongoing activity as "designing an experiment" on the immediate questionnaire but as "examining some data for an experiment" on the 9-month questionnaire was asked 16 months after the shuttle explosion what he was doing when he learned of the explosion. No information about his previous responses was given. The subject replied that he remembered vividly sitting at his desk looking at the data from an experiment. Shown his initial response, he was surprised, and confirmed that his current memory was inconsistent with his original report.

Although the 9-month responses scored as inconsistent were clearly discrepant with the corresponding immediate responses, none were grossly incongruent.[3] Thus, the inconsistencies do not imply that flashbulb memories are often complete confabulations, but instead suggest that these memories are subject to the same sorts of reconstructive errors that

seem to occur frequently for "ordinary" memories. That is, for flashbulb memories, as for other memories, inaccuracies may be introduced when information that cannot be retrieved from memory is filled in through inference or guesswork. Further, the reconstructed information may be stored in memory and recalled (perhaps with high confidence) on subsequent occasions.

In using subjects' immediate responses as the standard for assessing the accuracy of the 9-month responses, we are assuming that the immediate responses are accurate. Of course, this may not always be the case, given that the "immediate" questionnaires were completed between 3 and 7 days after the explosion. However, the risk we take in assuming that the immediate reports are accurate is one of underestimating the amount of inaccuracy at nine months: If immediate reports are sometimes inaccurate, then some 9-month reports that are the same as the corresponding immediate reports may be inaccurate.

More generally, our results should probably be viewed as placing a lower bound on the amount of forgetting and inaccuracy that occurred over the 9-month period following the shuttle explosion. In addition to the possibility that some of the immediate reports are inaccurate, it is possible that some of the responses that became more specific on the 9-month questionnaire did so through the importation of inaccurate information. Furthermore, when subjects give consistent but rather general responses on both occasions, these responses may conceal forgetting and inaccuracy. For example, if a subject reports on both questionnaires that he was walking to class with some friends when he learned of the shuttle explosion, we have no way of knowing whether he had the same particular friends in mind both times, or whether he even remembers who the friends were.

These points were brought home to us with some force when we described our study at an informal seminar attended by several of the individuals who had served as subjects. A discussion ensued about the particular flashbulb memories of some of the seminar participants, in the course of which it became apparent that the memories of our subjects, as well as those of other individuals who did not participate in the experiment, were often rather vague, and

---

[3]Similarly, Neisser's inaccurate memory for learning of the attack on Pearl Harbor is apparently not grossly inaccurate: Neisser recalls that he was listening to a baseball game on the radio, when in fact he was probably listening to a football game (see Neisser, 1982, 1986b; Thompson & Cowan, 1986). Linton (1975) describes another example of an inaccurate flashbulb memory, in which an acquaintance reported that Linton was the source of his information about the assassination of President Kennedy, when according to documentary evidence (and Linton's own memories), Linton was elsewhere at the time. However, no information is available about the circumstances in which Linton's acquaintance actually learned of the Kennedy assassination, and thus we have no way of knowing to what extent the memory was inaccurate.

frequently inconsistent with one another. (In the following account names have been changed to protect the forgetful.) Susan, one of the repeated-testing subjects, reported on the immediate questionnaire that she was eating lunch with some friends in the university cafeteria when she learned of the explosion. On the 9-month questionnaire, she stated that she was eating lunch in the cafeteria with John, Beth, and Jennifer. Thus, her 9-month response was scored as more specific than her immediate response. However, Tim, who was not a subject in the experiment, stated at the seminar that he was eating with John when he learned of the explosion, but did not remember Susan, Beth, or Jennifer being there. Beth, contacted by telephone, stated that she was elsewhere at lunch that day.

John, questioned after the seminar, reported that he was eating lunch with Susan and a few other people when he learned of the explosion, but did not remember Tim being there. Furthermore, John initially did not think that Jennifer was present at the lunch, although he later conceded that she may have been. (John, a repeated-testing subject, did not list his luncheon companions on either questionnaire, and his immediate and 9-month activity responses were scored as the same.) Jennifer, who was not a subject in the experiment, reported that she did eat lunch with John that day, but did not remember Susan being there and instead believed that Phil and Roger were present. Phil, a repeated-testing subject, stated that he ate lunch in his office that day, and learned of the explosion from the radio. Roger, who was not a subject in the study, also reported that he does not remember eating lunch in the cafeteria on the day of the shuttle explosion, and stated that he learned of the explosion in the psychology building when someone told him. Roger further indicated that he believed David was the person who gave him the news, but Linda states that she is the one who informed Roger. Asked whether it could have been Linda who told him, Roger conceded the possibility but stated that he did not specifically remember her telling him. Clearly, these accounts are not entirely complete and consistent.

The final point to be made about the data from the shuttle circumstances questions is that the forgetting and inaccuracy apparent in these data were not limited to responses about which the subject was uncertain on the immediate questionnaire. If we restrict the analysis to the 89 responses for which the subject gave a confidence rating of 7 on the immediate questionnaire, the pattern of results is almost identical to that for the full set of responses: 55 (61.8%) same responses, 6 (6.7%) more specific responses, 17 (19.1%) more general responses, 8 (9.0%) inconsistent responses, and 3 (3.4%) don't remember responses.

The Reagan assassination attempt. In addition to asking about the circumstances in which subjects learned of the space shuttle explosion, we also asked a single question about subjects' memories for their whereabouts at the time of the Reagan assassination attempt. The assassination attempt occurred on March 30, 1981, roughly 5 years prior to the present study. For the repeated-testing group, 13 of the 27 subjects (48.2%) gave a substantive response on the immediate questionnaire; 15 (55.6%) responded substantively on the 9-month questionnaire. (Interestingly, 2 subjects gave a don't remember response on the initial questionnaire and a substantive response 9 months later.) For the 9-month-only group, 17 of the 31 subjects (54.8%) gave a substantive response. Finally, for the 18 subjects who completed the immediate questionnaire but not the 9-month questionnaire, 9 (50%) gave a substantive response.

These percentages are considerably lower than those obtained by Pillemer (1984) for subjects questioned 1 and 7 months after the Reagan assassination attempt. Pillemer (personal communication) found that 96% of the subjects (80 of 83) tested 1 month after the assassination attempt and 85% of the subjects (70 of 82) tested at 7 months could report where they were when they learned of the incident.

Note that whereas Pillemer's (1984) subjects were faculty at Wellesley College, our subjects were faculty, students, staff, and others associated with the Johns Hopkins Psychology Department. Perhaps, then, differences between the subjects in the two studies are responsible for the lower incidence of flashbulb memories in our study than in Pillemer's. However, examination of our data provides no support for this interpretation. Eight of our subjects were university faculty at the time of Pillemer's study in

1981, and hence may reasonably be considered comparable to Pillemer's subjects. Only three of these subjects—37.5%—could report their whereabouts at the time of the Reagan assassination attempt.

Of course, caution must be exercised in comparing absolute performance levels across studies. However, the difference between studies in the incidence of flashbulb memories is sufficiently large to suggest that between the time of Pillemer's (1984) study a few months after the assassination attempt on Reagan, and the time of our study approximately 5 years later, considerable forgetting of the circumstances of learning about the assassination attempt occurred. (Note also that Pillemer's data show a decline over the interval between the 1- and 7-month questionnaire in the percentage of subjects who could report their location at the time of the assassination attempt.) Thus, the assassination attempt data argue against the claim that flashbulb memories are immune to forgetting.[4]

Our results for the assassination attempt question also provide further evidence that flashbulb memories may be inaccurate. Of the 13 repeated-testing subjects who gave a substantive response to the question on both the immediate and 9-month questionnaires, 2 (15.4%) gave inconsistent responses. For example, on the immediate questionnaire one subject responded as follows:

> I was in the Department of Hearing and Speech Sciences, University of _____. Specifically I was either in

my office or giving a speech therapy session when told. However, I can really only picture myself in the videotape room watching the assassination attempt on one of the video TV's. (That actually seems like where I was when I first learned about it, but I know that in reality I was only watching it at that time because I had already heard about it and wanted to hear/see what happened.)

On the 9-month questionnaire, the subject gave a somewhat different answer:

> I was rewinding a speech therapy tape in the TV room at the Univ. of _____. I believe it was in the morning (9:30–10:30) and I was watching TV and saw the news flash right away after it happened.

The television report, which the subject initially said she saw after being told of the assassination attempt, is now remembered as the original source of the news. Interestingly, at the time of the initial account the watching of the television report was apparently the most vivid part of the subject's memory and seemed "like where I was when I first learned about it." Note also that the second report corresponds more closely than the first to the stereotype of a flashbulb memory: The later account is more detailed and less tentative.

The subject was questioned again in June 1987, 8 months after completing the 9-month questionnaire. At this time she provided an account very similar to her 9-month report. When she was then informed of her previous accounts, she stated that she thought her initial report—that someone else told her of the assassination attempt—was incorrect, because she was the one who told everyone else. She also provided additional details, stating that she was in the TV room preparing to videotape an upcoming session with a client. Further, she said, she clearly remembered the client, a 12-year-old boy with a fluency disorder whom she always saw on Wednesdays. However, reference to a calendar indicated that Reagan was shot on a Monday. Furthermore, a check of speech therapy records revealed that whereas the assassination attempt occurred in the spring of 1981, the client our subject clearly remembers working with on the day of the incident was someone she first met the following fall.

---

[4]In October, 1982, Rubin and Kozin (1984) asked college students whether they had flashbulb memory for several events, including the Reagan assassination attempt. Fifty percent reported a flashbulb memory for the assassination attempt. However, in Rubin and Kozin's study the subject was first given a definition of a flashbulb memory (e.g., "A flashbulb memory occurs when your brain 'takes a picture' of an event. You have particularly vivid memories of these events long after they occur. You tend to remember your surroundings in exceptional detail"; Rubin & Kozin, 1984, p. 85), and was then asked for each of the events whether his or her memory for the event was a flashbulb memory. Thus, the Rubin and Kozin procedure defines a much higher criterion than our procedure, or that of Pillemer (1984). Presumably, to report a flashbulb memory for the Reagan assassination attempt, a subject in Rubin and Kozin's study not only had to remember the circumstances in which he or she learned of the event, but had to remember these circumstances vividly and in exceptional detail. Consequently, Rubin and Kozin's results cannot be compared directly with either our results or Pillemer's.

Discussion

In probing subjects' memories for the circumstances of learning about the space shuttle explosion and the Reagan assassination attempt, our principal aim was to assess the strong claims that flashbulb memories are complete, accurate, vivid, and immune to forgetting. In the following sections we discuss these claims in light of our results and the results of previous studies.

Accuracy and immunity to forgetting. Our data clearly indicate that flashbulb memories are neither uniformly accurate nor immune to forgetting. The results suggest that like other memories, memories for the circumstances of learning about a surprising, consequential event are subject to reconstructive errors, and to a decline over time in the amount of information that can be retrieved from memory.

In contrast, most previous studies of flashbulb memory (e.g., Brown & Kulik, 1977; Colegrove, 1899; Pillemer, 1984; Yarmey & Bull, 1978) have emphasized the longevity of the memories, and have assumed that they are accurate. However, the procedures used in these studies were simply not adequate to detect forgetting and inaccuracy. With the exception of Pillemer's (1984) study, previous flashbulb memory studies have probed subjects' memories only once, long after the event or events of interest. These studies have found that high proportions of subjects can report at least some information about the circumstances in which they learned of surprising, consequential events. This finding, which constitutes the major empirical basis for claims about the characteristics of flashbulb memories, was also obtained in the present study: Nine months after the space shuttle explosion, all of our subjects could report some information about the circumstances in which they learned of the event. However, the ability of subjects to report at least some information about the circumstances of learning about an event does not demonstrate that their memories for these circumstances are immune to forgetting; whatever information subjects report on a questionnaire may be far less than they could have reported at an earlier time. This is especially true when, as we found (see also Pillemer, 1984, p. 71), subjects' reports are often vague and general. Furthermore, as Neisser (1982) has argued, and our

findings amply illustrate, the ability of subjects to provide accounts of the circumstances in which they learned of surprising, consequential events does not ensure that these accounts are accurate.

Pillemer questioned subjects twice about the assassination attempt on Reagan, 1 month and 7 months after the event. He reported a high incidence of flashbulb memories, and emphasized that subjects' reports were quite consistent over the 6-month interval between questionnaires. However, Pillemer's results are actually quite consistent with our findings, and support our conclusion that flashbulb memories are subject to forgetting and inaccuracy. With regard to forgetting, the percentage of subjects who responded "yes" when asked if they recalled the circumstances in which they learned of the assassination attempt declined over the 6-month interval between Pillemer's 1- and 7-month questionnaires. Furthermore, even among the subjects who responded "yes" on both questionnaires, the mean number of canonical informational categories and the mean number of words provided in free reports of recollections decreased over the interval between questionnaires, as did the mean number of substantive responses to specific questions concerning the canonical categories. With regard to inaccuracy, comparison of 1-month and 7-month responses to the six specific questions about canonical information categories revealed inconsistency for an average of 1.12 of the 6 responses per subject (19%).

Completeness. The strong claims about characteristics of flashbulb memories hold that the flashbulb-memory mechanism creates a detailed record of all material to which the individual was attending immediately before, during, and immediately after learning of the event in question. This claim is entirely without empirical support, in part because the criteria that researchers have used to classify a memory as a flashbulb memory are orders of magnitude weaker than the claim would appear to require. Typically, a subject is classified as having a flashbulb memory for an event if the subject answers "yes" to a question of the form, "Do you recall the circumstances in which you first heard of [event]?", and provides any information in at least one of the six canonical informational categories defined by Brown and Kulik (1977; i.e., place, ongoing event, informant, own affect, affect in others, aftermath). Even if we ignore problems associated with potential inaccuracy in subjects' reports, these criteria obviously fail to ensure that a memory classified as a flashbulb memory is a detailed record of the individual's conscious experience around the time of learning about the event in question. The subject is not required to report information in all of the categories (which in any event were not selected on the basis of an analysis of the sorts of information the posited mechanism should record), or to provide detailed information in any category. Thus, for example, a subject whose report of the circumstances in which she learned of the Kennedy assassination consisted solely of the statement "I was at work" (or perhaps even "I was in Baltimore"; see Winograd & Killinger, 1983) would be scored as having a flashbulb memory.

The weakness of the classification criteria might be of little consequence if subjects typically provided accounts that were far more detailed and complete than required to meet the criteria. However, this does not appear to be the case. In the Brown and Kulik (1977) study, for example, subjects gave free reports of their recollections about 10 different events. The mean number of informational categories per report ranged from 1.6 to 5.6 across the 10 events; for most events the mean was less than 3. Thus, subjects did not uniformly or even typically provide information in all six categories.

Even when subjects provide information in a category, the information may be very vague and general. For example, Pillemer (1984) noted that his subjects' substantive responses to questions about canonical information categories were often "short and unspecific" (Pillemer, 1984, p. 71). As discussed earlier this was also true in the present study. Thus, the available data provide no basis for the claim that memories for the circumstances of learning about surprising, consequential events preserve the contents of awareness for a period extending from shortly before to shortly after learning of the event.

Of course, vague, incomplete responses to questionnaire items do not necessarily imply vague, incomplete memories; subjects may not report all of the details they recall when writing answers to questionnaire items. However, this point in no way alters the fact that the completeness claim is entirely without empirical support. Furthermore, several observations suggest that incompleteness is a characteristic not merely of subjects' questionnaire reports but also of the information they can recall. First, the "don't remember" responses given by some of our subjects to specific questionnaire items (e.g., What were you doing when you first learned of the explosion?; see Table 2) cannot readily be explained in terms of mere failure to report remembered details. Furthermore, in the interviews we conducted to follow up ambiguous questionnaire responses and to pursue apparent inconsistencies in the seminar discussion of flashbulb memories for the shuttle explosion, we encountered numerous instances in which individuals failed to remember, or were uncertain about, various aspects of the circumstances of learning about the explosion of the space shuttle. Finally, it is clear to us that our own flashbulb memories for the shuttle explosion, although generally quite detailed, have significant gaps. For example, Michael McCloskey remembers learning of the explosion when two colleagues came into his office around lunchtime, but cannot recall what he was doing when they walked in, or even which of them told him the news. Neal Cohen recalls that he learned of the explosion when someone listening to the radio shouted out the news, but does not remember whether he saw the person who shouted, or only heard the voice. Further, although Cohen remembers speaking to some other people immediately after learning of the explosion, he cannot remember who they were. Many of our other flashbulb memories, especially those for less recent events, are considerably more fragmentary. Similarly, Brown and Kulik (1977, p. 75) describe lacunae in their flashbulb memories for the assassination of President Kennedy.

It might be suggested that gaps in individuals' recollections reflect forgetting, and not incompleteness in the originally created memories. However, from the perspective of the strong claims about the characteristics of flashbulb memories this would constitute a step from the frying pan into the fire: In the attempt to save the completeness claim, the claim of immunity to forgetting is sacrificed. Alternatively, it might be argued that details missing from flashbulb memories are details that simply were not among the contents of awareness at the time of learning about the event in question, and so were never recorded by the special flashbulb memory mechanism. However, this argument is thoroughly unpersuasive; for example, it is hard to argue that McCloskey was unaware of which of his two colleagues told him of the shuttle explosion, or that Cohen was unaware of the identities of the people to whom he spoke just after learning of the explosion. Thus, the claim that flashbulb memories preserve a complete representation of the contents of awareness around the time of learning about a surprising, consequential event is not only unsupported, but in fact difficult to maintain in the face of the available evidence.

Vividness.   Most discussions of flashbulb memory repeatedly emphasize that these memories are exceptionally vivid (e.g., Brown & Kulik, 1978; Pillemer, 1984; Winograd & Killinger, 1983; Yarmey & Bull, 1978). For example, Brown and Kulik (1977) suggested that flashbulb memories for President Kennedy's assassination almost always have "a primary, 'live' quality that is almost perceptual" (p. 74). Hence, vividness has been treated as another attribute that distinguishes flashbulb memories from memories produced by ordinary mechanisms. However, once again the available data fail to motivate this claim; the criteria used by researchers to classify memories as flashbulb memories have typically not included any requirement that the memories be vivid. Furthermore, Rubin and Kozin (1984) have found that memories involving surprising, consequential events are not often among those reported by subjects who are asked to describe their most vivid memories.

To summarize, we have shown that contrary to the strong claims of accuracy and immunity to forgetting, flashbulb memories are subject to inaccuracy and forgetting. Moreover, we have argued that claims of completeness and vividness are, at best, entirely without empirical support. We conclude, therefore, that the strong claims about characteristics of flashbulb memories cannot be offered as grounds for postulating a special flashbulb-memory mechanism.

A potential counterargument.   Our conclusions might be called into question on grounds that we have failed to separate the wheat from the chaff in our data. Specifically, it might be argued that the special flashbulb-memory mechanism does not "fire" for everyone at the time of learning about an event such as the space shuttle explosion or even the assassination of President Kennedy; for some individuals the crierial levels of surprise and consequentiality may not be achieved. Thus, the data on which our conclusions are based may constitute a mixture of some memories created by the special flashbulb-memory mechanism and some memories created by ordinary memory mechanisms. If this were the case, it would not be surprising that the data show some inaccuracies, gaps, and decreases over time in the amount of information that could be reported. These findings would simply reflect the fact that some subjects with memories created by ordinary memory mechanisms were mixed with subjects having complete, accurate, vivid, and permanent memories created by the special flashbulb-memory mechanism.

This "wheat versus chaff" argument does not stand up to scrutiny. First, simply to dismiss as products of ordinary memory mechanisms any memories that do not evidence the characteristics posited on the strong construal of the special-mechanism hypothesis serves only to render the claim that flashbulb memories have these characteristics entirely circular. The argument merits serious consideration only if criteria independent of claims about characteristics of flashbulb memories can be specified for distinguishing true flashbulb memories (i.e., memories created by the presumed special mechanism) from memories created by ordinary memory mechanisms. It might of course be suggested that flashbulb and ordinary memories could be distinguished by assessing for each individual subject whether the subject experienced high levels of surprise and consequentiality. However, it has not been demonstrated that assessments of surprise and consequentiality (or any other criteria) would in fact partition memories into two distinct classes, one made up of true flashbulb memories that are complete, accurate, and immune to forgetting, and the other of ordinary memories that evidence gaps, forgetting, and inaccuracy. In the absence of such a demonstration the wheat versus chaff argument represents, at best, a promissory note.[5]

A second problem is that the argument offers no response whatever to one of our two major points. We asserted not only that our results provide evidence against some of the strong claims about characteristics of flashbulb memories, but also that even the data usually taken as support for these claims fail to motivate them. Even if the present data (or, for that matter, any other data showing inaccuracy and forgetting) could be dismissed as reflecting memory representations created by ordinary memory mechanisms, the strong claims about characteristics of flashbulb memories would remain unsupported: One will search the flashbulb-memory literature in vain for data demonstrating completeness, accuracy, vividness, and immunity to forgetting for a single memory in a single individual.

WEAKER CLAIMS AS A BASIS FOR THE SPECIAL-MECHANISM HYPOTHESIS

Given that the strong claims about characteristics of flashbulb memories are untenable, we may ask whether postulation of a special mechanism can be

---

[5]There is some evidence to suggest that surprise and consequentiality are correlated with amount of information remembered. For example, Brown and Kulik (1977) found that the percentage of subjects classified as having a flashbulb memory for an event, and the number of canonical informational categories included in free reports, were correlated with rated consequentiality. Furthermore, Pillemer (1984) found that rated surprise (but not rated consequentiality) was correlated with the number of canonical information categories represented in subjects' free reports of the circumstances of learning about the Reagan assassination attempt. However, these findings obviously fall far short of establishing a discontinuity between memories created under conditions in which both surprise and consequentiality are high, and memories created under other conditions. Furthermore, Neisser (1982) and Winograd and Killinger (1983) have pointed out that flashbulb-like memories occur for events that are not surprising in the sense of being unexpected, such as the landing on the moon in 1969, the resignation of Richard Nixon, or the death of General Franco, and Pillemer (1984) noted that flashbulb memories for the assassination attempt on President Reagan occurred even among subjects who rated the event as inconsequential. Finally, Pillemer (1984) interpreted his results as suggesting a graded effect of surprise or emotional reaction on the amount of information subjects can remember, and not an all-or-none effect of the sort that might be expected on the basis of the special-mechanism hypothesis.

motivated on the basis of weaker claims. Consider, then, the following formulation of the special-mechanism hypothesis: People can often provide, months or years after a surprising and consequential event, reasonably detailed, accurate, and vivid reports of the circumstances in which they learned about the event. Although imperfect, recall seems far better than would be expected if it were based upon memories created by ordinary memory mechanisms, and so points to the operation of a special flashbulb-memory mechanism.

Let us assume for the sake of argument that these weaker claims about the characteristics of flashbulb memories are defensible. Given this assumption, the central question is whether these characteristics clearly distinguish flashbulb memories from memories produced by ordinary memory mechanisms. To address this question we need to know what the special-mechanism hypothesis claims about the characteristics of memories produced by ordinary memory mechanisms, and we need to know the basis for the claims.

Brown and Kulik (1977) and Pillemer (1984) seem to have assumed that memories for the circumstances of learning about surprising, consequential events would, if created by ordinary memory mechanisms, be just like (i.e., just as poor as) memories for the humdrum circumstances of everyday life. Pillemer, for example, made the following statement:

> What is remembered about personal circumstances (as opposed to the actual newsworthy event) often is inconsequential, and is really nothing to recount to others (unless a psychologist happens by). Why these mundane, private experiences are remembered *at all* is what was in need of explanation in the first place. (Pillemer, 1984, p. 77, italics added)

This conclusion appears to reflect a tendency to view the circumstances of learning about a newsworthy event from within a framework that focuses narrowly on the event itself. Within this framework the circumstances of learning about the event are seen as incidental (relative to the central information about the event itself), and the significance of these circumstances is evaluated by applying the criteria used to assess the significance of the event itself. This perspective is illustrated clearly in a statement by Pillemer (1984):

But what information do these recollections [of learning about a surprising, consequential event] convey? They do not portray social or political consequences, but rather the individual's *own* behaviors and reactions at the time. One's location upon first hearing, what one was doing, how one found out, one's feelings— why are mundane personal circumstances so vividly remembered years later? (Pillemer, 1984, p. 65)

Viewed in this way, the circumstances of learning about a newsworthy event do indeed seem inconsequential and nonmemorable.

If we view matters from a slightly different perspective, however, it is no longer obvious that ordinary memory mechanisms would yield very poor memory for the circumstances of learning about a surprising, consequential event. Learning about such an event is itself an event: a personal experience. For example, a memory of the circumstances of learning about the space shuttle explosion is a memory for the experience of learning about the explosion. While the experience of learning about a surprising, consequential event does not have the same sort of public significance as the event itself, it may nonetheless have personal significance for the individual. For example, Neisser (1982) suggests that memories for the circumstances of learning about newsworthy public events perform the important function of tying one's personal "time line" to the time line of public events: "They are the places where we line up our own lives with the course of history itself and say 'I was there'" (Neisser, 1982, p. 48; see also Brewer, 1986, and Rubin & Kozin, 1984).

As well as being personally significant, experiences in which one learns of a surprising, consequential event are likely to be distinctive. For example, a meeting that is interrupted by the announcement that the President of the United States has been assassinated is, by virtue of the announcement alone, a very unusual meeting. The significant departures from routine that are likely to follow the announcement (e.g., the adjournment of the meeting, the seeking of additional information from radio or television) may contribute further to the distinctiveness of the experience.

Other factors might also be mentioned in this context. For example, experiences of learning about a surprising, consequential event may be rehearsed covertly as one thinks about the experience, or overtly as one recounts it to others (Neisser, 1982). Furthermore, experiences of learning about shocking events are, at the least, interesting personal experiences: The news itself, the shock we feel, the departures from routine that ensue, and so forth, clearly render these experiences more interesting than the mundane events of everyday life.

It is commonly accepted that the strength and durability of memories produced by ordinary memory mechanisms are influenced by factors such as the distinctiveness of the to-be-remembered material, the interest and significance it holds for the individual, and the extent to which it is rehearsed. If, then, experiences in which one learns of a surprising, consequential event are indeed more significant, distinctive, or interesting than the commonplace experiences of everyday life, or more often rehearsed, there is reason to expect that ordinary mechanisms would yield considerably better memory for the former than for the latter. More generally, experiences in which one learns about events may, as the events themselves are increasingly surprising and consequential, be increasingly significant, distinctive, and so forth, and therefore increasingly memorable.

As soon as we recognize that ordinary memory mechanisms would not necessarily yield very poor memory for the circumstances of learning about surprising, consequential events, we can see that the weak version of the special-mechanism hypothesis is in serious trouble. To the extent we accept that ordinary memory mechanisms could support reasonably good memory for experiences of learning about shocking events (and note that reasonably good recall, and not perfect recall, is what the weak claims assume), there is no need to postulate a special flashbulb memory mechanism.

Of course, our analysis of what can be expected from ordinary memory mechanisms is not beyond question. However, proponents of the special-mechanisms hypothesis clearly carry the burden of demonstrating that ordinary memory mechanisms could not support reasonably good memory for the circumstances of learning about surprising, consequential events. However, no such demonstration has been made. . . .

CONCLUDING REMARKS

In this article we have endeavored to assess the theoretical implications of flashbulb memories. On the basis of empirical observations and logical arguments, we have concluded that claims about characteristics of flashbulb memories strong enough to motivate positing a special flashbulb-memory mechanism are untenable, and that weaker, more defensible claims do not provide sufficient grounds for asserting that flashbulb memories are so special as to require postulation of a special memory mechanism.

As an alternative to the special-mechanism hypothesis, we have suggested that flashbulb memories may be viewed as memories for significant and distinctive personal experiences, and hence as memories explicable in terms of ordinary memory mechanisms. From this perspective, two final observations may be offered. First, our viewpoint (see also Rubin & Kozin, 1984) suggests that the distinction between the flashbulb memories and other sorts of autobiographical memories is an artificial and arbitrary one. Memories for experiences of learning about surprising, consequential events are continuous in their characteristics with other autobiographical memories, and conform to the same principles. The experience of learning about an event may be more significant, distinctive, and so forth—and therefore more memorable—as the event itself is more surprising and consequential, but there is no qualitative distinction to be drawn between memories for learning about shocking, important events, and memories for learning about expected, trivial events.

A related observation has to do with research on the flashbulb-memory phenomenon. By adopting as a starting point the position that a special memory mechanism is required to account for flashbulb memories, proponents of the special-mechanism hypothesis have stressed the disconnection between these memories and more "ordinary" memories, thus insulating the research from theory and data regarding normal memory. In contrast, the present analysis has led us to embrace a view in which flashbulb memories fall squarely within the domain of normal memory (see also Rubin & Kozin, 1984). Working within this framework, our conceptions of flashbulb memories must be informed by data and theory concerning normal memory; and conversely, the study of flashbulb memories should help to illuminate our understanding of normal memory.

REFERENCES

Brewer, W. F. (1986). What is autobiographical memory? In D. C. Rubin (Ed.), *Autobiographical memory* (pp. 25–49). Cambridge, England: Cambridge University Press.

Brown, R., & Kulik, J. (1977). Flashbulb memories. *Cognition, 5,* 73–99.

Colegrove, F. W. (1899). Individual memories. *American Journal of Psychology, 10,* 228–255.

Linton, M. (1975). Memory for real-world events. In D. A. Norman & D. E. Rumelhart (Eds.), *Explorations in cognition* (pp. 376–404). San Francisco: Freeman.

Neisser, U. (1982). Snapshots or benchmarks? In U. Neisser (Ed.), *Memory observed: Remembering in natural contexts* (pp. 43–48). San Francisco: Freeman.

Neisser U. (1986a). Nested structure in autobiographical memory. In D. C. Rubin (Ed.), *Autobiographical memory* (pp. 71–81). Cambridge, England: Cambridge University Press.

Neisser, U. (1986b). Remembering Pearl Harbor: Reply to Thompson and Cowan. *Cognition, 23,* 285–286.

Pillemer, D. B. (1984). Flashbulb memories of the assassination attempt on President Reagan. *Cognition, 16,* 63–80.

Rubin, D. C., & Kozin, M. (1984). Vivid memories. *Cognition, 16,* 81–95.

Thompson, C. P., & Cowan, T. (1986). Flashbulb memories: A nicer interpretation of a Neisser recollection. *Cognition, 22,* 199–200.

Winograd, E., & Killinger, W. A., Jr. (1983). Relating age at encoding in early childhood to adult recall: Development of flashbulb memories. *Journal of Experimental Psychology: General, 112,* 413–422.

Yarmey, A. D., & Bull, M. P. III. (1978). Where were you when President Kennedy was assassinated? *Bulletin of the Psychonomic Society, 11,* 133–135.

POSTSCRIPT

Like McCloskey, Wible, and Cohen, Bohannon (1988) studied subjects soon after the *Challenger* explosion. He found that only those subjects who had frequently retold the story of their hearing about the explosion and had had a strong emotional reaction upon hearing the news were likely to have a long-term flashbulb memory about the experience (specifically, one lasting at least eight months). The factors of retelling and emotional response did not affect memory for *Challenger* facts or memories for the event itself, such as the time at which the explosion occurred. Bohannon therefore believes, contrary to McCloskey, Wible, and Cohen's conclusion, that it is quite possible that flashbulb memories are special in some way (Schmidt & Bohannon, 1988; see Cohen, McCloskey, & Wible, 1988, for a reply to this argument).

Pillemer (1990) suggests that some of the controversy surrounding flashbulb memories arises from the use of the label *flashbulb*. He suggests that it would be less misleading to refer to such memories as *memories of personal circumstances*. Pillemer emphasizes that, rather than differing qualitatively from other kinds of memories, such memories vary in their completeness, accuracy, and persistence, as all memories do. Thus, he argues, flashbulb-memory research should focus on the factors that contribute to such variability (see Cohen, McCloskey, & Wible, 1990, for their response to Pillemer's arguments).

The phrase *flashbulb memory* does call to mind the popular concept of a photographic memory. The phenomenon closest to this concept studied by psychologists is that of eidetic images (Haber, 1979; Haber & Haber, 1988). Eidetic images do appear to be almost photographic, but aren't quite, and they generally last only a few minutes; it's unclear whether they should be classified as a type of true memory or not. (It's also interesting, although puzzling, that the majority of people in whom they are found are children.)

FOR FURTHER THOUGHT

1. In this article's study, why was the questionnaire given nine months after the event to people who had not received a questionnaire immediately after the event?
2. McCloskey and his colleagues noted that responses given by subjects nine months after the event were sometimes more general and sometimes more specific than those they gave immediately after the event. Why could this have been the case even if flashbulb memories are accurate and complete? Note, however, that McCloskey and his colleagues interpret this outcome

as indicating that flashbulb memories are neither particularly complete nor particularly accurate. Why?

3. McCloskey and his colleagues find evidence for some inconsistencies in flashbulb memories whether reported immediately or after some number of months (or years). What's responsible for these inconsistencies? Do these inconsistencies set flashbulb memories apart from ordinary (episodic, or maybe more specifically, autobiographical) memories or not?

4. One way to maintain that flashbulb memories are complete and immune to forgetting in the face of incompleteness in later reports is to argue that the missing information simply was not in consciousness at the time of the original "snapshot." What evidence do McCloskey and his colleagues offer against this possibility?

5. According to McCloskey, Wible, and Cohen, why is it not possible to simply equate flashbulb memories with especially vivid memories?

6. Why did McCloskey and his associates ask a question about people's memories for the Reagan assassination attempt? What problems in interpretation did those data present?

7. How do McCloskey and his associates explain why we seem to remember learning about surprising and/or consequential events better than we remember learning about most everyday events?

REFERENCES

Bohannon, J. N., III. (1988). Flashbulb memories for the Space Shuttle disaster: A tale of two theories. *Cognition, 29,* 179–196.

Cohen, N. J., McCloskey, M., & Wible, C. G. (1988). There is still no case for a flashbulb-memory mechanism: Reply to Schmidt and Bohannon. *Journal of Experimental Psychology: General, 117,* 336–338.

Cohen, N. J., McCloskey, M., & Wible, C. G. (1990). Flashbulb memories and underlying cognitive mechanisms: Reply to Pillemer. *Journal of Experimental Psychology: General, 119,* 97–100.

Haber, R. N. (1979). Twenty years of haunting eidetic imagery: Where's the ghost? *Behavioral and Brain Sciences, 2,* 583–629.

Haber, R. N., & Haber, L. R. (1988). The characteristics of eidetic imagery. In L. K. Obler & D. Fein (Eds.), *The exceptional brain: Neuropsychology of talent and special abilities* (pp. 218–241). New York: Guilford Press.

Pillemer, D. B. (1990). Clarifying flashbulb memory concept: Comment on McCloskey, Wible, and Cohen (1988). *Journal of Experimental Psychology: General, 119,* 92–96.

Schmidt, S. R., & Bohannon, J. N., III. (1988). In defense of the flashbulb-memory hypothesis: A comment on McCloskey, Wible, and Cohen (1988). *Journal of Experimental Psychology: General, 117,* 332–335.

INTRODUCTION

One area in which the study of cognitive phenomena has a practical application is that of the eyewitness report. How accurate are such reports? What factors affect their accuracy? These are among the issues raised by Elizabeth Loftus and John Palmer in "Reconstruction of Automobile Destruction: An Example of the Interaction between Language and Memory."

As you read this article, ask yourself what the implications are of Loftus and Palmer's findings for how interrogations for criminal investigations are conducted. What can be done to increase the likelihood that testimony given by eyewitnesses to an accident or crime is accurate?

Reconstruction of Automobile Destruction: An Example of the Interaction between Language and Memory

Elizabeth F. Loftus and John C. Palmer

University of Washington

How accurately do we remember the details of a complex event, like a traffic accident, that has happened in our presence? More specifically, how well do we do when asked to estimate some numerical quantity such as how long the accident took, how fast the cars were traveling, or how much time elapsed between the sounding of a horn and the moment of collision?

It is well documented that most people are markedly inaccurate in reporting such numerical details as time, speed, and distance (Bird, 1927; Whipple, 1909). For example, most people have difficulty estimating the duration of an event, with some research indicating that the tendency is to overestimate the duration of events which are complex (Block, 1974; Marshall, 1969; Ornstein, 1969). The judgment of speed is especially difficult, and practically every automobile accident results in huge variations from one witness to another as to how fast a vehicle was actually traveling (Gardner, 1933). In one test administered to Air Force personnel who knew in advance that they would be questioned about the speed of a moving automobile, estimates ranged from 10 to 50 mph. The car they watched was actually going only 12 mph (Marshall, 1969, p. 23).

Given the inaccuracies in estimates of speed, it seems likely that there are variables which are potentially powerful in terms of influencing these estimates. The present research was conducted to investigate one such variable, namely, the phrasing of the question used to elicit the speed judgment. Some questions are clearly more suggestive than others. This fact of life has resulted in the legal concept of a leading question and in legal rules indicating when leading questions are allowed (*Supreme Court Reporter*, 1973). A leading question is simply one that, either by its form or content, suggests to the witness what answer is desired or leads him to the desired answer.

In the present study, subjects were shown films of traffic accidents and then they answered questions about the accident. The subjects were interrogated about the speed of the vehicles in one of several ways. For example, some subjects were asked, "About how fast were the cars going when they hit each other?" while others were asked, "About how fast were the cars going when they smashed into each other?" As Fillmore (1971) and Bransford and McCarrell (1974) have noted, *hit* and *smashed* may involve specification of differential rates of movement. Furthermore, the two verbs may also involve differential specification of the likely consequences of the events to which they are referring. The impact of the accident is apparently gentler for *hit* than for *smashed*.

This research was supported by the Urban Mass Transportation Administration, Department of Transportation, Grant No. WA-11-0004. Thanks go to Geoffrey Loftus, Edward E. Smith, and Stephen Woods for many important and helpful comments. Reprint requests should be sent to Elizabeth F. Loftus, Department of Psychology, University of Washington, Seattle, Washington 98195.

SOURCE: *Journal of Verbal Learning and Verbal Behavior, 13,* 1974, pp. 585–589. Copyright © 1974 by Academic Press, Inc. Reprinted by permission.

EXPERIMENT I

Method

Forty-five students participated in groups of various sizes. Seven films were shown, each depicting a traffic accident. These films were segments from longer driver's education films borrowed from the Evergreen Safety Council and the Seattle Police Department. The length of the film segments ranged from 5 to 30 sec. Following each film, the subjects received a questionnaire asking them first to, "give an account of the accident you have just seen," and then to answer a series of specific questions about the accident. The critical question was the one that interrogated the subject about the speed of the vehicles involved in the collision. Nine subjects were asked, "About how fast were the cars going when they hit each other?" Equal numbers of the remaining subjects were interrogated with the verbs *smashed, collided, bumped,* and *contacted* in place of *hit*. The entire experiment lasted about an hour and a half. A different ordering of the films was presented to each group of subjects.

Results

Table 1 presents the mean speed estimates for the various verbs. Following the procedures outlined by Clark (1973), an analysis of variance was performed with verbs as a fixed effect, and subjects and films as random effects, yielding a significant quasi F ratio, $F'(5, 55) = 4.65, p < .005$.

Some information about the accuracy of subjects' estimates can be obtained from our data. Four of the seven films were staged crashes; the original

TABLE 1   Speed Estimates for the Verbs Used in Experiment I

Verb	Mean Speed Estimate
Smashed	40.8
Collided	39.3
Bumped	38.1
Hit	34.0
Contacted	31.8

purpose of these films was to illustrate what can happen to human beings when cars collide at various speeds. One collision took place at 20 mph, one at 30, and two at 40. The mean estimates of speed for these four films were: 37.7, 36.2, 39.7, and 36.1 mph, respectively. In agreement with previous work, people are not very good at judging how fast a vehicle was actually traveling.

Discussion

The results of this experiment indicate that the form of a question (in this case, changes in a single word) can markedly and systematically affect a witness's answer to that question. The actual speed of the vehicles controlled little variance in subject reporting, while the phrasing of the question controlled considerable variance.

Two interpretations of this finding are possible. First, it is possible that the differential speed estimates result merely from response-bias factors. A subject is uncertain whether to say 30 mph or 40 mph, for example, and the verb *smashed* biases his response towards the higher estimate. A second interpretation is that the question form causes a change in the subject's memory representation of the accident. The verb *smashed* may change a subject's memory such that he "sees" the accident as being more severe than it actually was. If this is the case, we might expect subjects to "remember" other details that did not actually occur, but are commensurate with an accident occurring at higher speeds. The second experiment was designed to provide additional insights into the origin of the differential speed estimates.

EXPERIMENT II

Method

One hundred and fifty students participated in this experiment, in groups of various sizes. A film depicting a multiple car accident was shown, followed by a questionnaire. The film lasted less than 1 min; the accident in the film lasted 4 sec. At the end of the film, the subjects received a questionnaire asking them first to describe the accident in their own words, and then to answer a series of questions about the accident. The critical question was the one that interrogated the subject about the speed of the vehicles. Fifty subjects were asked, "About how fast were the cars going when they smashed into each other?" Fifty subjects were asked, "About how fast were the cars going when they hit each other?" Fifty subjects were not interrogated about vehicular speed.

One week later, the subjects returned and without viewing the film again they answered a series of questions about the accident. The critical question here was, "Did you see any broken glass?" which the subjects answered by checking "yes" or "no." This question was embedded in a list totalling 10 questions, and it appeared in a random position in the list. There was no broken glass in the accident, but, since broken glass is commensurate with accidents occurring at high speed, we expected that the subjects who had been asked the *smashed* question might more often say "yes" to this critical question.

Results

The mean estimate of speed for subjects interrogated with *smashed* was 10.46 mph; with *hit* the estimate was 8.00 mph. These means are significantly different, $t(98) = 2.00$, $p < .05$.

Table 2 presents the distribution of "yes" and "no" responses for the *smashed*, *hit*, and control subjects. An independence chi-square test on these responses was significant beyond the .025 level, $\chi^2(2) = 7.76$. The important result in Table 2 is that the probability of saying "yes," P(Y), to the question about broken glass is .32 when the verb *smashed* is used, and .14 with *hit*. Thus *smashed* leads both to more "yes" responses and to higher speed estimates. It appears to be the case that the effect of the verb is mediated at least in part by the speed estimate. The question now

TABLE 2   Distribution of "Yes" and "No" Responses to the Question, "Did You See Any Broken Glass?"

	Verb Condition		
Response	Smashed	Hit	Control
Yes	16	7	6
No	34	43	44

TABLE 3   Probability of Saying Yes to, "Did You See Any Broken Glass?" Conditionalized on Speed Estimates

	Speed Estimate (mph)			
Verb Condition	1–5	6–10	11–15	16–20
Smashed	.09	.27	.41	.62
Hit	.06	.09	.25	.50

arises: Is *smashed* doing anything else besides increasing the estimate of speed? To answer this, the function relating P(Y) to speed estimate was calculated separately for *smashed* and *hit*. If the speed estimate is the only way in which effect of verb is mediated, then for a given speed estimate, P(Y) should be independent of verb. Table 3 shows that this is not the case. P(Y) is lower for *hit* than for *smashed*; the difference between the two verbs ranges from .03 for estimates of 1–5 mph to .18 for estimates of 6–10 mph. The average difference between the two curves is about .12. Whereas the unconditional difference of .18 between the *smashed* and *hit* conditions is attenuated, it is by no means eliminated when estimate of speed is controlled for. It thus appears that the verb *smashed* has other effects besides that of simply increasing the estimate of speed. One possibility will be discussed in the next section.

DISCUSSION

To reiterate, we have first of all provided an additional demonstration of something that has been known for some time, namely, that the way a question is asked can enormously influence the answer that is given. In this instance, the question, "About how fast were the cars going when they smashed into each other?" led to higher estimates of speed than the same question asked with the verb *smashed* replaced by *hit*. Furthermore, this seemingly small change had consequences for how questions are answered a week after the original event occurred.

As a framework for discussing these results, we would like to propose that two kinds of information go into one's memory for some complex occurrence. The first is information gleaned during the perception of the original event; the second is external information supplied after the fact. Over time, information from these two sources may be integrated in such a way that we are unable to tell from which source some specific detail is recalled. All we have is one "memory."

Discussing the present experiments in these terms, we propose that the subject first forms some representation of the accident he has witnessed. The experimenter then, while asking, "About how fast were the cars going when they smashed into each other?" supplies a piece of external information, namely, that the cars did indeed smash into each other.

When these two pieces of information are integrated, the subject has a memory of an accident that was more severe than in fact it was. Since broken glass is commensurate with a severe accident, the subject is more likely to think that broken glass was present.

There is some connection between the present work and earlier work on the influence of verbal labels on memory for visually presented form stimuli. A classic study in psychology showed that when subjects are asked to reproduce a visually presented form, their drawings tend to err in the direction of a more familiar object suggested by a verbal label initially associated with the to-be-remembered form (Carmichael, Hogan, & Walter, 1932). More recently, Daniel (1972) showed that recognition memory, as well as reproductive memory, was similarly affected by verbal labels, and he concluded that the verbal label causes a shift in the memory strength of forms which are better representatives of the label.

When the experimenter asks the subject, "About how fast were the cars going when they smashed into each other?", he is effectively labeling the accident a smash. Extrapolating the conclusions of Daniel to this situation, it is natural to conclude that the label, smash, causes a shift in the memory representation of the accident in the direction of being more similar to a representation suggested by the verbal label.

REFERENCES

Bird, C. The influence of the press upon the accuracy of report. *Journal of Abnormal and Social Psychology,* 1927, 22, 123–129.

Block, R. A. Memory and the experience of duration in retrospect. *Memory & Cognition,* 1974, 2, 153–160.

Bransford, J. D., & McCarrell, N. S. A sketch of a cognitive approach to comprehension: Some thoughts about understanding what it means to comprehend. In D. Palermo & W. Weimer (Eds.), *Cognition and the symbolic processes.* Washington, D.C.: V. H. Winston & Co., 1974.

Carmichael, L., Hogan, H. P., & Walter, A. A. An experimental study of the effect of language on the reproduction of visually perceived form. *Journal of Experimental Psychology,* 1932, 15, 73–86.

Clark, H. H. The language-as-fixed-effect fallacy: A critique of language statistics in psychological research. *Journal of Verbal Learning and Verbal Behavior,* 1973, 12, 335–359.

Daniel, T. C. Nature of the effect of verbal labels on recognition memory for form. *Journal of Experimental Psychology,* 1972, 96, 152–157.

Fillmore, C. J. Types of lexical information. In D. D. Steinberg and L. A. Jakobovits (Eds.), *Semantics: An interdisciplinary reader in philosophy, linguistics, and psychology.* Cambridge: Cambridge University Press, 1971.

Gardner, D. S. The perception and memory of witnesses. *Cornell Law Quarterly,* 1933, 8, 391–409.

Marshall, J. *Law and psychology in conflict.* New York: Anchor Books, 1969.

Ornstein, R. E. *On the experience of time.* Harmondsworth. Middlesex. England: Penguin, 1969.

Whipple, G. M. The observer as reporter: A survey of the psychology of testimony. *Psychological Bulletin,* 1909, 6, 153–170.

Supreme Court Reporter, 1973, 3: Rules of Evidence for United State Courts and Magistrates.

POSTSCRIPT

This is one of the earlier articles on eyewitness testimony; the literature has since grown enormously (see Buckhout, 1974; Kassin, Ellsworth, & Smith, 1989; and Loftus, 1979, for very readable summaries of that research; see Wells, 1993, and other articles in the same issue for more recent and somewhat more technical reviews). Aside from looking further at the immediate and subsequent impact of the wording of questions, psychologists have since looked at the following issues (among others): (1) the accuracy of eyewitness identification (Brown, Deffenbacher, & Sturgill, 1977) and how identification accuracy is affected by (a) the presence of a weapon (Tooley, Brigham, Maass, & Bothwell, 1987) and (b) the races of the witness and suspect (Brigham & Malpass, 1985); (2) the effects of the high emotions that typically accompany witnessing a crime or accident (Christianson, 1992); and (3) the relevance of eyewitnesses' confidence in their reports (Bothwell, Deffenbacher, & Brigham, 1987; Wells & Murray, 1984). Loftus' accounts of some of the more notorious trials for which she has provided expert testimony (Loftus & Ketcham, 1991) demonstrate how these issues arise in real-life criminal cases. It should be noted, however, that the usefulness and appropriateness of psychologists' providing expert testimony on eyewitness reports has been the subject of some debate (Loftus, 1983a, b; McCloskey & Egeth, 1983a, b).

There is also controversy about a more theoretical issue: just what is the effect that leading questions and subsequent discussion have on eyewitnesses' original memory? In this and subsequent articles, Loftus and her colleagues argue that the information that is either implied by leading questions or given directly to people after the event often will be integrated into and actually change or impair the original memory (Loftus & Hoffman, 1989; Loftus, Miller, & Burns, 1978). Others, however, have argued that the original memories remain intact; the inaccuracies of eyewitness reports for the most part simply reflect biases in responding introduced by leading questions or other aspects of the experimental design (McCloskey & Zaragoza, 1985; Zaragoza & Koshmider, 1989; Zaragoza, McCloskey, & Jamis, 1987). A series of comments on this controversy have been made by Belli (1989), Tversky and Tuchin (1989), Zaragoza and McCloskey (1989), and Loftus and Hoffman (1989). Metcalfe (1990) has developed a computer model that tries to account for both positions. Perhaps not surprisingly, that model is itself the focus of some controversy (see Lindsay, 1991; Metcalfe, 1991; Metcalfe & Bjork, 1991; Schooler & Tanaka, 1991).

The conclusions about the use of hypnosis to enhance witness reports, on the other hand, are somewhat less controversial: although people may be more willing to report details when hypnotized, their reports are not any more accurate (Sheehan & Tilden, 1983; Smith, 1983), primarily because they are more apt to be influenced by suggestions and assumptions presented in the course of their questioning (Sanders & Simmons, 1983). For this reason, several states bar testimony taken under hypnosis. Fortunately, encouraging subjects to imagine the context of the witnessed event does enhance recall, even without hypnosis (Geiselman, Fisher, MacKinnon, & Holland, 1985), a finding that is consistent with research on the specificity of encoding (see Reading 11). A closely related, but much more controversial, issue is the recovery of repressed memories (such as of early childhood abuse), which typically occurs in the course of psychotherapy. Loftus (1993) presents a broad and clear overview.

FOR FURTHER THOUGHT

1. In their introduction, Loftus and Palmer point out that speed estimates are generally quite inaccurate. In fact, Loftus and Palmer report mean speed estimates of 37.7, 36.2, 39.7, and 36.1 mph for films in which cars were going 20, 30, 40, and 40 mph, respectively. Given that the speed estimates were so inaccurate, how can they tell us anything about the effect of different verbs? If the accidents took place at different speeds, how do we know that the different accident speeds didn't account for the observed results?
2. Technically, a problem exists in Experiment 1: subjects questioned with different verbs also saw the films in different orders (see the last sentence of the Method section). Why is this a problem?
3. What ambiguity in the interpretation of the results from Experiment I was Experiment II intended to address? Explain how Experiment II addresses that ambiguity.
4. In Experiment II, some subjects were questioned about the speed of the cars with the word *smashed,* some with the word *hit,* and some were not questioned at all. Why was there a condition without a speed estimate question? Is it a problem that the other verbs used in Experiment I (*collided, bumped, contacted*) were not used? Why or why not?
5. In your own words, explain the data from Experiment II that are presented in Table 3. Why was this analysis necessary? What conclusion do these data lead to?
6. According to Loftus and Palmer, what cognitive processes occurred in Experiment II to explain the results they got?

REFERENCES

Belli, R. F. (1989). Influences of misleading postevent information: Misinformation interference and acceptance. *Journal of Experimental Psychology: General, 118,* 72–85.

Bothwell, R. K., Deffenbacher, K. A., & Brigham, J. C. (1987). Correlation of eyewitness accuracy and confidence: Optimality hypothesis revisited. *Journal of Applied Psychology, 72,* 691–695.

Brigham, J. C., & Malpass, R. S. (1985). The role of experience and contact in the recognition of faces of own- and other-race persons. *Journal of Social Issues, 41*(3), 139–155.

Brown, E., Deffenbacher, K., & Sturgill, W. (1977). Memory for faces and the circumstances of encounter. *Journal of Applied Psychology, 62,* 311–318.

Buckhout, R. (1974, December). Eyewitness testimony. *Scientific American,* pp. 23–31.

Christianson, S.-A. (1992). Emotional stress and eyewitness testimony: A critical review. *Psychological Bulletin, 112,* 284–309.

Geiselman, R. E., Fisher, R. P., MacKinnon, D. P., & Holland, H. L. (1985). Eyewitness memory enhancement in the police interview: Cognitive retrieval mnemonics versus hypnosis. *Journal of Applied Psychology, 70,* 401–412.

Kassin, S. M., Ellsworth, P. C., & Smith, V. L. (1989). The "general acceptance" of psychological research on eyewitness testimony. *American Psychologist, 44,* 1089–1098.

Lindsay, D. S. (1991). CHARMed but not convinced: Comment on Metcalfe (1990). *Journal of Experimental Psychology: General, 120,* 101–105.

Loftus, E. F. (1979). *Eyewitness testimony.* Cambridge, MA: Harvard University Press.

Loftus, E. F. (1983a). Silence is not golden. *American Psychologist, 38,* 564–572.

Loftus, E. F. (1983b). Whose shadow is crooked? *American Psychologist, 38,* 576–577.

Loftus, E. F. (1993). The reality of repressed memories. *American Psychologist, 48,* 518–537.

Loftus, E. F., & Hoffman, H. G. (1989). Misinformation and memory: The creation of new memories. *Journal of Experimental Psychology: General, 118,* 100–104.

Loftus, E. F., & Ketcham, K. (1991). *Witness for the defense.* New York: St. Martin's Press.

Loftus, E. F., Miller, D. G., & Burns, H. J. (1978). Semantic integration of verbal information into a visual memory. *Journal of Experimental Psychology: Human Learning and Memory, 4,* 19–31.

McCloskey, M., & Egeth, H. (1983a). A time to speak, or a time to keep silence? *American Psychologist, 38,* 573–575.

McCloskey, M., & Egeth, H. (1983b). Eyewitness identification: What can a psychologist tell a jury? *American Psychologist, 38,* 550–563.

McCloskey, M., & Zaragoza, M. S. (1985). Misleading postevent information and memory for events: Arguments and evidence against memory impairment hypotheses. *Journal of Experimental Psychology: General, 114,* 1–16.

Metcalfe, J. (1990). Composite Holographic Associative Recall Model (CHARM) and blended memories in eyewitness testimony. *Journal of Experimental Psychology: General, 119,* 145–160.

Metcalfe, J. (1991). Representations, predictions, and remembrances in CHARM: A reply to Lindsay (1991). *Journal of Experimental Psychology: General, 120,* 313–315.

Metcalfe, J., & Bjork, R. A. (1991). Composite models never (well, hardly ever) compromise: Reply to Schooler and Tanaka (1991). *Journal of Experimental Psychology: General, 120,* 203–210.

Sanders, G. S., & Simmons, W. L. (1983). Use of hypnosis to enhance eyewitness accuracy: Does it work? *Journal of Applied Psychology, 68,* 70–77.

Schooler, J. W., & Tanaka, J. W. (1991). Composites, compromises, and CHARM: What is the evidence for blend memory representations? *Journal of Experimental Psychology: General, 120,* 96–100.

Sheehan, R. W., & Tilden, J. (1983). Effects of suggestibility and hypnosis on accurate and distorted retrieval from memory. *Journal of Experimental Psychology: Learning, Memory, and Cognition, 9,* 283–293.

Smith, M. C. (1983). Hypnotic memory enhancement of witnesses: Does it work? *Psychological Bulletin, 94,* 387–407.

Tooley, V., Brigham, J. C., Maass, A., & Bothwell, R. K. (1987). Facial recognition: Weapon effect and attentional focus. *Journal of Applied Social Psychology, 17,* 845–859.

Tversky, B., & Tuchin, M. (1989). A reconciliation of the evidence on eyewitness testimony: Comments on McCloskey and Zaragoza. *Journal of Experimental Psychology: General, 118,* 86–91.

Wells, G. L. (1993). What do we know about eyewitness identification? *American Psychologist, 48,* 553–571.

Wells, G. L., & Murray, D. M. (1984). Eyewitness confidence. In G. L. Wells & E. F. Loftus (Eds.), *Eyewitness testimony: Psychological perspectives* (pp. 155–170). New York: Cambridge University Press.

Zaragoza, M. S., & Koshmider, J. W. (1989). Misled subjects may know more than their performance implies. *Journal of Experimental Psychology: Learning, Memory, and Cognition, 15,* 246–255.

Zaragoza, M. S., & McCloskey, M. (1989). Misleading postevent information and the memory impairment hypothesis: Comment on Belli and reply to Tversky and Tuchin. *Journal of Experimental Psychology: General, 118,* 92–99.

Zaragoza, M. S., McCloskey, M., & Jamis, M. (1987). Misleading postevent information and recall of the original event: Further evidence against the memory impairment hypothesis. *Journal of Experimental Psychology: Learning, Memory, and Cognition, 13,* 36–44.

INTRODUCTION

As Michael Ross and Fiore Sicoly point out in "Egocentric Biases in Availability and Attribution," we commonly need to judge the extent of our own and others' contribution to a joint project. Your own experience with such situations probably confirms one of Ross and Sicoly's findings: people tend to overestimate their personal contribution. Why does this happen? Ross and Sicoly argue that this egocentric bias in attribution stems from certain general characteristics of human decision making and judgment—in particular, how judgments are affected by the relative availability of different kinds of information.

References in the original article to the actor–observer difference in social perception have been excluded in this reading, as have Experiment 4 and some final comments on the pervasiveness of egocentric biases. As you read this article, think about the other sorts of judgments and decisions we are often called upon to make in the real world. Are all of these decisions always affected by an egocentric bias?

Egocentric Biases in Availability and Attribution

Michael Ross and Fiore Sicoly

University of Waterloo, Canada

One instance of a phenomenon examined in the present experiments is familiar to almost anyone who has conducted joint research. Consider the following: You have worked on a research project with another person, and the question arises as to who should be "first author" (i.e., who contributed more to the final product?). Often, it seems that both of you feel entirely justified in claiming that honor. Moreover, since you are convinced that your view of reality must be shared by your colleague (there being only one reality), you assume that the other person is attempting to take advantage of you. Sometimes such concerns are settled or prevented by the use of arbitrary decision rules, for example, the rule of "alphabetical priority"—a favorite gambit of those whose surnames begin with letters in the first part of the alphabet.

We suggest, then, that individuals tend to accept more responsibility for a joint product than other contributors attribute to them. It is further proposed that this is a pervasive phenomenon when responsibility for a joint venture is allocated by the participants. In many common endeavors, however, the participants are unaware of their divergent views, since there is no need to assign "authorship"; consequently, the ubiquity of the phenomenon is not readily apparent. The purpose of the current research was to assess whether these egocentric perceptions do occur in a variety of settings and to examine associated psychological processes.

In exploring the bases of such differential perceptions, we are not so naive as to suggest that intentional self-aggrandisement never occurs. Nonetheless, it is likely that perceptions can be at variance in the absence of deliberate deceit; it is from this perspective that we approach the issue.

To allocate responsibility for a joint endeavor, well-intentioned participants presumably attempt to recall the contributions each made to the final product. Some aspects of the interaction may be recalled more readily, or be more available, than others, however. In addition, the features that are recalled easily may not be a random subset of the whole. Specifically, a person may recall a greater proportion of his or her own contributions than would other participants.

An egocentric bias in availability of information in memory, in turn, could produce biased attributions of responsibility for a joint product. As Tversky and Kahneman (1973) have demonstrated, people use availability, that is, "the ease with which relevant instances come to mind" (p. 209), as a basis for estimating frequency. Thus, if self-generated inputs were indeed more available, individuals would be likely to claim more responsibility for a joint product than other participants would attribute to them.

There are at least four processes that may be operating to increase the availability of one's own contributions: (a) selective encoding and storage of information, (b) differential retrieval, (c) informational disparities, and (d) motivational influences.

This research was supported by a Canada Council grant to the first author. We are grateful to the following people for their comments on earlier versions of this article: Dick Bootzin, Leslie McArthur, Hildy Ross, Lee Ross, Shelley Taylor, Amos Tversky, and Mark Zanna. We thank Vicky Vetere for collecting the data in Experiment 5.

Requests for reprints should be sent to Michael Ross, Department of Psychology, University of Waterloo, Waterloo, Ontario, Canada N2L 3G1.

SOURCE: *Journal of Personality and Social Psychology, 37*(3), 1979, pp. 322–336. Copyright 1979 by the American Psychological Association. Reprinted by permission.

Selective Encoding and Storage

For a number of reasons, the availability of the person's own inputs may be facilitated by differential encoding and storage of self-generated responses. First, individuals' own thoughts (about what they are going to say next, daydreams, etc.) or actions may distract their attention from the contributions of others. Second, individuals may rehearse or repeat their own ideas or actions; for example, they might think out their position before verbalizing and defending it. Consequently, their own inputs may receive more "study time," and degree of retention is strongly related to study time (Carver, 1972). Third, individuals' contributions are likely to fit more readily into their own cognitive schema, that is, their unique conception of the problem based on past experience, values, and so forth. Contributions that fit into such preexisting schemata are more likely to be retained (Bartlett, 1932; Bruner, 1961).

Differential Retrieval

The availability bias could also be produced by the selective retrieval of information from memory. In allocating responsibility for a joint outcome, the essential question from each participant's point of view may be, "How much did I contribute?" Participants may, therefore, attempt to recall principally their own contributions and inappropriately use the information so retrieved to estimate their *relative* contributions, a judgment that cannot properly be made without a consideration of the inputs of others as well.

Informational Disparities

There are likely to be differences in the information available to the contributors that could promote egocentric recall. Individuals have greater access to their own internal states, thoughts, and strategies than do observers. Moreover, participants in a common endeavor may differ in their knowledge of the frequency and significance of each other's independent contributions. For example, faculty supervisors may be less aware than their student colleagues of the amount of time, effort, or ingenuity that students invest in running subjects, performing data analyses, and writing

preliminary drafts of a paper. On the other hand, supervisors are more cognizant of the amount and of the importance of the thought, reading, and so on that they put into the study before the students' involvement begins.

Motivational Influences

Motivational factors may also mediate an egocentric bias in availability. One's sense of self-esteem may be enhanced by focusing on, or weighting more heavily, one's own inputs. Similarly, a concern for personal efficacy or control (see deCharms, 1968; White, 1959) could lead individuals to dwell on their own contributions to a joint product.

The preceding discussion outlines a number of processes that may be operating to render one's own inputs more available (and more likely to be recalled) than the contributions of others. Consequently, it may be difficult to imagine a disconfirmation of the hypothesis that memories and attributions are egocentric. As Greenwald (Note 1) has observed, however, the egocentric character of memory "is not a necessary truth. It is possible, for example, to conceive of an organization of past experience that is more like that of some reference work, such as a history text, or the index of a thesaurus" (p. 4). . . .

Two studies offer suggestive evidence for the present hypothesis. Rogers, Kuiper, and Kirker (1977) showed that trait adjectives were recalled more readily when subjects had been required to make a judgment about self-relevance (to decide whether each trait was descriptive of them) rather than about a number of other dimensions (e.g., synonymity judgments). These data imply that self-relevance increases availability; however, Rogers et al. did not contrast recall of adjectives relevant to the self with recall of adjectives relevant to other people—a comparison that would be more pertinent to the current discussion. Greenwald and Albert (1968) found that individuals recalled their own arguments on an attitude issue more accurately than the written arguments of other subjects. Since the arguments of self and other were always on opposite sides of the issue, the Greenwald and Albert finding could conceivably reflect increased familiarity with, and memory for, arguments consistent with one's own attitude position rather than enhanced memory for self-generated statements (although the evidence for attitude-biased learning is equivocal, e.g., Greenwald & Sakumura, 1967; Malpass, 1969).

We conducted a pilot study to determine whether we could obtain support for the hypothesized bias in availability. Students in an undergraduate seminar were asked to estimate the number of minutes each member of the seminar had spoken during the immediately preceding class period. An additional 26 subjects were obtained from naturally occurring two-person groups approached in cafeterias and lounges The participants in these groups were asked to estimate the percentage of the total time each person had spoken during the current interaction.

It was assumed that subjects would base their time estimates on those portions of the conversation they could recall readily. Thus, if there is a bias in the direction of better recall of one's own statements, individuals' estimates of the amount of time they themselves spoke should exceed the average speaking time attributed to them by the other member(s) of the group.

The results were consistent with this reasoning. For seven of the eight students in the undergraduate seminar, assessments of their own discussion time exceeded the average time estimate attributed to them by the other participants ($p < .05$, sign test). Similarly, in 10 of the 13 dyads, estimates of one's own discussion time exceeded that provided by the other participant ($p < .05$, sign test). The magnitude of the bias was highly significant over the 13 dyads, $F(1, 12) = 14.85$, $p < .005$; on the average, participants estimated that they spoke 59% of the time. These data provide preliminary, albeit indirect, evidence for the hypothesized availability bias in everyday situations.

The principal objectives of the current research were (a) to assess the occurrence of egocentric biases in availability and attributions of responsibility in different settings; (b) to examine factors that were hypothesized to influence these biases; and (c) to offer preliminary evidence of a relation between a bias in availability and a bias in attributions of responsibility. Experiment 1 assessed the occurrence of egocentric biases in availability and allocations of responsibility in a natural setting and examined the relation between the two biases. Next, a laboratory was con-

ducted to address the issue of whether the quality of the group's performance affects the availability bias: Is the tendency for one's own inputs to be more available reduced substantially when the group's performance is poor, as a *motivational* interpretation would suggest? Experiment 3 further examined the effects of success and failure in a natural setting. The experimental manipulations in Experiments 4 and 5 were designed to influence availability, and changes in attributions of responsibility were assessed. The manipulation in Experiment 4 [excluded here] induced *differential encoding;* the manipulation in Experiment 5 varied the *retrieval* cues provided to the subjects.

EXPERIMENT 1

In this experiment, we wished to examine egocentric biases in naturally occurring, continuing relationships. Married couples appeared to represent an ideal target group. Spouses engage in many joint endeavors of varying importance. This circumstance would appear to be rife with possibilities for egocentric biases.

Accordingly, the first experiment was conducted (a) to determine if egocentric biases in allocations of responsibility occur in marital relationships; (b) to replicate, using a different dependent measure, the egocentric bias in availability obtained in the pretest; and (c) to correlate the bias in availability with the bias in responsibility. If the bias in responsibility is caused by a bias in availability, the two sets of data should be related.

Method

Subjects. The subjects were 37 married couples living in student residences. Twenty of the couples had children. The subjects were recruited by two female research assistants who knocked on doors in the residences and briefly described the experiment. If the couple were willing to participate, an appointment was made. The study was conducted in the couple's apartment; each couple was paid $5 for participating.

Procedure. A questionnaire was developed on the basis of extensive preliminary interviews with six married couples. In the experiment proper, the questionnaire was completed individually by the husband

and wife; their anonymity was assured. The first pages of the questionnaire required subjects to estimate the extent of their responsibility for each of 20 activities relevant to married couples by putting a slash through a 150-mm straight line, the endpoints of which were labeled "primarily wife" and "primarily husband."[1] The twenty activities were making breakfast, cleaning dishes, cleaning house, shopping for groceries, caring for your children, planning joint leisure activities, deciding how money should be spent, deciding where to live, choosing friends, making important decisions that affect the two of you, causing arguments that occur between the two of you, resolving conflicts that occur between the two of you, making the house messy, washing the clothes, keeping in touch with relatives, demonstrating affection for spouse, taking out the garbage, irritating spouse, waiting for spouse, deciding whether to have children.

Subjects were next asked to record briefly examples of the contributions they or their spouses made to each activity. Their written records were subsequently examined to assess if the person's own inputs were generally more "available." That is, did the examples reported by subjects tend to focus more on their own behaviors than on their spouses'? A rater, blind to the experimental hypothesis, recorded the number of discrete examples subjects provided of their own and of their spouses' contributions. A second rater coded one third of the data; the reliability (Pearson product-moment correlation) was .81.

Results

The responses of both spouses to each of the responsibility questions were summed, so that the total included the amount that the wife viewed as her contribution and the amount that the husband viewed as his contribution. Since the response scale was 150

mm long, there were 150 "units of responsibility" to be allocated. A sum of greater than 150 would indicate an egocentric bias in perceived contribution, in that at least one of the spouses was overestimating his or her responsibility for that activity. To assess the degree of over- or underestimation that spouses revealed for each activity, 150 was subtracted from each couple's total. A composite score was derived for the couple, averaging over the 20 activities (or 19, when the couple had no children).

An analysis of variance, using the couple as the unit of analysis, revealed that the composite scores were significantly greater than zero, $M = 4.67$, $F(1, 35) = 12.89$, $p < .001$, indicating an egocentric bias in perceived contributions Twenty-seven of the 37 couples showed some degree of overestimation ($p < .025$, sign test). Moreover, on the average, overestimation occurred on 16 of the 20 items on the questionnaire, including negative items—for example, causing arguments that occur between the two of you, $F(1, 32) = 20.38$, $p < .001$. Although the magnitude of the overestimation was relatively small, on the average, note that subjects tended to use a restricted range of the scale. Most responses were slightly above or slightly below the halfway mark on the scale. None of the items showed a significant underestimation effect.

The second set of items on the questionnaire required subjects to record examples of their own and of their spouses' contributions to each activity. A mean difference score was obtained over the 20 activities (averaging over husband and wife), with the number of examples of spouses' contributions subtracted from the number of examples of own contributions. A test of the grand mean was highly significant, $F(1, 35) = 36.0$, $p < .001$; as expected, subjects provided more examples of their own ($M = 10.9$) than of their spouses' ($M = 8.1$) inputs. The correlation between this self–other difference score and the initial measure of perceived responsibility was determined. As hypothesized, the greater the tendency to recall self-relevant behaviors, the greater was the overestimation in perceived responsibility, $r(35) = .50$, $p < .01$.

The number of words contained in each behavioral example reported by the subjects was also assessed to provide a measure of elaboration or richness of recall. The mean number of words per

---

[1]In the preliminary interviews, we used percentage estimates. We found that subjects were able to remember the percentages they recorded and that postquestionnaire comparisons of percentages provided a strong source of conflict between the spouses. The use of the 150-mm scales circumvented these difficulties; subjects were not inclined to convert their slashes into exact percentages that could then be disputed.

example did not differ as a function of whether the behavior was reported to be emitted by self ($M = 10.0$) or spouse ($M = 10.1$), $F < 1$. Further, this measure was uncorrelated with the measure of perceived responsibility, $r(35) = -.15$, *ns*.

In summary, both the measure of responsibility and the measure reflecting the availability of relevant behaviors showed the hypothesized egocentric biases. Moreover, there was a significant correlation between the magnitude of the bias in availability and the magnitude of the bias in responsibility. This finding is consistent with the hypothesis that egocentric biases in attributions of responsibility are mediated by biases in availability. Finally, the amount of behavior recalled seemed to be the important factor, rather than the richness of the recall.

EXPERIMENT 2

The data from Experiment 1 indicate that egocentric biases in availability and attributions of responsibility occur in ongoing relationships. The remaining experiments were designed to demonstrate the prevalence of these phenomena, and to investigate some of the factors that were expected to influence their magnitude.

The major purpose of Experiment 2 was to evaluate the self-esteem interpretation of the availability bias. If the availability bias is caused primarily by the motivation to enhance self-esteem, recall of a joint endeavor should facilitate an acceptance of personal responsibility after success and a denial of personal responsibility after failure. Consequently, the self-esteem interpretation implies that self-generated inputs should be more available after success than after failure. The evidence from past research that people accept more responsibility for a success than for a failure is consistent with this reasoning (e.g., Luginbuhl, Crowe, & Kahan, 1975; Sicoly & Ross, 1977; Wortman, Costanzo, & Witt, 1973).

In Experiment 2, subjects learned several days after participating in a problem-solving task that their group had performed either well or poorly. It was hypothesized that subjects would recall a greater proportion of their own statements when the group product was positively evaluated. Because we moved

to the laboratory for this experiment, it was possible to tape record the group's initial interaction. This recording provided a "reality base" against which to compare the subsequent recall of subjects.

Method

Subjects.   The subjects were 37 males and 7 females selected from lists of students living at the university. Subjects were paid $5 each. All of the subjects participated in both sessions.

Procedure.   The experiment was conducted in two sessions separated by a 3- or 4-day interval. Subjects reported for the first session in groups of two. They were told that the purpose of the study was to determine whether groups exhibit more social awareness than individuals. They were given 10 minutes to read a case study of Paula, a psychologically troubled person (selected from Goldstein & Palmer, 1975). Each subject in the dyad was provided with different portions of the case study. The subjects were next asked questions designed to assess their psychological understanding of Paula's difficulties. They were told to discuss each question and arrive at a joint response, taking into account the different information that each group member brought with him or her to the case. Subjects were told that their discussions were being tape recorded. The experimenter informed them that she would listen to the tapes following the sessions to evaluate the group's answers.

Subjects returned individually for the second session. In a random one half of the dyads, subjects were led to believe that their group had performed poorly relative to other groups in the experiment (third from the worst). In the remaining dyads, subjects were informed that their group had performed relatively well (third from the best). Subjects were then told, "Write down as much as you can recall of your group's discussion of Paula. You will only have a short time to do this, so it is unlikely that will be able to report all or even most of what was said. It is, therefore, important that you put things down in the order that they come to you. . . . If you remember the idea, but not the exact comment, rephrase it in your own words." Subjects were told not to record who said each statement. They were simply to write what was said.

Subjects were asked to stop writing at the end of 8 minutes and to go back over their responses to indicate who said each statement during the discussion. Finally, they were asked whether, in their opinion, each statement improved or lowered their group's score, or whether they were uncertain. Subjects were debriefed at the end of the second session.

An observer who was blind to the subjects' treatment conditions contrasted subjects' recall with their original comments on the tape to assess accuracy. A statement was judged to be accurate if it represented an idea that the subject expressed during the interaction, even though the actual words used during the discussion might have differed from the words recalled by the subject. A second rater scored a random one third of the tapes, and agreement was 93%.

Results and Discussion

Availability.   The proportion of statements that subjects attributed to themselves was calculated for each member of the dyad. The average proportion for each dyad served as the unit of analysis. In 21 of the 22 dyads, the subjects attributed the majority of the statements that they recalled to themselves ($p < .001$, sign test). The average proportion of subjects' own statements was .70 in the success condition and .60 in the failure condition. Each of these proportions was significantly greater than a .50 or chance expectancy, $t(10) = 9.09$, $p < .001$, and $t(10) = 3.22$, $p < .01$, respectively. Thus, in both the success and failure conditions, subjects attributed significantly more of the recalled statements to themselves than would be expected by chance. Nevertheless, as hypothesized, subjects attributed a greater proportion of the recalled statements to themselves after a success than after a failure, $F(1, 20) = 7.10$, $p < .025$. The total number of statements recalled (adding over statements attributed to self and the other person) did not differ significantly as a function of the group's performance ($F = 1.57$).

Accuracy.   Subjects' recall was compared with the taped record in a 2×2 between–within analysis of variance (Success vs. Failure × Self vs. Partner), with the dyad as the unit of analysis. Subjects recalled a higher percentage of their own actual statements ($M = 5.6\%$) than of their partner's actual statements ($M = 2.6\%$), $F(1, 19) = 18.37$, $p < .001$.[2] Although the means seem low, note that subjects were given only an 8-minute recall period. The group's performance level did not affect the percentage of actual statements recalled (main effect and interaction $Fs < 1$).

We also compared the accuracy of the statements subjects attributed to themselves with the accuracy of the statements they attributed to their partners. Sixty-nine percent of the statements that subjects attributed to self were accurate reflections of self-generated comments; 56% of the statements that subjects attributed to their partners were accurate. The difference between these two percentages was significant, $F(1, 19) = 7.06$, $p < .025$. The group's performance level did not significantly affect the accuracy of the attributed statements (success–fail main effect $F = 1.14$, interaction $F < 1$).

Most of the errors that subjects made were of two types: They recalled material from the case history that had not been mentioned in the discussion; they reported inferences and conclusions that were not contained in the case history or in the discussion. In only a few instances (approximately 2% of the errors) did subjects take credit for statements made by their partners.

Evaluations.   Finally, subjects' evaluations of the statements were transcribed onto a 3-point scale: +1 (improved the group's score), 0 (uncertain), and −1 (lowered the group's score). Two scores were obtained for each subject: the average rating of comments attributed to self and the average rating of statements attributed to the other person. An analysis of variance, with the dyad as the unit of analysis, revealed a main effect for success–fail, $F(1, 20) = 14.56$, $p < .005$, and a Success–Fail × Self–Other interaction, $F(1, 20) = 5.19$, $p < .05$.

The success–fail main effect indicated that statements were evaluated more positively following success ($M = .75$) than following failure ($M = .41$). The interaction revealed that whereas subjects' evaluations of their own comments were marginally lower in the failure condition than in the success condition

---

[2]The tapes from one of the failure groups were lost; this group is omitted from the analysis.

(M difference = .18, $t = 1.85$, $p < .10$), their evaluations of the other person's comments were significantly lower in the failure condition than in the success condition (M difference = .50, $t = 5.14$, $p < .01$).

In summary, the present study provided some evidence for the self-esteem maintenance hypothesis. Subjects attributed a higher proportion of the recalled comments to themselves after success than after failure; subjects' evaluations of the recalled statements suggested an attempt to shift the blame for failure onto their partners. On the other hand, contrary to the self-esteem interpretation, recall was egocentric even in the failure condition.

Note that the strong egocentricity obtained on the recall measure and the increased accuracy of self-generated statements may reflect, in part, the fact that subjects initially read different aspects of the case history. Since they subsequently presented this material to the other person in responding to the questions, subjects' own contributions may have received more "study time." Nevertheless, this differential is ecologically valid. A person's inputs are often derived from his or her previous history and experiences.

EXPERIMENT 3

In Experiment 3 we examined the effects of success and failure in a more natural setting. We had the players on 12 intercollegiate basketball teams individually complete a questionnaire in which they were asked to recall an important turning point in their last game and to assess why their team had won or lost.

It is a leap to go from the self–other comparisons that we have considered in the previous studies to own team–other team comparisons. There are, however, a number of reasons to expect that the actions of one's own team should be more available to the attributor than the actions of the other team: I know the names of my teammates, and therefore, I have a ready means of organizing the storage and retrieval of data relevant to them; our success in future games against other opponents depends more on our own offensive and defensive abilities than on the abilities of the opposing team. Consequently, I may attend more closely to the actions of my teammates, which would enhance encoding and storage. Also, there are informational disparities: The strategies of my own team are more salient than are the strategies of the opposing team (Tversky & Kahneman, 1973).

If the initiative of one's own team are differentially available, players should recall a turning point in terms of the actions of their team and attribute responsibility for the game outcome to their team. On the basis of the data from Experiment 2, it may be expected that these tendencies will be stronger after a win than after a loss.

Method

Subjects.   Seventy-four female and 84 male intercollegiate basketball players participated in the study. The team managers were contacted by telephone; all agreed, following discussions with their players, to have their teams participate in the study.

Procedure.   The questionnaires were administered after six games in which the teams participating in the study played each other. Thus, for the three male games chosen, three of the six male teams in the study were competing against the other three male teams. Similarly, the three female games selected included all six of the female teams. The questionnaires were administered at the first team practice following the target game (1 or 2 days after the game), except in one case where, because of the teams' schedules of play, it was necessary to collect data immediately after the game (two female teams). The questionnaires were completed individually, and the respondents' anonymity was assured. The relevant questions, from the current perspective, were the following:

1. Please describe briefly one important turning point in the last game and indicate in which period it occurred.
2. Our team won/lost our last game because. . . .

The responses to the first question were examined to determine if the turning point was described as precipitated by one's own team, both teams, or the other team. Responses to the second question were examined to assess the number of reasons for the win or loss that related to the actions of either one's own or the opposing team. The data were coded by a person who was unaware of the experimental hypotheses. A second observer independently coded the responses from 50% of the subjects. There was 100% agreement for both questions.

Results

There were no significant sex differences on the two dependent measures; the results are, therefore, reported collapsed across gender. Since team members' responses cannot be viewed as independent, responses were averaged, and the team served as the unit of analysis.

A preliminary examination of the "turning point" data revealed that even within a team, the players were recalling quite different events. Nevertheless, 119 players recalled a turning point that they described as precipitated by the actions of their own team; 13 players recalled a turning point that they viewed as caused by both teams; 16 players recalled a turning point seen to be initiated by the actions of the opposing team (the remaining 10 players did not answer the question). Subjects described such events as a strong defense during the last 2 minutes of the game, a defensive steal, a shift in offensive strategies, and so on.

The percentage of players who recalled a turning point caused by their teammates was derived for each team. These 12 scores were submitted to an analysis that compared them to a chance expectancy of 50%. The obtained distribution was significantly different from chance, $F(1, 11) = 30.25$, $p < .001$, with a mean of 80.25%. As hypothesized, most reports emphasized the actions of the players' own team.

The percentage of players who recalled a turning point caused by their teammates was examined in relation to the team's performance. The average percentage was higher on the losing team than on the winning team in five of the six games ($p < .11$, sign test). The mean difference between the percentages on losing ($M = 88.5$) and winning ($M = 72.0$) teams was nonsignificant ($F < 1$).

The players' explanations for their team's win or loss were also examined. Of the 158 participants, only 14 provided any reasons that involved the actions of the opposing team. On the average, subjects reported 1.79 reasons for the win or loss that involved their own team and .09 reasons that involved the opposing team, $F(1, 11) = 272.91$, $p < .001$. Finally, the tendency to ascribe more reasons to one's own team was nonsignificantly greater after a loss ($M = 1.73$) than after a win ($M = 1.65$), $F < 1$.

Discussion

The responses to the turning point question indicate that the performances of subjects' teammates were more available than those of opposing team members. Further, subjects ascribed responsibility for the game outcome to the actions or inactions of their teammates rather than to those of members of the opposing team. Thus, biases in availability and judgments of responsibility can occur at the group level. Rather and Heskowitz (1977) provide another example of group egocentrism: "CBS (news) became a solid Number One after the Apollo moonshot in 1968. If you are a CBS person, you tend to say our coverage of the lunar landing tipped us over. If you are a NBC person, you tend to cite the break-up of the Huntley–Brinkley team as the key factor" (p. 307).

Contrary to the data from Experiment 2, the availability bias in Experiment 3 was as strong after failure as after success. There are differences between the studies that may contribute to this discrepancy. The "egocentric" availability and attributions in the basketball experiment were team rather than self-oriented; as a result, responsibility for failure was more diffused, and subjects' self-esteem was threatened less directly. Also, unlike the group in the laboratory study, the basketball team had a future: The players could enhance their control over subsequent game outcomes by locating causality within their own team. Finally, and perhaps most important, unlike the laboratory group, the team also had a past. Team members recalled aspects of their behavior that changed and attributed the game outcomes to these variations (e.g., we win because of discipline and hustle; we lose because of a lack of discipline and hustle). What players seemed to ignore, however, was that the opposing teams might contribute to these fluctuations.

It seems likely that a tendency to perceive both teams as responsible for the game outcome might increase with the magnitude of the win or loss (assuming that large wins or losses are atypical). As Kelley (1973) noted, multiple causes are necessary to explain extreme outcomes. Although no such tendency was observed in the current study, there were too few data points (games) to provide an accurate determination. . . .

[Experiment 4 is excluded.]

EXPERIMENT 5

In Experiment 5, we again attempted to vary the individual's focus of attention so as to affect availability. In this experiment, however, we employed a manipulation designed to promote selective retrieval of information directly relevant to attributions of responsibility.

In our initial analysis, we suggested that egocentric attributions of responsibility could be produced by the selective retrieval of information from memory and that retrieval might be guided by the kinds of questions that individuals ask themselves. Experiment 5 was conducted to test this hypothesis. Subjects were induced to engage in differing retrieval by variations in the form in which questions were posed. Graduate students were stimulated to think about either their own contributions to their BA theses or the contributions of their supervisors. The amount of responsibility for the thesis that subjects allocated to either self or supervisor was then assessed. It was hypothesized that subjects would accept less responsibility for the research effort in the supervisor-focus than in the self-focus condition.

Method

Subjects.   The subjects were 17 female and 12 male psychology graduate students. Most had completed either 1 or 2 years of graduate school. All of these students had conducted experiments that served as their BA theses in their final undergraduate year.

Procedure.   The subjects were approached individually in their offices and asked to complete a brief questionnaire on supervisor-student relations. None refused to participate. The two forms of the questionnaire were randomly distributed to the subjects; they were assured that their responses would be anonymous and confidential.

One form of the questionnaire asked the subjects to indicate their own contribution to each of a number of activities related to their BA theses. The questions were as follows: (a) "I suggested _____ percent of the methodology that was finally employed in the study." (b) "I provided _____ percent of the interpretation of results." (c) "I initiated _____ percent of the thesis-relevant discussions with my supervisor." (d) "During thesis-related discussions I tended to control the course and content of the discussion _____ percent of the time." (e) "All things considered, I was responsible for _____ percent of the entire research effort." (f) "How would you evaluate your thesis relative to others done in the department?"

The second form of the questionnaire was identical to the above, except that the word *I* (self-focus condition) was replaced with *my supervisor* (supervisor-focus condition) on Questions 1–5. Subjects were asked to fill in the blanks in response to the first five questions and to put a slash through a 150-mm line, with endpoints labeled "inferior" and "superior," in response to Question 6.

Results and Discussion

For purposes of the analyses, it was assumed that the supervisor's and the student's contribution to each item would add up to 100%. Though the experiment was introduced as a study of supervisor–student relations, it is possible that the students may have considered in their estimates the inputs of other individuals (e.g., fellow students). Nevertheless, the current procedure provides a conservative test of the experimental hypothesis. For example, if a subject responded 20% to an item in the "I" version of the questionnaire, it was assumed that his or her supervisor contributed 80%. Yet the supervisor may have contributed only 60%, with an unspecified person providing the remainder. By possibly overestimating the supervisor's contribution, however, we are biasing the data against the experimental hypothesis: The "I" version was expected to reduce the percentage of responsibility allocated to the supervisor.

Subjects' responses to the first five questions on the "I" form of the questionnaire were subtracted from 100, so that higher numbers would reflect greater contributions by the supervisor in both conditions.

Question 5 dealt with overall responsibility for the research effort. As anticipated, subjects allocated more responsibility to the supervisor in the supervisor-focus ($M = 33.3\%$) than in the self-focus ($M = 16.5\%$) condition, $F(1, 27) = 9.05$, $p < .01$. The first four questions were concerned with different aspects of the thesis, and the average response revealed a similar result: supervisor-focus $M = 33.34$; self-focus $M = 21.82$; $F(1, 27) = 5.34$, $p < .05$. Finally, subjects tended to evaluate their thesis more positively in the self-focus condition than in the supervisor-focus condition: 112.6 versus 94.6, $F(1, 27) = 3.59$, $p < .10$.

The contrasting wording of the questions had the anticipated impact on subjects' allocations of responsibility. The supervisor version of the questionnaire presumably caused subjects to recall a greater proportion of their supervisors' contributions than did the "I" form of the questionnaire. This differential availability was then reflected in the allocations of responsibility. Note, however, that the questions were not entirely successful in controlling subjects' retrieval. The supervisor was allocated only one third of the responsibility for the thesis in the supervisor-focus condition.

In light of the present data, the basketball players' attributions of responsibility for the game outcome in Experiment 3 need to be reexamined. Recall that the players were asked to complete the sentence, "Our team won/lost our last game because. . . ." This question yielded a highly significant egocentric bias. With hindsight, it is evident that the form of the question—"*Our* team . . . *our* last game"—may have prompted subjects to focus on the actions of their own teams, even though the wording does not preclude references to the opposing team. The "turning point" question in Experiment 3 was more neutrally worded and is not susceptible to this alternative interpretation.

The leading questions in these studies emanate from an external source; many of our retrieval queries are self-initiated, however, and our recall may well be biased by the form in which we pose retrieval questions to ourselves. For example, basketball players are probably more likely to think in terms of "Why did *we* win or lose?" than in terms of a neutrally phrased "Which team was responsible for the game outcome?"

GENERAL DISCUSSION

The five studies employed different subject populations, tasks, and dependent measures. As hypothesized, the egocentric biases in availability and attribution appear to be robust and pervasive.

Determinants of the Availability Bias

Several processes were hypothesized to contribute to the increased availability of self-generated inputs. It is possible to consider how well each accounts for the existing data. *Selective encoding* and *storage* cannot have contributed to the effects of success versus failure on availability in Experiment 2 or of supervisor-versus self-focus in Experiment 5 (since these manipulations occurred long after encoding and storage took place). *Informational disparities* should not have contributed to the pretest results (subjects' time estimates were based solely on the preceding discussion), to the tendency to attribute a higher proportion of the recalled statements to oneself in the success as compared to the failure condition in Experiment 2, or to the effects of supervisor- versus self-focus in Experiment 5 (since neither performance level, as operationalized here, nor focus could affect the information initially available to the subjects). Two *motivational processes* were posited. Self-esteem maintenance does not seem pertinent to the results obtained from the two-person groups in the pretest. Nor does it account for (a) the over-recall of self-generated inputs in the failure condition of Experiment 2 and (b) the finding that players on losing basketball teams recalled the turning point of the game in terms of the actions of their teammates. The control motivation hypothesis fares somewhat better. Although focusing on one's own inputs in failure situations may lower self-esteem, it does permit one to perceive personal control over the activity. Hence, efficacy motivation could account for these results. Nevertheless, a desire for personal efficacy does not appear to explain all of the data. The two-person groups in the pretest seem to reveal a relatively "pure" information-processing effect: It is unlikely that people would feel a need to report that they dominated casual conversations. Also, the effect of supervisor- versus self-focus in Experiment 5 appears to be mediated by differential retrieval. Efficacy considerations may have induced the subjects to report that they were major contributors to their theses; nonetheless, motivational concerns do not dictate that focusing on the supervisor's contributions will reduce one's need to assume responsibility.

In summary, selective encoding and storage, informational disparities, and motivational influences do not appear to be necessary determinants of the egocentric bias in availability. The one remaining process that was posited, *selective retrieval,* is not precluded by any of the current data; further, it receives direct support from the findings in Experiments 2 and 5.

Nevertheless, it seems premature to eliminate any of the hypothesized processes as sufficient causes of the availability bias. The tendency of spouses to recall their own contributions in Experiment 1 may reflect informational disparities; the desire to maintain self-esteem may have contributed to the effect of performance level in Experiment 2; basketball players' responses to the turning point question in Experiment 3 may well have been influenced by selective encoding and by control motivation.

We suspect that, like many cognitive phenomena (cf. Erdelyi, 1974; Erdelyi & Goldberg, 1979; McGuire, 1973), biases in availability are multidetermined in real life. Multidetermination may seem an unsatisfying resolution; however, it is one that social psychologists shall probably confront increasingly as they begin to study cognitive phenomena in situ. Researchers in other sciences face parallel complexities. For example, similar cancers appear to have different etiologies, depending, among other factors, on the environment in which the patient lives (Goodfield, 1976).

The Link between Availability and Attributions of Responsibility

The focus of the present research has been on demonstrating that the hypothesized biases in availability and attribution exist and are relatively ubiquitous. It was also hypothesized, however, that the egocentric bias in attributions of responsibility would be mediated by the bias in availability. Although the data are

suggestive, we have no definitive evidence that the bias in availability *causes* the bias in responsibility. The strongest affirmative evidence is that the two biases were significantly correlated in the marriage study and that a manipulation designed to induce selective retrieval influenced attributions of responsibility (Experiment 5). In opposition, it might be contended that the covariation between the two biases is susceptible to a number of alternative causal interpretations and that there is no direct evidence that the retrieval manipulation in Experiment 5 affected availability. Conceivably, the attributions of responsibility in Experiment 5 were mediated by some other factor not yet identified. Further evidence will be required to establish whether the bias in responsibility is caused by the bias in availability. . . .

REFERENCE NOTE

1. Greenwald, A. G. *The tolitarian ego: Fabrication and revision of personal history.* Unpublished manuscript, 1978.

REFERENCES

Bartlett, F. C. *Remembering.* Cambridge, England: Cambridge University Press, 1932.

Bruner, J. S. The act of discovery. *Harvard Educational Review,* 1961, *31,* 21–32.

Carver, R. P. A critical review of mathagenic behaviors and the effect of questions upon the retention of prose materials. *Journal of Reading Behavior,* 1972, *4,* 93–119.

Cofer, C. N. On the constructive theory of memory. In I. A. Uzgiris & F. Weizmann (Eds.), *The structuring of experience.* New York: Plenum Press, 1977.

deCharms, R. C. *Personal causation: The internal affective determinants of behavior.* New York: Academic Press, 1968.

Erdelyi, M. H. A new look at the new look: Perceptual defense and vigilance. *Psychological Review,* 1974, *81,* 1–25.

Erdelyi, M. H., & Goldberg, B. Let's not sweep repression under the rug: Towards a cognitive psychology of repression. In J. F. Kihlstrom & F. J. Evans (Eds.), *Functional disorders of memory.* Hillsdale, N.J.: Erlbaum, 1979.

Goldstein, M. J., & Palmer, J. O. *The experience of anxiety.* New York: Oxford University Press, 1975.

Goodfield, J. *The siege of cancer.* New York: Dell, 1976.

Greenwald, A. G., & Albert, R. D. Acceptance and recall of improvised arguments. *Journal of Personality and Social Psychology,* 1968, *8,* 31–34.

Greenwald, A. G., & Sakumura, J. S. Attitude and selective learning: Where are the phenomena of yesteryear? *Journal of Personality and Social Psychology,* 1967, *7,* 387–397.

Jones, E. E., & Nisbett, R. E. *The actor and the observer: Divergent perceptions of the causes of behavior.* Morristown, N.J.: General Learning Press, 1971.

Kelley, H. H. The process of causal attribution. *American Psychologist,* 1973, *28,* 107–128.

Langer, E. J. Rethinking the role of thought in social interaction. In J. H. Harvey, W. J. Ickes, & R. F. Kidd (Eds.), *New directions in attribution research* (Vol. 2). Potomac, Md.: Erlbaum, 1978.

Loftus, G. R., & Loftus, E. F. *Human memory: The processing of information.* Hillsdale, N.J.: Erlbaum, 1976.

Luginbuhl, J. E. R., Crowe, D. H., & Kahan, J. P. Causal attribution for success and failure. *Journal of Personality and Social Psychology,* 1975, *31,* 86–93.

Malpass, R. S. Effects of attitude on learning and memory: The influence of instruction-induced sets. *Journal of Experimental Social Psychology,* 1969, *5,* 441–453.

McGuire, W. J. The yin and yang of progress in social psychology: Seven Koan. *Journal of Personality and Social Psychology,* 1973, *26,* 446–456.

Rather, D., & Heskowitz, M. *The camera never blinks.* New York: Ballantine Books, 1977.

Rogers, T. B., Kuiper, N. A., & Kirker, W. S. Self-reference and the encoding of personal information. *Journal of Personality and Social Psychology,* 1977, *35,* 677–688.

Sicoly, F., & Ross, M. The facilitation of ego-biased attributions by means of self-serving observer feedback. *Journal of Personality and Social Psychology,* 1977, *35,* 734–741.

Storms, M. D. Videotape and the attribution process: Reversing actors' and observers' points of view. *Journal of Personality and Social Psychology,* 1973, *27,* 165–175.

Taylor, S. E., & Fiske, S. T. Point of view and perceptions of causality. *Journal of Personality and Social Psychology,* 1975, *32,* 439–445.

Taylor, S. E., & Fiske, S. T. Salience, attention, and attribution: Top of the head phenomena. In L. Berkowitz (Ed.), *Advances in experimental social psychology* (Vol. 11). New York: Academic Press, 1978.

Tversky, A., & Kahneman, D. Availability: A heuristic for judging frequency and probability. *Cognitive Psychology,* 1973, *5,* 207–232.

White, R. W. Motivation reconsidered: The concept of competence. *Psychological Review,* 1959, *66,* 297–333.

Wortman, C. B., Costanzo, P. R., & Witt, T. R. Effect of anticipated performance on the attribution of causality to self and others. *Journal of Personality and Social Psychology,* 1973, *27,* 372–381.

POSTSCRIPT

Since this article was published, numerous other researchers have confirmed several aspects of Ross and Sicoly's work. For example, Christensen, Sullaway, and King (1983); Lerner, Somers, Reid, and Chiriboga (1991); Mullen (1983); and Thompson and Kelley (1981) have reported egocentric biases in attribution among couples or others in close relationships. Brawley (1984) found that the degree of egocentric bias on sports teams is relatively unaffected by event outcomes. Some research, however, has suggested some constraints on these conclusions. Fiedler, Semin, and Koppetsch (1991) found that egocentric bias is more pronounced when talking about behaviors as opposed to abstract descriptions, and Christensen and his colleagues (1983) reported that egocentric bias tends to lessen for negative behaviors as length of relationship increases, at least among married or dating couples. Furthermore, level of egocentric bias may be affected by subjects' level of self-consciousness (Sandelands & Stablein, 1986) and depression (Burger & Rodman, 1983).

Research and references on the more general issues of human judgments and decision making can be found in the Postscript to Reading 25.

FOR FURTHER THOUGHT

1. What is the difference between the selective encoding and retrieval and the differential retrieval alternatives that Ross and Sicoly identify as possible explanations for the egocentric bias?
2. What is the self-esteem interpretation of the availability bias? How is it like and unlike the concern for personal efficacy or control interpretation?
3. If Ross and Sicoly are interested in the causes of bias in availability, why do they measure subjects' judgments of their responsibility for joint products?
4. In Experiment 1, different measures are used for amount of behavior recalled and the richness of recall. What are those measures, and how are amount and richness (conceptually) distinguished?
5. In Experiment 1, Ross and Sicoly found that subjects overestimated their contribution to negative items (such as causing arguments) as well as to positive items. Is this finding consistent with, inconsistent with, or neutral with respect to the results of Experiment 2? with the results of Experiment 3 regarding the impact of winning or losing on biases in attribution? Explain why or why not for each case.
6. In Experiment 2, the success versus failure manipulation affected the pattern of availability but not the accuracy of subjects' recalled statements. What does this imply?
7. Ross and Sicoly point out that the egocentricity and accuracy of the information subjects gave in Experiment 2 may reflect, at least in part, the fact that they had a chance to read (and therefore contribute) only part of the information about the case. Why don't they worry very much about this observation when interpreting the results of their experiment?
8. In what ways are the results of Experiments 2 and 3 the same, and in what ways are they different? How do you account for this?

REFERENCES

Brawley, L. R. (1984). Unintentional egocentric biases in attributions. *Journal of Sport Psychology, 6,* 264–278.

Burger, J. M., & Rodman, J. L. (1983). Attributions of responsibility for group tasks: The egocentric bias and the actor-observer difference. *Journal of Personality and Social Psychology, 45,* 1232–1242.

Christensen, A., Sullaway, M., & King, C. E. (1983). Systematic error in behavioral reports of dyadic interaction: Egocentric bias and content effects. *Behavioral Assessment, 5,* 129–140.

Fiedler, K., Semin, G. R., & Koppetsch, C. (1991). Language use and attributional bias in close personal relationships. *Personality and Social Psychology Bulletin, 17,* 147–155.

Lerner, M. J., Somers, D. G., Reid, D., & Chiriboga, D. (1991). Adult children as caregivers: Egocentric biases in judgments of sibling contributions. *Gerontologist, 31,* 746–755.

Mullen, B. (1983). Egocentric bias in estimates of consensus. *Journal of Social Psychology, 121,* 31–38.

Sandelands, L. E., & Stablein, R. E. (1986). Self-consciousness and bias in social interaction. *Social Behavior and Personality, 14,* 239–252.

Thompson, S. C., & Kelley, H. H. (1981). Judgments of responsibility for activities in close relationships. *Journal of Personality and Social Psychology, 41,* 469–477.

CHAPTER TEN
Group and Individual Differences in Cognition

515

INTRODUCTION

As adults, much of our thinking seems to be like an internal dialogue. If so, this implies that differences in language should lead to differences in thinking. This is the central claim of the linguistic relativity hypothesis, also known as the Whorfian hypothesis or the Sapir–Whorf hypothesis. Curt Hoffman, Ivy Lau, and David Johnson investigate the applicability of the linguistic relativity hypothesis to thinking about people in their article "The Linguistic Relativity of Person Cognition: An English–Chinese Comparison."

Hoffman and his colleagues argue that language affects thought because it affects the formation and use of schemas, the organized units of information about different kinds of objects, events, and so on that provide the "basic building blocks" of cognition (Rumelhart, 1980). For example, I have a schema for dogs. It specifies (1) different things I know about dogs, such as that there are different breeds, that some breeds have long legs and others have short, that some breeds have a more exuberant temperament, and so on; (2) the relationships that hold among those pieces of knowledge, such as that length of legs is related to the purpose for which the breed was developed; and (3) how to use that knowledge, such as how to decide whether a dog is likely to be exuberant and how to interact with such a dog. According to schema theory (Rumelhart, 1980), people understand and interact with the world on the basis of the information in their schemas. Schematic processing—interpreting a situation in terms of a particular schema—enables a person to decide, among other things, what information is relevant to the situation, what relevant information is lacking, what assumptions or inferences can be made, what information must be obtained, and how such information might be obtained.

For example, once I know that Joe is a basset hound, I think about Joe in terms of my schema for basset hounds. Thus I would assume that, lacking information to the contrary, Joe has all of the attributes specified by my schema for basset hounds, such as having short legs and long ears. An interesting prediction of schema theory is that later I may be unable to remember whether I inferred such schema-congruent information or whether I was specifically given that information about Joe. If someone were to ask whether Joe's having long ears was inferred by me or given to me and I were to decide incorrectly that I had been given that information when I had in fact inferred it, I would have committed what is called a false alarm.

Schemas such as that for basset hound are directly coded in our language—that is, they have a familiar label and are therefore easy to access and activate. Schemas that are not directly coded in our language or categories for which we do not have schemas are more difficult to activate. This difficulty leads to the prediction that schematic processing is more likely in situations for which a directly coded schema is available. If no schema is directly coded in the language or if no schema at all is available for a situation, schematic processing is unlikely.

The predictions and results in this article are somewhat complex. One terminological problem that you may have is with *foil*. In a recognition test, the subject must identify the correct answer from several choices; the wrong choices are called *foils* (or *distractors*). As you read this article, carefully review the different subject groups and different stimulus conditions, and make sure you understand the predictions.

The Linguistic Relativity of Person Cognition: An English–Chinese Comparison

Curt Hoffman, Ivy Lau, and David Randy Johnson

University of Alberta, Canada

The idea that the particular language one speaks importantly affects the manner in which one perceives and thinks about the world—the linguistic relativity hypothesis—has a long but somewhat checkered history within the disciplines of psychology, anthropology, linguistics, and philosophy. Benjamin Lee Whorf, this century's most influential proponent of the linguistic relativity hypothesis, expressed its central proposition as follows:

> We dissect nature along lines laid down by our native languages. The categories and types that we isolate from the world of phenomena we do not find there because they stare every observer in the face; on the contrary, the world is presented in a kaleidoscopic flux of impressions which has to be organized by our minds—and this means largely by the linguistic systems in our minds. . . . We are thus introduced to a new principle of relativity, which holds that all observers are not led by the same physical evidence to the same picture of the universe, unless their linguistic backgrounds are similar, or can in some way be calibrated. (Whorf, 1956, pp. 213–214)

Whorf's writings were the primary inspiration for a small flurry of behavioral research on the language-cognition relation that arose in the 1950s and continued into the 1960s, most of which was concerned with the impact of language on color memory

We thank Igor Gavanski, Yvonne Ko, Judy Lau, Maria Tchir, and Mary Yu for their assistance with the research reported in this article.

Correspondence concerning this article should be addressed to Curt Hoffman, Department of Psychology, University of Alberta, Edmonton, Alberta, Canada T6G 2E9.

SOURCE: *Journal of Personality and Social Psychology, 51*(6), 1986, pp. 1097–1105. Copyright 1986 by the American Psychological Association. Reprinted by permission.

and object classification. By the 1970s, the linguistic relativity hypothesis had largely fallen into disfavor. This was due in part to the vague and sometimes extreme form in which Whorf had stated the hypothesis. It also occurred because anthropology had begun to accord more importance to linguistic and cultural universals than to linguistic and cultural differences (e.g., Berlin & Kay, 1969), and psychology had begun to question (both on empirical and on conceptual grounds) the assumption that categorization is arbitrary and was moving toward the view that the perceptual world contains its own built-in category structure (e.g., Rosch, 1974). Recently, however, there have been signs of renewed interest in the linguistic relativity hypothesis. More sophisticated theoretical analyses of the language-cognition relation (e.g., Bloom, 1981), as well as methodologically superior empirical work (e.g., Lucy & Shweder,1979), are helping to clarify the ways in which linguistic classifications and linguistic structures can and do partially shape the cognitive categories and processes by which we come to know the world.

This revival of interest in the linguistic relativity hypothesis is particularly timely in view of the central conceptual role currently accorded to the schema concept in cognitive, social, and developmental psychology. As Bloom (1981) has argued, language affects cognitive life in two general ways. First, it influences the development of our repertory of cognitive schemas:

> In addition . . . to developing a large number of schemas free of the influence of language, which never come to be labeled, and to developing a large number of schemas free of the influence of language, which come in time to be labeled, but whose internal organization remains unaffected by the fact that they receive labels, the child will construct or reconstruct a very large number of schemas expressly to meet the requirements of linguistic labels. (Bloom, 1981, p. 66)

An example of this last type of schema is that labeled by the word *dog;* dogs do not constitute an especially coherent or distinctive category, and were it not for the necessity of learning the correct use of the word *dog,* it is unlikely that the child would ever arrive at this particular equivalence class. Other, more abstract examples include the schemas labeled by the words *sister, amount,* and *tao.*

Second, those schemas that have linguistic labels enjoy a special status in our mental life. According to Bloom, this is because the use of verbal symbols not only is a prerequisite to overt social communication but also facilitates the covert self-communication in which we engage to structure our own thought processes.

> We seem to call specially upon those of our schemas that have names, via their names, when we want to disengage particular schematic perspectives from the collectivity of our interacting associations, ideas, and experiences and make use of those discrete, structured perspectives on reality as stable points of mental orientation to provide direction to our continuing cognitive activities. (Bloom, 1981, p. 76)

There is now a good deal of evidence attesting to the special role played by labeled schemas in such diverse cognitive activities as object classification (Carroll & Casagrande, 1958; Greenfield, Reich, & Olver, 1966), memory for forms (Carmichael, Hogan, & Walter, 1932), creative problem solving (Higgins & Chaires, 1980), and deductive reasoning (Clark, 1969), among others (see Bloom, 1981, for a review). Perhaps the best-known research on the power of linguistic labels to guide mental activity is the series of studies on color memory initiated by Brown and Lenneberg (1954). Collectively, this research has demonstrated that those colors that are most readily and most accurately codable (i.e., those that have accessible, accurate verbal labels) are also the colors that people are best able to remember when tested for their recognition memory (e.g., Brown & Lenneberg, 1954; Lantz & Stefflre, 1964; Lucy & Shweder, 1979; Stefflre, Castillo Vales, & Morley, 1966).

Furthermore, given that language affects the acquisition and use of our cognitive schemas, it follows that different languages, because they label certain perspectives on the world but not others, must affect their speakers' repertories of schemas in language-specific ways. This, of course, is simply the linguistic relativity hypothesis restated in contemporary terms.

Surprisingly, the linguistic relativity hypothesis has never, to our knowledge, been tested in the domain of social cognition. Indeed, it is ironic that researchers in the linguistic relativity tradition have typically sought to demonstrate effects of language on thought in domains (such as color memory) where language would seem intuitively to play only a minor role. If linguistic effects on cognitive activity can be demonstrated even here, however, then the effects of language on the more subjective, less perceptually grounded kinds of thinking involved in our transactions with the social world must almost certainly be still more pronounced. This study was therefore designed to test whether distinct languages (in this case, English and Chinese) are capable of exerting language-specific effects on people's impressions of and memory for other individuals.

One important way in which the social lexicons of languages vary is their codification of individual differences, that is, their repertories of labeled schemas for personality traits and types. No language has names for all possible behavior patterns, and the particular personality traits and types singled out for labeling differ somewhat from language to language. For example, what is the English term for the type of personality characterized by these attributes: worldly, experienced, socially skillful, devoted to his or her family, and somewhat reserved? Most readers will agree that there is no economical expression in English that names this particular constellation of attributes. On the other hand, it is just this constellation of attributes that is named by the Chinese term *shì gù*. Thus, Chinese possesses a relatively short, precise label summarizing a cluster of personality qualities that English can express only via a long string of adjectives. Does this linguistic difference imply that Chinese speakers have readier access to a cognitive schema corresponding to that personality type and would, when confronted with an individual displaying that configuration of attributes, be more likely to demonstrate the sorts of cognitive responses associated with schematic processing?

To address this question, we first identified two personality schemas that, like the one named by *shì gù*, have economical labels in Chinese but not in English, and two that have economical labels in English but not in Chinese. We then constructed parallel English- and Chinese-language descriptions of charac-

ters exemplifying these four personality types. Pretesting established that each character's personality was, in fact, more codable (i.e., more readily and accurately nameable) in one language than in the other. The following three groups of subjects were then presented with the descriptions and were later tested for their impressions of and memory for the characters: English monolinguals, Chinese–English bilinguals who read and responded in English, and Chinese–English bilinguals who read and responded in Chinese. We predicted that subjects working in English would show greater evidence of schematic thinking in the case of the two characters representing schemas labeled in English but not in Chinese, and that subjects working in Chinese would show greater evidence of schematic thinking in the case of the two characters representing schemas labeled in Chinese but not in English.

We looked for the following specific indicators of schematic processing in our study (see Fiske & Taylor, 1984). First, schematic processing typically involves "going beyond the information given" and, in the case of person cognition, leads the perceiver to infer schema-congruent attributes that were never directly observed. A second, related consequence of schematic processing is that it often leads the perceiver to misremember schema-congruent but never-seen attributes or behaviors as in fact having been displayed by the person and, more broadly speaking, often impairs the perceiver's later ability to distinguish presented and nonpresented information (e.g., in tests of recognition memory). Third, schematic processing has occasionally been demonstrated to facilitate free recall of information about the person (or at least the ability to reconstruct such information), particularly when the person is a highly prototypical example of the schema (e.g., Cantor & Mischel, 1979b; Forgas, 1983).

A note regarding our choice of subject groups is in order at this point. Most studies in the linguistic relativity tradition have compared monolingual, or nearly monolingual, speakers of different languages. A problem with this type of study is that one cannot separate any effects of language per se from effects due to nonlinguistic cultural differences between the groups. The vast majority of English and Chinese monolinguals, for example, differ in many ways in addition to the language they speak. Our solution to this problem was to assign Chinese–English bilinguals randomly to think and respond in one or the other language during the experiment. A group of English monolinguals from the same university population was also studied. (Unfortunately, a sample of Chinese monolinguals was not available to us, let alone a sample demographically similar to the other groups. The inclusion of such a group was not, however, essential to the logic of the design.) The advantages of this design are that it allows true experimental control over the linguistic variable (at least in the case of the bilinguals) and enables one to isolate linguistic effects from more general cultural effects. In other words, to the extent that any obtained results are due to language per se, the English monolinguals and the Chinese–English bilinguals working in English should respond similarly and should differ from the Chinese–English bilinguals working in Chinese. A hidden assumption underlying this type of design is that bilinguals possess two relatively separate language codes, and that when utilizing one code, there is no strong, automatic tendency to access the other code and its associated schematic knowledge. If, on the other hand, bilinguals do tend to access both codes more or less simultaneously, then of course no effects of language would be obtained with a design such as this.

PRETEST STUDIES: DEVELOPMENT OF THE STIMULUS CHARACTER DESCRIPTIONS

Method

The behavioral descriptions used as stimuli in the main experiment were developed through a series of pretest studies. In the first of these, 18 English monolinguals were presented with 16 English-language personality trait terms and were asked to list as many attributes as they could think of, such as typical behaviors, attitudes, abilities, likes and dislikes, and so forth, that are associated with each of these personality types (cf. Cantor & Mischel, 1979a). Similarly, 18 Chinese–English bilinguals listed (in Chinese) attributes associated with the personality types named by 16 Chinese-language trait terms. On the basis of

these data and our own intuitions concerning the connotative meanings of the terms, several personality types were selected for further study: two types named by English terms and two named by Chinese terms that appeared to have no corresponding label in the other language; two types that, although labeled in both English and Chinese, seemed to be missing an attribute in one language relative to the other; and two types that are labeled in both English and Chinese and appeared to have essentially identical attributional definitions in each language. After identifying clusters of related attributes associated with each of these eight personality types, we selected the three largest or most important clusters for each type and wrote 6 statements (each describing a specific behavior, attitude, ability, or other concrete attribute) for each cluster. In this way, character descriptions exemplifying the eight personality types were created, each of which consisted of 18 statements. All of the characters were young men identified only by an English first name.

The original drafts of these descriptions were written primarily in English, and great care was taken to use the most concrete language possible and to avoid the use of trait terms or other expressions that do not have more or less exact equivalents in Chinese. Next, each description was translated into Chinese. Changes to the English originals were made whenever necessary to achieve equivalence of meaning. As a final step, the Chinese translations were back-translated into English by bilinguals unconnected with our research, and these back-translated descriptions were compared with the original English versions (cf. Brislin, 1970). This step resulted in a number of further changes to the materials.

The remaining pretest studies were designed to test the correctness of our intuitions concerning the relative codability of the characters' personalities in English and Chinese. In the first of these codability studies, 10 English monolinguals and 8 Chinese–English bilinguals were presented with the English and Chinese versions of the descriptions, respectively. They were then asked to label each character with the best overall personality trait or type term they could think of, and also to rate how "accurately and completely" their term captured the character's personality. They then gave their second choice of descriptive term for each character, also rating how well it described him.

For the second codability study, we first compiled a list of all English terms and a list of all Chinese terms (both first and second choices) used to describe any of the eight characters by subjects in the first study. To each of these lists we added the nearest equivalent, where one existed, of each term on the other list not already appearing in a fairly close translation, as well as a number of additional terms culled from subjects' responses in the attribute-listing study. This brought the total number of terms in each list to 103. A new group of English monolinguals ($N = 20$) and one of Chinese–English bilinguals ($N = 19$) were then presented with either the English or Chinese versions of the character descriptions and the trait list and were asked to (a) pick the one trait from the list that best described each character, (b) rate how accurately and completely that trait described him, and (c) select the second- and third-best trait descriptor for each character (ratings were not obtained for these traits).

Results

On the basis of the results of the two codability studies (to be described shortly), four of the eight characters—those developed to exemplify the two English and the two Chinese trait terms having no close equivalent in the other language—were eventually used in the main experiment to test the research hypotheses.[1] The two personality types with economical labels in English but not in Chinese were the *artistic type* and the *liberal type*. The artistic character (David) was described with statements relating to the following categories of attributes (derived from the attribute-listing study described earlier): (a) artistic skills and interests, (b) the artist's cognitive style and temperament (intense, moody, imaginative, fantasy prone, etc.), and (c) the bohemian lifestyle (unconventional behavior, attitudes, possessions). The description of the liberal character (Richard) exemplified these attribute categories: (a) liberal (i.e., progressive, left-wing) social and political attitudes, (b) tolerance and open-mindedness, and (c) a humanitarian, people-oriented outlook. Although Chinese has separate terms for the three attribute categories comprising each of these two types, in neither case is there an economical expression that incorporates, in the way that the English terms *artistic type* and *liberal type* do, all three attribute categories (as well as others not directly represented in the character descriptions).

The two personality types with labels in Chinese but not in English were *shì gù* and *shēn cáng bú lòu*.[2] The description of the shì gù character (Steven) exemplified these attribute categories: (a) greater than average experience of the world (well traveled, varied job experience, etc.), (b) a strong family orientation (in particular, devotion to the immediate family), and (c) well-developed social and interpersonal skills (especially the ability to smooth out difficult interpersonal situations). The shēn cáng bú lòu character (Kevin) was described with statements relating to the following attribute categories: (a) very knowledgeable and skilled in a wide variety of areas, both practical and intellectual, (b) reluctant to display this knowledge and skill unless it is absolutely necessary to do so, and (c) inconspicuous to the point of frequently being ignored or forgotten by others. Again, although English possesses labels for the individual attributes associated with these two personality types, it lacks economical terms capable of unifying these attributes into single, coherent concepts. The Chinese terms *shì gù* and *shēn cáng bú lòu,* on the other hand, imply exactly these two constellations of attributes (in addition to other attributes not explicitly represented in the character descriptions).

---

[1]The two characters exemplifying trait terms with essentially identical meanings in the two languages were omitted from the main study to reduce subjects' memory load and because their inclusion was not essential to evaluate the hypotheses under study. The two characters exemplifying trait terms with a missing attribute in one language did not seem to be perceived in the intended manner by subjects in the pretest studies. Although modified versions of these two characters were included in the main study for exploratory purposes, they yielded no interpretable results and will therefore not be discussed further in this article.

---

[2]Chinese terms are given here in pīn yīn romanization kindly provided for us by J. S. Lin of the Department of East Asian Languages and Literatures, University of Alberta. Chinese-language materials in the actual studies were, of course, written in Chinese ideographs.

The data shown in Table 1 confirmed our intuitions regarding the differential codabilities of these four stimulus personalities in English versus Chinese. As can be seen, English-language subjects in both codability studies believed that their freely chosen descriptors for the two characters based on English-labeled schemas (artistic David and liberal Richard) were more accurate and complete than were their descriptors for the two characters based on Chinese-labeled schemas (shì gù Steven and shēn cáng bú lòu Kevin). Chinese-language subjects in both studies showed just the opposite pattern of ratings. Because the results of the two studies did not differ significantly (all F ratios for interaction effects involving study as a variable were less than 1), they were analyzed together to increase power (see the bottom panel of Table 1 for the combined means). This analysis revealed that the predicted Language of Processing × Language of Schema interaction was reliable, $F(1, 53) = 6.73$, $p < .02$, and that no other effects reached significance. In sum, then, these studies established that the four characters created to exemplify schemas having labels in one of the languages but not in the other are indeed more readily and accurately codable by speakers of that language.

TABLE 1 Subjects' Ratings of Their Freely Chosen Trait Descriptors in the Two Codability Studies

| | Language of Schema | |
Language of Processing	English[a]	Chinese[b]
Study 1		
English	6.95	6.12
Chinese	6.44	6.56
Study 2		
English	8.02	7.75
Chinese	7.79	8.47
Studies 1 and 2 combined		
English	7.49	6.94
Chinese	7.11	7.52

Note. In Study 1, ratings were made on scales of 1 to 9. In Study 2, ratings were made on scales of 1 to 11. The two studies were combined in an unweighted-means analysis of variance.

[a]The data in this column are averaged over the two characters based on English-labeled schemas.

[b]The data in this column are averaged over the two characters based on Chinese-labeled schemas.

The data of the second codability study were also examined for evidence of the predicted trait labelings, and the results generally confirmed that the characters were labeled in the intended manner. The label most frequently chosen for Steven by the Chinese-language subjects was, as predicted, shì gù, which was listed by the majority of subjects. The English-language subjects' most frequent choice of label for Steven was *considerate,* which, as the reader who will refer to the description of that character can verify, does not adequately capture the important elements of his personality. Also as predicted, the label most frequently chosen for Kevin by the Chinese-language subjects was shēn cáng bú lòu,, listed by a large majority of subjects. The English-language subjects most often chose *reserved,* which omits the skill/knowledgeability component of this character's personality, among other things.

The label most frequently selected for David by the English-language subjects was, as predicted, *artistic,* listed by a clear majority of subjects. Chinese-language subjects most often chose yì shù tiān fèn, which means *artistically talented,* particularly in the visual or musical arts. This term, however, refers narrowly to artistic skill and carries no stereotypic connotations regarding the person's temperament or lifestyle, unlike the English term *artistic type.* In the case of Richard, the English-language subjects apparently regarded *open-minded* as a somewhat better descriptor than *liberal* (we had the latter label in mind when constructing this character), but *liberal* was the second most frequently listed term. Chinese-language subjects most often listed sī xiǎng xīn cháo, which roughly translates as *trendy* and is not a particularly apt description of Richard's personality.

In general, we found the trait-labeling data quite encouraging in view of the fact that subjects had 103 trait terms from which to select in describing the characters. After taking into account these and other data from the pretest studies, we reduced each character description from 18 to 15 statements in length (deleting what in our judgment was the weakest statement in each cluster). We also made a few final adjustments to some of the English and Chinese wordings, and the descriptions were considered ready for use in the main experiment.

MAIN EXPERIMENT

Method

Twelve English monolinguals and 24 Chinese–English bilinguals, all undergraduates at the University of Alberta, Canada, participated in the experiment. The following three groups comprised the between-subjects variable in this study: (a) English monolinguals performing the experiment in English (hereinafter referred to as the *E–E* group), (b) Chinese–English bilinguals performing the experiment in English (the *CE–E* group), and (c) Chinese–English bilinguals performing the experiment in Chinese (the *CE–C* group). Bilingual subjects had previously been asked to rate, on a scale of 1 to 9, their fluency in both English and Chinese. Only those giving themselves a rating of 5 or greater for both languages were eligible to participate. The bilinguals were randomly assigned to the CE–E and CE–C conditions. There were 7 women and 5 men in each of the three groups. Each subject participated in two sessions conducted 5 days apart. The same bilingual experimenter conducted both sessions for subjects in all three groups.

In the E–E and CE–E conditions, all instructions (written and oral), stimulus materials, and response forms were in English, and subjects in the CE–E condition were asked to make every effort to think (and respond) exclusively in English during the experiment. Chinese instructions, stimulus materials, and response forms were used in the CE–C condition, and subjects were asked to think and respond exclusively in Chinese.

In the first session, subjects were given a booklet containing the character descriptions, with instructions to read them as many times as necessary to form a distinct impression of each character's personality and to remember each character's name. Subjects were told that they would be required to answer questions about each character's personality when they returned 5 days later, but they were led to believe that they would not be expected to remember the descriptions in literal detail. The order of character descriptions was counterbalanced across subjects.

In the second session, subjects performed the following four tasks in the order listed:

1. *Free impressions.* The subjects were given a list of the characters' names and were asked simply to write down their impressions of each character's personality. They were allowed 3 min per character in which to complete this task.

The English- and Chinese-language free-impression data were each coded by two independent judges. One bilingual judge coded both the English- and Chinese-language responses. A second bilingual judge coded only the Chinese-language responses, and an English monolingual judge coded only the English-language responses. The first step in coding the data was to segment the responses into information units, the smallest units of independent, meaningful information. For example, a sentence that described a character as "shy but intelligent" would be segmented into two information units: shy and intelligent. Whenever there was a subsidiary phrase that was meaningless without the main phrase, the two were counted together as one unit. Segmentation agreement was 85% for the English-language data and 92% for the Chinese-language data. Disagreements were decided by another judge.

The segmented impression units were then classified into three categories: (a) description-based items—those referring to attributes implicit in the original character description; (b) schema-congruent items—those referring to attributes contained in the personality schema on which the character was based but not directly represented in the character description (the attribute-listing data collected in the first pretest study served to define the contents of the personality schemas); for example, the attribute *unreliable* was not implicit in the description of David but is part of the *artistic type* schema and would therefore be scored as a schema-congruent item; and (c) miscellaneous items—this was a residual category for items referring to attributes not represented in the character description and not contained in the schema on which the character was based.

Classification agreement was 92% for the English-language data and 78% for the Chinese-language data. Disagreements were again decided by another judge. Preliminary inspection of these data indicated that, although our hypotheses had been strongly confirmed, the Chinese-language responses had apparently been scored according to a looser criterion than had the English-language responses. In particular, there was a higher overall proportion of schema-congruent classifications and a lower overall proportion of miscellaneous classifications in the Chinese-language data than in the English-language data. Therefore, the Chinese data were given to a new bilingual judge and the English data to a new monolingual judge. The Chinese-language judge was instructed to review the original classifications and to apply a stricter criterion for the schema-congruent category, that is, to reclassify borderline cases of schema-congruent items as miscellaneous items. The English-language judge was instructed to apply a looser criterion for the schema-congruent category, that is, to reclassify borderline cases of miscellaneous items as schema-congruent items. These revisions resulted in roughly comparable overall proportions of description-based, schema-congruent, and miscellaneous items in the Chinese- and English-language data.

2. *Free recall.*   Subjects were told to write down as many statements from the original descriptions as they could remember. They were given 4 min per character in which to complete this task.

The English- and Chinese-language recall data were each rated by two independent judges. The judges first decided if a given item could be matched with one of the stimulus sentences; if so, it was given a score of either 1 (the judge was barely able to match the recalled item with the original item), 2 (a fairly good reproduction, but one containing significant omissions, additions, or distortions), or 3 (an excellent reproduction except for minor details such as names, locations, etc.). Interjudge agreement was 82% for the English-language responses and 90% for the Chinese-language responses. Disagreements were decided by another judge.

3. *Recognition memory.*   Subjects were presented with 12 statements about each character and were asked to assign each statement a rating of either 1 ("I am certain this statement was not in the description"), 2 ("I think this statement was not in the description, but I'm not sure"), 3 ("I think this statement was in the description, but I'm not sure"), or

4 ("I am certain this statement was in the description"). Subjects had a total of 12 min in which to complete this task.

Of these 12 statements, 6 were taken from the original description (2 from each of the three attribute clusters) and 6 were new statements. Three of the new statements (schema-congruent foils) depicted behaviors consistent with the personality type on which the character was based. The other 3 new statements (schema-irrelevant foils) depicted behaviors unrelated to either the original character description or to the schema.

4. *Inference.*   Subjects were shown six entirely new statements pertaining to each character and were asked to rate the likelihood that each statement would be true of the character. Ratings were made on a 13-point scale ranging from 1 (*very unlikely*) to 13 (*very likely*). Three of the statements (description-based items) were based directly on the original character description; that is, they described attributes implicit in the stimulus materials. An example of a description-based item pertaining to the artistic character is, "David is more easily moved by music, art, and literature than is the average person." The other three statements (schema-congruent items) described attributes that were not implicit in the character description but were congruent with the schema on which the character was based. An example is, "David drinks heavily at times and likes to try out hallucinogenic drugs." Subjects were allowed a total of 12 min in which to complete this task.

Hypotheses

We advanced the following hypotheses, all of which take the form of a Language of Processing × Language of Schema interaction:

1. Subjects who had processed the stimulus information in English (E–E and CE–E groups) would have greater difficulty distinguishing presented and nonpresented items on the recognition-memory test for the characters based on English-labeled schemas, whereas subjects who had processed the stimulus information in Chinese (CE–C group) would have greater difficulty for

the characters based on Chinese-labeled schemas. This effect was predicted to be particularly evident in the recognition judgments made of the schema-congruent foils.

2. Subjects who had processed the stimulus information in English would recall more of the material presented about the characters based on English-labeled schemas, whereas subjects who had processed the stimulus information in Chinese would do so for the characters based on Chinese-labeled schemas.

3. Subjects who had processed the stimulus information in English would generate more schema-congruent items in the free-impression task, and assign higher likelihood ratings to the schema-congruent items on the inference test, for the characters based on English-labeled schemas, whereas subjects who had processed the stimulus information in Chinese would do so for the characters based on Chinese-labeled schemas.

Results

[Editor's note: Given the complexity of the results, you may find the following summary useful.

1. Recognition data were mixed, but tended to support Hypothesis 1.
   a. As predicted, bilinguals using Chinese were less accurate (less able to distinguish old information from new) with characters based on Chinese-labeled schemas, whereas English monolinguals were less accurate with English-labeled characters. Bilinguals using English did not differ significantly from English monolinguals, but were less accurate with Chinese-labeled characters (contrary to predictions).
   b. Surprisingly, subjects did not have much confidence in their recognition of old information about characters based on schemas directly labeled in their language of processing.
   c. The predicted schematic effects may have been present in false alarms to schema-congruent new information (technically, in false alarms to schema-congruent items minus

TABLE 2   Mean d' Scores from the Recognition-Memory Test

		Language of Schema	
Language of Processing	Group	English[a]	Chinese[b]
English	E–E	1.91	2.11
	CE–E	2.43	2.24
Chinese	CE–C	3.13	2.25

Note. E–E = English monolinguals using English. CE–E = Chinese–English bilinguals using English. CE–C = Chinese–English bilinguals using Chinese.

[a]The data in this column are averaged over the two characters based on English-labeled schemas.

[b]The data in this column are averaged over the two characters based on Chinese-labeled schemas.

false alarms to schema-incongruent items), but this result was not statistically significant.

2. Free-recall data did not support Hypothesis 2.

3. Free impression and inference data supported Hypothesis 3.]

Hypothesis 1, which pertains to the recognition-memory test, was partially supported. Table 2 presents subjects' mean scores on the measure d', which is an index of overall sensitivity to old versus new items. There was, first of all, a nearly significant but theoretically uninteresting main effect of language of schema, $F(1, 33) = 2.96$, $p < .10$, indicating that subjects tended to be less accurate for the characters based on Chinese-labeled schemas (mean $d' = 2.20$) than for the characters based on English-labeled schemas (mean $d' = 2.49$). In addition to this main effect of character type, however, a contrast testing the predicted Language of Processing × Language of Schema interaction was also significant, $t(33) = 2.47$, $p < .01$.[3] The CE–C group was much less accurate for

---

[3]The test for the Language of Processing × Language of Schema interaction, in this and all other analyses, was as follows. Because language of schema is a within-subjects variable, a difference score was first calculated for each subject by subtracting the mean score for the two characters based on Chinese-labeled schemas from the mean score for the two characters based on English-labeled schemas. The hypothesized interaction could then be tested by applying the following contrast to the difference scores just described: 1 (E–E), 1 (CE–E), –2 (CE–C). Because a directional pattern of means was predicted, one-tailed tests of significance were used.

TABLE 3   Mean Ratings of Previously Seen Recognition-Memory Items

Language of Processing	Group	Language of Schema	
		English[a]	Chinese[b]
English	E–E	3.25	3.42
	CE–E	3.32	3.52
Chinese	CE–C	3.54	3.46

Note. E–E = English monolinguals using English. CE–E = Chinese–English bilinguals using English. CE–C = Chinese–English bilinguals using Chinese.

[a]The data in this column are averaged over the two characters based on English-labeled schemas.

[b]The data in this column are averaged over the two characters based on Chinese-labeled schemas.

the characters based on Chinese-labeled schemas, the CE–E group was only slightly less accurate for those characters, and the E–E group was slightly less accurate for the characters based on English-labeled schemas. A further contrast comparing the two English-language conditions did not approach significance ($t < 1$).[4]

Surprisingly, however, these differences in accuracy were due more to differences in the ability to recognize old items of information than to differences in the tendency to give false alarms to schema-congruent foils. Table 3 presents subjects' mean recognition ratings of previously presented items. The Language of Processing × Language of Schema interaction was significant, $t(3) = 2.37$, $p < .05$. As the table shows, both groups of subjects working in English less confidently recognized information previously presented about the characters based on English-labeled schemas, whereas subjects working in Chinese less confidently recognized information previously presented about the characters based on Chinese-labeled schemas.

As it turned out, between-condition variability in the tendency to give false alarms to schema-congruent foils was very highly correlated with between-con-

dition variability in the tendency to give false alarms to schema-irrelevant foils (the correlation between the mean recognition ratings given to the two types of foils across the six cells of the design was $r = .87$). Because of this, it would not be appropriate to test the second part of Hypothesis 1 (which pertains to schema-congruent false alarms) directly on the schema-congruent false-alarm scores per se. Therefore a derived measure was constructed, namely the subject's mean rating of the schema-congruent foils minus his or her mean rating of the schema-irrelevant foils. This measure provided an index of the subject's tendency to falsely recognize schema-congruent material while simultaneously controlling for any tendency to give false alarms to all new items. The data for this relative false-alarm index are shown in Table 4. The hypothesized Language of Processing × Language of Schema interaction failed to reach significance, $t(33) = 1.43$, $.05 < p < .10$, although the pattern of means is more or less consistent with predictions (the E–E group showed a greater tendency to give false alarms for the characters based on English schemas, the CE–E group showed an equal tendency to give false alarms for both sets of characters, and the CE–C group showed a greater tendency to give false alarms for the characters based on Chinese-labeled schemas). The contrast comparing the two English-language conditions did not approach significance ($t < 1$).

TABLE 4   Mean Scores on the Recognition-Memory False-Alarm Index

Language of Processing	Group	Language of Schema	
		English[a]	Chinese[b]
English	E–E	.76	.62
	CE–E	.71	.71
Chinese	CE–C	.68	.93

Note. E–E = English monolinguals using English. CE–E = Chinese–English bilinguals using English. CE–C = Chinese–English bilinguals using Chinese. The index reported in this table is the subject's mean rating of the schema-congruent foils minus his or her mean rating of the schema-irrelevant foils.

[a]The data in this column are averaged over the two characters based on English-labeled schemas.

[b]The data in this column are averaged over the two characters based on Chinese-labeled schemas.

---

[4]The E–E and CE–E groups were compared by applying the following contrast to the difference scores described in Footnote 3: 1 (E–E), −1 (CE–E). Because no differences between these two groups were anticipated, two-tailed tests of significance were used.

In retrospect, we believe that the weakness of the false-alarm results stemmed from the nature of the schema-congruent foils themselves. In general, these foils tended to describe behaviors that were roughly similar to behaviors appearing in the original character descriptions. This in turn may have acted to minimize any effect of schematic processing on subjects' tendency to give false alarms to these foils. Had we used schema-congruent foils that were more clearly distinct from the originally presented information, we suspect that the Language of Processing × Language of Schema interaction would have been stronger.

Hypothesis 2 (that there would be a Language of Processing × Language of Schema interaction on the amount of freely recalled information about the characters) was not at all supported. In fact, the free-recall data showed no significant effects whatsoever on the number of items recalled, the accuracy with which items were recalled, or any other measure that we derived from these data. On the basis of this result, along with the finding that subjects less confidently recognized old information pertaining to characters based on labeled schemas in their language of processing, we may definitely conclude that schematic processing had no facilitative effect on memory for previously presented information in this study.

Tables 5 and 6 present the mean numbers of schema-congruent items in subjects' free impressions and mean ratings of the schema-congruent items on the inference test, respectively. Hypothesis 3 was

TABLE 5   Mean Numbers of Schema-Congruent Items in Subjects' Free Impressions

| Language of Processing | Group | Language of Schema | |
		English[a]	Chinese[b]
English	E–E	1.50	0.38
	CE–E	0.92	0.38
Chinese	CE–C	0.67	1.33

Note. E–E = English monolinguals using English. CE–E = Chinese–English bilinguals using English. CE–C = Chinese–English bilinguals using Chinese.

[a]The data in this column are averaged over the two characters based on English-labeled schemas.

[b]The data in this column are averaged over the two characters based on Chinese-labeled schemas.

TABLE 6   Mean Ratings of Schema-Congruent Attributes on the Inference Test

| Language of Processing | Group | Language of Schema | |
		English[a]	Chinese[b]
English	E–E	8.33	9.01
	CE–E	8.15	9.06
Chinese	CE–C	7.53	10.01

Note. E–E = English monolinguals using English. CE–E = Chinese–English bilinguals using English. CE–C = Chinese–English bilinguals using Chinese.

[a]The data in this column are averaged over the two characters based on English-labeled schemas.

[b]The data in this column are averaged over the two characters based on Chinese-labeled schemas.

strongly supported by both sets of results: Subjects' impressions contained more schema-congruent information, and subjects made stronger inferences regarding schema-congruent attributes, when the language in which they processed a stimulus character provided a label for the schema that the character exemplifies. The Language of Processing × Language of Schema interaction was significant both for the free-impression data, $t(33) = 4.09$, $p < .001$, and for the inference data, $t(33) = 2.72$, $p < .01$. The contrast comparing the two English-language conditions did not reach significance in either analysis, $t = 1.38$ and $t < 1$, respectively. (The inference-test data also showed a main effect of language of schema in that subjects tended to make stronger inferences about the characters based on Chinese-labeled schemas than about the characters based on English-labeled schemas. Again, however, this is a theoretically insignificant result that merely shows that the schema-congruent items written for the Chinese-schema characters happened to be somewhat more strongly linked to their personalities than the items written for the English-schema characters were linked to theirs. The important finding is that the tendency to make stronger inferences about the Chinese-schema characters was much more pronounced in the case of Chinese-language subjects.)

In contrast to the results just described, there was no Language of Processing × Language of Schema interaction in the case of description-based attributes, either in the free-impression data ($t < 1$) or in the inference data ($t < 1$).

DISCUSSION

This study tested whether languages with differing repertoires of labeled personality-type schemas are capable of exerting language-specific effects on their speakers' memory for and impressions of other people. It succeeded in demonstrating that both impressions and memory are affected when the target's personality and behavior conform to a labeled schema in the perceiver's language. These results should provide a broader, cross-linguistic perspective on current schema research in addition to extending the growing body of work on the language-cognition relation into the domain of social cognition (cf. Hoffman, Mischel, & Baer, 1984).

An interesting pattern of results emerged from the free-impression and inference tasks. There were significant Language of Processing × Language of Schema interactions on the number and strength of schema-congruent inferences but not of description-based inferences. Thus, ready access to an appropriate labeled schema facilitated "going beyond the information given" but did not act to strengthen impressions or predictions concerning attributes implicit in the targets' actual behavior.

The recognition-memory data provide further evidence of linguistic effects on thinking and also suggest a possible explanation for the pattern of results obtained with the free-impression and inference tasks. To restate the primary findings, subjects whose language of processing labels the schema on which a given character was based were less confident in recognizing previously presented items of information about the character and also tended (although nonsignificantly) to have greater difficulty in rejecting nonpresented but schema-congruent items of information. These findings suggest that the availability of a labeled schema may have led subjects to focus relatively less on the details of a target's behavior and instead rely more on their schematic knowledge of his personality type. Such a strategy has the advantage of greatly reducing the cognitive effort required of the

perceiver, but also has the obvious disadvantage of causing confusion in memory between presented and nonpresented information.

On the other hand, subjects without the benefit of a labeled schema apparently attended more closely to the target's behavior, as they exhibited superior recognition memory for previously presented information. This analysis can also explain the lack of a Language of Processing × Language of Schema interaction on description-based responses in the free-impression and inference tasks. Inferences about stimulus-based attributes could potentially have been reached in two ways—by consulting the appropriate schema or by consulting one's memory for the stimulus information—and the two strategies apparently yielded comparable results. In contrast, it is only by way of a schema that one can transcend the direct implications of the presented information, which accounts for the significant Language of Processing × Language of Schema interaction on schema-congruent responses in these tasks.

It is of some interest to compare our findings with the results of the research on language and color memory, which represents the most extensive body of work to date on the language-and-thought question. Except for the substitution of personality types for colors, the logic of our study was very similar to that of the color-memory experiments—particularly the study by Stefflre et al. (1966), in which an actual cross-linguistic comparison was made. In both cases, the research strategy involved looking for possible effects of the linguistic codability of stimuli on memory for the stimuli (and, in our study, on inferences about the stimuli as well). The color-memory research, however, has consistently shown that the availability of an appropriate verbal description results in more accurate recognition memory for a given color, whereas our study found that ready access to an appropriate labeled schema resulted in less accurate recognition memory for a target person's behavior.

These divergent findings may have stemmed in part from differences in the recognition-memory tasks used. In our study, subjects were required to recognize facts about the stimulus person, whereas in the color-memory research the task was simply to identify the stimulus in an array. Had our study also required subjects to identify the target person in a group of similar individuals, it is possible that a facilitative effect of schema availability would have been found. Intuitively, however, this seems unlikely. We tend to think that the differences in results stem from differences in the nature of the stimuli themselves. Many of the important attributes of social stimuli—personalities in particular—are hidden from the perceiver's view, and consequently there is a need, or at least the opportunity, to rely heavily on the inference process in fleshing out one's representation of the stimulus. This, of course, can lead to confusion in memory between observed and inferred attributes—all the more so to the extent that one can apply a schematic label to the stimulus. In the case of colors, there is obviously little if any need or even possibility for the perceiver to infer additional attributes of the stimulus, if indeed it makes sense to speak of colors as having attributes at all. Consequently, if one's descriptive label for a color is a reasonably good one in the first place, there is no reason to expect it to bias one's later memory for the color.

In many respects, color stimuli may be the exception rather than the rule. Certainly it seems to be true that most other nonsocial stimuli, including the natural objects studied by cognitive psychologists, more closely resemble most social stimuli than they do colors. There is, however, at least one fairly obvious difference in the effects of schematic processing on the representations that people form of social and nonsocial stimuli. This difference has to do not so much with the extent of people's inferences about the two types of stimuli but more with the accuracy of those inferences. In most cases where a natural object can be labeled with a relatively brief verbal expression at all, the label constitutes a highly useful description of the object, in the sense of being highly predictive of the object's attributes. Inferences about the important features of objects categorized as chairs, trees, or automobiles are very likely to be correct. In contrast, inferences about the attributes of persons categorized as artistic types or extraverts are nearly as likely to be wrong as to be right, if we accept the current wisdom regarding the generality and consistency of personality (or rather the lack thereof). People could pay a considerable price in accuracy by attempting to apply

the same type of categorical thinking that serves them so well in the object domain to the world of social experience.[5]

We believe that our study provides somewhat more conclusive evidence for an effect of language on thought than have most previous studies using a cross-linguistic design. We say this because the design of this study allowed us to evaluate the role of non-linguistic cultural differences between the groups as possible causes of the obtained effects, which is not the case with studies that simply contrast monolingual speakers of different languages or, more generally, with studies that limit their comparisons to two groups of subjects with differing cultural characteristics. Because the E–E and CE–E groups for the most part responded similarly but differed from the CE–C group, we have clear evidence for an effect of language per se. It is true, however, that although in no case did the difference between the E–E and CE–E groups reach significance, on some measures the CE–E group did tend to fall between the E–E and CE–C groups. This suggests that cultural differences also played a role in our results, albeit a smaller one than did the language-of-processing variable.

On the other hand, there are at least two respects in which this study furnishes only limited evidence in support of the linguistic relativity hypothesis, beyond the obvious fact that the results are consistent only with the weak Whorfian view (i.e., that a given language makes certain ways of thinking either easier or more difficult) and not with the strong view (i.e., that a given language makes certain ways of thinking either obligatory or impossible). In the first place, we are unsure if the effects of language demonstrated here generally characterize most real-world cases of

---

[5]Of relevance here is the distinction that Lingle, Altom, and Medin (1984) drew between *membership attributes* and *inference attributes*. Membership attributes are those that are (or can be) used to assign instances to categories in the first place, whereas inference attributes are those that are simply implied by the fact of category membership. According to Lingle et al., membership attributes and inference attributes tend to be the same for natural object categories but not for social categories, particularly person categories. If this is true, it provides an obvious explanation for the difference in inferential accuracy that, as we have argued, is probably associated with the two types of categories.

person cognition. Subjects in our study received relatively impoverished input about a relatively large number of stimulus persons and had to retain this information over a fairly long period of time. It is precisely under these difficult memory conditions that we would expect the effects of verbally labeled schemas to be most pronounced. When people are able to focus their attention in a more leisurely manner on the behavior of individual persons, their impressions may not be structured to the same degree, if at all, in terms of labeled schemas such as *artistic type*. In the second place, this study has demonstrated only that a language's repertory of labeled categories (its lexicon) affects the categorizing behavior of its speakers. Far more controversial, and also far more interesting, are the possible effects of a language's grammar on the thought patterns of its speakers. Whorf himself believed that a language's grammar embodies the linguistic community's world view. With few exceptions, however (e.g., Bloom, 1981; Carroll & Casagrande, 1958), the effects of grammar on thought and behavior have gone unstudied, probably because it is so difficult to operationalize and measure the sorts of effects hypothesized by Whorf. The possibility that these fascinating ideas will someday yield to empirical scrutiny nonetheless remains an exciting one.

REFERENCES

Berlin, B., & Kay, P. (1969). *Basic color terms: Their universality and evolution.* Berkeley: University of California Press.

Bloom, A. H. (1981). *The linguistic shaping of thought: A study in the impact of language on thinking in China and the West.* Hillsdale, NJ: Erlbaum.

Brislin, R. W. (1970). Back-translation for cross-cultural research. *Journal of Cross-Cultural Psychology, 1,* 185–216.

Brown, R., & Lenneberg, E. (1954). A study in language and cognition. *Journal of Abnormal and Social Psychology, 49,* 454–462.

Cantor, N., & Mischel, W. (1979a). Prototypes in person perception. In L. Berkowitz (Ed.), *Advances in experimental social psychology* (Vol. 12, pp. 3–52). New York: Academic Press.

Cantor, N., & Mischel, W. (1979b). Prototypicality and personality: Effects on free recall and personality impressions. *Journal of Research in Personality, 13,* 187–205.

Carmichael, L., Hogan, H. P., & Walter, A. A. (1932). An experimental study of the effect of language on the reproduction of visually perceived form. *Journal of Experimental Psychology, 15,* 73–86.

Carroll, J. B., & Casagrande, J. B. (1958). The function of language classifications in behavior. In E. E. Maccoby, T. M. Newcomb, & E. L. Hartley (Eds.), *Readings in social psychology* (3rd ed., pp. 18–31). New York: Holt, Rinehart & Winston.

Clark, H. H. (1969). Linguistic processes in deductive reasoning. *Psychological Review, 76,* 387–404.

Fiske, S. T., & Taylor, S. E. (1984). *Social cognition.* Reading, MA: Addison-Wesley.

Forgas, J. P. (1983). The effects of prototypicality and cultural salience on perceptions of people. *Journal of Research in Personality, 17,* 153–173.

Greenfield, P. M., Reich, L. C., & Olver, R. R. (1966). On culture and equivalence: II. In J. S. Bruner, R. R. Olver, & P. M. Greenfield (Eds.), *Studies in cognitive growth* (pp. 270–318). New York: Wiley.

Higgins, E. T., & Chaires, W. M. (1980). Accessibility of interrelational constructs: Implications for stimulus encoding and creativity. *Journal of Experimental Social Psychology, 16,* 348–361.

Hoffman, C., Mischel, W., & Baer, J. (1984). Language and person cognition: Effects of communicative set on trait attribution. *Journal of Personality and Social Psychology, 46,* 1029–1043.

Lantz, D., & Stefflre, V. (1964). Language and cognition revisited. *Journal of Abnormal and Social Psychology, 69,* 472–481.

Lingle, J. H., Altom, M. W., & Medin, D. L. (1984). Of cabbages and kings: Assessing the extendibility of natural object concept models to social things. In R. S. Wyer, Jr., & T. K. Srull (Eds.), *Handbook of social cognition* (Vol. 1, pp. 71–117). Hillsdale, NJ: Erlbaum.

Lucy, J. A., & Shweder, R. A. (1979). Whorf and his critics: Linguistic and nonlinguistic influences on color memory. *American Anthropologist, 81,* 581–615.

Rosch, E. (1974). Linguistic relativity. In A. Silverstein (Ed.), *Human communication: Theoretical explorations* (pp. 95–121). New York: Halstead Press.

Stefflre, V., Castillo Vales, V., & Morley, L. (1966). Language and cognition in Yucatan: A cross-cultural rep-

lication. *Journal of Personality and Social Psychology*, 4, 112–115.

Whorf, B. L. (1956). *Language, thought, and reality*. New York: Wiley.

POSTSCRIPT

The idea that differences in language would lead to differences in thinking seems very commonsensical, and examples that appear to support that idea abound, such as the number of words Eskimos have for snow (an example, by the way, that is not well founded; Martin, 1986, or Pullum, 1991). The linguistic relativity hypothesis in one form or another has had a long history (Penn, 1972; Schlesinger, 1991), although empirical tests of the hypothesis have taken place only in the last 40 years. Unfortunately, it's difficult to come to a conclusion about whether the experimental data support linguistic relativity or not, in part because there are so many interpretations of its predictions (Schlesinger, 1991). In general, however, experimental evidence supporting the linguistic relativity hypothesis has been quite weak.

For example, although research on the effects of terms for colors on peoples' perception and memory of color initially supported the linguistic relativity hypothesis (see Brown & Lenneberg, 1954), it is now generally accepted that color vocabulary has small, if any, effects (see Brown, 1976, for a summary; see Kay & Kempton, 1984, for a different emphasis). Bloom's (1981) research on the Chinese speakers' difficulty with counterfactual reasoning has been strongly criticized also (Au, 1983; Liu, 1985; Takano, 1989; see Bloom, 1984, for a reply, and Brown, 1986, for a thoughtful commentary on the controversy).

Speaking Chinese (or Japanese or Korean), however, apparently does lead to a different mental representation of numbers relative to speaking English. Kindergarten and first grade children who speak Chinese, Japanese, or Korean have been shown to have a better understanding than American children do of the base-10 nature of our counting system—for example that 31 means 3 groups of 10 plus 1 (Miura, Kim, Chang, & Okamoto, 1988). The "teens" in English pose a particular problem; the 10 + 2 nature of 12 is not apparent in the word *twelve*, whereas in the Asian languages studied the name for 12 is literally *ten-two*. Furthermore, *fourteen* is not as clearly distinguished from *forty* as *ten-four* is from *four-ten*, particularly when the numbers are spoken. In certain tasks, difficulty with "teens" can be seen in adults, including Chinese–English bilinguals when speaking English (Miller & Zhu, 1991). However, it is somewhat unclear whether these findings imply differential mathematical ability or achievement, particularly in adults. McCloskey, Sokol, and Goodman (1986), for example, have shown that number *naming* is a process distinct from *calculating* with numbers. On the other hand, Chinese speakers do seem to have an advantage in digit span, the number of numbers that can be held in working memory (see Reading 9); English numbers take longer to pronounce, and working memory appears to be temporally limited (Chen & Stevenson, 1988; Stigler, Lee, & Stevenson, 1986). The large differences in Chinese and English orthography (writing systems) also have a number of cognitive psychological ramifications (see Hoosain, 1991). (See the Postscript to Reading 33 and Saxe & Posner, 1983, for further discussion of the impact of language and culture on mathematical ability and achievement.)

Most scientists have concluded that the language one speaks does not completely determine or control one's perception and cognition, and most recent research emphasizes the universality of perceptual, linguistic, and other cognitive processes (Berry, Poortinga, Segall, & Dasen, 1992; Keil, 1979; van Riemsdijk & Williams, 1986). But this conclusion does not rule out the possibility that the language one speaks has some *influence* on one's perception and cognition. The problem with the latter claim is its vagueness, and therefore, its untestability. Hunt and Agnoli (1991) suggest that the influence claim can be clarified and that there are some areas, particularly in social cognition, in which support for the linguistic relativity hypothesis may be found (for example, this work by Hoffman et al. and work by Woll & Martinez, 1982).

One final issue worth mentioning is an area in which the veracity of the linguistic relativity hypothesis has particular social significance: the use of sexist language. Does using terms like *mankind* to refer to all people actually dispose people to think only about males? The empirical evidence (Hamilton, 1988; Hyde, 1984; MacKay, 1980; MacKay & Fulkerson, 1979; Moulton, Robinson, & Elias, 1978) confirms that adults and children are much more inclined to think of men when the pronoun *he* is used. But apart from these studies of pronouns, no published experiments investigating the general issue of the impact of sexist language on cognition appear to be available, despite the level of discussion the topic engenders (see Henley, 1989, for a description of a number of unpublished studies).

FOR FURTHER THOUGHT

1. Explain why it is reasonable to predict that language will have a greater effect on social categories than on perceptual ones.
2. What were the advantages and disadvantages in using Chinese–English bilinguals (rather than Chinese monolinguals) for this experiment? Are Hoffman, Lau, and Johnson's results directly comparable with those re-

ported by Preston and Lambert (Reading 20)? How do Hoffman, Lau, and Johnson's findings relate to (or not relate to) Preston and Lambert's?

3. What is the relevance of the language fluency of the subjects in this experiment; that is, how might different levels of fluency affect the interpretation of the researchers' results? What are the advantages and disadvantages of assessing language fluency in the way that they did?

4. Why did Hoffman and his colleagues report their pilot studies in such detail? Why were those studies necessary?

5. What is the difference between the free-recall and free-impressions tasks? between the free-impressions and the inference tasks?

6. Explain the rationale for each of Hoffman, Lau, and Johnson's hypotheses.

7. Why was the hypothesis regarding the tendency to commit false alarms to schema-congruent items actually tested on the derived measure (or index) of false alarms to schema-congruent items minus false alarms to schema-incongruent items? What possible explanation for the weakness of the false alarm data do Hoffman and his colleagues give?

8. Why was an effect found for schema-congruent attributes but not for description-based attributes in the free-impression and the inference data?

9. Why should it be that Hoffman and his associates found poorer performance on categories that correspond to directly coded schemas, whereas regarding the effect of language on color perception and memory, people do *better* with colors that are directly coded? What crucial differences are there between social and nonsocial categories (excluding color)?

REFERENCES

Au, T. K.-F. (1983). Chinese and English counterfactuals: The Sapir-Whorf hypothesis revisited. *Cognition, 15,* 155–187.

Berry, J. W., Poortinga, Y. H., Segall, M. H., & Dasen, P. R. (1992). *Cross-cultural psychology: Research and applications.* New York: Cambridge University Press.

Bloom, A. H. (1981). *The linguistic shaping of thought: A study in the impact of language on thinking in China and the West.* Hillsdale, NJ: Erlbaum.

Bloom, A. H. (1984). Caution—the words you use may affect what you say: A response to Au. *Cognition, 17,* 275–287.

Brown, R. (1976). Reference—In memorial tribute to Eric Lenneberg. *Cognition, 4,* 125–153.

Brown, R. (1986). Linguistic relativity. In S. H. Hulse & B. F. Green, Jr. (Eds.), *One hundred years of psychological research in America: G. Stanley Hall and the Johns Hopkins tradition* (pp. 241–276). Baltimore: Johns Hopkins University Press.

Brown, R., & Lenneberg, E. H. (1954). A study in language and cognition. *Journal of Abnormal and Social Psychology, 49,* 454–462.

Chen, C., & Stevenson, H. W. (1988). Cross-linguistic differences in digit span of preschool children. *Journal of Experimental Child Psychology, 46*, 150–158.

Hamilton, M. C. (1988). Using masculine generics: Does generic "he" increase male bias in the user's imagery? *Sex Roles, 19*, 785–799.

Henley, N. M. (1989). Molehill or mountain? What we know and don't know about sex bias in language. In M. Crawford & M. Gentry (Eds.), *Gender and thought: Psychological perspectives* (pp. 59–78). New York: Springer-Verlag.

Hoosain, R. (1991). *Psycholinguistic implications for linguistic relativity: A case study of Chinese.* Hillsdale, NJ: Erlbaum.

Hunt, E., & Agnoli, F. (1991). The Whorfian hypothesis: A cognitive psychology perspective. *Psychological Review, 98*, 377–389.

Hyde, J. S. (1984). Children's understanding of sexist language. *Developmental Psychology, 20*, 697–706.

Kay, P., & Kempton, W. (1984). What is the Sapir-Whorf hypothesis? *American Anthropologist, 86*, 65–79.

Keil, F. C. (1979). *Semantic and conceptual development: Ontological perspectives.* Cambridge, MA: Harvard University Press.

Liu, L. G. (1985). Reasoning counterfactually in Chinese: Are there any obstacles? *Cognition, 21*, 239–270.

MacKay, D. G. (1980). Psychology, prescriptive grammar and the pronoun problem. *American Psychologist, 35*, 444–449.

MacKay, D. G., & Fulkerson, D. C. (1979). On the comprehension and production of pronouns. *Journal of Verbal Learning and Verbal Behavior, 18*, 661–673.

Martin, L. (1986). Eskimo words for snow: A case study in the genesis and decay of an anthropological example. *American Anthropologist, 88*, 418–423.

McCloskey, M., Sokol, S. M., & Goodman, R. A. (1986). Cognitive processes in verbal-number production: Inferences from the performance of brain-damaged subjects. *Journal of Experimental Psychology: General, 115*, 307–330.

Miller, K. F., & Zhu, J. (1991). The trouble with teens: Accessing the structure of number names. *Journal of Memory and Language, 30*, 48–68.

Miura, I. T., Kim, C. C., Chang, C.-M., & Okamoto, Y. (1988). Effects of language characteristics on children's cognitive representation of number: Cross-national comparisons. *Child Development, 59*, 1445–1450.

Moulton, J., Robinson, G. M., & Elias, C. (1978). Sex bias in language use: "Neutral" pronouns that aren't. *American Psychologist, 33*, 1032–1036.

Penn, J. M. (1972). *Linguistic relativity versus innate ideas: The origins of the Sapir-Whorf hypothesis in German thought.* The Hague: Mouton.

Pullum, G. K. (1991). *The great Eskimo vocabulary hoax and other irreverent essays on the study of language.* Chicago: University of Chicago Press.

Rumelhart, D. E. (1980). Schemata: The building blocks of cognition. In R. J. Spiro, B. C. Bruce, & W. F. Brewer (Eds.), *Theoretical issues in reading comprehension* (pp. 33–58). Hillsdale, NJ: Erlbaum.

Saxe, G. B., & Posner, J. (1983). The development of numerical cognition: Cross-cultural perspectives. In H. P. Ginsburg (Ed.), *The development of mathematical thinking* (pp. 291–317). New York: Academic Press.

Schlesinger, I. M. (1991). The wax and wane of Whorfian views. In R. L. Cooper & B. Spolsky (Eds.), *The influence of language on culture and thought* (pp. 7–44).Berlin: Mouton de Gruyter.

Stigler, J. W., Lee, S.-Y., & Stevenson, H. W. (1986). Digit memory in Chinese and English: Evidence for a temporally limited store. *Cognition, 23,* 1–20.

Takano, Y. (1989). Methodological problems in cross-cultural studies of linguistic relativity. *Cognition, 31,* 141–162.

van Riemsdijk, H., & Williams, E. (1986). *Introduction to the theory of grammar.* Cambridge, MA: MIT Press.

Woll, S. B., & Martinez, J. M. (1982). The effects of biasing labels on recognition of facial expressions of emotion. *Social Cognition, 1,* 70–82.

INTRODUCTION

Cultural differences in practices and values are to a certain extent adaptations to local environments. Do such cultural or environmental differences have implications for cognitive functioning? Judith Kearins explores this question in "Visual Spatial Memory in Australian Aboriginal Children of Desert Regions."

Kearins gives her subjects, descendents of either nomadic desert Aborigines or of white European settlers, a task that requires remembering the locations of various objects. She is particularly interested in testing whether subjects use a purely visual strategy—one that involves remembering what the layout of objects *looks* like—or a strategy that includes verbal mediation, remembering verbal labels for the objects and their positions. Kearins believes that the desert environment favors a visual strategy.

In her introduction, Kearins carefully discusses many of the methodological problems that arise when trying to compare performance on cognitive tasks across cultures. As you read this article, make sure you understand what those problems are and how Kearins addresses them in her studies. Do you think she solves those problems? Do her methods raise problems of their own? (Most of Experiment 2, and all references to it, have been excluded in this selection.)

Visual Spatial Memory in Australian Aboriginal Children of Desert Regions

Judith M. Kearins
University of Western Australia

The experimental studies reported here arose from a hypothesis relating pressures of particular environments to cognitive strengths or biases of different human groups. The hypothesis has been extended to human cognitive research from suggestions made by Lockard (1971) for investigations in comparative animal psychology. Lockard contended that the arbitrary laboratory tasks frequently used to compare the relative ability of different animals were unlikely to provide information on special skills or behavioral strengths, since the tasks bore little or no relationship to the types of intelligent behavior required for survival in the natural habitat. Since particular ways of behaving are known to have adaptive significance (e.g., Tinbergen, 1953; Crook, 1970) and thus to be subject to selection pressures, it should be expected that those behaviors most closely related to survival in the natural environment will be the most important in any organism's repertoire. According to this view, experimental tasks are unlikely to reveal special skills or strengths unless they are derived from significant behavioral requirements of the natural environment.

Since all groups of humans belong to a single species and thus have far greater genetic similarities than differences (Tobias, 1972) it can perhaps be expected that group differences in human ability will be differences of extent rather than kind. But differences in skill biases and thus in patterns of ability (rather than in presence or absence of a characteristic) are to be expected between groups of widely different environments and related life-style, according to the view adopted here. Where a group has successfully inhabited a particular environment for a long period, differences between this and other groups may be especially marked. Such a group can be found in the large Western Desert region of Australia (Figure 1).

Aboriginal people, traditionally following a seminomadic hunting and gathering life-style, are thought to have occupied the large internal desert regions of Australia for at least 30,000 years (Mabbutt, 1971; Bowler & Thorne, 1976) and may have done so for much longer (Kirk, 1971). These regions are considered to be among the world's least hospitable habitats for man (e.g., Gould, 1969) and have been subject to little successful exploitation by later European settlers.

In common with nonindustrialized people elsewhere, Australian Aborigines have performed relatively poorly on more or less standard cognitive tests originating in Western culture. Even when such tests have been substantially modified in attempts to make them "culture-fair," as in the case of the Queensland Test (McElwain & Kearney, 1970), remote Aboriginal children have obtained very low scores. Since performances of urban children living in close contact with white Australians have, on the other hand, approximated those of low socioeconomic white groups, with intermediate contact groups performing accordingly, McElwain and Kearney (1973) conclude that "the test results are dependent to a considerable degree upon contact or some variable related to contact" (p. 47).

I am grateful to all the children who participated in this study for their friendly and willing cooperation and to their teachers, and to James Lumsden, Peter Livesey, Jay Birnbrauer, and John Watson for advice and criticism. Reprint requests should be sent to Dr. Judith Kearins, Department of Psychology, The University of Western Australia, Nedlands, 6009, Western Australia.

SOURCE: *Cognitive Psychology*, 13, 1981, pp. 434–460. Copyright © 1981 by Academic Press, Inc. Reprinted by permission.

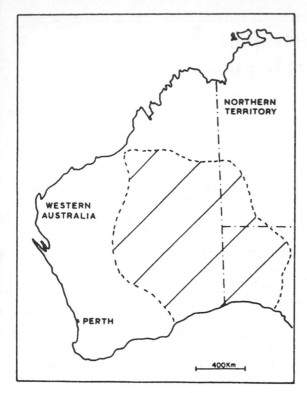

FIGURE 1   Map showing approximate boundaries of the Western Desert region of Australia (shaded).

Piagetian investigators of the development of certain logical concepts have found a similar effect of the European contact variable (de Lacey, 1970; Dasen, 1973a; Dasen, de Lacey, & Seagrim, 1973). Remote children and adults have been found to demonstrate all of the concepts in question at a much later age than is usual for Europeans, and "a more or less large proportion . . . do not develop these concrete operational concepts at all" (Dasen, 1973b, p. 400). Children living in urban communities, on the other hand, have been found to perform like European children.

In these investigations no attempts have been made to devise tasks reflecting cognitive requirements of Aboriginal culture or life-style, or to establish the possible relevance of any standard task requirements to the Aboriginal milieu. Although the more obviously alien components have been removed from tasks (e.g., language, in the case of the Queensland Test, and certain material items in the case of some

Piagetian tasks), actual task requirements have remained essentially unchanged from their standard European forms.

Even where theoretical attempts to take account of local cultural factors have occurred, environmental or cultural features of interest have tended to be global ones, and, in practice, tasks used have been Western tests apparently of no real relevance to local requirements. Berry (1971), for instance, attempted to relate a "hunting ecology" to performance on "spatial" tests, and found that Australian Aboriginal adults of central desert regions performed at levels well below those of Scottish samples. This finding is at variance with the many indications in popular belief and in anthropological literature (e.g., Lockwood, 1962, 1964; Lewis, 1976), that Aboriginal people are characterized by unusual spatial competence (e.g., in route-finding, tracking, etc.), and can presumably be attributed largely to the nature of the test requirements. It is not clear that the tests themselves (Kohs' Blocks, Embedded Figures Test, Raven's Progressive Matrices) are spatial measures even in their culture of origin (see, e.g., McFarlane-Smith, 1964; Bock & Kolakowski, 1973), and no attempt to relate their requirements to spatial behavior in a "hunting ecology" has been made by Berry. Following Berry, Dasen (1973b) hypothesized that Aboriginal children should develop Piagetian "spatial" concepts earlier than logicomathematical concepts, and found this to be the case for remote children. Again, however, European children acquired these "spatial" concepts earlier than the Aboriginal children. Further, Dasen points out that the less verbal nature of the "spatial" relative to the logicomathematical tasks may account for the apparent reversal of developmental sequence in Aboriginal children with low English competence, since all testing was done in English.

Attempts to interpret such results are fraught with difficulty. Berry (1971) suggests that since the effect of Western education is to increase test scores, lower scores on all tests for remote people are to be expected. But the effects of differential ability and test sophistication cannot then be disentangled. If such remote people are those living closest to environmental requirements postulated for the total group of interest, their scores on measures related to these requirements should presumably be the highest. No conclusions can reasonably be drawn when their scores are consistently the lowest, except perhaps those relating to standard test sophistication.

From psychological reports it is clear, then, that although desert Aboriginal people have successfully occupied for thousands of years country considered virtually uninhabitable by European settlers, they have not been shown to exhibit any particular skill on standard cognitive tests. Their performances on such tests have been consistently inferior to those of white Australians even where some attempt has been made to relate the tests to general views of Aboriginal strengths.

THE PRESENT STUDY

In this study, an attempt has been made to relate the requirements of the experimental tasks to a postulated important requirement of desert living—accurate memory for the spatial relationships between several environmental features. Under traditional desert living conditions, water supplies (dependent on the capricious and unreliable desert rainfall) ultimately determined the movement patterns of small foraging groups. Thus, for instance, regular routes could not be followed between often widely spaced sites when camp was shifted, so that particular sites, mostly visually unremarkable, would need to be located from any direction. Tonkinson (1974) points out that due to the uncertain distribution of rainfall "the pattern of movement within any particular year was never duplicated" (p. 19). Similarly, in the daily search for food, both hunting and gathering required that people should be able to move considerable distances in different directions from camp and frequently return by new and roundabout routes without getting lost (Gould, 1969). Memory for a single environmental feature would be unlikely to have been a reliable identifier of any particular spot, both because outstanding features are rare in this region of many recurring features, and because of the need for approach from any direction. But particular spatial relationships between several features could uniquely specify a location, more or less regardless of orientation. Accurate memory for such relationships is thus likely to have been of considerable value both in

movement between water sources and in daily foraging movements from a base camp.

Despite their derivation, the experimental tasks of the study are not especially "Aboriginal" in appearance, but relatively neat and geometrically arranged in the manner of many European tests. They differ from the latter mainly in that they were devised to reflect a cognitive skill, postulated on environmental and life-style considerations, for a particular non-European group. Thus there is here an attempt to match task requirements to long-term survival requirements. Standard tests, on the other hand, have not generally been aimed at reflecting any postulated survival skill, even within their culture of origin; in cross-cultural research, analogies between their particular cognitive or behavioral requirements and living requirements of a group of interest have tended not to be drawn.

In the experimental tasks children were asked to view a rectangular array of objects for 30 sec and then, when the objects were disarrayed, to reconstruct the original array. The basic task could be varied in a number of ways by the use of different categories and arrangements of objects. Arrays were constituted as 5×4 matrices in most cases, although two 4×3 matrices were used initially. In the first study, involving adolescents (Kearins, 1976), four tasks were used, which formed the basis of subsequent investigations of younger children.

These tasks were designed to control for differences in object familiarity, and to reveal possible group differences in task strategy. The question of object familiarity is important in relation to task equivalence for children of two cultures (desert Aboriginal and white Australian comparison groups). In this study the problem was avoided by the provision of two sets of materials, one to suit the experience of each group, but with both sets being presented to each group. These sets can be broadly classed "Artifactual" and "Natural." Thus, if item familiarity affected performance, Aboriginal children would be expected to perform better on Natural than on Artifactual tasks, while the reverse would be expected of white Australian children. Within each of these two broad divisions two memory arrays were constituted, one having items of different nominal categories and the other not. If verbal coding strategies were attempted by children of both groups, then similar patterns of performance could be expected, but if such strategies characterized white children (as suggested by other evidence, e.g., Conrad (1972)) and not Aboriginal children, the patterns should differ regardless of absolute levels of performance.

EXPERIMENT 1

Method

Subjects (N = 88)

Forty-four adolescents aged 12–16 years (27 boys, 17 girls) of desert Aboriginal origin and 44 adolescents (28 boys, 16 girls) of white Australian origin took part. The desert group constituted the total population of a school drawing children from several widely separated settlements of the Western Desert region, who had been reared among people living, for the most part, under semitraditional tribal conditions (fully traditional groups no longer exist). All spoke English of a nonstandard variety, as a second language, and wrote it with varying degrees of competence. The white Australian subjects were drawn from a large student population of a high school in an outer suburb of Perth. They were selected haphazardly by the guidance officer to match the Aboriginal group for age and sex. No further attempts at matching were made, since white subjects matched in material, educational, and social status with the desert children would be unusually socially depressed in circumstance relative to the total white Australian population. In language spoken (English), school progress, and family backgrounds, the group can be considered reasonably representative of the wider white population.

Testing Strategy

In this and all subsequent studies great care was taken to make the testing enterprise acceptable to Aboriginal children, for most of whom "standard" testing situations have many alien components. To this end, for instance, all children were individually invited to participate, rather than coerced in any way. No testing was done until children had had time and opportunity to ask questions informally under conditions of their choosing, and all such questions were openly an-

swered. No personal questions (age, name, and so on) were in turn directed at children. Only when children had indicated a willingness to take part, had shown an interest in the projected proceedings, and had begun to volunteer information did testing begin, and this was always done under informal conditions. Schoolrooms were not used for testing, for instance; the work was done entirely out of doors, under trees, or in partially enclosed playground sheds or verandahs when shelter was necessary, but always in places open to public view and to natural sights and sounds. Materials were set out at sitting rather than table height, allowing a top view, and experimenter and subject sat side by side rather than opposite each other. No time limits were suggested for actual performance and all testing was avoided during school breaks. Casual, quiet behavior (old clothes, soft voice, limited speech, unhurried movements) and "appropriate" demeanor for an outsider were maintained throughout. These measures were adopted to accord with both adult expectations of children and general notions of courtesy among desert people, and thus to provide maximum psychological and physical comfort for participants. (Full details are contained in Kearins (1977).)

For white Australian subjects, schoolrooms were likewise avoided. Otherwise, informal and friendly contacts were established with children and all appearance of mystery avoided, as with Aboriginal children.

Memory Tasks

The following four tasks were used:

1. *Artifactual different* (A/D). A heterogeneous collection of 20 small man-made objects likely to be familiar to white Australian children (knife, eraser, thimble, die, ring, scissors, matchbox, etc.), and able to be differentiated by name and differing from each other in at least one other way (color, size, shape, usage). Objects, selected for interest and visual appeal, were presented on a white plastic-covered card divided into 20 (8 × 8 cm) compartments (in a 5 × 4 matrix) by narrow black lines.

2. *Natural different* (N/D). A heterogeneous collection of 20 naturally occurring objects, likely to be familiar to desert children (feather, rock, bark,

leaf, small skull, wildflower, etc.). Objects were arranged and presented as for Task 1.

3. *Artifactual same (A/S).* Twelve small bottles arranged as a 4 × 3 matrix. Bottles differed in age, size, shape, color, but were not labeled and not commonplace, so that ready differentiation by name was unlikely.

4. *Natural same (N/S).* Twelve small rocks differing in size, shape, color, texture, arranged as a 4 × 3 matrix.

Procedure

The four (covered) memory arrays were set out on benches at the same height as the stool on which each child sat. Presentation was in one of two randomly determined orders: N/D, N/S, A/D, A/S or A/D, A/S, N/D, N/S. Subjects were instructed that on removal of the cover they should "look hard at all the things and try to remember where they all are," and that the subsequent task was reconstruction of the array. (Many Aboriginal subjects may have incompletely understood these instructions, thus perhaps causing first performances to suffer somewhat.) The cover was then removed, and 30 sec allowed for viewing. The subject was then asked to close his/her eyes while the objects were jumbled in a heap in the center of the board, after which reconstruction proceeded with no set time limit. When reconstruction was completed, placements were recorded, the subject was informed of any errors, and misplaced objects were relocated correctly. The next array was then uncovered.

Results and Discussion

On all four tasks the desert adolescents correctly relocated more objects than did white subjects (Figure 2, Table 1). Group differences for 20-item arrays and for 12-item arrays (analyzed separately by two-way analysis of variance) were highly significant (Table 2). A significant Tasks × Groups effect occurred for the 20-item arrays, and for the 12-item arrays there was a significant Tasks effect (Table 2).

Comparison between groups for each task separately, and between tasks within each group show that:

1. For all four tasks performances of the Aboriginal group were significantly superior (A/D, $t(86)$ = 2.3, $p < .02$; N/D, $t(86)$ = 4.1, $p < .001$; A/S, $t(86)$ = 4.1, $p < .001$; N/S, $t(86)$ = 4.6, $p < .001$). The least difference between groups occurred for the A/D array, the task on which the white group obtained its highest score.

2. While the Aboriginal group scored better on the Natural/Different than on the Artifactual/Different array, the difference was not significant ($t(43)$ = 0.59, $p > .40$). The white Australian group, on the other hand, did significantly better on the Artifactual/Different array than on the Natural/Different ($t(43)$ = 2.61, $p < .02$), hence the significant Tasks × Groups effect (Table 2) for 20-item arrays.

3. While both groups found one 12-item array, Natural/Same, more difficult than the other (hence the significant 12-item Tasks effect, Table 2), the score difference was significant for the white Australian group ($t(43)$ = 2.14, $p < .05$) and not for the Aboriginal group ($t(43)$ = 1.22, $p > .20$).

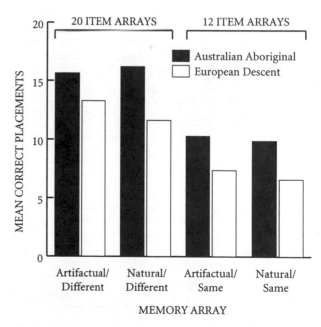

FIGURE 2   Mean correct placements on each of four visual spatial memory arrays for Australian Aboriginal and European-descent adolescents.

TABLE 1   Mean Correct Placements and Standard Deviations on Four Memory Tasks for Australian Aboriginal and White Australian Adolescents

	Task							
	A/D		N/D		A/S		N/S	
Group	Mean	SD	Mean	SD	Mean	SD	Mean	SD
Australian Aboriginal, N = 44	15.64	3.12	16.20	3.16	10.28	2.24	9.89	2.49
White Australian, N = 44	13.29	3.55	11.64	4.05	7.39	2.41	6.61	2.22

For many Aboriginal children the memory tasks seem to have been too easy. This was especially the case for the 12-item arrays, where on over half the performances (45 of 88) no errors were made. The 20-item arrays were apparently more difficult, although about one-fifth of performances were error free. From Table 3, showing error-free performances on all tasks for both groups, it is clear that the tasks were not too easy for white Australian children, and also that (in terms of error-free performances) the 12-item arrays were not any easier than the 20-item arrays. For this group, perfect performances accounted for less than 5% of total performances on both 20- and 12-item arrays. Frequency distributions (shown for both groups in Figure 3) show clearly the differential difficulty of 12-item arrays for the two groups, and for 12-item arrays in relation to 20-item arrays for the Aboriginal group. Where approximately normal distributions occur on both sets of tasks for white children, this is not so for Aboriginal children, and very much less so for 12- than 20-item arrays. As the data differences would suggest, the number of subjects contributing perfect performances differed markedly between the groups. Eight (18%) of the white Australian subjects managed one perfect score, and none obtained two or more perfect scores. Thirty-three (75%) of the desert children, on the other hand, made at least one perfect score, and 18 (41%) made at least two error-free performances. (Eight made no errors on two, nine made no errors on three, and one made no errors on four tasks.)

In addition to score differences, marked differences in behavior in relation to the tasks characterized the groups. Aboriginal subjects typically sat very still while viewing an array, and showed no signs of overt or covert vocalization. Their reconstructions were characterized by careful deliberation and a steady rate of progress. Most children were very effi-

TABLE 2   Summary of Analysis of Variance

	F[a]		
Comparison	Between Groups	Between Tasks	Groups×Tasks
20-item	33.945***	1.473 NS	6.140**
12-item	57.058***	4.008*	0.445 NS

[a] $df = 1,86$.
*$p < .05$.
**$p < .01$.
***$p < .001$.

TABLE 3   Frequency of Perfect Scores on Each Memory Task

Group	A/D f	A/D %	N/D f	N/D %	A/S f	A/S %	N/S f	N/S %
Australian Aboriginal, N = 44	6	13.6	11	25	24	54.5	21	47.7
White Australian, N = 44	2	4.5	2	4.5	2	4.5	2	4.5

cient and few location changes were made. Many sat, at some stage, holding an object and carefully scanning a section of the board before finally placing it in position. Most white Australian children, on the other hand, when viewing an array, moved about on the seat, picked up objects or turned them over, and muttered a great deal. Comments and questions relating to "same" or "natural" arrays frequently reflected a naming difficulty (e.g., "But how shall I know what to call them?"). In their reconstructions these children made many changes in location of objects. Many began the reconstruction with great haste, pushing the first four or five items quickly into position. There tended then to be a slowing down, and for the later items changes in item position tended to increase. (While this pattern characterized the majority, there were exceptions. A few children behaved and performed in similar ways to the Aboriginal children.)

Differences in both the scoring patterns and the task behavior of the two groups suggest differences in strategy. The still, absorbed, and silent behavior of the Aboriginal children suggests an essentially nonverbal approach, which is strongly suggested also by their

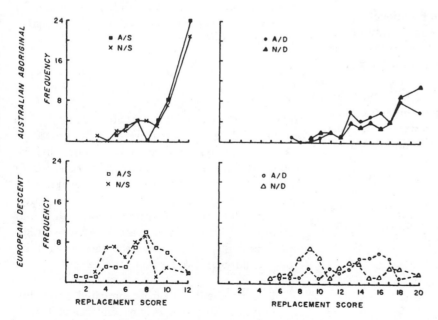

FIGURE 3   Frequency distributions of memory scores (correct replacements) for Australian Aboriginal and European-descent adolescents.

high scores on the same-name 12-item arrays. If the nominal class of objects was irrelevant to the strategy employed (which would be the case for a visual strategy), then it should not be surprising that the positions of 12 objects were easier to remember than the positions of 20, thus explaining the high proportion (51%) of error-free scores on these arrays. In this study arrays containing equal numbers of items in same name and different name categories could have been used for Aboriginal children, whose performance can be expected to have been equivalent for all arrays. For the white Australian group, on the other hand, the picture is rather different. They appear to have experienced as much difficulty in remembering the positions of 12 items having the same name as of 20 having different names, suggesting that attempts at differentiation by name occurred, or that verbal labels were clearly not irrelevant. Further, where objects can be expected to have been very familiar (thus lending themselves readily to a verbal strategy since all would have known names) performances were better than for less familiar (or less able to be differentiated by name) natural items.

The findings of this study can be summarized as follows:

1. Aboriginal adolescents of semitraditional desert-dwelling families scored at significantly higher levels than white Australian adolescents on visual spatial memory tasks derived from postulated desert survival requirements.

2. Since relative familiarity of materials did not influence Aboriginal scores but did influence white scores, and since a reduction in size of task combined with an increase in naming difficulty made tasks easier for Aboriginal children but not for whites, it seems highly likely that strategy differences characterized the two groups. A visual strategy is suggested for the Aboriginal subjects, while attempts at verbal mediation seem to have occurred for the white subjects. . . .

EXPERIMENT 2

Method

[Following are the descriptions of two of the three groups of children used in Experiment 2. (The third group of children were like those in Experiment 1.)

These descriptions are retained because those children or children like them are used in subsequent experiments. Experiment 2 itself is excluded.]

Subjects

(i) *Nontraditional Aboriginal group* (N = 46; 24 girls, 22 boys).   Children of this group, aged from 6 years 6 months to 11 years 10 months attended school in an old gold-mining town of a desert fringe area, in or around which they lived, either with their families or in a hostel during school terms. The sample consisted of all children attending the school of fully or predominantly Aboriginal descent. English (of a somewhat nonstandard variety) was the only language spoken by these children, the original local language having been lost for at least two generations. Pastoral activity in the 1880s, followed by the discovery of gold in the 1890s, led to the loss of cultural traditions and language. Today the people live on pastoral stations or in the small remaining "ghost" towns of the region, in a life-style resembling more that of poor whites of outback inland towns than that of the semitraditional desert settlement people. Men work at unskilled jobs, and food is bought from local stores. No gathering occurs, and hunting takes place only as recreation (in the same manner as that practiced by non-Aboriginal men of the locality—on weekends with rifles).

(ii) *White Australian group* (N = 46; 30 girls, 16 boys). Children of this group, aged from 6 years 11 months to 11 years 9 months attended a country school of approximately the same size as that attended by the Aboriginal children. An exhaustive sampling procedure was thus possible in both schools. Additionally, the school setting, in a small bush township 60 km from the capital, provided children with opportunity for maximum interaction with the natural world. Forty-two of the children were Australian born, while four were foreign born of migrant parents. All were of European descent, and all spoke standard English, although children of two farming families spoke Italian at home. . . .

[In Experiment 2, Kearins compared white children to nontraditional Aboriginal children and semitraditional Aboriginal students like those used in Experiment 1. She confirmed the white/Aboriginal differences, and found that the nontraditional and semitraditional Aboriginal children differed from one another only at the youngest ages.]

A number of smaller studies (Experiments 3, 4, 5) involving various manipulations of content and presentation within the same basic experimental procedure were directed at the question of task strategy. (Figure 4 provides a data summary.)

EXPERIMENT 3

This experiment was designed to differentiate between recognition of items previously seen and memory for spatial location.

Method

Subjects

Australian Aboriginal group. Subjects were 14 children (9 girls, 5 boys, aged from 10:0 to 12:0 years, mean age 11:6) who had been members, 18 months previously, of the nontraditional group of Experiment 2. They were selected as the only children between the ages of 10 and 12 years, at the time attending the school, who had participated in the previous study.

White Australian group. These were 14 children (8 girls, 6 boys, aged from 10:11 to 11:11 years, mean age 11:2) attending a suburban primary school. All were Australian born and had Australian parents, and were selected on this basis from a larger, more heterogeneous group of the same age. This group can be considered comparable to the 11-year-old white Australian group of Experiment 2; preliminary testing on the Natural/Different array of the previous experiments established that on this task there was no difference between the two groups (previous group, $N = 16$, N/D mean = 9.63, $SD = 3.91$; this group, $N = 14$, N/D mean = 9.5, $SD = 5.8$).

Testing Site

Essentially similar informal sites (open sheds on schoolgrounds) were employed for both groups, and bench seating was used to display material, while experimenter and subject sat side by side on small stools of the same height as the bench.

Materials and Procedure

The task had two elements—a spatial replacement requirement like those of previous experiments and an item recognition requirement. Twenty man-made items (small objects similar to those of the earlier A/D array, but none being the same) set out in a rectangular (5×4) array on the squared board described

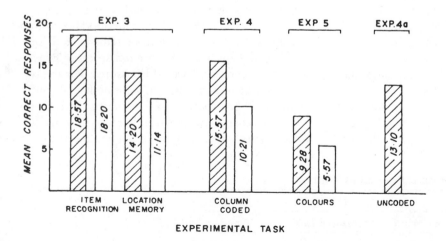

FIGURE 4   Summary of Experiments 3, 4, and 5.

previously, were viewed for 30 sec as before. These items were then removed from the board and mixed haphazardly with 20 other similar items on a neighboring clear Perspex tray. Children were required to select the items they had seen previously from the 40 items now displayed and to replace them in their original positions.

Results and Discussion

Neither group of children had any difficulty with the recognition task (Aboriginal mean = 18.64, $SD = 0.74$; white Australian mean = 18.21, $SD = 1.22$), while the Aboriginal group's location score was superior to that of the white group (mean = 14.21, $SD = 1.92$, as opposed to 11.14, $SD = 5.54$). These results indicate that the relatively low scores of white Australian children in previous experiments represented a specific difficulty in remembering spatial location of items rather than difficulty in item recognition. The location score difference between the groups ($t(26) = 1.96, p < .05$) is in line with other results. (Since the same subjects participated in Experiments 3, 4, and 5, a two-way analysis of variance with repeated measures was initially performed on the data. Table 4 provides a summary.)

Again, however (as the high white Australian variance indicates), some of the white Australian children obtained high location scores. (Scores ranged from 1 to 19, with two scores of 18 and one each of 16 and 19.) There is some evidence (Schulman, 1973) to suggest that a bipartite task such as this may lead to "incidental" gains in location scores—if the main task is selection of remembered items, recall of their location may be better than if the sole task is to remember location. In the present experiment the high location scorers of the white group tended to score better than on related (spatial) tasks. Overt behavioral differences between the groups were less marked in this experiment than in others, the white group tending to whisper less. Five of these children said nothing to indicate use of verbal labels, and for some others statements such as "there was a knife" may not have been more than incidental verbal accompaniments to selection and replacement. Even so, the mean location score in this experiment was virtually identical to the A/D score of the 11-year-old white group of Experiment 2, suggesting that for the white Australian group as a whole there was no incidental gain in the present experiment. (Likewise no such gain occurred for the Aboriginal group, whose mean location score of 14.21 matches the A/D score of 14.13 obtained by 11-year-old nontraditional children of Experiment 2.)

EXPERIMENT 4

This experiment concerned the use made of a readily available verbal strategy. In a 5×4 array, where all items in any one column were clearly of the same type (and each column easily named by its contents), would the obvious verbal strategy be adopted by white Australian children, and would it help or hinder? It might reasonably be assumed that verbal strategists would perceive and use the code provided. If they succeeded in memorizing the five column labels no items should be replaced in the wrong columns. Then if locations of only the top and bottom items of each column were to be remembered (predictable, perhaps, from the location scores of Experiment 3) a score of 10 would be assured. For the two middle items in each column, since no lateral confusions would be expected, half should be correctly replaced by chance (in practice, because they are five middle pairs, either four or six can be expected to be

TABLE 4   Summary of Analysis of Variance: Experiments 3, 4, and 5

Comparison	F values		
	Between Groups	Between Tasks	Groups × Tasks
Australian Aboriginal and Australian white	17.459*** (1,26)[a]	40.375*** (2,52)	1.351 NS (2,52)

[a]The degrees of freedom are given in parentheses.

***$p < .001$.

correctly located). Thus, if top and bottom items were to be learned along with column labels, the total score expected with chance gains would be 14 or 16. For the white Australian group, then, a higher score than on other tasks might be expected, while the Aboriginal groups' score should not be expected to change.

Method

Subjects and Testing Site

These were as described for Experiment 3.

Materials and Procedure

The array contained 20 items set out as before. Objects were of five broad categories (shells, nuts, beaten copper leaves, rocks, sticks) and were arranged by column so that each column contained objects of only one category. Within each category all items were clearly distinguished by shape and size. In some cases items also differed in color (mainly shells and rocks) although colors were generally subtle and fairly neutral (off-whites, mauve, browns, greys, copper). This task and that of the previous experiment were performed in the same session.

Results and Discussion

Again, the Australian Aboriginal children's scores were superior (Aboriginal mean = 15.57, SD = 2.82; white Australian mean = 10.21, SD = 2.35; $t(26)$ = 5.45, $p < .001$).

A total of seven children apparently failed to notice the columnar arrangement of objects by category in that they made errors across columns. Four of these were white Australian and three were Aboriginal children. At least two other Aboriginal children appeared not to have noticed, although they made no column errors.

The columnar categorization of objects appears to have aided the Australian Aboriginal children, whose performance on this array was somewhat better than on the location task of the previous experiment, rather than the white Australian children. For the latter group, if the scores (9, 9, 9, 5) of the four who failed to notice the column code are disregarded,

the mean score of 11.1 for the remaining 10 children is considerably lower than the predicted 14 or 16, and the number of locations actually having to be remembered to yield this score is even lower. A score of 10 could be expected, for instance, if the location of only 5 items, one in each column, were to be learned in addition to the column code—the additional 5 score points being gained through the correct location by chance of 1 of the 3 remaining items within each column. Thus it is possible that only 6 item locations were learned in this array. This compares unfavorably with the group's initial performance on the Natural/Different array (containing similar items), where memory of the correct locations of approximately 8.5 items would be required to yield the observed mean of 9.5 (given a chance gain of one score point, to be expected in an uncategorized array).

The reports of many white children suggest that the columnar arrangement of items did provide a verbal code. All 10 of the children who made no column errors reported (either spontaneously when first seeing the array, or when asked later, "Was this one like the others?") that the columns contained "shells, nuts, leaves, rocks, sticks" naming the categories in the correct order. Only two of the Australian Aboriginal children, on the other hand, named any category, and none did so spontaneously. When asked about the array, these children said "they all went together" or "they were all the same" or "they were all in a line" without naming object categories. While the failure to report naming does not mean that naming did not occur, of course, it seems safe to suggest that column-naming did not occur in the case of those children making cross-column errors. The high scores (18, 13, 15) of the Aboriginal children in this category indicate that the columnar arrangement may have had perceptual, rather than verbal, advantages. There is a clear perceptual neatness about an array having item types arranged by column which haphazardly constructed arrays do not have which may aid visual organization or learning.

To determine whether the columnar arrangement had in fact increased Aboriginal scores, a further small study (Experiment 4a) was performed. On a subsequent occasion (to attempt to avoid confusions caused by use of the same items) 10 subjects of the original group were presented again with this array, this time with no columnar arrangement. Scores in the experiment were significantly lower (column-coded mean = 15.9, SD = 2.51; uncoded mean = 13.1, SD = 3.11; $t(9)$ = 2.39, $p < .05$).

The columnar arrangement thus seems to have improved the scores of the Aboriginal group rather than, as predicted, those of the white Australian group. While it may be suggested both that a perceptual aid was provided, by the arrangement, for visual strategists and that active verbal rehearsal of an obvious verbal code perhaps interfered with effective learning for verbal strategists, the questions of differential practice effects should also be considered. Since all children attempted the Experiment 3 tasks in the same session as, and immediately prior to, Experiment 4, it is possible that, given different strategies for the two groups, the strategy employed by Aboriginal children led to greater practice benefits than that employed by white children.

EXPERIMENT 5

This experiment examined the effect on memory of a task in which items differed in essentially only one dimension or attribute, color.

For verbal strategists on the memory tasks it seems reasonable to suppose that (if verbal coding only is used) the reduction, to one, of differentiating physical dimensions should not adversely affect performance, provided adequate differentiation by name is possible (which it should be if color is the differentiating attribute).

It seems likely that children who use visual strategies, however, will store object/location relationships in some manner which takes account of more than one physical dimension of the stimuli. . . . In Experiment 5 all objects had the same shape. A further reduction in differentiating features was made by using objects of the same size. Aboriginal children, if relying on visual strategies, might therefore be expected to experience greater difficulty in this experiment than in others.

Method

Subjects, testing site, and conditions were as described for Experiment 3. Normal color vision was reported by teachers for all subjects.

Materials and Procedure

The array contained 20 objects set out as before. The objects were small two-strand Turks' head knots (such as are seen as knobs on leather whip handles, or on rope cables). Each was about 3 cm in diameter and about 2.5 cm high (with slight variation depending on thickness of material). Sixteen were made of plastic-coated electrical wiring cord of different colors, while four were made of various stringlike cords of comparable dimensions. These relatively complex items were chosen in an attempt to make the array visually interesting to children, despite the shape and size identity of items.

For three main colors more than one hue was provided (green, four shades; pink/red, three shades; brown, two shades) to facilitate detection of color-naming strategists.

Results and Discussion

Both groups of children found this task considerably more difficult than the previous one, but again the Aboriginal scores were the higher (Aboriginal mean = 9.28, SD = 2.3; white Australian mean = 5.57, SD = 3.3; $t(26)$ = 3.419, $p < .01$).

The relatively low scores indicate the importance of multidimensional cues to object location for both groups, and suggest that in previous experiments both must have used such cues to advantage. It also seems likely that verbal coding may have been easier and more useful in other experiments than in this one, where a straightforward nominal listing may have had to be attempted by verbal strategists.

Response patterns (Table 5) in this study contain indications of attempts at verbal coding by white children, but again, not by Aboriginal children. The first such indication is the relatively high number of confusions made by white children between items of the same name but different hues. A naming strategy would be expected to lead to such confusions, while the marked hue differences between items sharing each color name would be unlikely to confuse visual strategists. Fifteen confusions and thirty-two correct replacements of these items (1:2.1) were made by white children, whereas Aboriginal children made three confusions and 57 correct replacements (1:19).

TABLE 5   Correct Replacements of Color Items in Each Position

White Australian Group (N = 14)						Australian Aboriginal Group (N = 14)					
10	5^2	4^1	2^4	3^2	$(24)^9$	7	5^1	8	4^1	11	$(35)^2$
6	6	2	4^2	4^2	$(22)^4$	10^1	10	4	4	6	$(34)^1$
2	1	4	0	4	(11)	5	2	4	5	8	(24)
5	2^2	3	0	10	$(20)^2$	5	7	7	5	13	(37)

Note. Row totals are shown at the end of each row in parentheses. Superscript figures refer to same-name confusions.

It also seems likely, from inspection of the data (Table 5) that white children attempted a reading related strategy—probably the only way to deal with the location coding problem for those whose approach involved a sequential ordering of color names. In such a strategy, the top left corner is the obvious starting point. The color item in this location was disproportionately well remembered by white children, suggesting that they began here. A further indication of serial learning is the apparent concentration on the top two rows. If names were sequentially verbally rehearsed the many same-name confusions which occurred in those rows are understandable—if giving an item the correct general name had counted, the contribution of the top two rows to the total score would be nearly double that of the bottom two (59:33). Two other indications of such a verbal strategy are the low scores for presumably easily named colors if these occurred in the lower rows (e.g., blue, 3, orange, 2) and zero scores for perhaps hard to name colors in these rows (e.g., grey and mauve). The bottom right-hand item was as well remembered as the top left, again suggesting serial learning (although the bottom right item, being of gold string, may have been especially memorable).

The response patterns of the Australian Aboriginal children differ in several respects. Although the bottom row (rather than the top) made the greatest contribution to the overall score, correct replacements were more evenly distributed. Difficult-to-name colors were not ignored (for example, five correct replacements were made for each of grey and mauve which no white child correctly replaced); there were only three same-name confusions; there were four highly favored items, which were scattered over the board (unlikely if a serial strategy had been attempted); the top left item (yellow) was not one of these, and was no more favored than green and blue,

two colors presumably having equally familiar names (and located in the second and third positions of the bottom row).

It seems likely, therefore, that Aboriginal children did not attempt a verbal listing strategy in this experiment. Although the two groups thus apparently differed in approach it is nevertheless clear, from the relatively low scores of both groups in this experiment, that if the number of physical dimensions of array objects is severely restricted, memory for spatial relationships suffers for children of both white Australian and Australian Aboriginal groups. It thus seems likely that, even where verbal strategies were attempted by white children on less perceptually restricted arrays, some visual coding (probably in terms of outstanding features of items) also occurred.

CONCLUSIONS

The consistently superior performances of the Australian Aboriginal children who participated in this study appear to support the environmental pressures hypothesis from which the experimental tasks were derived. Of particular interest are the high scores of children from families some generations removed from a traditional Aboriginal cultural milieu. For such children, cultural pressures toward particular skill development cannot be expected to have been as marked as under more traditional conditions.

Even so, here as elsewhere, complex interactions between inheritance and learning must be postulated. It seems likely that individuals of any culture having a propensity for a particular skill will practice it spontaneously to a greater extent than others, so that learning differences may exist at relatively early ages between individuals who differ in natural endowment. Thus in the present context greater visual memory experience may be an inevitable and inextricable consequence of greater natural endowment, more or less irrespective of life-style.

A further complication concerns child-rearing practices. Those which characterize hunters and gatherers have been described as oriented toward self-reliance and assertion while in high food-accumulation (e.g., agricultural) societies, pressures upon children are toward obedience and conscientiousness (Barry, Child, & Bacon, 1959). Early upbringing may strongly influence the development of particular cognitive characteristics, perhaps especially in the way it affects learning style or habitual cognitive strategy. It is possible that marked differences still exist between the child-rearing practices of white Australian and nontraditional Aboriginal mothers; child-rearing practices may be especially resistant to change. Even where obvious traditional practices are no longer seen (maternal encouragement of Aboriginal toddlers to track beetles and small animals over the sand, for instance) there may yet be prolonged failure to introduce elements from the new culture. Thus while nontraditional Aboriginal families live in houses and no longer forage for a living, their attitude and behavior toward small children may not have altered much since traditional times. Preliminary observations suggest, for instance, that white Australian parents actively encourage verbal behavior in small children to a greater extent than do Aboriginal parents, that they expect small children to heed verbal instructions and begin early to teach them to count, while Aboriginal parents do not. By the time white Australian children reach 5 years or so, therefore, they may have had considerable training and practice in linear thinking, while Aboriginal children probably encounter it formally for the first time in school.

Within a wider context, it may be conjectured that child-rearing practices of traditionally settled groups invariably involve some encouragement of linear processing, especially if animal husbandry is practiced. Keeping livestock involves tallying, and thus concepts of linear invariance are likely to be learned early. Even so, the possibility of group differences in cognitive strategy, or processing mode preferences, should be investigated more widely, since educational practice arising largely within the Western European tradition may fail to provide children of many other groups with the materials and methods best suited to their cognitive skills and strategies.

REFERENCES

Barry, H., Child, I., & Bacon, M. Relation of child training to subsistence economy. *American Anthropologist,* 1959, 61, 51–63.

Berry, J. W. Ecological and cultural factors in spatial perceptual development. *Canadian Journal of Behavioral Science,* 1971, 3(4), 324–336.

Bock, R. D., & Kolakowski, D. Further evidence on sex-linked major-gene influence on human spatial visualising ability. *American Journal of Human Genetics,* 1973, 25, 1–14.

Bowler, J. M., & Thorne, A. G. Human remains from Lake Mungo. In R. L. Kirk & A. G. Thorne (Eds.), *The origin of the Australians.* Canberra: Australian Institute of Aboriginal Studies, 1976.

Conrad, R. Speech and reading. In J. F. Kavanagh & I. G. Mattingley (Eds.), *The relationships between speech and reading.* Cambridge, MA: MIT Press, 1972.

Crook, J. H. The socio-ecology of primates. In J. H. Crook (Ed.), *Social behaviour in birds and mammals.* New York/London: Academic Press, 1970.

Dasen, P. R. Cross-cultural Piagetian research: A summary. *Journal of Cross-Cultural Psychology,* 1972, 3, 23–40.

Dasen, P. R. Piagetian research in Central Australia. In G. E. Kearney, P. R. de Lacey, & G. R. Davidson (Eds.), *The psychology of Aboriginal Australians.* Sydney: Wiley, 1973. (a)

Dasen, P. R. The influence of ecology, culture, and European contact on cognitive development in Australian Aborigines. In J. W. Berry & P. R. Dasen (Eds.), *Culture and cognition: Readings in cross-cultural psychology.* London: Methuen, 1973. (b)

Dasen, P. R., de Lacey, P. R., & Seagrim, G. N. Reasoning ability in adopted and fostered Aboriginal children. In G. E. Kearney, P. R. de Lacey, & G. R. Davidson (Eds.), *The psychology of Aboriginal Australians.* Sydney: Wiley, 1973.

de Lacey, P. R. A cross-cultural study of classificatory ability in Australia. *Journal of Cross-Cultural Psychology,* 1970, 1, 293–304.

Gould, R. A. Subsistence behaviour among the Western Desert Aborigines of Australia. *Oceania,* 1969, 39(4), 253–274.

Kearins, J. Skills of desert Aboriginal children. In G. E. Kearney & D. W. McElwain (Eds.), *Aboriginal cognition, retrospect and prospect.* Canberra: Australian Institute of Aboriginal Studies, 1976.

Kearins, J. *Visual spatial memory in Australian Aboriginal children of desert regions.* Unpublished Ph.D. thesis, University of Western Australia, 1977.

Kirk, R. L. Genetic evidence and its implications for Aboriginal pre-history. In D. J. Mulvaney & J. Golson (Eds.), *Aboriginal man and environment in Australia.* Canberra: Australian National Univ. Press, 1971.

Lewis, D. Observations on route finding and spatial orientation among the Aboriginal peoples of the Western Desert region of Central Australia. *Oceania,* 1976, 46(4), 249–282.

Lockard, R. B. Reflections on the fall of comparative psychology: Is there a message for us all? *American Psychologist,* 1971, 26, 168–179.

Lockwood, D. *I, the Aboriginal.* Adelaide: Rigby, 1962.

Lockwood, D. *The lizard eaters.* Sydney: Cassell, 1964.

Mabbutt, J. A. The Australian arid zone as a pre-historic environment. In D. J. Mulvaney & J. Golson (Eds.), *Aboriginal man and environment in Australia.* Canberra: Australian National Univ. Press, 1971.

McElwain, D. W., & Kearney, G. E. *Queensland Test Handbook.* Melbourne: Australian Council for Educational Research, 1970.

McElwain, D. W., & Kearney, G. E. Intellectual development. In G. E. Kearney, P. R. de Lacey, & G. R. Davidson (Eds.), *The psychology of Aboriginal Australians.* Sydney: Wiley, 1973.

McFarlane-Smith, I. *Spatial ability.* London: Univ. of London Press, 1964.

Schulman, A. I. Recognition memory and the recall of spatial location. *Memory and Cognition,* 1973, 1(3), 256–260.

Tinbergen, N. *Social behaviour in animals.* London: Methuen, 1953.

Tobias, P. V. The meaning of race. In P. Baxter & B. Sansom (Eds.), *Race and social difference.* Harmondsworth: Penguin, 1972.

Tonkinson, R. *The Jigalong Mob.* Menlo Park, CA: Cummings, 1974.

POSTSCRIPT

Notice that Kearins is somewhat ambivalent in her conclusions about the relative contributions of biology—in the form of genetic selection over many generations—and learning—in the form of cultural experiences over an individual's lifetime—to the differences she observed in subjects' propensity to use a visual coding strategy with her tasks. In practice, of course, the two influences are extremely difficult to disentangle (see the Postscript to Reading 34), and Kearins properly suggests that some interaction of the two factors is probably involved. Furthermore, Kearins is careful to point out that the difference between Aboriginal and white children lies in a *propensity to use* a particular strategy, not in the presence or absence of a strategy (a conclusion confirmed in a later study by Klich & Davidson, 1983). This view is consistent with that of most cross-cultural researchers who believe that most general characteristics of human cognition are universal (Berry, Poortinga, Segall, & Dasen, 1992), with differences among cultures lying in differential use of particular strategies or in what is thought about (see D'andrade, 1989, or Shweder, 1990, for a different emphasis).

Kearins tested a specific cognitive ability: memory for spatial location. Other researchers have examined cross-cultural differences in other cognitive abilities (see Cole & Scribner, 1974; Laboratory of Comparative Human Cognition, 1982; or Segall, Dasen, Berry, & Poortinga, 1990, for reviews; see

Holland & Quinn, 1987, for a collection of in-depth investigations). Cross-cultural differences in cognitive style have also been researched. Cognitive style refers to a general manner or pattern in an individual's approach to cognitive tasks (Berry et al., 1992). Field dependence/independence (FDI) is a cognitive-style dimension that has been extensively studied across cultures and that manifests itself in a variety of ways as an individual deals with the physical and social environments (Witkin & Goodenough, 1981). Cultural differences in another dimension of cognitive style, Impulsive-Reflective, has been examined by Smith and Caplan (1988).

Attempts to compare the general intelligence of people in different cultures were once quite common but are much less so now (Laboratory of Comparative Human Cognition, 1982; Segall et al., 1990). Such attempts encounter severe methodological problems; not only is it extremely difficult to assure cross-cultural validity and comparability of intelligence tests, but different cultures have different notions of what makes for an intelligent person (Berry et al., 1992; Goodnow, 1976; Segall et al., 1990). However, Stevenson, Stigler, Lee, and their colleagues recently have conducted a massive and extremely careful comparison of the school achievement of American children and of children in several Asian countries (Stevenson, 1992; Stevenson et al., 1990; Stevenson, Lee, & Stigler, 1986; Stigler, Lee, & Stevenson, 1990; see also Geary, Fan, & Bow-Thomas, 1992). They have found that, in the area of mathematics particularly, Asian children perform better than American children do and that the gap increases as children progress through school. They conclude that these differences emerge largely because Asian schools are structured to be more enjoyable for children, Asian teachers are given much more preparation time, and Asian students and parents have higher expectations and a stronger belief that effort affects achievement. (See the Postscript to Reading 32 and Saxe & Posner, 1983, for further discussion of the effects of language and culture on mathematical ability and achievement.)

Given that the particular methods used in school (as well as parental attitudes) have an effect on children's performance, it is not surprising that there is an effect of formal schooling as such on children's cognition (Rogoff, 1981; Scribner & Cole, 1973). Somewhat more controversial is whether literacy as such, apart from formal schooling, also has an effect (Olson, 1986; Scribner & Cole, 1981; see also Stanovich, 1993, for a within-culture study). Sinha (1988) has found that urbanization and industrialization also affect cognition; more broadly, Goodnow (1990) argues that cognitive development must be understood as taking place within a general social context, leading her to emphasize the pervasiveness of social effects on cognition (see also Markus & Kitayama, 1991).

For comprehensive discussions of the methodological problems posed by cross-cultural psychological research, see Lonner and Berry (1986) or Triandis and Berry (1980).

FOR FURTHER THOUGHT

1. In earlier research, Dasen found that Aboriginal children develop spatial concepts before logico-mathematical ones (as predicted), but still lag behind European children. Why did Dasen predict that Aboriginal children would develop spatial concepts before logico-mathematical ones? What are some possible reasons for Dasen's finding that Aboriginal children lag behind European children in the development of spatial concepts?

2. In what ways are the methods Kearins uses in her experiments different from those of Dasen, Berry, and others? What are the pros and cons of the highly informal settings and interview procedures Kearins uses?

3. Why are there "Artifactual" and "Natural" conditions in Experiment 1? What would be implied if the relative performance of Aboriginal and white children were not affected by that variable? Why do you think that there was a same/different variable in addition to the Artifactual/Natural one? Explain Kearins' predictions about the relative performance of Aboriginal and white children on the same/different variable. Why did Kearins have 20 items in the "different" array and only 12 in the "same" array? Does that present any problems in analysis?

4. Given the findings of Experiment 1, why were Experiments 3, 4, and 5 carried out? In particular, what further information did Kearins gain from each experiment?

5. Summarize the evidence for the conclusion that the differences between Aboriginal and white children lay in the former using a visual strategy and the latter using a verbal mediation strategy. What evidence is there that Aboriginal children do not use a hybrid strategy that includes both some verbal mediation and some direct visual coding? Describe the steps involved in using a verbal mediation strategy to perform the task in Experiment 4, then describe the steps involved in using a visual strategy.

6. Explain Kearins' predictions for numbers of correctly placed items in Experiment 4.

7. What evidence is there for an effect of literacy in how the white children performed Kearins' tasks?

REFERENCES

Berry, J. W., Poortinga, Y. H., Segall, M. H., & Dasen, P. R. (1992). *Cross-cultural psychology: Research and applications.* New York: Cambridge University Press.

Cole, M., & Scribner, S. (1974). *Culture and thought: A psychological introduction.* New York: Wiley.

D'andrade, R. (1989). Cultural cognition. In M. I. Posner (Ed.), *Foundations of cognitive science* (pp. 795–830). Cambridge, MA: MIT Press.

Geary, D. C., Fan, L., & Bow-Thomas, C. C. (1992). Numerical cognition: Loci of ability differences comparing children from China and the United States. *Psychological Science, 3,* 180–185.

Goodnow, J. J. (1976). The nature of intelligent behavior: Questions raised by cross-cultural studies. In L. B. Resnick (Ed.), *The nature of intelligence* (pp. 169–188). Hillsdale, NJ: Erlbaum.

Goodnow, J. J. (1990). The socialization of cognition: What's involved? In J. W. Stigler, R. A. Shweder, & G. Herdt (Eds.), *Cultural psychology: Essays on comparative human development* (pp. 259–286). New York: Cambridge University Press.

Holland, D., & Quinn, N. (Eds.). (1987). *Cultural models in language and thought.* Cambridge: Cambridge University Press.

Klich, L. Z., & Davidson, G. R. (1983). A cultural difference in visual memory: On le voit, on ne le voit plus. *International Journal of Psychology, 18,* 189–201.

Laboratory of Comparative Human Cognition (1982). Culture and intelligence. In R. J. Sternberg (Ed.), *Handbook of human intelligence* (pp. 642–719). New York: Cambridge University Press.

Lonner, W. J., & Berry, J. W. (Eds.). (1986). *Cross-cultural research methodology series: Vol. 8. Field methods in cross-cultural research.* Newbury Park, CA: Sage.

Markus, H. R., & Kitayama, S. (1991). Culture and the self: Implications for cognition, emotion, and motivation. *Psychological Review, 98,* 224–253.

Olson, D. R. (1986). Intelligence and literacy: The relationships between intelligence and the technologies of representation and communication. In R. J. Sternberg & R. K. Wagner (Eds.), *Practical intelligence: Nature and origins of competence in the everyday world* (pp. 338–360). New York: Cambridge University Press.

Rogoff, B. (1981). Schooling and the development of cognitive skills. In H. C. Triandis & A. Heron (Eds.), *Handbook of cross-cultural psychology: Vol. 4. Developmental Psychology* (pp. 233–294). Boston: Allyn & Bacon.

Saxe, G. B., & Posner, J. (1983). The development of numerical cognition: Cross-cultural perspectives. In H. P. Ginsburg (Ed.), *The development of mathematical thinking* (pp. 291–317). New York: Academic Press.

Scribner, S., & Cole, M. (1973). The cognitive consequences of formal and informal education. *Science, 182,* 553–559.

Scribner, S., & Cole, M. (1981). *The psychology of literacy.* Cambridge, MA: Harvard University Press.

Segall, M. H., Dasen, P. R., Berry, J. W., & Poortinga, Y. H. (1990). *Human behavior in global perspective: An introduction to cross-cultural psychology.* New York: Pergamon Press.

Shweder, R. A. (1990). Cultural psychology—what is it? In J. W. Stigler, R. A. Shweder, & G. Herdt (Eds.), *Cultural psychology: Essays on comparative human development* (pp. 1–43). New York: Cambridge University Press.

Sinha, G. (1988). Exposure to industrial and urban environments and formal schooling as factors in psychological differentiation. *International Journal of Psychology, 23,* 707–719.

Smith, J. D., & Caplan, J. (1988). Cultural differences in cognitive style development. *Developmental Psychology, 24,* 46–52.

Stanovich, K. E. (1993). Does reading make you smarter? Literacy and the development of verbal intelligence. *Advances in Child Development, 24,* 133–180.

Stevenson, H. W. (1992, December). Learning from Asian schools. *Scientific American,* pp. 70–76.

Stevenson, H. W., Lee, S.-Y, Chen, C., Stigler, J. W., Hus, C.-C., & Kitamura, S. (1990). Contexts of achievement: A study of American, Chinese, and Japanese children. *Monographs of the Society for Research in Child Development, 55* (1–2, Serial No. 221).

Stevenson, H. W., Lee, S.-Y., & Stigler, J. W. (1986). Mathematics achievement of Chinese, Japanese, and American children. *Science, 231,* 696–699.

Stigler, J. W., Lee, S.-Y., & Stevenson, H. W. (1990). *Mathematical knowledge of Japanese, Chinese, and American elementary school children.* Reston, VA: National Council of Teachers of Mathematics.

Triandis, H. C., & Berry, J. W. (1980). *Handbook of cross-cultural psychology: Vol. 2. Methodology.* Boston: Allyn & Bacon.

Witkin, H. A., & Goodenough, D. R. (1981). *Cognitive styles: Essence and origins.* New York: International Universities Press.

INTRODUCTION

Some people seem to "catch on" to things more quickly and reason or solve problems better than others; they tend to excel at a variety of intellectual tasks. In our everyday "folk" psychology, we explain this observation by saying that such people are highly intelligent, or at least highly intelligent in particular ways. For example, a student who scores well on the verbal portion of the SAT might be described as being high in verbal intelligence, or high verbal. But what does it mean to be high verbal, aside from scoring well on the verbal portion of the SAT and often doing well in a variety of linguistic tasks? This is the question Earl Hunt, Clifford Lunneborg, and Joe Lewis address in their article "What Does It Mean to Be High Verbal?"

Hunt, Lunneborg, and Lewis's strategy is to compare people of high verbal ability and those of lesser verbal ability on a variety of tasks that involve basic cognitive processes such as those examined in Part I of this volume. These basic cognitive processes are assumed to function in the same fashion in all people. Thus, what Hunt and his colleagues are looking for are *quantitative* rather than *qualitative* differences in their subjects' performance. Some of the tasks Hunt and his associates use are quite familiar to cognitive psychologists—the audience for whom this article was originally written. Students less familiar with those tasks may find the following descriptions useful.

Hunt, Lunneborg, and Lewis's first experiment is essentially a replication of an earlier study that Hunt and his colleagues carried out, using a task originally developed by Michael Posner. In this task, the subject is given a pair of letters and must decide whether the two letters of the pair are the same or different. The letters may be in upper- or lowercase. There are two instructional conditions (physical identity and name identity) and three kinds of letter pairs. The letters in a pair may be physically identical (such as AA, aa, BB, or bb), they may have the same name but be in different cases (such as Aa, aA, Bb, or bB), or they may be different in either name or both name and case (as in AB, Ab). In the physical identity instructional condition, subjects need only to compare the letters physically; they do not need to figure out the names of the letters (that is, translate the physical, visual symbols into names). In the name identity instructional condition, subjects need not figure out the names of the letters if they are physically identical but must if the letters are not, because they may be the same letter in different cases. There are two parts to Hunt and his associates' first experiment. The first part uses presentation on a computer and only the name identity instructional condition. The second part uses presentation on cards and both the name identity and physical identity instructional conditions.

In this article, Experiments 2 and 3 involve the presentation of strings or sequences of letters. A string of three characters is sometimes referred to as a *trigram,* and a string of four characters as a *quadrigram.* Thus Hunt and his colleagues use the term *n-gram* to refer to strings or sequences of different lengths. The task used in Experiment 2 is novel and is explained fully in the article. The task used in Experiment 3, however, is a variation of a task originally developed by Peterson and Peterson and is assumed to be familiar to the reader.

In Hunt and his colleagues' version of this task, the subject is presented with a sequence of four letters on a computer screen; each letter is displayed, one at a time, for 400 msec. After a certain amount of time, the subject must recall the letters in the correct order. To prevent rehearsal during the retention period (see Reading 10) and to generate what is called retroactive interference, presentation of the four letters is followed by a series of numbers (each number is also displayed for 400 msec). (In retroactive interference, new material disrupts the retrieval of older material.) The subject is required to read the numbers aloud as they appear. The amount of time (and retroactive interference) between presentation of letters and recall depends on how many numbers the subject is given. Because acoustic confusions are common in experiments on short-term memory (see Reading 9), Hunt and his associates make sure that none of the letters in a sequence sound alike. The researchers identify two kinds of errors that subjects can make in recalling the letter strings: having one or more letters wrong or having the letters in the wrong order. If the subject has all the right letters but in the wrong order, a transpositional error is said to have occurred; otherwise the subject is said to have made a nontranspositional error.

Understanding Experiment 5 requires understanding the distinction between marked and unmarked word forms. Many words come in complementary pairs that label different values along some dimension. For example, *tall* and *short* indicate different values along the dimension of height. Often, one of the words in the pair is used as the "normal" or unbiased way to refer to values along the dimension; that word is called the "unmarked" form. In our example, *tall* is the unmarked form: one ordinarily asks "How tall is she?" or states "He is 5 feet tall." *Short* is the marked form: to ask "How short is she?" or to say "He is 5 feet short" presumes an unusual height. Following an analysis popular at the time, Hunt and his associates assume that marked forms are mentally represented as the unmarked form plus additional information. Thus (very simplistically) if *tall* is mentally represented as something like "of normal height or greater," then *short* is represented as "not of normal height or greater" or "not tall" (see Clark & Clark, 1977).

In their discussion, Hunt and his associates mention the work of Donders (see Reading 8)—specifically, the ideas of simple and choice reaction times. To measure simple reaction time, a subject may be given a single light to watch, a single button to push, and the instruction "Push the button as soon as the light comes on." In choice reaction time, the subject may be given two lights, two buttons, and the instruction "Push the left button as soon as the light on the left comes on and push the right button as soon as the light on the right comes on" (Lachman, Lachman, & Butterfield, 1979). Notice that the choice reaction time task requires the same steps as does the simple reaction time task plus the additional processes of categorizing the light and choosing the appropriate response.

In this reprint of the original article, an experiment on sensitivity to stimulus order involving presentation to different ears has been excluded, as has an experiment on speed of processing involving mathematical computations requiring translation into a novel code. A long section comparing a battery of cognitive tasks and a battery of intelligence tests has also been omitted. As you read this selection, ask yourself whether the tasks Hunt and his associates use really capture what you think of as verbal intelligence. If so, are there aspects of verbal intelligence that they do not capture? What other kinds of cognitive tasks that you're familiar with also capture verbal intelligence? If you think Hunt, Lunneborg, and Lewis's tasks do not capture verbal intelligence, what is problematic about the tasks? Are there cognitive tasks that do capture verbal intelligence?

What Does It Mean to Be High Verbal?

Earl Hunt, Clifford Lunneborg, and Joe Lewis
University of Washington

Almost twenty years ago Cronbach (1957) deplored the existence of two disciplines of scientific psychology; the psychometrician who measures differences between individuals without much concern for the process by which subjects attack tests, and the experimental psychologist who studies processes in general, without regard for the differences between individuals. At the time Cronbach wrote, intelligence tests, based on a sophisticated theory of multidimensional measurement, were often heralded as psychology's greatest technological achievement. There were several theories of how man processes information in general (e.g., the Gestalt view and various adaptations of S-R learning theory), but within experimental psychology the study of cognition was not considered a rapidly developing area. In hindsight, the psychometricians of the 1940s and 1950s were probably quite correct in being disinterested in explanations of individual differences based on the then-current theories of cognition.

Today the situation is drastically changed. Cognitive psychology has shifted its philosophical position to a world view of man as an information processor, and as a result it is a thriving field of scientific investigation. Psychometrics, by contrast, has remained fairly static. The dominant social attitude toward intelligence has changed from one of approval to one of censure. This, however, must reflect a change in society's values since little new evidence concerning the tests themselves has been obtained.

These observations present a challenge to scientists interested in the study of cognition. On both scientific and social philosophical grounds, it seems a dubious procedure to base decisions on a measure, without a theory of how the measure works. We ought to measure cognitive power by use of an instrument whose design is based on our understanding of the cognitive process. The current paper addresses this point, but somewhat indirectly. Directly we address ourselves to a related point. Does the present intelligence test (actually a composite of several specialized subtests) differentiate between individuals who also differ in ways in which a modern cognitive psychologist will find theoretically interesting? If they do, is this finding more than a tautology? Clearly we would have discovered little if we found that the tests a cognitive psychologist devises are, on their face, only slightly changed variants of the subtests of the present intelligence test. It would be more interesting if we found that the psychometric tests require one sort of ability, and the cognitive psychologist's tasks require another, but the same individuals who possess (or lack) one set of abilities possess or lack the other.

Intelligence is too global a term for such a discussion, since psychometrically defined intelligence consists of a number of separate factors. (Guilford and Hoepfner (1971) distinguish more than 100 separate components, and virtually all psychometric theories distinguish at least two kinds of intelligence.) We shall report studies of the information processing capabilities of people with varying degrees of *verbal ability* as defined by the Washington Pre-College Test

This research was sponsored by the National Institute of Mental Health, grant MH21795, to the University of Washington (Earl Hunt, principal investigator). We have benefited from the assistance of numerous colleagues in the design, execution, and analyses of the studies to be reported, and are happy to acknowledge the work of John Bolland, Hans Brunner, Judith Clark, Michelle Ellis, Jane Gaston, Steven Poltrock, Kathy McClure, and Philip Milliman. Martha Holland read and cogently criticized an earlier draft. Reprints may be requested from Earl Hunt, Department of Psychology NI-25, University of Washington, Seattle, WA 98195.

SOURCE: *Cognitive Psychology, 7,* 1975, pp. 194–227. Copyright © 1975 by Academic Press, Inc. Reprinted by permission.

(WPCT), a standard, group administered test used to evaluate the academic potential of high school juniors in the state of Washington.[1] The WPCT consists of several subtests, whose scores are combined in varying ways to yield different composites. The verbal composite score is a weighted sum of four subtests; English Usage, Spelling, Reading Comprehension, and Vocabulary. English Usage requires the student to detect errors in capitalization, punctuation, grammar, usage, diction, and idiom; Spelling calls for the recognition of misspellings; Reading Comprehension presents the student with a series of paragraphs each followed by a set of questions relating to the content of the paragraph; and Vocabulary asks that a synonym be selected from among a set of alternatives for each of a series of stem words. Each test is in multiple choice format. The composite "verbal ability" score is defined by

(1) Verbal Composite = (.22) English Usage
+ (.33) Spelling
+ (.29) Reading Comprehension
+ (.33) Vocabulary
− 8.94

Each of the four contributing scores is in standard form with a mean of 50 and standard deviation of 10 for the high school normative population. The resulting verbal composite is in that same metric. The weights are based upon a factor analysis of the WPCT, and define a verbal factor. Verbal Composite scores so defined are generally the best single predictors of academic success (Lavin, 1965). When we refer to "verbal ability" our operational definition will be the composite defined by (1).

Intuitively, a person with "high verbal ability" should be glib of tongue, quick to pick up nuances in the language, and generally alert to information conveyed by either written or oral speech. We also expect the "high verbal" to show superior performance in the basic perceptual and motor skills involved in speech. A contrasting, less pleasant picture can be drawn for the low verbal. But let us consider the op-

erational definition of verbal ability. Performance in the subtests of (1) is determined largely by what a person knows; the meaning of words, syntactic rules, and semantic relations between concepts denoted by words. None of the subtests measure aptitudes for recognizing letters or other highly overlearned codes, since all people taking the tests recognize these codes perfectly. The emphasis is on tests of knowledge.

In experimental psychology, by contrast, studies of cognition are usually designed so that extra-experimental knowledge will not be a factor in performance. The paradigm developed by Posner, Boies, Eichelman and Taylor (1969) is a good example. This task requires that the subject identify two printed letters as being "same" or "different" in accordance with their name, regardless of type case (e.g., A is the same as a). The only thing a subject must know is the alphabet, in upper and lower case. This information is possessed by a substantial majority of American university students.

Experimental psychologists do deal at considerable length with the processes by which people detect stimuli, locate them in time and space, and co-ordinate them with respect to stored representations of highly overlearned codes. Experimental psychologists also study the process by which people integrate sequences of stimuli over time to form a stable percept, and how they operate upon this percept, co-ordinate it with stored percepts, transform it during problem solving, and eventually abstract information from the percept and place it in long term memory. Let us refer to all these processes, collectively, as *Current Information Processing* (CIP). CIP obviously makes use of the particular information stored in long term memory (LTM), but experiments are generally designed so that performance depends only on LTM information held by all subjects.

CIP has been described by analogy to sets of memory buffers and attached processors in a computer system (Atkinson & Shiffrin, 1968; Atkinson & Westcourt, 1974; Hunt, 1971, 1973; Hunt & Poltrock, 1974). Very generally, these theorists see information as being received simultaneously on several channels, each of which has its attached buffer memories. The channel buffers may make direct, and parallel, contact with LTM to arouse learned codes describing the current stimuli, e.g., during the trans-

---

[1] For all practical purposes, the WPCT is interchangeable with the Educational Testing Service's more widely used Scholastic Achievement Test (SAT), the "College Board."

lation from an acoustic signal to a recognized word. At some point the stimulus will be coded to a level at which it enters conscious short term memory (STM). At this point a "time tag" is assigned to the perceived code. As items are assembled into STM they are temporally integrated into a coherent whole, as in the recognition of the meaning of a sentence. The argument is particularly striking for speech, although similar effects have been reported for other stimuli, including the perceptions built up from a sequence of visual scenes (Neisser, personal communication). Further manipulation of the internal representation may occur after the percept is formed, as in the transformation of mental images which occurs during certain types of spatial problem solving (Cooper & Shepard, 1973).

We shall focus our attention on the following characteristics of CIP activity; (a) the sensitivity of overlearned codes to arousal by incoming stimulus information, (b) the accuracy with which temporal tags can be assigned, and hence order information can be processed, and (c) the speed with which the internal representations in STM and intermediate term memory (ITM, memory for events occurring over minutes) can be created, integrated, and altered.[2] The remainder of this paper reports several studies relating these three CIP activities to one's verbal ability, as computed by Equation (1). There are two reasons for expecting to find relationships between psychometric intelligence and CIP capability. One is the intuitive expectation that, even if the intelligence test is not a direct measure of information processing, somehow we think that the more intelligent are also the more alert. We repeat our basic point. This may well be the case, but if so, it is an empirical fact to be established. The conclusion does not follow from a straightforward examination of psychometric intelligence tests. The second reason for expecting a relationship is more prosaic; preliminary work has indicated that such a relationship exists (Hunt, Frost, & Lunneborg, 1973). We shall first review the earlier studies, and then present some more complete data.

GENERAL PROCEDURE

Our general procedure has been to contrast groups of university students of varying intelligence. "High verbal" subjects were defined as those students scoring in the upper quartile of WPCT verbal composite scores in the University of Washington freshman class for 1971–1972 or 1972–1973. "Low verbals" were similarly defined by the lower quartile. Since the University of Washington's student body is generally selected for scholastic ability, "high verbals" as identified by us can be considered to be high verbal with respect to the general population. Our "low verbal" subjects are better described as being of average verbal ability with respect to the population at large. This is shown in Figure 1, which depicts the distribution of verbal ability scores for all college bound high school seniors in Washington state. Our "high" and "low" ranges are superimposed on this distribution.[3]

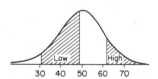

FIGURE 1 Ranges of low and high verbal university freshmen in the normal distribution of college bound high school juniors.

Students eligible to serve as subjects were contacted by telephone or mail, and offered employment at the prevailing hourly rate for unskilled student help. The amount of money each participant earned depended upon the particular experiments in which they served as subjects.

---

[2]We use the term intermediate term memory (ITM) to refer to the process of holding information for a period of minutes. It would be consistent with much current usage to refer to this as long term memory (LTM), but we prefer to reserve the latter term for the storage of information over days and even years. For elaboration of this viewpoint, see Hunt (1971, 1973) and Anderson and Bower (1973).

---

[3]As there is probably self selection of the high school students who take the WPCT, the distribution of Figure 1 is itself biased toward containing fewer low scores than would be expected in a random sample of all high school juniors.

OVERVIEW OF PREVIOUS RESULTS

[A portion of Hunt and his associates' summary of findings from earlier studies has been excluded here. One study, using a Sternberg task (see Reading 8), suggested that high verbals are able to search short-term memory more quickly than are low verbals. Another study suggested that high and low verbals are likely to differ in their sensitivity to semantic information (information about word meanings).]

The question of differential sensitivity to semantic information was attacked directly in a third study, based on a procedure developed by Posner, Boies, Eichelman, and Taylor (1969). The subject is shown two letters which may vary either in identity (A or B) or type case (A or a) or both (A or b). The task is to identify the letters as "same" or "different." In the *physical identity* condition the subject is instructed to respond "same" only if the two letters are exactly identical, i.e., one of the pairs (AA,aa,BB,bb). In the *name identity* condition characters are to be identified as identical if they refer to the same letter, regardless of type case. Posner *et al.* (1969) have found that it requires about 70 msec longer for a subject to make a name identification than a physical identification. This presumably reflects the added time required to retrieve the name associated with each character. Hunt *et al.* (1973) found that the corresponding values were 33 msecs for high verbal subjects and 86 msecs for low verbals. If reliable, this is an extremely interesting result, for it indicates that high verbals can access highly overlearned material in LTM more rapidly than can low verbals. (It does not seem reasonable to maintain that "low verbal" college students do not know the alphabet.) Unfortunately, Hunt *et al.* (1973) used very few subjects in their study, and the data were only marginally significant ($p < .08$ for the crucial comparison).

In summary, the sheer number of results of Hunt *et al.* (1973) indicates that there is a relation between psychometrically defined intelligence and information processing. The specific experiments can be accepted only with reservations. Our first concern, therefore, was to attempt to reach the same conclusions as Hunt *et al.* (1973), but by using either different techniques or technically more reliable designs. Our second concern was to gain further information about the relationship between psychometrically defined verbal ability and information processing capacity.

EXPERIMENTS ON NAME ACCESSING AND CODE AROUSAL

"Being verbal" implies an ability to interpret arbitrary stimuli as part of the speech system. In dealing with written speech one must make a translation from an arbitrary visual code to its name. We regarded the Posner *et al.* (1969) name vs. physical identity paradigm as the most direct test of this ability, and therefore our first concern was to repeat the experiment of Hunt *et al.* (1973) using this paradigm, in order to establish the reliability of their results.

The second experiment explored the ability to arouse long term codes in a slightly different way. We asked if subjects with high verbal ability were more adept at arousing a "name code" in a situation in which the code was created by integrating two different stimuli over time.

Experiment 1

Experiment 1 was basically a repetition of the previous study using the Posner *et al.* (1969) paradigm. A second condition of the experiment offered us a chance to draw the same sort of conclusion using a different experimental procedure.

Subjects.   The subjects were twenty high and twenty low verbals recruited in the manner described previously.

Procedure.   The experiment consisted of two separate parts which, although they used the same subjects and were addressed to the same question, can logically be thought of as two distinct experiments.

The *computer display* data were from a replication of the Posner *et al.* (1969) *name instruction* condition, using both physically identical and name-identical stimuli. That is, the subject was instructed to call two letters "identical" if they had the same name. The stimuli presented included physically identical (AA), name identical (aA) and different (aB) pairs. Posner *et*

TABLE 1   Means of Median Reaction Time for Same–Different Identifications Using Computer-Controlled Display (msec)

Subjects	(1) Name Identical Trials	(2) Physically Identical Trials	(1)–(2)
High verbals	588.1	524.5	63.6
Low verbals	631.7	542.8	88.9

al. (1969) have found that the difference in the reaction time to physically and name identical stimuli appears in this situation. Using the name identity instructions has the added advantage that the subject cannot adopt a "set" toward name or physical identification and still optimize performance.

The stimuli were presented on a computer driven display screen. Responses were made by pressing two keys marked "same" or "different". The subject's preferred hand rested on top of the keys as the stimuli were presented. Prior to beginning the experiment, subjects were given 40 practice trials, followed by 320 trials containing 80 name identical pairs, 80 physical identity pairs, and 160 trials with letter pairs that were not physically or name identical (i.e., a B and an A in either upper or lower case). Median reaction times (RTs) for each subject were computed for physical and name identical trials.

In the *card sorting* study, which followed immediately, subjects sorted 3 × 5 in. cards with two letters (A,B,a,b, as before) on each card. The cards were to be sorted into "identical" and "different" piles under either physical identity or name identity instructions. Cards were sorted in decks of twenty, chosen to have an equal number of "identical" and "nonidentical" pairs under the appropriate instructions. Each deck was sorted three times in succession, with the experimenter rearranging the cards after each sorting. The first two decks were sorted under physical identity instructions. The data from the first deck were disregarded, to weaken practice effects. The third deck was sorted under name identity instructions. The data reported are based on average times to sort each deck computed over three sortings.

Results.   Fewer than 5% errors were made in the identification of letter pairs in the computer display phase. No differences across type of subject were noted. Table 1 shows the means of the median reaction times for correct name and physical identity identifications. Table 2 shows similar data for the time required to sort card decks under name or physical identity instructions. Accuracy in card sorting was virtually perfect. In both cases an analysis of variance showed that the interaction between type of identity or instruction and verbal ability was significant at less than the .05 level. Combining these results with the previous work of Hunt *et al.* (1973) there can be little doubt about the statistical reliability of the phenomenon.

Experiment 2[4]

In Experiment 1 subjects were presented with a stimulus for which they had an overlearned code. In Experiment 2 we used a task in which two successive stimuli were presented. Each of them alone was meaningless, but when integrated they formed an overlearned code. Temporal integration of this sort is what is required when we recognize words; in many cases the individual phonemes are not meaningful, although they may be recognizable as word features. The specific experimental task, in fact, did require subjects to integrate pronounceable units into words.

Subjects were shown lists of letter *n*-grams, (*n*— varying from two to four) at rates of from .5–2 sec

---

[4]This experiment was designed and conducted by Hans Brunner as a Bachelor of Science Honors thesis.

TABLE 2   Mean Time in Seconds to Sort 20 Cards under Varying Instructions

Subjects	(1) Name Identification	(2) Physical Identification	(1)–(2)
High verbals	14.74	13.68	1.06
Low verbals	16.07	14.35	1.72

per exposure. Some of the *n*-grams were successive syllables of a word, as in *prob lem*. Lists without such adjacent pairs served as a control. All *n*-grams were pronounceable. To avoid circumlocutions, we shall refer to *syllables*. Following presentation of each sixteen syllable list, subjects were given a free recall test. The ability to integrate syllables into words should assist in the free recall task. We asked if high verbals were selectively aided, compared to low verbals, by the presence of integrable pairs in a list.

Subjects and procedure.   Eight high and eight low verbal subjects participated. Each subject served in five daily sessions, each lasting about one hour. In the first (practice) session subjects were shown nine lists containing either nonsense syllables only or nonsense syllables and words different from those used in the experiment. The first list contained only meaningless syllable combinations. Lists were presented by a computer controlled display, at the rate of 1.25 sec per syllable. Following the last syllable of each list sixty numbers appeared, one by one, on the display. The subject spoke the name of each number. This served as a distractor to prevent recall from immediate memory. The word "recall" then appeared, and the subjects spelled out as many syllables as they could remember. Guessing was encouraged. Responses were tape recorded for later scoring.

The procedure on the four following experimental days was similar. Each day the first list consisted solely of nonsense syllables. The following eight lists consisted of four with nonsense syllables only and four in which eight of the fifteen successive pairs of syllables made up a common word. The subjects were not told whether a list was a word list or not. The words used were taken from the list of words of Paivio *et al.* (1968) with rated imagery, and were balanced for imagery ratings.[5] The position of the words in the lists varied across the four lists, and the positions of the word lists in the sequence of lists was varied each day. The rate of presentation was either 0.5, 1.0, 1.5, or 2.0 sec per syllable for all lists presented on a given day. The order in which different rates were used was counterbalanced by a Latin Square design within groups of high and low verbal subjects.

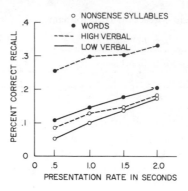

FIGURE 2   Proportion of word syllables or nonsense syllables recalled as a function of verbal ability and presentation rate.

Results.   The data to be reported are the mean proportion of syllables correctly recalled either for (a) all 80 syllables in the five nonsense syllable lists or (b) the 32 syllables that were parts of words in the word lists. Figure 2 displays these statistics as a function of presentation interval and type of subject. Recall was better at slower presentation rates for all groups and list types. High verbal subjects showed superior recall for word lists ($p < .01$ by the Mann–Whitney test, at all presentation rates). The only significant difference between groups on syllable list recall was at the 0.5 sec presentation rate ($.04 < p < .05$).

These results would, of course, be trivial if the low verbal subjects simply did not know that the words used were words. To test this hypothesis a test of word familiarity was given following the last experimental session. The words used in the experiment were combined with an equal number of distractors, i.e., combinations of syllables which followed English spelling rules but were not words. An example is *probfel*. High verbal subjects were reliably more successful in selecting words from nonwords, although only two low verbal subjects made more than three "misses" in word identification. Because of this result, two further analyses were conducted. An analysis of covariance was computed, using the number of words recalled on word lists as the dependent variable and the number of words identified in the word familiarity test as the covariate. The difference between groups remained. The data were also reanalyzed, omitting the two low verbal subjects who performed poorly on the word identification task. The difference between groups again remained. Finally, we report that in an earlier "pilot" experiment using a very similar design the main effects described here were found, but there was no difference between high and low verbal subjects on a word familiarity test. We conclude that the results cannot be explained in terms of differential word familiarity. They are consistent with the hypothesis that highly overlearned codes are somehow more accessible to high verbal subjects, and that the high verbal subject is more adept at integrating acoustic cues over time.

STUDIES OF SENSITIVITY TO ORDER

The next two experiments [only the first is included here] were designed to test the hypothesis that order information is better retained by high verbal subjects.

Experiment 3

This experiment assessed the ability to maintain order information in STM in a situation in which semantic content was not a variable. The paradigm used was a variation of the well known Peterson and Peterson (1959) technique. Four letters were shown, in sequence, on a computer display screen. The letters were followed by a variable number of digits. The subject spoke the name of each character ("shadowed") as it appeared. After the last digit was shown the word RECALL appeared. At this point the subject attempted to recall the letters in the order in which they had been presented. Estes (1972) has found that in this situation errors associated with phonetic confusability occur in the first one or two seconds following stimulus presentation, and that the effect of further shadowing is to introduce errors in recall of stimulus order.

Procedure and data analysis. Twenty-four high and 25 low verbal subjects were recruited as before. These subjects participated as part of a two day session in which they served as subjects in several experiments, to be reported below. Subjects were seen individually. The experiment was conducted using an IMLAC Corporation PDS-1 display station, on which the appropriate characters were displayed at the rate of 400 msec per character. The four alphabetic characters were followed by either 1, 3, 6, 12, 24, or 36 digits. Each alphabetic string was constructed by choosing not more than one consonant from each of the following sets:

1. {R}
2. {L}
3. {Y}
4. {H}
5. {N ,M}
6. {Y,W}
7. {J,K}
8. {F,S,S}
9. {G,D,V,B,T,P,Z}.

As a result, acoustic confusions would not be expected for letters within a stimulus quadrigram.

Responses were analyzed by position within the list of recalled items and by length of the intervening string of digits. Two types of errors were identified, transposition errors (correct letter out of place) and nontransposition errors (letter reported that was not shown).

Results. Low verbal subjects made more errors of both types than did high verbal subjects. Table 3 presents point biserial correlations[6] between the mean number of errors for each letter position and the low

---

[6] The point biserial correlation coefficient, r_{pbs}, has been used instead of the more conventional Student's t statistic, in order to present an idea of the size of the difference between groups, relative to the total variance in the dependent variable. The point biserial correlation coefficient (r_{pbs}) can be transformed into a t statistic by the equation $t_{n-2} = ((r_{pbs}^2 \bullet (N-2))/(1 - r_{pbs}^2))^{1/2}$ where N is the number of subjects in the two groups, combined.

TABLE 3   Point Biserial Correlations between Verbal Ability and Number of Errors Made, by Type and Temporal Position[a]

Temporal Position	Transposition Errors	Non-transposition Errors
1	−.27	− .28
2	−.31	−.38
3	−.30	− .43
4	−.38	− .47

[a]For this size group $/r/ > .27$, $p < .05$, and $/r/ > .36$, $\dot{p} < .01$.

TABLE 4[a] Relative Frequency of Errors and Point Biserial Correlations between Verbal Ability and Errors as a Function of Error Type and Amount of Retroactively Interfering Material[a]

Number of Intervening Digits	Mean Proportion of Errors					
	Transposition			Non-transposition		
	Low Verbal	High Verbal	r_{rbs}	Low Verbal	High Verbal	r_{pbs}
1	.13	.04	−.42	.06	.02	−.38
3	.16	.07	−.34	.06	.04	−.22
6	.21	.14	−.31	.16	.07	−.42
12	.27	.21	−.23	.31	.23	−.33
24	.32	.24	−.24	.48	.43	−.20
36	.30	.26	−.20	.49	.46	−.12

[a]For significance of point biserial correlation coefficients see Table 3.

verbal–high verbal dichotomy. Table 4 presents data on the frequency of transpositional and nontranspositional errors as a function of the number of digits presented in the interfering task. Point biserial correlations are presented for each length of digit string. High verbal subjects made substantially fewer errors of both types, regardless of the amount of retroactively interfering material. It is also of interest to note that the number of nontranspositional errors increased as the amount of intervening material increased. . . . Thus, while high verbal subjects were more sensitive to order information than low verbal subjects, they were not differentially more sensitive. The results of this study are consistent with the hypothesis that high verbal subjects have a generally better short term memory. . . .

EXPERIMENTS ON SPEED OF PROCESSING

The next two experiments [only the first experiment is included here] represent direct tests of the proposition that high verbal subjects are more rapid at processing information in simple verbal tasks where knowledge is not a problem. For the most part speed was the only question in the tasks we used, for the subjects were all quite capable of perfect information processing if time pressures were removed. We assert this because all our subjects were university students and, as will be seen, the accuracy demands of these tasks were quite low.

Experiment 5. Processing Statements about Pictures[7]

The task used was a modification of a task first proposed by Clark and Chase (1972). The subject read a simple assertion about a picture, then looked at a picture and determined whether the assertion was an accurate description of the picture, or not. The times taken to read the assertion and to make the true–false judgment were recorded, and analyzed as a function of the complexity of the assertion and its accuracy.

Procedure and subjects. Ten high and 10 low verbal subjects were recruited in the usual manner. Subjects were seen individually. Stimuli were projected on a milk glass screen, using a Kodak carousel projector. The back projection method was used, so that the subject sat in front of the screen, with the projector behind the screen out of the subject's sight. The index finger of the subject's preferred hand was posed over a button. In addition, the subjects wore a "voice key" throat microphone. Each trial was initiated by displaying on the screen a statement of the form.

    * ABOVE +
    + NOT ABOVE *;

etc. There are eight such sentences, constructed from all possible combinations of * or + in the subject po-

---

[7]This experiment was planned by Earl Hunt and carried out by Michelle Ellis.

sition, NOT present or absent, and the prepositions ABOVE and BELOW. In our analyses we disregarded the * or + distinction, thus providing four sentence types. The subject was instructed to press the button after the sentence was comprehended. This advanced the slide projector to display one of two possible pictures, either ⁺⁄ or ⁺⁄. The subject then stated whether the sentence was TRUE or FALSE with reference to the picture. Subject response activated the voice key, stopping a clock. Thus two measures were provided for each trial; *encoding time,* measured from the display of the first slide until the subject pressed the button indicating comprehension, and *decision time,* measured from the onset of the second slide until the subject responded TRUE or FALSE. Only a very few errors were made, and these were not systematically distributed across groups or conditions. All further analyses refer to times computed for correct trials only.

Combining the four sentence types with the two possible pictures produces eight trial types, and sixteen possible sentence–picture combinations. Each subject was run for 64 trials, using, in sequence, four randomly chosen orders of the 16 sentence–picture combinations, i.e., eight of each trial type.

Analysis and results. Each trial type can be described by stating whether the sentence is true or false with reference to the picture (the *true–false* dimension), whether the sentence contains the unmarked preposition "above" or the marked preposition "below," and whether or not the sentence contains "not" (the *negation* dimension). All of these dimensions might affect reaction time. A number of studies have found that, at least for untrained subjects, "true" responses are made more rapidly than "false" responses (Trabasso, 1972). Clark and Chase have pointed out that comparatives such as "above" and "below" have a marked and unmarked (normal) form. They argue that the marked form is more complex, in that it is represented internally by the unmarked form plus a qualification. Thus, in the present example, "below," the marked form, would be stored as "above," and thus be more difficult to process. Clark and Chase's experimental work has confirmed this prediction, although the effect is a small one. Finally, several studies have shown that the presence of a negation in-

creases processing time (Clark and Chase, 1972; Trabasso, 1972; Trabasso *et al.*, 1971; Wason and Johnson-Laird, 1972). In the present study these three dimensions provide within-subjects variables in a $2 \times 2 \times 2 \times 2$ design, with the fourth variable being level of verbal ability.

An analysis of variance of decision and encoding times indicated that virtually all the variance was due to (a) the true–false distinction (decision times only), (b) the negation effect, and (c) the interaction of the negation effect with verbal ability. The marking effect did not reach statistical significance. The size of the negation effect for an individual subject can be determined by subtracting the decision time (or encoding time) for a sentence containing a negation from the decision time (or encoding time) for a semantically equivalent sentence without the negation. In making this computation for decision time, one must also ensure that the two sentences are both either TRUE or FALSE with respect to the picture displayed. Figure 3 shows mean negation times obtained for high and low verbals in both the encoding and decision operations. There is a statistically reliable difference between groups ($p < .05$) in both cases, in spite of the relatively small size of this experiment. Furthermore, the low verbals take almost twice as long as the high verbals to process a negation.

A comment on the theoretical interpretation of this finding is in order. This task requires that the subject convert the sentence into an internal representation, convert the picture into an internal representation, and finally compare the two. The fact that a high verbal would be more rapid than a low verbal

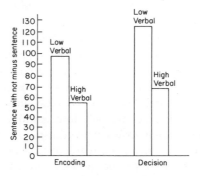

FIGURE 3 Negation time for encoding and deciding truth of sentences as a function of verbal ability.

in converting a complex sentence into an internal representation is not surprising in itself. What is interesting is the fact that the difference between high and low verbals in the ability to process a negation also appears in the analysis of decision time, i.e., when the physical stimulus is the picture. Trabasso *et al.* (1971) present data strongly indicating that experimentally naive subjects, such as were used in this study, convert sentences containing negations into more complex representations than those for comparable affirmative assertions. The negation effect, at the decision stage, therefore, is the discrepancy between comparing a complex or noncomplex sentence representation (but no longer a sentence) to the same picture representation. The added logical processing imposes less of a burden on high verbals than it does on low verbals. . . .

[In a long section excluded here, Hunt and his associates investigate the possibility of using information processing tasks to distinguish high verbals and low verbals. They succeed in doing so, and find that the ability to retrieve a name rapidly and the ability to retain information in short-term memory are the two measures that most clearly distinguish high and low verbals.]

DISCUSSION

University students who obtain high scores on a conventional paper and pencil test of verbal ability do unusually well on a variety of CIP tasks. We conclude that although a verbal intelligence test is directly a measure of what people know, it is indirectly a way of identifying people who can code and manipulate verbal stimuli rapidly in situations in which knowledge *per se is* not a major factor.

One of the most interesting superior abilities displayed by the high verbal is the ability to make a rapid conversion from a physical representation to a conceptual meaning, e.g., to recognize a particular visual pattern as a word or letter. Atkinson and Westcourt (1974) remark that this is a basic step in cognition, since the world impinges on us with physical stimuli, but our cognition is based on the manipulation of concepts. Another interesting superior ability of the high verbal is the ability to retain in STM informa-

tion about the order of stimulus presentation. We have not explored the ramifications of this to any great extent. We do note, however, that this ability is assumed and used heavily in all psycholinguistic models of speech comprehension (e.g., Schank, 1973). We do not claim that "low verbals" cannot retain order information, for they obviously can. To do so, however, low verbals may have to spend more time recovering order information from the context of the situation, while the high verbals can rely on an internally assigned time tag. This would allow the high verbal subjects more time to deploy their mental machinery upon the task of extracting meaning from the input. Finally, the high verbal subjects appear to be more rapid in the manipulation of data in short term memory, as evidenced by their performance on scanning and simple computational tasks. Considering the number of such transformations that speech requires, this is certainly a useful ability.

Many of the tasks we have used conform to the classical "Donders task," in that they consist of a base component and, in some conditions, an added component. The physical identification-name identification task is a good example. Before retrieving a name code one clearly must recognize a physical code. Our interest has focused upon the interaction between groups of subjects and the increased amount of information processing required by the "added component" task. It should be noted that we consistently find small, though not statistically significant, differences between high and low verbal subjects on the base task as well as upon the added component. This is not in conflict with the classical finding that intelligence is not related to "simple" reaction time, because each of our base tasks typically contains an element of choice. Keele has speculated that although motor reaction times are not correlated with intelligence, choice reaction times may be (Keele, 1973, p. 80). Our data are certainly not compelling evidence for this speculation, but they are consistent with it.

It apparently would be possible to distinguish low verbal university students from high verbals by the use of information processing tasks alone. It is hard to see why one would do this, since presently available psychometric measures are quite adequate for this purpose and much easier to administer. Using an information processing test to identify verbal ability seems to us to be putting the cart before the horse. . . . Besides, we regard information processing capacity as being a more basic mental ability than the composite of skills lumped under the title "verbal aptitude."

This brings us to some speculations which, we believe, follow from our research. The first concerns the meaning of intelligence test scores. We know that these scores are, for some reason, moderately successful predictors of success in a variety of situations (Herrnstein, 1973). The statistical fact is hardly in doubt, although there is great controversy concerning the reason behind it. In our terms verbal intelligence tests *directly* tap a person's knowledge of the language, and *indirectly* tap CIP ability. Success in different tasks is probably dependent upon a host of factors, including both acquired knowledge and CIP ability. In many situations success may be achieved either by relying on prior knowledge or CIP ability to do the current task. We note that in the psychometric literature a similar distinction has been made by Cattell (1971), who argues that with increasing age cognitive style appears to shift from the fixing of new information (his "fluid intelligence") to the utilization of old information ("crystallized intelligence").

It seems plausible to believe that high verbal subjects know more about the linguistic aspects of their culture because they are more rapid in CIP tasks, rather than the reverse. To illustrate, imagine two individuals, one with high CIP abilities and one with low abilities, both of whom are given the same exposure to linguistic information. Unless the exposure is such that the low CIP individual can abstract all the information from this presentation, the high CIP individual will fix more information in long term memory. If, by contrast, the initial exposure of information were individualized so that both persons were brought to the same level of immediate information fixation, then long term retention should be equated. Indeed, we have previously reported that there is no correlation between verbal ability and retention of information over a period of weeks, providing that individual learning is equated (Hunt *et al.*, 1973).

Another question which arises from our research is "What does it mean to know something?" At face value, "knowing something" is an either/or state of affairs. Either a piece of information is in long term memory or it is not. This, of course, is too naive a view, since on occasion information can be recovered only with the aid of prompts. The amount of prompting required will vary from individual to individual and from time to time. Our results on differential accessibility of codes (e.g., the names of letters) indicate that even highly overlearned codes may be differentially available. At present there is no information to indicate whether this is because certain people have better "machinery" for retrieving information, suggesting a biological explanation, or because they have learned better coding and retrieval schemes.

Because of the interest in the social aspects of intelligence testing, we further point out that the results we have reported here have *no* implications for the debate over either social class or racial determinants of intelligence. None of our studies have contrasted CIP abilities in different racial or social groups. We have argued that *given roughly comparable cultural experiences,* differences in the amount of linguistic knowledge acquired and tested directly in an intelligence test are associated with differences in CIP abilities. If the cultural backgrounds of subjects are not comparable, then we would expect the correlation between CIP abilities and intelligence test scores to be reduced *unless* the groups involved also differed in CIP abilities. Whether such differences exist is an open question.

Although we would not advocate using the information processing tasks we have described as replacements for conventional scholastic aptitude tests, we do feel that such tasks have an important role in the measurement of individual differences. A test of current information processing ability should be useful in determining the manner in which information should be presented to a specific person, in order to maximize the probability of the information's being retained. We believe that the aptitude treatment interactions much sought after by educators are more likely to be found if "aptitude" is defined by the parameters of the information processing process than if it is defined by one's relative standing in a population. We also believe that information processing measures appear more suitable than psychometric instruments in assessing the effects of inter-individual differences, such as sex or age, and intra-individual differences, such as stress or drug intake, upon cognitive functioning. We hope that these conjectures will shortly be re-examined in the light of the data that must be obtained.

REFERENCES

Anderson, J., & Bower, G. *Human associative memory.* New York: Academic Press, 1973.

Atkinson, R. & Westcourt, K. Some remarks on a theory of memory. *Acta Psychologica,* 1974 (in press).

Atkinson, R. C., & Shiffrin, R. M. Human memory: A proposed system and its control processes. In K. Spence & J. Spence (Eds.), *The psychology of learning and motivation* (Vol. 2, pp. 89–195). New York: Academic Press, 1968.

Carroll, J. B. A new "structure of intellect." For presentation at the LDRC Conference on the Nature of Intelligence. Pittsburgh, PA, March 4–6, 1974.

Cattell, R. B. *Abilities: their structure, growth, and action.* Boston: Houghton-Mifflin, 1971.

Clark, H., & Chase, W. On the process of comparing sentences against pictures. *Cognitive Psychology,* 1972, **3**, 472–517.

Cooper, L. A., & Shepard, R. N. Chronometric studies of the rotation of mental images. In W. G. Chase (Ed.), *Visual information processing.* New York: Academic Press, 1973.

Cronbach, L. J. The two disciplines of scientific psychology. *American Psychologist,* 1957, **12**, 671–684.

Day, R. S., Cutting, J., & Copeland, P. Perception of linguistic and nonlinguistic dimensions of dichotic stimuli. Paper presented at 12th annual meeting of the Psychonomic Society. November 1971.

Estes, W. K. An associative base for coding and organization in memory. In A. Melton & E. Martin (Eds.), *Coding processes in human memory.* Washington, DC: Winston-Wiley, 1972.

Gazzaniga, M. *The bisected brain.* New York: Appleton, 1970.

Guilford, J. P., & Hoepfner, R. *The analysis of intelligence.* New York: McGraw-Hill, 1971.

Herrnstein, R. J. *I.Q. in the meritocracy.* Boston: Little, Brown, 1973.

Hunt, E. What kind of computer is man? *Cognitive Psychology,* 1971, **2**, 57–98.

Hunt, E. B. The memory we must have. In R. Schank & K. Colby (Eds.), *Computer models of thought and language.* San Francisco: Freeman, 1973.

Hunt, E. B., & Poltrock, S. Mechanics of thought. In B. Kantowitz (Ed.), *Human information processing: Tutorials in performance and cognition.* Hillsdale, NJ: Erlbaum, 1974.

Hunt, E. G., Frost, N., & Lunneborg, C. L. Individual differences in cognition: A new approach to intelligence. In G. Bower (Ed.), *Advances in learning and motivation.* Vol. 7. New York: Academic Press, 1973.

Keele, S. *Attention and human performance.* Los Angeles: Goodyear, 1973.

Lavin, D. E. *The prediction of academic performance.* New York: Russel Sage, 1965.

Mackworth, J. F. The relation between the visual image and post perceptual immediate memory. *Journal of Verbal Learning and Verbal Behavior,* 1963, **2**, 75–85.

Massaro, D. W. Preperceptual and synthesized auditory storage. Technical report 72–1. University of Wisconsin, Department of Psychology, 1972.

Newell, A. & Simon, H. A. *Human problem solving.* Englewood Cliffs, NJ: Prentice Hall, 1972.

Paivio, A., Yuille, J., & Madigan, S. Concreteness, imagery, and meaningfulness for 925 nouns. *Journal of Experimental Psychology* (Monograph) 1968, **76**, (1, 2) 1–21.

Peterson, L., & Peterson, M. J. Short term retention of individual verbal items. *Journal of Experimental Psychology,* 1959, **58**, 193–198.

Posner, M. I., Boies, S. J., Eichelman, W. H., & Taylor, R. L. Retention of visual and name codes of single letters, *Journal of Experimental Psychology* (Monograph) 1969, **79**, 1–16.

Robb, G. P., Bernardoni, L. C., & Johnson, R. W. *Assessment of individual mental ability.* Scranton, PA: Intext Educational Publishers, 1972.

Schank, R. C. Identification of conceptualizations underlying natural language. In R. C. Schank & K. M. Colby (Eds.), *Computer models of thought and language* (pp. 187–247). San Francisco: Freeman, 1973.

Sperling, G. The information available in brief visual presentations. *Psychological Monographs,* 1960, **74**, (Whole No. 498).

Sternberg, S. High speed scanning in human memory. *Science,* 1965, **153**, 652–654.

Sternberg, S. Memory scanning: Mental processes revealed by reaction time experiments. In J. Antrobus (Ed.), *Cognition and affect.* Boston: Little, Brown, 1970.

Tatsuoka, M. *Multivariate analysis.* New York: Wiley, 1971.

Trabasso, T. Mental operations in language comprehension. In J. B. Carroll & R. V. Freedle (Eds.), *Language comprehension and the acquisition of knowledge.* Washington, DC: Winston-Wiley, 1972.

Trabasso, T., Rollins, H., & Shaunessey, E. Storage and verification stages in processing concepts. *Cognitive Psychology,* 1971, 2, 239–289.

Wason, P. & Johnson-Laird, P. *Psychology of reasoning.* Cambridge, MA: Harvard University Press, 1972.

Wickens, D. Characteristics of word encoding. In A. Melton & E. Martin (Eds.), *Coding processes in human memory.* Washington, DC: Winston-Wiley, 1972.

POSTSCRIPT

Because the study of intelligence is so controversial, it's appropriate in the limited space of this Postscript only to provide some references and point to some general trends. Some very useful resources for understanding recent research on intelligence are the edited volumes by Sternberg (1982) and Wolman (1985) and the book by Sternberg (1985). Carroll's work (1988) is also very thoughtful but quite technical. Kail and Pellegrino (1985) and Sternberg (1988a, b) provide less technical coverage. A taste of the variety of viewpoints about intelligence among contemporary researchers can found in Sternberg and Detterman (1986). Sternberg, Conway, Ketron, and Bernstein (1981) describe laypeople's conceptions of intelligence. Snyderman and Rothman (1987, 1988) compare expert and public opinions of the controversy over IQ.

Several trends in the study of intelligence are worth mentioning here. This article by Hunt and his colleagues helped begin one trend: the rise of the information-processing approach to the study of intelligence and the decline of the psychometric approach that dominated research on intelligence until the mid- to late-1970s.

The psychometric approach is grounded in the observation described in the introduction: people who are good at one intellectual task tend to be good at others. In the psychometric approach, a statistical method called factor analysis is applied to scores on intelligence tests in an attempt to understand this correlation (see Kline, 1991, for a modern, relatively accessible account of this view). The usefulness of this procedure hinges on the assumption that correlations in performance on different intellectual tests arise because those tests are imperfect or impure measures of the same underlying factor or factors. Factor analysis allows one to determine the extent to which each test is correlated with that underlying factor (or factors). Researchers who argue that there is one main factor common to all tests call that factor *g*. Lately, Jensen (1987) has suggested that *g* corresponds to processing speed.

In contrast, this article by Hunt and his associates was one of the earliest attempts to understand differences in intelligence as differences in the efficiency or effectiveness with which an individual can apply the processes that characterize human cognition or in the capacity or organization of an individual's cognitive structures. Rather than linking the study of intelligence to an analysis of intelligence tests, the information-processing approach construes the study of intelligence as a part of cognitive psychology. In the past 15 years, this approach has become dominant (at least in the United States).

A second trend in the study of intelligence is the elaboration of the information-processing approach to suggest that different *kinds* of cognitive processes, typically called components, work in concert to produce intelligent behavior. Sternberg's (1985, 1988b) triarchic theory is the best known instance of this view. Sternberg suggests that intelligent behavior depends on (1) metacomponents that enable us to plan, monitor, and evaluate performance; (2) performance components, which roughly correspond to basic cognitive processes, such as those studied by Hunt, Lunneborg, and Lewis, that actually carry out the cognitive tasks; and (3) knowledge-acquisition components.

A third trend is a greater emphasis on intelligent behaviors in everyday settings (e.g. Sternberg & Wagner, 1986; Scribner, 1984) and a greater recognition of the roles of social context and noncognitive factors (such as personality traits) in intelligent behavior (Baron, 1982; Sternberg & Detterman, 1986).

A fourth trend is a more explicit recognition of different kinds of human intelligence. Perhaps the theory that best embodies this trend is Gardner's (1983) theory of multiple intelligences. Gardner argues that there are at least seven distinct kinds of intelligences, including the linguistic, musical, logical-mathematical, spatial, bodily-kinesthetic, interpersonal, and intrapersonal. Similarly, concepts related to intelligence have received added attention (for example, giftedness, Sternberg & Davidson, 1986; wisdom, Sternberg, 1990; and creativity, Perkins, 1988, and other references in the Postscript to Reading 27).

Finally, a fifth trend has been to turn more attention to the links between intelligence and biology. This has taken two forms: the use of psychophysiological indices to measure intelligence (Dillon, 1989) and more sophisticated studies of the contributions of genetics and environment to intelligence (Bouchard, Lykken, McGue, Segal, & Tellegen, 1990; McGue & Bouchard, 1989). Interestingly however, since the eruption of the controversy over claims about race differences in intelligence (Jensen, 1980, Modgil & Modgil, 1987; Snyderman & Rothman, 1988), psychologists have tended not to examine specifically the effects of race or sex on intelligence. This may stem in part because of the movement of the field away from a reliance on standard IQ tests for understanding the nature of intelligence (the controversy has been over reasons for differential performance on IQ tests). But the political ramifications of such research undoubtedly play a part (see Scarr, 1981, for some commentary).

FOR FURTHER THOUGHT

1. Why did Hunt and his associates use a composite of scores from several intelligence tests as their measure of verbal ability?
2. In the name identity instructional condition, subjects take longer to respond to Aa than to AA. What accounts for that time difference?
3. In the second part of Experiment 1, subjects always first sorted the cards twice under physical identity instructions, then sorted them once under the name identity condition. Why were the results for the first sorting for each subject not analyzed? What advantages and disadvantages can you see to having the subjects always do two physical identity sorts followed by a name identity sort?
4. In Experiment 2, Hunt and his associates predict that the ability to integrate syllables into words should increase performance on the free recall task. Why? Why was it important at the end of this task to test all subjects' familiarity with all the words used? Why did the researchers reanalyze the results of Experiment 2 upon measuring subjects' familiarity with the words?
5. Why were reaction times not analyzed on trials in which subjects made errors (for example, in Experiment 5)?
6. What are the four variables in the design of Experiment 5? How is encoding time measured in Experiment 5? decision time? What is the subject supposed to be doing during those two time periods?
7. Why is it reasonable to expect that people high in CIP abilities will do well on verbal intelligence tests if the latter directly measure what people know rather than their abilities as such?

REFERENCES

Baron, J. (1982). Personality and intelligence. In R. J. Sternberg (Ed.), *Handbook of human intelligence* (pp. 308–351). New York: Cambridge University Press.

Bouchard, T. J., Jr., Lykken, D. T., McGue, M., Segal, N. L., & Tellegen, A. (1990). Sources of human psychological differences: The Minnesota study of twins reared apart. *Science, 250,* 223–228.

Carroll, J. B. (1988). Individual differences in cognitive functioning. In R. C. Atkinson, R. J. Herrnstein, G. Lindzey, & R. D. Luce (Eds.), *Stevens' handbook of experimental psychology* (2nd ed.). New York: Wiley.

Clark, H. H., & Clark, E. V. (1977). *Psychology and language: An introduction to psycholinguistics.* New York : Harcourt Brace Jovanovich.

Dillon, R. F. (1989). Information processing and intelligence. In R. J. Sternberg (Ed.), *Advances in the psychology of human intelligence* (Vol. 5, pp. 135–155). Hillsdale, NJ: Erlbaum.

Gardner, H. (1983). *Frames of mind: The theory of multiple intelligences.* New York: Basic Books.

Jensen, A. R. (1980). *Bias in mental testing.* New York: Free Press.

Jensen, A. R. (1987). Differential psychology: Towards consensus. In S. Modgil & C. Modgil (Eds.), *Arthur Jensen: Consensus and controversy* (pp. 353–399.). New York : Falmer Press.

Kail, R., & Pellegrino, J. W. (1985). *Human intelligence: Perspectives and prospects.* New York: W. H. Freeman.

Kline, P. (1991). *Intelligence: The psychometric view.* New York: Routledge.

Lachman, R., Lachman, J. L., & Butterfield, E. C. (1979). *Cognitive psychology and information processing: An introduction.* Hillsdale, NJ: Erlbaum.

McGue, M., & Bouchard, T. J., Jr. (1989). Genetic and environmental determinants of information processing and special mental abilities: A twin analysis. In R. J. Sternberg (Ed.), *Advances in the psychology of human intelligence* (Vol. 5, pp. 7–45). Hillsdale, NJ: Erlbaum.

Modgil, S., & Modgil, C. (Eds.). (1987). *Arthur Jensen: Consensus and controversy.* New York: Falmer Press.

Perkins, D. N. (1988). Creativity and the quest for mechanism. In R. J. Sternberg & E. E. Smith (Eds.), *The psychology of human thought* (pp. 309–336). New York: Cambridge University Press.

Scarr, S. (1981). *Race, social class, and individual differences in I.Q.* Hillsdale, NJ: Erlbaum.

Scribner, S. (1984). Studying working intelligence. In B. Rogoff & J. Lave (Eds.), *Everyday cognition: Its development in social context* (pp. 9–40). Cambridge, MA: Harvard University Press.

Snyderman, M., & Rothman, S. (1987). Survey of expert opinion on intelligence and aptitude testing. *American Psychologist, 42,* 137–144.

Snyderman, M., & Rothman, S. (1988). *The IQ controversy, the media and public policy.* New Brunswick, NJ: Transaction, Inc.

Sternberg, R. J. (Ed.). (1982). *Handbook of human intelligence.* New York: Cambridge University Press.

Sternberg, R. J. (1985). *Beyond IQ.* New York: Cambridge University Press.

Sternberg, R. J. (1988a). Intelligence. In R. J. Sternberg & E. E. Smith (Eds.), *The psychology of human thought* (pp. 267–308). New York: Cambridge University Press.

Sternberg, R. J. (1988b). *The triarchic mind: A new theory of intelligence.* New York: Penguin Books.

Sternberg, R. J. (Ed.). (1990). *Wisdom: Its nature, origins, and development.* New York: Cambridge University Press.

Sternberg, R. J., Conway, B. E., Ketron, J. L., & Bernstein, M. (1981). People's conceptions of intelligence. *Journal of Personality and Social Psychology, 41,* 37–55.

Sternberg, R. J., & Davidson, J. E. (1986). *Conceptions of giftedness.* New York: Cambridge University Press.

Sternberg, R. J., & Detterman, D. K. (Eds.). (1986). *What is intelligence?* Norwood, NJ: Ablex.

Sternberg, R. J., & Wagner, R. K. (1986). *Practical intelligence: Nature and origins of competence in the everyday world.* New York: Cambridge University Press.

Wolman, B. B. (Ed.). (1985). *Handbook of intelligence: Theories, measurements and applications.* New York: Wiley.

INTRODUCTION

Experts are much more effective in solving problems in their domain of expertise than novices are. What is responsible for this difference? This is the question examined by Michelene Chi, Paul Feltovich, and Robert Glaser in "Categorization and Representation of Physics Problems by Experts and Novices."

Chi and her associates make extensive use of technical terminology in their description of problem solving. To read this article, you must understand (1) the distinction between bottom-up, or data-driven, and top-down, or conceptually driven, processes (see Readings 5 or 6); (2) the concept of a schema (plural of *schema* is either *schemas* or *schemata*; see the Introduction to Reading 32), and (3) the spatial metaphor for problem solving (see the Introduction to Reading 27). It's also helpful if you understand the distinction between declarative and procedural knowledge and are familiar with earlier research with chess experts.

Declarative knowledge is sometimes described as "knowing that"; in contrast, procedural knowledge is sometimes described as "knowing how." *Knowing that* Bernese Mountain Dogs belong to the group of working dogs is declarative knowledge. *Knowing how* to classify a particular dog as an instance or noninstance of a Bernese Mountain Dog is procedural knowledge; we would say in the latter case that someone has a procedure or a production rule for classifying dogs (Schacter, 1989). By theory, procedural and declarative knowledge are integrated in schemas (Winograd, 1975), which are sometimes regarded as the basic building blocks of cognition (Rumelhart, 1980). Chi and her associates argue that what distinguishes experts from novices are the schemas that they have for solving physics problems and the schemas they elect to use when faced with any particular problem.

Chi, Feltovich, and Glaser often allude to studies of chess experts. Those studies (see Chase & Simon, 1973, for example) found that although chess experts do not consider more possible moves than novices do, the moves that they do consider tend to be better than the alternatives novices consider (but see Charness, 1981). Furthermore, experts seem to perceive the layout of pieces during a chess game differently than novices do. Whereas novices see individual pieces on specific squares, experts see meaningful configurations of pieces, such as a set of pawns and a knight in a particular defensive array or a rook and a bishop in a particular offensive array. This is sometimes described as perceptual chunking (see Reading 9). Much as our schemas for faces allow us to see a whole face at once rather than as separate features that happen to lie close together, chess experts have their schemas for different kinds of defensive and offensive configurations in chess that allow them to quickly perceive larger chess chunks than novice players do. (See Holding, 1985, for a full discussion of expertise in chess.)

Two experiments and some technical discussion from the original article have been excluded in this selection. As you read this article, think about some area in which you have some expertise, such as using a computer or playing a sport. How does your problem solving in that area now—or more generally, your thinking about that area now—compare to the time before you developed your expertise? How does it compare to an area in which you have no expertise? Are the differences just quantitative or are they qualitative—that is, is it just that you're faster or do you seem to approach things in an entirely different fashion?

Categorization and Representation of Physics Problems by Experts and Novices

Michelene T. H. Chi, Paul J. Feltovich, and Robert Glaser
University of Pittsburgh

CATEGORIZATION AND REPRESENTATION OF PHYSICS PROBLEMS BY EXPERTS AND NOVICES

This paper presents studies designed to examine differences in the ways expert and novice problem solvers represent physics problems and to investigate im-

This research program, conducted at the Learning Research and Development Center, is supported in part by contract No. N00014-78-C-0375, NR 157-421 of the Office of Naval Research, and in part by the National Institute of Education. Portions of this paper were presented by the first author at the meeting of the American Educational Research Association, San Francisco, April 1979, and at the meeting of the Psychonomic Society, Phoenix, November 1979. The authors are grateful for the help of Andrew Judkis, Ted Rees, and Christopher Roth, for comments, data collection, analysis, and editing. We particularly appreciate the generosity of the physics professors and graduate students who contributed their time, especially Ned S. VanderVen. Jill Larkin deserves special thanks for her contributions and insightful comments to Study Four. Reprint requests should be sent to Michelene Chi, Learning Research and Development Center, University of Pittsburgh, Pittsburgh, Pa. 15260.

plications of these differences for problem solution. A *problem representation* is a cognitive structure corresponding to a problem, constructed by a solver on the basis of his domain-related knowledge and its organization. A representation can take a variety of forms. Greeno (1977), for example, has proposed the representation of a problem as a constructed semantic network containing various components. Some of these correspond closely with the problem as stated, including the initial state (i.e., the "givens"), the desired goal, and the legal problem-solving operators (Newell & Simon, 1972). In addition, a representation can contain embellishments, inferences, and abstractions (Heller & Greeno, 1979). Since embellishment is one way of judging a solver's "understanding" of a problem (Greeno, 1977), it is possible that with increasing experience in a domain, the representation becomes more enriched. The research described here explores the changes in problem representation that emerge as a result of developing subject-matter expertise. . . .

SOURCE: *Cognitive Science, 5,* 1981, pp. 121–152. Copyright 1981 by Ablex Publishing Corporation. Reprinted by permission.

The hypothesis guiding the present research is that the representation is constructed in the context of the knowledge available for a particular type of problem. The knowledge useful for a particular problem is indexed when a given physics problem is categorized as a specific type. Thus, expert-novice differences may be related to poorly formed, qualitatively different, or nonexistent categories in the novice representation. In general, this hypothesis is consistent with the "perceptual chunking" hypothesis for experts (e.g., Chase & Simon, 1973) and its more general cognitive ramifications (e.g., Chase & Chi, 1981), which suggest that much of expert power lies in the expert's ability to quickly establish correspondence between externally presented events and internal models for these events.

More particularly, some evidence already exists in the literature to suggest that solvers represent problems by category and that these categories may direct problem solving. First, Hinsley, Hayes, and Simon (1978) found that college students can categorize algebra word problems into types, and that this categorization can occur very quickly, sometimes even after reading just the first phrase of the problem statement. For example, if subjects were to hear the words "a river steamer," then they might surmise that the problem was one about current, perhaps comparing the rates of going upstream and downstream. The ability to categorize problems quickly suggested to Hinsley et al. (1978) that "problem schemata" exist and can be viewed as interrelated sets of knowledge that unify superficially disparate problems by some underlying features. Secondly, in chess research, it appears that experts' superiority in memorizing chessboard positions arises from the existence of a large store of intact and well-organized chess configurations or patterns in memory (Chase & Simon, 1973). It is plausible that a choice among chess moves (analogous to physics solution methods) results from a direct association between move sequences and a configural (chunked) representation of the surface features of the board. Finally, from research in medical diagnosis, there is evidence to suggest that expert diagnosticians represent particular cases by general categories, and that these categories facilitate the formation of hypotheses during diagnosis (Pople, 1977; Wortman, 1972).

The accumulation of evidence for the importance of categorization in expert problem solving leads us to examine the role of categorization in expert physics problem solving: particularly, to investigate the relationships between such categorization and subsequent attempts at solution. The following series of studies attempts to determine: the categories that experts and novices impose on physics problems (Studies One and Two); the knowledge which these categorical representations activate in the problem solver (Study Three); and the cues or features of problems which subjects use to choose among alternative categories (Study Four). [Only Studies One and Three are reprinted here.]

STUDY ONE: PROBLEM SORTING

The objective of the first study was to determine the kinds of categories subjects (of different experience) impose on problems. Using a sorting procedure, we asked eight advanced PhD students from the physics department (experts) and eight undergraduates (novices) who had just completed a semester of mechanics, to categorize 24 problems selected from Halliday and Resnick's (1974) *Fundamentals of Physics,* beginning with Chapter 5, Particle Dynamics, and ending with Chapter 12, Equilibrium of Bodies. Three problems were selected from each chapter, and these were individually typed on 3 × 5 cards. Instructions were to sort the 24 problems into groups based on similarities of solution. The subjects were not allowed to use pencil and paper and, thus, could not actually solve the problems in order to sort them. As a test of consistency, subjects were asked to re-sort the problems after the first trial. Following this, they were asked to explain the reasons for their groupings. The time taken to sort on each trial was also measured.

ANALYSIS OF GROSS QUANTITATIVE RESULTS

No gross quantitative differences between the sorts produced by the two skill groups were observed. There were no differences in the number of categories produced by each group (8.4 for the experts and 8.6 for the novices), and the four largest categories produced by each subject captured the majority of the problems (80 percent for the experts and 74 percent for the novices). Likewise, experts and novices were equally able to achieve a stable sort within the two trials, that is, their second sort matched their first sort very closely. This suggests that their sorting pattern was not ad hoc, but rather, was based on some meaningful representation.

There were, however, some differences in the amount of time it took experts and novices to sort the problems. In fact, experts took longer (18 minutes or 45 seconds per problem, on the average) to sort the problems in the first trial than novices (12 minutes or 30 seconds). Both groups were relatively fast at sorting the second trial (4.6 minutes for the experts and 5.5 minutes for the novices). The speed with which the problems were sorted on the second trial (about 12 seconds per problem) suggests that subjects probably did not have to go through the entire process of "understanding" each problem again. Since the problems were all categorized after the first trial, the subjects probably needed only to identify the cues that elicited category membership.

In general, these quantitative data suggest that both experts and novices were able to categorize problems into groups in a meaningful way. Other than the difference in the time taken to sort on the first trial, there was little difference between skill groups. The critical question then becomes: what are the bases on which experts and novices categorize these problems?

QUALITATIVE ANALYSIS OF THE CATEGORIES

Analyses of Four Pairs of Problems

A cluster analysis (Diameter method) was performed on the problems grouped together by the experts and those by the novices. Such an analysis shows the degree to which subjects of each skill group agree that certain problems belong to the same group. One way to interpret the cluster analysis is to examine only those problems that were grouped together with the highest degree of agreement among subjects.

Our initial analysis centered on four pairs of problems. Figures 1 and 2 contain the diagrams of pairs of problems that were grouped together by the

novices and the experts, respectively. These diagrams can be drawn to depict the physical situations described in the problem statements, and are sometimes given along with a problem statement (although no diagrams were given to the subjects in our studies). All eight novices grouped the top pair (Figure 1) together, and seven of the eight novices grouped the bottom pair. Both pairs of problems (Figure 2) were grouped together by six of the eight experts.

Examination of the novice pairs (Figure 1) reveals certain similarities in the surface structures of the problems. By "surface structures," we mean: (a) the objects referred to in the problem (e.g., a spring, an inclined plane); (b) the literal physics terms mentioned in the problem (e.g., friction, center of mass); or (c) the physical configuration described in the problem (i.e., relations among physical objects such as a block on an inclined plane). Each pair of problems in Figure 1 contains the same object components and configurations—circular disks in the upper pair, blocks on an inclined plane in the lower pair.

The suggestion that novices categorize by surface structure can be confirmed by examining subjects' verbal descriptions of their categories. (Samples are given in the figures.) Basically, according to their explanations, the top pair of problems involves "rotational things" and the bottom two problems "blocks on inclined planes."

To reiterate, the novices' use of surface features may involve either keywords given in the problem statement or abstracted visual configurations, that is, the presence of identical keywords (such as friction) is one criterion by which novices group problems as similar. Yet, novices were also capable of going beyond the word level to classify by types of physical objects. For example, "merry-go-round" and "rotating disk" are classified as the same object, as is the case for the top pair of problems in Figure 1.

For experts, surface features do not seem to be the bases for categorization. There is neither great similarity in the keywords used in the problem statements, nor visual similarity apparent in the diagrams depictable from each pair of problems shown in Figure 2. Nor is the superficial appearance of the equations that can be used on these problems the same. Only a physicist can detect the similarity underlying the expert's categorization. It appears that the experts

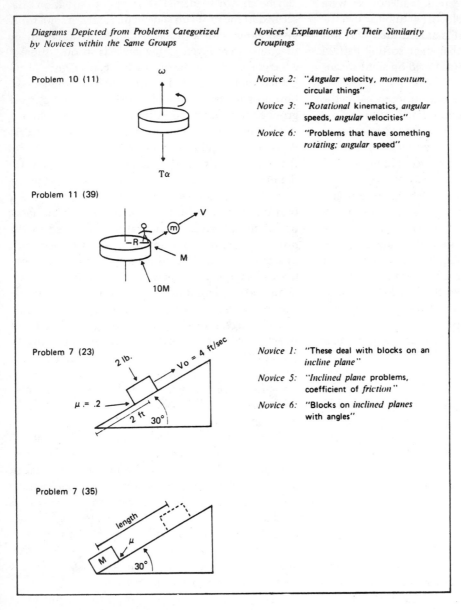

Diagrams Depicted from Problems Categorized by Novices within the Same Groups

Problem 10 (11)

Problem 11 (39)

Problem 7 (23)

Problem 7 (35)

Novices' Explanations for Their Similarity Groupings

Novice 2: "*Angular* velocity, *momentum,* circular things"

Novice 3: "*Rotational* kinematics, *angular* speeds, *angular* velocities"

Novice 6: "Problems that have something *rotating; angular* speed"

Novice 1: "These deal with blocks on an *incline plane*"

Novice 5: "*Inclined plane* problems, coefficient of *friction*"

Novice 6: "Blocks on *inclined planes* with angles"

FIGURE 1   Diagrams depicted from two pairs of problems categorized by novices as similar and samples of three novices' explanations for their similarity are provided. Problem numbers given represent chapter, followed by problem number from Halliday and Resnick (1974).

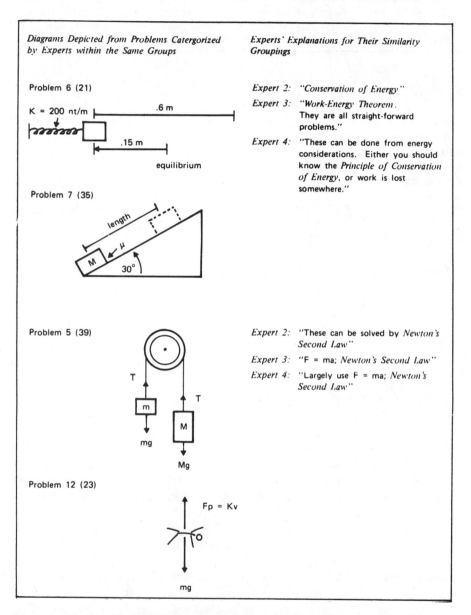

Diagrams Depicted from Problems Catergorized by Experts within the Same Groups

Problem 6 (21)

K = 200 nt/m   .6 m

.15 m

equilibrium

Problem 7 (35)

length   μ

M   30°

Problem 5 (39)

T   T

m   M

mg   Mg

Problem 12 (23)

Fp = Kv

O

mg

Experts' Explanations for Their Similarity Groupings

Expert 2:   *"Conservation of Energy"*

Expert 3:   *"Work-Energy Theorem.*
They are all straight-forward problems."

Expert 4:   "These can be done from energy considerations. Either you should know the *Principle of Conservation of Energy*, or work is lost somewhere."

Expert 2:   "These can be solved by *Newton's Second Law"*

Expert 3:   *"F = ma; Newton's Second Law"*

Expert 4:   *"Largely use F = ma; Newton's Second Law"*

FIGURE 2   Diagrams depicted from pairs of problems categorized by experts as similar and samples of three experts' explanations for their similarity are provided. Problem numbers given represent chapter, followed by problem number from Halliday and Resnick (1974).

TABLE 1   Expert Categories

Category Labels	Number of Subjects Using Category Labels ($N_1 = 8$)	Average Size of Category ($N_2 = 24$)	Number of Problems Accounted for ($N_1 \times N_2$)
Second law	6	6.0	36
Energy principles (Conservation of Energy considerations, Work-Energy Theorem)†	6	5.5	33
*Momentum principles (Conservation of Momentum, Conservation of Linear Momentum, momentum considerations)†	6	5.0	30
*Angular motion (angular speed, rotational motion, rotational kinematics, rotational dynamics)†	6	3.0	18
Circular motion	5	1.6	8
*Center of mass (center of gravity)†	5	1.4	7
Statics	4	1.0	4
Conservation of Angular Momentum	2	1.5	3
*Work (work and kinetic energy, work and power)†	2	1.5	3
Linear kinematics (kinematics)†	2	1.5	3
Vectors	2	1.0	2
*Springs (spring and potential energy, spring and force)†	2	1.0	2

*Indicates the categories used by both novices and experts.

†When multiple descriptors across subjects were treated as equivalent, these are given in parentheses.

classify according to the major physics principle governing the solution of each problem. The top pair of problems in Figure 2 can be solved by applying the Law of Conservation of Energy; the bottom pair is better solved by applying Newton's Second Law (F = MA). The verbal justification of the expert subjects confirms this analysis. If "deep structure" is defined as the underlying physics law applicable to a problem, then, clearly, this deep structure is the basis by which experts group the problems.

Analysis of Categories

Further insight into the ways subjects categorize problems is given by the descriptions subjects gave for the categories they created. Tables 1 and 2 show the category descriptions (Column 1) used by more than one expert or novice. These category labels apply to all

problems within each of their sorted piles.[1] Column 2 shows the number of subjects who used the category label. Column 3 shows the average size of the category among subjects who used it. And, Column 4 gives the total number of problems (out of 192, 24 problems for each of 8 subjects) according to category.

There are several things to note about these data which confirm our initial analyses of the four pairs of problems. First, there is little overlap between expert and novice categories. Only five of 20 distinct categories (marked with asterisks) are shared by the two groups. Second, if one considers the four predominant categories (the upper four in the tables in

---

[1]For example, if a subject said of a problem group: "These all involve inclined planes, some with a frictional surface, some frictionless," the label "inclined planes" was counted since it applied to all problems in the set.

TABLE 2 Novice Categories

Category Labels	Number of Subjects Using Category Labels ($N_1 = 8$)	Average Size of Category ($N_2 = 24$)	Number of Problems Accounted for ($N_1 \times N_2$)
*Angular motion (angular velocity, angular momentum, angular quantities, angular speed)[†]	7	5.6	39
*Springs (spring equation, spring constant, spring force)[†]	6	2.8	17
Inclined planes (blocks on incline)[†]	4	3.8	15
Velocity and acceleration	2	5.5	11
Friction	2	5.0	10
Kinetic energy	4	2.0	8
*Center of mass (center of gravity)[†]	5	1.4	7
Cannot classify (do not know equations, do not go with anything else)[†]	4	1.8	7
Vertical motion	2	3.5	7
Pulleys	3	2.0	6
*Momentum principles (Conservation of Momentum)[†]	2	3.0	6
*Work (work, work plus Second Law, work and power)[†]	4	1.0	4
Free fall	2	1.0	2

*Indicates the categories used by both novices and experts.

[†]When multiple descriptors across subjects were treated as equivalent, these are given in parentheses.

each subject group, ranked by total number of problems in each), the only overlap is in the category "angular motion." In particular, for these predominant classifications, the novices' descriptions are mostly objects and other surface characteristics of problems, whereas descriptions given by experts all involve laws of physics. Third, although both experts and novices classify a large number of problems (61 percent for the experts, 43 percent for the novices)[2] into four categories, there is a slight difference in the distribution of the problems across categories, which may suggest greater variability in novices' classifica-

tion. Three major categories accounted for a sizable number (33 on the average) of experts' problems, whereas only one major category accounted for a large number (39) of novices' problems. This again suggests that experts are able to "see" the underlying similarities in a great number of problems, whereas the novices "see" a variety of problems that they consider to be dissimilar because the surface features are different. . . .

[In Study Two, Chi and her associates tested how two advanced novices as well as an expert and a novice categorized problems. The performance of the expert and novice replicated the results from Study One. Although the categories of the advanced novices were based (imperfectly) on underlying characteristics, those of the less experienced of the two were still influenced somewhat by surface characteristics of the problems.]

---

[2]The percentages here do not correspond to those mentioned on page 579. Those were based on the largest sorting piles given by each subject, regardless of their contents or what they were labeled. Percentages here (Tables 1 and 2) are based on the sizes of specifically labeled categories when they were used by subjects.

DISCUSSION OF THE NATURE OF THE REPRESENTATION

The results of the first two studies clearly indicate that the categories into which experts and novices sort problems are qualitatively different. However, neither group is classifying *solely* on the basis of the literal description of the problem statement. Both are able to read and gain some understanding of the problem, that is, to construct a somewhat enriched internal representation of it.

What is the relation between categorization and a subject's representation of problems? There are at least two plausible interpretations. One, that after the reading of a problem statement, a representation is formed, and based on that representation, the problem is categorized. The taxonomy of representations proposed by McDermott and Larkin (1978) offers a plausible interpretation for the present results. These authors have proposed that the problem solver progresses through four stages of representations as s/he solves a problem. The first stage is a literal representation of the problem statement (containing relevant keywords) and the fourth stage is the algebraic representation that results once equations are produced. The middle two are the most important. The second stage ("naive") representation contains the literal objects and their spatial relationships as stated in the problem and is often accompanied by a sketch of the situation (Larkin, 1980).[3] Such a representation and the accompanying sketch is "naive" because it can be formed by a person who is relatively ignorant of the domain of physics. The third stage ("scientific") representation contains the idealized objects and physical concepts, such as forces, momenta, and energies, which are necessary to generate the equations of the algebraic representation. This stage is related to the solution method. A plausible interpretation based on this framework is to postulate that novices' categori-

zation is based on the construction of "naive" representations, with some limited elements of a "scientific" representation. Experts, on the other hand, may have constructed a more "scientific" representation, and based their categorizations on the similarities at this third level of representation. Such an interpretation would be consistent with the timing data of Study One: it could explain why experts actually took longer initially to classify the problems. They had to process the problems more "deeply" to a scientific representation in order to determine the principle underlying a problem.

An alternative interpretation for the nature of problem representation and its relation to categorization is to postulate more interaction among "stages" of representation than is proposed by McDermott and Larkin (1978). Under this interpretation, a problem can be at least tentatively categorized after some gross preliminary analyses of the problem features. After a potential category is activated, then the remainder of the representation is constructed for solution with the aid of available knowledge associated with the category. This interpretation is supported by the evidence that a problem can be categorized quickly (within 45 seconds, including reading time) and that it can often be tentatively categorized after reading just the first phrase of the problem (Hinsley et al., 1978; and our own results from Study Four). According to this interpretation, a problem representation is not *fully* constructed until after the initial categorization has occurred. The categorization processes can be accomplished by a set of rules that specify problem features and the corresponding categories that they should cue.

The second interpretation is our initial preferred hypothesis for the process of representing a problem for solution. It suggests that a problem representation is constructed in the context of the knowledge available for a problem type which constrains and guides the final form which the representation will take. A category and its associated knowledge within the knowledge base constitute a "schema," in Rumelhart's sense (1980), for a particular problem type. It is the content of these problem schemata (plural for *schema*) that ultimately determines the quality of the problem representation. Because the character of problem categories is different between experts and

---

[3]In the McDermott and Larkin (1978) paper, they referred to the second stage of representation as the accompanying or produced diagram and to the third stage as the abstracted free body diagram. We took the liberty of corresponding the "naive" representation as the second stage and the "scientific" representation as the third stage, although Larkin (1980) has developed the ideas of "naive" and "scientific" representations beyond that of the diagram and the free body diagram.

novices, we postulate that their problem schemata contain "different" knowledge. The next study presents a somewhat more direct look at the knowledge accessed by the category labels used by experts and novices.

STUDY THREE: CONTENTS OF SCHEMATA

We presume that the category descriptions provided by experts and novices (Tables 1 and 2) represent labels they use to access a related unit of knowledge, i.e., a schema. To assess the kind of knowledge that might be associated with these schemata, a selected set of 20 category labels, ranging from those generated predominantly by experts (e.g., Newton's Second Law, see Table 1) to those provided by novices (e.g., block on incline, see Table 2), was presented to two experts (M. G., M. S.) and two novices (H. P., P. D.). Subjects were given three minutes to tell everything they could about problems involving each category label and how these might be solved.

ANALYSIS OF PROTOCOLS AS NODE-LINK STRUCTURES

The protocols of one expert's (M. G.) and one novice's (H. P.) elaboration of the category label "inclined plane" can be grossly diagrammed in the form of a node-link structure (Figures 3, 4). The network depiction shown in Figure 3 indicates that the novice's representation for "inclined plane" is very well developed. His representation contains numerous variables that can be instantiated, including the *angle* at which the *plane* is inclined with respect to the horizontal, whether there is a *block* resting on a plane, and the *mass* and *height* of the block. Other variables mentioned by the novice include the *surface property* of the plane, whether or not it has *friction,* and if it does, what the *coefficients of static and kinetic friction* are. The novice also discussed possible *forces* that may act on the block, such as possibly having a *pulley* attached to it. The novice did not discuss any physics principles until the very end, where he mentioned the pertinence of Conservation of Energy. However, his mentioning of the Conservation of Energy principle was not elicited as an explicit solution procedure that is applicable to a

configuration involving an inclined plane, as will be seen later in the case of the expert.

The casual reference to the underlying physics principle given by the novice in the previous example is in marked contrast to the expert's protocol in which she immediately mentioned general alternative basic physics principles, Newton's laws of Force and Conservation of Energy, that may come into play for problems containing an inclined plane (Figure 4). The expert not only mentioned the alternative methods, but also the conditions under which they can be applied (dotted enclosures in Figure 4). Therefore, the expert appears to associate her principles with procedural knowledge about their applicability.

After elaboration of the principles and the conditions of their applicability to inclined plane problems (depicted in the top half of Figure 4), Expert M. G. continued her protocol with descriptions of the structural or surface features of inclined plane problems (lower half of Figure 4), much like the description provided by Novice H. P. in Figure 3. Hence, it appears that this knowledge is common to subjects of both skill groups, but the expert has additional knowledge pertaining to solution procedures based on major physics laws.

ANALYSIS OF PROTOCOLS IN THE FORM OF PRODUCTION RULES

An alternative way to analyze the same set of protocols is to convert them directly into "production rules" (Newell, 1973). This can be done simply by converting all statements that can be interpreted as reflecting *if–then* or *if–when* structures in the protocols. This transformation is quite simple and straightforward and covers a majority of the protocol data. Tables 3 and 4 depict the same set of protocols as do Figures 3 and 4, except these also include the data of the other two subjects. Such an analysis captures differences between the expert and novice protocols in a more pronounced way, and other differences also become more apparent.

As suggested earlier, the experts' production rules (Table 3) contain explicit solution methods, such as "use F = MA," "sum all the forces to 0." These procedures may be considered as calls to action schemata (Greeno, 1980).

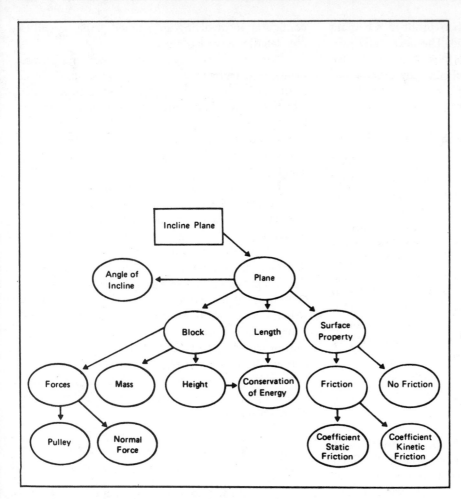

FIGURE 3   Network representation of Novice H. P.'s schema of an inclined plane.

None of the novices' rules depicted in Table 4 contain any actions that are explicit solution procedures. Their actions can be characterized more as attempts to find specific unknowns, such as "find mass" (see rules H. P. 2 and P. D. 1 in Table 4). In addition, one novice (H. P.), exhibited a number of production rules that have no explicit actions. This suggests that he knew what problem cues are relevant, but did not know what to do with them, that is, if we think of the protocols as reflecting contents of an inclined plane schema, the novice's schema may contain fewer explicit procedures.

Finally, our network analyses (Figures 3 and 4) suggested that the mentioning of Conservation of Energy by Novice H. P. was somehow different from the mentioning of Conservation of Energy by the Expert M. G. This difference can now be further captured by this second mode of analysis. In Table 4, it can be seen that Novice H. P.'s statement of Conservation of Energy (Rule 8) was part of a description of the condition side of a production rule, whereas the statement of this principle by both experts (Table 3, see rules M.S. 2 and M.G. 2) is described on the action side of the production rules—supporting our previous interpretation of a difference in the way "Conservation of Energy" was meant when mentioned in the protocols of Novice H. P. (Figure 3) and Expert M. G. (Figure 4). . . .

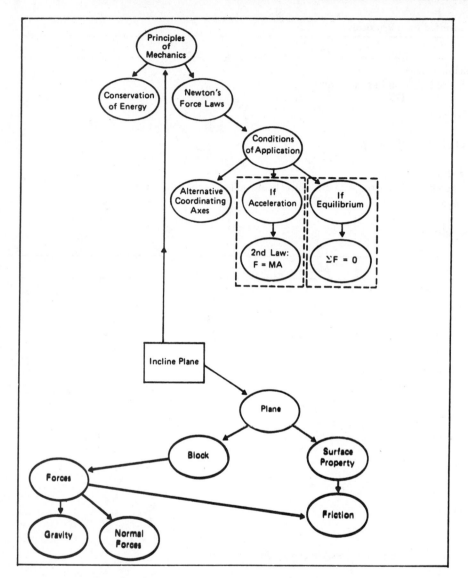

FIGURE 4   Network representation of Expert M. G.'s schema of an inclined plane.

[In Study Four, Chi and her associates examined the features of the problems on which experts and novices based their categorizing. They found that the features used were similar for the two groups, but, in the case of experts, problem features elicited characterizations not literally present in the problem (for example, descriptions such as "no external forces"). This suggests that, for the experts, problem features activate schemas that link surface features to other characteristics that help in the identification of underlying principles.]

GENERAL DISCUSSION

Our research goal has been to ultimately understand the difference between experts and novices in solving physics problems. A general difference often found in the literature (Larkin, McDermott, Simon, & Simon,

TABLE 3   Expert Productions Converted from Protocols

M.S.

---

1. IF problem involves an inclined plane
    THEN a) expect something rolling or sliding up or down;
            b) use F = MA;
            c) use Newton's 3rd Law.
2. IF plane is smooth
    THEN use Conservation of Mechanical energy.
3. IF plane is not smooth
    THEN use work done by friction.
4. IF problem involves objects connected by string and one object being pulled by the other
    THEN consider string tension.
5. IF string is not taut
    THEN consider objects as independent.

M.G.

---

1. (IF problem involves inclined plane)*
    THEN a) use Newton's Law;
            b) draw force diagram.
2. (IF problem involves inclined plane)*
    THEN can use energy conservation.
3. IF there is something on plane
    THEN determine if there is friction.
4. IF there is friction
    THEN put it in diagram.
5. (IF drawing diagram)*
    THEN put in all forces—gravity, force up plane, friction, reaction force.
6. IF all forces in diagram)*
    THEN write Newton's Laws.
7. IF equilibrium problem
    THEN a)$\Sigma F = 0$
            b) decide on coordinate axes.
8. IF acceleration is involved
    THEN use F = MA.
9. IF "that's done" (drawing diagram, putting in forces, choosing axes)*
    THEN sum components of forces.

---

*Statements in parentheses were not said explicitly by the subjects but are indicated by the context.

1980; Simon & Simon, 1978) and also in our own study (Study Four, examining the processes of arriving at a "basic approach") [excluded here] is that experts engage in qualitative analysis of the problem prior to working with the appropriate equations. We speculate that this method of solution for the experts occurs because the early phase of problem solving (the qualitative analysis) involves the activation and confirmation of an appropriate principle-oriented knowledge structure, a schema. The initial activation of this schema can occur as a data-driven response to some fragmentary cue in the problem. Once activated, the schema itself specifies further (schema-driven) tests for its appropriateness (Bobrow & Norman, 1975). When the schema is confirmed, that is, the expert has decided that a particular principle is

TABLE 4   Novice Productions Converted from Protocols

H.P.

1. (IF problem involves inclined plane)*
   THEN find angle of incline with horizontal.
2. IF block resting on plane
   THEN   a) find mass of block
             b) determine if plane is frictionless or not.
3. IF plane has friction
   THEN   determine coefficients of static and kinetic friction.
4. IF there are any forces on the block
   THEN . . .
5. IF the block is at rest
   THEN . . .
6. IF the block has an initial speed
   THEN . . .
7. IF the plane is frictionless
   THEN the problem is simplified.
8. IF problem would involve Conservation of Energy and height of block, length of plane, height of plane are known
   THEN could solve for potential and kinetic energies.

P.D.

1. (IF problem involves an inclined plane)*
   THEN   a) figure out what type of device is used;
             b) find what masses are given;
             c) find outside forces besides force coming from pulley.
2. IF pulley involved
   THEN try to neglect it.
3. IF trying to find coefficient of friction
   THEN slowly increase angle until block on it starts moving.
4. IF two frictionless inclined planes face each other and a ball is rolled from a height on one side
   THEN ball will roll to same height on other side.
5. IF something goes down frictionless surface
   THEN can find acceleration of gravity on the incline using trigonometry.
6. IF want to have collision
   THEN can use incline to accelerate one object.

*Statements in parentheses were not said explicitly by the subject but are indicated by the context.

appropriate, the knowledge contained in the schema provides the general form that specific equations to be used for solution will take. For example, once the problem solver has decided to use an energy conservation approach, the general form of the solution equation involves energy terms equated at two points. The solver then needs only to specify these terms for the problem at hand. Such initial qualitative analysis would naturally lead to a more forward-working character (Larkin et al., 1980) of problem solving for the expert, in that the equations used depend more on the way the problem is represented than on the "unknown." Although the problem unknown obviously cannot be ignored by the experts, the status of the unknown in the expert solution method appears secondary to that of deciding which physics principles have their conditions of applicability met in the problem. Hence, analogous to the way that a chess expert's initial classification yields a small set of "good" alternative moves, which must then be investigated analytically (Chase & Simon, 1973), the physics expert's initial categorization restricts search for a particular solution to a small range of possible operations.

Consistent with this point of view, the exploratory studies reported here suggest that problem solving in a rich knowledge domain begins with a brief analysis of the problem statement to categorize the problem. The first [study] showed that experts tended to categorize problems into types that are defined by the major physics principles that will be used in solution, whereas novices tend to categorize them into types as defined by the entities contained in the problem statement. We view the categories of problems as representing internal schemata, with the category names as accessing labels for the appropriate schemata. Although it is conceivable that the categories constructed by the novices do not correspond to existing internal schemata, but rather represent only problem discriminations that are created on the spot during the sorting tasks, the persistence of the appearance of similar category labels across a variety of tasks gives some credibility to the reality of the novices' categories even if they are strictly entities related. . . .

Furthermore, we presume that once the correct schema is activated, knowledge—both procedural and declarative—contained in the schema is used to further process the problem in a more or less top-down manner. The declarative knowledge contained in the schema generates potential problem configurations and conditions of applicability for procedures which are then tested with what is presented in the problem statement. The procedural knowledge in the schema generates potential solution methods that can be used on the problem. . . .

In order to ascertain whether our initial hypothesis about the contents of the problem schemata is correct, Study Three attempted to assess their contents by asking subjects to elaborate on them. Such initial analyses have begun to show clear differences between the problem schemata of experts and those of novices: Experts' schemata contain a great deal of procedural knowledge, with explicit conditions for applicability. Novices' schemata may be characterized

as containing sufficiently elaborate declarative knowledge about the physical configurations of a potential problem, but lacking abstracted solution methods.

REFERENCES

Bobrow, D. G., & Norman, D. A. Some principles of memory schemata. In D. G. Bobrow & A. M. Collins (Eds.), *Representation and understanding: Studies in cognitive science.* New York: Academic Press, 1975.

Chase, W. G., & Chi, M. T. H. Cognitive skill: Implications for spatial skill in large-scale environments. In J. Harvey (Ed.), *Cognition, social behavior, and the environment.* Hillsdale, N.J.: Erlbaum, 1981.

Chase, W. G., & Simon, H. A. Perception in chess. *Cognitive Psychology,* 1973, *4,* 55–81.

de Kleer, J. Multiple representations of knowledge in a mechanics problem solver. *Proceedings of the 5th International Joint Conference on Artificial Intelligence.* Cambridge, Mass.: MIT Press, 1977.

Greeno, J. G. Process of understanding in problem solving. In N. J. Castellan, D. B. Pisoni, & G. R. Potts (Eds.), *Cognitive theory* (Vol. 2). Hillsdale, N.J.: Erlbaum, 1977.

Greeno, J. G. *Development of processes for understanding problems.* Paper presented at the Heidelberg Conference, Germany, July 1980.

Halliday, D., & Resnick, R. *Fundamentals of physics.* New York: Wiley, 1974.

Hayes, J. R., & Simon, H. A. The understanding process: Problem isomorphs. *Cognitive Psychology,* 1976, *8,* 165–190.

Heller, J. I., & Greeno, J. G. Information processing analyses of mathematical problem solving. In R. W. Tyler & S. H. White (Eds.), *Testing, teaching, and learning: Report of a conference on research on testing.* Washington, D.C.: U. S. Department of Health, Education, and Welfare, National Institute of Education, October 1979.

Hinsley, D. A., Hayes, J. R., & Simon, H. A. From words to equations: Meaning and representation in algebra word problems. In P. A. Carpenter & M. A. Just (Eds.), *Cognitive processes in comprehension.* Hillsdale, N.J.: Erlbaum, 1978.

Larkin, J. H. *Understanding, problem representations and skill in physics* (Tech. Rep. Applied Cognitive Psychology No. 2). Pittsburgh: Carnegie-Mellon University, Department of Psychology, November 1980.

Larkin, J. H., McDermott, J., Simon, D. P., & Simon, H. A. Expert and novice performance in solving physics problems. *Science,* 1980, *208,* 1335–1342.

McDermott, J., & Larkin, J. H. Re-representing textbook physics problems. *Proceedings of the 2nd National Conference of the Canadian Society for Computational Studies of Intelligence.* Toronto: University of Toronto Press, 1978.

Newell, A. Production systems: Models of control structures. In W. G. Chase (Ed.), *Visual information processing.* New York: Academic Press, 1973.

Newell, A., & Simon, H. A. *Human problem solving.* Englewood Cliffs, N.J.: Prentice-Hall, 1972.

Novak, G. S., Jr. Representations of knowledge in a program for solving physics problems. *Proceedings of the 5th International Joint Conference on Artificial Intelligence.* Cambridge, Mass.: MIT Press, 1977.

Novak, G. S., Jr., & Araya. A. A. *Research on expert problem solving in physics* (Tech. Rep. NL-40). Austin: University of Texas, Department of Computer Sciences, June 1980.

Pople, H. E. The formation of composite hypotheses in diagnostic problem solving: An exercise in synthetic reasoning. *Proceedings of the 5th International Joint Conference on Artificial Intelligence.* Cambridge, Mass.: MIT Press, 1977.

Reif, F. *Cognitive mechanisms facilitating human problem solving in a realistic domain: The example of physics.* (Manuscript submitted for publication, 1979.)

Rumelhart, D. E. Schemata: The building blocks of cognition. In R. Spiro, B. Bruce, & W. Brewer (Eds.), *Theoretical issues in reading comprehension.* Hillsdale, N.J.: Erlbaum, 1980.

Simon, D. P., & Simon, H. A. Individual differences in solving physics problems. In R. S. Siegler (Ed.), *Children's thinking: What develops?* Hillsdale, N.J.: Erlbaum, 1978.

Wortman, P. M. Medical diagnosis: An information processing approach. *Computers and Biomedical Research* 1972, *5,* 315–328.

POSTSCRIPT

Subsequent studies have confirmed Chi, Feltovich, and Glaser's characterization of the differences in problem representation by experts and novices (see Chi, Glaser, & Farr, 1988, for a collection of articles on expertise in different areas). For example, Novick (1988) found that shared underlying structure enhanced spontaneous analogical transfer between problems for experts but not for novices, and that inappropriate transfer is likely in novices but not in experts when surface features are shared and underlying structure is not (see Reading 26 and its Postscript for a discussion of analogical transfer).

In an interesting follow-up to this work, Schoenfeld and Herrmann (1982) argued that examining the impact of experience on knowledge organization and problem solving by comparing the performance of experts and novices leads to some problems of interpretation. In particular, experts generally have greater aptitude and/or motivation in their area of expertise than do novices. Schoenfeld and Herrmann therefore compared subjects' categorization of mathematical problems before and after taking a course on mathematical problem solving. They found that subjects tended to sort on the basis of surface features before the course and on the basis of deeper principles, much as experts do, after the course, thus supporting Chi and her associates' original conclusion. Elio and Scharf (1990) describe a computer model that simulates this novice-to-expert/surface-structure-to-underlying-structure shift. Bransford, Sherwood, Vye, and Rieser (1986) and Eylon and Reif (1984) discuss the importance of the development of proper representations in teaching people how to solve problems.

Anderson (1983, 1987) offers a slightly different view of the development of expertise, one that sees it as the development of cognitive skill. Basically, he suggests that problems and the methods for their solution are first represented as declarative memories. Through practice, procedural representations (that is, certain cognitive skills) that solve problems more efficiently are developed. With even more practice, these procedural representations are combined or streamlined, making them even more efficient (see also Klahr, Langley, & Neches, 1987). Computer programs called expert systems use production rule representations to give expert advice in a variety of areas, including medical diagnosis (Edmunds, 1988; Harmon & King, 1985).

None of the results discussed above should be taken to imply that all novices are alike and that all experts are alike or that the distinction between experts and novices is cut-and-dried. Hardiman, Dufresne, and Mestre (1989) found that under certain conditions, surface features can negatively affect experts' problem solving. Furthermore, in the course of learning to solve problems, some novices are more likely to notice or make use of underlying structural characteristics or to explain to themselves why certain procedures apply to particular examples. Those who do tend to be more successful at solving problems than are those who don't (Chi, Bassok, Lewis, Reimann, & Glaser, 1989).

Incidentally, the representations of the physical world that people without any formal training construct, called their naive physics beliefs, have been widely studied (see McCloskey, 1983; Proffitt, Kaiser, & Whelan, 1990). Mental representations of physical systems or events are sometimes called mental models (see the Postscript to Reading 24).

FOR FURTHER THOUGHT

1. What information did Chi and her colleagues gain by having subjects in Study One sort cards twice? What alternative explanation does this information help rule out?
2. Give some examples of the characteristics novices apparently use to categorize physics problems. Give some examples of the characteristics experts apparently use.
3. Early in their description, Chi and her associates point out that there were no gross differences either in the number of categories that experts and novices used on average (8.4 and 8.6, respectively) or in the percentage of problems put into the four largest categories (80 and 74%, respec-

tively). But they conclude that (in addition to the distinction raised in question 2) experts and novices categorize physics problems very differently. What observation led to this conclusion?

4. According to McDermott and Larkin, what are the four stages of representation formation in solving physics problems? How might the results of Study One be interpreted in terms of these stages, and what evidence supports this interpretation? What alternative interpretation do Chi and her associates describe, and what evidence supports this alternative? What kinds of evidence might help confirm a choice between these two alternatives?

5. What evidence does Study Three provide for arguing that concepts like "Conservation of Energy," which occur in both experts' and novices' protocols, play very different roles in experts' and novices' representations of physics?

6. If Chi and her associates want to know about subjects' schemas, why do they focus on categorization?

7. Chi and her associates use very few subjects; is this acceptable? Why or why not? (Consulting Reading 19 may be helpful.)

REFERENCES

Anderson, J. R. (1983). *The architecture of cognition.* Cambridge, MA: Harvard University Press.

Anderson, J. R. (1987). Skill acquisition: Compilation of weak-method problem solutions. *Psychological Review, 94,* 192–210.

Bransford, J., Sherwood, R., Vye, N., & Rieser, J. (1986). Teaching thinking and problem solving. *American Psychologist, 41,* 1078–1089.

Charness, N. (1981). Search in chess: Age and skill differences. *Journal of Experimental Psychology: Human Perception and Performance, 7,* 467–476.

Chase, W. G., & Simon, H. A. (1973). Perception in chess. *Cognitive Psychology, 4,* 55–81.

Chi, M. T. H., Bassok, M., Lewis, M. W., Reimann, P., & Glaser, R. (1989). Self-explanations: How students study and use examples in learning to solve problems. *Cognitive Science, 13,* 145–182.

Chi, M. T. H., Glaser, R., & Farr, M. J. (Eds.). (1988). *The nature of expertise.* Hillsdale, NJ: Erlbaum.

Edmunds, R. A. (1988). *The Prentice-Hall guide to expert systems.* Englewood Cliffs, NJ: Prentice-Hall.

Elio, R., & Scharf, P. B. (1990). Modeling novice-to-expert shifts in problem-solving strategy and knowledge acquisition. *Cognitive Science, 14,* 579–639.

Eylon, B.-S., & Reif, F. (1984). Effects of knowledge organization on task performance. *Cognition and Instruction, 1,* 5–44.

Hardiman, P. T., Dufresne, R., & Mestre, J. P. (1989). The relation between problem categorization and problem solving among experts and novices. *Memory & Cognition, 17,* 627–638.

Harmon, P., & King, D. (1985). *Expert systems: Artificial intelligence in business.* New York: Wiley.

Holding, D. H. (1985). *The psychology of chess skills.* Hillsdale, NJ: Erlbaum.

Klahr, D., Langley, P., & Neches, R. (1987) (Eds.). *Production system models of learning and development.* Cambridge, MA: MIT Press.

McCloskey, M. (1983, April). Intuitive physics. *Scientific American,* pp. 122–130.

Novick, L. R. (1988). Analogical transfer, problem similarity, and expertise. *Journal of Experimental Psychology: Learning, Memory, and Cognition, 14,* 510–520.

Proffitt, D. R., Kaiser, K. K., & Whelan, S. M. (1990). Understanding wheel dynamics. *Cognitive Psychology, 22,* 342–373.

Rumelhart, D. E. (1980). Schemata: The building blocks of cognition. In R. J. Spiro, B. C. Bruce, & W. F. Brewer (Eds.), *Theoretical issues in reading comprehension* (pp. 33–58). Hillsdale, NJ: Erlbaum.

Schacter, D. L. (1989). Memory. In M. I. Posner (Ed.), *Foundations of cognitive science* (pp. 683–725). Cambridge, MA: MIT Press.

Schoenfeld, A. H., & Herrmann, D. J. (1982). Problem perception and knowledge structure in expert and novice mathematical problem solvers. *Journal of Experimental Psychology: Learning, Memory, and Cognition, 8,* 484–494.

Winograd, T. (1975). Frame representations and the declarative procedural controversy. In D. G. Bobrow & A. M. Collins (Eds.), *Representation and understanding: Studies in cognitive science* (pp. 185–210). New York: Academic Press.

INDEX

TO THE OWNER OF THIS BOOK:

We hope that you have found *Experimenting with the Mind* useful. So that this book can be improved in a future edition, would you take the time to complete this sheet and return it? Thank you.

School and address: _____

Department: _____

Instructor's name: _____

_____

1. What I like most about this book is: _____

_____

2. What I like least about this book is: _____

_____

_____

3. My general reaction to this book is: _____

_____

4. The name of the course in which I used this book is: _____

_____

5. Were all of the chapters of the book assigned for you to read? _____

   If not, which ones weren't? _____

6. In the space below, or on a separate sheet of paper, please write specific suggestions for improving this book and anything else you'd care to share about your experience in using the book.

_____

_____

_____

_____

_____

_____

_____

Optional:

Your name: _____ Date: _____

May Brooks/Cole quote you, either in promotion for *Experimenting with the Mind* or in future publishing ventures?

       Yes: _____ No: _____

       Sincerely,

       Lloyd K. Komatsu

- -

FOLD HERE

BUSINESS REPLY MAIL

FIRST CLASS   PERMIT NO. 358   PACIFIC GROVE, CA

POSTAGE WILL BE PAID BY ADDRESSEE

ATT: _____ *Lloyd K. Komatsu* _____

Brooks/Cole Publishing Company
511 Forest Lodge Road
Pacific Grove, California 93950-9968

- -

FOLD HERE